PRINCIPLES OF FINANCIAL MANAGEMENT

PRINCIPLES OF FINANCIAL MANAGEMENT

SECOND EDITION

BENTON E. GUP

The University of Alabama

John Wiley & Sons

New York   Chichester   Brisbane   Toronto   Singapore

Library of Congress Cataloging in Publication Data:

Gup, Benton E.
  Principles of financial management.

  Bibliography: p.
  Includes index.
  1. Business enterprises—Finance.   2. Corporations
—Finance.   I. Title.
HG4026.G88   1987   658.1′5   86-28937
ISBN 0-471-81203-X

Printed in the United States of America

10 9 8 7 6 5 4 3 2 1

To my sons: Lincoln, Andrew, and Jeremy, may they grow
and prosper in a peaceful world

ABOUT THE AUTHOR

Dr. Benton E. Gup is a professor of finance and holds the Chair of Banking at the University of Alabama. He has held banking chairs at the University of Virginia and the University of Tulsa. His graduate and undergraduate degrees are from the University of Cincinnati. He has written extensively in the field of finance. His books include: *The Basics of Investing,* 3rd. ed., John Wiley & Sons; *Cases in Bank Management* (with Charles Meiburg), Macmillan Co.; *Financial Intermediaries,* 2nd. ed., Houghton Mifflin; *Guide to Strategic Planning,* McGraw-Hill; and *Management of Financial Institutions,* Houghton Mifflin. Dr. Gup's articles have appeared in *The Journal of Finance, The Journal of Financial and Quantitative Analysis, Financial Management,* and elsewhere. He is a nationally known lecturer in executive development programs and seminars and serves as a consultant to business and government.

Preface

Financial management is a dynamic, exciting discipline. It is dynamic because its body of knowledge is evolving as new theories are presented and tested. Advances in computer technology have made it possible to explore new areas of interest and use data bases that were not available until recently. The net result is a better understanding of the way business concerns and investors operate. In the past, for example, financial management focused on the practices of mature firms in smokestack industries. But that is not what the world is like. Today we recognize that the financial practices of growing firms are different from those of mature firms. We also live in a world where service firms, such as television stations and health care providers, are becoming increasingly important. Therefore, it is necessary to understand how to cope with the financial needs of businesses as they grow in our economic environment.

Financial management is exciting because it deals with decisions that can make or break a company. Not every decision is that dramatic. Nevertheless, most decisions made by business concerns have financial implications. What appears to be a fantastic marketing campaign may be a financial disaster if the firm cannot finance the expansion needed to sell the additional goods or services. Hiring, firing, buying, and selling all affect the bottom line—profit or loss. So no matter what your position is in a business, you should understand financial management.

Principles of Financial Management uses MPT—finance jargon for *modern portfolio theory*. However, I have borrowed those initials and altered their meaning somewhat. In this book, it means *modern, practical,* and *teachable*. This book is modern because it incorporates the latest thinking in finance that is appropriate for an introductory course. The organization is modern because the sections on valuation, investment decisions, and capital structure are given a preeminent place in the beginning of the text. This is important because increasing the value of the firm for the benefit of their owners is the primary goal of financial management.

The book is practical because it explains how to make financial decisions. In fact, the emphasis in this book can be summarized in two words—*practical* and *decisions*. The decisions we make are about which financial policies are best.

The book is teachable because it is written with both students and their professors in mind. At the beginning of each chapter is an outline and a statement about the teaching objectives of the chapter. New concepts and terms are explained when they are introduced, and examples are used to illustrate each point. At the end of each chapter is a summary and a listing of important concepts, as well as questions and problems. The extensive glossary at the end of the book contains brief definitions of the important concepts. Answers to selected problems are available in quantity from the publisher. In addition, microcomputer applications of selected problems are available on disk. Finally, there is a student Study Guide that will help sharpen your financial skills and understanding. Chapter 3 and other chapters were revised to incorporate changes resulting from the new 1986 tax guidelines.

Writing a book about financial management requires the efforts of many people. This is the time and the place to thank them for their contributions, suggestions, and support. Without their help, this book would not have been possible. Those who contributed to the first edition are: Gordon Bonner, Patrick Casabona, Tom Conine, Alan W. Frankle, Patrick Hennessee, Chris Hessel, Joanne Hill, Robert D. Hollinger, Ron E. Hutchins, R. Larry Johnson, Terry Maness, Israel Shaked, Hany Shawky, Richard J. Teweles, John Wachowicz, Tony R. Winger, and R. Douglas Womack.

Contributors to the second edition are: Kathleen Brown, David Cleeton, Pamela K. Coats, Julie Gerdsen, J. L. Hexter, James F. Jackson, Ravindra R. Kamath, Theodor Kohers, Duncan Kretovich, Jaroslaw Komarynsky, Harlan D. Platt, Dennis Proffitt, Yash Puri, William D. Samson, Gary C. Sanger, Fred Seigel, C. Lankford Walker, Michael C. Walker, Ralph Collins Walter III, and Howard Van Auken. Special thanks are due to Mona Gardner, who was responsible for all the end-of-chapter questions, and the Instructor's Manual. William "Lew" Randolph did the microcomputer applications for the students. Finally, thanks go to Sally-Jo Wright for preparing the Student Study Guide.

Finally, I want to thank Richard Esposito and Joe Dougherty, the editors who worked so hard to make this book a success, and Beverly Peavler for her excellent job of copy editing.

Benton E. Gup

Contents

An Overview of Financial Management

The first part of this book provides an overview of financial management and the environment in which it operates.

Change is a recurring theme in the first two chapters. Chapter 1 explains how the study of financial management has been changing; it also introduces the goals and functions of financial management. Chapter 2 describes how firms, industries, and products evolve through a life cycle and how business policies change during the various phases of the business cycle.

Chapters 3 and 4 complete the overview. Chapter 3 explains the operating environment of businesses, including organization forms and taxes. Chapter 4 introduces several sources of funds but focuses on the corporate securities markets.

Introduction to Financial Management

All major business decisions have financial implications. A small manufacturing firm, for example, may begin receiving orders to produce more than its facilities can handle. Should the firm expand? What would be the best way to finance an expansion? Other kinds of organizations must make similar decisions. The local transit authority may have to decide whether to buy new buses for the city bus line or to improve the city's airport facilities and charge landing fees. Which proposal would generate more revenue? Which would result in the greatest long-term benefit to the community? To help managers make basic decisions—what to produce, where and how to produce it, and what price to charge for it—finance scholars and professionals have developed a body of theory and a set of tools. These are the principles of financial management that form the subject of this text.

After reading this chapter, you should know the following.

1. **How financial management today differs from financial management in the past.**
2. **Why wealth maximization is so important.**
3. **What investment and financing decisions involve.**
4. **Why people study financial management.**
5. **How this book is organized.**

Development of Financial Management

Today, we define **financial management** as the process of making optimal use of financial and real, or physical, resources to increase the value of the firm. Managing finances has always been part of managing organizations, but finance first appeared as an academic discipline in the early 1900s. Since then, both the teaching and the practice of financial management have changed considerably. Table 1–1 lists some major changes in the content of financial management courses. These changes are described in the following discussion.

From Descriptive to Analytical   Finance as a subject of study is an outgrowth of institutional economics—a field that attempted to explain the economic behavior of various institutions by describing their activities. Around the turn of the century, the growth of giant industrial combinations, such as U.S. Steel and Standard Oil, was an important economic phenomenon. Therefore, early finance courses described mergers, combinations, and the issuance of securities—important financial activities of these giant corporations. During the depression of the 1930s, when many large-scale bankruptcies took place, finance courses described liquidity, profitability, and corporate reorganization.

With post-World War II economic expansion came a gradual pedagogical shift away from description and toward analysis. The increased use of com-

Table 1–1

Content of Financial Management Courses—Past and Present

Past Content	Present Content
Was descriptive	Is analytical
Emphasized fund raising, mergers, liquidity, etc.	Emphasizes optimal use of resources
Assumed a static environment	Assumes a dynamic environment
Was taught from perspective of outsider looking in	Is taught from perspective of financial manager making decisions

puters in the 1960s and the development of mathematical models and statistical techniques contributed to the emphasis on analysis. Today, financial managers make extensive use of quantitative techniques to solve problems and make decisions.

A Change in Emphasis As finance became more analytical, the optimal use of resources in the form of assets and liabilities was stressed. On the asset side of the balance sheet, mathematical models were developed to help firms optimize their use of cash, inventories, and receivables. Quantitative techniques were introduced to aid in the selection of long-term investments. (This process of asset selection is called **capital budgeting**.) In addition, **portfolio theory**—a method of asset selection that considers the combined risk of all assets held by the firm—became an increasingly important tool as the relationship between risk and return became better appreciated and understood.

On the liability side, theories dealing with the optimal capital structure and theories of valuation began to receive considerable attention. In addition, high interest rates and difficulties in raising funds have contributed to an interest in liability management. In general, modern financial management focuses on using all the firm's resources in the most efficient manner.

From Static to Dynamic In the past, finance focused on the problems of large manufacturing firms operating in a static or very slowly changing environment. In contrast, contemporary finance recognizes that different financial strategies are required by small, medium, and large companies, by manufacturers and producers of services, by rapidly growing companies and established, mature firms. Equally important has been the realization that all firms operate in an economic environment characterized by business cycles and by external shocks, such as fuel shortages. Financial decisions are thus made in a dynamic setting.

A Change in Perspective Descriptive finance was taught from the perspective of an outsider, such as a banker, looking in on the operations of a company. Today, financial management is taught from the perspective of a decision maker within the firm. The goals of outsiders and insiders may differ. For example, the banker is interested in the firm's ability to repay a loan. In contrast, the financial manager of a firm is concerned with wealth maximization.

Goals of Financial Management

Like other forms of management, financial management must start with clearly defined goals and objectives. While growth of assets and earnings and maximization of profits sometimes served as acceptable goals in the past, today's professional financial managers hold the maximization of the firm's total value to be the objective of all decision making. This concept is more commonly expressed as the **maximization of shareholder wealth**.

Wealth Maximization Throughout this text, maximizing shareholder wealth is stressed as a firm's appropriate financial goal. The term *shareholder* refers to an owner of a corporation or any other type of business concern. Shareholder wealth is measured by the market value of the corporation's stock, which depends on expectations about the corporation's profitability in the future. Maximizing shareholder wealth means making financing and investment decisions, for both the long run and the short run, that maximize the market value of the stock. Substantially different decisions might be made if the goal were **profit maximization**.

Profit Maximization versus Wealth Maximization It is important to recognize how the goals of profit maximization and wealth maximization differ. Otherwise, you might inadvertently focus on profits when you should be focusing on shareholder wealth. We will examine four areas of difference: risk, timing, measurement, and short-term versus long-term objectives.

Risk. Profit maximization does not recognize risk; wealth maximization takes risk into account. In general terms, **risk** refers to the possibility that actual returns may be less than expected returns. As a rule, projects with the potential for high returns also carry high risks of failure. Betting the company's capital on a project with a small chance of showing big returns may sometimes suit the goal of profit maximization but may not be in the best interest of shareholders.

Timing. Profit maximization does not take into account the timing of receipts; wealth maximization does take timing into account. Consider the following example, which shows the receipts a company expects from two competing projects, A and B. Both projects will have the same total returns—$300. Profit maximizers are indifferent between the two projects, since total returns are the same. But those who maximize shareholder wealth are not indifferent, because the returns from Project A will not be realized until the third year, whereas the returns from Project B will be distributed equally over the three years.

Year	Project A	Project B
1	$ 0	$100
2	0	100
3	300	100
	$300	$300

You can easily understand why timing should be taken into account if you ask yourself whether you would rather receive $100 today or a year from now. Probably, like most people, you would prefer to receive the money today. Investors, too, prefer current receipts; so they will place a higher value on shares of the company's stock if it accepts Project B than if it accepts Project A. Therefore, the value of the shareholders' stock will be increased if the company uses wealth maximization, not profit maximization, as its criterion for making investment decisions.

Measurement. A major problem in using profit maximization as the financial goal of the firm is variability in the way firms measure profits. Any firm's profits can be changed appreciably by changes in accounting techniques. To demonstrate, let's examine three generally accepted methods of accounting for inventory costs—first-in, first-out (FIFO); last-in, first-out (LIFO); and average cost—and their impact on profits.

Let's say that a firm purchases 10 items for inventory at $5 each and then 10 more items at $8 each, as shown in Table 1–2. (For simplicity's sake, we'll also say the firm had no inventory before it made these purchases.) If the firm uses FIFO, it will assume that items are sold from this inventory in the order in which they were purchased. Thus, if 15 items are sold, 10 items will be

Table 1–2
Effect of Inventory Accounting on Profit

Inventory Costs during Period

	FIFO	LIFO	Average Cost
First inventory purchase (10 items at $5 each)	$ 50	$ 50	$ 50
Second inventory purchase (10 items at $8 each)	80	80	80
Total inventory purchases	$130	$130	$130
Cost of goods sold (15 items)	10 at $5 = $50	10 at $8 = $80	15 at $6.50[a] = $97.50
	5 at $8 = $40	5 at $5 = $25	
Total cost of goods sold	$90	$105	$97.50

Inventory Balance at End of Period

Beginning inventory (assumed)	$ 0	$ 0	$ 0
Total inventory purchases	130	130	130.00
Less total cost of goods sold	90	105	97.50
Value of ending inventory	$ 40	$ 25	$ 32.50

Profit

Gross sales (15 items at $12 each)	$180	$180	$180.00
Less total cost of goods sold	90	105	97.50
Gross profit	$ 90	$ 75	$ 82.50

[a]Average cost of units is $6.50 ($5.00 + $8.00 = $13.00/2 = $6.50).

assigned a cost of $5 each, and 5 items will be assigned a cost of $8 each. The total cost of goods sold is $90, as you can see in the first column of Table 1-2. Because inventory purchases total $130 and the cost of goods sold totals $90, remaining inventory is valued at $40. Let's say the 15 items sold were priced at $12 each, giving a gross sales figure of $180. With cost of goods sold at $90, profit is $90.

If, instead, the firm uses LIFO, the results are quite different, as shown in the second column of Table 1–2. Here, the cost of the last items purchased is assigned first. Profit under the LIFO method is $75.

Finally, if the firm uses the average cost method, it will determine inventory cost by calculating the arithmetic average of inventory purchases. Profit when this method is used equals $82.50, as shown in the third column of the table.

Short-Run versus Long-Run Objectives. Profit maximization tends to demand short-run planning strategies, which may not maximize wealth in the long run. For example, to maximize profit a firm may cut costs—perhaps by reducing the quality of its output. Cost cutting was the course chosen by managers of the Joseph Schlitz Brewing Company in the early 1980s. Schlitz managers decided to increase profits by lowering the quality of the ingredients used in the company's beer. It did not take long for customers to recognize the difference in quality, however, and the reputation of the firm was harmed. The changed attitude of consumers influenced investors, and many sold their Schlitz stock, depressing share prices and decreasing shareholder wealth. (Later, Schlitz recognized the errors it had made and changed its policies.)

An extreme case of short-run profit maximization would be a firm's selling all its earning assets (plant, equipment, and so on), paying off its liabilities, and distributing the remainder to the shareholders. Clearly, that would not be the best course for shareholders of a business with good long-term prospects. It is important to note, however, that it might benefit shareholders of a firm in a declining industry (buggy whips, for example), because it might produce more wealth than continuing to operate would. Thus, short-run profit maximization is not always incompatible with wealth maximization.

A related problem involves shareholders' goals. Shareholders are concerned about the distribution of earnings. Cash dividends are the only financial return they realize until they sell their stock. On the other hand, distributing all earnings as cash dividends would not be in the best long-run interests of the shareholders, because it would reduce the firm's ability to grow in value. Consequently, financial managers know there must be a trade-off between the amount of earnings retained to finance corporate growth and the amount paid out to shareholders in the form of cash dividends. Firms that are growing rapidly and that must borrow large sums to support that growth will probably pay little or no cash dividends. Firms that are growing at a slower pace may share more of their earnings with stockholders. Management must balance long-term against short-term needs of shareholders and choose the course of action that will maximize shareholder wealth.

Conflicting Goals Although maximizing shareholder wealth is stressed throughout the text as the firm's appropriate financial goal, we must recognize that other groups make claims on firms that affect shareholder wealth adversely. Four readily identifiable claimant groups are management, labor, consumers, and government.

As business concerns grow, ownership becomes increasingly separated from management; that is, the owners of large firms—the shareholders—are not likely to be the firms' managers. One effect of this phenomenon is to create costs for the owners. The owners' costs of monitoring the behavior of managers, limiting their activities, and compensating them are called **agency costs**. Another effect is to separate the owners from the everyday decision making of the firm. Firms such as General Electric and Exxon employ thousands of people around the world; it is difficult to imagine that the goal of each of these employees is to maximize the wealth of an unknown shareholder living in Gordo, Alabama. To get the cooperation of everyone involved, the owners receive audited reports of the firm's activities and offer incentives in the form of management contracts.

Functions of Financial Management

The goals of financial management are addressed through the functions of financial management, which can be placed in three categories: investment decisions, financing decisions, and analysis and planning. Let's examine these broad categories in more detail.

Investment Decisions **Investment decisions** involve the allocation of resources among various types of assets. What proportion of the firm's funds should be invested in **financial assets**, such as cash, securities, and receivables, and what proportion in **real assets**, such as inventories and plant and equipment? The asset mix affects the amount of income the firm can earn. For example, a manufacturer is in business to earn income with real assets—such as machinery—not with financial assets. However, placing too high a percentage of its assets in a new building or new machinery may leave the firm short of cash to meet an unexpected need or exploit a sudden opportunity. The firm's financial manager must invest enough in real assets, but not too much. Besides determining the asset mix, financial managers must also decide what types of financial and real assets to acquire.

Financing Decisions **Financing decisions** involve raising funds for the firm. Thus, while investment decisions are related to the asset side of the balance sheet, financing decisions are related to the liabilities and equity side, as shown in Figure 1–1. When firms make financing decisions, they must consider a number of factors, in-

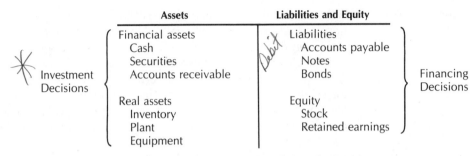

Figure 1–1   Balance Sheet Related to Investment and Financing Decisions

cluding capital structure, risk, cost of funds, availability of funds, timing, and distribution of earnings.

Capital Structure.   The **capital structure** of a firm is its mix of debt and equity. Financial managers decide which mix is best. Several factors affect a firm's capital structure; one of them involves the firm's expected earnings. Generally, firms that expect stable earnings can borrow proportionately more funds than firms whose earnings are less predictable. Lenders may worry that firms with unstable earnings will experience shortfalls in revenue and fail to repay their debt. Debt requires the firm to make interest and principal payments as scheduled or face bankruptcy. Suppliers of funds recognize the risk this involves and take it into account when deciding how much to lend.

Risk.   The concept of risk is especially important in decisions concerning capital structure. When a firm borrows funds, the lender expects to be repaid according to the terms of the lending agreement. If a firm is unable to raise sufficient revenue over time by selling its products or services to repay the borrowed funds, it will go bankrupt—the ultimate risk for a firm.

Cost.   One function of financial management is to minimize the cost of funds in order to maximize shareholder wealth. That involves examining all alternative sources of financing. A firm may, for example, decide to issue bonds instead of stock. Bonds are a form of debt and thus represent more risk than stock. On the other hand, bonds cost less than stock, for reasons that will be explained in later chapters. Here, the firm accepts the risk of borrowing in exchange for a lower cost of funds.

Availability.   During periods of credit restraint, or tight money—such as the early 1980s—banks and other financial institutions restrict the amount of funds they will lend to some businesses. During such periods, the availability of funds may be a more important consideration than their cost.

Timing.   Knowing when to borrow may be difficult. Suppose interest rates are high but are expected to decline within three months' time. Should the firm borrow all the funds it needs now by taking a long-term loan at current interest rates? Or should it take a short-term loan now and hope to refinance the borrowing with a long-term loan if interest rates decline? Making the correct decision may make the difference between profit and loss, success and bankruptcy.

Distribution of Earnings.   As mentioned earlier, shareholders may expect to receive some part of the firm's earnings as cash dividends. However, earnings that are retained may represent an important source of funds to the firm. Financial managers must decide how much of the firm's earnings should be paid out and how much retained.

Analysis and Planning   To make effective investment and financing decisions, financial management must analyze and plan. **Analysis** is the process of monitoring the current performance of the company. Analyzing trends and key financial indicators often helps financial managers detect potential problems. In addition to serving as an early warning system, analysis provides a useful means of comparing the firm's performance with that of others in the same industry.

Planning includes the evaluation of major opportunities and threats facing the company. Evaluating potential acquisitions and formulating strategies to avoid being acquired are part of the planning process. One benefit of planning is that it shortens the reaction time to events. For example, having prepared in advance for a corporate "raid" will help a firm react quickly if it learns that T. Boone Pickens is about to attempt an unfriendly takeover.

Another advantage of planning is that it lets the firm know when financial decisions will have to be made. For example, a company that plans to increase its sales at a rate of 25 percent per year should double in size in about 3 years. Knowing that, financial management can make arrangements at the appropriate time to finance this growth by negotiating for lines of credit at banks and perhaps by selling additional bonds and stock. These funds might be earmarked to expand present facilities or to build a new plant to satisfy increasing demand. Evaluating such financing and investment decisions is part of the planning process.

Why Study Financial Management?

The chapter began by saying that all major business decisions have financial implications. The discussions of financial management's goals and functions should have illustrated this point. It follows, then, that understanding financial management is important for all managers.

Basic Knowledge Studying financial management, like studying political science or economics, helps people understand how the world works and helps them make better decisions in daily life. Financial management also forms the basis for other subjects. Broadly defined, the field of finance includes investment, security analysis, international finance, financial institutions, real estate finance, insurance, and the rapidly growing field of personal financial planning. A course in financial management only scratches the surface of finance as a field of study, but mastery of its principles is the foundation for more specialized pursuits.

Importance in the Firm Understanding the principles of financial management is, of course, crucial to financial managers. Let's look briefly at how financial managers fit into the firm's organizational structure. Figure 1–2 shows a typical organization chart. In this firm, the vice-president of finance is the highest-ranking financial manager. (Many firms call their highest-ranking financial manager the Chief Fi-

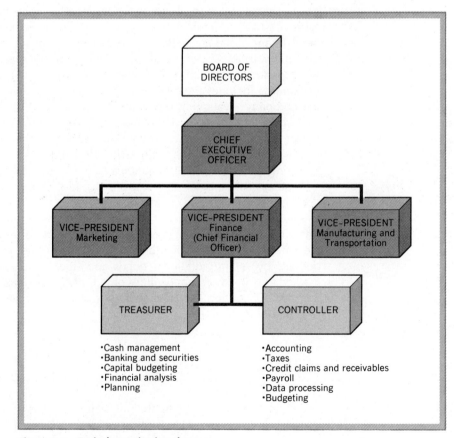

Figure 1–2 Typical organization chart.

nancial Officer, or CFO.) Our firm's vice-president of finance holds direct authority over the treasurer and the controller, whose areas of responsibility are listed in the figure. Although the responsibilities of treasurer and controller may vary from organization to organization, the major areas outlined in Figure 1–2 generally come under the control of a firm's financial manager. They include managing cash flow, arranging bank loans, purchasing and selling securities, supervising the capital budgeting process, and carrying out financial analysis and planning, as well as holding responsibility for accounting, taxes, credit, payroll, and data processing.

Financial managers interact with others in the firm. Accordingly, managers in other functional areas will be able to contribute more meaningfully to the overall management process if they understand the basic tools and concepts of financial management. For example, a marketing manager may see an exciting opportunity to launch a new product. Developing the product may require taking on new debt. However, an expected rise in interest rates may make borrowing unwise. Understanding this basic fact of financial management will make the marketing manager a more productive member of the management team. Again, virtually all decisions made in a company affect the value of the firm. Any decision—to expand into new markets, to modernize equipment, to change health insurance benefits for employees, even to add a new water fountain—affects the wealth of shareholders.

Organization of the Book

This book is divided into eight parts. An examination of the subjects of these parts reveals that most of the book is concerned with investment and financing decisions for business concerns.

Part 1. An Overview of Financial Management
Part 2. Valuation and the Cost of Capital
Part 3. Capital Investment Decisions
Part 4. Capital Structure
Part 5. Tools for Financial Analysis and Planning
Part 6. Working Capital Management
Part 7. Sources of Funds
Part 8. Special Topics

Let's look briefly at each part.

An Overview of Financial Management The first part of the book, which includes this chapter and the next three, describes the environment within which businesses operate. Chapter 2 looks at the cycles that affect business, including the product life cycle and business cycles. Chapter 3 explains the various forms of business organization and the taxes each must pay. Finally, Chapter 4 discusses the financial system and the corporate securities markets, where businesses raise a substantial portion of their funds.

Valuation and the Cost of Capital　As mentioned earlier, increasing the value of the firm is of primary importance to the financial manager. But what is value? Part 2 comprises three chapters that address that question. Chapter 5 explains the time value of money—a concept that must be understood before value can be discussed. Chapter 6 explains the meaning of value and describes the kinds of returns investors can expect. Chapter 7 discusses the cost of capital—a specific rate of return used in valuation and in making investment decisions.

Capital Investment Decisions　Economists use the term **capital investment** to describe goods used in the production of commodities or other goods. **Capital** includes plant, equipment, and other large-scale investments. Part 3, which includes Chapters 8 and 9, evaluates capital budgeting techniques, which may be used to determine whether a given capital investment is economically feasible.

Capital Structure　Capital structure, as mentioned earlier, is a firm's mix of debt and equity. Firms that have a great deal of debt relative to equity are said to be highly leveraged, a condition that affects both earnings per share and the risk of bankruptcy. Chapter 10, the first chapter in Part 4, examines some of the implications of financial leverage. Chapter 11 deals with dividend policy. Dividend policy affects capital structure because retaining earnings adds to equity.

Tools for Financial Analysis and Planning　Every trade has its tools. Part 5 presents some of the basic tools used in financial management. Chapter 12 discusses break-even analysis, a technique for examining the relationship of a firm's revenues, costs, and profits. The analysis of financial statements is covered in Chapter 13, and Chapter 14 describes forecasting and planning.

Working Capital Management　Investment decisions, you may remember, involve the allocation of financial assets. The assets listed first on a firm's balance sheet include cash and investments in securities, receivables, and inventories, which make up the firm's working capital. Part 6 explains various methods for using these resources most effectively. Chapter 15 discusses working capital policy, while Chapters 16, 17, and 18 examine the components of working capital—cash and short-term securities, accounts receivable, and inventories.

Sources of Funds While the first six parts of the book are largely concerned with making the best investment and financing decisions, Part 7 focuses on sources of funds. Where does a firm obtain external funds? Part of that question is answered in Chapter 4, where the corporate securities markets are examined. In Chapters 19 to 23, the rest of the answer is revealed in a detailed analysis of the other sources of funds. Chapter 19 describes various short-term and intermediate-term sources of financing. Leasing, bonds, and stocks are discussed in Chapters 20, 21, and 22; and Chapter 23 examines convertibles, warrants, and rights.

Special Topics Part 8 contains two chapters. The first, Chapter 24, explains how some firms grow externally by acquiring other firms and why some firms may decide to reduce their size by selling off part of their operations. The book's final chapter, Chapter 25, discusses international business finance, an area that is becoming increasingly important as more firms invest and borrow funds outside their own countries.

Summary

Financial management is the process of making efficient use of financial and real resources to increase the value of the firm. As the practice of financial management has changed over time, so has the way financial management is taught. The content of financial management courses has shifted from descriptive to analytical, from an emphasis on various specific aspects of finance toward an emphasis on the best use of all resources, from the assumption of a static environment to the assumption of a dynamic one, and from the perspective of an outsider to the perspective of a decision maker in the firm.

Financial management must start with goals and objectives. The maximization of shareholders' wealth, measured by the market value of the company's shares, is the objective of today's professional financial managers. It is superior to profit maximization as a goal because it recognizes risk, takes timing into account, is less susceptible to problems of measurement, and emphasizes long-term objectives.

Basically, financial managers perform three functions as they work to meet their objectives. They make investment decisions, which involve the selection of assets, and financing decisions, which deal with the acquisition of funds. They also are involved in analysis and planning.

Because all business decisions have financial implications, understanding financial management is important for all managers and, of course, particularly important for financial managers. The rest of this book offers theory and tools that will help you understand and practice the fundamentals of financial management.

Important Terms

Agency cost | Financing decision
Analysis | Investment decision
Capital | Maximization of shareholder wealth
Capital budgeting | Planning
Capital investment | Portfolio theory
Capital structure | Profit maximization
Financial asset | Real asset
Financial management | Risk

Questions

1. Define *financial management.*
2. How does the modern study of finance differ from that of the past?
3. What is the appropriate goal of financial management? In what way is the achievement of this goal measured?
4. Compare and discuss profit maximization and wealth maximization.
5. Why is timing of receipts an important consideration in achieving the goals of financial management?
6. Give an example of a financial decision in which *risk* is involved.
7. Explain the effects on profit measurement of the LIFO, FIFO, and average cost methods of accounting for inventory.
8. Give an example of the ways in which long-term goals may be sacrificed for short-term goals.
9. Explain the three main functions of the financial manager.
10. Discuss what is meant by *investment decision* and *financing decision.*
11. What issues must be considered in the capital structure decision. Why?
12. What is the purpose of financial analysis and planning and how does the financial manager use these techniques to improve decision making?
13. What is the usual role of the treasurer of a firm? Of the controller?

Problems

1. Bookstore X and Bookstore Y each sold 1,000 finance textbooks at $30 apiece in 1987. Both stores purchased the textbooks they sold from the publisher in three lots of 400 books per lot. The first 400-book lot cost $22.50 per book; the second lot cost $24.50 per book; and the third order cost $25 per book. Bookstore X uses the FIFO method of accounting for inventory, whereas Bookstore Y uses LIFO.
   (a) Which store was more profitable in 1987?
   (b) Was this same store more successful at maximizing shareholder wealth? Explain.
2. Suppose instead that Firm X used the average cost method for inventory accounting. How would your answers to Problem 1 change?

The Dynamic Environment

Knowing when to do something is often as important as knowing what to do. Knowing when is of crucial importance for financial management, because the conditions under which firms operate are always changing. One reason for change is that firms grow and mature over time, evolving through stages of development that resemble a life cycle. Another reason for change involves the economy. In some respects, economic activity is similar to the tides in the ocean; it perpetually ebbs and flows. Such movements are called business cycles. Inflation also creates changes that affect costs and profits. Finally, government policies, which affect all businesses, undergo frequent changes. This chapter examines life cycles, business cycles, inflation, and the role of government in the economy, as well as the impact of all these factors on financial management.

After reading this chapter, you should know the following.

1. **What a product life cycle is.**
2. **How the phases of the product life cycle affect financial policies.**
3. **What problems business cycles pose for financial decision makers.**
4. **What strategies financial managers use during each phase of a business cycle.**
5. **How inflation affects investment and financing decisions.**
6. **How government affects business.**

The Product Life Cycle

All products, companies, and industries evolve through certain stages of development. By convention, these stages are grouped under the name **product life cycle**, although they apply not only to products but to companies and other forms of organization and to entire industries. The concept of the life cycle is particularly important for financial management because companies' financial needs and financial constraints change as the companies develop over time. Early recognition of these needs and constraints enables the financial manager to make better policy decisions. The product life cycle is used throughout this book to illustrate the interaction between financial policies and corporate growth.

The Typical Life Cycle
The typical product life cycle is shown in Figure 2–1.[1] The vertical axis represents dollar amounts expressed in real terms—that is, the effects of inflation are not taken into account. The horizontal axis represents time and is divided into four phases of development: pioneering, expansion, stabilization, and decline. The figure tracks price per unit, total sales, and profits over the course of a typical life cycle.

The Pioneering Phase. The **pioneering phase** of the life cycle is characterized by the introduction of a new product by a limited number of firms. Because the volume of production and sales is low and development costs must be recovered, the market price of the new product tends to be high. Another result of high costs and low volume is that firms in this phase of development frequently experience losses on the product.

The personal computer industry offers a good example of this life-cycle phase. The industry's principle innovator was Apple Computer, Inc., founded in 1977. Apple introduced its Apple I personal computer in 1978. At that time, the price for an Apple I with a relatively small amount of memory and no disk drives or monitor was about $1,800. The product enjoyed instant success and the firm introduced the Apple II the following year. From 1977 to 1979, Apple's net profit went from zero to $5.1 million.

The Expansion Phase. The **expansion phase** of the life cycle is characterized by increasing competition, declining prices, and rising industry profits. It is a period of spectacular successes—and spectacular failures. Only the fittest firms will survive.

[1]Charles Hofer, "Toward a Contingency Theory of Business Strategy," *Academy of Management Journal*, December 1975, pp. 784–810. This article is an excellent reference for students who want to learn more about life cycles as they relate to business problems.

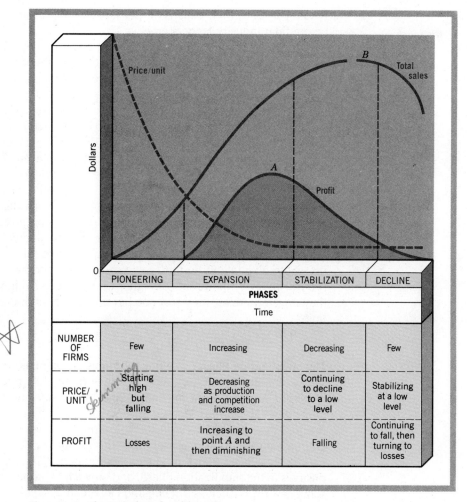

	PIONEERING	EXPANSION	STABILIZATION	DECLINE
NUMBER OF FIRMS	Few	Increasing	Decreasing	Few
PRICE/ UNIT	Starting high but falling	Decreasing as production and competition increase	Continuing to decline to a low level	Stabilizing at a low level
PROFIT	Losses	Increasing to point A and then diminishing	Falling	Continuing to fall, then turning to losses

Figure 2–1   The typical product life cycle.

In the personal computer industry, Apple's profits reached $44 million in 1985. By then, its success had attracted more than 150 competitors, including Tandy (Radio Shack), IBM, Hewlett-Packard, Digital Equipment, and others. Increased production and sales of personal computers drove prices down. In one 18-month period (December 1981 to June 1983), prices of personal computers fell 75 percent.[2] By 1985, about $1,300 would buy an Apple with a disk drive, a monitor, and four times as much memory as the Apple that cost $1,800 in 1978. Lower prices, along with poor management decisions, contributed to the failure of Osborne Computer Corporation, Archieves Inc., and Victor Technologies, Inc., to name a few. Because the personal computer

[2]Bro Uttal, "Sudden Shake-Up in Home Computers," *Fortune*, July 11, 1983, pp. 105–106.

industry is still in the expansion phase of the life cycle, other firms may fail before final industry leaders emerge.

Although costs are not depicted in Figure 2–1, they should be mentioned here in connection with profit. Microeconomic theory tells us that a firm's profit is highest when marginal revenue equals marginal cost—that is, when the revenue from the last unit sold equals the cost of producing the unit. The point of greatest profit, marked Point A on Figure 2–1, occurs during the expansion phase. Beyond that point, the cost of each unit sold is greater than the revenue it produces, and total profit declines. Notice that total sales revenue continues to increase after total profit has peaked. Therefore, the point of maximum profit, Point A, precedes the point of maximum sales, Point B.

Cost is also important in pricing, and pricing affects profit. IBM, for example, mass-produces personal computers in automated factories where a computer is made about every 45 seconds. Low production cost gives IBM an advantage over higher-cost producers. Recall that profit is the difference between revenue and cost. If IBM cut prices, revenue per unit would fall; but if IBM's costs per unit were also falling by the same amount, the company could maintain its profit. However, the profits of higher-cost producers might be endangered. If they lowered prices, their revenue per unit could fall more than their cost per unit.

The Stabilization Phase.   During the **stabilization phase** of the life cycle, total sales continue to increase, but at a slower rate, while prices decline to a low level and profits fall. At the same time, the number of firms in the industry continues to decline. Because the personal computer industry has not yet reached this phase, let's turn to the automobile industry for an illustration. During the expansion phase of this industry's life cycle, about 1,500 companies in the United States produced automobiles.[3] Today, the automobile industry is in the stabilization phase, and only a few producers remain. Although some new firms (such as Bricklin and DeLorean) have tried to enter the industry in recent years, all have stopped production because of financial difficulties.

The fact that a wide variety of automobile models is available today at relatively low prices tells us something about the firms that survived the stabilization phase. Each firm has three essential characteristics.

1. Sufficient *capital* to finance expansion and continue operations in spite of falling prices.
2. Sufficient *technology* to provide a continuous stream of new products.
3. Sufficient *scale*, or size, to allow mass production at the lowest possible cost.

[3]Donald L. Kemmerer and C. Clyde Jones, *American Economic History* (New York: McGraw-Hill, 1959), p. 325.

At the top of the sales curve shown in Figure 2–1 is a break in the line. This break represents the fact that the stabilization phase may last longer for some products, firms, or industries than for others. For electric utilities, for example, this phase may go on for many years. In some high-technology industries, it may last for a year or less.

The Declining Phase. The **declining phase** of the life cycle is characterized by decreasing sales and falling profits that ultimately turn into losses. As this process occurs, the number of firms in the industry continues to drop. However, firms in decline need not go out of business, a fact that will be explained in the following discussion of alternate shapes for the life cycle.

Alternate Shapes for the Life Cycle Not all life cycles look like the standard one depicted in Figure 2–1. Figures 2–2, 2–3, and 2–4 show three life cycles with different shapes. Unlike Figure 2–1, these figures show only the sales curve of the life cycle.

Fads. Figure 2–2 shows one possible life-cycle shape for fad products, such as Cabbage Patch dolls, Hula-Hoops, and Frisbees. The sales of such products increase rapidly, then drop abruptly when the fad ends. After a sharp decline, sales may continue to fall, at a more gradual rate, until the product disappears from the market.

Rejuvenation. Figure 2–3 illustrates the effect of **rejuvenation** on the life cycle. Let's consider ceiling fans as an example. Ceiling fans were widely used for cooling homes during the early part of this century; but when air conditioning became popular, they nearly disappeared from use. Ceiling fans were

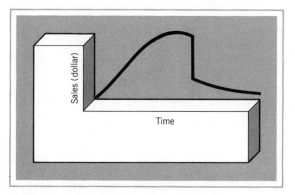

Figure 2–2   A life-cycle shape for a fad product.

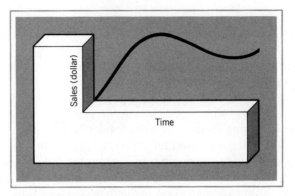

Figure 2–3   The effect of rejuvenation on the life cycle.

rejuvenated when soaring energy costs in the late 1970s and early 1980s forced consumers to seek less expensive means of cooling.

There are two important lessons to be learned here. First, external factors, such as changes in technology, may have a major influence on the ability of well-managed firms to survive. Air conditioning altered the need for ceiling fans; automobiles altered the need for horse-drawn wagons; hand-held calculators altered the need for slide rules; and so on. Second, industries, firms, or products in the declining phase of the life cycle may be rejuvenated. Ceiling fans are only one example. It is not difficult to imagine how fuel shortages and higher energy costs might rejuvenate railroads, windmill manufacturing, and coal mining.

Extending the Term.   Figure 2–4 illustrates the effects of new products on a company's life cycle. In this example, we see how the Quarter Pounder, the Egg McMuffin, and a growing list of new products have affected McDonald's growth. The cumulative effect of such new products is to extend the life cycle

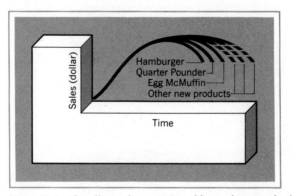

Figure 2–4   The effects of new McDonald's products on the firm's life cycle.

and prolong growth. Thus, the life cycle of a firm may incorporate the life cycles of many products.

Financial Aspects of the Life Cycle Knowing a company's location on the life cycle provides useful information about the company's financial requirements and some of its prospects for the future. Figure 2–5 shows the approximate locations of four companies on the life cycle.[4]

The first company, Advanced Micro Devices, Inc. (AMD), manufactures microprocessors, computer memories, and other high-technology computer and communications equipment. Its position in the expansion phase of the life cycle suggests that its sales will continue to grow rapidly. It also suggests that the firm faces a high degree of risk, because many firms do not survive the intense competition of this phase.

The second firm, McDonald's Corporation (MCD), has survived the competition. McDonald's is the leader in the fast-food business, with more than 8,000 outlets. The location of this firm in the stabilization phase indicates that its sales will continue to grow, but at a slower pace than before.

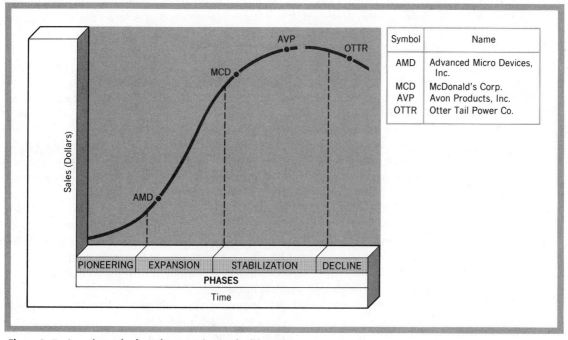

Symbol	Name
AMD	Advanced Micro Devices, Inc.
MCD	McDonald's Corp.
AVP	Avon Products, Inc.
OTTR	Otter Tail Power Co.

Figure 2–5 Locations of selected companies on the life cycle.

[4]Information on the companies described here can be found in the *Value Line Investment Survey*, Standard and Poor's, and Moody's Investment Services, which are available in most university libraries.

Table 2–1
Selected Financial Aspects of the Life Cycle

	Phases of the Life Cycle			
	Pioneering	**Expansion**	**Stabilization**	**Decline**
Cash needs	Heavy	Heavy, but increasing at a lower rate	Declining; some companies generate more cash than they need	Continuing to decline; companies may generate cash for a time but eventually experience losses
Dividend policies	No cash dividend	Small but increasing cash dividend	Increasing cash dividend	Large cash dividend until losses occur
Systematic risk	High	High	Average	Low

Avon Products (AVP), the world's largest manufacturer of cosmetics and toiletries, is the third firm. It is a mature company that entered the stabilization phase some time ago. Because of its position, Avon's future growth will probably be relatively slow.

The fourth firm, Otter Tail Power Company (OTTR), has entered the declining phase of the life cycle. Otter Tail Power supplies electricity to customers in Minnesota, North Dakota, and South Dakota. Otter Tail's management has estimated its growth at about 4 percent per year for the rest of the 1980s and at a lower rate after that.

It is important to keep certain cautions in mind when considering a firm's placement on the life cycle. One is that placement on the life cycle is to some extent a matter of judgment; no precise method exists for making that determination. Moreover, the phases of the life cycle are functional measures that do not represent specific amounts of time. Thus, Avon Products could remain in the stabilization phase of the life cycle for many years to come. It is also possible that some external factor, such as new industrial growth in its geographical area, could alter Otter Tail's projections and rejuvenate that firm. In other words, each firm must be judged according to its own unique situation, not just according to its position in the life cycle.

Against this background, let's consider the cash needs, the dividend policies, and the riskiness of each of the four companies. These financial aspects of the life cycle are summarized in Table 2–1.

Cash Needs. Companies in the pioneering phase of the life cycle need a great deal of cash to finance research and development and to market new products. (The term **cash** is used here in a general sense, to mean all the funds a firm has at its disposal.) During the expansion phase of the cycle, a strong demand for cash still exists. Cash is needed to fund new plant and equipment and to provide working capital (such as inventory) to increase the market share. When the company enters the stabilization phase, the demand for cash tapers off. The company is well established, and expansion occurs at a reduced rate. Some firms in this phase of the life cycle generate more funds than they need to finance their continued operations. (Such firms are sometimes called **cash cows**.) Many companies in the declining phase of the life cycle also generate large amounts of cash, but they finally experience losses.

Dividend Policies.   Cash dividend policies reflect both cash requirements and the ability to generate cash. During the pioneering phase of the life cycle, companies generally experience losses and have no earnings from which to pay cash dividends. During the expansion phase, earnings increase and companies may have more funds than they need to finance growth. Accordingly, dividends tend to be small in the early part of the expansion phase and to increase steadily as the company matures through the life cycle.

A term used in discussions of dividend policy is **dividend payout ratio**, which is the cash dividend per share expressed as a percentage of earnings per share. Table 2–2 lists some dividend payout ratios for our four companies. Advanced Micro Devices, in the early part of the expansion phase, pays no cash dividend. AMD retains all its earnings to help finance its growth rather than paying out some of them to stockholders. McDonald's is in the early stabilization phase of the life cycle. The firm paid its first cash dividend in 1976, when it was in the expansion phase. Since then, McDonald's has evolved into the stabilization phase, and the dividend payout ratio has increased over the years. As mentioned, companies' dividend payout ratios tend to increase as the companies mature. This certainly seems to be the case for Avon and Otter Tail Power, whose dividend payout ratios are quite high.

Risk.   The trade-off between risk and expected returns is a theme that is stressed throughout this text. In the context of a life cycle, we know that new

Table 2–2

Dividend Payout Ratios for Companies from Figure 2–5

Company: Phase: Year	AMD Expansion	MCD Stabilization[a] (%)	AVP Stabilization (%)	OTTR Decline (%)
1975	Nil	Nil	65	82
1980	Nil	13	74	90
1986[b]	Nil	18	89	78

[a]MCD moved from the expansion phase to the stabilization phase during this 10-year period.
[b]Projected.

firms and small firms are more likely to fail than larger, mature firms that have survived the trials of competition. Firms fail for many reasons: adverse changes in economic conditions, changes in technology that eliminate the need for their products, bad management, insufficient revenue or funds to cover expenses, and excessive debt are just a few of them. Thus, firms face many kinds of risk.

Recall that risk was defined in the preceding chapter as the chance that future returns would be different from what was expected. This chapter uses one measure of risk, called systematic risk, to illustrate how risk changes over the course of a life cycle. **Systematic risk** is risk common to all firms. For example, a major economic depression would have an adverse affect on all businesses' returns.

Systematic risk is measured by a statistic called the **beta coefficient,** or beta. This statistic is explained in more detail in later chapters. For the moment, it is sufficient to say that it measures the sensitivity of one stock's returns compared with the returns for the entire stock market. (Here, **returns** equal cash dividends plus changes in the market price of the stock.) A stock with a beta of 1.00 behaves the same as the stock market as a whole, as represented by the Standard & Poor's index or some other measure of stock market activity. A stock with a beta of more than 1.00 is considered subject to higher systematic risk than the market, because its returns tend to fluctuate more in either direction than those of the market as a whole. A beta of less than 1.00 means that a stock is less volatile—less risky—than the market.

In general, systematic risk is greatest during the early phases of the life cycle and then diminishes as the cycle evolves. Table 2–3 lists betas for our four companies. The table shows that Advanced Micro Devices, which is in the expansion phase of the life cycle, has a beta of 1.65. This high beta suggests considerable systematic risk, but we can expect the risk to diminish if the company survives. By the time companies have reached the stabilization phase of the life cycle, their systematic risk has decreased substantially. McDonald's beta coefficient is 1.10, and those for Avon and Otter Tail Power are lower yet.

Beta coefficients and dividend payout ratios offer two examples of how financial characteristics change as firms mature. Later discussions in this book will demonstrate how life cycle changes affect working capital needs, as well as investment and financing decisions.

Table 2–3
Systematic Risk of Companies from Figure 2–5

Company	Phase	Beta
AMD	Expansion	1.65
MCD	Stabilization	1.10
AVP	Stabilization	0.95
OTTR	Decline	0.65

Business Cycles

The **business cycle,** like the life cycle, affects financial management. The economic expansions and contractions that make up business cycles are inherent in capitalist economic systems. However, business cycles do not affect

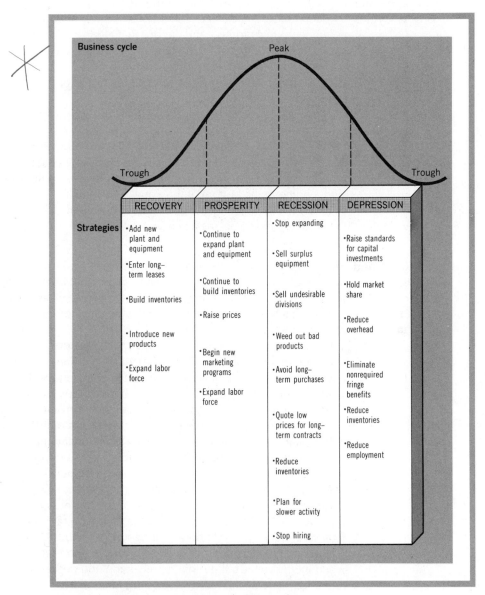

Figure 2–6 Selected strategies during business cycles.

all sectors of the economy in the same way. For example, cattle prices do not necessarily rise or fall at the same time as housing and automobile prices. Nevertheless, we can get a general idea of how business cycles affect management decisions by looking at Figure 2–6 on the previous page.

Management Decisions and Business Cycles As shown in Figure 2–6, the business cycle is divided into four phases: recovery, prosperity, recession, and depression. During the **recovery** phase, as economic activity is expanding, strategies include expansion of plant, equipment, inventories, and labor. Recovery is a time to enter long-term leases, because costs are relatively low. Business activity continues to expand during the **prosperity** phase of the business cycle, but at a reduced rate. Strategies for this phase include continued expansion of plant, equipment, inventories, and labor.

As signals begin to appear that expansion is slowing and that the peak of the cycle is in sight, managers must prepare for **recession**, when economic contraction begins. This is the time to begin reducing real assets by cutting back on excessive inventories and equipment and avoiding contracts that would commit the firm to high future costs. Recession then slides into **depression**, ending in the bottom of the trough. Now the firm must cut costs as much as it can without losing its market share. Eventually, the depression ends and the recovery phase begins again.

Interest Rates and Business Cycles Figure 2–7 illustrates the relationship between business cycles and short-term and long-term interest rates. The figure shows that interest rates tend to follow the general pattern of business activity. That is, when business activity increases, interest rates tend to rise; and when business activity declines, interest rates tend to fall.

Interest rates are an important concern for financial managers. Suppose, for example, that you are the financial manager of a large firm that wants to raise $50 million to build a new plant and buy new equipment. The business cycle is in the recovery phase. Should you borrow the $50 million in short-term funds or in long-term funds? As you can see from the figure, the short-term rate is lower than the long-term rate. However, as other chapters of this book will explain, it is sound financial policy to match the maturity of the liabilities with the maturity of the assets. Therefore, because you are financing long-lived assets, you may want to borrow long-term funds—and borrow them now, before both long-term and short-term rates rise higher.

Consider this problem. At the peak of the business cycle, your firm wants to borrow $75 million for 10 years. The long-term rate is lower than the short-term rate; so should you borrow long-term or short-term funds? In this case, you may be better off borrowing at the higher short-term rate. Why? Because when interest rates fall during the recession and depression to come, you can refinance the loan and borrow long-term funds at a lower rate for the remainder of the 10-year period. More will be said about such financing decisions in later chapters.

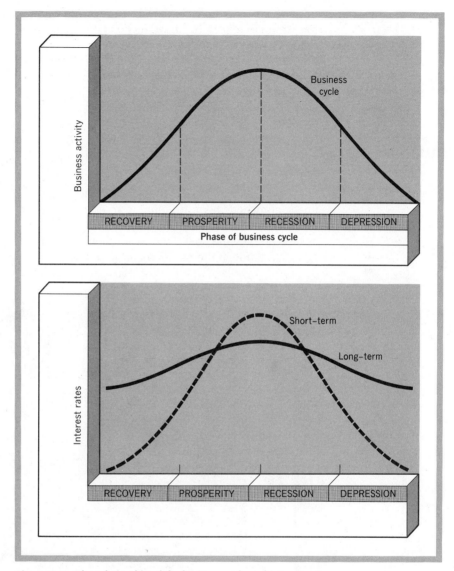

Figure 2–7   The relationship of the business cycle and interest rates.

Mergers and Another sort of decision affected by business cycles involves **mergers**, com-
Business Cycles binations of firms. In 1980, National Steel Corporation predicted boom times
for the steel industry.[5] The company spent millions of dollars to automate and
modernize its facilities and sought new markets for its steel. As part of its
expansion, National Steel diversified by buying savings and loan associations

[5]"Natural Intergroup: A New Name to Stress the Shift Away from Steel," *Business Week,* September 26, 1983, p. 82.

in San Francisco and Florida. The firm even changed its name to National Intergroup to reflect the new directions it planned to take. The plan was good, but the timing was bad. National Steel did not take the forthcoming recession into account. When the economy began to contract, demands for steel and home financing declined sharply. The company, after posting an $86 million profit in 1982, lost $144 million in 1983. It pays to watch the business cycle.

Inflation

Inflation is another aspect of economic activity that must be considered by financial management. **Inflation** is an erosion of the purchasing power of the dollar that results from price increases. As shown in Figure 2–8, U.S. prices as measured by the consumer price index (CPI) tripled during the period 1967 to 1986, although the rate of increase has slowed.

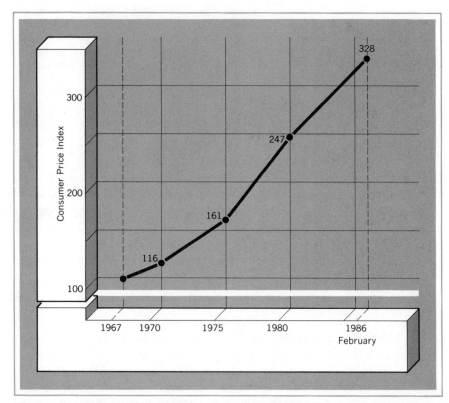

Figure 2–8 Inflation in the United States, 1967–1986. Although drawn as a straight line, the inflation rate between any two points on the graph, such as 1970 and 1975, varied from year to year.

Inflation affects the cost of funds as well as the prices of goods and services. The interest rate on Aaa (high-quality) bonds, for example, increased from 5.5 percent in 1967 to 15.5 percent in 1981, then declined to 9 percent in early 1986. Inflation also affects unit labor costs, which increased 60 percent faster than output per man hour during the 1967 to 1985 period. In other words, labor costs rose faster than productivity. These facts about inflation have important implications for financial management:

The cost of funds must be taken into account when capital investment decisions are made.

Fear of inflation and recessions creates uncertainty and some unwillingness to make capital investments. However, additional capital investment is necessary to increase productivity and profits.

Capital investment should replace marginal labor, thereby holding down future labor costs.

In an environment of inflation and recessions, deciding when to borrow becomes increasingly difficult. Therefore, financial strategies such as those suggested earlier, in Figure 2–6, should be employed.

Government and Business

Companies operate in a system bounded by laws, social expectations, and other constraints. In this section, we examine selected aspects of the role of government, beginning with the government's influence on economic activity.

Monetary and Fiscal Policies

Monetary policy—the Federal Reserve System's handling of the money supply—and **fiscal policy**—the government's spending and taxing—are to a large extent responsible for economic booms and busts. Because government policies influence the progress of business cycles and inflation, which in turn affect investment and financing decisions, financial managers must monitor monetary and fiscal policies and understand the implications of those policies for the future course of economic activity.

For example, an extended period of expansive monetary policy—that is, a period in which the money supply grows at an abnormally high rate—will drive the level of interest rates down in the short run. It would be easy to misinterpret the information conveyed by the lower interest rates and make bad financial decisions. Here's what might happen: The financial manager, associating the low interest rates with low inflation, might decide to invest in financial assets such as fixed-rate mortgages or bonds. That would be a bad decision because, in the long run, expansive monetary policies result in higher interest rate levels, inflation, and higher prices. When prices and interest rates increase, the value of such financial assets as fixed-rate mortgages and bonds decreases. A better decision would be to borrow funds at relatively low fixed rates and buy real assets that will appreciate in value in inflationary times.

Regulated Industries Certain industries that are "clothed with the public interest" are subject to public regulation. In 1887 the Interstate Commerce Commission was created to regulate the railroads, and later its jurisdiction was extended to include common and contract motor carriers. Some other federal regulatory agencies include the Federal Maritime Board, the Civil Aeronautics Board, the Federal Power Commission, and the Federal Communications Commission. The principal regulated industries are banks, railroads, gas and electric companies, and radio and television stations. In the case of the banking industry, regulations limit entry; they limit the extent to which banks can engage in other lines of business, such as insurance and leasing; they specify the amount of capital banks must have; and so on.

Under President Ronald Reagan's administration, the federal govenment has moved toward **deregulation** under the assumption that the public is better served by competition arising from the free market than by the prices and services delivered by some regulated industries.

Consider, for example, the case of the airline industry. For almost 50 years, it existed as a regulated industry. Both routes and prices were protected. Therefore, airlines had little incentive to hold down costs. The increased costs were passed on to consumers, who didn't have many choices of airlines or prices when they wanted to fly from New York to Miami, for example. Then, in the early 1980s, the rules under which the airline industry operated were changed. Routes and prices were no longer protected. Regulation was out and free-market competition was in. More than three-fourths of existing airlines' controllable costs were labor costs, and these costs were very high. But new entrants, which paid workers less, had lower labor costs and could offer lower prices. This upset the entire industry.

To make matters worse, deregulation's effects occurred during the 1982 to 1983 recession, the most severe since the 1930s. Continental Airlines finally declared bankruptcy, shut down for two days, and then began flying a reduced schedule, with about 35 percent of its former employees working for half their previous wages. Eastern Airlines also asked its employees to take a wage cut to avert corporate bankruptcy. For the airline industry, a regulatory environment seems to have contributed to management policies and practices that did not serve the long-run interests of the stockholders.

Antitrust Regulations Another area of government regulation involves laws meant to curb anticompetitive practices. The principal antitrust laws are listed here:

1. The **Sherman Antitrust Act** (1890) was designed to protect trade and commerce against unlawful restraint and monopoly.

2. The **Clayton Antitrust Act** (1914) supplemented the Sherman Act. One of the key provisions is Section 7, which forbids any corporation to acquire stock of any other corporation when the effect of the acquisition might be to substantially lessen competition or restrain trade.
3. The **Robinson-Patman Act** (1936) made certain types of price discrimination illegal.
4. The **Celler-Kefauver Act** (1950) strengthened Section 7 of the Clayton Act.

Although this listing is not complete, it is sufficient to suggest some of the major concerns of antitrust legislation. The federal government may prosecute companies it considers to be in violation of these laws. Many antitrust cases have involved large, well-known companies such as DuPont, IBM, and AT&T.

Government as a Buyer   The U.S. government affects businesses in yet another way: It is the largest single buyer of goods and services in the nation's economy. In 1985, the U.S. government spent $355 billion on goods and services. Of that total, $262 billion was spent for national defense. Major contracts involve millions of dollars, generating intense competition among bidders. In addition, many companies produce items primarily for government consumption.

Summary

Financial managers must take into account the dynamic environment within which businesses operate. That environment includes life cycles, business cycles, inflation, and government.

Every business evolves through stages of development that form a life cycle. During the pioneering phase of the cycle, businesses experience losses. Profits expand rapidly during the expansion phase and taper off during the stabilization phase. Unless the business expands its list of products or finds some method of rejuvenation, profits can be expected to decline during the declining phase. Similar patterns related to the life cycle affect cash requirements, dividend policies, risk, and other key financial variables.

The economic history of the United States records many wide swings in economic activity called business cycles. The four phases of the cycle are recovery, prosperity, recession, and depression. Firms should build inventories during the first two phases of the cycle and liquidate them over the remainder of the cycle. Other financial decisions must also take the business cycle into account, in part because of its effect on interest rates.

Inflation must be considered, too. The economic history of the United States suggests that the nation has periodically suffered from inflation. Because this is so, the rising cost of funds must be considered when financial decisions are made.

Finally, government plays an integral role in the U.S. economy. Government monetary and fiscal policies, as well as government regulations, affect every business concern. Government also affects businesses in its role as a buyer of goods and services.

Important Terms

Beta coefficient	Merger
Business cycle	Monetary policy
Cash	Pioneering phase
Cash cow	Product life cycle
Celler-Kefauver Act	Prosperity
Clayton Antitrust Act	Recession
Declining phase	Recovery
Depression	Rejuvenation
Regulation	Return
Dividend payout ratio	Robinson-Patman Act
Expansion phase	Sherman Antitrust Act
Fiscal policy	Stabilization phase
Inflation	Systematic risk

Questions

1. In general, why is it necessary for financial managers to understand the concept of the life cycle?
2. Do all firms have a life cycle? How might a manager determine the firm's current phase in the life cycle?
3. Which two phases of the life cycle are likely to be characterized by few firms and by anticipated losses? In what important ways are these two phases different?
4. Characterize the expansion phase of the life cycle with respect to unit price levels, potential profits, and cash needs.
5. In which phase of the life cycle is it probable that the number of firms will begin to diminish? Why is this so?
6. What three features are present in firms that survive the stabilization phase of the life cycle?
7. What strategy may firms use to postpone their entry into the declining phase of the life cycle?
8. In what phase of the life cycle is a firm likely to generate the most cash? How does this often affect shareholders?

9. Explain the term *systematic risk*? What is the measure of systematic risk called? How is the systematic risk of a firm affected by its stage in the life cycle?
10. What is the business cycle? Why must financial managers know about business cycles?
11. Explain the typical relationship between interest rate movements and phases of the business cycle.
12. Is it always best to borrow at the lowest possible interest rate, regardless of the maturity of the debt? Why or why not?
13. What are several ways in which inflation affects financial decision making?
14. Identify and explain the two major types of government policy that affect interest rates, inflation, and the business cycle.

Problems

1. Hawk Corporation reported earnings of $12 per share in 1988. Calculate the dividend payout ratio if cash dividends are $4 per share. The earnings not paid out are retained; what is the retention ratio? [Retention ratio = (1 − dividend payout ratio)].
2. Catoosa, Inc., is entering the stabilization phase of the life cycle and has established a dividend policy such that the firm's target payout ratio is 40 percent. Calculate the dividend per share stockholders will receive if the company earns $10 million in after-tax net income and if there are 1 million shares of common stock outstanding. (There is no preferred stock outstanding.)

The Operating Environment

Consider the various types of business concerns you deal with. The gas station is part of a large corporation. The fast-food restaurant is most likely a franchise. Your doctor may operate as a sole proprietor, as a partner in business with other physicians, or as a corporation. The university is a nonprofit organization. Understanding these forms of business organization is important for financial managers, because the form of an organization affects its ability to raise funds and its tax obligations.

After reading this chapter, you should know the following.

1. **What advantages and disadvantages are connected with the major forms of business organization.**
2. **What corporate and personal income tax rates are.**
3. **Why average tax rates are lower than marginal tax rates.**
4. **How depreciation affects taxes.**
5. **How, in general, to use the ACRS.**

The Structure of Business Organizations

Joe Bloch worked for IBM for 5 years before he decided to start his own business. He was in charge of a regional office that marketed IBM services to small and medium-sized business concerns. Joe discovered a gap in the services that were being offered and suggested to top managers that they explore the possibility of filling it. They rejected the idea; but Joe was convinced of its worth and viewed it as a golden opportunity for a new business—his business.

Joe established a sole proprietorship, a business he owned by himself, and called it Southwest Computing Services (SCS). SCS specialized in providing computing services for professional persons, such as doctors and lawyers. Because capital was limited, Joe did everything from sweeping to sales to programming. As the business grew, he hired people to take over some of these jobs and moved into larger quarters. That meant he had to put more money into the business to support its growth.

Joe began spending too much time on personnel problems, and the business needed more capital than he could muster. Sales were declining and bills were mounting. To alleviate these problems, he decided to take a partner into the business who had both management skills and capital. Joe found such a person and with her formed a partnership to operate SCS.

As the business continued to expand over the years, both partners recognized that the original partnership agreement between them had flaws that would inhibit the growth of SCS. They wanted to acquire other companies, but the partnership form of organization limited their ability to do so, for reasons that will soon be explained. Consequently, they decided to form a corporation—a legal organization chartered by the state to conduct business. One advantage of a corporation is that it has rights, privileges, and liabilities that are distinct from those of its owners, the shareholders. SCS could, as a legal entity, sell stocks and bonds to raise the additional capital required for future growth.

The SCS story illustrates part of the life cycle of an organization that evolved from a sole proprietorship at its birth, to a partnership as it grew, and finally to a corporation as it became a large business. (Of course, many companies begin as corporations.) The story also introduces the three major forms of business organization in the United States: sole proprietorships, partnerships, and corporations.

The sole proprietorship is the most common form of business organization in the United States. As shown in Figure 3–1, 70 percent of all business concerns are sole proprietorships. However, they account for only 20 percent of total profit. This fact suggests that most sole proprietorships are small, and that is indeed the case. In 1981, 81 percent of all proprietorships had profits of less than $50,000. Fewer than 10 percent had profits of more than $100,000.[1]

[1]Data on corporate profits and number of firms by type of organization are published annually in the *Statistical Abstract of the United States.*

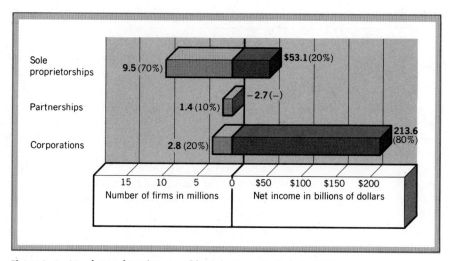

Figure 3–1   Number and net income of business organizations in 1981.

In contrast, although their numbers are relatively small, corporations account for 80 percent of total profits. This figure suggests that all corporations are large, but that is not the case. About 15 percent of all corporations account for 99 percent of total corporate profits. In other words, corporate profits are concentrated in a few large companies, whereas most companies make substantially smaller profits or suffer losses. Almost three-fourths of all corporations have profits of less than $500,000.

Finally, Figure 3 - 1 reveals that there are relatively few partnerships. Most partnerships are small; and their losses outweighed the incomes of more profitable partnerships. The result is that partnerships show a net loss in the figure.

Each of the three basic forms of organization has characteristics that give it certain advantages and disadvantages. Some of the major advantages and disadvantages are presented here.

Sole Proprietorships   The word *proprietor* means owner. The term **sole proprietorship** refers to a business owned by one person. Although sole proprietorships greatly outnumber other forms of business organization, they tend to be small businesses, such as local drug stores, home building and repair services, and restaurants. Doctors, lawyers, and accountants may also be sole proprietors.

Advantages of Sole Proprietorships

Ease of Formation.   There are no organizational requirements for establishing a sole proprietorship. Proprietors may have to obtain licenses from appropriate authorities to perform certain services. For example, doctors, lawyers, and others must be certified by the state to practice their trades (as they would if they practiced in partnerships or corporations). On a local level, licenses are required to operate taxicabs, restaurants, and many other types of business concerns. Aside from educational requirements, licensing many kinds of businesses is relatively simple and inexpensive.

Control. Being one's own boss is one of the greatest advantages of sole proprietorship. Many people like the freedom of selecting their own hours and establishing their own working conditions. Of course, there is usually some relationship between the amount of labor one puts into a business and the profit that results from that labor. Some proprietors work harder and longer hours on their own businesses than if they worked for others.

Retention of Profits. The business's profits belong to the proprietor and are taxed as ordinary income. Frequently (but not always), the tax rate that applies to ordinary income is lower than the tax rate for corporations. Because taxes are so important to business concerns and their owners, they will be examined in detail later in this chapter.

Disadvantages of Sole Proprietorships

Unlimited Liability. The major disadvantage of sole proprietorship is the **unlimited liability** of the proprietor. If the business experiences legal or financial difficulties, the owner's entire wealth may be lost to satisfy the claims of creditors or others. This is so because the owner and the business are legally one and the same.

Limited Capital. The ability to raise capital is limited to the wealth of the owner and the earning power of the business. Recall that in the case of SCS, presented earlier in this chapter, Joe Bloch was forced to take a partner into his business to raise additional capital.

Lack of Continuity. When the owner of a sole proprietorship dies, the business may go out of existence. The relatively short lifespan of sole proprietorships has some definite disadvantages. First, it makes attracting employees who want long-term careers in the same business difficult. Second, lenders are reluctant to make long-term loans to businesses that may not exist long enough to repay them.

Heavy Management Responsibilities. The typical sole proprietor is deeply involved in the daily activities of the business. Little time may remain for planning and evaluating future threats and opportunities. Further, some proprietors are good at sales, engineering, or some other speciality but do not understand the basic principles of management or finance. This is one reason why many sole proprietorships fail.

Partnerships A **partnership** consists of two or more people who engage in business for profit. The partnership is usually based on a partnership agreement that outlines the responsibilities of each partner, the distribution of income or losses, and the procedures to be followed for the addition of new partners or the withdrawal of existing ones. Detailed written agreements are helpful to avoid misunderstandings between partners and to settle legal disputes.

Forms of Partnership. The three major forms of partnership are general partnership, limited partnership, and joint venture. In a **general partnership**, each partner's liability is unlimited, like a sole proprietor's. The general partnership form of organization is widely used in small-scale manufacturing concerns and in professional organizations in the fields of medicine, law, and accounting.

In a **limited partnership**, at least one partner has unlimited liability. Other partners may have **limited liability**—that is, they are liable only for the amount they have invested in the business. Those with limited liability are so-called "silent partners," because they cannot be active in the management of the business and their names cannot appear in the name of the firm. This form of organization is well suited to those who want to invest capital in, for example, real estate development or oil drilling while avoiding the risk of general partnership and the responsibility of management. It should be clear by now that the role of silent partners is to provide capital.

A **joint venture** is an agreement between business concerns to enter into partnership for a specific project, such as the development of an oil field or the handling of a real estate transaction. One form of joint venture, called a **syndicate**, is widely used by investment banking firms in the distribution of securities. In such a syndicate, a group of investment bankers go together to purchase securities from the issuing corporation and then resell those securities to the public. When the securities have been sold, the syndicate is ended.

Advantages of Partnerships

Ease of Formation. Partnerships are relatively easy to establish. The organizational requirements for the operation of a partnership are generally spelled out in a partnership agreement.

Pooling of Skills. A partnership permits the pooling of skills in the operation of the business. For example, a lawyer who specializes in probate may form a partnership with one who concentrates on corporate law and another who handles antitrust cases. This is why many law firms and other partnerships have three or more persons listed in their names.

Enhanced Ability to Obtain Capital. The amount of capital that can be raised by a partnership depends on the wealth of the partners. Because more than one person is involved, however, it is presumed that their collective wealth is greater than that of a sole proprietor. Accordingly, it is easier for a partnership to obtain capital than a sole proprietorship.

Disadvantages of Partnerships

Unlimited Liability. The major disadvantage of a general partnership is the unlimited liability of the partners. As a result of this disadvantage, corporations have become more common in many fields in which partnerships have been a traditionally favored form of organization. This is particularly noticeable in medicine, where malpractice lawsuits may create huge liabilities.

Lack of Continuity. The partnership may be dissolved upon the death or withdrawal of a partner, depending on the terms of the partnership agreement. The limited lifespan of some partnerships may affect their ability to borrow funds. However, many partnership agreements avoid this problem by providing for the business's continued operation even after withdrawal of one or more partners from the firm.

Other Limitations. There is an ever-present possibility that partners may disagree and break up the partnership. The potential for this occurrence increases with the number of partners. Moreover, in firms with nationwide or international operations, effective communication among partners becomes increasingly difficult. Finally, it may be difficult for a partnership to acquire companies that want to exchange shares of stock instead of dealing for cash. Partnerships do not issue stock.

Corporations Corporations account for 80 percent of the profits earned by business organizations. Moreover, the bulk of the profits are concentrated in a small handful of very large corporations. Corporations clearly play a major role in the U.S. economy. What, then, is a corporation? In 1819, Chief Justice John Marshall provided the classic definition of a corporation, which states that a **corporation** is an artificial being existing only in the eyes of the law and possessing only those properties that the charter of its creation confers upon it. It may act as a single individual to manage its own affairs and to hold property, and it is immortal.[2]

Corporate Organization. Large corporations operated for profit are typically organized in three layers—the shareholders, the board of directors, and the chief executive officer. As shown in Figure 3–2, these three layers can be thought of as a pyramid.

[2]*Trustees of Dartmouth College v. Woodward*, 4 Wheaton (U. S.) 518 at 634 (1819).

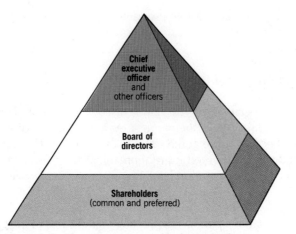

Figure 3–2   The corporate pyramid of organization.

Shareholders.   The bottom layer of the pyramid consists of the many **share-holders** of common and preferred stock who own the corporation. Millions of individual shareholders have invested in the major U.S. corporations. American Telephone and Telegraph Corporation has more than 3 million shareholders, for example, and General Motors has 1 million.

In theory, shareholders own and control corporations. In reality, very few shareholders are interested in controlling the companies whose shares they own. Shareholders want their stocks to go up in value and they want to receive their dividends. Generally, as long as managers do a reasonable job in running the corporation, they are safe from being thrown out of office by shareholders.

Holders of **common stock** have certain basic rights with respect to the corporation. These rights are:

1. To vote, usually on the basis of one vote for each share, in the election of directors and on other important issues, such as mergers.
2. To receive dividends if they are declared.
3. To participate in the distribution of assets if the company is liquidated.
4. To purchase a proportionate number of new stock issues if stated in the corporate charter or required by law.
5. To obtain up-to-date information about the company and inspect its records.
6. To sell their stock and transfer ownership of the shares.
7. To enjoy immunity from personal liability in connection with corporate acts.

Holders of **preferred stock** own an interest in the firm, just as holders of common stock do. However, the preferred shares take preference over the common shares with respect to dividends and the distribution of assets if the firm is dissolved. Stated another way, preferred shareholders get paid before common shareholders. However, preferred shareholders are not accorded the same rights as common shareholders. Their dividends are generally fixed, and they may not be able to vote. These differences affect the riskiness and expected returns on preferred stock.

Directors. The **board of directors** has the ultimate responsibility for supervising the operations of the organization, determining major operating goals and policies, and hiring the principal operating officers. In practice, some boards take these responsibilities seriously, and others serve as "rubber stamps" for the chief executive officer.

Chief Executive Officer. The **chief executive officer (CEO)** is responsible for the daily operations of the company and its strategic planning. The CEO supervises other officers who are in charge of carrying out corporate policies. The financial manager, for example, may report directly to the CEO.

Advantages of Corporations

Limited Liability. A corporation, you recall, is considered an artificial *corpus* (body or person) that is separate from its owners. This distinction is important, because the corporation shields the shareholders from liabilities arising from corporate actions. Thus, the most that shareholders can lose is the amount they have invested in the corporation.

Continuity. The continued existence of a corporation does not depend on the lives of persons; therefore, it may have an unlimited lifespan.

Liquidity of Shares. The stocks of many large companies are actively traded in the securities markets. The existence of such markets provides **liquidity**—the ability of an investor to convert shares to cash on short notice with little or no loss in current value. Both the limited liability of shareholders and the continuity of the corporate form of organization help maintain this liquidity.

Corporations can use the market for corporate securities to raise long-term funds from investors, while individual investors can use these markets to sell their securities to others and so can treat investments in securities as short-term investments. This important point is one reason why it is easier for corporations to raise capital funds than for any other form of business organization. Securities markets will be described in more detail in Chapter 4.

Availability of Management Pool. Corporations attract talented managers because these managers recognize the continuity of the corporation and its ability to acquire funds and grow. Thus, prospective employees are encouraged by the potential for long-term employment opportunities.

Disadvantages of Corporations

Relative Difficulty of Formation.   Although organizing a corporation is not especially difficult, it is more complex than organizing a sole proprietorship or a partnership. Each state has its own rules regarding the establishment of corporations. In general, corporations are required to file articles of incorporation, a certificate of incorporation, and a corporate charter. **Articles of incorporation** are executed by the incorporators, as a legal instrument, for the purpose of creating a corporation. The **certificate of incorporation** is evidence of compliance with the requirements for incorporation, and the **corporate charter** comprises the articles and certificate of incorporation along with the corporation's bylaws and a statement of its powers. Such documents are usually prepared by attorneys. In addition to lawyers' fees, some small fees usually must be paid to the state in connection with incorporation.

Requirement for Public· Disclosure.   Corporations whose shares are sold in more than one state and which have ten or more shareholders are required to file periodic reports with the Securities and Exchange Commission. These reports, which are open to public scrutiny, contain financial data and other information concerning the affairs of the company.

Nonprofit Corporations.   So far, the discussion of corporations has assumed that they are organized for profit. However, some corporations that actively participate in the economy do not have profit as a goal. Collectively, these are called **nonprofit corporations**. Nonprofit corporations are divided into two broad categories: public and private. Public nonprofit corporations are created by a public authority to perform governmental functions. For example, many cities, such as New York City, are incorporated by the state. The Tennessee Valley Authority and the Federal Deposit Insurance Corporation are but two of many public nonprofit corporations. Private nonprofit corporations are usually established to pursue religious, charitable, educational, or social goals. For example, the Financial Management Association, a professional organization whose goal is to enhance the development of financial management, is operated under the auspices of a private nonprofit corporation.

Incorporated mutual associations and cooperative societies, such as mutual life insurance companies and farm cooperatives, are also legally considered private nonprofit corporations. The question of whether they operate for profit is debatable, however, since they operate for the financial benefit of specific groups.

Franchises.   A popular form of organization is the franchised business. A **franchise** is an agreement by which a **franchiser** grants an individual, called the **franchisee**, the right to use the franchiser's name, equipment, and other processes in a certain geographic area. Most franchisers are corporations—McDonald's and Holiday Inns, for example. The franchisee pays the franchiser an initial fee and other payments based on sales. This system enables individuals to go into business with corporations. Gasoline service stations are one of the oldest franchise systems.

Some franchises are very profitable; others are not. For every franchise that is successful—such as Wendy's—many others—such as Minnie Pearl's Fried Chicken—fail. Minnie Pearl's was a fast-food franchise that grew rapidly in the late 1960s and then went bankrupt in 1970. In spite of such failures, almost one-third of all retail sales in the United States today are made through franchise outlets.

Corporate Income Taxes

George Bernard Shaw is supposed to have said that "for every complex problem, there is a simple solution, and it is wrong." The U.S. income tax system is complex; therefore, any simple treatment of it would lead to wrong conclusions. Accordingly, no attempt is made here to provide all the tax information financial managers should have at their disposal. Instead, certain important features of income taxes are presented to emphasize their importance in financial management. Remember as you read this material that tax laws and regulations change frequently. For a summary of the latest changes, refer to *Prentice-Hall Federal Taxes*, available in most accounting libraries.

Tax Reform Act of 1986 The Tax Reform Act of 1986 was the most extensive overhaul of the U.S. tax code since World War II. It was signed by the president on October 22, 1986, just as Congress was about to adjourn. Therefore corrections had to await the next Congress. The information presented here briefly describes selected aspects of the law that was passed in 1986.

This section focuses on those aspects of corporate and personal income taxes that will help you understand the process of making financial and investment decisions. For simplicity, some of the nuances of the new law are overlooked, and few comparisons are made with previous tax laws.

Investment Tax Credit. Because the new law is radically different from old tax regulations in many regards, *transition rules* permitting selected aspects of the new to be phased in over a period of years were included in it. The **investment tax credit (ITC)** is one example. The ITC permitted taxpayers investing in certain tangible assets to deduct up to 10 percent of the assets' value from their income taxes. The ITC has been repealed for new investments but is being phased out in stages for investments made before 1986 and will not be completely eliminated until the early 1990s. The ITC may be reinstated in the future. This book will use it in some examples to familiarize you with the concept.

Capital Gains or Losses. The transition rules do not apply to **capital gains or losses** for corporations or individuals. Under the prior law, certain capital assets that were held for more than six months and were sold for a profit were taxed at preferential (lower) rates. The preferential rate for capital gains has been repealed, and the profits are now taxed at the regular rates. However, certain capital losses are deductible. For corporations, such losses are deductible only against capital gains, but individuals may deduct up to $3,000 net capital losses from their ordinary income. Although preferential tax rates have been repealed, the structure of capital gains remains intact in case Congress wants to reinstate a capital gains differential in the future.

Corporate Tax Rates

As shown in Table 3–1, corporate income tax rates range from 15 percent on the first $50,000 of taxable income, to 25 percent on the next $25,000, to 34 percent on taxable income of more than $75,000. An additional surtax of 5 percent is imposed on taxable income of $100,001 to $335,000. The maximum surtax is $11,750.

Because the successively higher tax rates are paid only on incremental, or marginal, taxable income, they are called **marginal tax rates.** The marginal tax rates may not be the same as the **average tax rate**, which is equal to the total tax liability divided by total taxable income. The following examples show how to compute both marginal and average tax rates.

Example 1 assumes that a corporation's total taxable income is $150,000, as shown in Table 3–2. We compute the tax liability for each increment of income by multiplying that amount by the marginal tax rate. For example, the first $50,000 of income is multiplied by a marginal tax rate of 15 percent, resulting in a tax liability of $7,500. The tax liabilities for the other increments are calculated in a similar manner. Additionally, the 5 percent surtax applies

Table 3–1
Corporate Income Tax Rate Structure[a]

Taxable Income	Taxable Amount	Tax Rate	
$0–50,000	$50,000	15%	7500
50,000–75,000	25,000	25	6250
75,000 and over	—	34	8500
100,001–335,000	225,000	5	surtax[b]

[a]Based on the 1986 Tax Reform Act.

[b]The maximum surtax is $11,750.

Table 3–2

Examples of Calculating Average Tax Rates for Corporations

Taxable Income (1)	Marginal Tax Rate (2)	Tax Liability (3) = (1) × (2)	Average Tax Rate (4) = (3)/(1)
Example 1			
$50,000	15%	$7,500	
25,000	25	6,250	
75,000	34	25,500	
	5% surtax on $50,000	2,500	
$150,000		$41,750	$41,750/$150,000 ≈ 27.8%
Example 2			
$50,000	15%	7,500	
25,000	25	6,250	
1,175,000	34	399,500	
	Maximum surtax	11,750	$425,000/$1,250,000 = 34.0%
$1,250,000		$425,000	

in this example to the $50,000 of income in excess of $75,000. The total tax liability is $41,750. The average tax rate (total tax liability/total taxable income) is 27.8 percent.

Example 2 illustrates the tax rates that apply to taxable income of $1,250,000. The tax liabilities are computed just as in Example 1. However, because of the amount of taxable income, the maximum surtax of $11,750 is applied. The total tax liability is $425,000, and the average tax rate is 34 percent. (Notice that as taxable income increases, the average tax rate approaches—and eventually reaches—the highest marginal tax rate, 34 percent.)

Corporations generally pay a minimum tax (called the *alternative minimum tax*) based on 20 percent of their alternative minimum taxable income (AMTI) above $40,000 after certain adjustments have been made. The tax rate is reduced by 25 percent of the amount by which the AMTI exceeds $150,000 and is phased out once the AMTI reaches $310,000. We will not be using the alternative minimum tax in this text.

Depreciation and Cost Recovery Corporations reduce their tax liabilities in many ways; depreciation is one example. **Depreciation**, or cost recovery, is an accounting procedure for allocating the cost of tangible capital assets, such as buildings or machine tools, over their useful lives. The idea behind depreciation accounting is to permit business concerns to recapture a sufficient amount of dollars to provide for replacement of the asset and to recover the original investment.

Here is how it works. Federal tax laws permit business concerns (sole proprietorships and partnerships as well as corporations) to deduct depreciation charges from revenues when computing income taxes. Thus, depreciation charges lower taxable income. Depreciation, then, provides a source of funds in that it reduces income tax liabilities, perhaps putting a business concern in a marginal tax bracket lower than the one it would be in otherwise.

It is important to keep in mind that depreciation *must* offset income to qualify as a source of funds. For example, the depreciation expense from a factory does not serve as a source of funds if no revenue is being earned. That is because depreciation charges are **noncash outlays**, which are created by accounting entries. The usefulness of depreciation is in its ability to shield operating income from income taxes with expenses that do not require cash outlays.

It should also be noted that companies are permitted to use different methods of depreciation for computing taxes, for reporting to stockholders, and for internal use. Because the Internal Revenue Service (IRS), financial managers, financial analysts, accountants, and stockholders all require different kinds of information, the use of different methods of reporting is helpful to them. It may create advantages for the company, too. For example, by using different reporting methods, a company can report higher earnings (resulting from lower depreciation expenses) to its shareholders than it reports to the IRS.

Accelerated Cost Recovery System   The Economic Recovery Tax Act of 1981 introduced the **accelerated cost recovery system (ACRS)**, a type of accelerated depreciation. The ACRS was intended to stimulate economic growth by standardizing accelerated depreciation and thus encouraging its use. Other methods of accelerated depreciation, such as sum-of-the-year digits, were replaced by ACRS. However, the straight-line method was still allowed. Neither the ACRS nor the straight-line method takes salvage value into account.

Table 3–3
ACRS Class of Recovery Property

Class	Depreciation Rate	ADR Midpoints[a] and Examples of Property Included	Convention
3-year	200% declining balance	ADR midpoints of 4 years or less Small tools, machinery	Half-year
5-year	200% declining balance	ADR midpoints of 4–10 years Autos, light trucks, research equipment	Half-year
7-year	200% declining balance	ADR midpoints of 10–16 years Office furniture, commercial aircraft	Half-year
10-year	200% declining balance	ADR midpoints of 16–20 years Certain manufacturing assets	Half-year
15-year	150% declining balance	ADR midpoints of 20–25 years Telephone distribution equipment, billboards	Half-year
20-year	150% declining balance	ADR midpoints of 20–27.5 years Sewer pipes	Half-year
27.5-year	straight-line	Residential rental property	Midmonth
31.5-year	straight-line	Nonresidential property	Midmonth

[a]ADR is asset depreciation range.

Under the law, assets were grouped by the U.S. Treasury into classes, or **asset depreciation ranges (ADRs)**, based on their useful lives. The Treasury used the *midpoint* life of each ADR as a guideline in defining the classes. For example, as shown in Table 3–3, 3-year class assets have ADR midpoints of 4 years or less. This group includes small tools and machinery. Assets in the 5-year class have ADR midpoints of 4 to 10 years and include automobiles, light trucks, and certain research equipment. You do not have to be concerned with ADRs because we will only refer to classes (for example, the 5-year class) in the rest of the book.

ACRs created eight classes of capital assets (tangible personal property) for purposes of depreciation. The ACRS for the first four classes is based on the 200 percent declining balance method with a switch to the straight-line method sometime during the life of the asset. Consider an asset costing $100,000 that has a 5-year life. Under the straight-line method, 20 percent of the asset's *book value* (in this case, $100,000) is depreciated each year. Under the 200 percent method, 40 percent of the asset's *depreciable value* (its book value at the beginning of each year) is depreciated annually. This is twice (or 200 percent) the rate used under the straight-line method.

Year	Straight-Line Method (0.20 × $100,000 Book Value)	200 Percent Declining Balance Method	
		Beginning-of-Year Book Value	Amount of Depreciation (0.40 × Beginning-of-Year Book Value)
1	$20,000	$100,000	$40,000
2	20,000	60,000	24,000
3	20,000	36,000	14,400
4	20,000	21,600	8,640
5	20,000	12,960	5,184
	$100,000		$92,224[a]

[a]The book value is not fully recovered under this depreciation method. (See text.)

If the asset had been depreciated over a 10-year period, the rate for the straight-line method would have been 10 percent, and the rate for the 200 percent method would have been twice that, or 20 percent. The 200 percent method always uses twice the rate of the straight-line method, which varies depending on the number of years involved.

As shown in the table just presented, when the 200 percent method is used, the value of the asset cannot be reduced to zero by successive applications of a constant rate of depreciation. In other words, the book value will gradually approach zero, but it will never make it. As a practical matter, this is not a problem, because most firms switch to a straight-line method when there is a tax advantage in doing so.

Table 3–3 reveals that two ACRS classes use the 150 percent declining balance method. Here, we determine the amount of depreciation by multiplying the straight-line rate by 150 percent. Applying this to the previous example, we find that the depreciation rate is 30 percent (150 percent of the 20 percent rate used in the straight-line method).

	150 Percent Declining Balance Method	
Year	Beginning-of-Year Book Value	Amount of Depreciation
1	$100,000	$30,000
2	70,000	21,000
3	49,000	14,700
4	34,300	10,290
5	24,010	7,203
		$83,193

Again, since the full value of the asset is not recovered under the declining balance method, most firms switch to the straight-line method sometime during the asset's life.

Table 3–3 also lists conventions related to depreciation. The **half-year convention** means that only one-half of the first year's depreciation is taken in the first year. Under this convention, property is considered to be placed in service or disposed of at the midpoint of that year. A midquarter convention applies where more than 40 percent of the property is placed in service or disposed of during the last three months of the tax year. Midmonth conventions apply to real estate.

Applying the half-year convention to our example using the 200 percent method, we can see that only $20,000 of depreciation is allowed in the first year. Note that the amount depreciated in each year is different, and that six years are required to depreciate the asset, with a half-year's depreciation taken in the sixth year.

	200 Percent Declining Balance Method			
	Without Half-Year Convention		With Half-Year Convention	
Year	Beginning-of-Year Book Value	Amount of Depreciation	Beginning-of-Year Book Value	Amount of Depreciation
1	$100,000	$40,000	$100,000	$20,000
2	60,000	24,000	80,000	32,000
3	36,000	14,400	48,000	19,200
4	21,600	8,640	28,800	11,520
5	12,960	5,184	17,280	6,912
6			10,368	2,074
		$92,224[a]		$91,706[a]

[a]The book value is not fully recovered under this depreciation method. (See text.)

For your convenience, the ACRS schedule for 3-year, 5-year, and 7-year classes with the half-year convention are presented in Table 3–4. The table shows a switch to the straight-line method.

Table 3–4
ACRS Schedule for Selected Classes of Investments[a]

	Class of Investment		
Year	3-Year	5-Year	7-Year
1	33.333%	20.000%	14.286%
2	44.444	32.000	24.490
3	14.815	19.200	17.493
4	7.408	11.520	12.495
5		11.520	8.925
6		5.760	8.925
7			8.925
8			4.462
	100.000%	100.000%	100.000%

[a]With half-year convention and switch to straight-line depreciation. The switch occurs where the percentage remains the same as in the preceding year.

Dividend Received Deduction Corporations are allowed to deduct 80 percent of the dividends they receive from other domestic and selected foreign corporations. Dividends received from certain other companies (Small Business Investment Companies) are eligible for a 100 percent deduction.

Net Operating Losses Current net operating losses can be used to reduce future income tax liabilities and to obtain refunds on taxes that have already been paid. This is so because income tax losses can be carried back 3 years and forward 15 years. For example, suppose that a company had a net operating loss in 1988. The company could recompute its taxes for the previous three years (1985–1987) in order to obtain refunds on taxes it had already paid. The losses are applied to the earliest year first. If income in the previous years was not sufficient to offset all the losses, the remainder could be carried forward 15 years, or until the losses were eliminated, whichever came first. If losses are not eliminated during this period, there is no further tax recourse for recovering them.

Under the new tax law, there are significant limitations on the amount of carryforward allowed following a change in corporate ownership. Discussion of those changes is beyond the scope of this book.

Subchapter S Corporations Subchapter S of the Internal Revenue Code permits certain small business concerns to enjoy some of the advantages of corporations and partnerships at the same time. The major advantage of Subchapter S is the avoidance of so-called *double taxation*, which occurs when corporate earnings are taxed and then taxed again when they are distributed to shareholders. **Subchapter S corporations** generally pay no income taxes, because their taxable income is passed on to shareholders. In order to qualify as a Subchapter S corporation, a company must apply to the Internal Revenue Service, observe limits on income from passive investments such as stocks and bonds, and meet certain other requirements.

Personal Income Taxes

Eighty-four percent of all business concerns are sole proprietorships or partnerships. Their owners must file personal income tax returns that reflect the businesses' taxable income. As you will see, personal income tax rates are different from corporate income tax rates.

Personal Tax Rates Beginning in 1988, there will be two tax rates for individuals, 15 percent and 28 percent. In addition, a third tax rate of 33 percent will apply to individuals whose taxable income reaches a certain level. The purpose of the 33 percent rate is to phase out the tax benefits to high-income individuals from the 15 percent rate and from personal and dependency exemptions. The tax rates for a single individual with no dependents are shown in Table 3–5.

When discussing average corporate income tax rates, we used one corporation with taxable income of $150,000 and another with taxable income of $1,250,000 (see Table 3–2). Now we'll use these same amounts in determining the average tax rate for a single individual. As shown in Example 1, Table 3–6, the individual paid 15 percent tax on the first $17,850 of taxable income, 28 percent on the next $25,300 of taxable income, and so on. The total tax liability of $42,546 on a taxable income of $150,000 gives an average tax rate of 28.4 percent. This is slightly higher than the average tax rate for the corporation (27.8 percent) with the same amount of taxable income. Example 2, however, reveals that the average tax rate for the individual taxpayer with $1,250,000 taxable income is 28.0 percent, substantially lower than that for the corporation with the same amount of income (34.0%). The marginal tax rates for individuals are lower than the marginal tax rates for corporations.

Table 3–5
Income Tax Rate Structure for Single Individuals[a]

Taxable Income	Taxable Amount	Tax Rate	
$0–$17,850	$17,850	15%	2677.5
17,850–43,150	25,300	28	7,084.
43,150–100,480	57,330	33	18,918.
100,480 and over	—	28	

[a]Beginning in 1988; assumes no dependents.

Table 3–6
Examples of Calculating Average Tax Rates for Individuals

Taxable Income (1)	Marginal Tax Rate (2)	Tax Liability (3) = (1) × (2)	Average Tax Rate (4) = (3)/(1)
Example 1			
$17,850	15%	$2,677.50	
25,300	28	7,084.00	
57,330	33	18,918.90	
49,520	28	13,865.60	
$150,000		$42,546.00	$42,546/$150,000 = 28.4%
Example 2			
$17,850	15%	$2,677.50	
25,300	28	7,084.00	
57,330	33	18,918.90	
1,149,520	28	321,865.60	
$1,250,000		$350,546.00	$350,546/$1,250,000 = 28.0%

Summary

The three major forms of business organization in the United States are sole proprietorships, partnerships, and corporations. Sole proprietorships are the most numerous. Their advantages include ease of formation and the owner's ability to completely control the firm and keep the profits. Disadvantages include unlimited liability, limited capital, limited lifespan, and heavy management responsibilities.

Types of partnerships include general partnerships, limited partnerships, and joint ventures. Among the advantages are ease of formation, pooling of skills, and increased ability to raise external funds. Disadvantages include unlimited liability, limited lifespan, and potential conflicts among partners.

Corporations account for most of the profits earned by U.S. business concerns. Although corporations are owned by shareholders, control is generally exercised by boards of directors and chief executive officers. Corporations enjoy several advantages over other forms of organization. Shareholders have limited liability for the acts of the company. Corporations also have unlimited lifespans and access to capital markets for fund raising. Consequently, they attract talented managers. On the other hand, disadvantages include relative difficulty of formation and the need to provide information to shareholders.

The Tax Reform Act of 1986 was a major overhaul of the U.S. tax system. Under the act, marginal income tax rates for corporations range from 15 percent to 34 percent. In order to reduce their taxes, corporations use a variety of accounting devices, including the ACRS. Marginal income tax rates for individuals are 15 percent and 28 percent. Some knowledge of personal tax rates is important, because the incomes of sole proprietorships and partnerships are taxed as personal income.

Important Terms

Accelerated cost recovery system (ACRS)
Articles of incorporation
Asset depreciation range (ADR)
Average tax rate
Board of directors
Book value
Capital gain
Capital loss
Certificate of incorporation
Chief executive officer (CEO)
Common stock
Corporate charter
Corporation
Depreciation
Franchise
Franchisee
Franchiser

General partnership
Half-year convention
Investment tax credit (ITC)
Joint venture
Limited liability
Limited partnership
Liquidity
Marginal tax rate
Noncash outlay
Nonprofit corporation
Partnership
Preferred stock
Shareholder
Sole proprietorship
Subchapter S corporation
Syndicate
Unlimited liability

Questions

1. The majority of business firms are established according to what legal form of organization? What form of organization accounts for the most profits?
2. Which form of organization is the easiest to establish? Under which form is it the easiest to raise funds? Under which form do owners have the most control?
3. Identify some inherent difficulties in the proprietorship form of organization.
4. Explain the difference between a general partnership, a limited partnership, and a joint venture.
5. What are franchises?
6. In what major ways do the rights of common and preferred shareholders differ?
7. Explain how an ownership interest in a large corporation provides the liquidity that other forms of ownership do not.
8. Distinguish between marginal and average tax rates.
9. What is the major financial impact of a noncash accounting entry like depreciation? Under what circumstances may it be said that depreciation is a "source of funds"? When does depreciation *not* generate funds?
10. Describe in general the structure of ACRS. Why was it developed?
11. From the standpoint of taxation, are long-term or short-term capital gains more beneficial? Explain.
12. A firm lost money on its operations this year and therefore paid no corporate income taxes. Assuming the firm returns to profitability in the future, how can this loss result in a tax savings?

13. Contrast the impact of an investment tax credit on taxable income versus the impact of a depreciation deduction on taxable income.
14. What is the major advantage of a Subchapter S corporation?
15. How does bracket creep affect taxpayers?

Problems

1. Lard Corporation generated earnings in 1987 of $168,000 before taxes.
   (a) Calculate its tax liability.
   What is its marginal tax rate?
   (c) What is its average tax rate?

2. A corporation had a tax bill of $42,500 on its 1987 earnings. What were its taxable earnings for the year?

3. A small corporation had $275,000 in ordinary income this year. What taxes are owed? What are the firm's marginal and average tax rates?

4. Benjamin Corporation recently decided to sell the company car its president had been driving. The automobile had been purchased 4 years before at a cost of $10,000. At that time, it was estimated to have a useful life of 5 years and was depreciated on a straight-line basis. Since that time, however, this car model has come to be considered a "classic" by car buffs. Therefore, its current market value is $15,000. How much income will be taxed at Benjamin's ordinary income tax rate? How much at the capital gains rate?

5. Refer to Problem 4. If, instead, the car has a current market value of $3,500, how much income will be taxed at the ordinary income tax rate? How much at the capital gains rate?

6. Mansfield, Inc., bought a large snow machine for $50,000 in 1986 to produce synthetic snow for its ski trails. The machine was thought to have a 5-year life and was depreciated using the straight-line method over 5 years. The expected salvage value was $5,000. Four years later, in 1990, the firm was considering replacing the machine with a newer and larger model. Assuming a capital gains rate of 28 percent and an ordinary tax rate of 46 percent, answer the following questions:
   (a) What is the book value of the original snow machine in 1990?
   (b) What taxes would be paid on the sale of the machine if the sales price were $14,000? $5,000? $30,000? $60,000?

7. Little Abner's Restaurant is contemplating the purchase in January 1988 of a new and improved bun warmer. The current warmer cost $4,000 in 1983 and had an expected life of 10 years with no estimated salvage value. Otto's Emporium has offered Abner's $6,000 for the warmer. What will be Abner's net after-tax gain or loss on the sale if it has a 40 percent marginal tax rate on ordinary income and a 28 percent capital gains tax rate? Assume straight-line depreciation.

8. Hazel Drilling purchased a new machine 8 years ago for $150,000. This machine is being depreciated using the straight-line method over a 20-year period with an expected salvage value of $10,000. Assuming a 28 percent capital gains rate and a 46 percent marginal tax rate on ordinary income, answer the following:
   (a) What is the machine's current book value?
   (b) Calculate Hazel's tax liability if the machine is sold 8 years after purchase at a price of $50,000; $94,000; $200,000.

9. Solvent, Inc., had a net operating loss of $600,000 for 1987 after having before-tax profits of $300,000 in 1986, $250,000 in 1985, and $200,000 in 1984. To what tax refund would Solvent be entitled? Why? Assume a tax rate of 40 percent.

10. Jordan and Jordan, Inc., is attracted by the tax savings opportunities involved in the purchase of a new computer for research purposes. The firm is currently in the 40 percent marginal tax bracket. The computer it wishes to acquire costs $25,000 and qualifies for a 6 percent investment tax credit. Assuming the machine has a 3-year useful life for tax purposes, calculate the total tax savings that will result in the year of purchase. Assume ACRS will be used.

11. Flynn Flour Mills has pretax income before depreciation of $500,000.
    (a) Suppose the firm is eligible for an additional $10,000 tax deduction. Calculate taxes owed by Flynn.
    (b) Suppose the firm is eligible for a $10,000 tax credit instead. Calculate taxes owed.

12. College Productions bought a new piece of equipment in 1988 for $400,000 with an expected life of 10 years. How much will its 1988 tax bill change because of investment tax credits? What if the estimated life of the equipment is 3 years? What will happen in each case if the equipment is sold after 2 years?

13. Bob's Chicken House bought three new pieces of equipment in 1987. The first piece has a life of 3 years and cost $10,000; the second cost $20,000, with a 5 year expected life. The third had an estimated life of 10 years, and cost $30,000. Calculate the investment tax credit generated by these purchases in 1987.

14. Assuming that the purchases made by Bob's Chicken House and described in the previous question qualify for ACRS depreciation, what total tax savings resulted from the purchase of the 3-year equipment in 1987? From the 10-year equipment? Assumed Bob's is in the 30-percent tax bracket.

15. Sam Hill, the most eligible bachelor in town, has a taxable income of $45,000. Using the personal tax rates given in the chapter, calculate Sam's tax bill.

16. Barbara McCloud is the sole proprietor of a business. In 1987, the business earned $40,000 before taxes.
    (a) Calculate Barbara's tax bill.
    (b) Assume she has an equal partner with whom she must share the $40,000 and recalculate her taxes.

17. Jenny Jones, a single physician specializing in open-heart surgery, expects to earn taxable income of $200,000 this year. What income taxes will she pay if her practice is organized as a sole proprietorship?

18. Suppose Dr. Jones, in Problem 17, incorporates herself. What taxes will she pay?

4

The Financial System and Corporate Securities Markets

Business concerns raise money in the financial markets to fund their daily activities and to grow faster than they could if they depended only on earnings they retained. The U.S. financial markets encompass all the debt and equity securities and loans that are bought or sold by government, business concerns,

After reading this chapter, you should know the following.

---

1. **What the U.S. financial system includes.**
2. **What the corporate securities markets are and what advantages they offer.**
3. **What investment bankers do.**
4. **Who buys and sells securities.**
5. **What stockbrokers and dealers do.**
6. **How the structure of the stock market is changing.**
7. **What makes markets efficient.**
8. **Why an investor may not be able to earn better-than-average returns in the stock market.**

---

financial intermediaries, and individuals. The principal function of the financial markets is to allocate financial resources in the U.S. economic system. A detailed analysis of the economic system and the financial markets is beyond the scope of this book; however, this chapter gives an overview of the financial system and then focuses on aspects of the corporate securities markets, where debt and equity securities are bought and sold.

The Financial System

A simplified view of the U.S. financial and economic system appears in Figure 4–1. The figure shows three types of economic units: business concerns, individuals, and financial intermediaries. To keep this discussion of the system within manageable limits, the role of government is not examined. The following description, then, is not complete; but it should give you a basis for understanding how the system works.

As shown in Figure 4–1, business concerns pay individuals rent and wages for the use of their land, labor, and other resources. For example, suppose businesses pay individuals a total of $100—that is, that $100 is the total income (Y) in our economic system. The individuals can use the $100 for consumption, (C), to purchase goods and services from the businesses. The process by which businesses pay individuals who, in turn, use the funds to buy goods and services from the businesses is called the **circular flow of money**. Accordingly, total income Y is equal to total consumption C.

$$Y = C \qquad\qquad (4\text{--}1)$$
$$\$100 = \$100$$

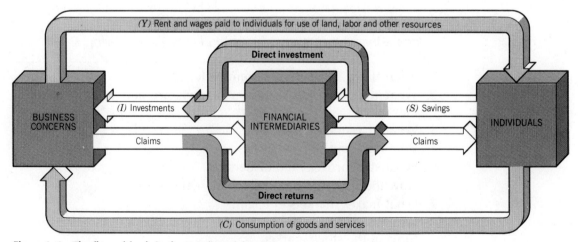

Figure 4–1   The flow of funds in the U.S. financial system.

In reality, money does not flow in a perfect circle between business concerns and individuals, because individuals save some of their earnings. Savings *(S)* are the difference between income and consumption. If savings are $10, then consumption is $90:

$$S = Y - C \qquad (4\text{--}2)$$
$$\$10 = \$100 - \$90$$

Savings reduce the amount of funds that individuals return to business concerns in the form of consumption. However, as shown in the inside loop of Figure 4–1, savings are channeled into financial intermediaries, which invest those funds in business concerns. Stated otherwise, investment *(I)* is also equal to income less consumption.

$$I = Y - C \qquad (4\text{--}3)$$
$$\$10 = \$100 - \$90$$

It follows, therefore, that savings must equal investment.

$$S = I \qquad (4\text{--}4)$$
$$\$10 = \$10$$

A large part of the savings and investment process takes place through **financial intermediaries**. They bring savers and borrowers together by selling claims (such as deposits) to savers for money and investing that money or lending it to borrowers. Financial intermediaries include such financial insti-

Table 4–1

Financial Intermediaries and Their Specialties

Type	Specialties
Commercial banks	Making short- and intermediate-term business loans, mortgage loans, consumer loans, and others.
Savings and loan associations	Primarily making home mortgage loans; sometimes making commercial and industrial mortgage loans.
Finance companies	Financing plant and equipment as well as providing funds for daily operations.
Life insurance companies	Making commercial and industrial mortgage loans and purchasing corporate bonds.
Money market funds	Providing short-term investments with high liquidity.
Pension plans	Purchasing corporate bonds and stocks as well as some mortgages.
Leasing companies	Leasing plant and equipment.
Investment bankers	Underwriting securities (discussed in detail later in this chapter).
Investment companies	Pooling investors funds and inverting in securities.
Quasi-government agencies	Some government agencies, such as the Small Business Administration, provide funds for business and guaranty loans.

tutions as banks, savings and loan associations, and others, as listed in Table 4–1. Although the listing in the table is not exhaustive, it covers many of the financial intermediaries that affect business concerns. Of these intermediaries, businesses use banks most.

Commercial Banks Business concerns depend heavily on commercial banks, both as borrowers and lenders. They borrow short-term funds (for less than 1 year) and intermediate-term funds (for 1 to 5 years) from banks to buy plant and equipment and run their daily operations. (More information about bank loans is presented in Chapter 19.) Businesses act as lenders when they deposit funds in banks—in effect, lending the banks the money.

Specialized Lenders Many financial intermediaries specialize in making particular types of loans or buying particular types of securities. Table 4–1 provides some information about the specialties of various types of intermediaries. As you can see, commercial banks specialize in making business loans, but they also deal in mortgages, consumer loans, and other kinds of lending. They have a broader range of lending powers than any other financial institution.

In contrast, savings and loan associations specialize in mortgages, although they do make some business and consumer loans. Thus, if you wanted to borrow funds to build a new factory, you could borrow from a bank or a savings and loan association. You might even borrow from a life insurance company that specialized in large real estate projects. If you wanted to lease equipment, you would go to a leasing company that offered the type of equipment you needed.

In addition to the traditional financial intermediaries, many other business concerns have begun to offer financial services. General Electric Credit Corporation, for example, makes business loans and extends consumer credit. Armco Steel has an affiliate that sells insurance. National Intergroup (formerly National Steel) owns savings and loan associations. Exxon is in the credit card business, and a large portion of Sears, Roebuck's income comes from financial services.

The entry of these business concerns into the financial services industry offers borrowers a more competitive environment. Today, business borrowers can deal with banks, other traditional financial intermediaries, and a host of less conventional lenders.

External Sources of Funds

The sources of funds for a firm can be classified according to two broad categories: internal and external sources. Internal sources of funds include liquidation of assets (the sale of inventory for cash, for example), retained earnings, and several other sources. These sources are considered in other chapters.

External sources of funds include debt and the sale of stock. Over the years, the amount a company borrows far exceeds the amount it raises through the sale of stock. Companies can borrow money by using any of a number of debt instruments, including the following:

Corporate bonds. Long-term debt issued by corporations. You will learn more about corporate bonds later in this chapter and in Chapter 21.

Revenue bonds. Bonds issued by municipalities to finance corporations' expenditures for plant and equipment. The local government hopes to attract new industries and thus encourage growth by providing the funds for industries to move to its area. Revenues from the corporation are used to pay off the bonds. Interest income that investors earn from such bonds is not exempt from federal income tax.

Mortgages. Long-term borrowings backed by real estate.

Loans from banks, finance companies, and U.S. government agencies.

Commercial paper. Short-term, unsecured promissory notes issued by major corporations.

Banker's acceptances. Negotiable form of accounts receivable used in trade, where payment is guaranteed by a commercial bank.

Business concerns also incur short-term loans when they buy goods and services on credit and when they accrue wages and taxes that are due, giving rise to accounts payable. These important sources of funds are examined later, in Chapters 15 through 18, which deal with working capital.

Corporate Securities Markets

The market for corporate securities, depicted in Figure 4–2, is divided into the primary market, which deals in new security issues, and the secondary market, which deals in outstanding securities. Before examining these markets, we'll look more closely at the securities offerings themselves.

Characteristics of Corporate Securities Offerings

Volume. The total dollar volume of new corporate securities offered varies widely from year to year, depending on conditions in the economy and the securities markets. In 1985, the gross proceeds from corporate public offerings amounted to $154 billion, compared with $85 billion 3 years earlier.

Issuers. The major corporate issuers are manufacturing concerns, financial and real estate firms, and public utilities, not necessarily in that order. The order changes depending on the needs in those industries.

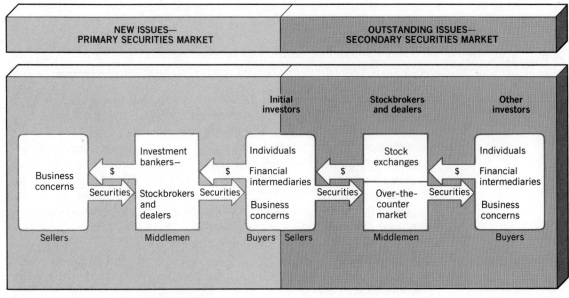

Figure 4–2 The corporate securities markets.

Types of Securities. The principal securities traded in the primary and secondary markets are stocks and bonds. Stocks—both common and preferred—represent ownership in a corporation. Some characteristics of stocks were described in Chapter 3, and they will be discussed further in Chapter 22.

Bonds, as mentioned earlier in this chapter, are long-term debt instruments. Most corporate bonds pay interest twice each year and pay the principal amount when they mature. The principal amount, typically $1,000, is frequently referred to as the **face value**, **face amount**, or **par value**.

There are many different types of bonds. Some, called **zero-coupon bonds**, pay no interest. They are sold at less than face value—called a **discount** from face value—and pay face value at maturity. (For example, a zero-coupon bond with a face value of $1,000 might be sold for $800 and pay $1,000 at maturity.) Other bonds have interest rates that vary over time. Some bonds are backed by real estate **(mortgage bonds)**; assets pledged in this way are called **collateral**. Some bonds are backed by the creditworthiness of the issuer **(debentures)**, others can be converted into some other security, such as common stock **(convertible bonds)**, and so on. Bonds will be discussed in more detail in Chapter 21.

As mentioned earlier, debt is the principal external source of funds for corporations. In 1985, the debt represented by bonds accounted for 77 percent of the total dollar volume of new corporate securities sold. In 1982, debt accounted for only 64 percent of the total. New stock issues accounted for the remainder.

Table 4–2

Holders of Corporate Stocks and Bonds at Year-End 1984 (billions of dollars)

	Stocks[a]		Bonds[a]	
Households	$1,272.6[b]	69.0%	$ 70.1	10.8%
Foreign investors	79.5	4.3	61.0	9.4
Commercial banks	——	——	17.8	2.7
Mutual savings banks	3.4	——	20.5	3.1
Life insurance companies	59.5	3.2	240.9	37.0
Private pension funds	213.1	11.5	77.1	11.9
State and local government retirement plans	92.8	5.0	116.2	17.9
Other insurance companies	43.7	2.3	21.6	3.3
Mutual funds	69.4	3.7	18.1	2.8
Brokers and dealers	9.5	1.0	7.4	1.1
	$1,842.5	100.0%	$650.7	100.0%

Source: Board of Governors of the Federal Reserve System, Flow of Funds Accounts, Assets and Liabilities Outstanding, 1959–1982. Data for 1984 were estimated from the Flow of Funds Accounts, First Quarter 1985.

[a]Stocks are valued at market value; bonds, at book value.
[b]Figure includes mutual fund shares.

Other types of securities are traded in the corporate securities markets, as well. These include rights, warrants, and options. You will learn more about these types of securities in Chapter 23.

Investors.   Table 4–2 shows who holds the stocks and bonds corporations sell. Households, or private investors, account for 69 percent of the ownership of common stocks. Private pension funds are next, accounting for 12 percent of the total. Bondholders present a substantially different picture. Life insurance companies and state and local government retirement funds are the largest holders of corporate debt. Together, these two institutions hold 55 percent of the total amount outstanding. Households are next, with only 11 percent of the total.

An Overview of the Primary and Secondary Markets   In the **primary securities market**, new security issues are sold to investors for the first time. In the **secondary securities market**, investors can sell securities they already hold to other investors. The primary and secondary markets are interdependent. In fact, many firms that deal in the primary market also deal in the secondary market—Merrill Lynch Pierce Fenner & Smith, Salomon Brothers Inc., and The First Boston Corporation, for example. It is easy to see why the secondary market depends on the primary market, where securities issues originate. Let's look more closely at how the secondary market affects the primary market.

The secondary market provides a means of reselling outstanding securities.

This is important because it encourages short-term investors to provide long-term capital to corporations. Short-term investors are willing to buy long-term securities because they know they can resell the securities if they wish to do so. For example, Philadelphia Electric Company sold 5 million shares of preferred stock to investors in the primary market. Some investors will hold the shares for years, whereas others will sell them within a few days because they want the money for other purposes. Philadelphia Electric and other companies would find it difficult and costly to sell long-term securities if investors had to hold debt securities until they matured and equity securities forever.

Another way to explain this is to say that the secondary market provides liquidity for investments. As you recall, that means investors can sell their securities on short notice with little or no loss from the current market price. If their investments were not liquid, investors would require higher rates of return because of the increased risk of holding the securities and the inconvenience of not being able to sell them.

A later part of this chapter will explain how the secondary securities market works. First, we'll consider the primary securities market.

The Primary Securities Market

Firms that deal in the primary market, where new securities are sold, are called investment bankers or underwriters. These firms provide a number of services to companies issuing new securities. Some of these services are described below.

Investment Bankers   **Investment bankers**, or underwriters, such as Merrill Lynch and The First Boston Corporation, bring together organizations that need capital with organizations or individuals that have funds to invest. In this way, they help to allocate financial resources; and by helping companies raise capital, they help the economy grow. The principal functions of investment bankers—helping borrowers and selling securities—are explained next. In addition, investment bankers help companies buy and sell other companies. More will be said about these mergers and divestitures in Chapter 24.

How Investment Bankers Help Borrowers.   Business concerns that need long-term capital can get advice from investment bankers about securities and current market conditions. For example, suppose a corporation wants to sell bonds. The investment banker may advise the company that it would be better off selling a first mortgage bond (a bond backed by a first mortgage on real estate) than a debenture, because the interest costs would be lower. Investment bankers also consider the timing and pricing of a new issue and prepare a prospectus where required. Through these services, investment bankers help corporate borrowers obtain long-term funds at the lowest possible cost. Investment bankers provide similar services for corporate borrowers who sell commercial paper, a short-term source of funds.

Timing. Timing may be very important in the issuing of securities. For example, say that an examination of the corporate bond calendar, which gives the dollar volume of bonds offered monthly, indicates that $2 billion worth of new bond offerings are expected to be sold in March, but that only $1.1 billion of new bonds are expected in April. April appears to be a better time to sell bonds than March, because competition will be less. Timing is also important for stock issues. Investors are more receptive to new stock issues when stock prices are rising than when they are declining.

The Securities and Exchange Commission (SEC) requires that registration statements be filed for new securities issues; and this, together with other requirements, could delay the sale of new securities. However, an SEC rule (Rule 415) permits companies to register a security and then sell it at any time within the next 2 years. This procedure is called **shelf registration**. In essence, it allows a company to put a security offering "on the shelf" until the most advantageous time to sell it; then the offering can be sold on very short notice to investment bankers.

Pricing. Pricing new issues involves setting the price or interest rate at which they will be sold to investors. Let's say that a stock is thought to have an intrinsic value (that is, an estimated value based on an analysis of the firm) of $25 per share. In order to make the issue attractive to investors, the investment banker may suggest selling it at $23 per share. When the stock is **undervalued** (that is, worth more than the current price) investors will want to buy it, because they will believe its price will go up as soon as it is issued. But to price it too low would alienate the issuer, who wishes to raise as much money as possible. Thus, the stock price must be fair to the seller and attractive to the buyer. It is hoped that the price will assure the company of obtaining the capital it needs while creating demand for the stock.

Prospectus. As previously mentioned, registration statements have to be filed with the SEC; and before large issues of new securities can be sold, the SEC requires that prospective investors be given a prospectus. According to the Securities Act of 1933, a **prospectus** must contain the following information to provide prospective investors with sufficient information so that they can make an intelligent decision about buying the security.

1. Price to the public, commissions and discounts to underwriters, and net proceeds to the issuer.
2. Names of underwriters and amounts underwritten.
3. Uses to which the proceeds from the offering will be put.

4. Financial statements of the issuer.
5. Organizational form of the registrant (corporation, trust, and so on) and name of state or jurisdiction where organized.
6. List of controlling interests of the registrant.
7. Description of business and property.
8. History of the organization if less than 5 years old.
9. Pending legal actions.
10. Description of the type of security being registered and provisions that are pertinent to investors.
11. List of directors and executive officers and their remuneration.
12. Information about options to purchase securities from the registrant or its subsidiaries.
13. Principal holders of the type of security being issued.
14. Interests of management and others in certain transactions.

A **preliminary prospectus** is sometimes issued to investors so that they can become acquainted with most of the details well in advance of the **offering**—that is, the sale of the new issue. A final prospectus is issued when it is available. The preliminary prospectus is commonly called a **red herring**, because some statements on the front page are printed in red ink to warn prospective investors that the prospectus is incomplete. For example, the price at which the security will be offered is missing.

How Investment Bankers Sell Securities.   Investment bankers sell new securities to investors in four ways: through underwriting, best efforts, standby underwriting, and private placements. They also sell blocks of outstanding securities to investors. This is known as a secondary distribution.

Underwriting.   **Underwriting** is the most common method of selling new securities to investors. In this case, one or more investment bankers, or underwriters, buy a new security issue from a firm and resell it to investors. The underwriters' profit, if any, is the difference between the price they pay the issuer and the price at which they sell the securities to the public. Investment bankers also earn fees, which range from less than 1 percent to more than 10 percent, depending on the size of the offering and the effort and degree of risk to the investment banker. In general, it costs relatively more to underwrite a small issue than a large one. The reason is that about the same amount of work is required for both.

Underwriting securities can be a risky business. Consider the case of a $1 billion note and bond offering by IBM. Salomon Brothers was the lead underwriter and Merrill Lynch was the comanager of an underwriting syndicate of 225 firms working together to sell the issues. The underwriters' fee was $6.25 per $1,000 of bond or note issued. From that $6.25, Salomon Brothers and Merrill Lynch took $1.25 as managers, and another $1.25 went to the other underwriters. The remaining $3.75 was paid to the stockbrokers who work for the underwriters and who sold the securities to the public. The anticipation of earning these fees was the good news.

The bad news was that soon after the underwriters bought the billion-dollar issue, for which they paid IBM $987,625,000, market interest rates increased sharply. This occurred before the entire issue had been sold to investors. When market interest rates increase, the price of outstanding bond issues declines. (Chapter 6 will explain why this happens.) Accordingly, the prices offered for the unsold bonds held by the underwriters fell below the price they had paid for them. Estimates of their losses ranged from $10 million to $15 million![1]

Best Efforts.   When the second method of selling new securities is used, the underwriters do not buy the securities from the issuing firm. Instead, they agree to use their **best efforts** to sell the firm's new issue of securities. If they are unable to do so, the firm will own the unsold securities instead of the underwriters. This method shifts the risk from the underwriter to the issuing corporation.

Standby Underwriting.   **Standby underwriting** is used when a corporation wants to sell additional securities through a **rights offering**, in which securities are offered directly to existing security holders. In this case, the underwriter agrees to buy the unsold portion of the new issue. For example, a corporation may give existing shareholders the right to buy additional stock from a new issue. The underwriter will buy the shares not taken by the shareholders, thereby guaranteeing the success of the offering. Subsequently, the underwriter will sell the new shares to other investors.

Private Placement.   Some securities are sold directly to large institutional investors, such as pension plans and life insurance companies, instead of being sold to the public. These **private placements** accounted for about 33 percent of corporate security offerings in 1984. One advantage of a private placement is that the underwriting fees are less than for a public issue. Another advantage is that bond issues can be custom tailored to meet the needs of both the borrower and the lender. For example, suppose a company is raising funds to build a new factory that will not be completed for 3 years. The lender may agree to defer interest payments for the first 3 years.

Secondary Distribution.   Investment bankers also handle large transactions involving existing shares. Recently, for example, an estate wished to sell 750,000 shares of United Airlines common stock. If this large block of stock had been sold on the open market, the price of the stock might have been

[1]Walter Guzzardi, Jr., "The Bomb IBM Dropped on Wall Street," *Fortune,* November 19, 1979, pp. 52–56. The IBM bonds and notes were issued in October 1979. By March 1980, their market value was 75 percent of their face value. The "collapse" of the bond market occurred because of soaring interest rates and had nothing to do with the creditworthiness of IBM.

depressed. To avoid driving the stock price down, an investment banker made a **secondary distribution**—the sale of a large block of stock—at a reduced price. Investors were able to buy the shares at a discount from the current market price.

The Secondary Securities Market

Let's look again at the secondary securities market—the market for existing securities. The participants and the activities in this market are shown in Figure 4–3. The investors are the same as in the primary market, but the organization and operation of the two markets are different.

Stockbrokers and Dealers   Investors who want to buy and sell securities in the secondary market usually do so through stockbrokerage firms. Such firms act in two capacities in the secondary market: as dealers and as brokers. As mentioned earlier, investment bankers are often part of stockbrokerage firms, which provide retail outlets for the securities they underwrite, selling to individuals and other investors. In this capacity, stockbrokerage firms are **dealers**. They trade for their own accounts and hope to make a profit by buying securities at a low price and selling them at a higher price.

Stockbrokerage firms also act as **brokers** in the secondary market. Brokers are agents for their customers, instead of being principals in the transactions. This means that they have no financial interest in the transaction and only

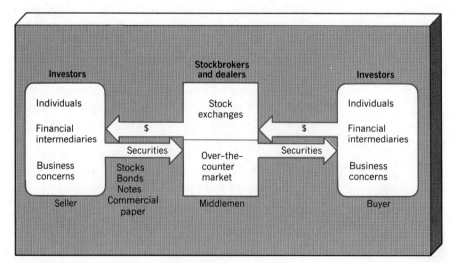

Figure 4–3 The secondary securities market.

receive a commission for their services. A stockbrokerage firm cannot act as both a broker and a dealer in the same transaction.

Not all stockbrokerage firms offer the same services. Some, like E. F. Hutton, offer such a wide variety of services that they might more appropriately be called financial supermarkets or securities firms than stockbrokerage firms. At the other end of the spectrum are **discount brokers**. These brokerage firms handle securities transactions for their clients at relatively low commission rates because they do not provide research and other costly services. In a sense, they are like discount self-service gas stations, where prices are lower because fewer services are offered. Some banks and other organizations have working arrangements with discount brokers or have their own subsidiaries that offer discount brokerage services.

Financial managers take the size and services offered by stockbrokerage firms into account when selecting a firm to underwrite their securities. Companies with international operations, such as IBM, select managing underwriters that can organize a syndicate to distribute the securites nationwide and that have the financial resources to handle such an issue. Smaller companies that do not require the same financial commitment or national scope for distribution may find regional firms or small local firms suitable to underwrite their issues.

Structure of the Secondary Securities Market

Transactions in the secondary market take place on a stock exchange or in the over-the-counter market. However, this market structure is slowly changing, as you will see.

Stock Exchanges. A **stock exchange** is a place where member stockbrokerage firms trade securities on behalf of themselves and their clients. Ten stock exchanges are registered with the Securities and Exchange Commission. The **New York Stock Exchange (NYSE)** is by far the largest, accounting for more than 80 percent of the total dollar volume of trading activity. The securities of about 1,500 companies are traded on the NYSE, including those of such giants as IBM, General Motors, Exxon, and General Electric. For a company, being **listed** on the NYSE—that is, having its securities traded there—is prestigious. (There is prestige associated with being listed on the other exchanges, too—but not as much.) The other registered stock exchanges are the American Stock Exchange, the Boston Stock Exchange, the Chicago Board Options Exchange, the Cincinnati Stock Exchange, the Midwest Stock Exchange, the Philadelphia Stock Exchange, the Pacific Stock Exchange, the Intermountain Stock Exchange, and the Spokane Stock Exchange. Stocks can be listed on more than one exchange.

Over-the-Counter Market. All securities that are not traded on an organized stock exchange are traded in the **over-the-counter (OTC) market**. In this system, securities brokers and dealers located throughout the world transact business by telephone, teletype, or some other means of communication. More than 40,000 issues are traded over the counter. They include U.S. government securities, state and local government obligations, corporate securities, foreign securities, bank and insurance company securities, and others. The quality of the securities traded in the OTC market ranges from very low quality to the highest quality possible. Even some stocks listed on stock exchanges are traded in the OTC market periodically. This generally happens when financial institutions are trading large **blocks of stock** (10,000 shares or more) among themselves to minimize commission costs.

The major difference between trading stock on a stock exchange and in the OTC market is technical in nature. Transactions on the major stock exchanges take place on an **auction** basis; that is, in a stock exchange, stocks are sold to the highest bidder on the trading floors. Because all the buyers and sellers of the stock are standing together, they can communicate easily. However, buyers and sellers in the OTC market may be at opposite ends of the country. Brokers and dealers have to **negotiate** the final price by telephone or teletype.

National Market System.   The existing market structure of stock exchanges and over-the-counter market are evolving into a **national market system**—a nationwide computer-based information system that will make price and volume data available to all interested parties. Any qualified broker or dealer registered with the Securities and Exchange Commission will have access to it. The system will reduce the relative importance of stock exchanges and increase the relative importance of small securities firms that were previously excluded from participating directly in the market.

Parts of the national market system are already in place. However, it will take many years to make the system fully operational. One reason is that many legal and technical barriers have to be overcome. Another is that some major participants in the stock market are reluctant to see their relative importance decline with the rise of the national market system.

The Continuous Market   The evolution of the securities markets is important because it will help ensure a smoothly functioning **continuous market** for securities, which in turn facilitates corporate financing. A continuous market has five attributes: high trading volume, narrow spread between the prices at which securities are bought and sold, minimal price changes, liquidity, and prompt execution. Together, these characteristics make it possible for short-term investors to deal in long-term securities.

High Trading Volume.   On one day in 1986, 200 million shares were traded on the New York Stock Exchange, and 100-million-share days are not uncommon on the NYSE. This high trading volume means that shares can be bought and sold at any time during the hours of operation of the exchange. (It should be noted, though, that some stocks are traded rarely, if at all. Such securities are uncommon on the New York Stock Exchange but common in the over-the-counter market.)

Narrow Spread.   The **spread** is the difference between the bid price and the asked price. The **bid price** is the price at which dealers are willing to buy the security from investors (investors can sell the security at that price); and the **asked price** is the price at which dealers will sell to investors (investors can buy the security at that price). For example, assume that a stock is being traded at $15 bid/$16 asked. This means investors can buy the stock at $16 per share or sell it at $15 per share. The $1 spread is considered relatively small and conducive to trading. If the stock were quoted at $15 bid/$22 asked, the $7 spread would inhibit trading. As a rule, relatively small spreads characterize actively traded securities.

Minimal Price Changes.   Price changes between transactions tend to be relatively small when trading is active and spreads are relatively small. A security traded at $16.50, for example, might next be traded at $16.75 or $16.25. Price changes of less than $0.50 are common. Price changes in higher-priced stocks seem larger, of course. The price for a stock trading at $515 bid/$530 asked may change by $10 or more between transactions. But the $0.50 change in the $16.50 stock is a 3 percent change, while the $10 change in the $515 stock is only a 1.9 percent change. Therefore, the $10 price change is small relative to the stock's price.

Liquidity.   Continuous markets provide liquidity. Investors can sell securities within minutes after the order to do so has been given. Compare the liquidity of a marketable security with that of a parcel of real estate. It may take months to find a buyer for the real estate and even longer to consummate the transaction.

Prompt Execution.   Orders to buy or sell securities in continuous markets are executed promptly. It takes about 2 or 3 minutes from the time an order is received by a stockbroker until it is executed on the New York Stock Exchange. The time is somewhat longer in the over-the-counter market.

Market Information   Readily available information about securities prices and dividends is another advantage associated with continuous securities markets. Such information is published daily in many newspapers and reported as sales are transacted by some cable television stations. Let's look at the way market information is expressed.

Stock Quotations.   Table 4–3 shows a listing of NYSE stock transactions from the *Wall Street Journal*. Consider the information for Black & Decker Manufacturing as an example. Black & Decker, known for its portable electric tools, is identified in the table by the abbreviation *BlackD*.

The first two columns in the row for Black & Decker show that during the 52 weeks that ended on September 23, 1985—the date of this quotation—the company's stock was traded at a high of 26 7/8 per share and a low of 17 1/4 per share. Most stock prices are reported to 1/8 of a point. A **point** is $1.00; so 1/8 is $0.125. Black & Decker shares, then, traded at a high of $26.875 and a low of $17.25.

The next column shows the dividend at 0.64, which means that Black & Decker had paid or declared a $0.64 cash dividend within the previous 12 months. The dividend is followed by the **current yield**—the cash dividend divided by the current market price, which is the **closing price** for the day, shown in the tenth column. The current yield for Black & Decker was 3.6 percent ($0.64/$17.75 = 3.6%).

Next is the **price/earnings (P/E) ratio**. The *Wall Street Journal* determines the P/E ratio by dividing the market price per share by the amount of earnings per share (which is reported by the company but not shown in this table). Black & Decker was selling at 15 times earnings. The average P/E ratio for stocks at that time was 12 times earnings. Therefore, Black & Decker stock had a relatively high P/E ratio. High P/E ratios are frequently associated with good prospects for growth.

The next column reports the number of shares traded, expressed in hundreds; 1,500 shares of Black & Decker stock were traded on September 23, 1985. During the day the highest price per share was 18, the lowest was 17 5/8, and the stock's final price of the day, as mentioned earlier, was 17 3/4. The last column, labeled **net change**, shows that this closing price was up $0.25 from the previous trading session's closing price.

Bond Quotations.   Table 4–4 shows a partial listing of bond quotations from the *Wall Street Journal*. Some of the terms at the heads of columns, such as *high*, *low*, and *close*, have the same meanings as in stock quotations. However, for bonds, volume is expressed in thousand-dollar units and prices are expressed as a percentage of face value. Most bonds, as mentioned earlier, have a face value of $1,000. Therefore, a price of $92 means 92 percent of $1,000, or $920.

To illustrate the reading of bond quotations, let's look at the Dow bonds in the table. *Dow* is Dow Chemical Company, which has several bonds outstanding, issued over a period of several years. We'll consider the bonds described

Table 4–3

New York Stock Exchange Transactions, September 23, 1985

NEW YORK STOCK EXCHANGE COMPOSITE TRANSACTIONS

Monday, September 23, 1985

Quotations include trades on the Midwest, Pacific, Philadelphia, Boston and Cincinnati stock exchanges and reported by the National Association of Securities Dealers and Instinet

Source: *Wall Street Journal*, September 24, 1985, p. 62.

Table 4–4
New York Exchange Bonds, September 23, 1985

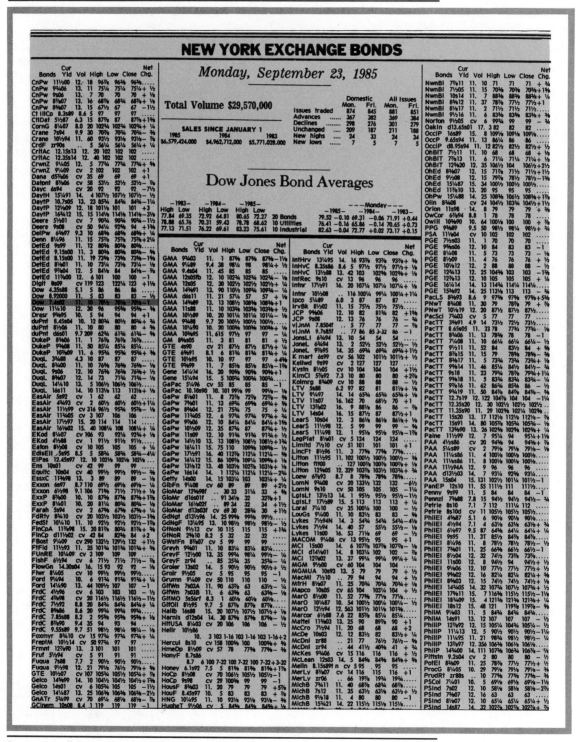

in the third entry for Dow. The second column in this row reads 7.4s02. That means the bond has a 7.4 percent *coupon rate* (each $1,000 face value of bond pays $74 interest per year), and it matures in the year 2002. The current yield on the bond is about 11 percent. This figure was determined by dividing the dollar amount of interest paid on the bond by the bond's current market price—again, the closing price ($74/$701.25 = 10.55%). The highest price for the bond was 70 1/2, which translates into $705. The lowest was 70 1/8, or $701.25. The net change from the previous trading session's close was −1—down $1.00. Notice that although bond prices are expressed as percentages of face value, the net change is expressed in dollar terms.

Efficient Markets   In theory, the proliferation of information about business concerns gives investors sufficient information to price securities correctly. The current prices of stocks, in other words, can fully reflect all information that is available. If this is so, then current and past prices of a security give no information about future price movements, and sequential price changes are independent of each other. That is, the fact that a security's price increases today is no indication that it will increase—or decrease—tomorrow. The net result of this and other conditions is that the stock market is said to be **efficient**. This means that, on the average, investors will not be able to outperform the market.

Analysts disagree about how efficient markets are. Three degrees of efficiency—weak, semistrong, and strong—have been postulated.

Weak Form.   According to the **weak form** of the efficient market hypothesis, each stock price change is independent of previous price changes; stock prices are said to follow a *random walk*. Therefore, investors are not able to predict future price changes by examining past stock market prices. In other words, the history of a stock's price changes tells us nothing about future changes in that stock's price.

Semistrong Form.   While the weak form of the efficient market hypothesis focuses on stock prices, the **semistrong form** incorporates a wider range of information. It considers publicly available information, such as financial statements and reports and investment advisory reports, for example. According to the semistrong form hypothesis, current stock prices fully reflect such information.

Strong Form.   The **strong form** of the efficient market hypothesis asserts that no amount of information, public or private, is of use, because the market anticipates all information, which is fully reflected in the current price.

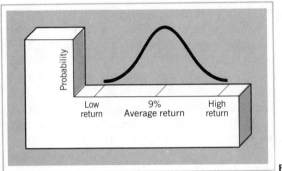

Figure 4–4   Stock market returns.

Implications of Market Efficiency.   The degree of efficiency in the securities markets is debatable. Nevertheless, a substantial body of literature indicates that the stock market is reasonably efficient. This suggests that, on the average, stock market investors can expect to earn only an average rate of return. The past average annual compound return for stocks was about 9 percent; for bonds, about 4 percent (see Chapter 6 for details).[2] However, these figures are subject to wide variations.

Figure 4–4 shows an average return in the stock market of about 9 percent. Most investors, as you can see, will earn about 9 percent; but a few will earn a high return of 30 percent or more, while others will earn nothing. It is the different degrees of risk as well as the random chance of earning high returns that attract many investors and speculators to the stock market.

Summary

The U.S. financial system includes three types of economic units: business concerns, individuals, and financial intermediaries. Financial intermediaries help savers channel their funds into investments in business concerns and others. Banks are the financial intermediaries used most by businesses. Other financial intermediaries, such as savings and loan institutions and life insurance companies, offer more specialized services.

Firms use both internal and external sources for the funds they need. External sources include debt and the sale of stock; debt is the major external source of funds. Firms often turn to the corporate securities markets to raise funds. In the primary securities market, new issues are sold; and in the secondary securities market, outstanding securities are resold to other investors. The exis-

[2]The average annual return for the Standard & Poor 500 index, including reinvestment of dividends over a 56-year period, was 9.1 percent measured by the geometric mean and 11.5 percent measured by the arithmetic mean.

tence of the secondary market provides liquidity for investments and thus encourages short-term investors to provide long-term capital to corporations.

Firms that help corporations sell securities in the primary market are investment bankers, or underwriters. They provide advice about securities issues and also help sell securities through underwriting, best efforts, stand-by underwriting, private placements, and secondary distributions.

Investors who want to buy and sell securities in the secondary market do so through stockbrokerage firms. The secondary market consists of stock exchanges and the over-the-counter market, but this structure is evolving into a national market system that will make price and volume information more widely available. This evolving system will enhance the continuous nature of securities markets, which facilitates corporate financing.

In theory, the proliferation of information about business concerns gives investors sufficient information to price securities correctly. Because securities' prices reflect their value, investors will not, on the average, be able to outperform the market.

Important Terms

Asked price
Auction basis
Best efforts
Bid price
Block of stock
Bond
Broker
Circular flow of money
Closing price
Collateral
Continuous market
Convertible bond
Current yield
Dealer
Debenture
Discount
Discount broker
Efficient markets
Face value or amount
Financial intermediaries
Investment banker
Listed (on an exchange)

Mortgage bond
National market system
Negotiated basis
Net change
New York Stock Exchange (NYSE)
Offering
Over-the-counter (OTC) market
Par value
Point
Preliminary prospectus
Price/earnings (P/E) ratio
Primary securities market
Private placement
Prospectus
Red herring
Rights offering
Secondary distribution
Secondary securities market
Semistrong form of efficient market hypothesis
Shelf registration
Spread

Standby underwriting
Stock exchange
Strong form of efficient market hy-
    pothesis
Undervalued

Underwriting
Weak form of efficient market hy-
    pothesis
Zero-coupon bond

Questions

1. Describe the circular flow of money.
2. In what two ways are household savings channeled to business firms?
3. Identify four major financial intermediaries and their traditional specialties.
4. What are two major internal sources of funds for businesses? What are two major external sources of funds? Which form accounts for the most funds raised externally?
5. What is the major difference between primary and secondary securities markets?
6. What does it mean to say that secondary markets provide liquidity?
7. Investment bankers are important financial intermediaries. Discuss their functions and explain their importance to corporations and to the financial system as a whole.
8. What are some factors to be considered in pricing a new issue of stock?
9. Explain why underwriting securities is risky business.
10. What general kinds of information must be included in a prospectus?
11. Contrast best efforts selling with standby underwriting.
12. What does SEC Rule 415 permit?
13. Explain two major advantages of private placement of securities.
14. Under what circumstances does a secondary distribution of securities occur? What impact does such a distribution have on the price of the stock involved?
15. What groups of investors are the major owners of corporate stock? Of corporate bonds?
16. Identify the two major types of secondary markets and two key differences between them.
17. Explain the difference between brokers and dealers.
18. Contrast an auction with a negotiated market.
19. What is the national market system?
20. Is there any relationship between the volume of trading in a stock and dealers' spreads on trades in that stock? Explain.
21. Explain the characteristics of a continuous market.
22. Consider information on the common stock of Delta Airlines (DeltaAr), in Table 4–3. What was the most recent 12-month dividend? Dividend yield? How many shares were traded on Monday, September 23? At what price did the final trade on that day occur?
23. What is a point?
24. Examine Table 4–4. How many Exxon 6s97 traded on September 23? What was the closing price? By how many dollars did this price differ from the previous day's close? What is the current yield? Is this bond selling at a discount? Explain.

25. There is an old Wall Street saying: "The markets have no memory." What is a more sophisticated term for this market characteristic? Explain.
26. What are the implications of efficient markets theory for investors who seek to earn above-average profits? Why?
27. Compare and contrast the weak, semistrong, and strong forms of the efficient markets hypothesis.

PART 2

Valuation and the Cost of Capital

Maximizing shareholder wealth is an objective emphasized throughout this book. In general, it means that financial managers, and other managers as well, should make decisions that enhance the value of the company. But how do they determine value?

The three chapters of Part 2 deal directly and indirectly with determining value. Chapter 5 explains the time value of money—the concept that money received today is worth more than the same amount received in the future. The concept underlies the theories of valuation discussed in Chapter 6. In Chapter 7, we turn our attention to the cost of capital, a rate of return widely used in valuation decisions.

The Time Value of Money

When we talk about the **time value of money**, we recognize that people prefer to receive a given amount of money now rather than at some time in the future. Consider the case of Al's Truck Leasing Company (a lessor) and Maria Ortiz (a lessee). Al wants Maria to give him a year's lease payment in advance rather than at the end of the year. If he receives the money now, he can invest it.

Maria Ortiz, however, is no fool. She does not want to pay the entire amount now. Maria has explained to Al that she will pay the year's rent in advance only if she can get a price reduction. Maria argues that she can invest her funds in a bank for a year and get a 12 percent return; so if Al wants the entire rent now, he should be willing to take 12 percent less. In the end, Al agrees because he knows that he too can invest the money for a 12 percent return.

This example illustrates two important concepts used throughout this book. The first is that investors want to get monetary returns (such as Al's lease payments) as soon as possible. Second, investors must consider the returns they can receive on alternative investments (such as putting funds in the bank) to determine how much they will pay for the funds. In this example, Al was willing to give a 12 percent discount to receive the lease payment today instead of waiting 1 year to get it. In other words, the time value of money was 12 percent.

After reading this chapter and its appendixes, you should know the following.

1. What *compound interest* is.
2. What *future value* means.
3. What impact high interest rates have.
4. What makes compounding powerful.
5. What *reinvestment rates* are.
6. What *present value* means.
7. How to use annuities to save time in working problems.
8. How to use future value, present value, and annuity tables.
9. How to use time value of money equations for other purposes.
10. How to use a calculator to solve present and future value problems.

Future Value

Future value is central to the concept of time value of money. To understand future value, it is necessary to understand compound interest. **Compound interest** is paid not only on the principal but also on the interest already earned. As an illustration, suppose you deposit $100 (the **principal amount**) in a bank. At the end of one year, the bank will pay 8 percent interest. Therefore, the **future value** of your $100 at the end of one year—in other words, the dollar amount that will be available at the end of the first period—is $108, the principal amount plus $8 interest. This relationship between time and money can be written in equation form as follows.

$$\text{Future value at end of 1 year} = \$100 \, (1 + 0.08) = \$108$$

$$FV_1 = PV_0 \, (1 + i)$$

where

FV_1 = Future value at end of 1 period
PV_0 = Present value (the principal amount in this example)
i = Interest rate

If the entire amount were left on deposit for 2 years, the future value at the end of the second year would include interest paid on the principal and interest paid on the first year's interest payment.

$$FV_2 = PV_0 (1 + i)(1 + i)$$
$$= PV_0 (1 + i)^2$$
$$= \$100 (1 + 0.08)^2$$
$$= \$116.64$$

The future value at the end of 3 years would be calculated as follows.

$$FV_3 = PV_0 (1 + i)(1 + i)(1 + i)$$
$$= PV_0 (1 + i)^3$$
$$= \$100 (1 + 0.08)^3$$
$$= \$125.97$$

The procedure by which the future value is found is called **compounding**. You can see that this compounding procedure could become cumbersome when many periods were involved. It is easier to use the following general equation for compounding.

$$FV_n = PV_0 (1 + i)^n \qquad (5\text{--}1)$$

where

FV_n = Future value at end of n periods
PV_0 = Present value
i = Interest rate
n = Number of periods

Equation 5–1 can be used to determine the future value at the end of any period. Suppose the original principal amount of $100 were left on deposit at 8 percent per year for 15 years. The future value at the end of 15 years would be calculated as follows.

$$FV_{15} = \$100 (1 + 0.08)^{15}$$
$$= \$100 (3.172)$$
$$= \$317.20$$

Table 5-1
Future Value of $1 Received at End of Period
$FV_n = PV_0 (1 + i)^n$

Year	1%	2%	3%	4%	5%	6%	7%	8%	9%	10%	15%	20%
1	1.010	1.020	1.030	1.040	1.050	1.060	1.070	1.080	1.090	1.100	1.150	1.200
2	1.020	1.040	1.061	1.082	1.102	1.124	1.145	1.166	1.188	1.210	1.322	1.440
3	1.030	1.061	1.093	1.125	1.158	1.191	1.225	1.260	1.295	1.331	1.521	1.728
4	1.041	1.082	1.126	1.170	1.216	1.262	1.311	1.360	1.412	1.464	1.749	2.074
5	1.051	1.104	1.159	1.217	1.276	1.338	1.403	1.469	1.539	1.611	2.011	2.488
6	1.062	1.126	1.194	1.265	1.340	1.419	1.501	1.587	1.677	1.772	2.313	2.986
7	1.072	1.149	1.230	1.316	1.407	1.504	1.606	1.714	1.828	1.949	2.660	3.583
8	1.083	1.172	1.267	1.369	1.477	1.594	1.718	1.851	1.993	2.144	3.059	4.300
9	1.094	1.195	1.305	1.423	1.551	1.689	1.838	1.999	2.172	2.358	3.518	5.160
10	1.105	1.219	1.344	1.480	1.629	1.791	1.967	2.159	2.367	2.594	4.046	6.192
11	1.116	1.243	1.384	1.539	1.710	1.808	2.105	2.332	2.580	2.853	4.652	7.430
12	1.127	1.268	1.426	1.601	1.796	2.012	2.252	2.518	2.813	3.138	5.350	8.916
13	1.138	1.294	1.469	1.665	1.886	2.133	2.410	2.720	3.066	3.452	6.153	10.699
14	1.149	1.319	1.513	1.732	1.980	2.261	2.579	2.937	3.342	3.797	7.076	12.839
15	1.161	1.346	1.558	1.801	2.079	2.397	2.759	3.172	3.642	4.177	8.137	15.407
16	1.173	1.373	1.605	1.873	2.183	2.540	2.952	3.426	3.970	4.595	9.358	18.488
17	1.184	1.400	1.653	1.948	2.292	2.693	3.159	3.700	4.328	5.054	10.761	22.186
18	1.196	1.428	1.702	2.026	2.407	2.854	3.380	3.996	4.717	5.560	12.375	26.623
19	1.208	1.457	1.754	2.107	2.527	3.026	3.617	4.316	5.142	6.116	14.232	31.948
20	1.220	1.486	1.806	2.191	2.653	3.207	3.870	4.661	5.604	6.728	16.367	38.338
25	1.282	1.641	2.094	2.666	3.386	4.292	5.427	6.848	8.623	10.835	32.919	95.396
30	1.348	1.811	2.427	3.243	4.322	5.743	7.612	10.063	13.268	17.449	66.212	237.376

Note: More detailed tables are presented in Appendix A at the back of the book.

The factor $(1 + i)^n$ in Equation 5–1 is the **future value interest factor**, which we will call $FVIF_{i,n}$. Calculations of $FVIF_{i,n}$ for various interest rates and time periods are shown in Table 5–1. For example, we can find the future value interest factor for 8 percent and 15 years (3.172) by reading down the 8 percent column until we reach the row for 15 years. The expression $FVIF_{i,n}$ can be substituted for $(1 + i)^n$ in Equation 5–1.

$$FV_n = PV_0 (FVIF_{i,n}) \qquad (5\text{–}2)$$

We can use the restated equation and the table to find the future value in another situation. Suppose a business concern with total assets of $50 million dollars is growing at a rate of 9 percent per year. What will the firm's total assets be at the end of 5 years? In this example, $50 million is the principal amount (PV); the interest rate (i) is 9 percent; and the number of periods (n) is five. Therefore, the future value at the end of five years is calculated as follows.

$$FV_5 = PV_0(FVIF_{9\%,\ 5\ \text{years}})$$

$$= \$50 \text{ million } (1.539)$$

$$= \$76.95 \text{ million}$$

It is important that the financial managers of this business concern know that it will grow more than 50 percent over the next 5 years. Firms facing such growth must consider adding personnel and equipment and arranging for financing before the need actually arises.

The Power of Compounding   The fact that compounding could make a company's assets grow more than 50 percent in 5 years gives some idea of its power. The power of compounding is particularly noticeable when interest rates are high for long periods of time. Figure 5–1 gives a graphic illustration of how the power of compounding increases as interest rates and time increase. The figure shows the growth of $1 compounded at 5, 10, and 20 percent over a number of years. The dollar compounded at 5 percent for 20 years grows to $2.65; compounded at 20 percent, it grows to $38!

Another illustration appears in Table 5–2, where $1,000 is compounded at 8, 14, and 20 percent for various periods of time. At the end of 5 years, the $1,000 will grow to $1,469 when compounded at 8 percent and to $2,488 when compounded at 20 percent. The differences among the future values become increasingly great as the years pass. At the end of 100 years, the future value of $1,000 is $2,199,761 at 8 percent and $82,817,974,520 at 20 percent.

Most investment and financing decisions involve shorter time horizons. However, even over shorter periods there are significant differences between

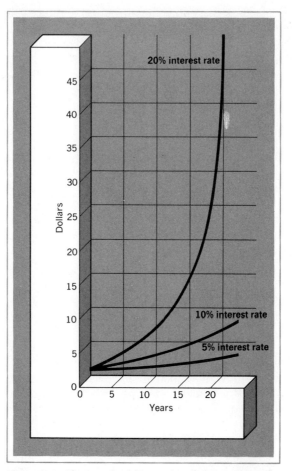

Figure 5–1   The growth of $1 compounded at various rates.

Table 5–2

The Growth of $1000 Compounded at 8, 14, and 20 Percent Annually

Year End	8%	14%	20%
5	$ 1,469	$ 1,925	$ 2,488
10	2,159	3,707	6,192
20	4,661	13,743	38,338
50	46,902	700,233	9,100,438
100	2,199,761	490,326,238	82,817,974,520

the future values of funds invested or borrowed at high interest rates and at low interest rates. These differences explain why many business concerns that borrow large sums study interest rate forecasts. They want to borrow at the lowest possible interest rates so that the future values they will have to pay are relatively small.

It should be noted that the future values shown in Table 5–2 assume that all interest payments are reinvested at the compounding rate (8, 14, or 20 percent). If the interest payments were withdrawn, the amounts received at the ends of the periods would be substantially less. For more discussion of this **reinvestment rate** assumption, read Appendix 5A, at the end of this chapter.

Present Value

The preceding section explained that future value is based on a compounding process. Now we will look at that same process in reverse to learn about present value. **Present value** is the current value of dollars that will be received in the future. A simple example will illustrate the concept. Suppose you are offered the chance to invest in a real estate development that will provide a future value of $50,000 when it is completed and sold at the end of 2 years. How much is earning $50,000 in 2 years worth to you today? In other words, what is the present value of $50,000 to be received at the end of 2 years?

Before we can answer that question, we must determine the rate of return you can receive on alternative investments. This rate of return is called the **opportunity cost**. Let's say your choices are to invest in marketable securities that provide a 10 percent rate of return or to invest in the real estate venture. You can do one or the other, but not both. Therefore, your opportunity cost for investing in the real estate venture is 10 percent. It is the minimum rate of return you must earn on the real estate venture before you will consider investing in it; thus, in this example, it is your **required rate of return**.

The required rate of return is also called the **discount rate**. Finding the present value of dollars that will be received in the future is often referred to as **discounting** or as finding the **discounted cash flow**. The equation used in this procedure is as follows.

$$PV_0 = FV_n \left[\frac{1}{(1 + i)^n} \right] \tag{5-3}$$

where

PV = Present value
FV_n = Future value at end of n periods
i = Interest rate (discount rate)
n = Number of periods

We can find the present value of the real estate venture by substituting $50,000 for the future value in the equation and discounting that amount by 10 percent for 2 years.

$$PV_0 = FV_n \left[\frac{1}{(1 + i)^n} \right]$$

$$= \$50,000 \left[\frac{1}{(1 + 0.10)^2} \right]$$

$$= \$50,000 \, (0.826)$$

$$= \$41,300$$

An amount of $50,000 to be received in 2 years is worth $41,300 today. In theory, if the discount rate is 10 percent, the investor would be indifferent between receiving $41,300 today and receiving $50,000 at the end of 2 years.

The factor $1/(1 + i)^n$ in the present value equation is called the **present value interest factor**, or $PVIF_{i,n}$. As with the future value interest factor, we can substitute the new expression into the basic equation.

$$PV_0 = FV_n(PVIF_{i,n}) \tag{5-4}$$

Like future value interest factors, present value interest factors can be found in tables, such as Table 5–3. To find the present value interest factor for the

Table 5–3
Present Value of $1 Received at End of Period

$$PV_0 = FV_n \left[\frac{1}{(1 + i)^n} \right]$$

Years	6%	8%	10%	12%	14%	16%	20%
1	0.943	0.926	0.909	0.893	0.877	0.862	0.833
2	0.890	0.857	0.826	0.797	0.769	0.743	0.694
3	0.840	0.794	0.751	0.712	0.675	0.641	0.579
4	0.792	0.735	0.683	0.635	0.592	0.552	0.482
5	0.747	0.681	0.621	0.567	0.519	0.476	0.402
6	0.705	0.630	0.564	0.507	0.456	0.410	0.335
7	0.665	0.583	0.513	0.452	0.400	0.354	0.279
8	0.627	0.540	0.467	0.404	0.351	0.305	0.233
9	0.592	0.500	0.424	0.361	0.308	0.263	0.194
10	0.558	0.463	0.386	0.322	0.270	0.227	0.162
11	0.527	0.429	0.350	0.287	0.237	0.195	0.135
12	0.497	0.397	0.319	0.257	0.208	0.168	0.112
13	0.469	0.368	0.290	0.229	0.182	0.145	0.093
14	0.442	0.340	0.263	0.205	0.160	0.125	0.078
15	0.417	0.315	0.239	0.183	0.140	0.108	0.065

Note: More detailed tables are presented in Appendix C at the back of the book.

real-estate venture problem solved above, we would simply look in the 10 percent column and the row for 2 years.

Let's use the present value table for a more complex problem. The financial manager of Plush Furniture Company wants to know the present value of expected cash flows over the next 5 years. As shown in Table 5–4, cash flows are expected to increase for 3 years and then decline. This pattern follows the long-range economic forecast used in the company's strategic plan.

Plush Furniture uses a 14 percent discount rate, which means it requires a 14 percent return. We can find the present value of the expected cash flow for each of the 5 years by multiplying that expected cash flow by the appropriate present value interest factor from Table 5–3. For example, the present value of the first year's expected cash flow is calculated as follows.

$$PV_0 = FV_1(PVIF_{14\%, \ 1 \ year})$$

$$= 10 \ (0.877)$$

$$= \$8.77$$

The results of calculations for all 5 years appear in Table 5–4. Over the 5-year period, Plush Furniture expects total cash flows of $63 million. The present value of those cash flows discounted at 14 percent is $43 million.

If Plush Furniture used some other discount rate, of course, the present value would be different. If the discount rate were reduced to 12 percent, for example, the present value would increase to about $45 million. Conversely, if the discount rate were increased to 16 percent, the present value would decline to about $41 million. This example demonstrates an important point: *Higher discount rates result in lower present values; lower discount rates result in higher present values.*

If, as suggested earlier, we think of the discount rate as an opportunity cost—that is, the rate that could be earned on alternate uses of the money—the relationship between present value and discount rates makes more sense. If

Table 5–4
Present Value of Expected Cash Flows for Plush Furniture Company

Year End	Expected Cash Flows (millions of dollars)	×	Present Value Interest Factor at 14% (from Table 5–3)	=	Present Value (millions of dollars)
1	$10		0.877		$ 8.770
2	14		0.769		10.766
3	15		0.675		10.125
4	13		0.592		7.696
5	11		0.519		5.709
	$63 million				$43.066 million

Plush can earn 16 percent, it will need fewer dollars today to produce the expected cash flows than if it could earn only 12 percent. Therefore, present value at 16 percent is lower than present value at 12 percent.

Relationship between Future Value and Present Value

The present value equation (Equation 5–3) is based on the future value equation (Equation 5–1). In fact, the present value interest factor is the reciprocal of the future value interest factor. That is, as you may have noticed, the present value interest factor, $1/(1 + i)^n$, is simply 1 divided by the future value interest factor, $(1 + i)^n$. Multiplying one factor by the other yields 1.

The values shown in Table 5–3, then, are the reciprocals of the values shown in Table 5–1. For example, Table 5–1 shows the future value of $1 compounded at 10 percent for 2 years to be 1.210. The reciprocal of this amount is 1/1.210, or 0.826, which is the present value of $1 discounted at 10 percent for 2 years. The reciprocal of 0.826 is, of course, 1.210 (1/0.826 = 1.210). Thus, we can determine the present value interest factor by taking the reciprocal of the future value interest factor, and vice versa. For more on this point and a method for using a calculator to determine interest factors that are not available in tables, see Appendix 5B at the end of this chapter.

Figure 5–2 should help clarify the relationship between present value and future value. This figure shows that the present value of $50,000 discounted at 10 percent for 2 years is $41,300. It also shows another way of looking at these figures; $41,300 compounded at 10 percent for 2 years is $50,000. Keep

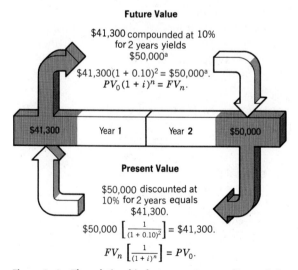

Future Value

$41,300 compounded at 10% for 2 years yields $50,000[a]

$41,300(1 + 0.10)^2 = $50,000[a].
$PV_0(1 + i)^n = FV_n$.

| $41,300 | Year 1 | Year 2 | $50,000 |

Present Value

$50,000 discounted at 10% for 2 years equals $41,300.

$50,000 \left[\frac{1}{(1 + 0.10)^2} \right] = $41,300.

$FV_n \left[\frac{1}{(1 + i)^n} \right] = PV_0$.

Figure 5–2   The relationship between compounding and discounting.

in mind that discounting (finding the present value) is the reverse of compounding (finding the future value), and vice versa.

One word of caution about compounding and discounting: The numbers shown in the future value and present value tables are rounded. For example, look at the bottom part of Figure 5–2, where the present value of $50,000 has been calculated. In the calculation, the value 0.826 is used for the factor $1/(1 + 0.10)^2$. Table 5–3 also gives 0.826 as the present value interest factor for $1 discounted at 10 percent for 2 years. However, the unrounded value is $0.82644628+$, which would yield a present value of $41,322.31. The difference caused by rounding in this example is only about $22. However, when we use high rates of interest and compound or discount over long periods of time, rounding errors can result in large differences. Where possible, use the complete number to make your calculations.

Annuities

So far, we have examined the present and future values of uneven cash flows. That is, the payments expected in future periods were unequal in size. Now we are going to examine even cash flows, or annuities, in which the payments expected are the same in each period. To be exact, an **annuity** is a series of periodic payments of equal amounts occurring over a specified period of time. Lease payments and interest payments on bonds are examples of annuities. In some cases, the cash flows from investment projects are annuities. Understanding how to value annuities makes it easier to solve certain problems involving equal cash flows.

There are several types of annuities. For the sake of simplicity, the examples used in this book are **ordinary annuities** unless otherwise specified. This means that periodic payments and interest payments are made at the end of each payment period and that the term of the annuity is specified—for example, 5 years.

Present Value of an Annuity We can determine the present value of an annuity by using a table or an equation. Let's look first at the table, Table 5–5, which is based on the present value table (Table 5–3). The following example will demonstrate how the 2 tables are related.

Suppose you want to know the present value of a lease that will pay $1,000 per year for 3 years. The lease payments are an annuity. The discount rate, or opportunity cost, is 16 percent. One way to solve the problem is to find the present value for each year using the procedure already described. Multiply the appropriate interest factor from the present value table by the future value—the receipt for each year.

End of year	Receipts (Future Value)	×	Present Value Interest Factors from Table 5–3 (16%)	=	Present Value
1	$1,000	×	0.862	=	$ 862
2	1,000	×	0.743	=	743
3	1,000	×	0.641	=	641
			2.246		$2,246

A time line showing this information is presented in Figure 5–3. The sum of the interest factors is 2.246—the same number Table 5–5 gives as the present value of an annuity at 16 percent for 3 years. In other words, we can obtain the same results with less effort by multiplying the periodic payment of $1,000 by the 2.246 interest factor for the present value of an annuity.

We can also refer to Table 5–5 when we use the following equation to determine the present value of an annuity.[1]

$$PV_a = PMT \sum_{t=1}^{n} \left[\frac{1}{(1 + i)^t} \right]$$

(5–5)

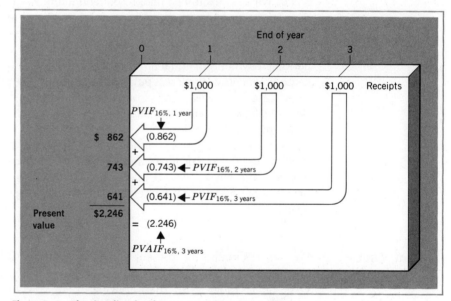

Figure 5–3   The time line for the present value of an annuity.

---

[1]An alternate form of the equation, which may be used when no PV_a tables are available,

$$PV_a = PMT \left[\frac{1 - (1 + i)^{-n}}{i} \right]$$

Table 5–5
Present Value of an Annuity of $1

$$\text{PMT} \sum_{t=1}^{n} \left[\frac{1}{(1 + i)^t} \right]$$

Years	6%	8%	10%	12%	14%	16%	20%
1	0.943	0.926	0.909	0.893	0.877	0.862	0.833
2	1.833	1.783	1.736	1.690	1.647	1.605	1.528
3	2.673	2.577	2.487	2.402	2.322	2.246	2.106
4	3.465	3.312	3.170	3.037	2.914	2.798	2.589
5	4.212	3.993	3.791	3.605	3.433	3.274	2.991
6	4.917	4.623	4.355	4.111	3.889	3.685	3.326
7	5.582	5.206	4.868	4.564	4.288	4.039	3.605
8	6.210	5.747	5.335	4.968	4.639	4.344	3.837
9	6.802	6.247	5.759	5.328	4.946	4.607	4.031
10	7.360	6.710	6.145	5.650	5.216	4.833	4.192
11	7.887	7.139	6.495	5.988	5.453	5.029	4.327
12	8.384	7.536	6.814	6.194	5.660	5.197	4.439
13	8.853	7.904	7.103	6.424	5.842	5.342	4.533
14	9.295	8.244	7.367	6.628	6.002	5.468	4.611
15	9.712	8.559	7.606	6.811	6.142	5.575	4.675

Note: More detailed tables are presented in Appendix D at the back of the book.

where

$$
\begin{aligned}
PV_a &= \text{Present value of an annuity} \\
PMT &= \text{Payment per period} \\
i &= \text{Interest (discount) rate per period} \\
n &= \text{Number of periods} \\
\sum_{t=1}^{n} \left[\frac{1}{(1 + i)^t} \right] &= \text{The sum of the interest factors for periods 1 through } n
\end{aligned}
$$

The last expression in the list above is the interest factor supplied in Table 5–5. We can also refer to it as $PVAIF_{i,n}$—the interest factor for the present value of an annuity.

$$\sum_{t=1}^{n} \left[\frac{1}{(1 + i)^t} \right] = PVAIF_{i,n}$$

Consequently, we can restate Equation 5–5 as follows.

$$PV_a = PMT\ (PVAIF_{i,n}) \tag{5–6}$$

To illustrate the use of this equation, we'll assume that Delta Industries can invest in a car wash franchise that promises to pay $60,000 per year for 3 years. The expected cash flows at the end of the 3 years can be thought of as an ordinary annuity. Delta's required rate of return (its discount rate) is 20 percent. Using the interest factor from Table 5–5, we find that the present value of the annuity is $126,360.

$$PV_a = PMT \ (PVAIF_{20\%, \ 3 \ years})$$

$$= \$60,000 \ (2.106)$$

$$= \$126,360$$

In other words, Delta would be willing to pay $126,360 to invest in the car wash franchise.

It should be noted that the interest factors listed in Table 5–5 can be used only when the payments are the same for each period. If the payments were uneven—for example, $1,000, $2,000, and $3,000—we would have to use the present value table (Table 5–3) or the present value equation (Equation 5–3).

Future Value of an Annuity   Delta Industries is concerned about funding its pension plan. Management wants to know how much the pension plan will be worth at the end of 5 years if the firm contributes $100,000 per year and invests the funds at 15 percent. This is the same as determining the future value of a stream of payments compounded at 15 percent. The equation used to solve this problem calculates the future value of an annuity.[2]

$$FV_a = PMT \left[\sum_{t=1}^{n} (1 + i)^{n-t} \right] \tag{5–7}$$

The interest factor for the future value of an annuity may also be expressed as $FVAIF_{i,n}$. (These interest factors may be found in Appendix B at the back of the book.)

$$\sum_{t=1}^{n} (1 + i)^{n-t} = FVAIF_{i,n}$$

Equation 5–7, then, can be restated as follows.

$$FV_a = PMT \ (FVAIF_{i,n}) \tag{5–8}$$

[2]An alternate equation, which may be used when no FV_a tables are available, is

$$FV_a = PMT \left[\frac{(1 + i)^n - 1}{i} \right]$$

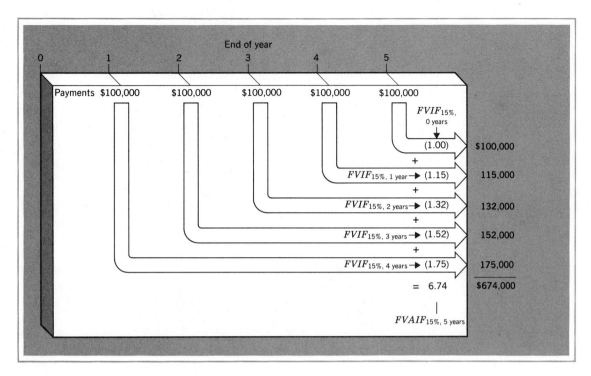

Figure 5–4 The time line for the future value of an annuity.

Accordingly, the management of Delta Industries can use the following calculation to determine the future value of an annuity at 15 percent for 5 years.

$$FV_a = PMT \, (FVAIF_{15\%, \; 5 \; years})$$

$$= \$100,000 \, (6.74)$$

$$= \$674,000$$

As shown in Figure 5–4, a payment is made at the end of each year. The time line shows that the first payment is compounded for 4 years, the second payment is compounded for 3 years, and so on. There is no compounding of the final payment.

Annuities Due The previous example, you recall, illustrated an ordinary annuity because payments were made at the *ends* of periods. When a payment is made at the *beginning* of each period, the annuity is an **annuity due**. Here, the first payment is made at Time 0 (instead of at the end of Year 1) and so is compounded for one more year, as are the other payments. Equation 5–6 can be modified to accommodate annuities due. We need only multiply the interest factors by $(1 + i)$ to take the extra compounding period into account.

$$FV_a \text{ (annuity due)} = PMT\ (FVAIF_{i,n})\ (1 + i) \qquad (5\text{–}9)$$

If we applied this equation to Delta Industries' situation, we would find the future value of the company's payments to be $775,100 instead of $674,000 because of the earlier payments and extra compounding.

$$FV_a = PMT\ (FVAIF_{i,n})\ (1 + i)$$
$$= \$100,000\ (6.74)\ (1 + 0.15)$$
$$= \$775,100$$

Present Value of a Perpetuity Some annuities, called **perpetuities**, begin on a definite date and never end. Consols, special bonds issued by the British government in the eighteenth century and still outstanding, are an example of a perpetuity. In some respects, a preferred stock is similar to a perpetuity, because it pays a fixed dividend forever or until it is retired. We determine the present value of a perpetuity by dividing the periodic payment by the discount rate.

$$PV_a^* = \frac{PMT}{i} \qquad (5\text{–}10)$$

where

PV_a^* = Present value of a perpetuity
PMT = Payment per period
i = Interest (discount) rate

For example, assume that a preferred stock pays a cash dividend of $2 per year forever and that investors require a 10 percent return. The value of one share of that preferred stock is calculated as follows.

$$PV_a^* = \frac{PMT}{i}$$
$$= \frac{\$2.00}{0.10}$$
$$= \$20.00$$

You will run into this concept again when we discuss the value of preferred stock in Chapter 6.

Related Topics

Future Values for Intrayear Periods So far, the examples of future values have assumed that compounding took place once a year. What about compounding for periods of less than a year? These so-called **intrayear** periods are important because cash flows from investments, bonds, and loans are frequently paid or received on an intrayear basis. The equation used for intrayear compounding is based on the future value equation (Equation 5–1). The difference is that the interest rate is divided by the number of intrayear periods, m; and the number of compounding periods, n, is multiplied by the same number. The equation for determining future value when intrayear compounding occurs is as follows.

$$FV_n = PV_0 \left(1 + \frac{i}{m}\right)^{nm} \tag{5–11}$$

Let's focus on the interest rate portion of the equation. If values are compounded only once a year, m is equal to 1, and the following equation results.

$$FV_n = PV_0 (1 + i)^n$$

This is the basic equation for future value. For example, if funds are compounded once a year at 16 percent, the annual yield is as follows.

$$FV_n = PV_0 (1 + 0.16)^n = 16.0\%$$

Suppose funds are compounded quarterly at 16 percent. In this case, there are four intrayear periods, and the annual yield is calculated as follows.

$$FV_n = PV_0 \left(1 + \frac{0.16}{4}\right)^{n \cdot 4} = 16.99\%$$

In this example of quarterly compounding, one-fourth of the interest is paid four times per year. With monthly compounding, one-twelfth of the interest is paid twelve times per year.

The data presented in Table 5–6 reveals that the number of times interest is paid per year is directly related to the annual yield. When 16 percent interest is paid once a year, the annual yield is 16 percent. However, the yield increases as the number of compounding periods increases. When interest is paid monthly, the annual yield is 17.23 percent; when it is paid weekly, the annual yield is 17.32 percent. The maximum yield of 17.35 percent is obtained with daily and continuous compounding.[3]

---

[3]The continuous yield is determined by calculating $e^{in} = (2.718)^{(0.16)(1)} = 17.35$ percent, where e is Euler's constant, and where e^{in} is the limit of $(1 + i/m)^{nm}$.

Table 5–6
Annual Yields Associated with Various Intrayear Compounding Periods When Interest Rate Is 16%[a]

Compounding Period	Times per Year (m)	Annual Yield
Annual	1	16.00%
Semiannual	2	16.64
Quarterly	4	16.99
Monthly	12	17.23
Weekly	52	17.32
Daily	365	17.35
Continuous[b]		17.35

[a]Based on the equation $FV_n = PV_0 (1 + i/m)^{nm}$.
[b]Continous yield $= e^{in}$.

Calculating Growth Rates and Number of Periods   Several ways in which time value equations are related have already been suggested. We should note that one basic equation can be used not only to determine future value and present value but also to find interest rates and number of periods. Look at the future value equation (Equation 5–1).

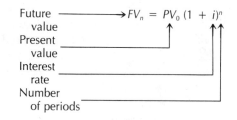

Future value ⟶ $FV_n = PV_0 (1 + i)^n$
Present value
Interest rate
Number of periods

Manipulation of this basic equation will allow us to solve for any one of its factors. Because we have already examined present value and future value,

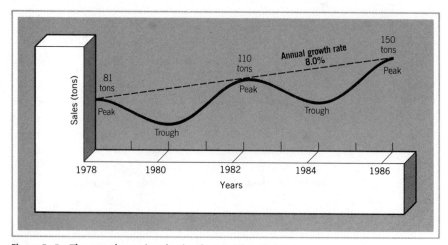

Figure 5–5   The growth rate in sales for the Ion Chemical Company.

the following examples show how to use the equation to find the interest rate (which can also be thought of as the growth rate) and the number of periods. The examples also show that the time value equations can be used for calculations that do not involve money.

Interest (Growth) Rate.   The financial manager of Ion Chemical Company was reviewing company sales in preparation for a meeting with the board of directors. As shown in Figure 5–5, chemical sales are cyclical. Ion's sales were 81 tons at the peak of the cycle in 1978 and 110 tons at the peak in 1982; 1986 sales are 150 tons. The financial manager wanted to compute the compound growth rate of sales and report that rate to the directors. Here, the compound growth rate can be thought of as the interest rate in the future value equation.[4]

$$\text{Interest (growth) rate per period} = i = \left[\frac{FV_n}{PV_0}\right]^{1/n} - 1 \qquad (5\text{--}12)$$

We can determine Ion Chemical's growth rate in sales in the following manner. Suppose the financial manager wants to know the growth rate from 1982 to 1986. In that case, the level of sales in 1986 is considered the future value, and the sales level during the 1982 peak is considered the present value. Accordingly, the growth rate can be calculated as follows.

$$i = \left(\frac{FV_n}{PV_0}\right)^{1/n} - 1$$

$$= \left(\frac{150}{110}\right)^{1/4} - 1$$

$$= (1.3636)^{0.25} - 1$$

$$= 1.0806 - 1$$

$$= 0.0806$$

$$\simeq 8\%$$

[4]The equation is derived as follows.

$$FV_n = PV_0 (1 + i)^n$$

$$\frac{FV_n}{PV_0} = (1 + i)^n$$

$$\left(\frac{FV_n}{PV_0}\right)^{1/n} = 1 + i$$

$$i = \left(\frac{FV_n}{PV_0}\right)^{1/n} - 1$$

The growth rate could have been measured from the peak in 1978 to the peak in 1982 or to the current level of sales. The rate would still have been 8 percent.

Number of Periods. At the meeting, one of the directors asked how many years it would take until Ion Chemical's level of sales reached 500 tons, the maximum capacity the company's manufacturing facilities can handle. That can be determined by solving the time value equation for n, the number of periods. We can start with this equation.

$$(1 + i)^n = \frac{FV_n}{PV_0} \tag{5-13}$$

The future value in this example is 500 tons and the present value is 150 tons. Because we know the company is growing at 8 percent per year, we can use 8 percent for i. Substituting these numbers into Equation 5–13 yields the following equation.

$$(1 + 0.08)^n = \frac{500}{150}$$

$$= 3.333$$

Recall that $(1 + i)^n$ is the future value interest factor, $FVIF_{i,n}$. Therefore, 3.333 is the future value interest factor at 8 percent for some year ($FVIF_{8,n}$). That year is n. To find n, we read down the 8 percent column in Table 5–1 (the future value table) to find the interest factors close to 3.333. An examination of the table reveals that 3.333 occurs between Year 15 and Year 16. Therefore, Ion Chemical should reach a sales level of 500 tons in 15 to 16 years.[5]

---

[5]Greater precision can be obtained by interpolating the interest factors. We do this by subtracting the interest factor for Year 15 from the interest factor for Year 16, which gives 0.254. We then subtract the interest factor for Year 15 from 3.333, which gives 0.161. By dividing 0.161 by 0.254, we obtain 0.634 years, which is added to 15 years; this results in a total of 15.6 years. Interpolation:

Step 1.	Year 16 interest factor	3.426
	less	
	Year 15 interest factor	-3.172
		0.254
Step 2.	Year n interest factor	3.333
	less	
	Year 15 interest factor	-3.172
Step 3.	$\dfrac{0.161}{0.254} = 0.634$ years	0.161
Step 4.	15 years + 0.634 years = 15.6 years	

Table 5–7
Summary of Equations

	Equation	Interest Factor and Location of Interest Factor Table	Equation Number
Future value	$FV_n = PV_0 (1 + i)^n$	$FVIF_{i,n}$ (Appendix A)	(5–1)
or	$FV_n = PV_0 (FVIF_{i,n})$		(5–2)
Present value	$PV_0 = FV_n \left[\dfrac{1}{(1 + i)^n} \right]$	$PVIF_{i,n}$ (Appendix C)	(5–3)
or	$PV_0 = FV_n (PVIF_{i,n})$		(5–4)
Present value of an annuity	$PV_a = PMT \sum\limits_{t=1}^{n} \left[\dfrac{1}{(1 + i)^t} \right]$	$PVAIF_{i,n}$ (Appendix D)	(5–5)
or	$PV_a = PMT (PVAIF_{i,n})$		(5–6)
or (when no tables are available)	$PV_a = PMT \left[\dfrac{1 - (1 + i)^{-n}}{i} \right]$		
Future value of an annuity	$FV_a = PMT \left[\sum\limits_{t=1}^{n}(1 + i)^{n-t} \right]$	$FVAIF_{i,n}$ (Appendix B)	(5–7)
or	$FV_a = PMT (FVAIF_{i,n})$		(5–8)
or (when no tables are available)	$FV_a = PMT \left[\dfrac{(1 + i)^n - 1}{i} \right]$		
Future value of an annuity due	FV_a (annuity due) $= PMT (FVAIF_{i,n}) (1 + i)$		(5–9)
Future value of a perpetuity	$FV_a^* = \dfrac{PMT}{i}$		(5–10)
Future value with intrayear compounding	$FV_n = PV_0 \left(1 + \dfrac{i}{m} \right)^{nm}$		(5–11)
Interest (growth) rate per period	$i = \left(\dfrac{FV_n}{PV_0} \right)^{1/n} - 1$		(5–12)
Number of periods (solve for n)	$(1 + i)^n = \dfrac{FV_n}{PV_0}$		(5–13)

---

[5]continued

The term n may also be determined from the following equation. This equation uses natural logarithms; therefore, you must have a table of natural logs or a calculator with natural log capability to use it.

$$n = \frac{\ln(FV_n/PV_0)}{\ln(1 + i)}$$
$$= \frac{\ln(500/150)}{\ln(1 + 0.08)}$$
$$= \frac{1.2039}{0.07696}$$
$$= 15.6 \text{ years}$$

Finally, an explanation of how to use a hand-held calculator to compute compound interest factors is presented in Appendix 5B.

Summary

The time value of money takes account of the fact that investors prefer to receive a given amount of money in the present than in the future. The concept is widely used in making investment and financing decisions.

Future value—the result of compounding—is central to the concept of time value of money. The equation for future value forms the basis for all the other time value equations discussed in this chapter. These important equations are summarized in Table 5–7.

The effects of compounding are particularly powerful when interest rates are high and long periods of time are involved. However, it is important to remember that future value computations assume that all funds are reinvested at the compounding rate.

Discounting is the reverse of compounding. It involves finding the present value of dollars that will be received in the future. When the cash flows to be compounded or discounted are made up of equal payments, they are annuities. Equations for the present and future values of annuities provide shortcuts in solving some financing and investment problems.

The basic time value equation can also be solved for interest (growth) rate and number of periods and can be used in some situations that do not involve money.

Important Terms

Annuity
Annuity due
Compound interest
Compounding
Discount rate
Discounted cash flow
Discounting
Future value
Future value interest factor
($FVIF_{i,n}$)
Intrayear period

Opportunity cost
Ordinary annuity
Perpetuity
Present value
Present value interest factor
($PVIF_{i,n}$)
Principal amount
Reinvestment rate
Required rate of return
Time value of money

The Reinvestment Rate Assumption

The reinvestment rate assumption is one of the most important concepts presented in this chapter and one of the cornerstones of the capital budgeting techniques presented in Chapter 8. Simply stated, it means that time value equations assume that *all* funds are reinvested at the relevant interest rate. Let's consider the implications of this statement.

The future values shown in the body of Table 5A–1 assume that all interest payments are reinvested at 8, 14, or 20 percent. If interest payments are not reinvested, compounding loses its power. In order to understand this very important point, consider the data presented in Table 5A–2. The top part of the table shows an original balance of $1,000 and the future value of that amount if all the interest payments are retained and invested at 20 percent. At the end of 5 years, the future value is $2,488.32; $1,488.32 interest has been earned.

The lower part of Table 5A–2 shows future values and interest payments if none of the funds are reinvested. At the end of 5 years, the future value is still $1,000 and the interest payments amount to $1,000. Failure to reinvest the interest payments reduces the total return by $1,488.32!

Let's look at this same issue from a different perspective. Assume that an investor buys a $1,000 bond that pays 10 percent interest per year and matures in 15 years. Further assume that the interest payments are made at the end of each year. Our question is: What annual compound interest rate, or *annual realized rate of return*, does the investor receive when the interest payments are withdrawn and when they are reinvested at various rates?[1]

---

[1] Because the cash flow, or coupon income, from a bond is the same each year, the total income is equivalent to the future value of an ordinary annuity (FV_a). After n periods, the total addition to income is

$$FV_a = PMT\ (FVAIF_{i,n})$$

or

$$FV_a = PMT\ \frac{(1 + i)^{n-1}}{i}$$

where

$$PMT = \text{Periodic payments}$$
$$i = \text{Interest rate}$$
$$n = \text{Number of periods}$$

Table 5A–1

Growth of $1,000 Compounded Annually at 8, 14, and 20 Percent

Year End	8%	14%	20%
5	$ 1,469	$ 1,925	$ 2,488
10	2,159	3,707	6,192
20	4,661	13,743	38,338
50	46,902	700,233	9,100,438
100	2,199,761	490,326,236	82,817,974,520

Table 5A–2

Reinvestment Compared with Failure to Reinvest

	Interest Reinvested at 20 Percent	
Year End		Interest
0	PV = $1,000.00	$ 0.00
1	FV = 1,200.00	200.00
2	FV = 1,440.00	240.00
3	FV = 1,728.00	288.00
4	FV = 2,073.60	345.60
5	FV = 2,488.32	414.72
		Total = $1,488.32
	Interest Withdrawn	
0	PV = $1,000	$ 0.00
1	FV = 1,000	200.00
2	FV = 1,000	200.00
3	FV = 1,000	200.00
4	FV = 1,000	200.00
5	FV = 1,000	200.00
		Total = $1,000.00

[1]continued

FV_a is Column 2 in Table 5A–3. The annual compound return investors receive from their original investment over the holding period is called the annual realized return (a), which may be determined with the following equation.

$$\frac{FV_a + F}{F} = (1 + a)^n$$

where

FV_a = Amount of an ordinary annuity
F = Face value of the bond payable at maturity
a = Interest rate per period, the annual realized rate of return
n = Number of periods

The annual realized return (a) is Column 3 in Table 5A–3.

Table 5A–3

Selected Returns from a 10 Percent Coupon Bond with 15 Years to Maturity

Reinvestment Rate (1)	Total Income from Coupons and Interest Earned over 15 Years	Annual Realized Rate of Return
0%	$1,500	6.3%
6	2,328	8.3
8	2,715	9.1
10	3,177	10.0
12	3,728	10.9
14	4,394	11.9

As Table 5A–3 shows, if no interest payments are reinvested, the investor will receive $1,500 over the life of the bond, and the annual realized rate of return will be 6.3 percent. If the interest income is reinvested at 6 percent, the investor will receive a total income of $2,328 and the annual realized rate of return will be 8.3 percent. Only when all funds are reinvested at 10 percent does the investor receive an annual realized rate of return of 10 percent. If all funds are reinvested at higher rates, the realized rate of return will increase commensurately.

The annual realized rate of return is also influenced by maturity. For example, if no funds are reinvested, the annual realized rate of return will range from 7.2 percent for 10 years to 5.6 percent for 20 years.

Two important lessons may be learned from these examples.

1. The reinvestment rate assumption applies every time future value, present value, or any of their variants are used.
2. Very high rates of return suggested by discounting techniques may be misleading if the funds earned are reinvested at lower rates.

Using a Calculator to Determine Interest Factors for Future and Present Value

Calculators that have exponent and reciprocal capability can be used to determine interest factors for future and present value, thereby eliminating the need for tables.

To determine the interest factor $(1 + i)^n$ used in the future value equation (Equation 5–1) use the following method.

$$FV_n = PV_0 (1 + i)^n$$

Example:

Determine the interest factor for 8.75 percent compounded for 5.25 years.

Action	Press Calculator Keys	Display Reads
1. Clear calculator	clear	—
2. Enter 1 plus interest rate	1.0875	1.0875
3. Raise to 5.25 power	$\boxed{y^z}$ 5.25 $\boxed{=}$	1.5533
		This is the compound interest factor $(1 + i)^n$.

To determine the interest factor $1/(1 + i)^n$ used in the present value equation (Equation 5–3) use the following method.

$$PV_0 = FV_n \frac{1}{(1 + i)^n}$$

Example:

Determine the interest factor for 8.75 percent discounted for 5.25 years. Use Steps 1 through 3 in the previous example.

Action	Press Calculator Key	Display Reads
4. Take the reciprocal of compound interest factor 1.5533	1/x	0.6438 This is the present value interest factor $1/(1 + i)^n$.

Also remember that the reciprocal of the present value interest factor is the future value interest factor, and vice versa.

Action	Press Calculator Key	Display Reads
5. Take the reciprocal of present value interest factor	1/x	1.5533

Answers on some calculators may differ slightly from these because of rounding of numbers.

Questions

1. Explain the phrase "the power of compound interest."
2. What is meant by the term *discount rate*? List some synonymous terms.
3. Define the term *reinvestment rate* and explain why it is important to a corporate finance manager or an investor.
4. Contrast the terms *present value* and *future value*. How are they related?
5. Define *annuity*. Give some examples of investments that usually provide returns in the form of annuities.
6. How does the present value of an annuity vary when the discount rate increases or decreases? How does the future value of an annuity vary with discount rate changes?
7. Contrast an *ordinary annuity* with an *annuity due*. Give an example of a financial instrument with payments in the form of an annuity due.
8. What is a perpetuity?
9. How can the factor for calculating the future value of an ordinary annuity be modified to calculate the future value of an annuity due with the same number of payments?
10. Can an ordinary annuity factor be used to compute present value as of Year 0 if the first cash flow begins at a time later than the end of Year 1? If so, explain how such a computation could be made. If not, why not?
11. If the highest stated interest rate you could receive was 8 percent, would you prefer yearly, semiannual, or monthly compounding of the 8 percent rate? Why?
12. Explain, in general, how present and compound value formulas can be used to solve for growth (interest) rates or for the number of periods.

Problems

1. Calculate the future value of the following sums *without* using the tables at the back of the book.
   (a) $450 on deposit for 5 years at 10 percent.
   (b) $800 on deposit for 10.5 years at 5 percent.
   (c) $100 on deposit for 8 years at 12.5 percent.
2. Using the tables, calculate the future value of the following sums:
   (a) $750 on deposit for 6 years at 15 percent.
   (b) $25,000 on deposit for 20 years at 8 percent.
   (c) $5000 on deposit for 2 years at 20 percent.
3. Determine the future value of a $1,000 deposit in your savings and loan association, compounded at an interest rate of 8 percent, as of the end of
   (a) 2 years.
   (b) 4 years.
   (c) 10 years.
4. The sales of a corporation have been growing more rapidly in recent years than in the past. Current sales have reached a level of $2 million annually. If they grow at a rate of 7 percent per year for the next 5 years, what will annual sales be at the end of that time?
5. In how many years will the sales of the firm in Problem 4 double? In how many years will they triple? If you do not have a calculator with logarithms, show how you would find an exact solution without giving a final answer. Then, estimate an answer from the tables.
6. Calculate the future value of $5,000 in 5 years when invested at 3, 8, 15, and 25 percent. What general principle is illustrated by your calculations?
7. Calculate the future value of $5,000 invested at 8 percent for 2, 5, 10, 25, and 40 years. What general principle is illustrated by your calculations?
8. If your opportunity cost is 10 percent, would you prefer $10,000 today, $17,000 at the end of 5 years, or $30,000 at the end of 10 years?
9. A credit union will lend you $10,000 today if you repay $18,000 at the end of 4 years. What is the effective rate of interest you would pay on the loan?
10. How much is $1,000 worth at the end of 5 years at a compound interest rate of
    (a) 0 percent.
    (b) 10 percent.
    (c) 100 percent.
11. Calculate the value of the following investments at the end of 5 years.
    (a) $100 invested at 10 percent compounded annually.
    (b) $100 invested at 10 percent with interest withdrawn when paid each year.
    (c) $100 invested at 10 percent with interest withdrawn when paid and deposited in an account earning 5 percent annually.
12. Calculate the present value of $1,000 to be received at the end of 10 years if the interest rate is
    (a) 0 percent.
    (b) 10 percent.
    (c) 100 percent.

13. Without using tables, calculate the present value of the following future amounts.
   (a) $400 at the end of 5 years at 7 percent.
   (b) $400 *per year* at the end of each of the next 5 years at 7 percent.
   (c) $200 at the end of 2 years at 10.5 percent.
   (d) $500 at the end of 2 years, 6 months at 10 percent.

14. In your analysis of Saranac Corporation, you find that current earnings per share are $5 and that most analysts are projecting a growth rate of 12 percent annually. What will earnings per share be at the end of 7 years?

15. If the earnings of Saranac in Problem 14 actually reach $8 per share at the end of 7 years, at what rate will they have grown? Show how you would solve mathematically for an exact answer *and* estimate and answer using the tables.

16. When you were in high school, your parents wished to provide for your college education by establishing a fund from which you could withdraw $10,000 per year at the beginning of each undergraduate year. Assuming you planned to enroll in a typical 4-year program, how much should they have invested at the beginning of your senior year in high school to make this financial plan possible? Assume they could have earned 14 percent on their investment.

17. What is the present value of an investment that promises to pay $10,000 at the end of the first 5 years and $20,000 per year at the end of each of the next 5 years? Use a discount rate of 18 percent.

18. Suppose the 10 payments described in Problem 17 occurred at the beginning of each year rather than at the end. Calculate their total present value at a discount rate of 18 percent.

19. How much would a person just turning 35 need to invest each year at 10 percent to accumulate $100,000 by age 60? Assume an ordinary annuity, with the first payment to be made on the saver's 36th birthday and the last payment on his 60th.

20. Calculate the value of $180,000 at the end of 2 years at an interest rate of 12 percent.
   (a) Compounded annually.
   (b) Compounded semiannually.
   (c) Compounded quarterly.
   (d) Compounded monthly.

21. Slinger, Inc., has issued bonds paying the holder $50 semiannually for 10 years and an additional $1,000 at the end of 10 years. At what price will a bond sell if investors can earn 12 percent annually on similar investments? (*Hint:* The bond price will be the total present value of all cash flows.)

22. Sellzar Corporation currently has sales of $100 million, and its marketing department is projecting sales of $800 million in 4 years.
   (a) What rate of growth in sales is being projected?
   (b) What would you expect the effects of such a growth rate to be on the finance function of the firm? (*Hint:* Think about the functions of the financial manager as discussed in earlier chapters.)

23. Elizabeth Palmer is 25 years old today and expects to live to be exactly 90. How much must she deposit at the end of each year, beginning on her 26th birthday and lasting until (and including) her 65th birthday, in order to receive an annuity of $30,000 from her 66th birthday to her 80th birthday and $20,000 per year from her 81st birthday until her death on her 90th birthday? She expects to be earning 8 percent interest annually throughout the entire period.

24. Russell Morgan has been married for exactly 5 years. He is planning to surprise his wife, Theresa, on their 30th wedding anniversary by taking her on an around-the-world trip. Until that time, including a final deposit on his 30th wedding anniversary, he will save $1,000 at the end of each year beginning on his 6th anniversary and will earn 9 percent. While on the trip, he expects their expenses to be $15,000 per year and hopes to earn 8 percent per year on their savings. Given Russell's savings plan, for how many years will they be able to travel?

25. If Russell Morgan in Problem 24 began his savings plan with an initial payment on his 5th wedding anniversary, how much would he accumulate by his 30th wedding anniversary? In this case, assume the last $1,000 payment will be made on his 29th anniversary.

Valuation, Rates of Return, and Risk

Beauty is in the eye of the beholder. One person may look at an abstract painting and see order and meaning. Another person looking at the same work of art may view it as random swirls of colors. To some extent the beauty of the painting depends on the insights and objectives of the viewer.

Similarly, two or more people can evaluate the same company and get different values. For example, an accountant may be interested in the company's book value, which is the value of the shareholders' equity. A tax assessor may be interested in the value of the firm's assets. Both these values differ from the liquidation value of a firm that is being dissolved and from the market value of a potentially profitable firm. The liquidation value is the value that will be received if the firm goes out of business. Under these circumstances, assets are frequently sold for less than they would be worth to a **going concern**—that is, a business whose operations are expected to continue. The value of a going concern is reflected in its market value—the price that willing buyers and sellers agree upon in an open market, such as the stock market.

113

This chapter is about the valuation of business concerns and the returns that people receive when they invest in business concerns.

After reading this chapter, you should know the following.

1. **How to use the basic model to determine the value of a going concern.**
2. **How interest rates and maturities affect bond prices.**
3. **How to apply the dividend valuation model.**
4. **How to apply the capital asset pricing model.**
5. **What returns investors in stocks and bonds have received for more than 50 years.**

The Value of a Going Concern

A valuation model provides a good starting point for determining the value of a firm that is a going concern. The **market value** of a going concern is equal to the market value of the firm's debt plus the market value of its equity.

$$V = B + S \qquad\qquad (6\text{--}1)$$

where

V = Market value of a going concern
B = Market value of the firm's debt (represented here by bonds)
S = Market value of the firm's common and preferred stock

We will use bonds as a proxy, or substitute, for the debt of a firm, although debt may also include mortgages, leases, and loans.

The market value of a publicly held corporation—the price its bonds and equity actually bring—is easy to determine. As you recall, corporations and others report to the public such matters as stock and bond prices. The following sections of this chapter describe how to determine the **intrinsic value** of a firm's bonds and its common and preferred stock. This value may differ from actual market value because it is a theoretical measure based in part on analysis and judgment. However, for simplicity, *we will assume that the intrinsic value is a reasonable approximation for the market value.*

The valuation process consists of using the time value of money concepts explained in Chapter 5 to calculate the present value of the expected cash flows from bonds and stock. The discount rates used in the calculations are the rates of return that investors in the firm's bonds and stock require.

Valuation of Bonds

Bonds, as you recall, are one type of long-term debt instrument. The market value of a bond—its price—is the sum of the discounted cash benefits, or returns, investors expect to receive over the life of the bond. Bondholders expect to receive two kinds of returns: interest payments over the life of the bond and a face value (typically $1,000) when the bond reaches maturity. Interest payments are usually made twice a year, but for simplicity, we'll assume one interest payment is made at the end of each year. Under this assumption, the price of a bond may be determined by the following equation.[1]

$$P_0 = \sum_{t=1}^{n} \left[\frac{I}{(1 + k_{db})^t} \right] + \frac{F}{(1 + k_{db})^n} \qquad (6-2)$$

where

P_0 = Price at time 0
I = Annual Interest payment
F = Face value of bond, payable at maturity
n = Number of years to maturity
t = Time (1 to n)
k_{db} = Current market rate of interest on newly issued bonds with similar characteristics, such as default risk and maturity

Notice that this equation adds two factors. The first factor describes the present value of the bond's interest payments.

$$\sum_{t=1}^{n} \left[\frac{I}{(1 + k_{db})^t} \right]$$

These payments, which are equal and regular, represent an annuity. Recall from Chapter 5 that to find the present value of an annuity we multiply the periodic payment by the appropriate interest factor from the table for present value of an annuity (see Appendix D at the back of this book for such a table). Thus, the first factor in the equation above can be restated as $I(PVAIF_{i,n})$, where I represents the annual interest payment and n represents the number of years

---

[1] If interest payments are made twice each year, the general equation for determining P_0 is as follows:

$$P_0 \sum_{t=1}^{2n} \left[\frac{I/2}{(1 + k_{db}/2)^{2t}} \right] + \frac{F}{(1 + k_{db}/2)^{2n}}$$

to maturity, as above, and i represents k_{db}, the current market rate of interest on newly issued bonds with similar characteristics.

The second factor, $F/(1 + k_{db})^n$, describes the present value of the bond's face value, F. We can find the present value by multiplying the future value by the appropriate present value interest factor (see the present value table in Appendix C at the back of this book). Here, the future value is F, the amount the bond will pay at maturity. The second factor in the equation, then, can be restated as $F(PVIF_{i,n})$.

Adding these two factors together gives the present value of all the returns investors expect from the bond. Restated, the equation is as follows.

$$P_0 \ I(PVAIF_{i,n}) + F(PVIF_{i,n}) \qquad (6\text{–}3)$$

This equation is used in the following manner. Suppose that a bond with a $1,000 face value and a 9 percent coupon interest rate was issued 5 years ago and that 15 years remain until maturity. As you may remember, the 9 percent coupon rate means that the bond pays $90 interest each year ($1,000 X 0.09 = $90). If the current interest rate on newly issued bonds with similar characteristics, such as risk and maturity, is also 9 percent, the price of the outstanding bond can be calculated as follows.

$$
\begin{aligned}
P_0 &= I \ (PVAIF_{i,n}) + F \ (PVIF_{i,n}) \\
&= \$90 \ (PVAIF_{9\%, \ 15 \ years}) + \$1,000 \ (PVIF_{9\%, \ 15 \ years}) \\
&= \$90 \ (8.0607) + \$1,000 \ (0.27454) \\
&= \$725.46 + \$274.54 \\
&= \$1,000
\end{aligned}
$$

The result—$1,000—is the amount investors will pay for the bond. The price and the face amount of the bond in this example are the same because the bond's coupon rate is equal to the current market rate of interest—9 percent. When the coupon rate differs from the market rate of interest, the price of the bond will change.

Interest Rates and Prices Market interest rates are always changing, so it is unlikely that the rates paid on bonds issued 5 years ago are the same as the rates paid today. What would happen to the price of the outstanding bond if current interest rates increased from 9 percent to 12 percent? In that case, the price of the bond would be calculated as follows.

$$
\begin{aligned}
P_0 &= \$90 \ (PVAIF_{12\%, \ 15 \ years}) + \$1,000 \ (PVIF_{12\%, \ 15 \ years}) \\
&= \$90 \ (6.8109) + \$1,000 \ (0.18270) \\
&= \$612.98 + \$182.70 \\
&= \$795.68
\end{aligned}
$$

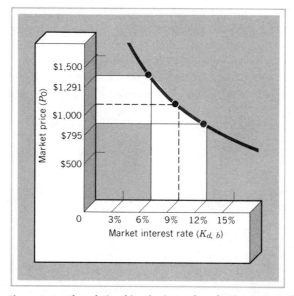

Figure 6–1   The relationship of price and market interest rate for a $1000 9 percent bond with 15 years to maturity.

The 9 percent bond would be selling at a deep discount from its face value.

On the other hand, what would happen to the price of the bond if interest rates fell to 6 percent? The price of the bond would be calculated as follows.

$$P_0 = \$90 \ (PVAIF_{6\%, \ 15 \ years}) + \$1,000 \ (PVIF_{6\%, \ 15 \ years})$$

$$= \$90 \ (9.7122) + \$1,000 \ (0.41726)$$

$$= \$874.10 + \$417.26$$

$$= \$1,291.36$$

The bond would be selling at a premium above its face value.

These examples demonstrate a very important point. Market interest rates and market prices of outstanding bonds are inversely related. Stated otherwise, when interest rates *increase* from 9 percent to 12 percent, the price of the bond *declines* from $1,000 to $795.68. Conversely, when interest rates *decline* from 9 percent to 6 percent, the price of the bond *increases* from $1,000 to $1,291.36. This relationship is shown in Figure 6–1.

Yield to Maturity   We can see from the preceding example that investors value bonds on the basis of current market rates of interest for similar bond issues. The market rate of interest, in turn, becomes the rate of return investors require if they hold the bond until maturity, or k_{db}. This rate of return is frequently referred to as the **yield to maturity**, or YTM.[2] YTM is the average rate of return on income and changes in price that investors will receive if the bond is held to maturity: It takes both interest income and capital gains or losses into account.

If we know the dollar amount of interest payments (I) and the current market price of the bond (P_0) we can determine the YTM precisely by solving Equation 6–2 (the bond valuation equation) for k_{db}. However, this method is cumbersome without the aid of a sophisticated calculator or a computer. The YTM can be approximated by the following equation.

$$YTM = \frac{I + [(F - P_0)/n]}{(F + P_0)/2} \qquad (6\text{–}4)$$

where

P_0 = Price at time 0
I = Annual interest payments
F = Face value of the bond, payable at maturity
n = Number of years to maturity

To illustrate the equation's use, we'll find the YTM for the bond described earlier as having 15 years to maturity, selling for $1,291.36, and paying $90 interest per year. We can calculate yield to maturity, using Equation 6–4, as follows.

$$YTM = \frac{\$90 + [(\$1,000 - \$1,291.36)/15]}{(\$1,000 + \$1,291.40)/2} = 6.16\%$$

Maturities and Prices   The extent to which changes in market rates of interest affect bond prices depends to a large degree on the maturity of the bonds.[3] When market rates of interest change, bonds with long-term maturities experience greater price changes than those with short-term maturities. Consider again the bond with a 9 percent coupon rate and 15 years to maturity. When the market rate of interest increased from 9 percent to 12 percent, the value of the bond declined to about $796. As shown in Figure 6–2, the price would have been $831 if 10 years had remained until maturity and $973 if 1 year had remained until maturity. Similarly, when market interest rates fell to 6 percent, the bond with

---

[2]The YTM should not be confused with the current yield, which is the interest income divided by the market price of the bond, or I/P_0. The current yield in the example above is $90/$1,291.40 = 6.97%.

[3]It can also be shown that a change of one percentage point in the market rate of interest will cause greater changes in bonds with low coupon rates than in bonds of the same maturity with higher coupon rates. For additional information, see Sidney Homer and Martin L. Leibowitz, *Inside the Yield Book: New Tools for Bond Market Strategy* (Englewood Cliffs, N.J.: Prentice-Hall, 1972), Chapter 3.

15 years to maturity had a price of $1,291. However, the price declines toward the face value as the years to maturity diminish. The lesson to be learned is that a change in market interest rates has a greater impact on the price of long-term bonds than on the price of short-term bonds when the coupon rates are the same.[4]

Bond valuation helps analysts determine the value of a firm. Remember, the firm's value is equal to the value of its debt plus the value of its equity. Suppose we were attempting to determine the value of Pulpo Fisheries, a corporation that specializes in seafood delicacies. Pulpo Fisheries has one

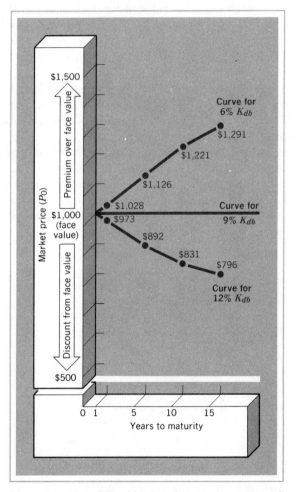

Figure 6–2   The relationship of market price, maturity, and market interest rate for a $1000 9 percent bond.

[4]The impact of changes in market interest rates on convertible bonds is not considered here. Convertible issues are examined in Chapter 23.

bond issue outstanding—$1 million worth of 9 percent bonds issued 5 years ago. The current rate of interest is 12 percent and the bonds will reach maturity in 15 years. The market value of the bonds is $795,680. Let's turn next to the equity side of the valuation equation.

Valuation of Stock

The method used for determining the value of stocks is similar to the method used for determining the value of bonds. Both methods discount the cash flows investors expect to receive by their required rates of return. However, the dollar amount of the cash flows investors receive from stocks varies widely. This is so because investors do not hold stocks for a set time period before selling them at a gain or a loss. Equally important, the cash dividends a firm pays may vary in amount from year to year, depending on its needs. In theory, the value of common stock is based on expected returns from cash dividends.

The basic dividend valuation model (commonly called the **Gordon model** because it was developed by Myron J. Gordon) assumes that the value, or price, of most common stock can be determined by discounting all the expected cash dividends of the firm. In this model, D_1, D_2, and so on represent cash dividends paid in every year in the future. These dividends are discounted by k_e, the rate of return required by investors in common stock. According to the model, then, the price of a share of common stock is the present value of an infinite stream of dividends.

$$P_0 = \frac{D_1}{(1 + k_e)} + \frac{D_2}{(1 + k_e)^2} + \cdots + \frac{D^\infty}{(1 + k_e)^\infty}$$

$$= \sum_{t=1}^{\infty} \left[\frac{D_t}{(1 + k_e)^t} \right] \tag{6-5}$$

where

P_0 = Price at time 0
D_t = Dividends per share expected in period t
k_e = Rate of return required by shareholders

Common Stock with Dividends Growing at a Constant Rate Let's assume that dividends are expected to grow at a constant rate, g. In that case, each dividend payment (D_t) is equal to the one before (D_0) plus g percent of D_0. D_t can be expressed as follows.

$$D_t = D_0 (1 + g)^t$$

Here, as suggested, D_0 is the dollar amount of the cash dividend at Time 0, and Time 0 can be thought of as the most recent period.

To accommodate this situation, Equation 6–5 can be rewritten as follows.

$$P_0 = \sum_{t=1}^{\infty} \left[\frac{D_0(1 + g)^t}{(1 + k_e)^t} \right] \qquad (6\text{–}6)$$

It can be further simplified to the following.[5]

$$P_0 = \frac{D_1}{k_e - g} \qquad (6\text{–}7)$$

This simplified equation is easy to use. Consider, for example, the stock of Standard Electric Company (SEC), a manufacturer of industrial electrical parts. SEC's stock is expected to pay a $1 cash dividend in the next period (D_1) and the growth rate of dividends (g) is expected to be 15 percent. SEC's investors require a 20 percent return. Using these figures and Equation 6–7, we find that a share of SEC is worth $20.

$$P_0 = \frac{D_1}{k_e - g}$$

$$= \frac{\$1.00}{0.20 - 0.15}$$

$$= \frac{\$1.00}{0.05}$$

$$= \$20.00$$

[5] Here is the simplification process. First, state Equation 6–6 as follows.

$$P_0 = D_0 \left[\frac{(1 + g)}{(1 + k_e)} + \frac{(1 + g)^2}{(1 + k_e)^2} + \cdots + \frac{(1 + g)^n}{(1 + k_e)^n} \right]$$

Multiply both sides of this equation by $(1 + k_e)/(1 + g)$.

$$\left[\frac{(1 + k_e)}{(1 + g)} \right] P_0 = D_0 \left[1 + \frac{(1 + g)}{(1 + k_e)} + \frac{(1 + g)^2}{(1 + k_e)^2} + \cdots + \frac{(1 + g)^{n-1}}{(1 + k_e)^{n-1}} \right]$$

Subtract the original equation from the result.

$$\left[\frac{(1 + k_e)}{(1 + g)} - 1 \right] P_0 = D_0 \left[1 - \frac{(1 + g)^n}{(1 + k_e)^n} \right]$$

$$\left[\frac{(1 + k_e) - (1 + g)}{(1 + g)} \right] P_0 = D_0 \left[1 - \frac{(1 + g)^n}{(1 + k_e)^n} \right]$$

Assume $k_e > g$ as n approaches infinity,

$$\left[1 - \frac{(1 + g)^n}{(1 + k_e)^n} \right]$$

Common Stock In reality, the growth rate of dividends on common stock varies over the life
with Dividends cycle of a firm and may also vary with business conditions. Figure 6–3 shows
Growing at a how cash dividends may vary over the course of a typical life cycle and a
Variable Rate business cycle. In general, as you may remember from Chapter 2, firms do
not pay cash dividends during the pioneering phase of the life cycle, because
they are not yet profitable. Dividends increase as the firm matures. Furthermore, many companies increase their cash dividends when business is good
in the recovery and prosperity phases of the business cycle and reduce them
or hold them steady when business activity declines. Accordingly, the growth
rate of dividends should be expected to vary over time.

Suppose that a firm's stock is expected to grow at rate g_x for a certain period
of time and at rate g_y thereafter. The value of the stock is determined by the
following equation.

$$P_0 = \begin{array}{c}\text{Present value}\\\text{of dividends}\\\text{growing at rate } g_x\end{array} + \begin{array}{c}\text{Present value}\\\text{of dividends}\\\text{growing at rate } g_y\end{array}$$

$$= \sum_{t=1}^{n} \left[\frac{D_0 (1 + g_x)^t}{(1 + k_e)^t} \right] + \sum_{t=n+1}^{\infty} \left[\frac{D_n(1 + g_y)^{t-n}}{(1 + k_e)^t} \right] \qquad (6\text{–}8)$$

where

g_x = Growth rate of dividends for n years
g_y = Growth rate of dividends for years $n + 1$ and beyond

This equation can be simplified.

$$P_0 = \sum_{t=1}^{n} \left[\frac{D_0 (1 + g_x)^t}{(1 + k_e)^t} \right] + \frac{D_{n+1}}{k_e - g_y} \left[\frac{1}{(1 + k_e)^n} \right] \qquad (6\text{–}9)$$

The equation can be expanded to include any number of growth rates or time
periods. The ability to change growth rates allows us to value stock over the
life cycle of a firm as the rate of growth changes.

To illustrate the use of the multiple growth rate dividend valuation model,
let's consider Pulpo Fisheries again. The company paid its first cash dividend
of $0.08 today and dividends are expected to grow at a rate of 30 percent per

---

approaches 1, which leaves the following.

$$\left[\frac{(1 + k_e) - (1 + g)}{(1 + g)} \right] P_0 = D_0$$

This may be simplified as follows.

$$(k_e - g) P_0 = D_0 (1 + g) = 1 \qquad D_1 = D_0 (1 + g)$$

$$\therefore P_0 = \frac{D_1}{k_e - g}$$

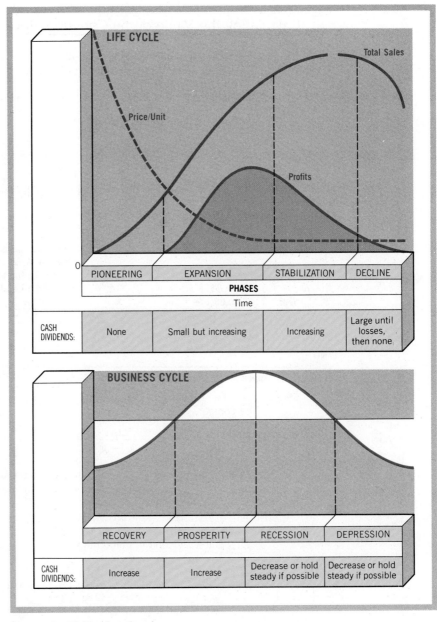

Figure 6–3   Dividends and cycles.

Table 6–1

Calculating the Value of the Common Stock of Pulpo Fisheries

Step 1 Assumptions:
1. The initial dividend $= D_0 = \$0.08$.
2. The rate of return required by equity investors $= k_e = 15$ percent.
3. The growth rate of D for the first 3 years $= g_x = 30$ percent per year.
4. The growth rate of D thereafter $= g_y = 10$ percent per year.

Use these assumptions and equation 6–7.

$$P_0 = \sum_{t=1}^{n} \frac{D_0 (1 + g_x)^t}{(1 + k_e)^t} + \frac{D_{n+1}}{k_e - g_y} \left[\frac{1}{(1 + k_e)^n} \right]$$

Step 2 Calculate the present value of dividends for the first 3 years.

$$\sum_{t=1}^{n} = \frac{D_0 (1 + g_x)^t}{(1 + k_e)^t}$$

Year	Dividend $D_0 (1 + g_x)^t =$ $\$0.08(1 + 0.30)^t$	×	Present Value Interest Factor for 15% Required Rate of Return $(PVIF_{15\%,\,n})^a$	Present Value of Dividends
1	0.104		0.870	$0.090
2	0.135		0.756	0.102
3	0.176		0.658	0.116
				$\Sigma = \$0.308$

^{a}From Appendix C, rounded to three decimal places.

Step 3 Calculate value of dividends from the end of 3 years for the remaining life of the company.

$$\frac{D_{n+1}}{k_e - g_y} \left[\frac{1}{(1 + K_e)^n} \right]$$

Step 3a Find P_3, the present value of all future dividends at the end of the third year.

$$P_3 = \frac{D_{n+1}}{k_e - g_y}$$

D_{n+1} is the dividend in the fourth year.

$$D_4 = D_3 (1 + g_y)$$
$$= \$0.176 (1 + 0.10)$$
$$= \$0.1936.$$

Thus,

$$P_3 = \frac{D_4}{k_e - g_y}$$
$$= \frac{\$0.1936}{0.15 - 0.10}$$
$$= \frac{\$0.1936}{0.05}$$
$$= \$3.87$$

Step 3b   Discount the present value at the end of the third year (P_3) by the required rate of return $k_e = 0.15$ to find the present value of P_3 today.

$$P_3 \left(\frac{1}{1 + k_e} \right)^3 = \$3.87 \, (0.658) = \$2.546$$

Step 4   Add the present value of dividends for the first 3 years (Step 2) to the present value of dividends beyond the third year (Step 3) to find the present value per share (P_0).

$$P_0 = \overset{\text{Step 2}}{\$0.308} + \overset{\text{Step 3}}{\$2.546} = \$2.85$$

Step 5   Multiply the number of shares outstanding (1,000,000) by the price per share ($2.85) to determine the total value of the common stock. $2.85 million

year for the next 3 years. Thereafter, cash dividends are expected to grow at 10 percent per year. Shareholders require a 15 percent return on their investments. Based on these assumptions, we can use the steps presented in Table 6–1 to calculate the value of Pulpo Fisheries' common stock.

The assumptions used in solving the problem are listed in Step 1 of the table. They include information about cash dividends, required returns, and growth rates. Step 2 shows how to calculate the present value of the cash dividends for the first 3 years, when they are growing at 30 percent per year. This is accomplished by the summing of the present values of the dividends for these 3 years. As shown in the table, the present value of the dividends for the first 3 years is $0.308.

Step 3 calculates the value of the dividends that will be paid beyond the third year. After the third year, the dividends are expected to grow at a constant rate of 10 percent per year. Using the second term of Equation 6–9, we find that their value at the end of the third year is $3.87. Because that is their value 3 years from now, we must determine how much they are worth today. Accordingly, we must next determine the present value of that amount, which is $2.546.

Step 4 adds the present value of the dividends for the first three years ($0.308) to the present value of the dividends thereafter ($2.546) to arrive at a $2.85 price per share.

Pulpo has 1 million shares of common stock outstanding; so the total value of the common stock is $2.85 million, as is determined in Step 5.

Recall that the market value of a firm is equal to the market value of the bonds plus the market value of the stock ($V = B + S$). Earlier in this chapter we found the market value of Pulpo's bonds to be $795,680. Therefore, the market value of Pulpo Fisheries can be totaled as follows.

Market value of bonds	$ 795,680
Market value of stock	2,850,000
Total	$3,645,680

Pulpo has no preferred stock. If it had any, the value of preferred stock would have been included in the market value of the firm.

Preferred Stock Although the growth rate of cash dividends can be expected to vary over the course of a life cycle for common stock, there is generally no growth rate in the cash dividends paid on preferred stock. We can determine the value of preferred stock by using a slightly modified version of Equation 6–7 and by recognizing that the growth rate of dividends is zero ($g = 0$). For example, suppose that a firm's preferred stock pays a $5 dividend per share and that the preferred shareholders require a 15 percent rate of return. Their required rate of return is indicated by the symbol k_p. The value of one share of preferred stock is $33.33, determined as follows.

$$P_0 = \frac{D_1}{k_p - g}$$

$$= \frac{\$5.00}{0.15 - 0}$$

$$= \$33.33 \qquad (6\text{–}10)$$

Rates of Return and Risk

Finding the values of stocks involves using some rate of return for k_e. How is that rate estimated? One way to estimate it is to solve the Gordon dividend valuation equation for k_e. Another method uses the capital asset pricing model, which expressly takes risk into account. Keep in mind that there is a trade-off between risk and return. Investors expect returns that are commensurate with the risks they incur.

The Gordon Model To estimate the required rate of return, k_e, from Equation 6–7, the simplified
and the Required form of the Gordon dividend valuation model, we need only rewrite the equa-
Rate of Return tion this way.

$$K_e = \frac{D_1}{P_0} + g \qquad (6\text{–}11)$$

Suppose a firm's financial manager knows that her company's shares are expected to pay a $2 dividend in the next period (D_1), that they sell at $20 ($P_0$), and that the company expects dividends to grow at a constant rate of 5 percent (g). Substituting these values into Equation 6–11, the financial manager can easily estimate the rate of return currently being required by investors in the firm's stock.

Unfortunately, this equation can be used to estimate k_e only when dividends are expected to grow at a constant rate, g, and when k_e is greater than g. Furthermore, because g is an estimate, k_e is ultimately based on the subjective judgment of the analyst. We will consider the advantages and disadvantages of this method again later in this chapter.

Capital Asset Pricing Model The **capital asset pricing model** (CAPM) is another tool that can be used to estimate k_e. However, the CAPM approaches the problem of estimating k_e differently from the Gordon model. One difference is that the Gordon model focuses on the dividend growth of one stock. In contrast, the CAPM compares the returns of one stock (that is, dividends plus changes in price) with the returns of a **portfolio**, or a large number of stocks. The portfolio is usually represented by Standard and Poor's composite stock index or some other stock market measure. (Different stock market measures give different results, but that is a shortcoming we must live with.) Another difference between the two approaches is that the CAPM gives explicit recognition to risk with an index called the beta coefficient. We will explore the concept of risk further after the general form of the CAPM has been introduced.

The CAPM states that the rate of return required by equity investors is equal to the risk-free rate of return, R_f, plus a **risk premium** determined by multiplying the beta coefficient by the difference between the return on the market portfolio and the risk-free rate.

$$k_e = R_f + \text{Risk premium}$$

$$= R_f + b(k_m - R_f) \qquad (6-12)$$

where

R_f = Risk-free rate of return
b = Beta coefficient
k_m = Rate of return on a market portfolio

To illustrate the use of this equation, we'll assume that Pulpo Fisheries' stock has a beta of 1, that the risk-free rate of return is 10 percent, and that the market return is 15 percent. Using these figures, we find the required rate of return on Pulpo Fisheries' stock as follows.

$$k_e = R_f + b\,(k_m - R_f)$$

$$= 0.10 + 1\,(0.15 - 0.10)$$

$$= 0.10 + 0.05$$

$$= 15\%$$

In simple terms, the *CAPM* tells us that the rate of return required by investors depends on the degree of risk as measured by beta. The higher the beta (risk), the higher the required rate of return. Examining the terms used in the *CAPM* should make that idea clearer.

Risk The term **risk**, as used here, refers to the variability of returns. Chapter 9 tells how to measure variability. For the present, however, let it suffice to say that the greater the variability, the greater the risk. We should note here that it makes sense to assume that investors take risk into account when they determine the rate of return they require. We would expect investors to require higher rates of return for riskier investments, and that's what the *CAPM* tells us they do. The rate against which the returns of prospective investments are compared in the *CAPM* is the risk-free rate.

The Risk-Free Rate.   The **risk-free rate** is the rate investors can earn if they place their funds in assets such as U.S. government securities that involve little or no risk of **default**, or failure to pay. (The U.S. Treasury will pay its financial obligations even if it has to print the money to do so.) If Treasury securities pay a return of, for example, 10 percent, investors will demand a higher rate of return from riskier investments. The extra return forms the basis for the risk premium in the *CAPM*.

The risk-free rate of return is generally measured by the returns on 90-day Treasury bills. However, some investors match the maturity of the risk-free asset to their investment horizon. For example, if their investment horizon is 1 year, they use the 1-year rate on U.S. Treasury securities as the risk-free rate.

Unsystematic Risk and Diversification.   As mentioned above, risk refers to the variability of returns. The total variation of returns—or total risk—is divided into two categories: systematic risk and unsystematic risk. **Unsystematic risk** is unique for each security or firm. For example, a fire or a labor strike at one firm does not mean that all firms will experience fires or strikes.

Because unsystematic risk is unique for each security, investors who hold portfolios of securities can eliminate it by diversifying. **Diversification** means holding assets whose returns are not perfectly related. For example, a portfolio consisting of General Motors, Ford, and Chrysler shares would not be well diversified. Because all these are automotive companies, the variations in their returns would be similar. In contrast, a portfolio consisting of General Motors, Dr. Pepper, Proctor & Gamble, Wendy's, and other unrelated firms would be well diversified, because variations in the returns would not be similar. More will be said about diversification in Chapter 9.

Systematic Risk and Beta. You may recall from Chapter 2 that **systematic risk** is common to all securities. It results from common causes, such as inflation or recessions, that affect all securities' returns. Because systematic risk affects all securities, it cannot be eliminated by diversification.

Systematic risk is measured by the beta coefficient, or **beta**.[6] As applied to stocks, beta is an index of volatility that compares the return on one stock with the return on a market portfolio of stocks. (The concept of beta can be applied to other types of assets as well, as you will learn in Chapter 9.)

Although investors cannot eliminate systematic risk by diversifying, they can use beta to gauge the degree of risk they face. For example, because the common stock of Pulpo Fisheries has a beta of 1, on the average, the returns on that stock are as volatile as the returns on a market portfolio of stocks. A beta greater than 1 means that, on the average, the returns on a stock are more volatile than the returns on the market portfolio; and a beta less than 1 means that they are less volatile. However, it should be noted that a stock's beta does not establish a precise numerical relationship between the stock's returns and market returns. That is, the returns on a stock with a beta of, for example, 1.5 do not change exactly 1.5 times as much as market returns change.[7]

Remember that, according to the *CAPM*, the rate of return required by investors depends on the degree of risk as measured by beta. We found earlier that Pulpo Fisheries' stock, with a beta of 1, had a required rate of return of

---

[6]The beta coefficient can be determined by use of the following equation.

$$b = \frac{\text{Cov }(k_j, k_m)}{\text{Variance }(k_m)} = \frac{\text{covariance returns of the asset with market returns}}{\text{variance of market returns}}$$

where

k_j = Percentage return on the stock
k_m = Percentage return on the market
Cov = Correlation between two variables multiplied by the standard deviation for each; thus, Cov = $r_{xy}\, \sigma_x \sigma_y$
Variance (k_m) = Variance of the market return

The numerator of this equation includes the statistical term *covariance*, which refers to the extent to which two sets of numbers move up and down together. In this case, the two sets of numbers are the returns from an asset and the returns from the market. The denominator includes the statistical term *variance*, a statistical measure of dispersion. As used here, it refers to the dispersion of returns of the market around the average return for the market.

[7]This can be demonstrated by use of the *CAPM* equation. Assume that the risk-free rate is 10 percent, the rate of return on the market portfolio is 15 percent, and the beta for a stock is 1.5. The required rate of return on this stock is 17.5 percent.

$$k_e = R_{rf} + b(k_m - R_{rf})$$
$$= 0.10 + 1.5\,(0.15 - 0.10)$$
$$= 17.5\%$$

If the return on the market portfolio increased from 15 percent to 20 percent (a 33 percent increase), the required rate of return on the stock would increase from 17.5 pecent to 25 percent (a 42 percent increase). The stock's return would have changed about 1.3 times as much as the market return.

15 percent, which was the same as the market return. A stock with a higher beta would be riskier; so investors would require a rate of return higher than the market rate if they were to buy that stock. A lower beta would result in a lower required rate of return.

The betas discussed above are positive—that is, the stock's returns move in the same direction as the market's returns. Occasionally, beta can be zero or a negative number. If beta is zero, the returns on the stock are not related to market returns. If beta is a negative number, the returns on the asset tend to move in the opposite direction to market returns; that is, when the market goes up, the returns on stocks with negative betas tend to go down. Assets with betas that are zero or negative are rare.

CAPM: Theory versus Practice In theory, the CAPM works as described in Equation 6–12. Investors consider the risk-free rate, the market rate of return, and an individual stock's beta when determining their required rate of return on the stock. However, some practical measurement problems appear when we try to calculate k_e. Two of the problems have been briefly mentioned: (1) different market measures and (2) different risk-free rates of interest can be used for the calculations. Thus, the numerical value of k_e depends on the measures used to calculate it. For our purposes, Standard & Poor's composite stock index and the 90-day Treasury bill rate are reasonable proxies for the market portfolio and the risk-free rate.

The third problem concerns the suitability of using historical stock market data, such as a composite stock index, in the CAPM to calculate k_e. The problem is that historical (or **ex post**) returns may not be the same as future returns. This is important because k_e represents the rate of return equity investors *expect* to earn in the future (**ex ante**), not the returns investors have earned in the past.

To avoid this problem, we can use the *expected* market return k_m (k hat) instead of the historical return k_m. Expected market returns can be obtained from economists and analysts who specialize in forecasting them. The CAPM equation that specifically takes expected returns into account is the following.

$$k_e = R_f + b\,(k_m - R_f)$$

If the historical returns are the same as the returns forecast by economists, then k_m is equal to k_m and k_e is equal to k_e. To simplify future discussions, we will assume that they are equal.

Security Market Line The relationship between expected returns and systematic risk is represented by the **security market line**, or SML, depicted in Figure 6–4. The SML is the graphic representation of the CAPM. It uses beta to measure systematic risk—as you recall, low betas suggest low systematic risk and high betas suggest high systematic risk. SML's are positively sloped, which means that investors expect a higher return as systematic risk increases.

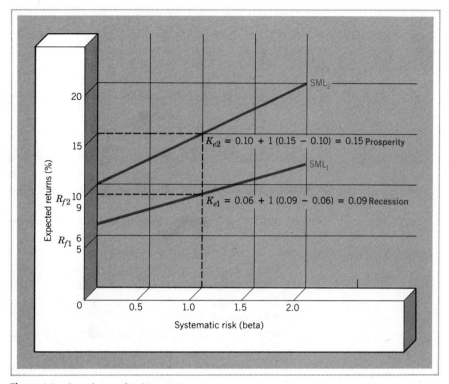

Figure 6-3 Security market line (SML).

Figure 6–4 shows two *SML*'s representing two economic conditions that may face the firm—prosperity and recession. When economic conditions change, the risk-free rate (R_f) changes. Consequently, $b(k_m - R_f)$, which is used in the *CAPM* to calculate the risk premium, changes. These changes result in different slopes for the *SML*.

SML_1 estimates conditions during a recession, when market interest rates are low and the risk-free rate is, for example, 6 percent. Investors believe that the recession and subsequent depression will be extensive, so the expected return on the market is 9 percent. The beta for Pulpo's common stock, you recall, is 1, which means that it has average risk—that is, the same as that of the market. According to the *CAPM*, investors expect a 9 percent return on their equity investments in Pulpo when market returns are 9 percent.

As you know, economic conditions can change dramatically. Suppose that instead of a depression there is a strong demand for goods and services, which results in prosperity (SML_2). Because the economy is booming, the level of interest rates rises and investors expect a higher return on their investments. Accordingly, the *CAPM* indicates that the expected rate of return on equity investments in Pulpo is now 15 percent.

This example demonstrates that the expected rate of return can change over time. You already know that dividends, too, can change over time. The timing of these changes is not known with certainty; so investors have different perceptions of the future.

Comparing Methods for Determining Rates of Return The Gordon dividend valuation model and the capital asset pricing model have different assumptions, advantages, and disadvantages, which are outlined in Table 6–2 and discussed below.

Assumptions. The basic assumptions underlying the Gordon model are that dividends will grow at a constant rate forever and that the required rate of return, k_e, is greater than the growth rate of dividends, (g).

The *CAPM* assumes efficient capital markets, which were briefly discussed in Chapter 4. Here, the term **efficient capital markets** implies the following conditions:

- There are many investors, and investors are profit maximizers.
- Investors have access to all relevant information concerning securities. The information comes to them in a random fashion; and they react to it as soon as possible.
- Securities prices reflect all available information.

The *CAPM* also deals explicitly with expected (ex ante) returns to investors.

Comparison of Gordon Model and Capital Asset Pricing Model

Gordon Model:

$$k_e = \frac{D_1}{P_0} + g$$

Capital Asset Pricing Model:

$$k_e = R_f + b(k_m - R_f)$$

Assumptions

Gordon Model	Capital Asset Pricing Model
• Constant growth rate of dividends	• Efficient capital markets
• $k_e > g$	• Ex ante

Advantages

Gordon Model	Capital Asset Pricing Model
• Is relatively easy to use	• Explicit recognition of systematic risk
• Can be adjusted for flotation costs	• Applies to any stock or portfolio
• Approximates actual behavior of many business firms over time	• Can be used to: 　• Adjust discount rates in capital budgeting 　• Determine divisional cost of capital 　• Manage large portfolios

Disadvantages

Gordon Model	Capital Asset Pricing Model
• Assumptions not entirely realistic	• Assumptions not entirely realistic
• Does not apply when $g \geq k_e$ or when no cash dividends are expected to be paid in the near term	• Betas may not be stationary over time
	• Difficult to measure accurately

These assumptions provide a starting point and a frame of reference. Recognizing that both models have limitations, the real issue is their usefulness in decision making. We can resolve this issue by acknowledging that both models add to our store of financial tools and that each has its own applications.

Advantages. The basic advantages of the Gordon model are that it is relatively easy to use and that the market price of the stock can be adjusted for the costs of underwriting it. Furthermore, over a period of time the Gordon model may approximate the actual behavior of many business firms. Therefore, it is used to calculate the cost of capital of retained earnings, which is explained in the next chapter.

The advantages of the *CAPM* are that it explicitly recognizes systematic risk and can be applied to any common stock. In addition, it can be used to risk-adjust discount rates for capital budgeting, to determine divisional cost of capital, and to manage large portfolios of securities. (These uses will come up again in later chapters.)

Disadvantages. One disadvantage of the Gordon model is that it cannot be used when the required rate of return, k_e, is not greater than the growth rate of dividends (g) or when no cash dividends are expected in the near term. Disadvantages of the *CAPM* include the fact, mentioned earlier, that betas may not remain stationary over time.

The major disadvantage of both models is that their assumptions are not entirely realistic; however, the disadvantages of the models are outweighed by their advantages and the fact that they can be used in practical applications. Equally important, difficulties in applying the models are not a fault of the models per se, but lie in our inability to forecast future benefits precisely and to measure certain data accurately. We must recognize the limitations of these and other models and apply judgment in their application and interpretation. Although there is no formal model for "sound judgment," it is clearly the most important tool at our disposal.

Arbitrage Pricing Theory. As mentioned in Chapter 1, the discipline of finance is evolving and new theories are emerging to overcome the shortfalls of existing ones. The **arbitrage pricing theory** (*APT*) is an emerging theory of asset pricing. The part of the theory of interest here concerns the number of factors that affect a security's return. The *CAPM* is considered a single-factor model because it considers only one factor—beta. The *APT*, on the other hand, argues that a security's return depends on a number of factors. Some of the factors that have been tested are unanticipated changes in inflation, in industrial production, in certain bond yields, and in certain interest rates. As this theory develops, it too will be added to our financial tool kit.

Historical Returns

Expected returns are uncertain; but we can calculate the returns investors have received in the past, and it is constructive to do so. A study by Ibbotson and Singuefield examined the returns from stocks and bonds during the period from 1926 to 1981. In the study, returns were represented by holding period yields.

Holding Period Yields. The **holding period yield** (*HPY*) is the sum of the dividend yield plus the yield of the change in capital value during a given period. It can be calculated as follows.

$$HPY = \frac{D_1 + (P_1 - P_0)}{P_0}$$

(6–14)

where

D_1 = Dividends received or expected during the holding period
P_0 = Price at the beginning of the holding period
P_1 = Price or expected price at the end of the holding period

Note that we need not use only historical data when calculating *HPY*. For example, assume that a stock is currently selling for $50 per share and that analysts believe that it will sell at $65 a year from now. The company is currently paying a $1.50 cash dividend that is not expected to change. If the analysts are correct, the *HPY* will be 33 percent for a 1-year holding period.

$$HPY = \frac{\$1.50 + (\$65 - \$50)}{\$50} = +0.33$$

The length of the holding period is arbitrary, but annual and monthly returns are commonly used. In this example, the *HPY* was positive. Had the price of the stock declined enough to offset the cash dividend, the return would have been negative.

We can also use the *HPY* equation to calculate bond returns; here, interest payments are substituted for dividends.

Historical Returns and Risk Premiums for Common Stock. When they examined *HPY*'s for common stock over the years 1926 to 1981, Ibbotson and Singuefield found that the average return was 9.1 percent compounded annually for the Standard & Poor's 500 stock index.[8] However, returns varied widely from year to year. In 1931, the return was −43.3 percent; in 1933, it was +53.99. The return was −0.99 percent in 1953 but was +52.63 percent in the following year.

The total return on common stock is the sum of a risk-free return plus a risk premium. According to Ibbotson and Singuefield, during the 1926 to 1981 period, the average risk premium was 5.9 percent compounded annually. However, the risk premium was highly variable from year to year—much more so than the risk-free return. From this and other information, the authors concluded that the risk premium followed a **random walk**. That is, risk premiums of previous years could not be used to predict risk premiums for future years. Other investigators have found a similar pattern in stock prices.[9]

Variability of Returns on Common Stock.   For another perspective on returns, consider the variations in stock prices depicted in Figure 6–5. The top line, representing stock prices, is characterized by constant fluctuation. This line measures the price movements of all the stocks traded on the New York Stock Exchange.

There is a saying that "there is no such thing as the stock market; there is a market of stocks." In other words, investors do not buy an average representing the entire stock market; they buy individual stocks that may perform differently from the market as a whole. To demonstrate this variabililty, we can turn to the table in Figure 6–5 and examine the stock exchange indexes for all stocks (the composite index), for industrial stocks, for transportation stocks, and for the others listed there. All the indexes have a base of 50. For the week ending February 8, 1986, the industrial index was 140.16, the transportation index was 121.71, and the utility index was 63.80. The differences among these indexes indicate that the industrial stocks were outperforming the transportation and utility stocks by a wide margin.

Historical Returns on Bonds.   The study by Ibbotson and Singuefield also revealed that the average return on long-term corporate bonds during the 1926 to 1981 period was 3.6 percent. Sharp increases in interest rates since the mid-1960s have resulted in lower bond prices for the long-term bonds that are outstanding. Consequently, the holding period yields were negative in some years. For example, in 1978, the *HPY* was −1.16 percent. However, the

[8]Roger G. Ibbotson and Rex A. Singuefield, *Stocks, Bonds, Bills and Inflation: The Past and the Future,* 1982 edition (Charlottesville, Va.: Financial Analysts Research Foundation, 1982), pp. 15, 26, 36. The data shown are the geometric means with all dividends reinvested. The arithmetic mean was 11.5 percent.

[9]Despite this variability, some practitioners use a risk premium of about 6 percent when they estimate the risk premium for the *CAPM*.

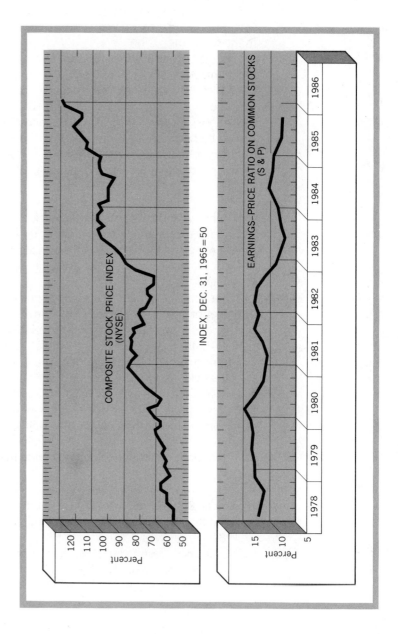

COMPOSITE STOCK PRICE INDEX
(NYSE)

INDEX, DEC. 31, 1965 = 50

Percent

120
110
100
90
80
70
60
50

EARNINGS–PRICE RATIO ON COMMON STOCKS
(S & P)

Percent

15
10
5

1978 1979 1980 1981 1982 1983 1984 1985 1986

Period	Common stock prices[1] New York Stock Exchange indexes (Dec. 31, 1965 = 50)[2]					Dow-Jones industrial average[3]	Standard & Poor's composite index (1941–43 = 10)[4]	Common stock yields (percent)[5]	
	Composite	Industrial	Transportation	Utility	Finance			Dividend–price ratio	Earnings–price ratio
1980	68.10	78.70	60.61	37.35	64.25	891.41	118.78	5.26	12.66
1981	74.02	85.44	72.61	38.91	73.52	932.92	128.05	5.20	11.96
1982	68.93	78.18	60.41	39.75	71.99	884.36	119.71	5.81	11.60
1983	92.63	107.45	89.36	47.00	95.34	1,190.34	160.41	4.40	8.03
1984	92.46	108.01	85.63	46.44	89.28	1,178.48	160.46	4.64	ʳ10.02
1985	108.09	123.79	104.11	56.75	114.21	1,328.23	186.84	4.25	......
1985: Jan.	99.11	113.99	94.88	51.95	101.34	1,238.16	171.61	4.51	......
Feb.	104.73	120.71	101.76	53.44	109.58	1,283.23	180.88	4.30	......
Mar	103.92	119.64	98.30	53.91	107.59	1,268.83	179.42	4.37	9.07
Apr.	104.66	119.93	96.47	55.51	109.39	1,266.36	180.62	4.37	......
May	107.00	121.88	99.66	57.32	115.31	1,279.40	184.90	4.31	......
June	109.52	124.11	105.79	59.61	118.47	1,314.00	188.89	4.21	8.12
July	111.64	126.94	111.67	59.68	119.85	1,343.17	192.54	4.14	......
Aug	109.09	124.92	109.92	56.99	114.68	1,326.18	188.31	4.23	......
Sept	106.62	122.35	104.96	55.93	110.21	1,317.95	184.06	4.32	8.03
Oct	107.57	123.65	103.72	55.84	112.36	1,351.58	186.18	4.28	......
Nov	113.93	130.53	108.61	59.07	122.83	1,432.88	197.45	4.06	......
Decʳ	119.33	136.77	113.52	61.69	128.86	1,517.02	207.26	3.88	......
1986: Jan.	120.16	137.13	115.72	62.46	132.36	1,534.86	208.19	3.90	......
Week ended:									
1986: Jan 4	121.25	138.91	113.65	62.96	131.05	1,546.02	210.61	3.82	......
11	120.48	137.72	112.90	62.71	131.86	1,534.33	208.90	3.89	......
18	119.90	137.09	114.05	61.97	131.90	1,529.04	207.84	3.88	......
25	118.80	135.50	116.44	61.71	130.94	1,517.41	205.50	3.97	......
Feb 1	121.05	137.57	120.49	63.20	135.25	1,555.23	209.72	3.84	......
8	123.12	140.16	121.71	63.80	137.81	1,598.95	213.55	3.80	......

[1]Average of daily closing prices.
[2]Includes all the stocks (more than 1,500) listed on the NYSE.
[3]Includes 30 stocks.
[4]Includes 500 stocks.
[5]Standard & Poor's series. Dividend-price ratios based on Wednesday closing prices. Earnings–price ratios based on prices at end of quarter.

NOTE.—All data relate to stocks listed on the New York Stock Exchange (NYSE).

Sources: New York Stock Exchange, Dow-Jones & Company, Inc., and Standard & Poor's Corporation.

Figure 6–5 Common stock prices and yields. Stock prices rose again in January.

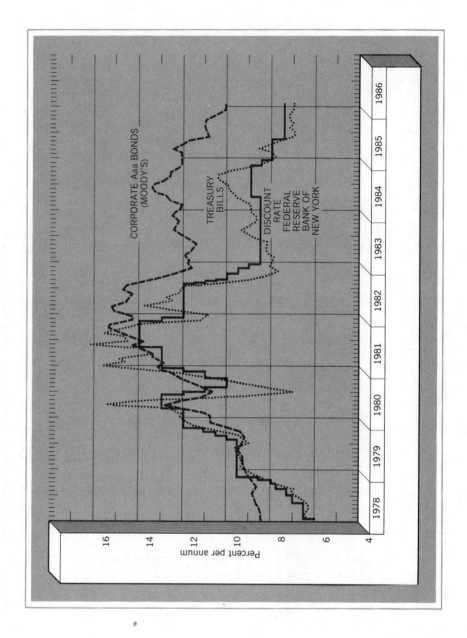

[Percent per annum]

| Period | U.S. Treasury security yields | | | High-grade municipal bonds (Standard & Poor's)[3] | Corporate Aaa bonds (Moody's)[4] | Prime commercial paper, 6 months[5] | Discount rate (N.Y.F.R. Bank)[6] | Prime rate charged by banks[6] | New-home mortgage yields (FHLBB)[7] |
| | 3-month bills[1] | Constant maturities[2] | | | | | | | |
		3-year	10-year						
1980	11.506	11.55	11.46	8.51	11.94	12.29	11.77	15.27	12.66
1981	14.029	14.44	13.91	11.23	14.17	14.76	13.41	18.87	14.70
1982	10.686	12.92	13.00	11.57	13.79	11.89	11.02	14.86	15.14
1983	8.63	10.45	11.10	9.47	12.04	8.89	8.50	10.79	12.57
1984	9.58	11.89	12.44	10.15	12.71	10.16	8.80	12.04	12.38
1985	7.48	9.64	10.62	8.18	11.37	8.01	7.69	9.93	......
							Open-close	Open-close	
1985: Jan	7.76	10.43	11.38	9.55	12.08	8.15	8.00–8.00	10.75–10.50	12.27
Feb	8.22	10.55	11.51	9.66	12.13	8.69	8.00–8.00	10.50–10.50	12.21
Mar	8.57	11.05	11.86	9.79	12.56	9.23	8.00–8.00	10.50–10.50	11.92
Apr	8.00	10.49	11.43	9.48	12.23	8.47	8.00–8.00	10.50–10.50	12.05
May	7.56	9.75	10.85	9.08	11.72	7.88	8.00–7.50	10.50–10.00	12.01
June	7.01	9.05	10.16	8.78	10.94	7.38	7.50–7.50	10.00–9.50	11.75
July	7.05	9.18	10.31	8.90	10.97	7.57	7.50–7.50	9.50–9.50	11.34
Aug	7.18	9.31	10.33	9.18	11.05	7.74	7.50–7.50	9.50–9.50	11.24
Sept	7.08	9.37	10.37	9.37	11.07	7.86	7.50–7.50	9.50–9.50	11.17
Oct	7.17	9.25	10.24	9.24	11.02	7.79	7.50–7.50	9.50–9.50	11.09
Nov	7.20	8.88	9.78	8.64	10.55	7.69	7.50–7.50	9.50–9.50	11.01
Dec	7.07	8.40	9.26	8.51	10.16	7.62	7.50–7.50	9.50–9.50	10.94
1986: Jan	7.04	8.41	9.19	8.06	10.05	7.62	7.50–7.50	9.50–9.50	10.87
Week ended: 1986: Jan 4	7.04	8.25	9.03	8.41	9.92	7.59	7.50–7.50	9.50–9.50	......
11	7.05	8.39	9.16	8.05	9.95	7.58	7.50–7.50	9.50–9.50	......
18	7.23	8.57	9.35	8.10	10.18	7.71	7.50–7.50	9.50–9.50	......
25	6.98	8.46	9.24	8.10	10.13	7.64	7.50–7.50	9.50–9.50	......
Feb 1	6.92	8.29	9.09	7.99	10.00	7.59	7.50–7.50	9.50–9.50	......
8	6.99	8.21	9.02	7.81	9.90	7.55	7.50–7.50	9.50–9.50	......
15	7.18	....	....	....	....	....	7.50–	9.50–	......

[1]Rate on new issues within period; bank-discount basis.
[2]Yields on the more actively traded issues adjusted to constant maturities by the Treasury Department.
[3]Weekly data are Wednesday figures.
[4]Series excludes public utility issues for January 17, 1984 through October 11, 1984 due to lack of appropriate issues.
[5]Bank-discount basis. Prior to November 1, 1979, data are for 4–6 months paper.
[6]Average effective rate for year; opening and closing rate for month and week.
[7]Effective rate (in the primary market) on conventional mortgages, reflecting fees and charges as well as contract rate and assumed, on the average, repayment at end of 10 years. Rates beginning January 1973 not strictly comparable with prior rates.
Sources: Department of the Treasury, Board of Governors of the Federal Reserve System, Federal Home Loan Bank Board, Moody's Investors Service, and Standard & Poor's Corporation.

Figure 6–6 Interest rates and bond yields. Interest rates fell in January.

erratic upward movement of interest rates was punctuated with some sharp declines. During those periods, both bond prices and HPY's increased. In 1976, for example, the HPY was 16.75 percent. These figures suggest the wide variations that have occured in HPY's for long-term corporate bonds.

Figure 6 - 6 shows interest rate movements of both long-term and short-term debt securities in recent years. Notice that short-term interest rates are more volatile than long-term interest rates. Nevertheless, price changes on long-term bonds are greater than price changes on Treasury bills.

Summary

In theory, the value of a firm depends on the dollar returns investors expect to receive over time discounted by their required rates of return. That means we must determine the market value of the stock and the market value of the debt, represented here by bonds, to determine the market value of a firm.

The value of a bond is the sum of the discounted cash benefits investors

Table 6–3
Summary of Equations

	Equation	Equation Number
Value of a going concern	$V = B + S$	(6–1)
Price of a bond	$P_0 = \sum\limits_{t=1}^{n} \left[\dfrac{I}{(1 + k_{db})^t} \right] + \dfrac{F}{(1 + k_{db})^n}$	(6–2)
or	$P_0 = I\,(PVAIF_{i,n}) + F(PVIF_{i,n})$	(6–3)
Yield to maturity (YTM)	$YTM = \dfrac{I + (F - P_0)/n}{(F + P_0)/2}$	(6–4)
Price of common stock (Gordon model)	$P_0 = \sum\limits_{t=1}^{x} \left[\dfrac{D_t}{(1 + k_e)^t} \right]$	(6–5)
with dividends growing at a constant rate	$P_0 = \sum\limits_{t=1}^{x} \left[\dfrac{D_0\,(1 + g)^t}{(1 + k_e)^t} \right]$	(6–6)
or	$P_0 = \dfrac{D_1}{k_e - g}$	(6–7)
with dividends growing at a variable rate	$P_0 = \sum\limits_{t=1}^{n} \left[\dfrac{D_0\,(1 + g_x)^t}{(1 + k_e)^t} \right] + \sum\limits_{t=n+1}^{x} \left[\dfrac{D_n\,(1 + g_y)^{t-n}}{(1 + k_e)^t} \right]$	(6–8)
or	$P_0 = \sum\limits_{t=1}^{n} \left[\dfrac{D_0\,(1 + g_x)^t}{(1 + k_e)^t} \right] + \dfrac{D_{n+1}}{k_e - g_y} \left[\dfrac{1}{(1 + k_e)^n} \right]$	(6–9)
Price of preferred stock	$P_0 = \dfrac{D_1}{k_p - g}$	(6–10)
Required rate of return based on Equation 6–7	$k_e = \dfrac{D_1}{P_0} + g$	(6–11)
Capital asset pricing model (CAPM) with expected returns	$k_e = R_f + b\,(k_m - R_f)$ $\hat{k}_e = R_f + b\,(\hat{k}_m - R_f)$	(6–12) (6–13)
Holding period yield (HPY)	$HPY = \dfrac{D_1 + (P_1 - P_0)}{P_0}$	(6–14)

expect to receive over the life of the bond. The equations to determine a bond's value (or price) along with the other equations presented in this chapter are summarized in Table 6–3. Both interest rates and maturity affect bond prices.

The Gordon dividend valuation model is used to determine the value of a stock. It is also based on discounted cash flows investors expect to receive. The model can accommodate situations in which dividends grow at a constant rate and situations in which dividends grow at a variable rate.

Part of the valuation process consists of estimating the rates of return required by investors. The basic stock valuation model and the capital asset pricing model offer two approaches to estimating investors' required rates of return. Each approach involves advantages and disadvantages. An important advantage of the *CAPM* is that it takes risk into account; it holds that required returns on a stock include a risk-free rate plus a risk premium.

An examination of the returns investors have received since 1926 provides some insight into historical returns. The data show that the average annual compound return for stocks was about 9 percent and for bonds was about 4 percent. It was found that the average annual compound risk premium for stocks was about 6 percent. However, all these figures were subject to wide variations over the years.

Important Terms

Beta	Market value
Capital asset pricing model (*CAPM*)	Portfolio
Default	Random walk
Diversification	Risk
Efficient capital markets	Risk-free rate
Ex ante	Risk premium
Ex post	Security market line (*SML*)
Going concern	Systematic risk
Gordon model	Unsystematic risk
Holding period yield (*HPY*)	Yield to maturity (*YTM*)
Intrinsic value	

Questions

1. Compare the following concepts of value: book value, liquidation value, market value, intrinsic value.
2. What information is needed to calculate the intrinsic value of a bond? How is the information used in the calculation?
3. Discuss the relationship between market interest rates and the market price of

bonds. Is the effect of interest rate changes on bond prices identical for all bonds? Why or why not?

4. What is meant by the *yield to maturity*? How is it determined?
5. In what ways does stock valuation differ from bond valuation?
6. According to the Gordon model, on what is the market value of a share of common stock based? What assumptions underlie this model?
7. Discuss the adaptations required to use the Gordon model to value a firm over a typical life cycle.
8. Can the Gordon model be used to value a share of preferred stock on which dividends are not expected to increase? If so, how?
9. Define *risk* in general, *systematic risk,* and *unsystematic risk.*
10. In what sense are United States government securities risk free?
11. What is the mathematical expression for the *CAPM*? Explain each term and interpret the overall model.
12. According to *CAPM*, how is the risk premium on an investment determined?
13. How can diversification reduce risk?
14. What interpretation can be given to beta coefficients of zero and negative beta coefficients?
15. Contrast the terms *ex post* and *ex ante*. What is the problem with using *ex post* data to forecast *ex ante* returns?
16. Graph and explain the security market line.
17. Would you expect the *SML* to have the same slope year after year? Why or why not?
18. Compare and contrast the advantages of the Gordon Model with those of *CAPM*.
19. Compare and contrast the disadvantages of the Gordon Model with those of *CAPM*.
20. What is meant by the *holding period yield*?

Problems

1. Nolan, Inc., has an outstanding $1,000 bond paying a coupon rate of 12 percent annually. The bond was issued 5 yeas ago and now matures in 15 years.
   (a) Calculate the market value of these bonds if the current required rate of return on bonds with similar characteristics is 8 percent; 12 percent; 16 percent. Explain why the market value changes.
   (b) If the remaining maturity of the Nolan bonds is only 5 years, calculate the market value of the bond if bonds with similar characteristics are yielding 8 percent; 12 percent; 16 percent.
   (c) Explain the difference in your answers to parts a and b.
2. Suppose the bond in Problem 1a paid interest semiannually. Calculate the price of the bond if the current market yield is 10 percent; 12 percent; 14 percent.
3. Calculate the price of a $1,000 face value bond that has an annual coupon of 8 percent and is currently selling at a yield of 14 percent if its remaining maturity is 1 year; 10 years; 30 years; infinite.
4. Samuels Manufacturing Company has issued 12 percent coupon, $1,000 bonds with 10 years remaining to maturity.

(a) If interest is paid annually, what is the yield to maturity on these bonds if they are currently selling at $95; $80; $105?

(b) What is the current yield on the bonds at each of those prices?

5. Puget Bay Fisheries has an outstanding preferred stock issue with a dividend of $10 per share. At what price will the preferred trade if investors require an annual return of 10 percent; 15 percent; 20 percent?

6. Oswego Corporation has common stock outstanding that now pays a dividend of $2 per share. Your broker projects a continuing growth rate of 10 percent annually. The stock is currently selling for $30 per share. If you buy this stock, what is your expected rate of return (k_e)?

7. What price would you pay for Cocker, Inc., stock if its most recent dividend was $3.50 per share and if dividends are projected to grow at 12 percent per year? Your required rate of return is 22 percent.

8. The Borg Corporation currently pays its stockholders $1.50 per share in dividends. Analysts are forecasting the growth of Borg's dividends to continue at an annual rate of 10 percent. Borg stockholders require a rate of return of 20 percent.

(a) What is the market value of Borg stock?

(b) At what price will Borg sell if its dividends next year are increased to $2 per share and expected growth remains at 10 percent?

(c) If, instead, Borg cuts the dividend to $0.50 per share next year to fund high-growth investments, analysts will revise the anticipated growth rate to 18 percent. Calculate the market value of the stock under these assumptions.

9. Tallahassee Timber has experienced earnings and dividend growth of 8 percent for the last 10 years; this rate is expected to continue.

(a) If Tallahassee currently pays a dividend to common shareholders of $1.00 per share, calculate the market value of the stock if shareholders require a rate of return of 10 percent; 15 percent; 20 percent.

(b) What relationship do you find between investors' required rates of return and the stock price? Why?

 10. JCA Corporation is a high-tech firm expected to grow at a 40 percent rate for 5 years, then at 15 percent thereafter. The firm currently pays a $0.50 per share dividend, and stockholders require a 24 percent rate of return. Calculate the current price of JCA stock.

11. Elsewhere Limited is expected to grow for 4 years at a rate of 50 percent, followed by a sharp decline in the popularity of its product. After 4 yeas, a negative growth rate of 5 percent is expected indefinitely. The current dividend is $1 per share, and investors' required rate of return is 18 percent. Calculate the market value of the stock under these forecasts.

12. Columbia International has estimated the following growth pattern: 30 percent for the first 5 years; 0 percent for the following 5 years; a permanent 10 percent growth rate thereafter. With a current dividend of $5 per share and a required rate of return of 16 percent, determine the value of this stock to shareholders.

13. Calculate the required rate of return on Niagara Sausage Company, given a risk-free rate of 12 percent, an expected market return of 20 percent, and a beta for Niagara of: 1.5, 0.5, −0.5.

14. Using the following information, calculate the beta for a stock:

$$k_e = 25 \text{ percent}$$
$$k_m = 22 \text{ percent}$$
$$R_f = 13 \text{ percent}$$

15. (a) Gallenkamp's stock has been estimated to have a beta of 1.2. If the expected rate of return on the market portfolio is 11.9 percent and the risk-free rate is 7.5 percent, what is the expected risk premium on Gallenkamp stock? What is the stock's expected return?

(b) Suppose the expected return on the market portfolio increases to 14 percent. By how much would the expected return on Gallenkamp's stock change?

(c) Suppose the beta for Gallenkamp is 0.83. What is its expected risk premium if the market portfolio is expected to return 11.9 percent?

16. Suppose the beta for Gallenkamp in Problem 15 is -0.2. If the risk-free rate is 8 percent and the expected rate of return on the market is 12 percent, what is the expected return on Gallenkamp stock?

17. The covariance between the returns on the market and the returns on Mallard Corporation's stock is 0.0206. The variance of expected returns on the market portfolio is 0.0190. What is the beta coefficient for Mallard?

18. (a) Sketch the security market line for R_f of 9 percent and k_m of 14 percent.

(b) Now suppose investors expectations of increased inflation lead them to require a 3 percent higher return on all investments. Sketch the new *SML* on the same graph.

(c) Suppose, instead, that investors in general are more reluctant to invest in risky investments, so that R_f remains at 9 percent, but k_m increases to 16 percent. What effect will this have on the *SML*, compared with the one you sketched in part a?

19. Wilson Imports issued 200 25-year $1,000 bonds 10 years ago. The bonds have a coupon rate of 14 percent paid annually, but current market yields on similar bonds are 12 percent.

There are 4,000 shares of common stock outstanding, on which the most recent dividend was $5 per share. The dividend growth rate is expected to be only 5 percent for the next 3 years but to increase to a permanent level of 9 percent after that time. Investors now require a rate of return of 16 percent.

Calculate the total market value of Wilson's securities.

20. Calculate the annual holding period return for California Prune Company if the dividend is expected to be $10 per share, the current price of the stock is $60 per share, and the price in 1 year is expected to be $50; $60; $70; $100.

21. Leslea, Inc., has an outstanding bond with a 12 percent coupon and a $1,000 par that is currently priced at $1,000 and matures in 10 years. Calculate the 1-year holding period yield on this bond if interest is paid annually and the bond is sold in 1 year at a price of $1,050; $1,150; $1,300.

7
Cost of Capital

Cost of capital is used extensively in managerial finance. It is used in the previous chapter in connection with the valuation of firms and their capital structures. It will be used as the minimum rate of return that a firm will accept on certain capital budgeting projects. It is also used in evaluating the performance of divisions of large companies and in regulating industries to justify the rates that they charge. In short, the cost of capital affects investment decisions (the left side of the balance sheet), financing decisions (the right side of the balance sheet), the value of firms, and pricing decisions. Because of its crucial role in decision making, it deserves our very careful attention.

After reading this chapter, you should know the following.

1. How to define *cost of capital* in two ways.
2. Why component costs of capital differ from the returns required by investors.
3. How to calculate the cost of debt before and after taxes.
4. How to calculate the cost of preferred stock.
5. How to calculate the costs of retained earnings and common stock.
6. Why target value weights are better than market value weights and book value weights for determining the firm's weighted average cost of capital.
7. How cost of capital is related to capital structure.

Basic Concepts

You learned in Chapter 6 that the value of a firm depends on the dollar returns investors expect over time discounted by their required rates of return. The valuation equation given in Chapter 6 was $V = B + S$. Let's consider that equation again to determine its relation to the cost of capital. For now, we will make several assumptions to simplify the task. The assumptions will be relaxed later. First, we will assume that investors hold only long-term bonds and common stock. These investors' required rates of return are k_{db} and k_e, as in Chapter 6. In addition, the following assumptions are made.

There are no corporate income taxes.
All earnings available to common stock are paid out as cash dividends.
There is no growth in earnings before interest and taxes.
All investors have the same expectations about the firm's operating income.
Business risk (the risk inherent in operating a business) is constant and independent of financial risk (the risk that a business might not be able to meet its financial obligations).
There are no flotation (underwriting) costs associated with new issues of securities.

Because we are assuming that there are no taxes and that no earnings are retained, we can assume that the firm's **earnings before interest and taxes** (*EBIT*) are divided between bondholders and shareholders. The bondholders receive interest payments, and the shareholders receive the remainder in the form of cash dividends.

Earnings before interest and taxes = Interest payments + Dividend payments
$$EBIT = I \qquad\qquad + (EBIT - I)$$

Bondholders and shareholders discount their returns by k_{db} and k_e. Because k_{db} and k_e represent costs to the firm, we can think of them from the firm's point of view as the *cost of debt* and the *cost of equity*, respectively. The average return for both classes of investors is the weighted average cost of capital for the firm (k). The weights are based on the amounts of debt and equity valued at the market price. (More will be said about weights later.) Thus, the value of a firm can be calculated as follows.

$$\text{Value of firm*} = \text{Value of debt} + \text{Value of equity}$$

$$V^* = \frac{I}{k_{db}} + \frac{EBIT - I}{k_e}$$

$$= \frac{EBIT}{k} \tag{7-1}$$

where

V^* = Value of firm under assumptions of no taxes, no earnings retained, and no flotation costs

k = Firm's weighted average cost of capital

k_{db} = Cost of debt before taxes; rate of return required by bondholders, which is the market rate of interest on newly issued bonds with similar characteristics, such as risk and maturity

k_e = Cost of equity; rate of return required by common stockholders

The value of a firm (V^*) under the assumptions outlined earlier is defined in Equation 7-1 as being equal to its *EBIT* discounted by its cost of capital, which is the subject of this chapter.

Cost of Capital Defined

The term *cost of capital* contains two key words—capital and cost. The word *capital* refers to a firm's **capital structure**—that is, its permanent long-term financing. The simple illustration in the preceding section assumed that capital structure included only bonds and common stock. However, as you can see in Table 7-1, it is made up of long-term debt, preferred stock, common stock, and retained earnings. These are the principal sources of funds used to acquire permanent assets.

Each component of the capital structure has a cost attached to it. The costs are based on the returns required by debtholders (k_{db}) and stockholders (k_p and k_e) but differs from them because of income taxes in the case of debt (interest expense is deductible from taxable income) and flotation (underwriting) costs in the case of new debt and equity securities. Collectively, the costs for all the components comprise the cost of capital for the firm.

Table 7–1

Rates of Return Required by Firm and Investors on Various Components of Capital Structure

Component of a firm's capital structure	Firm's required rate of return, component cost (%)[a]	Investors' required rate of return (%)[a]	Investors
Long-term debt	k_d	k_{db}	Bondholders[b]
Preferred stock	k_{pr}	k_p	Preferred stockholders
Common stock	k_s	k_e	Common stockholders
Retained earnings	k_r		
Weighted average cost of capital	k		

[a]The difference between the rate of return required by the firm (component cost) and the rate of return required by investors is due to flotation costs on new securities issues and tax deductions from interest expense on debt.

[b]The term *bondholder* is used here to represent holders of various types of debt.

It follows that a firm must earn enough to cover the costs of debt and preferred and common stocks. This is because both debt and equity investors expect to receive a certain return. If, for example, the debtholders do not receive their required interest payments, the firm could be forced into bankruptcy. Accordingly, the **cost of capital** can be defined as the minimum rate of return a firm must earn on its assets to satisfy its investors.[1]

The cost of capital may also be defined as that rate of return on assets at which the market value of the firm remains unchanged. By way of illustration, assume that a new firm begins with $1 million in assets. For simplicity, assume that it is entirely financed by common stock held by a few private investors and that there are no underwriting costs. The shareholders require a return of 10 percent on their investment in the form of cash dividends, and all earnings are paid out as cash dividends. The market value of the firm is determined by dividing the cash dividends by the cost of common stock. Table 7–2 shows the value of the firm for several rates of return on assets.

As shown in the table, when the firm earns a 10 percent return on its assets, it has earnings and cash dividends of $100,000. The market value of the firm is determined by dividing the $100,000 by 10 percent, the rate of return required by investors (k_e). Thus, the market value is $1 million—the same market value as the original investment.

If the firm earns 8 percent on its assets, the earnings and dividends equal

---

[1]We should note that, while depreciation and short-term liabilities are also important sources of funds, they are *not* included in the cost of capital calculations. Depreciation is part of the total funds of a firm that are available to make payments to holders of debt and equity. Therefore, its cost to investors is an opportunity cost, which we assume is the same as the opportunity cost for the firm. In other words, the cost of depreciation is the same as the firm's cost of capital, k.

In the case of short-term liabilities, they may not be a permanent part of the financial structure, and no explicit payments from them are made to long-term investors. Moreover, although it is possible to estimate the cost of not paying accounts payable on time, the cost of, say, accrued wages is not clear. The costs associated with short-term liabilities are explained later in this book.

Table 7–2
Market Value of Hypothetical Firm at Various Rates of Return on Assets

Rate of Return on Assets (%)	Assets $1 million Earnings = Dividends	Equity (Common stock) $1 million	Market Value $= \dfrac{\text{Dividends}}{k_e = 10\%}$
10	$100,000		$\dfrac{\$100,000}{0.10} = \$1,000,000$
8	$ 80,000		$\dfrac{\$\,80,000}{0.10} = \$\ \ 800,000$
13	$130,000		$\dfrac{\$130,000}{0.10} = \$1,300,000$

$80,000 and the market value is $800,000. In this case, the rate of return on assets is less than the cost of capital. Hence, the market value of the firm declines so that investors can still earn 10 percent ($80,000/$800,000 = 10%). In contrast, if the firm earns 13 percent on its assets, the market value increases to $1.3 million to keep the shareholders' return at 10 percent ($130,000/$1,300,000 = 10%).

The market value in this simple example, where all earnings are paid out as cash dividends, remains unchanged only when the rate of return on the firm's assets is the same as the investors' required rate of return—10 percent. Thus, 10 percent is the cost of capital.

Underlying Assumptions   Two assumptions underlie calculations of cost of capital. The first involves corporate risk; the second, new funds.

Corporate Risk.   The cost of capital is determined for a particular degree of risk. Stated otherwise, if risks faced by the firm change, the cost will have to be recalculated. Business concerns face a business risk and a financial risk; together, these equal total corporate risk.

Business Risk.   **Business risks** are inherent in the firm's operations and are influenced by management policies, economic conditions, consumer demands, and other factors that contribute to variations in *EBIT*. The decision by the management of Chrysler to build large cars when consumers wanted small cars involved business risk. As a result of the decision, Chrysler's earnings declined sharply and hindered its ability to raise additional capital. Earnings rebounded after Chrysler changed its product mix.

Financial Risk.   Variations in *EBIT* caused by business risk may give rise to **financial risk**—that is, risk that involves the firm's ability to meet fixed financial obligations, such as interest on borrowed funds and preferred stock dividends.

The degree of financial risk depends on the proportion of borrowed funds in the firm's capital structure and the variability of revenues. Firms financed entirely with common stock have no financial risk. Those with a high proportion of long-term debt have a high degree of financial risk.

New Funds. The second assumption is that the cost of capital is applicable to all *new* funds raised by the firm. Expenses associated with new funds have already been mentioned. Let's consider them in more detail. When business concerns sell new securities, they sometimes sell directly to investors; however, they generally engage the services of an investment banking firm. As noted in Chapter 4, investment bankers may underwrite large security issues, which means that they buy a security issue from the company and sell it to investors. The fee they receive for their services, as noted earlier, is the underwriting or **flotation cost**, which amounts to the difference between the price investors pay for a security and the amount the company receives. Flotation costs also include legal fees and other expenses associated with the new issue. For example, when an investor buys a bond for $1,000, the company may receive $960 of that amount. The flotation cost is $40, or 4 percent of the face value of the bond. Similarly, there are underwriting fees for preferred and common stock. New funds that do not involve underwriting fees are current earnings retained by the firm.

Against this general background, we will now consider the components of cost of capital—the costs of debt, preferred stock, retained earnings, and common stock.

Rate of Return Required by the Firm: Component Cost of Debt

Before-Tax Cost of Debt   In theory, the **before-tax cost of debt**, k_{db}, is easy to understand and easy to compute. It is the interest rate on borrowed funds. Suppose a firm borrows $100,000 for 1 year and is expected to repay the principal and $9,000 interest at the end of the year. The interest rate can be calculated as follows.

$$k_{db} = \frac{\text{Interest expense}}{\text{Principal}}$$

$$= \frac{\$9,000}{\$100,000}$$

$$= 9\%$$

In practice, the before-tax cost of debt is somewhat more difficult to compute. The difficulty arises because interest is computed on the **net proceeds** available to the company rather than on the principal amount. In the case of bank loans, for example, the net proceeds may differ from the principal amount because the bank requires a **compensating balance**. Here, the bank requires the firm to maintain a checking account balance equal to, for example, 10 percent of the amount of the loan outstanding. Therefore, a firm borrowing $100,000 would in effect have use of only $90,000 over the life of the loan. In the case of bonds, the difference between the principal amount and the net proceeds is the flotation cost.

The before-tax cost of debt is the yield to maturity, which equates the net proceeds to the present value of periodic payments and principal over the life of the debt. For simplicity, think of debt as bonds. The before-tax cost of bonds can be derived from the following equation.

$$P_0 = \sum_{t=1}^{n} \frac{I}{(1 + k_{db})^t} + \frac{F}{(1 + k_{db})^n}$$

where

P_0 = Net price (price less flotation costs) at Time
I = Interest payment
F = Face value
k_{db} = Rate of return required by bondholders
n = Number of years to maturity

This equation can be simplified as follows.

$$P_0 = I\,(PVAIF_{kdb}) + F\,(PVIF_{kdb}) \qquad (7-2)$$

You may recognize that Equation 7–2 is the same as Equation 6–2, which was used in Chapter 6 to determine the price of bonds.[2] (Although bonds generally pay interest twice each year, for simplicity we assume that interest is paid once, at the end of each year.) The before-tax cost of debt is the rate of return required by bondholders: It is the yield to maturity.

To illustrate the use of Equation 7–2 to estimate k_{db}, assume that Jupiter Company sells a $1,000 bond that matures in 20 years. The annual interest payments are $90 and the firm's net proceeds from the sale of the bond are $956.71. The before-tax cost of debt, k_{db}, can be calculated as follows.

$$P_0 = I\,(PVAIF_{kdb}) + F(PVIF_{kdb'})$$

$$\$956.71 = \$90\,(8.82105) + \$1,000\,(0.16282)$$

$$k_{db} = 9.49\%$$

Mechanically, we solve this problem by using a calculator or a computer or by using the trial-and-error method to determine the correct k_{db}. Although

---

[2]For simplicity, we assume here that the market price of a bond, P_0, and the net price, the price of the new issue less the flotation cost, are the same.

we can use the present value tables (Appendixes C and D) to calculate the first portion of the equation, it is an arduous problem to solve by the trial-and-error method.

Equation 7–3 provides an alternate method to find k_{db} that produces approximately the same answer with substantially less effort. This is the same equation that was used to estimate yield to maturity (Equation 6–4) in Chapter 6. It gives a percentage based on the average repayment divided by the average amount borrowed.

$$k_{db} = \frac{I + \dfrac{F - P_0}{n}}{\dfrac{F + P_0}{2}} \qquad (7\text{–}3)$$

where

P_0 = Net price at Time 0
I = Annual interest payments
F = Face value of the bond, payable at maturity
n = Number of years to maturity

Using the numbers from the previous example and Equation 7–3, we can find the before-tax cost of debt for Jupiter.

$$k_{db} = \frac{I + \dfrac{F - P_0}{n}}{\dfrac{F + P_0}{2}}$$

$$= \frac{\$90 + \dfrac{\$1,000 - \$956.71}{20}}{\dfrac{\$1,000 + \$956.71}{2}}$$

$$= \frac{\$92.16}{\$978.35}$$

$$= 9.42\%$$

In practice, bankers, investors, and others use bond value tables, calculators, and computers to determine bond yields.

After-Tax Cost of Debt Because interest payments are deductible from income subject to federal income taxes, the actual cost of debt to the firm is less than the before-tax cost of debt. Stated otherwise, the **after-tax cost of debt** (k_d) is less than the before-tax cost of debt (k_{db}) because of corporate income taxes. The appropriate measure to use in cost of capital calculations is the after-tax cost of debt, which is equal to the before-tax cost of debt times (1 − marginal tax rate).

$$k_d = k_{db} (1 - t) \qquad (7\text{--}4)$$

In the previous example, the before-tax cost of debt was found to be about 9.4 percent. If Jupiter Company is in the 40 percent marginal income tax bracket, its after-tax cost of debt is as follows.

$$k_d = k_{db} (1 - t)$$

$$= 0.094 (1 - 0.40)$$

$$= 0.0564$$

$$= 5.64\%$$

The federal government is in effect subsidizing profitable business organizations by reducing the percentage cost of their interest payments by the amount of the tax rate.

Rate of Return Required by the Firm: Component Cost of Preferred Stock

Although preferred stock represents ownership, it is not considered equity for purposes of calculating the cost of capital. It is treated as if it were debt, because its fixed dividend payments, which extend over an infinite number of years, are similar to the interest payments on unsecured perpetuities, described in Chapter 5.

There are, however, two important differences between preferred stock and unsecured bonds. First, if a corporation fails to meet its interest obligations on a bond, it may be forced into bankruptcy. However, if the corporation fails to make its dividend payments on preferred stock (in which case the stock is said to be in **arrears**) the firm will not be forced into bankruptcy for that reason. (It may go bankrupt for other reasons, but not because it failed to pay preferred stock dividends.)

The second difference is that, while bond interest payments are deductible from income subject to federal income taxes, dividend payments are not deductible. Since the government does not subsidize dividend payments, it is usually more costly for a corporation to pay $1 of preferred dividends than to pay $1 interest on a bond.

The required rate of return for preferred stockholders, k_p, is as follows.

$$k_p = \frac{\text{Preferred dividend}}{\text{Market price of preferred stock}}$$

$$= \frac{D_p}{P_m} \tag{7–5}$$

The cost of preferred stock for the firm, k_{pr}, is as follows.

$$k_{pr} = \frac{D_p}{P_{pn}} \tag{7–6}$$

where

P_{pn} = Net price received by the issuer after flotation costs

To illustrate calculating the costs of preferred stock, assume that Jupiter Company sold preferred stock through its investment banker at $20 per share and that the stock pays $2 per year in dividends. The investment banker's fee was $1 per share, so the net proceeds to Jupiter are $19 per share. Using Equation 7–5, we can find the investors' required rate of return, k_p.

$$k_p = \frac{D_p}{P_m}$$

$$= \frac{\$2.00}{\$20.00}$$

$$= 10\%$$

Using Equation 7–6, we can determine Jupiter's cost for the preferred stock.

$$k_{pr} = \frac{D_p}{P_{pn}}$$

$$= \frac{\$2.00}{\$19.00}$$

$$= 10.5\%$$

The difference between the rate of return required by shareholders of preferred stock and the cost of preferred stock to the firm is due to the flotation cost.

Rate of Return Required by the Firm: Component Costs of Retained Earnings and Common Stock

Component Cost of Retained Earnings   Although retained earnings are kept by the firm instead of paid out as cash dividends, they belong to the common shareholders, who are the owners of the firm. By permitting a firm to retain earnings, common shareholders incur an opportunity cost because they give up cash dividends. In essence, they expect the firm to earn the same rate of return on the retained earnings as it provides on common stock. That means *the component cost of retained earnings* (k_r) *is equal to the rate of return on common stock* (k_e).[3]

$$k_r = k_e$$

As shown in Chapter 6, the required rate of return on common stock can be estimated by use of the Gordon stock valuation model or the capital asset pricing model (*CAPM*).

Gordon Model.   The Gordon model can be used to estimate the rate of return investors require on equity when dividends are expected to grow at a constant rate forever and k_e is greater than g, the growth rate of dividends. This formulation of the Gordon model can be expressed as follows.

$$k_e = \frac{D_1}{P_0} + g \qquad\qquad (7\text{--}7)$$

where

P_0 = Price at Time 0
D_1 = Cash dividend per share in Period 1
g = Growth rate of dividends

Assume, for example, that Jupiter Company is selling a new issue of common stock to investors at $15 per share. The firm expects to pay a $1.50 cash

[3]This statement ignores flotation costs for new shares. If they are considered, the cost of new shares is higher than the cost of retained earnings. This issue will be covered in Equation 7–9. Another reason why the cost of new shares may be higher than the cost of retained earnings involves income taxes. Cash dividends on common stock are taxed at higher rates than the capital gains that may result if the price of the shares appreciates because of increased earnings on the funds that were retained. At this introductory level, however it is sufficient to assume that $k_r = k_e$.

dividend next year, and the cash dividends are expected to grow at a rate of 5 percent per year in the foreseeable future. The required rate of return on Jupiter's common stock and retained earnings is calculated as follows.

$$k_e = \frac{D_1}{P_0} + g$$

$$= \frac{\$1.50}{\$15.00} + 0.05$$

$$= 15\%$$

Capital Asset Pricing Model.   The rate of return investors require can also be estimated by use of the capital asset pricing model (*CAPM*). Recall that according to the *CAPM*, the required rate of return on equity is equal to the risk-free rate plus a risk premium that consists of the firm's beta times the difference between the expected market rate of return and the risk-free rate.[4]

$$k_e = R_f + b(k_m - R_f) \tag{7-8}$$

where

R_f = Risk-free rate of return
b = Beta coefficient
k_m = Expected rate of return on the market portfolio

Assume that the risk-free rate of return is 10 percent, that the beta for Jupiter's common stock is 1.25, and that the expected market return is 14 percent. Using these figures and Equation 7–8, we can find the required rate of return on Jupiter's common stock and retained earnings.

$$k_e = R_f + b(k_m - R_f)$$

$$= 0.10 + 1.25(0.14 - 0.10)$$

$$= 0.10 + 0.05$$

$$= 15\%$$

Component Cost of Common Stock   The rate of return on common stock required by stockholders (k_e) understates the cost to the firm of newly issued common stock (k_s) because of flotation costs. Thus, to determine the cost of common stock to the firm, we substitute

[4]Expected rates of return are often expressed as $\hat{k}_e$ and $\hat{k}_m$; but recall from Chapter 6 that we are assuming, for simplicity, that historical rates are an acceptable proxy for expected rates.

k_s (the component cost of common stock) for k_e (the rate of return required by common stockholders) and P_n (net proceeds) for P_0 (market price) in the Gordon model (Equation 7–7). For example, suppose the Jupiter Company stock that was sold to investors at $15 per share resulted in net proceeds of $14 per share to the firm, the difference being the flotation cost of the new issue. If we assume again that the firm expects to pay a $1.50 dividend next year and to grow at a rate of 5 percent per year, we find that the component cost of Jupiter's common stock is as follows.

$$k_s = \frac{D_1}{P_n} + g$$

$$= \frac{\$1.50}{\$14.00} + 0.05$$

$$= 15.7\% \tag{7–9}$$

It is worthwhile to note that flotation costs for small new issues can be substantial, sometimes exceeding 20 percent of total proceeds. In contrast, they may be 1 percent or less for large issues from well-established firms.

It should also be noted that the key to calculating the cost of capital is correct valuation of common stock. David Durand made this point clear when he said, "we can measure the cost of capital about as accurately as we can measure the value of common stock, and any of us who think that stock appraisal is a form of crystal gazing should prepare to include research on the cost of capital in this same category."[5]

Component Weights

The previous sections explained how to calculate the cost for each component of the capital structure. We determined these component costs for the Jupiter Company.

After-tax cost of long-term debt $= k_d = 5.64\%$.

Cost of preferred stock $\quad = k_{pr} = 10.50\%$

Cost of common stock $\quad = k_s = 15.70\%$

Cost of retained earnings $\quad = k_r = 15.00\%$

[5]David Durand, "Cost of Debt and Equity Funds for Business: Trends and Problems of Measurement," in *The Management of Corporate Capital*, ed. Ezra Solomon (New York: Free Press, 1959), p. 91.

Next, the component costs must be combined in some fashion to determine the cost of capital for the firm. *The cost of capital* (k) *for the firm is the weighted average cost of the individual components.* This is called the **weighted average cost of capital** (WACC).

$$k = WACC = w_1 k_d + w_2 k_{pr} + w_3 k_s + w_4 k_r \qquad (7\text{--}10)$$

where

w_1 = Proportion of long-term debt
w_2 = Proportion of preferred stock
w_3 = Proportion of common stock
w_4 = Proportion of retained earnings

The sum of the various proportions must equal 100 percent.

The problem before us is whether the proportions (or weights) of the components should be measured by book value, market value, or target value.

Book Value Weights   The **book value**, or historical cost, is the amount shown in the balance sheet. As shown in Table 7–3, the book value of the Jupiter Company amounts to $10 million. The weighted average cost of capital is determined by multiplying the proportion of each component by its cost and summing the results. In this example, the WACC is 11.62 percent.

The principal advantage of using book value weights is that the values are readily obtainable from the firm's balance sheet. The principal disadvantage is that the weights may misstate the WACC if the market values of the debt and equity have changed. Typically, as stock prices increase, the WACC calculated with book value weights becomes understated. This will result in distortions in decisions involving the cost of capital.

Market Value Weights   The market values shown in Table 7–4 are based on the current market prices of long-term debt and stocks. The **market value** of common and preferred

Table 7–3
Cost of Capital for Jupiter Company Based on Book Value

	Amount (1)	Proportion (2)	Component Cost (3)	Average (4) = (2) × (3)
Long-term debt	$ 3,500,000	35%	5.64%	1.97%
Preferred stock	1,000,000	10	10.50	1.05
Common stock	5,000,000	50	15.70	7.85
Retained earnings	500,000	5	15.00	0.75
	$10,000,000	100%		11.62%

Weighted average cost of capital = 11.62%

Table 7–4
Cost of Capital for Jupiter Company Based on Market Value

	Amount (1)	Proportion (2)	Component Cost (3)	Average (4) = (2) × (3)
Long-term debt	$ 2,600,000	17%	5.64%	0.96%
Preferred stock	8,000,000	5	10.50	0.52
Common stock	12,000,000	78	15.70	12.25
	$15,400,000	100%		13.73%

Weighted average cost of capital = 13.73%

stock equals the number of shares outstanding times the current price per share. The value of retained earnings is embodied in the market value of the common stock. The market value of long-term debt is the sum of the market values of the firm's bonds outstanding.

A comparison of Tables 7–3 and 7–4 reveals that the market values of the long-term debt and preferred stock for Jupiter Company are substantially lower than the book values and that the market value of the common stock is more than double the book value. When market value weights are used, the WACC is 13.73 percent.

Intuitively, market value weights are more appealing than book value weights for several reasons. First, as mentioned, book value weights may understate the WACC. Second, investors expect a return based on the current value of the firm, not the historical value. Stated otherwise, shareholders of common stock know that their holdings are worth $12 million today, not the $5 million shown on Jupiter's books. Being rational investors, they want a 15 percent return on the current market value or they will sell their shares and invest elsewhere.

One drawback of using market value weights is that the market prices of securities are constantly changing for a variety of reasons that may have nothing to do with the company. To some extent, this drawback is overcome when average market values over, for example, a 6-month period are used to smooth out undesirable fluctuations. Another shortcoming is that the proportions reflected in the market value (or the book value) may not be the proportions the company uses in raising new capital. This brings us to target values.

Target Value Weights One basic assumption underlying the cost of capital is that it applies to new funds being raised by a firm. Therefore, the weights used in estimating cost of capital should reflect the composition of new funds. Book values and market values reflect the composition of the existing capital structure; however, **target values** are based on the capital structure the firm wishes to maintain as it raises new funds.

To illustrate, suppose the financial manager of the Jupiter Company has reviewed the mix of the firm's capital structure and has decided to raise 30 percent of new funds from long-term debt, 10 percent from preferred stock,

Table 7–5
Cost of Capital for Jupiter Company Based on Target Value

	Proportion (1)	Component Cost (2)	Average (3) = (1) × (2)
Long-term debt	30%	5.64%	1.60%
Preferred stock	10	10.50	1.05
Common stock	60	15.70	9.42
	100%		12.16%
Weighted average cost of capital = 12.16%			

and 60 percent from common stock. These proportions reflect the financial structure the manager believes to be the best for Jupiter. As shown in Table 7–5, the WACC based on these target values is 12.16 percent.

Target value weights should be used in calculating the WACC because they reflect the desired mix of funds. If it is impossible to use target value weights, market value weights should be used. Although target value weights and market value weights are preferable to book value weights, many firms persist in using book value weights because they are easy to determine.

As a practical matter, determining the costs of various sources of capital and the appropriate capital structure weights involves a substantial amount of judgment and conjecture. For that reason, it may be worthwhile to approximate the cost of capital by using several of the previously described methods. There may or may not be substantial differences in the results. Even though the calculation of cost of capital is not precise, the resulting approximation is of value because the cost of capital is important in a number of decisions.

WACC and the Marginal Cost of Capital

The term *marginal*, as used in finance, means next. The **marginal cost of capital** (MCC) is the cost of obtaining the next funds to be raised at a certain time—in other words, the cost of raising new funds. The MCC is another name for the WACC.

The MCC shown graphically in the top panel of Figure 7–1 represents the various increments of the new funds that can be raised by Jupiter Company. For example, Jupiter can raise $2 million of new funds in the target proportions listed in Table 7–5 at a cost of 12.1 percent. An additional $1 million costs 13 percent. These increments, and their costs, were estimated by Jupiter's investment bankers.

New funds are raised in relatively large chunks rather than a few dollars at a time. This is because investors prefer to make one large investment of, for example, $1 million rather than a thousand small investments of $1,000 each. Furthermore, the origination costs (flotation costs, lawyers' fees, paperwork, and so on) of raising funds is about the same for large or small investments. Therefore, the origination cost per dollar of funds raised can be reduced by increasing the size of the offering.

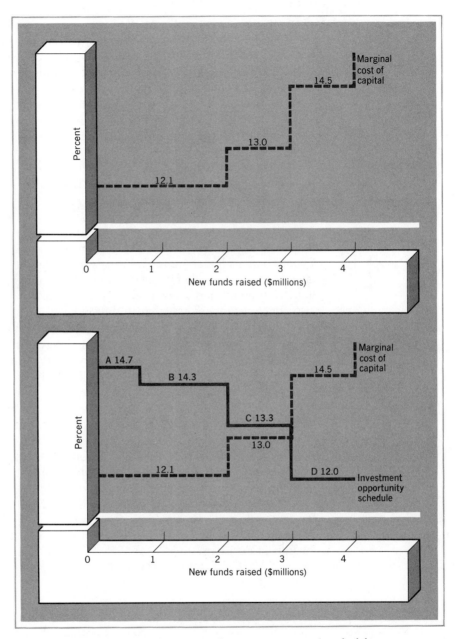

Figure 7–1   The marginal cost of capital and investment opportunity schedules.

The figure shows that the MCC increases as the total dollar amount of new funds raised increases. There are several reasons why this occurs. One is that the target weights may change in favor of higher-cost stock issues. Notice that Jupiter Company's cost is flat for the first $2 million of new funds. As mentioned, this cost reflects the target proportions listed in Table 7–5. But suppose Jupiter's investment bankers suggest that Jupiter should change the target mix and sell more stock, at higher costs. The increments in the figure reflect a mix continuing to change in favor of higher-cost stock as the amount of new funds raised increases.

Another reason the MCC for some firms increases concerns the amount of debt and equity they hold. As you know, the financial risk of a firm increases as it takes on more debt. Both debt and equity investors expect to be compensated for the increased risk.

Investors also wish to be compensated for the costs of monitoring or limiting the risks the firm takes. This is one example of the **agency costs** mentioned in Chapter 1. Recall that the goals of shareholders (principals) and management (agents) may differ. Shareholders incur costs in monitoring management's actions with audits and reports from the firm or from other sources. They are also concerned about contractual obligations, such as bond issues, that may affect their wealth. All of these costs are reflected in the MCC.

The lower panel of Figure 7–1 shows an **investment opportunity schedule** (IOS) that depicts the expected returns and costs of investment opportunities that face the firm. Jupiter can invest $500,000 in proposal A and expect to earn 14.7 percent. Likewise, it can invest $1.5 million in proposal B and expect to earn 14.3 percent. In order to invest in any of the proposals shown, Jupiter must raise new funds at the costs depicted in the figure.

Should Jupiter invest in proposals C and D? The answer is yes and no. It should raise $3 million and invest in proposals A, B, and C, because their expected returns exceed the MCC. It should *not* invest in proposal D, because the expected return (12 percent) is less than the MCC (14.5 percent) necessary to fund it. The lesson to be learned here is that the firm should raise funds to the point where the marginal return on investments is equal to or greater than the marginal cost of funds. Later chapters discuss other methods for making investment decisions.

Cost of Capital and Capital Structure

Although target weights should be used to calculate the WACC, the existing capital structure affects the cost of new funds. For example, we know from the capital asset pricing model that the rate of return investors require on common stock is equal to the risk-free rate of return plus a risk premium. To some extent, the risk premium reflects the degree of financial risk a firm faces.

The beta in the risk premium is affected by **financial leverage**, which is the use of debt in the firm's capital structure. Betas for firms with debt are generally higher than those for firms without debt. The beta for firms with financial leverage may be expressed as follows.

$$\text{Beta}_L = \text{Beta}_U[1 + B/S(1 - t)] \qquad (7\text{–}11)$$

where

Beta_L = Beta for firm with debt
Beta_U = Beta for firm with no debt (all equity)
B/S = Market value of debt to market value of equity
t = Corporate tax rate

Of course, most firms have some debt. These firms can use Equation 7–11 to determine what their betas would be in the absence of financial leverage. For example, suppose that market data shows a certain firm's beta to be 1.51. The proportion of debt to equity in the firm's capital structure (the debt-to-equity, or B/S, ratio) is 0.85, and its tax rate is 40 percent. If the firm were financed only by equity, its beta (Beta_U) could be calculated as follows.

$$\text{Beta}_L = \text{Beta}_U[1 + B/S(1 - t)]$$

$$1.51 = \text{Beta}_U[1 + 0.85(1 - 0.40)]$$

$$\text{Beta}_U = \frac{1.51}{[1 + 0.85(1 - 0.40)]}$$

$$\text{Beta}_U = 1.00$$

As mentioned earlier in this chapter, financial risk is measured by a firm's ability to meet its financial obligations, and that risk is assumed constant when the cost of capital is calculated. What happens if the degree of financial risk changes? When a firm changes its financial structure, the financial risk does change. Because the B/S ratio is one measure of financial risk, we can use it to observe how different levels of financial risk affect the cost of capital.

Assume that a firm has a capital structure amounting to $10 million consisting of debt and equity. For simplicity, also assume that the component cost of common stock is the same as the shareholders' required rate of return ($k_s = k_e$). By changing the mix of debt and equity, we can study the impact of debt and equity on the firm's cost of capital. Three B/S mixes are depicted in Figure 7–2. The first is low; the capital structure is 30 percent debt and 70 percent equity. Because the financial risk is relatively small, the required rate of return on common stock is relatively low ($k_e = 15\%$) and the WACC is 12 percent.

As the B/S ratio increases to 50 percent debt and 50 percent equity, share-

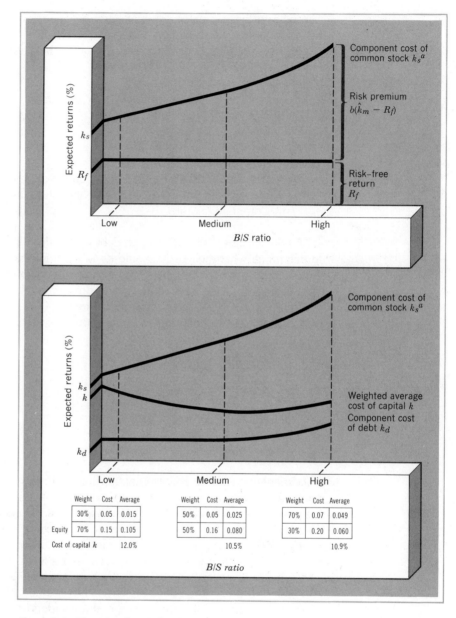

Figure 7–2 The cost of capital with various *B/S* ratios.
[a]For simplicity, it is assumed that $k_s = k_e$.

holders of common stock perceive increased financial risk and require a higher return of 16 percent. However, bondholders do not require a higher return. The result is that, because a larger portion of the capital structure is financed with low-cost debt, the *WACC* declines to 10.5 percent.

The increased use of debt will lower the *WACC* to some point. Beyond that unspecified point, bondholders will recognize the increased financial risk and also require higher returns. Thus, when the debt-to-equity ratio is, for example, 70 percent debt and 30 percent equity, the cost of debt increases. In the figure, the cost of debt increases to 7 percent and the cost of equity to 20 percent. At this point the *WACC* is 10.9 percent, somewhat higher than before. The reason that the average cost of capital is not substantially higher is that, although the cost of debt has increased, it is still much lower than the cost of equity.

Some Controversy   The extent to which the proportions of debt and equity affect the value of a firm has been debated for many years. According to Franco Modigliani and Merton Miller, if there were no corporate taxes, a firm's cost of capital would be constant, and the composition of the capital structure would have no effect on the value of the firm.[6] They argue that under the tax-free condition the cost of capital is constant because increases in the cost of equity offset the advantages of using additional low-cost debt.

When income taxes are considered, however, the cost of capital declines with the increased use of debt, because interest payments are a tax-deductible expense. Therefore, firms should use as much debt as possible to lower their costs of capital and increase their values.

The popular view today is that capital structure does affect value. The judicious use of debt lowers the cost of capital and enhances the value of the firm. For example, suppose that a firm has an *EBIT* of $1 million, no debt, and a cost of capital of 15 percent. Using Equation 7–1, we estimate the value of the firm as follows.

$$V^* = \frac{EBIT}{k}$$

$$= \frac{\$1,000,000}{0.15}$$

$$= \$6,666,667$$

By using some debt, the firm might be able to reduce the cost of capital to

[6]Franco Modigliani and Merton Miller wrote several classic articles dealing with this subject. See "The Cost of Capital, Corporation Finance and the Theory of Investment," *American Economic Review,* June 1958, pp. 261–297; and "Taxes and the Cost of Capital: A Correction," *American Economic Review,* June 1963, pp. 433–443. In addition, see replies to these articles in the *American Economic Review,* September 1958, pp. 655–669, and June 1965, pp. 524–527.

12 percent, which would raise the value of the firm to $8,333,333 ($1,000,000/0.12 = $8,333,333). However, if the firm increased debt too much, its financial risk would increase to such an extent that both bondholders and shareholders would demand higher rates of return. As a result, the cost of capital would increase and the value of the firm would be reduced.

In practice, financial managers recognize the important effect of capital structure on the cost of funds and the value of the firm. For example, TRW, Inc., a large manufacturer of aerospace equipment and other high-technology products, had a capital structure with approximately 40 percent debt and 60 percent equity. This ratio was one factor that helped determine the A rating on TRW's debt securities. Bonds with an A rating are considered upper-medium grade in terms of risk and they carry higher interest rates than AA (high-grade) and AAA (highest-grade) bonds. TRW recently decided to reduce its debt-to-equity ratio to about 30 percent debt and 70 percent equity, which produced the following benefits: First, the change reduced the firm's financial risk, because the proportion of debt to equity fell. Second, the reduced financial risk helped improve the company's bond rating, moving it from A toward AA, which lowered the interest cost on new debt issues. The more conservative capital structure and higher rating were recognized by both bondholders and shareholders and thus reduced the cost of capital and increased the value of the firm.

Optimum Capital Structure   In theory, the optimum mix of debt and equity is the one that provides the lowest *WACC* and the highest value for the firm. In practice, we do not know where that point is, and it may shift over time. Moreover, the optimum debt-to-equity ratio may vary from industry to industry. Among electric utility companies, for example, it is common practice to have high debt-to-equity ratios. One reason for this is that electric utility companies frequently have fairly predictable sources of income, and the prices they charge are determined by administrative fiat. In contrast, manufacturers of cotton products tend to have low debt-to-equity ratios; their revenues and prices are determined by the whims of the market. A firm's position on the life cycle is another factor affecting both the cost and the proportion of its debt financing.

Life Cycle, Capital Structure, and Cost of Capital   The capital structure of a firm changes over the course of its life cycle. For example, consider the typical life cycle depicted in Figure 7–3. The proportion of debt to equity changes as the firm matures. As a general rule, firms in the early phases of the life cycle depend more on debt to finance expansion of plant and equipment than firms in the later phases.

It follows that the costs of debt and equity will also vary as a firm's debt-to-equity ratio and business risks change. Both business risk and financial risk are highest during the pioneering and early expansion phases of the life cycle. It is not surprising, then, that rates of return required by both debt and equity

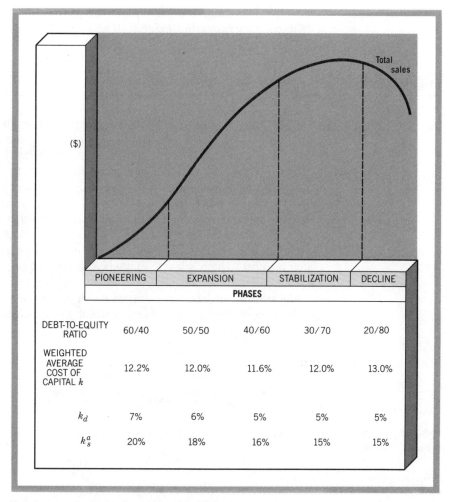

Figure 7–3   The life cycle and cost of capital[a].
[a]For simplicity, it is assumed that $k_s = k_e$.

investors are higher during these phases than after the firm has matured. For example, investors would consider a company just entering the personal computer market with a new product to have greater risk than IBM, the market leader.

The *WACC* in Figure 7–3 is based on the debt-to-equity ratios and the required rates of return shown in the figure. For simplicity, we assume again that k_s equals k_e. The *WACC* is high during the early phases of the life cycle because of the high financial leverage and the high returns required by both debt and equity investors. As the firm survives and matures, both financial risk and business risk diminish and the *WACC* declines. Later, as the firm continues to mature, high-cost equity becomes relatively more important than debt in the capital structure and the *WACC* increases again. More will be said about debt-to-equity mixes in Chapters 10 and 11.

Summary

The cost of capital may be defined as the minimum rate of return a firm must earn on its assets to satisfy its investors or as the rate of return on assets at which the market value of the firm remains unchanged. The cost of capital is determined for a particular degree of risk and applies to new funds being raised by the firm. Component costs that make up the cost of capital are the costs of debt, preferred stock, retained earnings, and common stock. Equations to estimate these costs, along with other important equations from the chapter, are summarized in Table 7–6.

The appropriate cost of debt to be used in cost of capital calculations is the after-tax cost, which is less than the before-tax cost because interest payments are deductible from taxable income. Although preferred stock shares some characteristics of debt, payments of dividends on preferred stock are not tax deductible. In theory, cost of equity—both common stock and retained earn-

Table 7–6
Summary of Equations

	Equation	Number
Value of firm	$V* = \dfrac{I}{k_{db}} + \dfrac{EBIT - I}{k_e} = \dfrac{EBIT}{k}$	(7–1)
Value of bond; used to find before-tax cost of debt	$P_0 = I(PVAIF_{k_{db},n}) + F\,(PVIF_{k_{db},n})$	(7–2)
Before-tax cost of debt, alternate method	$k_{db} = \dfrac{I + \dfrac{F - P_0}{n}}{\dfrac{F + P_0}{2}}$	(7–3)
After-tax cost of debt	$k_d = k_{db}\,(1 - t)$	(7–4)
Rate of return required by preferred shareholders	$k_p = \dfrac{D_p}{P_m}$	(7–5)
Component cost of preferred stock	$k_{pr} = \dfrac{D_p}{P_{pn}}$	(7–6)
Rate of return required by common shareholders, derived from Gordon model	$k_e = \dfrac{D_1}{P_0} + g$	(7–7)
Rate of return required by common shareholders, derived from *CAPM*	$k_e = R_f + b\,(k_m - R_f)$	(7–8)
Component cost of common stock, derived from Equation 7–7	$k_s = \dfrac{D_1}{P_n} + g$	(7–9)
Weighted average cost of capital for firm	$k = WACC = w_1 k_d + w_2 k_{pr} + w_3 k_s + w_4 k_r$	(7–10)
Beta for leveraged firm	$Beta_L = Beta_U\,[1 + B/S\,(1 - t)]$	(7–11)

ings—is the most difficult component to estimate. The Gordon model and the capital asset pricing model are used to estimate the cost of equity.

Once component costs have been determined, they should be weighted according to their proportions in the firm's capital structure. Book values, market values, or target values may be used in this process. Target values, which reflect the firm's desired capital structure, are preferable to book and market values.

The extent to which the proportion of debt to equity affects the value of a firm has been debated for many years. The popular view today is that capital structure does affect value. The judicious use of debt lowers the cost of capital and enhances the value of the firm; however, too much debt results in increased risk, an elevated cost of capital, and lower value for the firm.

Important Terms

Agency cost	Financial leverage
After-tax cost of debt	Financial risk
Arrears	Flotation cost
Before-tax cost of debt	Investment opportunity schedule
Book value	(*IOS*)
Business risk	Marginal cost of capital (*MCC*)
Capital structure	Market value
Compensating balance	Net proceeds
Cost of capital	Target value
Earnings before interest and taxes	Weighted average cost of capital
(*EBIT*)	(*WACC*)

Questions

1. Business risk and financial risk affect the cost of capital. Explain what is meant by these two terms.
2. What is a firm's capital structure?
3. Identify two ways of defining the cost of capital. Are these definitions consistent? Why or why not?
4. What two factors cause a firm's component costs to be different from investors' required rates of return?
5. What are two major differences between preferred stock and unsecured bonds? How do these differences affect the cost of preferred stock relative to the cost of debt?
6. Explain why there is a cost associated with retained earnings.
7. How does the component cost of retained earnings differ from the component cost of new common stock?

8. Compare the advantages and disadvantages of using book value versus market value weights to calculate the cost of capital. How and why is k likely to differ with the use of book versus market values?

9. What is meant by the target capital structure? Will this always be different from existing book or market values?

10. What is the marginal cost of capital?

11. Explain how and why stock betas are affected by the firm's use of financial leverage.

12. Define the terms *optimum capital structure* and *minimum cost of capital*. Graphically illustrate these concepts.

13. Explain this statement: Lowering the cost of capital can increase the value of the firm.

14. If there is an optimum capital structure, why is it expected to vary from.industry to industry?

15. How does the life cycle of the firm affect the firm's cost of capital?

Problems

1. Parade Corporation is planning a 12 percent, 20-year bond issue, with annual interest payments and a face value at maturity of $1,000. The firm will net $967 per bond and has a marginal tax rate of 40 percent. What are the before-tax and after-tax costs of this debt? Use both the trial and error and the approximation methods to make these calculations.

2. Suppose the Parade Corporation in Problem 1 expected to net $1,050 from the sale of its bonds. What are the before- and after-tax costs of debt under these conditions? Use the approximation period.

3. Harper Company has issued a new $25 million, 10 percent preferred stock issue that sold to investors for $100 per share. Investment bankers claimed 10 percent of the sales price as flotation costs. If Harper is in the 46 percent tax bracket, compute the required rate of return for Harper's preferred shareholders and the cost of preferred stock for Harper.

4. Technicast Studios plans an issue of preferred stock at a price of $60 per share and issuance costs of $4 per share. The dividend will be $9 per share. Calculate the cost of preferred stock and the required rate of return for Technicast's shareholders.

5. Walker Media has just issued new common stock with a market price of $26 per share and an expected dividend in the first year of $1.20. The dividend growth rate is expected to be 10 percent annually, and flotation costs were 10 percent of the sales price.
   (a) What is the component cost of Walker's common stock?
   (b) What is the required rate of return for the firm's shareholders?
   (c) What is the cost of retained earnings for the firm?

6. Shamrock Hotel Corporation is planning an expansion in which retained earnings will be used as one of the sources of financing. What is the cost of retained earnings if the firm has a beta of 1.8, the risk-free rate is 8 percent, and the expected return on the market is 13 percent?

7. The Rutter Company's management has collected the following information.

Bonds	$4 million face value	$3.6 million market value
Preferred stock	$1 million face value	0.8 million market value
Common stock	$5 million book value	7.6 million market value

Calculate book value and market value weights for Rutter's capital structure.

8. Miller Corporation has the following book value capital structure as of year-end 1989.

Bonds (14 percent, due 2004, $1000 face value)	$40 million
Preferred (11 percent, $50 par value)	10 million
Common stock	
Par value (20 million shares at $1 each)	20 million
Paid-in capital	40 million
Retained earnings	40 million

Calculate Miller's book value weights.

9. Suppose the bonds of Miller Corporation in Problem 8 are selling for $850 each, preferred stock is selling for $46 per share, and common stock is selling for $12 per share. Calculate Miller's market value weights. What are the major reasons for the difference in your answers to Problems 8 and 9?

10. Patty's Pancake Houses are going national. To finance the expansion, the firm needs $80 million. Calculate the weighted average cost of capital, given the following information.

Target Weights
Debt	30%
Preferred stock	10%
Common equity	60%

New debt having a coupon rate of 13 percent and a 15-year maturity can be issued at the face value of $1,000 and flotation costs of $15 per bond. Preferred stockholders currently expect a 15 percent return. Flotation costs on new preferred will reduce the proceeds to the firm by 5 percent of the $100 market price.

Common stock currently pays a dividend of $1.60 per share on a market price of $37. An expected growth rate of 12.5 percent is projected for the indefinite future. Issuance costs will be 10 percent of the market price. Patty's is in the 40 percent marginal tax bracket.

11. John Zincke Equipment has projected a capital budget of $2.5 million for 1990. The target capital structure is 30 percent debt, 10 percent preferred stock, 10 percent new common stock, and 50 percent retained earnings. The following information has been collected about the new securities that will be issued to finance the projects.

Debt: 20-year maturity, 12 percent coupon rate, net proceeds of $984 on a $1,000 face value bond.

Preferred stock: Par $100, 11 percent dividend, net proceeds of $95 per share.

Common stock: Market price $43, current dividend $2, expected growth rate 14 percent, flotation costs of 10 percent.

Assuming a marginal tax rate of 40 percent, calculate Zincke's weighted average cost of capital.

12. Babcock Grain Elevators is estimating financing needs over the next investment period. Planned funds sources include the following.

Debt	$10 million
Preferred stock	5 million
New common stock	20 million
Retained earnings	7 million

Debt: 15-year maturity, 14 percent coupon rate, net proceeds of $992 on a $1,000 face value bond

Preferred stock: Par value $50, $6 dividend, net proceeds of $46 per share.

Common stock: Market price $85, current dividend $6, expected growth rate 10 percent, flotation costs of $10 per share.

The firm's tax rate is 40 percent. Calculate the weighted average cost of capital.

13. Selma's Craft Supplies has never calculated its cost of capital before. Now, however, the firm is expanding and must estimate the total cost of raising new funds. Management has made the following policy decision and collected the following information.

Target Weights

Debt	40%
Preferred stock	10%
Common equity	50%

Investors are expected to require a rate of return of 14 percent on new bond issues, and flotation costs are expected to be minimal. The firm's marginal tax bracket is 30 percent.

Preferred stockholders currently expect a 15 percent return. Flotation costs will reduce the proceeds to the firm by 5 percent of the market price, which is $75.

The common stock has a beta of 1.5. The risk-free rate is 10 percent, and the expected return on the market as a whole is 18 percent. No new common stock will be sold, so all additions to equity will be made through retained earnings.

(a) Calculate the weighted average cost of capital for Selma.

(b) If Selma's managers decided to change the firm's major line of business to automobile manufacturing, would the cost of capital remain the same? Why or why not?

14. Wenders Corporation is an all-equity financed firm with a beta of 0.8. The expected market rate of return is 15 percent and the risk-free rate is 9 percent.

(a) What is Wenders' cost of capital?

(b) Suppose Wender's management decides to change the capital structure to include 20 percent debt, increasing the beta to 0.96. If the after-tax cost of debt for Wenders is 8 percent, would you recommend the change? Why or why not?

15. Millrace Limited currently has a target capital structure of 40 percent debt, 60 percent equity. The beta of the firm's common stock is 1.3. The expected market rate of return is 12 percent, and the risk-free rate is 7 percent. The firm's bonds are yielding 11 percent before tax, and the firm is in the 46 percent marginal tax bracket.

(a) What is Millrace's cost of capital?

(b) If management decides on a new target capital structure of 50 percent debt, 50 percent equity, what will the firm's new beta be?

(c) If, under the revised capital structure, the after-tax cost of debt is 6 percent, what is the firm's new cost of capital? Is the new capital structure optimum? Why or why not?

16. Preston Properties is negotiating to build a large business complex in a fast-growing Arizona city. The firm plans to raise the necessary funds in the following proportions.

Debt	40%
Preferred stock	10%
Common equity	50%

The firm's marginal tax bracket is 40 percent. Data on the new securities issues are as follows.

Debt: A privately placed bond issue with a large insurance firm at an interest rate of 13 percent; no flotation costs.

Preferred stock: Issued to yield 12 percent on a market price of $100. Flotation costs are 5 percent of the price.

Common stock: Current market price is $62, with dividends of $5 per share and an expected growth rate of 10 percent. Flotation costs are $5 per share.

(a) Calculate the cost of capital for Preston Properties, assuming that all equity financing will be provided from the sale of new common stock.

(b) Calculate the cost of capital for Preston, assuming that all the equity financing will be provided through retained earnings.

17. Information on Moser, Incorporated's current capital structure has been collected.

Bonds: 10 percent annual coupon rate, 20 years to maturity, face value $1,000, current price $800, number of bonds outstanding, 1,000. The tax rate is 35 percent.

Preferred stock: $10 dividend, par value $100, current price $90, 500 shares outstanding.

Common stock account: 8,000 shares outstanding, originally sold at $50 per share.

Retained earnings: $600,000

Current market price of common stock: $120 per share, growth in dividends 15 percent per year, next expected dividend $5.

(a) Calculate book and market value weights for Moser.

(b) Calculate the weighted average cost of capital using both sets of weights. Assume that new common stock will be sold to generate equity capital and that flotation costs for both preferred and common stock will be $5 per share. Flotation costs for new debt are $10 per bond.

18. Consider the following estimates for the after-tax cost of debt and cost of equity for the Adams Apple Farm under various capital structures.

Percent Debt in Capital Structure	k_d (%)	k_a (%)
0.00	————	12.00
0.10	5.00	12.50
0.25	5.25	13.25
0.30	5.25	13.50
0.40	6.25	14.00
0.50	7.25	14.50
0.75	9.00	17.00
0.80	10.00	17.50
0.90	11.00	20.00
0.95	12.00	25.00

(a) Calculate the cost of capital for Adams Apple under these capital structures.

(b) Plot your results on a graph (use the percent of debt in the capital structure on your horizontal axis) and determine the location of the optimum capital structure for this firm.

19. If a firm expects *EBIT* of $200,000, calculate its total value if the cost of capital is 12 percent; 15 percent; 20 percent. What idea is illustrated by these calculations? (Assume there are no taxes.)

20. Fisher Shoe Company is financed entirely with equity and intends to remain that way. The firm has a beta of 2.5, indicating a high level of systematic risk. The risk-free rate is 10 percent, and the expected return on the market portfolio is 16 percent. The firm's tax rate is 30 percent, and all after-tax earnings are paid as dividends.

What is the market value of the firm if *EBIT* is expected to be $60,000 indefinitely? If *EBIT* is expected to be $75,000? $90,000?

Capital Investment Decisions

C apital investment decision is a broader term than capital budgeting. Capital budgeting usually involves evaluating investment proposals to acquire plant and equipment. Capital investment decisions encompass a wider range of investment proposals. The same tools are used in both tasks, but in capital investment decision making they are applied to evaluating the purchase of other companies, evaluating marketing proposals, and making a host of other decisions necessary in the daily operations of a firm.

The first chapter of Part 3, Chapter 8, explains the major capital budgeting techniques. The second, Chapter 9, deals with the issue of making investment decisions under uncertainty. That is, how do we make decisions today that affect the future when we do not know what the future will be?

Capital Budgeting Techniques

Eaton Corporation paid $350 million to acquire Cutler - Hammer, Inc.; and Northwest Industries, Inc., paid $205 million to acquire Coca-Cola Bottling Company of Los Angeles.[1] Both acquiring companies used discounted cash flow techniques to help determine the prices they would pay. Traditionally, discounted cash flow techniques have been used to evaluate capital investment decisions concerning plant and equipment. That is why these techniques are commonly called **capital budgeting techniques**. A better name might be investment decision techniques, because they can be used not only for capital budgeting but for evaluating acquisitions and various lines of business as well as for many other purposes. Some capital budgeting techniques consider the time value of money and can also be adjusted to take risk into account. The point is, modern methods for evaluating investment decisions, as described in this chapter and the next one, have a wide variety of business applications; they are not limited to evaluation of investments in plant and equipment.

---

[1]"The Cash-Flow Takeover Formula," *Business Week*, December 18, 1978, pp. 86–87.

After reading this chapter, you should know the following.

1. **What investment outlays and after-tax cash flows are.**
2. **How cash flows and profits differ.**
3. **How depreciation affects cash flow.**
4. **How mutually exclusive and independent proposals differ.**
5. **What strengths and weaknesses the payback method involves.**
6. **How to use the net present value, the profitability index, and the internal rate of return.**
7. **Why net present value is such a valuable tool.**
8. **Why discounted cash flow methods don't always agree, and what to do about it.**

Basic Information

The capital budgeting process begins with an estimation of how much cash is going to be spent on an investment proposal and how much cash the investment is expected to generate over time. The amount of cash spent is called the **investment outlay**, and the expected net returns (the funds available to the firm after all expenses have been accounted for) are called **after-tax cash flows**.

Capital budgeting focuses on cash outflows and inflows (in contrast to accrual accounting procedures, which recognize expenses when they are incurred rather than when they are paid and recognize revenues when a sale is made, not when cash is collected). Emphasizing the timing of the cash flow—the actual inflows and outflows of funds available to the firm—recognizes the fact that, for example, making a sale and collecting the receipts are two different things. A correct specification of cash outflows and inflows is essential in capital budgeting. Therefore, the following sections provide a detailed explanation of investment outlays and after-tax cash flows.

Investment Outlay Tru-Cut Company produces machined metal parts that are used in the automobile replacement parts industry. The company has been deluged with orders and is considering buying a new automated machine tool that will replace an older machine and add to the company's productive capacity. The financial manager has been given the task of evaluating the costs and benefits of the new machine. He began by preparing a list of the various types of costs associated with buying the new machine. The list is shown in Table 8–1. It includes a cash outlay for the machine, increases in working capital, and other expenses. The disposition of the machine being replaced must also be considered.

Table 8–1
Investment Outlays for Tru-Cut Company

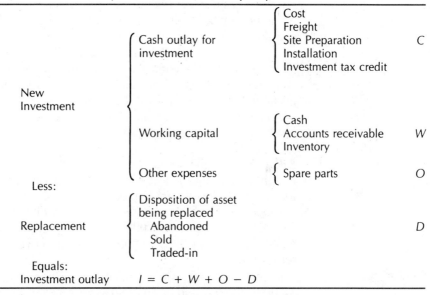

Cash outlay for investment
- Cost
- Freight
- Site Preparation   C
- Installation
- Investment tax credit

Working capital
- Cash
- Accounts receivable   W
- Inventory

Other expenses
- Spare parts   O

Less: Replacement
Disposition of asset being replaced
- Abandoned   D
- Sold
- Traded-in

Equals:
Investment outlay $I = C + W + O - D$

Cash Outlay. The **cash outlay** for the new machine includes the cost of the machine, the cost of shipping it, the cost of hardening the floor to support its weight, and the installation costs for the wiring. The investment tax credit, which is 10 percent of the purchase price and is deducted from Tru-Cut's tax liability in the year when the asset is purchased, is also considered, because it reduces the cash outlay. The investment tax credit was repealed by the Tax Reform Act of 1986. Since the ITC has come and gone several times in the past, we will retain it to familiarize you with it.

Working Capital. The new machine tool will require an inventory of metal bars to be cut and will produce an inventory of finished parts to be sold. Therefore, the addition of the machine will be accompanied by an increase in inventories and by an increase in accounts receivable when the parts are sold. Inventories and accounts receivable are part of the firm's **working capital**. (When the machine is replaced, the level of working capital and operating expenses may decline, resulting in reduced outlays at that time.)

Other Expenses. The new machine tool requires an inventory of spare parts (belts, gears, and so on) to keep it operating. The cost of the spare parts can be depreciated.

Disposition of Replaced Asset.   The final consideration involves the **disposition** of the machine that is being replaced. The firm can (1) abandon it, (2) sell it for cash, or (3) trade it in on the new machine. Each course of action has important tax implications. Because tax laws are so complex, only a general notion of the tax consequences is presented here.

Abandonment.   If the machine is abandoned and has no book value, no loss will occur. **Book value**, as you recall, is the original cost of the asset less its accumulated depreciation. If the asset has some book value, there will be an ordinary income tax loss that will reduce the firm's income tax payments, resulting in a net after-tax cash flow.

Sale.   The income tax paid if the asset is sold for more than book value (or the amount deducted if it is sold for less than book value) represents a tax adjustment to income for depreciating the asset too fast (or too slowly).

Suppose a machine with an original cost of $30,000 and a book value of $10,000 was sold for $35,000. As shown in Table 8–2, ordinary income tax would be paid on the $20,000 difference between the book value and the selling price.

If the machine was sold for less than book value—for example, $7,000—there would be an ordinary income tax loss on the $3,000 difference between the book value and the selling price. The loss would result in a reduction in the firm's income tax payment.

Returning to the Tru-Cut example, assume that the company's old machine is sold for $22,000, which is $12,000 more than the book value. Tru-Cut is in the 30 percent income tax bracket, so it will have to pay $3,600 income tax ($12,000 × 0.30 = $3,600) on the sale of the machine.

The dollar value of the disposition is the amount of cash received from the sale of the asset less the tax impact.

$$D = S - t(S - B) \qquad\qquad (8\text{–}1)$$

where

D = Dollar value of disposition
S = Cash from the sale of the asset
t = Applicable tax rate on gain or loss
B = Book value of asset being replaced

Because the machine is sold for $22,000, the net benefit to Tru-Cut can be calculated as follows.

$$D = S - t(S - B)$$
$$= \$22,000 - 0.30(\$22,000 - \$10,000)$$
$$= \$18,400$$

Table 8–2
Examples of Tax Results of Selling Asset

Value	Selling Price	Tax Consequence	Tax
Example 1			
$30,000 (original cost) $10,000 (book value)	$35,000	Ordinary income tax on $25,000	Ordinary income tax
Example 2			
$10,000 (book value)	$ 7,000	Ordinary income tax *loss* on $3,000	Loss
Tru-Cut Example			
$10,000 (book value)	$22,000	Ordinary income tax on $12,000	Ordinary income tax

Trade-in. If the asset is traded in, the book value of the new asset is calculated as the book value of the old asset plus any additional cash expenses.

Collectively, as shown in Table 8–1, the investment outlay includes the cash outlay plus increases in working capital and other expenses, less the disposition of the asset being replaced.

$$I = C + W + O - D \qquad (8\text{–}2)$$

where

I = Investment outlay
C = Cash outlay for the investment
W = Increase (or decrease) in working capital
O = Increase (or decrease) in other expenses
D = Dollar value of disposition of asset being replaced

Substituting Equation 8–1 into Equation 8–2 results in the following.

$$I = C + W + O - [S - t(S - B)]$$

Use this part
for a new investment.

Use entire equation if
replacement is involved. $\qquad (8\text{–}3)$

Using Equation 8–3, Tru-Cut's financial manager has determined that the investment outlay for the new machine tool is as follows.

$$
\begin{array}{lr}
C \text{ (cash outlay for investment)} & \$150,000 \\
W \text{ (increase in working capital)} + & 20,000 \\
O \text{ (increase in other expenses)} + & 18,000 \\
D \text{ (disposition of old machine)} - & 18,400 \\
\hline
I \text{ (investment outlay)} & = \$169,600
\end{array}
$$

Simplifying Assumption.   Throughout this chapter, we make the simplifying assumption that the investment outlay occurs instantly, in Time 0 (t_0). This is done to make the examples easier to understand. In reality, investment outlays can occur at any time. It may take years to build a large office building, for example. Similarly, airlines have to make periodic cash outlays on the aircraft they own to rebuild engines and other parts. Remember that, although we assume investment outlays are made at Time 0, they are often made at other times.

After-Tax Cash Flow   As mentioned earlier, the capital budgeting process begins with a determination of the investment outlay and the expected net returns, which are called after-tax cash flows. **Cash flow** is simply cash inflow less cash outflow over a given period of time.

Profit versus Cash Flow.   After-tax cash flow is not the same as accrual accounting profit, or net income. In order to distinguish between the two, consider the information presented in Table 8–3. The financial manager of Tru-Cut has estimated that the cash income realized from the sale of the parts produced by the new automated machine tool will be $100,000 in the first year. To determine the accounting profit, we deduct operating expenses, depreciation, and taxes from that amount, resulting in a net income of $10,500.

In computing the after-tax cash flow, however, only cash inflows and outflows are taken into account. The $100,000 income is the inflow and the $70,000 operating expense and $4,500 taxes are the outflows, giving a cash flow of $25,500. The difference is depreciation, a noncash outflow.

It is also possible to approximate after-tax cash flow by adding net income to depreciation.

$$\text{After-tax cash} = \text{Net income} + \text{Depreciation} \qquad (8\text{--}4)$$

Net income of $10,500 and depreciation of $15,000 give a cash flow of $25,500.

Table 8–3
Net Income and Cash Flow from New Machine Tool in First Year

	Income Statement	Cash Flow
Cash income	$100,000	$100,000
Less: Operating expenses other than depreciation	− 70,000	− 70,000
Less: Depreciation (straight-line with half-year convention)	15,000	
Earnings before taxes (net operating income)	$ 15,000	
Less: Income taxes (30%)	− 4,500	− 4,500
Net income	$ 10,500	
		$ 25,500

Depreciation Although depreciation is a noncash expense, it has a major impact on cash flow because it reduces the cash payment of income taxes. Consider the difference in impact of straight-line depreciation and the accelerated cost recovery system (ACRS) on tax payments.

Suppose Tru-Cut's financial manager has determined that the automated machine tool, which had an original cost of $150,000, would be used for 5 years. To calculate the amount of depreciation using the straight-line method, we can use the following equation.

$$\text{Dollar amount of depreciation per year} = \frac{\text{Depreciable value}}{\text{Useful life}}$$

$$= \frac{\$150,000}{5 \text{ years}}$$

$$= \$30,000/\text{year}$$

Of the $30,000 depreciation for the first year, $15,000 is taken in the first year and $15,000 in the sixth year, because of the half-year convention.[2] This is the depreciation amount shown in Table 8–3. Taxes in the first year amount to $4,500, as the table shows.

If the firm used the ACRS, the depreciation expense in the first few years would be higher and the tax payment lower. Table 8–4 shows that when the ACRS is used, the depreciation expense in the first year is $30,000 and income taxes are reduced from $4,500 to $0. Reduced taxes result in a higher cash

[2]Under the tax act of 1981, only one-half of the first year's straight-line depreciation is taken in the first year; the remainder is taken at the end of the recovery period. Salvage value need not be included in the calculations.

Table 8–4
Net Income and Cash Flow from New Machine Tool in the First
Year When ACRS Is Used

	Income Statement	Cash Flow
Cash income	$100,000	$100,000
Less: Operating expenses other than depreciation	− 70,000	− 70,000
Less: Depreciation (ACRS of 20%)	− 30,000	
Earnings before taxes (net operating income)	$ 0	
Less: Income taxes (30%)	− 0	− 0
Net Income	$ 0	
		$ 30,000

flow—$30,000, compared with $25,000 when the straight-line method was used.[3]

Interest Expense Borrowed funds have not been mentioned in the Tru-Cut example because interest expense is not included in cash flow calculations. This means that the method of financing a specific project is ignored when expected returns, or cash flows, are assessed. That is, the financing decision is separate from the investment decision. However, as a later part of this chapter will explain, the method of financing is taken into account in the net present value method of analysis, where cash flows are discounted by the cost of capital.

Differential Cash Flow So far, the discussion has focused on the after-tax cash flow from a single investment proposal. Frequently, one investment proposal may affect the after-tax cash flows from other investments. When this occurs, it is best to use the **differential cash flow**, or **incremental cash flow**—the difference between the cash flows of the firm with and without the investment proposal's being implemented.

For example, suppose a manufacturer is considering an investment proposal to produce a new soap. Its current Brand A soap has an after-tax cash flow of $20 million per year. The proposed Brand B soap has an expected after-tax cash flow of $10 million per year. However, if the firm produces Brand B, it expects the demand for Brand A to decline and the cash flow for Brand A to

[3]Recall that firms can use different accounting methods for "tax" and "book" purposes. Thus, a firm may use straight-line depreciation for book purposes, to report earnings, and accelerated depreciation for tax purposes, to keep taxes low. The difference between the two methods is shown as *deferred taxes* on the balance sheet. It may appear either as a liability or as an asset, depending on the timing of reported depreciation.

be reduced to $17 million per year. The expected $3 million reduction in Brand A's cash flow must be considered in evaluations of Brand B. Brand B's differential cash flow can be calculated as follows.

Brand A			Brand B	Differential
Expected Cash Flow (1)	Change due to Brand B (2)	Net Cash Flow (3) = (1) − (2)	Expected Cash Flow (4)	Cash Flow (5) = (3) − (4)
$20,000,000	− $3,000,000	$17,000,000	$10,000,000	$7,000,000

The differential cash flow for Brand B is $7 million per year.

Investment Proposals

Before we go on to a discussion of how investment proposals are evaluated and ranked, we'll examine some general information about them. Some business concerns classify investment proposals as mandatory, replacement, or expansion. **Mandatory proposals** are required for the continued operation of the firm. For example, the jet engines on airliners must be replaced periodically or the airplanes cannot fly.

Replacement proposals involve the replacement of existing equipment that results in no major increase in revenues. Some considerations involved in replacement decisions are illustrated by a Coca-Cola bottling company that had to replace a bottle-scrubbing machine. The company could buy a new machine identical to the one being replaced or it could buy one that cost more but was more efficient. In this case, the bottler evaluated the savings from both pieces of equipment. One would save the company money because it cost less; the other would save money because it operated more efficiently. It is important to note that the benefits from some replacement decisions are reduced costs (that is, savings) instead of increased revenues.

Expansion proposals are expected to add substantially to revenues. The soap company's Brand B proposal is an example of an expansion project.

It is also useful to classify investment proposals as either mutually exclusive or independent. **Mutually exclusive proposals** involve "either-or" situations in which only one project can be selected, but not all. For example, a firm can build a factory or an office building on a parcel of land but cannot build both on the same site. In contrast, any number of **independent proposals** may be selected as long as there are funds to pay for them.

The categories mentioned above are, as noted, useful in allocating capital. Firms may also allocate capital according to the economic feasibility of the available investment proposals. Four methods are used for evaluating the economic feasibility of investment proposals and for ranking them. The first method, which uses the payback period, has been used for many years. This method does not use discounted cash flows. In contrast, the other three methods—net present value, profitability index, and internal rate of return—do use discounted cash flows. We will examine all four methods in some detail. For now, we will assume that firms have enough funds to accept all economically feasible proposals; so choices need only be made when mutually exclusive proposals are involved.

The Payback Period Method

The **payback period** is defined as the number of years required to recover the investment outlay. The shorter an investment proposal's payback period, the better. The payback period method is widely used for evaluating investment proposals because it is both easy to calculate and easy to understand. However, it does have some serious shortcomings, as the following example will show.

The information presented in Table 8–5 lists the investment outlays and after-tax cash flows for two mutually exclusive investment proposals—only one can be selected. The investment outlay for Project A is $45,000 and the annual after-tax cash flows are $20,000 per year—an annuity. We can determine the payback period for this project, in which the cash flows comprise an annuity, by dividing the investment outlay by the annual cash flow.

$$\text{Payback period} = \frac{\text{Investment outlay}}{\text{Annual cash flow (annuity)}} \qquad (8\text{--}5)$$

The payback period for Project A is 2.25 years ($45,000/$20,000 = 2.25).

Project B calls for an investment outlay of $100,000, and the annual after-

Table 8–5
Cash Flows for Two Projects

Investment Outlay	Project A $45,000		Project B $100,000	
End of Year	After-Tax Cash Flow	Cumulative Cash Flow	After-Tax Cash Flow	Cumulative Cash Flow
0		$-45,000		$-100,000
1	$20,000	-25,000	$35,000	- 65,000
2	20,000	- 5,000	30,000	- 35,000
3	20,000	15,000	25,000	- 10,000
4	20,000	35,000	20,000	10,000
5			15,000	25,000
6			40,000 (asset sold)	65,000

tax cash flows vary from year to year. We find the payback period when cash flows are uneven by adding successive cash flows (**cumulative cash flows**) until it is obvious that the project will pay for itself sometime in the next year. To find the fraction of that year needed to reach payback, we divide the dollar amount needed to reach payback by the dollar amount to be received that year. For example, by the end of Year 3, Project B will have a cumulative cash flow of −$10,000; only $10,000 will be needed to reach payback. Since a cash flow of $20,000 is expected during Year 4, the project will pay for itself sometime during that year. The fraction of the year is found as described above: $10,000/$20,000 = 0.5. We would expect a payback period of 3.5 years for Project B. Because this is longer than Project A's payback period, we would prefer Project A over Project B.

Advantages.   This example demonstrates the principal advantages of the payback period: It is easy to calculate and it is easy to understand that it will take 2.25 years to recover the investment outlay for Project A and 3.5 years for Project B. Ease of use makes the payback period suitable as an initial screening

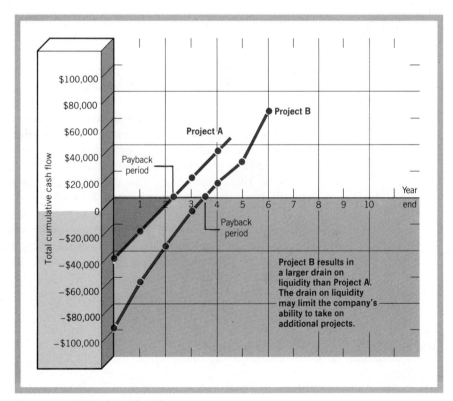

Figure 8–1   Payback and liquidity.

device for investment proposals. It is also useful when time is important in the decision process. For example, a mining company located in a politically unstable country wants to invest in projects that will pay back as soon as possible to minimize the risk of having the project taken over by an unfriendly government.

Another advantage is that the payback method can be used to assess the effect of an investment proposal on **liquidity**—the firm's ability to meet its financial obligations. Cash, along with certain other assets, such as securities, provides liquidity; so a drain on cash flows reduces liquidity. Figure 8–1 depicts the cumulative cash flows from Project A and Project B, which are listed in Table 8–5. Examination of the figure reveals that Project B results in a greater drain on liquidity than Project A. Stated otherwise, Project B produces larger negative cash flows, for a longer period, than Project A. Thus, acceptance of Project B might preclude other investment outlays in, for example, Year 2, because of lack of liquidity. Using the payback method in this manner is useful when major projects are being considered that might affect the liquidity of the firm. However, this advantage does not outweigh the method's disadvantages.

Disadvantages. One disadvantage of the payback method is that it does not measure profitability, because it ignores cash flows beyond the payback period. As Table 8–5 shows, Project A is expected to produce additional cash flows of $35,000 and Project B, to produce additional cash flows of $65,000. If these additional cash flows are considered important, Project B should be preferred to Project A.

Another disadvantage is that the payback period does not take the time value of money into account. The expected returns in the first year are weighed equally with expected returns in subsequent years, even though, as you recall from Chapter 5, $100 received today is worth more than $100 received a year from now. This is particularly important for capital investment projects, which typically involve cash flows over several years.

A third disadvantage is that the payback period measures only the number of years it takes to pay back the investment outlay, which may not relate to the objective of financial management—maximizing shareholder wealth. Finally, the payback method ignores risk as well as the cost of financing the new projects.

Discounted Cash Flow Methods

The discounted cash flow (DCF) methods for making investment decisions overcome many disadvantages of the payback period method. For example, they take the time value of money into account. They can also be used to evaluate investment proposals that have different lives, sizes, and degrees of risk. However, as we shall see, these methods have their weaknesses, too.

Net present value (NPV) is the present value of cash flows discounted at the cost of capital, less the investment outlay. (Chapter 7 described how the cost of capital—the firm's required rate of return, k—is estimated.) The equation for calculating net present value is as follows.

Net present value = Present value of cash flows − Investment outlay

$$NPV = \sum_{t=1}^{n} \left[\frac{CF_t}{(1 + k)^t} \right] \qquad - I_0 \qquad\qquad (8\text{–}6)$$

where

CF_t = After-tax cash flow in Year t
k = Cost of capital (required rate of return for the project)
I_0 = Investment outlay at Time 0

The equation can be restated.

$$NPV = \sum_{t=1}^{n} [CF_t (PVIF_{k,n})] - I_0 \qquad\qquad (8\text{–}7)$$

Table 8–6
Net Present Value with Even Cash Flows

Method 1

$$NPV = \sum_{t=1}^{n} [CF_t(PVIF_{k,n})] - I_0$$

Years (1)	After-Tax Cash Flows of Project C (2)	$PVIF_{12\%,n}$[a] (3)	Present Value (4) = (2) × (3)
1	$50,000	0.893	$ 44,650
2	50,000	0.797	39,850
3	50,000	0.712	35,600
4	50,000	0.636	31,800
5	50,000	0.567	28,350
		3.605	$180,250
		Less: Investment outlay −	100,000
		Net present value =	$ 80,250

Method 2

NPV	=	Annual cash flow	×	$(PVAIF_{12\%,\ 5\ years})$	−	Investment outlay
	=	$ 50,000	×	3.605	−	$100,000
	=	$180,250			−	$100,000
	=	$ 80,250				

[a]Rounded to three decimal places.

Even Cash Flows. Table 8–6 shows two methods for calculating *NPV* when cash flows are the same in every year. In this example, after-tax cash flows are $50,000 per year for 5 years and the cost of capital is 12 percent. Method 1 calculates the *NPV* by multiplying the appropriate interest factor from the present value table (see Appendix C) by the cash flow in each year, summing those amounts, and subtracting the investment outlay of $100,000. The net present value of the project is $80,250.

Because the cash flows are the same in every year, they are an annuity. Chapter 5 explained that the present value of an annuity interest factor may be used as a time-saving device, and this is the place to use it. The interest factor for the present value of an annuity for 5 years is the sum of the present value interest factors for 5 years. Allowing for rounding, the sum of the interest factors used in Method 1 (3.605) is the same as the interest factor listed in the present value of an annuity table (found in Appendix D). Using Method 2, we multiply the annual cash flow by the interest factor for the present value of an annuity and subtract the investment outlay to obtain the *NPV*.

$$
\begin{array}{lllll}
\text{Net} & \text{Annual} & \text{Interest factor} & & \\
\text{present} = & \text{cash} & \times \text{ for present} & - & \text{Investment} \\
\text{value} & \text{flow} & \text{value of annuity} & & \text{outlay} \\
NPV & = CF & (PVAIF_{k,n}) & & - I_0 \\
& = \$50,000 \times & 3.605 & & - \$100,000 \\
& = \$80,250 & & & \hspace{3em} (8\text{--}8)
\end{array}
$$

Table 8–7
Net Present Value with Uneven Cash Flows

	Project D			Project E		
Years	Cash Flows (1)	$PVIF_{12\%,n}$[a] (2)	Present Value (3) = (1) × (2)	Cash Flows (4)	$PVIF_{12\%,n}$[a] (5)	Present Value (6) = (4) × (5)
1	$ 1,000	0.893	$ 893	$ 7,000	0.893	$ 6,251
2	2,000	0.797	1,594	5,000	0.797	3,985
3	4,000	0.712	2,848	4,000	0.712	2,848
4	8,000	0.636	5,088	3,500	0.636	2,226
5	10,000	0.567	5,670	2,000	0.567	1,134
	$25,000		$16,093	$21,500		$16,444
Present value		PV	$16,093			$16,444
Less: Investment outlay		$-I_0$	− 15,000			15,000
Equals: Net present value		= NPV	$ 1,093			$ 1,444

[a]Rounded to three decimal places.

Uneven Cash Flows.   Method 1, just described, is also used to calculate the NPV when cash flows are uneven. Let's use that method to evaluate two investment proposals—Projects D and E—as shown in Table 8–7. Both projects call for the same investment outlay of $15,000, but their cash flows differ from year to year. Because this is so, it is necessary to multiply the cash flow for each year by the appropriate interest factor from the present value table and then sum the present values for all the years. The NPV, again, is the difference between the present value and the investment outlay. Accordingly, the NPVs for Projects D and E are $1,093 and $1,444, respectively.

Acceptance and Ranking Criteria.   In the examples used so far, the NPV has been positive, which means that the present value of the benefits (the cash flows) exceeds the cost (the investment outlay); thus, the projects are economically feasible. Stated otherwise, the expected return from the investment proposal exceeds the required rate of return. If the NPV were equal to zero, it would mean that the project earned the required rate of return—no more and no less. If the NPV were negative, it would mean that the project earned less than the required rate of return. It is important to understand that a negative NPV does *not* mean that the project would result in a financial loss, only that the project would not earn the required rate of return. Even though it would not necessarily produce a loss, the project with a negative NPV should be rejected (except as noted below) because it would be uneconomical and would reduce the value of the firm.

The acceptance of proposals whose NPVs are equal to or greater than zero increases the value of the firm. Such proposals add to wealth because they earn more than the cost of capital. In contrast, the acceptance of proposals with negative NPVs reduces the value of the firm because the proposals earn less than the cost of capital. Use the following as a general rule.

$$NPV \geq 0 \text{ Accept}$$

$$NPV < 0 \text{ Reject}$$

It should be noted that some uneconomical projects are accepted on other grounds. Recall that mandatory investment proposals are required for the continued operation of the firm. Suppose, for example, the Environmental Protection Agency orders a business to install an antipollution device or shut down its operations. In some cases, the antipollution device costs more than the business is worth and the firm must shut down. In most cases, businesses in this position acquire the uneconomical, but mandatory, antipollution devices. Such businesses may be able to minimize their costs by choosing, from available antipollution devices, the one with the smallest negative NPV.

In the case where a decision must be made between two or more mutually exclusive proposals, the project with the highest NPV should be chosen, because it will add the greatest wealth to the firm.

Other Considerations

Timing of Returns.   Projects D and E, which were described in Table 8–7, can be used to demonstrate the importance of the timing of cash flows. For Project D, the largest cash flows are expected during the last few years. In contrast, for Project E, the largest cash flows occur during the first few years. As a result, the firm gets more immediate cash benefits from Project E than from Project D. This is particularly important when the time value of money is taken into account and the discount rates are high.

The timing of the cash benefits may be just as important as the *NPV*, depending on the cash needs of the company. If the company needs cash *now*, it may favor projects that provide immediate cash over those that provide cash in the future, disregarding the *NPVs* if the differences are not very large.

Investments with Different Lives.   Another type of timing problem occurs when a firm must choose between investment proposals that have substantially different project lives. For example, one project may have a life of 3 years and another a life of 9 years. One solution is to develop a theoretical construct called a **replacement chain** to equate the lives of the two projects. This assumes that each project, if necessary, will be replaced at the end of its life with another project having the same financial characteristics. In other words, the projects will be duplicated in all respects until their lives are equal.

To determine when the projects' lives are equal, we first find the lowest common denominator for the number of years. The lowest common denominator for the example just given is 9 years. In this case, the financial characterstics for the 3-year project can be duplicated twice to equate the lives of both projects.

For projects with lives of 11 and 13 years, the lowest common denominator is 143 years. Here it is more reasonable simply to select a terminal year based on judgment. The selection of the terminal year depends to some extent on the discount rate that is used. If the discount rate is high—for example, 25 percent—the present value of cash flows received 10 years from now will be worth only about 10 percent of their undiscounted value. On the other hand, if the discount rate is low—for example, 7 percent—the present value of cash flows received 10 years from now will be worth about 50 percent of their undiscounted value. More will be said about timing later in the chapter.

Advantages.   The *NPV* method has certain advantages that make it particularly useful. First, it takes the time value of money into account. Second, it discounts cash flows by the cost of capital, which gives explicit recognition to financing costs and the returns required by shareholders. Third, the *NPV* is expressed in dollar amounts. As previously noted, if capital is limited, managers may be more interested in dollars than percentages. Fourth, *NPVs* of various projects are additive, so the *NPV* for a number of projects is easy to calculate. Fifth, the net present value method can be modified to consider risk, which we will take up in the next chapter. Finally, accepting projects with the highest NPVs maximizes the value of the firm, all other things being equal.

Disadvantages

Reinvestment Rate Assumption. One disadvantage of all discounted cash flow techniques concerns the **reinvestment rate assumption**. As noted in Chapter 5, a reinvestment rate is assumed every time compound interest—which includes net present value—is used. The NPV method assumes that funds are reinvested at the cost of capital. The actual reinvestment rate may differ from the cost of capital, thereby distorting the NPV.

Changes in the Cost of Capital. The second disadvantage is that the cost of capital is assumed to remain constant throughout the life of the project. This problem can be addressed by changing the rate used in calculations to reflect expected changes in the actual cost of capital.

Confusion about Concept. A third disadvantage is that the concept of NPV is confusing for some managers. For example, an investment proposal with an NPV of zero can be accepted. The zero means the project produces the required rate of return, and no more. It does not mean that the project has a zero dollar return.

Difficulty with Projects of Different Sizes. The final disadvantage occurs because the NPV may be difficult to interpret when investments are of substantially different size. For example, consider two more projects—Projects F and G. Project F, with an NPV of $500, is ranked higher than Project G, with an NPV of $400—even though Project F requires an investment outlay of $1 million while Project G requires only a $5,000 investment outlay. Project G gives a larger return for every dollar invested, but it does not maximize shareholder wealth by producing the larger NPV.

Present value of cash inflow	$-$	Investment outlay	$=$	NPV
$\sum_{t=1}^{n} [CF_t \ (PVIF_{k,n})]$	$-$	I_0	$=$	NPV
Project F: $1,000,500	$-$	$1,000,000	$=$	$500
Project G: $ 5,400	$-$	$ 5,000	$=$	$400

On balance, these problems are relatively minor. Its advantages are such that the NPV method is one of the principal techniques used for determining economic feasibility and for ranking investment proposals.

Profitability Index The **profitability index** (*PI*) gives the return for each dollar invested. We calculate it by dividing the present value of benefits by the investment outlay. Thus, it is a benefit/cost ratio. An examination of the *PI* equation reveals that the *PI* is a variant of net present value.

$$PI = \frac{\sum\limits_{t=1}^{n} \left[\dfrac{CF_t}{(1 + k)^t} \right]}{I_0} \qquad (8-9)$$

where

CF_t = After-tax cash flow in Year t
k = Cost of capital
I_0 = Investment outlay at Time 0

The equation can be restated in two ways.

$$PI = \frac{\sum\limits_{t=1}^{n} \left[CF_t(PVIF_{k,n}) \right]}{I_0} \qquad (8-10)$$

or

$$PI = \frac{\text{Present value of cash inflows}}{\text{Investment outlay}}$$

For example, Project F, just described, has the following *PI*.

$$\text{Project F: } PI = \frac{\$1,000,500}{\$1,000,000} = 1.0005$$

Acceptance and Ranking Criteria.   The acceptance criteria for the *PI* ratio are easy to understand. Because it is a benefit/cost ratio, it indicates that projects should be accepted if the discounted benefits are equal to or exceed the cost. In other words, use the following general rule.

$$PI \geq 1 \text{ Accept}$$

$$PI < 1 \text{ Reject}$$

The *NPV* and the *PI* give the same accept/reject decisions but may give different rankings. For example, the *PI* for Project G is calculated as follows.

$$\text{Project G: } PI = \frac{\$5,400}{\$5,000} = 1.0800$$

This indicates that, according to the *PI*, Project G should be preferred to Project F, even though Project F's *NPV* is higher. When such conflicts arise, it is appropriate to select the project with the largest *NPV*, because it maximizes shareholder wealth.

Internal Rate of Return The **internal rate of return** (***IRR***) is that rate of interest that equates the present value of cash flows to the investment outlay.[4] It is a widely used method for ranking investment proposals. Today, computer programs are sometimes used for computing the *IRR*, because computing it is a more tedious process than computing the *NPV*. Nevertheless, calculation of the *IRR* will be demonstrated here.

$$I_0 = \frac{CF_1}{(1 + r)} + \frac{CF_2}{(1 + r)^2} + \frac{CF_3}{(1 + r)^3}$$

$$+ \cdots + \frac{CF_n}{(1 + r)^n}$$

$$= \sum_{t=1}^{n} \left[\frac{CF_t}{(1 + r)^t} \right] \qquad (8\text{--}11)$$

where

I_0 = Investment outlay at Time 0
CF_t = After-tax cash flow in Year t
r = Internal rate of return

The equation can be restated.

$$I_0 = \sum_{t=1}^{n} \left[CF_t \, (PVIF_{r,n}) \right] \qquad (8\text{--}12)$$

The equation must be solved for r, the interest rate that equates the present value of the benefits (*CF*) with the cost (*I*).

The *IRR* may also be defined as that rate of interest that causes the sum of the discounted cash flows, less the investment outlay, to equal zero.

$$\sum_{t=1}^{n} \left[\frac{CF_t}{(1 + r)^t} \right] - I_0 = 0 \qquad (8\text{--}13)$$

This equation uses basically the same formulation as *NPV* (Equation 8–6). Therefore, the *IRR* is the discount rate that causes the *NPV* to equal zero.

---

[4]It is interesting to note that the yield to maturity, discussed in Chapter 6 in connection with bond prices, is the same as the *IRR*.

When this occurs, the discount rates (k and r) in the equations are equal. Stated somewhat differently, then, the cost of capital equals the internal rate of return when NPV equals zero. This will be shown graphically in Figures 8–2 and 8–3 later in this chapter.

Let's return to Equation 8–12. We can use a trial-and-error method to solve the equation for r. Refer to Table 8–8, which shows cash flows for 4 years and an investment outlay of $29,863 for Project H. The first step in solving for the IRR is to make an educated guess about the correct discount rate. If using that interest rate results in a present value that is more than the investment outlay, try a higher rate. Increasing the discount rate will lower the present value. Similarly, if the trial rate results in a present value that is too low, try a lower rate; the lower discount rate will increase the present value. Continue this trial-and-error process until a discount rate is found that equates the present value of the cash flows to the investment outlay. That rate is the IRR. If the cash flows are even, use the present value of an annuity table to save time.

In Table 8–8, 12 percent is the first interest rate selected. Because the cash flows are uneven, interest factors for each year are required; they may be obtained from the present value table (see Appendix C). The present value of the cash flows discounted at 12 percent is $31,148, which is more than the $29,863 investment outlay. Therefore, a higher rate is used next to lower the present value. When the cash flows are discounted at 16 percent, the present value is $28,680. This time, the present value is less than the investment outlay. When the cash flows are discounted at 14 percent, the present value equals the investment outlay. Therefore, the IRR is 14 percent.

Table 8–8
Finding the *IRR* for Project H

Solution: $\sum_{t=1}^{n}$ (Cash flows $\times$ $PVIF_{r,n}$) = Investment outlay

Given: Investment outlay = $29,863

Year	Cash Flows	12% Discount Rate		Present Value	16% Discount Rate		Present Value	14% Discount Rate		Present Value
1	$ 9,000	0.893	=	$ 8,037	0.862	=	$ 7,758	0.877	=	$ 7,893
2	11,000	0.797	=	8,767	0.743	=	8,173	0.769	=	8,459
3	13,000	0.712	=	9,256	0.641	=	8,333	0.675	=	8,775
4	8,000	0.636	=	5,088	0.552	=	4,416	0.592	=	4,736
				$31,148			$28,680			$29,863

$$NPV = \sum_{t=1}^{n}\left[CF_t\,(PVIF_{k,n})\right] - I_0$$

NPV at 12% = $31,148   − $29,863 = $1,285
NPV at 16% = $28,680   − $29,863 = − $1,183
NPV at 14% = $29,863   − $29,863 = $ 0

[a]Present value interest factors are from Appendix C, rounded to three decimal places.

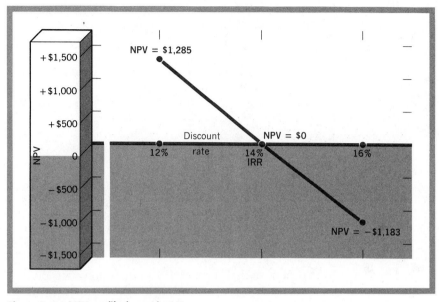

Figure 8–2   *NPV* **profile for project H.**

Figure 8–2 shows some of the same information as Table 8–8. As you can see, when the discount rate is 14 percent—the *IRR*—*NPV* is equal to zero. When the discount rate is less than the *IRR*, *NPV* is positive; and when it is more than the *IRR*, *NPV* is negative.

Acceptance and Ranking Criteria.   The *IRR* is an interest rate that represents the compound rate of return on an investment; thus, acceptance and ranking of investment proposals can involve comparing the *IRRs* with the cost of capital or some other rate. In general, if the *IRR* for a proposal is equal to or greater than the cost of capital or some other chosen rate (a **hurdle rate**), the project should be accepted. If it is less than the chosen rate, the project should be rejected:

$$IRR \geq \text{Cost of capital or hurdle rate Accept}$$

$$IRR < \text{Cost of capital or hurdle rate Reject}$$

When it is necessary to choose among mutually exclusive investment proposals, the highest *IRR* should receive the highest ranking. However, sound judgment must be used here. Recall that one disadvantage shared by all *DCF* methods involves the reinvestment rate assumption. Suppose a project is determined to have an *IRR* of 45 percent. This figure is based on the assumption that all funds are reinvested at that same 45 percent rate of interest. If they are not, the annual realized rate of return (which was explained in Appendix 5A, following Chapter 5) will be substantially different.

Advantages.   Like the *NPV* and the *PI*, the *IRR* takes the time value of money into account. In addition, it provides a compound rate of return on investment that can be compared with the cost of capital or some other hurdle rate.

Disadvantages.   One disadvantage of the *IRR* is that the trial-and-error process used to calculate it can become unmanageable if many investment proposals with long durations are involved. Fortunately, calculators and computer programs are available to solve *IRR* problems in seconds instead of hours.

Another disadvantage is that, under some circumstances, the equation for *IRR* produces multiple rates of return. Multiple solutions occur when the cash flows reach a certain size and alternate in sign from positive to negative.[5] Although such problems can be solved, the most expedient solution at this level of study is to use *NPV* to make the decision.

Still another disadvantage is that the *IRR* does not reflect the scale, or dollar size, of various investment proposals. In addition, the *IRR* and *NPV* may give different rankings for some investment proposals. Let's consider these situations in more detail.

We noted earlier that the *PI* and the *NPV* may give different rankings, although they give the same accept/reject decision. As mentioned, *IRR* and *NPV* also provide the same accept/reject decisions but, under some conditions, different rankings. Conditions that contribute to conflicting rankings include situations in which the investment outlay for one project is much larger than that for the other project (scale effect), situations in which the largest cash flows of one project occur during the early years and the largest cash flows from the other project occur during the later years (timing effects), and situations in which the projects have unequal lives.

The following example illustrates the conflict that can result from differences in scale. In this example, Project I and Project J are mutually exclusive proposals. Project I calls for an investment outlay of $500, and Project J for an investment outlay of $1,500. No alternative investments are available. The life of both projects is one year, and the cost of capital is 12 percent. The following table show the projects' *NPVs* and *IRRs*.

Project	Investment Outlay I_0	Cash Flow CF_1	Present Value at 12%	NPV = (PV − I)	IRR
I	$ 500	$ 625	$ 558	$58	25%
J	$1,000	$1,770	$1,580	$80	18%

[5]According to Descartes' rule of signs, every time signs change there is a new root. Equations 8–12 and 8–13 are polynomials of *n* with *n* roots, and each root can produce a different solution. For additional information about this issue, refer to James H. Lorie and Leonard J. Savage, "Three Problems in Rationing Capital," *Journal of Business,* October 1955, pp. 236–237.

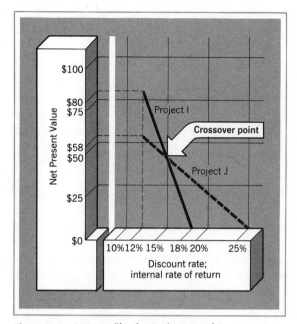

Figure 8–3 *NPV* profiles for Projects I and J.

The data reveal that Project I has an *NPV* of $58 and an *IRR* of 25 percent and that Project J has an *NPV* of $80 and an *IRR* of 18 percent. Which project should be accepted?

The *NPVs* and *IRRs* for both projects are depicted in Figure 8–3. Whenever the crossover point shown in the figure is greater than the cost of capital, the *NPV* and *IRR* give conflicting rankings. The better choice in this example is Project J, the project with the higher *NPV*, because it adds the greatest wealth to the company.

Suppose we also consider the projects' *PIs*. Project I has a *PI* of 1.116 ($558/$500 = 1.116), whereas Project J has a *PI* of 1.053 ($1,580/$1,500 = 1.053). The *PI* also indicates that Project I is preferable to Project J. As you can see, under some circumstances, results of discounted cash-flow analyses can be confusing. If no better choices for investments are available, it is appropriate to select the project that provides the greatest increase in wealth over the years. In this example, Project J is still the better choice, since there are no investment alternatives.

Appropriate Rate. Another way to solve conflicting rankings is to determine which reinvestment rate (*k* or *r*) is more appropriate. Keep in mind that the *NPV* assumes that all funds are invested at *k*—the cost of capital. If funds are reinvested at a higher rate, *NPV* will understate the value of the investment. Similarly, the *IRR* assumes that funds are reinvested at *r*. If funds are reinvested at a different rate, the *IRR* will misstate the compound return from that project.

Capital Rationing

Capital rationing occurs when funds that can be spent on investments are limited. As mentioned, this chapter has assumed that the firm could fund any proposal, except where proposals were mutually exclusive. In this case, when there is no constraint on the amount of capital and the cost of capital is not expected to change, a firm's value is maximized when it accepts all projects with an *NPV* greater than zero. (Its wealth is maintained when it accepts projects with an *NPV* of zero.)

When the amount of capital available for investment projects is limited, the firm cannot maximize its value, because it must forgo some pofitable projects. Therefore, it can only maximize its value subject to the amount of capital that is available. Under these circumstances, the selection of investment proposals becomes more complex. Linear programming may be used to determine the best solutions; short of that, the firm can select those projects that fit the budget and add the largest combined *NPV*.

Summary

Cash outflows and inflows are the focus of capital budgeting. The process begins with estimations of the investment outlay required for a project and the project's after-tax cash flows. Equations used in arriving at these estimations are summarized in Table 8–9, along with other equations from this chapter.

Estimations of cash inflows and outflows are used in the evaluation and ranking of investment proposals. Four techniques commonly used to evaluate and rank proposals are the payback period, net present value, profitability index, and internal rate of return methods.

The payback period method, which tells how soon the investment will pay for itself, is easy to calculate and to understand. It is useful as an initial screening device and in some other situations as well. On the other hand, its failure to take cash flows into account beyond the payback period and the time value of money are two among several serious disadvantages.

The other three methods, called discounted cash flow methods, do take the time value of money into account. They also assume all funds will be reinvested at a certain rate—a potential disadvantage, since reinvesting at this rate may not be possible. Each method also involves its own advantages and disadvantages.

The net present value method measures the present value of cash flows discounted at the cost of capital, less the investment outlay. In general, firms should invest in proposals with net present values equal to or greater than zero. The profitability index, a variant of the net present value, gives the return for each dollar invested in the form of a cost/benefit ratio. Proposals with a profitability index greater than or equal to 1 should generally be accepted. The internal rate of return, the most difficult method to calculate, equates the present value of cash flows to the investment outlay in the form of a percentage rate. In general, the firm should accept projects with internal rates of return greater than or equal to the cost of capital or any other chosen hurdle rate.

The discounted cash flow methods support the same accept/reject decisions but may give different rankings. In these cases, it is appropriate to prefer the project that provides the greatest increase in wealth over the years. Under conditions of capital rationing, where a firm may not be able to invest in all profitable projects, the firm may choose the projects that fit the budget and add the largest combined net present value.

Table 8–9
Summary of Equations

	Equation	Equation Number
Disposition of asset	$D = S - t(S - B)$	(8–1)
Investment outlay	$I = C + W + O - D$	(8–2)
or	$I = C + W + O - [S - t(S - B)]$	(8–3)
After-tax cash flow	After-tax cash flow = Net income + Depreciation	(8–4)
Payback period	Payback period $= \dfrac{\text{Investment outlay}}{\text{Annual cash flow (annuity)}}$	(8–5)
Net present value	$NPV = \sum\limits_{t=1}^{n} \left[\dfrac{CF_t}{(1 + k)^t} \right] - I_0$	(8–6)
or	$NPV = \sum\limits_{t=1}^{n} [CF_t(PVIF_{k,n})] - I_0$	(8–7)
Net present value (annuity)	$NPV = CF(PVAIF_{k,n}) - I_0$	(8–8)
Profitability index	$PI = \dfrac{\sum\limits_{t=1}^{n} \left[\dfrac{CF_t}{(1 + k)^t} \right]}{I_0}$	(8–9)
or	$PI = \dfrac{\sum\limits_{t=1}^{n} [CF_t(PVIF_{k,n})]}{I_0}$	(8–10)
Internal rate of return (solve for r)	$I_0 = \sum\limits_{t=1}^{n} \left[\dfrac{CF_t}{(1 + r)^t} \right]$	(8–11)
or	$I_0 = \sum\limits_{t=1}^{n} [CF_t(PVIF_{r,n})]$	(8–12)
or	$\sum\limits_{t=1}^{n} \left[\dfrac{CF_t}{(1 + r)^t} \right] - I_0 = 0$	(8–13)

Important Terms

After-tax cash flow
Book value
Capital budgeting techniques
Capital rationing
Cash flow
Cumulative cash flow
Differential cash flow
Disposition of asset
Expansion proposal
Hurdle rate
Incremental cash flow
Independent proposals

Internal rate of return (*IRR*)
Investment outlay
Liquidity
Mandatory proposal
Mutually exclusive proposals
Net present value (*NPV*)
Payback period
Profitability index (*PI*)
Reinvestment rate assumption
Replacement chain
Replacement proposal
Working capital

Questions

1. In its broadest sense, what is meant by capital budgeting?
2. Compare cash flow with accounting profit.
3. Additions to working capital must be considered when determining an investment outlay. Explain why and provide examples of this type of expenditure.
4. In a replacement decision, what alternatives are available for disposition of existing assets? In general, what are the tax consequences of each alternative?
5. Compare the effects of accelerated depreciation and straight-line depreciation on after-tax cash flow.
6. Why is interest expense from financing a project not considered a cash outflow for capital budgeting purposes?
7. What are incremental cash flows?
8. Distinguish between mutually exclusive and independent projects.
9. Explain the advantages and disadvantages of using the payback method to select investments.
10. What is the net present value of an investment? What decision rules apply to its use as a capital budgeting technique?
11. Explain the advantages and disadvantages of using net present value to select investments.
12. What is a replacement chain and when is its use appropriate?
13. What is the profitability index? What decision rule applies to its use as a capital budgeting technique?
14. Provide two definitions for *internal rate of return*.
15. What is a hurdle rate? Is the cost of capital ever a hurdle rate?
16. Under what circumstances may conflicting project rankings result from different discounted cash flow techniques? When conflicts occur, on what basis should investment decisions be made?
17. What is capital rationing? What special problems does it present in capital budgeting?

Problems

1. Citation Corporation is purchasing a new piece of equipment to expand production. Its purchase price is $100,000 and its useful life is 10 years. Additional costs include: freight and installation, $10,000; working capital support, $20,000; and site preparation, $5,000. If a 10 percent investment tax credit will be taken in the year of purchase, what investment outlay is required?

2. Suppose, instead, that Citation Corporation is replacing an existing machine with the one described in Problem 1. The old machine has a book value of $40,000 and a market value of $60,000. It has been depreciated at a rate of $10,000 per year for 5 years. If the firm's marginal tax rate is 40 percent and if the capital gains rate is 28 percent, what investment outlay will be required for the replacement decision?

3. Suppose, instead, that the current market value for the old machine described in Problem 2 was $30,000. Calculate the investment outlay required for the replacement decision.

4. HoJo's Restaurants, Inc., has an opportunity to sell a fully depreciated clam shucker that is currently being carried on the books at its $1,200 salvage value. The original cost was $13,000. Because of the machine's historical significance, the American Restaurant Association has offered to buy it for $25,000, to add to its museum collection. If HoJo is in the 40 percent marginal tax bracket with a 20 percent capital gains tax rate, what will be the impact of the sale on the firm's cash flow?

5. Lynx, Inc., is purchasing a new machine for $10,000 in 1990. Expected effects of the purchase include an annual sales increase of $20,000 over a 10-year period and an increase in expenses of $1,400 per year over the same period. If straight-line depreciation is used and if there is no anticipated salvage value, calculate the annual cash flows expected in each year as a result of the purchase. Lynx is in the 30 percent marginal tax bracket.

6. Bloomington Tire Company is studying the possibility of replacing a 5-year-old machine with an original life of 15 years, a cost of $75,000, and no anticipated salvage value. The new machine has an installed cost of $100,000 and a 10-year anticipated life. It is expected to increase sales by $10,000 and to decrease costs by $5,000 annually.

   The current market value of the old machine is $30,000. Assuming the use of straight-line depreciation, a 10 percent investment tax credit, and a marginal tax rate of 30 percent, calculate the investment outlay and the annual cash inflows associated with this replacement decision. For simplicity, ignore the half-year convention in calculating the book value of the old machine, although you should include it in calculating the after-tax cash inflows as a result of purchasing the new machine.

7. Suppose that Bloomington Tire's old machine, described in Problem 6, has a market value of $90,000. Calculate the investment outlay under these conditions. The capital gains tax rate is 20 percent.

8. Cosmos Cola is planning a new advertising campaign that will have a net cost, considering all tax effects, of $300,000 in January 1992.

   Expected benefits from the campaign include an annual sales increase of $60,000 from the end of 1992 through the end of 2002. Because the campaign is not dependent upon celebrity endorsements of the product, a decrease in expenses of $20,000 per year over the same period is anticipated. Cosmos is in the 46 percent marginal tax bracket and uses discounted cash flow techniques to evaluate all long-term expenditures. If the required rate of return is 15 percent, is the campaign worth its cost?

 9. Consider the following information.

End of Year	Project X Cash Flows	Project Y Cash Flows
0	– $10,000	– $10,000
1	4,000	6,000
2	4,000	4,000
3	4,000	3,000
4	4,000	2,000
5	4,000	1,000

Maximum acceptable payback for the firm is 3 years.
Minimum acceptable rate of return is 10 percent.

(a) Calculate the payback period for each project.
(b) If the projects are independent, which should be accepted using the payback criterion?
(c) If the projects are mutually exclusive, which should be accepted?

10. (a) Using the data in Problem 9, calculate the NPV of the two projects.
(b) If the projects are independent, which should be accepted using the NPV criterion?
(c) If they are mutually exclusive, which should be accepted?

11. (a) Using the data in Problem 9, develop a net present value profile of the two projects. Plot your profiles on a graph.
(b) By examining the NPV profiles, estimate the IRR of each project.
(c) Using the estimates you made in part b, determine which project is acceptable using the IRR criterion if the projects are independent? If they are mutually exclusive, which is acceptable?

12. Calculate the NPV and profitability index for the following 10-year projects, assuming a cost of capital of 12 percent.
(a) Initial outlay, $100,000; after-tax cash flow, $15,000 per year.
(b) Initial outlay, $50,000; after-tax cash flow, $10,000 per year.
(c) Initial outlay, $40,000; after-tax cash flow, $5,000 per year.
(d) If the projects in parts a through c are independent, which are acceptable?
(e) If they are mutually exclusive, which are acceptable?

13. Calculate the payback period, net present value, profitability index, and internal rate of return for the following project. The cost of capital is 9 percent.

Year	Cash Flows
0	– $36,000
1	9,000
2	12,000
3	6,000
4	12,000
5	8,000

14. Given net cash flows for these mutually exclusive projects, answer the following questions.

Year	Project A Cash Flows	Project B Cash Flows
0	$ – 800	$ – 800
1	50	300
2	200	300
3	300	300
4	400	300
5	500	100

(a) Develop and graph a net present value profile for each project.
(b) Estimate the *IRR* for each project using the graph.
(c) Calculate the *IRR* for each project using the trial-and-error method.
(d) At what cost of capital would you be indifferent between the two projects?
(e) Which project should be selected at a discount rate of 16 percent? At a discount rate of 10 percent?

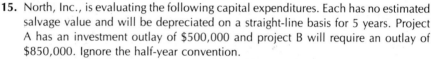

15. North, Inc., is evaluating the following capital expenditures. Each has no estimated salvage value and will be depreciated on a straight-line basis for 5 years. Project A has an investment outlay of $500,000 and project B will require an outlay of $850,000. Ignore the half-year convention.

End of Year	Profit A Profit after Taxes	Project B Profit after Taxes
1	$120,000	$170,000
2	120,000	170,000
3	100,000	170,000
4	80,000	170,000
5	50,000	170,000

(a) Calculate the payback period for each investment.
(b) Calculate *NPVs* at a hurdle rate of 15 percent.
(c) Calculate the profitability index for each project at 15 percent.
(d) Calculate the *IRR* of each project.
(e) Which project is preferred? Explain.

16. Zappa, Inc., is considering two projects, X and Y. X will cost $5,000 at the end of Year 0 and will generate net cash benefits of $2,000 per year at the end of Years 1 through 4. Y will cost $8,000 at the end of Year 0 and will generate net cash benefits of $2,000 per year at the end of Years 1 through 6.

(a) Assuming the firm employs the replacement chain concept to evaluate these investments, prepare a table with the required cash flow data. (*Hint*: Remember that if a project is replaced at the end of its life, a new cash outflow will be required before any new benefits can be received.)
(b) If X's cash flows are expected to last for 9 years instead, over how many years would the chain extend?

17. Bayless Industries has been asked by its employees' union to air-condition a plant. One system would require a $120,000 cash outlay and would have an after-tax operating cost of $7,500 per year. Another system would cost $150,000 but would have an after-tax operating cost of only $3,000 per year. Which system should be selected? Assume the tax effects of depreciation have already been included in the after-tax operating cost figures and that the cost of capital is 12 percent.

18. Western Hardware plans to spend $40,000 this year to update its computer in order to achieve better inventory control. If the expected after-tax cash flows from the decision are $9,000 per year, what is the minimum number of years these benefits must be received in order for the investment to be worthwhile? Western's cost of capital is 12 percent and discounted cash flow techniques are the basis for all its investment decisions.

19. Sunya, Inc., is evaluating whether to replace an old machine. The information in the table below has been collected.

	Old Machine	New Machine
Installed cost		$100,000
Estimated life		5 years
Remaining life	5 years	
Book value	$25,000	
Depreciation	$ 3,000 per year	ACRS
Market value	$ 5,000	
Estimated cost		
savings		$18,000 annually
Marginal tax rate:	40%	
Cost of capital:	10%	
Investment tax credit:	10%	

Should the old machine be replaced? (*Hint*: Consult the ACRS tables in Chapter 3 to determine the relevant annual depreciation percentages for the new machine.)

20. Suppose the new machine in Problem 19 had an estimated salvage value of $10,000 at the end of Year 5. How would your answer change?

Capital Budgeting under Uncertainty

Uncertainty is so pervasive in the world we live in that managers must take it for granted when making investment and financing decisions. Some multinational firms borrow and invest overseas, where they face political instability that may adversely affect their business activities. Domestic firms buying and selling goods in international markets have similar concerns. There is plenty of uncertainty on the domestic scene, too. High federal budget deficits cause concern over interest rates and federal defense budgeters can make or break a firm with the award or denial of a multi-million-dollar contract. New technology eliminates the market for some products and creates new markets for others. Even cool summers and warm winters affect retail sales and the use of energy for cooling and heating. All these factors and more contribute to uncertainty.

A variety of techniques have been developed to help financial managers accommodate risk when they make investment decisions.[1] Table 9–1 lists methods for taking risk into account when the net present value method to determine the cost of capital is used for investment decisions. The first method is to improve estimates of projected cash flows; the second is to adjust the

[1]The terms *risk* and *uncertainty* are used interchangeably here.

discount rate; and the third is to efficiently diversify assets. (The first and third methods can also be used with the internal rate of return.) This chapter describes these three methods of accommodating risk in capital budgeting.

After reading this chapter, you should know the following.

1. **How to calculate expected cash flows.**
2. **How to identify two types of probability distributions.**
3. **What risk means and how it is measured.**
4. **How to develop a hurdle rate.**
5. **How to use the capital asset pricing model.**
6. **How to test the sensitivity of net present value to different discount rates.**
7. **What two ways can be used to diversify and reduce risk.**

Improving Estimates of Cash Flows and Measuring Risk

The principal theme of this book is that business concerns operate in a dynamic environment. In terms of capital budgeting, this means financial managers must make investment decisions today based on estimates of cash flows for future periods about which little is known with certainty. Therefore, projected cash flows for distant periods are probably less reliable than projections for the next few years. One way to reduce the risk associated with projections is to better determine the expected cash flow. This does not reduce the risk of the project per se. However, it permits the financial manager to assess the degree of risk.

Expected Cash Flows The term **expected cash flow** refers to average cash flow, a statistical concept used throughout this chapter. Do not confuse expected cash flows with **projected cash flows**—that is, estimates of what cash flows may be under various circumstances. The following example will clarify the difference.

Happy Days, a large amusement park, is evaluating the economic feasibility of acquiring a roller coaster, and the financial manager must estimate cash

Table 9–1
Adjusting Net Present Value for Risk

$$\text{Net present value} = \sum_{t=1}^{n} \frac{\text{Cash flows}_t}{(1 + \text{Cost of capital})^t} - \text{Investment outlay}$$

Methods for Taking Risk Into Account
1. Improve estimates of cash flows.
2. Adjust discount rate to take risk into account.
3. Diversify assets.

flows for the next 4 years. Based on past experience, the manager knows that business conditions affect attendance at the park and, in turn, revenues from the rides. The information presented in Table 9–2 shows the projected revenues for different phases of the business cycle. During the recovery phase, projected revenues, or cash flows, are $80,000; during the recovery phase, $100,000; and during the recession and depression phases, $60,000 and $40,000, respectively.

The probabilities that the various phases of the business cycle will occur, which are shown in the table, are based on current economic forecasts. In Year 1, there is a 0.5, or 50 percent, probability that the economy will be in the recovery phase. The probability is 0.3, or 30 percent, that it will be in the prosperity phase, 0.1 that it will be in the recession phase, and 0.1 that it will be in the depression phase. Collectively, the probabilities must sum to 1, or 100 percent. The probabilities for the remaining years indicate that the economy will probably continue to expand in the second year and then slide into a recession.

Projected cash flows and probabilities are used to calculate expected cash flows. As shown in Table 9–2, the probabilities are multiplied by the projected cash flows and summed to determine the expected cash flows. The expected cash flow, then, is the weighted *average* cash flow. The following equation is used to calculate expected cash flow.

$$E[x] = \sum_{i=1}^{n} [x_i P_i] = \bar{x} \qquad (9–1)$$

where

$E[x]$ = Expected return or value, such as cash flow
x_i = Possible (projected) value i
P_i = Probability associated with value i

n = Number of observations for which $\sum_{i=1}^{n} P_i = 1$

$\bar{x}$ = Average (mean) value

As you can see from the table, Happy Days' expected cash flows peak in Year 2 ($86,000) and then decline as the probability of recession increases.

Probability Distributions The projected cash flows and their respective probabilities for Year 1 are depicted in Figure 9–1. Two types of probability distributions are shown in the figure. The vertical bars represent a **discrete probability distribution**. It is called discrete because only a finite number of possible outcomes are shown, corresponding to the four phases of the business cycle. For example, the proba-

Table 9–2
Business Cycles and Cash Flows

Phase of Business Cycle	Year 1			Year 2			Year 3			Year 4		
	Prob-ability	Projected Cash Flows	Expected Cash Flow	Prob-ability	Projected Cash Flows	Expected Cash Flow	Prob-ability	Projected Cash Flows	Expected Cash Flow	Prob-ability	Projected Cash Flows	Expected Cash Flow
Recovery	0.5 ×	$ 80,000		0.2 ×	$ 80,000		0.0 ×	$ 80,000		0.0 ×	$ 80,000	
Prosperity	0.3 ×	100,000		0.6 ×	100,000		0.3 ×	100,000		0.1 ×	100,000	
Recession	0.1 ×	60,000		0.1 ×	60,000		0.4 ×	60,000		0.5 ×	60,000	
Depression	0.1 ×	40,000		0.1 ×	40,000		0.3 ×	40,000		0.4 ×	40,000	
	1.0		$80,000	1.0		$86,000	1.0		$66,000	1.0		$56,000

$$\text{Expected cash flows} = \sum_{i=1}^{n} \text{Probability}_i \times \text{Projected cash flow}_i$$

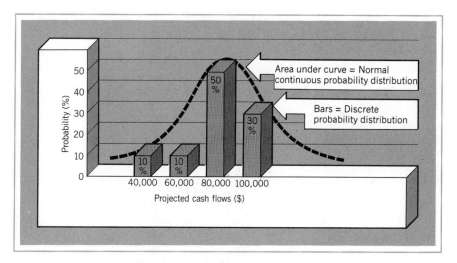

Figure 9–1   Discrete and normal continuous probability distributions.

bility of having a cash flow of $80,000 is 50 percent and the probability of having a cash flow of $40,000 is 10 percent. As mentioned, the probabilities for the four phases of the business cycle must sum to 100 percent.

In reality, an infinite number of business conditions could be depicted for Happy Days. In that case, the probability distribution might appear as a bell-shaped curve or as some other shape. The bell-shaped curve depicted in the figure is a normal **continuous probability distribution**. The area under the curve represents probability and equals 100 percent. More will be said about this later in the chapter.

Standard Deviation: A Measure of Risk One way to define **risk** is to say that it is a deviation from an expected or average value. We know that the expected cash flow from the roller coaster in Year 1 is $80,000. The extent to which cash flows may differ from that amount is risk, and it is measured by the standard deviation.

The **standard deviation** (σ or sigma) is a statistical tool that serves as a proxy (or substitute) for risk. The larger the standard deviation, the higher the risk. Using the standard deviation allows us to quantify and compare the riskiness of various assets. It is widely employed in this way because it can be used in mathematical operations.

The method for calculating the standard deviation of Happy Days' cash flows in Year 1 is shown in Table 9–3. The expected return ($80,000) is subtracted from each of the projected cash flows. Then, the differences are squared to eliminate the negative signs. Next, the squared differences are multiplied by their respective probabilities and summed. The sum is a weighted average called **variance**, which is also a measure of deviation. The

Table 9–3
Calculating Standard Deviation of Happy Days' Projected Cash Flows in Year 1

Business Cycle Condition	Projected Cash Flows		Expected Cash Flows	Difference (1)	Difference Squared (2) = (1)²	Probability (3)	Weighted Average (4) = (2) × (3)
Recovery	$ 80,000	—	$80,000 =	$ 0	0	0.5	$ 0
Prosperity	100,000	—	80,000 =	20,000	400,000,000	0.3	120,000,000
Recession	60,000	—	80,000 =	−20,000	400,000,000	0.1	40,000,000
Depression	40,000	—	80,000 =	−40,000	1,600,000,000	0.1	160,000,000
						1.0	$320,000,000 = Variance

$$\text{Standard deviation } \sigma = \sqrt{\text{Variance}}$$
$$= \sqrt{\$320,000,000}$$
$$= \$17,888$$

standard deviation is the square root of the variance, or $17,888. The equation for the standard deviation is as follows.

$$\sigma = \sqrt{\sum_{i=1}^{n} (x_i - \bar{x})^2 \, P_i}$$

(9–2)

where

x_i = Possible (projected) value i
$\bar{x}$ = Average (mean) value
P_i = Probability associated with value i

Normal Distribution Curve and Standard Deviation. Now, look again at Figure 9–1. Note that the shape of the discrete probability distribution is not symmetrical—it does not fit the shape of the normal curve. Nevertheless, we are going to assume that it is normal so that we can take advantage of the properties of a normal curve and because the complex mathematical calculations necessary to fit this distribution to a normal curve are beyond the scope of this book.

The area under a normal curve may be described in terms of standard deviations or percentages that represent probabilities. One-half of the area lies on either side of the expected value. We have already determined that the expected value of Happy Days' cash flow in Year 1 is $80,000 and that the standard deviation is $17,888. As shown in Figure 9–2, one standard deviation to the right of the expected value ($80,000 + $17,888) and one to the left ($80,000 − $17,888) encompass 68 percent of the area under the curve. This means that chances are 68 out of 100 that the actual cash flow will be greater than $62,112 and less than $97,888.

Two standard deviations from the expected value include 95 percent of the area under the curve, and three standard deviations include 99.7 percent of the area. Therefore, chances are 99.7 out of 100 that the actual cash flow will be between $26,336, which is three standard deviations to the left of the expected value, and $133,664, which is three standard deviations to the right of the expected value. However, $100,000 is the maximum projected income; so it is the upper limit in our example.

Shape of the Curve and Risk. Some symmetrical probability distributions are spread out more than others. Figure 9–3 shows two symmetrical distributions that have the same expected value ($80,000), but one has a standard deviation of $17,888 and the other has a standard deviation of $5,000. The one with the smaller standard deviation—Distribution B—is less risky than the other; as mentioned, the larger the standard deviation, the higher the risk. Chances are 68 out of 100 that the actual cash flow for Distribution B will be between

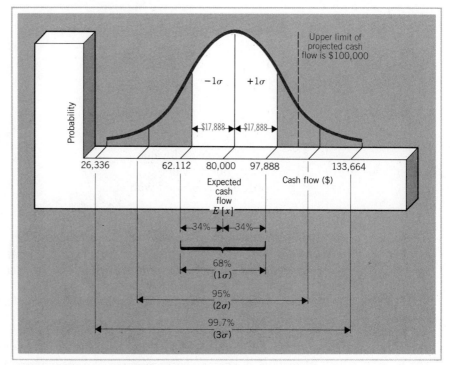

Figure 9–2   Normal curve and standard deviation.

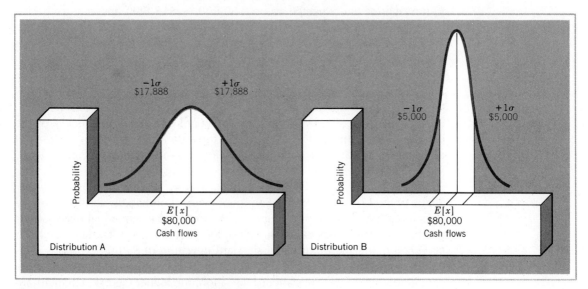

Figure 9–3   Two shapes for symmetrical distributions.

$75,000 and $85,000; whereas there is an equal chance that the cash flows for Distribution A could range from $62,112 to $97,888.

At this point, you may be wondering why receiving higher cash flows than expected is considered risky. The answer is that the standard deviation measures deviation on *both* sides of the expected value. In a statistical sense, higher than expected cash flows (although usually welcomed when they materialize) are just as much a risk as lower than expected cash flows.

Using Z to Find Probabilities.   As mentioned, the area under a normal curve is measured in terms of standard deviations. The statistic **Z**, computed by the following equation, is a useful tool for relating the standard deviation to the area under the curve.

$$Z = \frac{x_i - \bar{x}}{\sigma} \qquad (9\text{--}3)$$

where

Z = The standardized Z statistic, which relates the area under a normal curve
to standardized deviations from the expected value
$\bar{x}$ = Average (mean) value
x_i = Possible (projected) value i
σ = Standard deviation

Selected values of Z are presented in Figure 9–4, and a complete table of values appears at the end of the book in Appendix E. For purposes of illustration, we can again use Happy Days' roller coaster project. We know that the expected cash flow is $80,000 and that the standard deviation is $17,888. For x_i, one possible cash flow, we can use $97,888. (This figure is different from the figures for x_i given earlier in the chapter because, as mentioned, we are now using the Happy Days example as if it represented a normal distribution.) Using these numbers and Equation 9–3, we can find the value of Z in this situation.

$$Z = \frac{x_i - \bar{x}}{\sigma}$$

$$= \frac{\$97,888 - \$80,000}{\$17,888}$$

$$= 1.0$$

As shown in Figure 9–4, a Z of 1.0 accounts for 34.13 percent of the area under the curve on one side of the expected value. This tells us that chances are about 34 percent that the actual value of the cash flow will be greater than $80,000 and less than $97,888. The area covered by Z is depicted in Figure

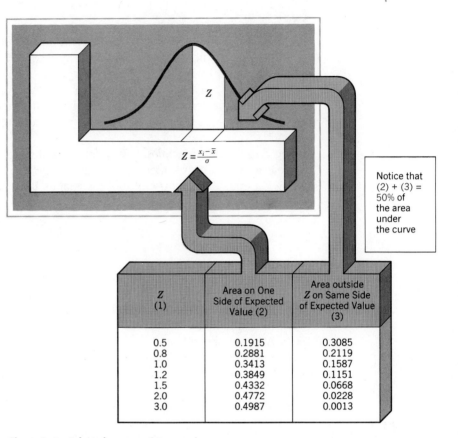

Figure 9–4   Selected areas under normal curve.
Note: (2) + (3) = 50 percent of the area under the curve. Column (2) values can be + or − in sign.

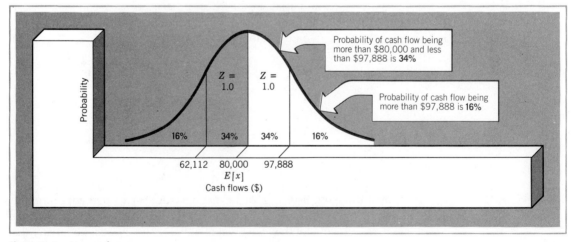

Figure 9–5   Area under curve.

9–5. Figures 9–4 and 9–5 also reveal that chances the cash flow will exceed $97,888 are about 16 percent (15.87 percent). Adding the 34 percent and the 16 percent yields 50 percent—or half the area under the curve.

Now let's use Z to solve the following problem. The management of Happy Days needs a cash flow of at least $53,168 in Year 1 to cover expenses if the roller coaster is purchased. What is the probability that Year 1's cash flow will be *less* than that amount? The problem is solved by calculating the value of Z and determining the area to the *left* of Z under the normal curve. The value of Z is calculated as follows.

$$Z = \frac{x_i - \bar{x}}{\sigma}$$

$$= \frac{\$53,168 - \$80,000}{\$17,888}$$

$$= -1.5$$

The negative sign indicates that the area described is to the left of the mean value. According to Figure 9–4, a Z of −1.5 is equivalent to 43.32 percent of the area under the curve. Because the possible cash flow ($53,168) is less than the expected cash flow ($80,000), the probability that the cash flow will be *more* than $53,168 is 93 percent (43% + 50% = 93%), as shown in Figure 9–6. The probability that the cash flow will be *less* than $53,168 is 7 percent (100% − 93% = 7 percent). Thus, management can expect a 93

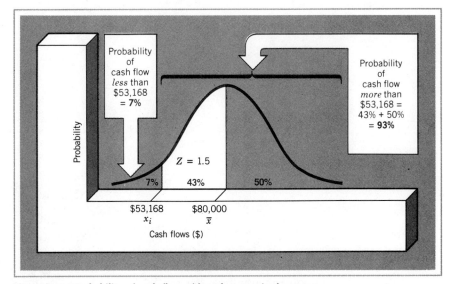

Figure 9–6 Probability of cash flow of less than required amount.

percent chance that Happy Days will achieve the necessary cash flow in Year 1.

Coefficient of Variation: A Measure of Risk   The standard deviation, then, is used as an indicator of risk. However, the standard deviation by itself is a misleading indicator of risk when management must compare investment projects of substantially different sizes and expected cash flows. For example, the financial manager of Happy Days is also evaluating the construction of a giant swimming pool that has an expected cash flow of $390,000 and a standard deviation of $75,000 in Year 1. Is the cash flow from the swimming pool more or less risky than the cash flow from the roller coaster, which has an expected cash flow of $80,000 and a standard deviation of $17,888?

	Swimming Pool	Roller Coaster
$\sigma =$	$ 75,000	$17,888
$\bar{x} =$	$390,000	$80,000

If the standard deviation is the criterion for measuring risk, the swimming pool appears to be riskier than the roller coaster, because its standard deviation is larger. However, the difference in size between the two projects distorts the relative importance of the standard deviations. To remove the effects of size, we use the **coefficient of variation (CV)**, which provides a relative measure of risk. As used here, it measures risk per dollar of expected return. The following equation defines the coefficient of variation.

$$CV = \frac{\sigma}{\bar{x}} \qquad\qquad (9\text{–}4)$$

where

σ = Standard deviation
$\bar{x}$ = Average (mean) value

The coefficients of variation for the roller coaster and swimming pool are 0.22 and 0.19, respectively.

$$CV \text{ (roller coaster)} = \frac{\$17,888}{\$80,000} = 0.22$$

$$CV \text{ (swimming pool)} = \frac{\$74,000}{\$390,000} = 0.19$$

This means that the roller coaster is relatively more risky than the swimming pool, because the roller coaster has the larger coefficient of variation.

Adjusting the Discount Rate

The standard procedure for calculating net present value is to use the firm's cost of capital as the discount rate—that is, the minimum rate of return a firm must earn to satisfy its investors. However, the discount rate may be adjusted for individual projects to reflect differences in risk. In other words, very risky projects might be discounted by a higher rate than less risky projects. This can be accomplished by using a **hurdle rate** for discounting the expected cash flows.

The reason for using a hurdle rate different from the cost of capital is straightforward. As you already know, there is a relationship between risk and return. Investors expect higher returns for risky projects than for those that are less risky. (In other words, they are *risk averse*.) It follows, then, that management should use higher discount rates on high-risk projects than on low-risk projects. The cost of capital is, of course, the minimum discount rate that should be used in making most capital budgeting decisions.

Although the reason for using a hurdle rate is simple, the determination of hurdle rates requires considerable thought. Two methods for determining hurdle rates are presented here. The first, which involves the development of a risk profile, is based on judgment; the second, which uses the capital asset pricing model, is based on theory.

Risk Profile For purposes of illustrating the first method, consider the **risk profile** used by Happy Days' management to determine the hurdle rate for the roller coaster project. This procedure, as mentioned, is based on judgment. It should be noted that this is only one of a variety of methods that can be used to organize judgments about risks in order to determine hurdle rates.[2]

An infinite number of factors can affect the risk of a project, but such possibilities as a meteor hitting the roller coaster can be eliminated and a list of realistic concerns developed. The management of Happy Days developed the list of **risk elements** presented in Table 9–4 some time ago to evaluate all the firm's projects; some elements, such as political risks in foreign nations, are not applicable to the roller coaster project. Table 9–4 also shows the **risk class** for each risk element. The classes range from low (1) to high (5). The degree of risk that applies to each risk element is determined by judgment.

The eight risk elements applicable to the roller coaster project are ranked according to risk class. For example, the dollar cost of the roller coaster is $200,000, which is average for Happy Days' investments; so the financial manager checked 3. Happy Days equates dollar cost with risk. Its management

---

[2]The method is described in Benton E. Gup and Samuel W. Norwood III, "Divisional Cost of Capital: A Practical Approach," *Financial Management*, Spring 1982, pp. 20–24. For an alternate approach, see R. Fuller and H. Kerr, "Estimating the Divisional Cost of Capital: An Analysis of the Pure Play Technique," *Journal of Finance*, December 1981, pp. 997–1009.

Table 9–4
Relative Risk Profile for Roller Coaster

Selected Risk Elements	Not Applicable	Low 1	Medium 2	Medium 3	Medium 4	High 5	
Dollar cost				3			
Replacement of existing project	✓						
Political risk in foreign nation	✓						
Customer base		1					
Exposure to legal action						5	
Seasonal factors						5	
Business conditions					4		
Equipment failure			2				
Environmental considerations		1					
Skilled labor				3			
Totals		2	2	6	4	10	**24**

Total score

$$\textbf{Average risk class} = \frac{\text{Total score}}{\text{Number of applicable risk elements}}$$

$$= \frac{24}{8}$$

$$= 3$$

believes that projects whose dollar cost is low constitute a small risk to the firm, whereas projects with huge dollar costs may present a major threat to the firm if they fail. Consumer base is the second risk element ranked. Because the park is located next to a major metropolitan area, there is a large consumer base to ride the roller coaster. Hence, risk for that element is low. However, risk of legal action is high; just last year, someone fell from a roller coaster and sued the amusement park and the manufacturer of the equipment for damages. The risk classes for the remaining elements were determined in the same manner—that is, by use of judgment.

The totals shown at the bottom of Table 9–4 are the sums of the values for applicable risk elements. The total score is 24. The average risk class for the roller coaster project is determined by dividing this total by the number of

Table 9–5
Risk-Adjusted Discount Rate

	Risk Class (1)	Project Premium[a] (2)	Rise-Adjusted Discount Rate (Cost of Capital = 12%) (3) = (2) × 12% = $k*$
Low	1	1.0	12.0%
	2	1.1	13.2
Average	3	1.2	14.4
	4	1.3	15.6
High	5	1.5	18.0

[a]For a derivation multiple risk index, see Benton E. Gup and Samuel W. Norwood III, "Divisional Cost of Capital: A Practical Approach," *Financial Management,* Spring 1982, pp. 20–24.

applicable risk elements. Accordingly, the roller coaster belongs in risk class 3 (24/8 = 3).

Project Premiums. The management of Happy Days has established project premiums for each risk class. The **project premium** reflects management's judgment about the additional returns it requires above the cost of capital to invest in any projects except the least risky ones. The project premium in this

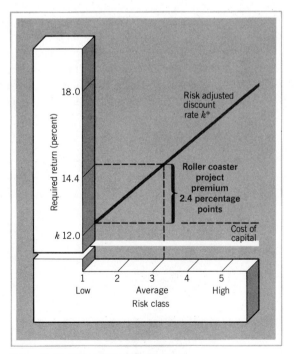

Figure 9–7 Risk-adjusted discount rate.

example is a multiple of the cost of capital and is used in determining net present value. The cost of capital for Happy Days is 12 percent.

As shown in Table 9–5, there is no project premium for projects with the lowest risk—risk class 1. Remember that the cost of capital is the lowest discount rate that should be used for most projects. That means the cost of capital is applied to the lowest-risk projects. Projects in risk class 2 carry a project premium of 1.1 times the cost of capital, which results in a **risk-adjusted discount rate** (k^*) of 13.2 percent $(0.12 \times 1.1 = 0.132)$. The roller coaster is in risk class 3, which means that the risk-adjusted discount rate for that project is 14.4 percent. It has an average risk. The highest risk class (5) is associated with a discount rate of 18 percent.

Figure 9–7 is a graphic representation of the relationship between required rates of return and risk classes. As noted, the cost of capital for Happy Days is 12 percent. For projects in risk class 1, the financial manager uses the cost of capital as the discount rate. For the roller coaster, which is in risk class 3, a risk premium of 2.4 percentage points is added to the cost of capital, which gives a discount rate of 14.4 percent.

Net Present Value.   Now that management knows the expected cash flows and the adjusted discount rate, it can determine the net present value for the roller coaster. Table 9–6 shows net present values for the roller coaster using the cost of capital and the risk-adjusted discount rate. The net present value using the cost of capital $(k = 12\%)$ is $22,558; the net present value using the risk-adjusted rate $(k^* = 14.4\%)$ is $12,415.

The net present value using the risk-adjusted rate is lower because the risk-adjusted rate is higher than the cost of capital. Higher discount rates result in lower *NPVs*. That means risky projects will be rejected before projects discounted at lower rates. If the investment outlay for the roller coaster had been,

Table 9–6
Net Present Value for Roller Coaster

Year	Expected Cash Flow (from Table 9–2) (1)	$PVIF_{12\%,n}$ (2)	Present Value of Expected Cash Flows (3) = (1) × (2)	$PVIF_{14.4\%,n}$ (4)	Present Value of Expected Cash Flows (5) = (1) × (4)
		Cost of Capital k		**Risk-Adjusted $k*$**	
1	$80,000	0.8929	$ 71,432	0.8741	$ 69,928
2	86,000	0.7972	$ 68,559	0.7641	65,713
3	66,000	0.7118	46,979	0.6679	44,081
4	56,000	0.6355	35,588	0.5838	32,693
	Totals		$222,558		$212,415
	Less: Investment outlay		200,000		200,000
	Equals: Net present value		$ 22,558		$ 12,415

[a]Refer to Appendix 5B for an explanation of how to use hand-held calculators for determining interest factors.

say, $220,000, the risk-adjusted project would have been rejected, because the investment outlay would have exceeded the present value of the expected cash flows by $7,585. However, the same project discounted at the cost of capital would have been accepted, because its net present value would have been $2,558:

	Discount Rate $=k$	Discount Rate $=k*$
Present value of cash flows	$222,558	$212,415
Investment outlay	$220,000	$220,000
Net present value	$ 2,558	−$ 7,585

Using the cost of capital instead of the appropriate risk-adjusted discount rate would have caused the firm to accept a project mistakenly. The financial manager must choose the discount rate very carefully.

Capital Asset Pricing Model The second method used to establish a hurdle rate involves the capital asset pricing model (*CAPM*). We used the *CAPM* in Chapter 6 to determine the rate of return investors require on common stock (k_e). The cost represented to the firm by k_e is one component of the cost of capital (k), used as the discount rate in calculating net present value. Financial managers also use the *CAPM* to establish hurdle rates for investment projects.

Remember that according to the *CAPM* the required rate of return is equal to the risk-free rate of return plus a risk premium:

$$k_e = R_f + \text{Risk premium}$$

$$= R_f + b(k_m - R_f) \qquad (9-5)$$

where

k_e = Required rate of return
R_f = Risk-free rate of return
b = Beta
k_m = Expected rate of return on a market portfolio

Although so far we have used the *CAPM* only to find shareholders' required rates of return, it can be used to help determine the firm's required rate of return on a project. In this case, beta represents the project's systematic risk. As before, the yield on short-term government securities represents the risk-free rate, and the return on the stock market represents the market portfolio.

To illustrate the use of the *CAPM* to establish a hurdle rate, we'll consider the following example. Suppose the management of Happy Days is considering buying controlling interest in a company that operates 10 amusement parks in Europe and the Orient. Management is treating the purchase of that

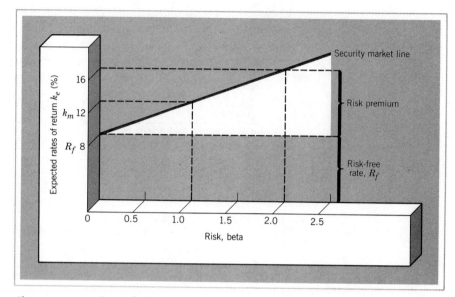

Figure 9–8   Security market line.

company's stock as a capital budgeting problem. Such uses of capital budgeting techniques are becoming increasingly popular.

The security market line in Figure 9–8 shows the required returns associated with several betas when the risk-free rate is 8 percent. Notice that, when beta is 1, the required rate of return is 12 percent. Even though a beta of 1 represents average risk, Happy Days' management will require a 4-percentage-point premium over the risk-free rate to invest in the project. If Happy Days determines that the proposed investment is riskier than average, the firm will require an even higher return. For example, a beta of 2 will raise the required rate of return to 16 percent. The required rate of return will be used to determine the net present value of the project. Using the *CAPM* in this way is feasible so long as management believes systematic risk, as measured by beta, is the most important risk to adjust for.

Sensitivity   Because different discount rates may be applied to the same project, it is useful to test the **sensitivity** of a project to changes in discount rates. For example, suppose Happy Days is evaluating two mutually exclusive projects, Space Ride and Haunted House. The investment outlays and expected cash flows for both projects are listed in Table 9–7. The table also lists the net present values for both projects when the discount rates are 10 percent, 12 percent, and 14 percent. The net present values from Table 9–7 were used to plot the profiles in Figure 9–9. The profiles show that Space Ride is more responsive, or sensitive, to changes in the discount rate than Haunted House. Stated other-

Table 9–7

Selected Net Present Values for Two Projects

	Year		Expected Cash Flows	Discount Rates		
				10%	12%	14%
Space ride						
Investment outlay	0	−	$15,000			
Cash flows	1	+	1,000			
	2	+	2,000			
	3	+	4,000			
	4	+	8,000			
	5	+	10,000			
Net present values				$2,239	$1,093	$ 47
Haunted house						
Investment outlay	0	−	$15,000			
Cash flows	1	+	7,000			
	2	+	5,000			
	3	+	4,000			
	4	+	3,500			
	5	+	2,000			
Net present values				$2,133	$1,442	$799

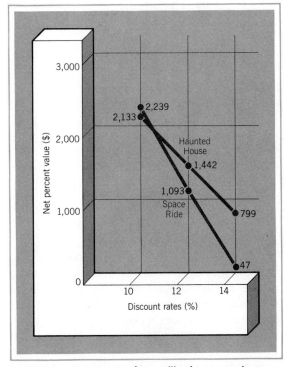

Figure 9–9   Net present value profiles for two projects.

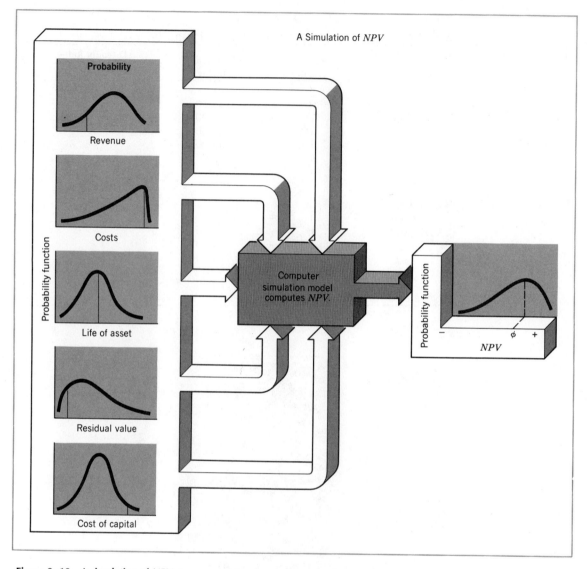

Figure 9–10   A simulation of *NPV*.

wise, if the discount rate increases substantially, Space Ride will lose more (have a lower net present value) than Haunted House.

One reason for the differences in sensitivity is the timing of the projects' cash flows. Haunted House produces its largest cash flows during the first few years. In contrast, Space Ride's largest cash flows occur during the latter years.

Simulation The sensitivity of net present value to differences in discount rates, revenues, costs, and other variables that affect cash flows may be determined by computer simulation models. Such models allow us to test "what if" questions. For example, what happens to *NPV* if revenues are lower than expected and costs are higher than expected? Figure 9–10 depicts some of the factors that may be considered in a simulation that addresses this question. The computer program picks at random various combinations of values from the factors shown in the figure and computes the *NPV* for each combination. The process of random selection and computation is repeated many times and the final product is a distribution of various *NPVs*. The distribution shown in the figure suggests that the project under consideration has a high probability of having an *NPV* less than zero.

Portfolio Risk and Diversification

The preceding sections of this chapter examined selected aspects of risk associated with single investment projects. This section examines the risks associated with combinations of projects, or **portfolios**, because many firms invest in several projects at the same time. The section shows how different combinations of assets affect risk.

Types of Risk As you may recall from Chapter 6, two types of risk must be considered—systematic risk and unsystematic risk. Together, they make up the total risk of an asset, its deviation from its expected return. The types of risk are summarized in Table 9–8. **Systematic risk** is attributable to a common factor, such as general economic conditions, that affects all assets similarly. Therefore, it cannot be eliminated by diversification. However, we will see how average portfolio betas—which measure systematic risk for entire portfolios—can be altered. **Unsystematic risk** is unique to a particular asset and can be eliminated by diversification. The possibility of a failure of the motor that drives Happy Days' roller coaster is one example of unsystematic risk. Although the roller coaster could not be used until the motor was repaired, other projects would continue to operate and provide cash flows.

Figure 9–11 graphically depicts the relationship among total risk, its com-

Table 9–8
Types of Risk

Total Risk of Asset	
Systematic Risk	**Unsystematic Risk**
• Due to *common* factor	• Due to *unique* factor
• Affects *all* securities	• Affects *one* security
• *Cannot* be eliminated by diversification, but can be altered	• Can be eliminated by diversification
• Measured by beta	

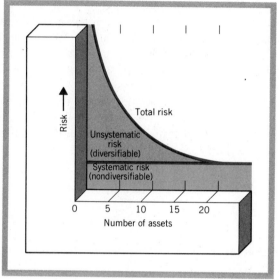

Figure 9–11   Portfolio risk.

ponents, and the number of assets in a portfolio. The figure shows that total risk declines sharply as the number of assets is increased. Most unsystematic risk is eliminated from a portfolio that holds 12 or more assets. As the number of assets is increased, total risk gradually approaches the level of systematic risk of the portfolio. As you will see, the extent to which the combination of assets affects risk depends on the correlation of the cash flows of the assets involved.

Diversification of Assets   Against this background, let's consider the expected cash flows and risks (represented by standard deviations) of the four projects listed in Table 9–9. Project A has even cash flows during a 5-year period and a standard deviation of 0. The cash flows from Projects B and C are the same in every year. Thus, they are said to have a **perfect positive correlation**—a statistical term that means both series of data change in exactly the same manner.[3] In contrast, the cash flows from Projects C and D are said to have a **perfect negative correlation**—that is, they change in exactly opposite manners. The cash flow from Project C declines by $100 each year and the cash flow from Project D increases by the same amount. The standard deviations of the cash flows from Projects B, C, and D are $158.

Now, let's consider what happens when two projects are combined in a portfolio. Table 9–9 shows three different combinations of projects. Portfolio BC, which contains the two projects whose cash flows have a perfect positive

---

[3]The correlation coefficient r ranges from $+1$ for perfect positive correlation to -1 for perfect negative correlation. When r is 0, no correlation exists between the data.

Table 9–9
Portfolio Returns and Risks[a]

| | | | Expected Cash Flows | | | | | | |
| | | | Single Projects | | | | Portfolios of Projects | | |
	Years		A	B	C	D	AB	BC	CD
	1		$500	$500	$500	$100	$1,000	$1,000	$600
	2		500	400	400	200	900	800	600
	3		500	300	300	300	800	600	600
	4		500	200	200	400	700	400	600
	5		500	100	100	500	600	200	600
Average cash flow	$\bar{x}$	=	500	300	300	300	800	600	600
Risk (represented by standard deviation)	σ	=	0	158	158	158	158	316	0

[a]P_i of each cash flow = 0.5.

correlation, has the largest standard deviation ($316) and thus the highest risk. The reason for the large standard deviation is that changes in the cash flows of the two projects reinforce each other because they move in the same direction.

Portfolio CD, which consists of the projects with cash flows that have a perfect negative correlation, has the smallest standard deviation (0) and risk. In this case, the changes in the cash flows offset each other because they move in opposite directions. Finally, Portfolio AB, which consists of assets whose cash flows are not perfectly related, has a standard deviation of $158.

The three examples of perfect correlations presented here are special cases. More commonly, the cash flows of a firm's projects have some correlation with each other, but not a perfect one. Nevertheless, these sample portfolios suggest the following guidelines for portfolio construction.

1. To eliminate risk, select assets whose expected returns have perfect negative correlations.
2. To maximize risk, select assets whose expected returns have perfect positive correlations.
3. For an intermediate position, select assets whose returns are not perfectly correlated.

Diversification involves selecting assets whose returns are *not* perfectly positively correlated. The result is reduction or elimination of unsystematic risk.

Portfolio Beta Although systematic risk cannot be eliminated from a portfolio, the degree of systematic risk can be changed by changes in the proportions of assets held. For example, assume that a company owns four subsidiaries—E, F, G, and H—as depicted in Figure 9–12. The figure reveals that Subsidiaries G and F are in the pioneering and expansion phases of the life cycle and have betas of 2 and 1.8, respectively. Subsidiaries H and E are mature; their betas are 0.7 and 0.5.[4]

As shown at the top of Table 9–10, the company originally invested 25 percent of its assets in each subsidiary. In this situation, the **average portfolio beta**—the weighted average beta for the entire company—is 1.25.[5] This means the returns on the stock of the company will change 12.5 percent on the average when the stock market changes 10 percent.

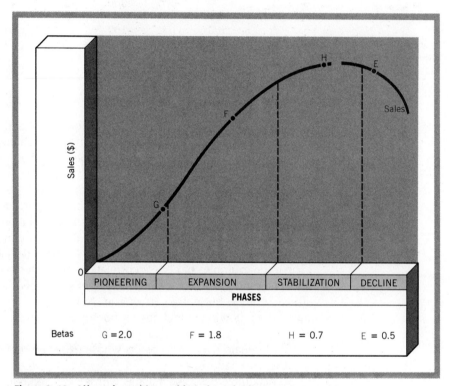

Figure 9–12   Life cycle position and beta for Subsidiaries E, F, G, and H.

[4]For details on estimating betas for industry segments, see John A. Boquist and William T. Moore, "Estimating the Systematic Risk of an Industry Segment: A Mathematical Programming Approach," *Financial Management*, Winter 1983, pp. 11–18.

[5]The following is the formula for portfolio beta.

$$b_p = \sum_{t=1}^{n} b_i w_i$$

where

b_p = Portfolio beta
b_i = Beta of Asset i
w_i = Percent of total investment in Asset i

Table 9–10
Average Portfolio Betas

Asset (1)	Proportion of Portfolio (2)	Beta (3)	(4) = (2) × (3) (4)	
Original Portfolio				
E	25%	0.5	0.125	
F	25%	1.8	0.450	
G	25%	2.0	0.500	
H	25%	0.7	0.175	
			1.250	= Average portfolio beta
Rearranged Portfolio				
E	50%	0.5	0.250	
F	10%	1.8	0.180	
G	10%	2.0	0.200	
H	30%	0.7	0.210	
			0.840	= Average portfolio beta

Management has decided it wants to reduce the company's systematic risk. It can accomplish this by reducing the proportion of high-risk assets held and increasing the proportion of low-risk assets held. Table 9–10 shows a rearranged portfolio in which the proportions of high-beta Subsidiaries F and G have been reduced from 25 percent each to 10 percent each, while the proportions of low-beta Subsidiaries E and H have been increased. The net result is that the average beta for the rearranged portfolio is 0.84.

Another result of reducing systematic risk by shifting the portfolio in favor of the mature subsidiaries is to slow the company's rate of growth. Had management decided to increase the company's growth rate, it could have rearranged the portfolio in favor of the subsidiaries in the pioneering and expansion phases of the life cycle. That would have *increased* portfolio risk.

The expected returns on the subsidiaries were not shown in Table 9–10. When management decided to reduce systematic risk for the company, it recognized that expected returns would decline.

Summary

Financial managers must make decisions today based on what they think will happen in the future. Because the future is uncertain, they must use techniques designed to accommodate risk. Three ways of taking risk into account in the capital budgeting process are to improve estimates of cash flows, to adjust the discount rate, and to diversify assets. The first two methods apply to single assets; the third, to portfolios of assets.

Managers can improve estimates of cash flows by calculating expected cash

Table 9–11
Summary of Equations

	Equation	Equation Number
Expected Value	$E[x] = \sum_{i=1}^{n} [x_i P_i] = \bar{x}$	(9–1)
Standard deviation	$\sigma = \sqrt{\sum_{t=1}^{n} (x_i - \bar{x})^2 \, P_i}$	(9–2)
Z (standardized area under normal curve)	$Z = \dfrac{x_i - \bar{x}}{\sigma}$	(9–3)
Coefficient of Variation (CV)	$CV = \dfrac{\sigma}{\bar{x}}$	(9–4)
CAPM	$k_e = R_f + b(k_m - R_f)$	(9–5)
Porfolio beta	$b_p = \sum_{t=1}^{n} b_i w_i$	

flows and measuring some of the risks associated with them. Risk can be measured by use of the standard deviation. The coefficient of variation provides a relative measure of risk useful in comparisons of projects with different sizes and different expected cash flows. The formulas for various risk measurements appear in Table 9–11, along with the other equations from this chapter.

The firm's discount rate—its required return on a project—may be adjusted to accommodate various levels of risk. To determine hurdle rates, managers can develop a project's risk profile, which is based on judgment; or they can use the capital asset pricing model.

Diversification of assets offers a way to reduce unsystematic risk in a portfolio. Expected returns from the assets that make up the portfolio must not be perfectly positively correlated. Systematic risk for the portfolio can be reduced when the composition of the portfolio favors low-beta assets.

Important Terms

Average portfolio beta
Coefficient of variation (CV)
Continuous probability distribution
Discrete probability distribution
Diversification
Expected cash flow
Hurdle rate

Perfect negative correlation
Perfect positive correlation
Portfolio
Project premium
Projected cash flow
Risk
Risk-adjusted discount rate

Risk class   Systematic risk
Risk element   Total risk
Risk profile   Unsystematic risk
Sensitivity   Variance
Standard deviation   Z

Questions

1. When net present value is used to make capital budgeting decisions, in what three ways may risk be incorporated in the analysis?
2. Distinguish between the terms *projected cash flow* and *expected cash flow*.
3. How is expected cash flow calculated? Identify all data necessary and explain how they are used.
4. What is the difference between a discrete and a continuous probability distribution?
5. Define *risk* in a statistical sense. Explain how the standard deviation of expected cash flows can be used as a measure of risk. What data are required to calculate the standard deviation of expected cash flows?
6. Assuming a normal distribution, what is the chance that the actual cash flow from a project will be within one standard deviation of the expected cash flow? Within two standard deviations? Draw a probability distribution that illustrates your answers.
7. Explain how Z values can be used to find the probability that actual cash flows will be less than or greater than a particular dollar amount.
8. Under what circumstances is the standard deviation misleading as a measure of risk? Why? What alternative risk measure is available when the standard deviation is inappropriate?
9. Explain, in general, the steps required to assess the riskiness of a project using managerial judgment.
10. What are project premiums? How are they used in developing risk-adjusted discount rates?
11. What is meant by the term *risk-averse*?
12. Consider a project of above-average risk. Will the use of a risk-adjusted discount rate result in a higher or lower *NPV* than if the cost of capital was used? Why?
13. How can the capital asset pricing model be used to determine a project's risk-adjusted required return? When a risk-adjusted rate is chosen in this way, what risk is considered the most important?
14. Explain the use of net present value profiles to estimate the sensitivity of projects to changes in the required rate of return.
15. How can simulation be used as a risk-assessment technique?
16. In what way can diversification reduce portfolio risk? What type of risk cannot be eliminated through diversification? Why?
17. How can the systematic risk of a diversified portfolio be lowered? What impact will this action have on the portfolio's expected return? Why?

Problems

1. Calculate the expected annual cash flow, variance, and standard deviation of the following investments. Each investment has a 5-year life. Cash flow projections and their probabilities are estimated to be the same each year.

Project A		Project B	
Probability	Projected Cash Flow	Probability	Projected Cash Flow
0.10	$100	0.10	$100
0.20	200	0.20	200
0.40	300	0.30	300
0.20	400	0.40	400
0.10	500		

2. Using the data from Problem 1, draw probability distributions for the projected cash flows from each investment. On this basis, which project is riskier? Why?

3. Tassa Equipment is planning a new product introduction. The following is the forecast of projected cash flows at the end of each year of the product's 3-year life.

State of the Economy	1993		1994		1995	
	Probability	Cash Flow	Probability	Cash Flow	Probability	Cash Flow
Improving	0.4	$ 700	0.2	$ 800	0.1	$ 900
Good	0.1	1,000	0.3	1,200	0.4	1,500
Declining	0.4	500	0.3	600	0.3	700
Depressed	0.1	200	0.2	300	0.2	400

(a) Calculate the expected cash flows in each year.
(b) Calculate the standard deviation of the cash flows in each year.
(c) Which year is expected to be the riskiest for this project?
(d) Assuming an investment outlay of $2,000 at the beginning of 1993 and a discount rate of 10 percent, should this product be introduced?

4. Bonnie Raines is a financial planner for a large computer company. The following investments are mutually exclusive, and Bonnie is doing a preliminary screening based on project risk. Which project is riskiest? Explain your choice of risk measures.

	Project A	Project B
Expected cash flows	$400,000	$250,000
Standard deviation	150,000	112,000

5. Reagan Supply Company is dominated by conservative managers. If only the least risky projects will be considered for additional analysis, which one of the following proposals will be considered further? The projections represent expected annual cash flows for each year of their anticipated 10-year lives.

Project 1		Project 2		Project 3	
Probability	Cash Flow	Probability	Cash Flow	Probability	Cash Flow
0.2	$30,000	0.25	$20,000	0.1	$20,000
0.3	36,000	0.25	35,000	0.4	40,000
0.3	44,000	0.25	45,000	0.4	50,000
0.2	50,000	0.25	60,000	0.1	60,000

6. Refer to the information in Problem 5. Suppose, instead, management planned to evaluate each project and to select the one with the highest *NPV*. Each project costs $240,000. The least risky project will be evaluated at a discount rate of 10 percent, the next riskiest at 12 percent, and the riskiest at 15 percent. Which of the three, if any, should be selected?

7. Steve Streets, a newly graduated finance major, is conducting a risk analysis for his employer. The following forecasts have been made for the annual cash flows from two 5-year projects.

Dynamo		Cyclone	
Probability	Cash Flow	Probability	Cash Flow
0.05	− $1,000	0.03	− $2,000
0.10	− 500	0.07	− 1,000
0.15	0	0.10	0
0.20	500	0.13	1,000
0.20	1,000	0.17	2,000
0.15	1,500	0.17	3,000
0.10	2,000	0.13	4,000
0.05	2,500	0.10	5,000
		0.07	6,000
		0.03	7,000

(a) For each project, compute the expected annual cash flow, its standard deviation, and its coefficient of variation.
(b) Draw probability distributions for the projected annual cash flows.
(c) Assuming a normal distribution, what is the probability that each project will return at least $565 annually?

8. Appletree Pub is estimating its cash flow for the coming year. Management has compiled the following information.

Economic Forecast	Probability	Cash Flow
Poor	0.15	$100,000
Fair	0.35	150,000
Good	0.35	200,000
Great	0.15	250,000

(a) Calculate expected cash flow and its standard deviation.
(b) What is the probability that the pub will generate a cash flow greater than $12,000; greater than $225,000; less than $120,000?

9. Providence Pottery is considering a new kiln to fire its products. In order to be acceptable, the kiln must have at least a 75 percent chance of generating $90,000 in its first year of operation. Based on the cash flow estimates below, is purchasing the kiln advisable?

Economic Outlook	Probability	Cash Flow
Poor	0.1	$ 0
Mediocre	0.2	100,000
Fair	0.4	150,000
Good	0.2	200,000
Excellent	0.1	300,000

10. Frame Corporation is investigating the possibility of exploring a gold mine in Arizona. The company's current business is concentrated in baked goods, for which it uses a 10 percent cost of capital in evaluating expansion proposals. Using the framework provided by Table 9–4, prepare a risk profile for the gold mining project. Based on your analysis, would a 15 percent required return be appropriate for the project?

11. Suppose that Frame Corporation, in Problem 10, establishes a risk class of 4 for the gold mine project relative to a class of 1 for its normal operations. Each successive risk class adds 0.2 to the project premium required. The required rate of return for class 1 is 10 percent. Calculate the NPV for the gold mine if the initial outlay totals $193,000 and if expected cash flows are $58,000 per year for 10 years.

12. Suppose, instead, that Frame Corporation in Problem 10 is considering a substantial investment in United States Treasury bills. If 15 percent is the normal cost of capital, should that rate be used to evaluate the potential investment in Treasury bills? Why or why not?

13. Melba Toast, Inc., has two mutually exclusive opportunities to invest $100,000. The expected cash flows from each project over their anticipated 6-year lives are presented in the table below.

Year	Project R	Project S
0	$ – 100,000	$ – 100,000
1	70,000	10,000
2	20,000	10,000
3	20,000	20,000
4	20,000	20,000
5	10,000	50,000
6	10,000	70,000

(a) Calculate the NPV of each project at a discount rate of 8 percent, which is management's best estimate of the cost of capital. Which project is preferable?

(b) Calculate the NPV of each project at a discount rate of 4 percent, 12 percent, 16 percent, 20 percent, and 28 percent. Prepare an NPV profile of each project based on your results.

(c) Suppose Melba's managers are uncertain about the firm's true cost of capital because of changes the firm has recently been undergoing. Which project would recommend in that case? Why?

14. Jensen Corporation, a firm financed entirely by equity, is contemplating the purchase of a Western clothing division now owned by a major competitor. In determining the proper price to pay for the division, Jensen is using the capital asset pricing model to estimate the required rate of return. The risk-free rate is 10 percent, Jensen's beta is 1.2, the beta of the division is 2 percent and the expected return on the market is 18 percent.

(a) Calculate Jensen's cost of capital.

(b) Calculate the risk-adjusted discount rate to use in evaluating the Western clothing division.

(c) If the division is expected to return a cash flow of $260,000 indefinitely, what price should Jensen offer?

15. Calculate risk-adjusted rates of return for the following investments if $R_f = 8$ percent and $k_m = 15$ percent.

Project	Beta
1	−0.5
2	0.0
3	0.9
4	1.0
5	1.2

16. Suppose the projects in Problem 15 were combined into a portfolio. If the projects are of equal size, what is the beta of the resulting portfolio?

17. Common Corporation has three projects of equal size in its capital budget. The expected cash flows of each project are provided below.

Year	Project A	Project B	Project C
1	$100	$300	$100
2	200	200	250
3	300	100	400
4	400	50	600

Which pair of projects would provide the least diversification benefit? Why?

18. Consider the expected cash flows for the following four projects.

Year	Project L	Project M	Project N	Project O
1	$500	$100	$500	$300
2	500	200	400	400
3	500	300	300	500
4	500	400	200	650
5	500	500	100	700

Comment on the relative diversification potential of each of the six pairs of projects available.

19. Kemp Corporation is an aspiring conglomerate. It has invested the following amounts in each of six product lines.

	Investment	Beta
Igloo Ice Creams	$ 5,000	1.4
Bruiser Skates	10,000	1.8
Sampson Steel	40,000	0.9
Coney Calculators	20,000	1.2
Pryor Electric Ovens	30,000	0.7
Enid Telephone	20,000	1.0

Calculate the resulting portfolio beta.

20. A firm has invested in 10 projects, each valued at $111,000. The beta of the resulting portfolio of projects is 0.8. What will happen to the beta of the portfolio if one of the original projects, having a beta of 0.6, is dropped and replaced with a $111,000 project with a beta of 1.2?

Capital Structure

oes the amount of debt a firm has matter? It certainly
does. Having the proper mix of debt and equity can make
the difference between extinction and survival. The mix of
debt and equity that makes up the firm's capital structure is the
subject of Part 4. Chapter 10 explains how firms can use debt
and equity to grow faster. Chapter 11 examines stock dividends
with particular attention to the firm's decision to pay dividends
or retain earnings.

Financial Leverage and Growth

Business concerns borrow funds to grow faster than they could if they relied on retained earnings alone. Borrowing gives rise to financial leverage. This chapter examines various aspects of financial leverage and its effects on the growth of firms. It also explains why financing growth with debt involves risk.

After reading this chapter, you should know the following.

---

1. **Why growth is important.**
2. **What *experience* means.**
3. **How the management of costs is related to survival.**
4. **Why borrowing may be a good idea and paying dividends a bad idea if rapid growth is desired.**
5. **Why financial leverage is a double-edged sword.**
6. **How investors can use personal financial leverage.**

The Rationale for Growth: Survival

This chapter is about managing capital in order to grow faster. But why grow faster? For one thing, firms must grow to survive. In addition, growth enhances shareholders' wealth. To understand these answers better, consider the life cycle shown in Figure 10–1. By now, you should be familiar with the life cycle, but a brief review is in order.

Assume that the life cycle in Figure 10–1 is that of a new industry that produces exotic computers. During the pioneering phase of the life cycle, there are only a few firms in the industry. Developmental and promotional costs make the price of the computer $100,000. Even so, the product is an instant success, because it is faster and more powerful than older types of computers that cost three times as much.

The success of the new computer attracts other firms into the industry and thus ushers in the expansion phase. One of the important characteristics of the expansion phase is that only a few firms will survive it to enter the stabilization phase. Therefore, one objective of a firm located at Position X in the figure, in the pioneering phase of the life cycle, should be to *survive* in order to get to Position Y in the expansion phase. To survive, a firm must manage its *costs* and its *financial structure* properly. As you will see, given the proper

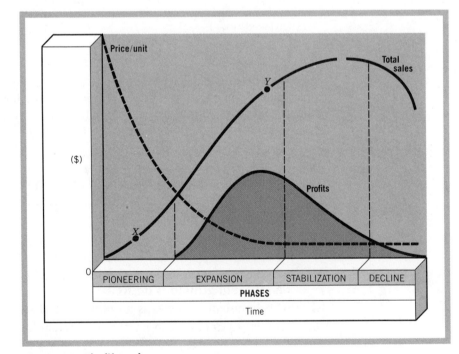

Figure 11-1   The life cycle.

financial structure, a firm can acquire sufficient assets to produce enough output to drive its costs below those of its competitors.

Costs   During the expansion phase of the life cycle, prices of the new computers decline as the additional supply from new entrants into the industry is brought forth. Stated otherwise, revenue per unit declines during the expansion phase. Recall that a firm's profit is equal to revenue less costs.

$$\text{Profit} = \text{Revenue} - \text{Cost} \qquad (10\text{--}1)$$

Firms with low-cost production will make greater profits (that is, have higher earnings) and survive, whereas those with high costs may not survive.

Learning Curves.   To some extent, costs are related to the accumulated volume of production, sometimes called **experience**. Firms that produce the most have the greatest accumulated volume of production and tend to have the lowest costs. The reason is that the more times you produce something, the more proficient you become. The **learning curve** in Figure 10–2 shows how cost per unit declines as the volume of production increases. If cost per unit declines 20 percent every time output doubles, a **learning rate** of 80 percent is said to occur. Figure 10–2 shows an 80 percent learning curve. It is plotted on a graph that produces a straight line when unit cost declines by a fixed percentage each time the cumulative volume doubles. As a general rule, most learning curves range from 70 to 90 percent, which means that the cost per unit declines from 30 to 10 percent every time cumulative output doubles.

Texas Instruments (TI) is one of many companies that uses learning curves as an aid to decision making. TI's basic strategy is to strive for industry leadership (and thus survival) by producing as much volume as possible to lower costs and enhance earnings.[1] For example, TI applied the learning curve principle to the semiconductor business. In 1960, a simple functional circuit cost $10. Today, one silicon chip accommodates 20,000 functions at a cost of less than 1 cent per function. TI estimates that by 1990 a single silicon chip will contain 10 million or more functions and cost less than one-hundredth of a cent per function.

The point of all this is that firms must acquire assets in order to produce

[1]"Texas Instruments Shows U.S. Business How to Survive in the 1980s," *Business Week*, September 18, 1978, p. 68. For additional information on learning experience curves, see Boston Consulting Group, *Perspectives on Experience* (1968) and *Experience Curves as a Planning Tool* (1970); and K. Hartley, "The Learning Curve and Its Applications to the Aircraft Industry," *Journal of Industrial Economics*, March 1965, pp. 112–118. To see how experience curves are integrated into corporate strategies, see Benton Gup, *Guide to Strategic Planning* (New York: McGraw-Hill, 1980), Chapter 11. Finally, see Malcolm B. Coate, "Elementary Portfolio Planning Models," in *Portfolio Planning and Corporate Strategy*, ed. Thomas H. Naylor and Michele H. Mann (Oxford, Ohio: Planning Executives Institute, 1983), pp. 1–7.

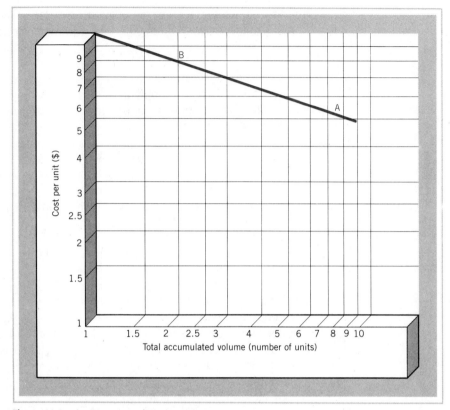

Figure 11-2   An 80 percent learning curve.

more and to gain experience, thereby reducing their costs. Consider two firms, A and B. Firm A is a well-managed, aggressive company that has been in its industry for some time and has acquired many assets. Firm B, a new entrant into the industry, has a relatively small asset base. The result, shown in Figure 10–2, is that Firm A has lower unit costs than Firm B. This gives a major advantage to A. Recall that during the expansion phase of the life cycle, prices fall rapidly and earnings are difficult to maintain. It follows that firms with low costs can tolerate declining prices better than those with high costs. In fact, if Firm A can produce a sufficient volume, it can drive prices down and force its high-cost competitors out of the market. Therefore, the offensive strategy is to have sufficient resources (assets) to be able to produce and sell a large volume quickly, thereby undercutting competition.

It is important to note that new entrants into an industry are not always high-cost producers. For example, at the end of World War II, the United States helped finance new steel mills in Japan and Germany. The new mills were more efficient than the old steel mills in the United States; so they were able to produce steel at lower unit costs than the U.S. mills, thereby undercutting U.S. producers' prices and markets.

The remainder of this chapter explains how financial leverage can be used to achieve a rapid expansion of assets that will allow the firm to produce large volumes of a product at low cost. If the product sells, the firm will be profitable and survive. **Financial leverage**, you may recall, involves debt; more precisely, it is the relationship of total debt to equity. (Some analysts consider preferred stock in the same category as debt.)

We should note that using leverage to grow is compatible with the primary goal of management—maximizing shareholder wealth. Ensuring the firm's survival is of obvious benefit to shareholders. Managing costs as described above also benefits stockholders in another way: When a firm is able to reduce expenses relative to total assets, both the return on assets and the return on equity increase. (These two measures of returns on shareholders' investments will be described in Chapter 13.) This, in turn, contributes to increased investment values, which benefit shareholders.

Financial Structure As mentioned, financial structure as well as costs must be managed properly if the firm is to grow. Table 10–1 shows how the financial structure of a firm, as reflected in its debt-to-equity ratio and its dividend payout ratio, evolves over its life cycle. Keep in mind that the relationships are generalizations and so may not fit every company. Nevertheless, this model serves as a useful basis for discussion. Thus, we can usually say that the proportion of debt to equity in the financial structure, or the **debt-to-equity ratio**, is high during the pioneering and expansion phases of the life cycle. This is what we would expect based on the discussion of learning curves. Once the firms have matured, the ratio declines as relatively more equity is added to their capital structures.

You may recall that the **dividend payout ratio** is the cash dividend per share expressed as a percentage of earnings per share. **Earnings per share** (*EPS*) is derived by dividing earnings available for holders of common stock by the number of shares outstanding. Earnings can be paid to shareholders as cash dividends or retained and added to equity capital. Typically, more earnings are paid out to shareholders as firms mature. Next, we will examine the impact

Table 10–1
Life Cycle and Financial Structure

Financial Ratios	Phases of Life Cycle			
	Pioneering	Expansion	Stabilization	Decline
Debt-to-equity ratio	High	High	Decreasing	Low
Dividend payout ratio	None	Small, increasing	Increasing, large	Large until losses occur

on growth of both the debt-to-equity ratio and the proportion of earnings paid out as dividends.

Growth with No Debt

The term **growth** as used here refers to the growth of the total assets of a firm. To examine the impact of financial structure on growth, we will begin with a simple financial structure and then add complexities. First, we will consider a hypothetical firm financed entirely with equity. It pays no cash dividends and no taxes. Incidentally, although most firms have debt, some have little or none. For example, DeBeers Consolidated Mines, Ltd., a South African Mining Company, is 97 percent equity-financed. Closer to home, the Communications Satellite Corporation (Comsat) was 100 percent equity-financed for many years. The company added some debt, but in 1980 it was still 99.5 percent equity-financed. Disney Productions and Mesabi Trust, which owns iron ore properties, have no long-term debt.

To illustrate the growth of assets in our hypothetical company, consider the example presented in Table 10–2. At the beginning of Year 1, earnings are $12 and the firm retains the entire amount. Because the company pays no dividends, interest, or income taxes, its assets increase by the amount of the retained earnings and equal $112 at the end of the year. The growth rate of assets, then, is 12 percent. The same pattern occurs in the second and third years.

The growth rate of assets ultimately depends on the **operating return on assets**—earnings before interest payments and taxes divided by total assets.[2] In this example, the operating return on assets is 12 percent ($12/$100 =

Table 10–2
Growth of Assets with No Debt or Dividends

	Years		
	1	**2**	**3**
Total assets at the beginning of each year	$100.00	$112.00	$125.44
Equity	$100.00	$112.00	$125.44
Earnings	$ 12.00	$ 13.44	$ 15.05
Earnings retained	$ 12.00	$ 13.44	$ 15.05
Total assets at the end of each year	$112.00	$125.44	$140.49
Growth rate of assets	12.0%	12.0%	12.0%

[2]When, as here, no interest or taxes are paid, operating return on assets is the same as return on equity (that is, net income divided by shareholders' equity).

12%). The growth rate of assets of a firm that has no debt and pays no dividends or taxes is equal to the operating return on assets.

$$g = r$$

where

g = Growth rate of assets
r = Operating return on assets

Effect of Dividends What happens to the growth rate if the firm pays a cash dividend? Assume that the company pays a cash dividend equal to 50 percent of its earnings, which means that its dividend payout ratio is 50 percent. As shown in Table 10–3, the company earns $12 in the first year and pays a cash dividend of $6. The remaining $6 is added to the firm's capital, and assets grow 6 percent during the year. The pattern is repeated in the next 2 years; so the growth rate of assets continues to be 6 percent. Here, the growth rate depends on the proportion of earnings retained by the firm as well as on the operating return on assets. We determine the rate of growth as follows.

$$g = br$$

where

g = Growth rate of assets
b = Proportion of earnings retained by the firm after cash dividends have been paid (retention ratio)
r = Operating return on assets

The degree to which the proportion of earnings paid out as dividends affects the growth rate of assets is shown in Table 10–4. The operating return on

Table 10–3
Growth of Assets with No Debt and 50 Percent Dividend Payout Ratio

	Years		
	1	2	3
Total assets at the beginning of each year	$100.00	$106.00	$112.36
Equity	$100.00	$106.00	$112.36
Earnings	$ 12.00	$ 12.72	$ 13.48
Dividend	$ 6.00	$ 6.36	$ 6.74
Earnings retained	$ 6.00	$ 6.36	$ 6.74
Total assets at the end of each year	$106.00	$112.36	$119.10
Growth rate of assets each year	6.0%	6.0%	6.0%

Table 10–4
Effect of Dividends on Growth Rate

Growth Rate of Assets		Proportion of Earnings Retained by the Firm		Operating Return on Assets
g	$=$	b	$\times$	r
0%		0.00		0.12
3%		0.25		0.12
6%		0.50		0.12
9%		0.75		0.12
12%		1.00		0.12

assets is assumed to be 12 percent. As you can see, the growth rate of assets increases directly with the proportion of earnings retained. The growth rate is zero when the firm pays out all of its earnings as dividends and retains nothing; if the company retains half its earnings, the growth rate is 6 percent. The maximum growth rate of assets for the equity-financed firm is achieved when all earnings are retained.

Growth with Debt

Now let's examine the effect of financial leverage on growth. Table 10–5 illustrates the growth of our hypothetical firm when it is financed equally with debt and equity and pays no cash dividends. The firm's debt-to-equity ratio is 1:1 (50% debt to 50% equity = 1:1) and the operating return on assets is

Table 10–5
Growth of Assets with Equal Debt and Equity but No Dividends

	Years		
	1	2	3
Total assets at beginning of each year	$100.00	$118.00	$139.24
Debt	$ 50.00	$ 59.00	$ 69.62
Equity	$ 50.00	$ 59.00	$ 69.62
Operating earning before interest $r = 0.12$	$ 12.00	$ 14.16	$ 16.70
Interest $i = 0.06$	$ 3.00	$ 3.54	$ 4.18
Earnings after interest	$ 9.00	$ 10.62	$ 12.52
Earnings retained	$ 9.00	$ 10.62	$ 12.52
Additional debt	$ 9.00	$ 10.62	$ 12.52
Total new investment = Additional debt + Earnings retained	$ 18.00	$ 21.24	$ 25.04
Total assets at the end of each year	$118.00	$139.24	$164.28
Growth rate of assets each year	18.0%	18.0%	18.0%

again 12 percent. Because the firm has debt, it must pay interest; the interest rate on the debt is 6 percent.

As the table shows, we assume again that assets at the beginning of the first year are $100 and earnings for the year are $12. Interest payments of $3 (0.06 × $50 = $3) are deducted from the earnings to obtain $9 earnings after interest. Because there are no cash dividend payments, the $9 is retained as equity. To maintain a constant debt-to-equity ratio of 1:1, the firm borrows an additional $9; so new investment in the firm totals $18. Therefore, the assets at the end of the year are $118 and the growth rate of assets is 18 percent. The same process is followed in the next 2 years.

You can see that the use of financial leverage has increased the growth rate of the firm's assets from 12 percent when it was financed entirely with equity and paid no dividend to 18 percent with a 1:1 debt-to-equity ratio. The effect of debt on the growth rate of assets can be determined by use of the following equation. This equation builds on the simpler equations given earlier but takes interest payments and financial leverage into account.[3]

$$g = b \left[r + (r - i)\frac{L}{E} \right] \qquad (10\text{--}2)$$

where

g = Growth rate of assets
b = Proportion of earnings retained by the firm after cash dividends have been paid (retention ratio)
r = Operating return on assets
i = Interest rate on borrowed funds
L = Total liabilities (debts)
E = Total equity

Applying Equation 10–2 to the data in Table 10–5 yields a growth rate of assets of 18 percent.

$$g = b \left[r + (r - i)\frac{L}{E} \right]$$

$$= 1.0 \left[0.12 + (0.12 - 0.06)\frac{\$50.00}{\$50.00} \right]$$

$$= 0.18$$

$$= 18\%$$

[3]Appendix 10A at the end of this chapter explains the development of Equation 10–2.

If the debt-to-equity ratio increased from 1:1 to 2:1, the growth rate of assets would be 24 percent.

$$g = 1.0 \left[0.12 + (0.12 - 0.06) \frac{\$100.00}{\$50.00} \right]$$

$$= 0.24$$

$$= 24\%$$

Increasing the debt-to-equity ratio to 3:1 would result in a growth rate of 30 percent.

Financial Leverage and Earnings per Share So far, this discussion of financial leverage has concentrated on the growth of assets; but financial leverage also has a marked effect on earnings per share. Financial leverage increases the volatility of earnings per share and the financial risk of the firm. Both these effects are illustrated in Table 10–6, which shows three companies with different proportions of financial leverage. The proportions of leverage are indicated by the debt-to-equity ratios. Company A has no financial leverage; it is financed entirely by common stock and has a debt-to-equity ratio of 0:1. Company B is financed equally by debt and equity and so has a debt-to-equity ratio of 1:1. Finally, Company C has a 4:1 debt-to-equity ratio, which indicates that it is highly leveraged.

Earnings per share for the companies are calculated in the following manner: Interest payments, which amount to $1 per bond, are deducted from earnings, and the remainder is divided by the number of shares of common stock outstanding. If each company earned $100 before interest, their respective shareholders would earn $1 per share, calculated as follows.

	Company A	Company B	Company C
Earnings before interest	$100	$100	$100
Less: Interest payments	− 0	− 50	− 80
Equals: Earnings after interest	$100	$ 50	$ 20
Divided by: Number of shares	÷ 100	÷ 50	÷ 20
Equals: Earnings per share	$1	$1	$1

Financial leverage boosts *EPS* when earnings before interest payments increase. If earnings before interest increased from $100 to $200, for example, earnings would be $2 per share for Company A, $3 per share for Company B, and $6 per share for Company C. As long as total earnings are increasing, financial leverage has a beneficial effect on earnings per share.

We know, however, that business conditions are cyclical, and what goes up must come down. Unfortunately, financial leverage also magnifies the effects of lower earnings or losses on earnings per share. As Table 10–6 shows, if total earnings before interest payments declined from $100 to $50, Company A's shareholders would earn $0.50 per share; Company B's would

Table 10–6
Financial Leverage and *EPS*

	Company A	Company B	Company C
Number of shares of stock (equity)	100	50	20
Number of bonds (debt)	0	50	80
Debt-to-equity ratio	0/1	1/1	4/1
Fixed interest charges ($1/bond)	0	$50	$80
Earnings per share			
with earnings before interest of $100	$1.00	1.00	1.00
with earnings before interest of $200	$2.00	$3.00	$6.00
with earnings before interest of $50	$0.50	$0.00	Deficit of $1.50 per share

earn nothing; and Company C, with a $30 deficit, would not be able to cover its interest payments. In that case, the firm would go bankrupt.

This example demonstrates the fact that financial leverage is a double-edged sword. When earnings before interest payments increase 100 percent, Company C's earnings increase 600 percent. However, when earnings before interest payments decline 50 percent, Company C is unable to meet its financial obligations and may be forced into bankruptcy.

The sort of information given in Table 10–6 can be presented graphically in what is commonly called an **EBIT-EPS chart**, which relates earnings before interest and taxes (*EBIT*) to earnings per share (*EPS*). *EBIT-EPS* charts are used to evaluate the impact on earnings of various capital structures. The relationship between earnings per share and earnings before interest and taxes is defined as follows.

$$EPS = \frac{(EBIT - \text{Interest expense})(1 - \text{Tax rate}) - \text{Preferred dividends}}{\text{Number of shares of common stock outstanding}}$$

(10–3)

The examples we have considered so far have included no taxes and no preferred dividends. Nevertheless, Equation 10–3 can be applied to them.

The data concerning *EPS* and *EBIT* from Table 10–6 are plotted in Figure 10–3. (Table 10–6 used the term *earnings before interest* instead of *earnings before interest and taxes* because we assumed there were no taxes.) Notice that the relationship between *EPS* and *EBIT* for each firm's method of financing is a straight line. We can plot such a line by determining any two of its points. It is common practice to place one of those points where earnings per share equal zero. This point is also called the **break-even EBIT**. It can be determined

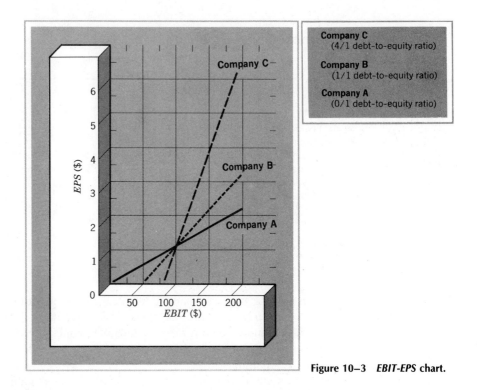

Figure 10–3   *EBIT-EPS* chart.

by setting earnings per share equal to the after-tax expense plus the preferred dividend payments.

Break-even *EBIT* = Interest expense + [Preferred dividends/(1 − Tax rate)]

(10–4)

Although preferred dividends are a financial obligation of the firm, they are not a tax-deductible expense. That is why an adjustment is made to put them on a pretax basis.

Figure 10–3 shows that when *EBIT* is less than $100, the shareholders of Company A and Company B have higher earnings per share than those of the highly leveraged Company C. However, when *EBIT* exceeds $100, the shareholders of the highly leveraged Company C are better off than those of Companies A and B.

Management can use such analyses as an aid to decision making. Suppose, for example, that the management of our hypothetical firm considered A, B, and C in Figure 10–3 as three options for the firm's target capital structure. If management believed that earnings over $100 were more likely than earnings under $100, it could maximize the value of the firm—albeit with greater financial risk—by using more financial leverage. On the other hand, if earnings less than $100 were considered more likely, management could choose an all-equity capital structure.

Growth, Financial The combined effects of financial leverage and dividend policy on the growth
Leverage, and rate of assets for Companies A, B, and C are shown in Table 10–7. An
Dividends examination of the data reveals that growth rates increase as the percent of
earnings retained and financial leverage increase. If no earnings are retained
(b = 0), the growth rate of assets is zero no matter how much financial
leverage is involved! If the retention rate is 25 percent, growth rates range
from 3 percent for Company A, which is financed entirely with equity, to 9
percent for Company C, which has a 4:1 debt-to-equity ratio. The growth rates
in the table were determined by use of Equation 10–2 under the assumptions
that r equals 12 percent and i equals 6 percent. For example, the growth rate
for Company C when the retention rate is 25 percent is as follows.

$$g = b \left[r + (r - i) \frac{L}{E} \right]$$

$$= 0.25 \left[0.12 + (0.12 - 0.06) \frac{4}{1} \right]$$

$$= 0.09$$

$$= 9\%$$

When all the earnings are retained (that is, when b equals 1), the growth rate
of assets ranges from 12 percent for Company A to 36 percent for Company C.

The same relationships are depicted graphically in Figure 10–4. The assets
at the beginning of the year are $100. The upward-sweeping line represents
the assets at the end of one year when various debt-to-equity ratios are used.
Figure 10–4 shows the dramatic effect of very high debt-to-equity ratios on
the growth rate of assets. If the ratio is 9:1, the assets will be $166 at the end
of one year.

The price to be paid for growth with leverage is high financial risk—the risk
that the firm may not be able to meet its financial obligations. Some firms are
willing to take on such risk. According to *RMA Annual Statement Studies*, for

Table 10–7
Growth, Financial Leverage, and Dividends

	Growth Rate of Assets, g		
Percent of Earnings Retained, b	**Company A (0:1 Debt-to-Equity Ratio)**	**Company B (1:1 Debt-to-Equity Ratio)**	**Company C (4:1 Debt-to-Equity Ratio)**
0.00%	0.00%	0.00%	0.00%
0.25	3.00	4.50	9.00
0.50	6.00	9.00	18.00
0.75	9.00	13.50	24.00
1.00	12.00	18.00	36.00

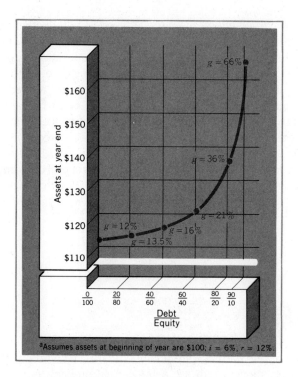

Figure 10–4   Assets and financial leverage.

example, in one recent year small firms (those with assets up to $250,000) in the metal stamping industry had debt-to-equity ratios of 27:1, while larger firms in this industry (those with assets of $250,000 to $1 million) had ratios of 3:1. Similarly, small manufacturers of cutlery and hand tools had debt-to-equity ratios of 18:1 and larger firms had ratios of 2.3:1. If the revenues of the highly leveraged firms decline, they may not be able to cover their financial obligations and may as a result go bankrupt.

Simulating Growth[4]

One way to observe the effects of leverage and dividend policy on the growth of firms is to simulate them—that is, run an experiment trying various combinations of dividend policies and leverage for a number of hypothetical firms

[4]This portion of the chapter is based on Benton E. Gup, "The Financial Consequences of Corporate Growth," *Journal of Finance,* December 1980, pp. 1257–1265.

over a long period of time. To perform such an experiment, it is necessary to establish values for each of the variables in the following equation.

$$g = b(1 - t)\left[r + (r - i)\frac{L}{E}\right] \qquad (10\text{--}5)$$

where

g = Growth rate of assets after taxes
b = Proportion of earnings retained after cash dividends
t = Income tax rate
i = Interest rate on borrowed funds
r = Operating return on assets
L = Total liabilities
E = Total equity

The astute reader will recognize that the only difference between this equation and Equation 10–2 is the addition of an income tax factor $(1 - t)$.[5] This model includes variables that are influenced by management (b, L/E, and r), as well as externally controlled variables (t and i). It can be used to determine the after-tax growth rate of a firm in any period, assuming that the debt-to-equity ratio remains constant during that period.

A simulation involving 50 hypothetical firms was performed using the variables listed in Table 10–8. As you can see, the proportion of earnings retained ranged from zero to all earnings, taxes varied from 30 percent to 50 percent, and so on.

A total of 250 simulations were run for each of 50 firms in a hypothetical industry. In each of the simulation runs, values for the variables were selected at random from the data presented in Table 10–8. The results of the simulations revealed that the fastest-growing firms had higher retention rates (r), higher returns on assets (r), and higher financial leverage (L/E) than firms that grew at a slower pace. This is what we would expect based on the information presented earlier in the chapter.

Table 10–8
Parameters for the Model

Variables	Values		
	Minimum	Most Likely	Maximum
b	0.00	0.60	1.00
t	0.30	0.40	0.50
r	0.04	0.08	0.12
i	0.03	0.05	0.08
L/E	0.80	1.40	3.00

[5]Appendix 10A shows how this equation is developed.

Personal Financial Leverage

Investors can incur some of the benefits—and risks—associated with financial leverage by borrowing funds to buy securities. To illustrate how this works, assume that an investor wants to buy shares of Company A for $100 each. Company A is financed entirely by equity and pays no cash dividends. The return on assets is 12 percent, so the stock is worth $112 at the end of 1 year. If the investor sells the stock at the end of 1 year, the gain will be $12. (If the stock had paid cash dividends, they would be considered part of the return.)

The rate of return on the investor's equity investment depends on the proportion of funds that are borrowed. If the investor finances the entire purchase with equity, the rate of return is 12 percent ($12 gain/$100 initial investment = 12%). However, if the investor borrows 50 percent of the initial investment and if the interest cost is 6 percent of the borrowed funds, the investor's rate of return on equity is 18 percent.

Profit from sale of stock	$12.00
Less: Interest on borrowed funds (0.06 × $50.00)	3.00
	$ 9.00
Divided by: Equity investment	÷$50.00
Equals: Rate of return on equity	18%

Similarly, if the investor borrows 90 percent of the funds, the rate of return on equity is 66 percent.

Profit from sale of stock	$12.00
Less: Interest on borrowed funds (0.06 × $90.00)	5.40
	$ 6.60
Divided by: Equity Investment	÷$10.00
Equals: Rate of return on equity	66%

Thus, investors can use personal borrowing power to achieve about the same effects of leverage as a corporation can achieve.

The practice of borrowing money to buy securities is widespread in the stockbrokerage industry. Investors can borrow funds from stockbrokerages or other financial institutions by opening **margin accounts**. The proportion of funds that can be borrowed is determined by the Board of Governors of the Federal Reserve System. At present, the margin requirement is 50 percent. That means investors must deposit 50 percent of the value of the securities they purchase in the margin account. If they buy $10,000 worth of stock, for example, they must deposit $5,000 cash (or $10,000 worth of eligible securities for collateral).[6]

[6]For additional information on margin accounts, see Benton E. Gup, *The Basics of Investing* 3rd ed., (New York: Wiley, 1986), Chapter 6.

Table 10–9
Summary of Equations

	Equation	Equation Number
Profit	Profit = Revenue − Cost	(10–1)
Growth of assets[a]	$g = b \left[r + (r - i) \dfrac{L}{E} \right]$	(10–2)
Earnings per share (EPS)	$EPS = \dfrac{(EBIT - \text{Interest expense})(1 - \text{Tax rate}) - \text{Preferred dividends}}{\text{Number of shares of common stock outstanding}}$	(10–3)
Breakeven EBIT	Breakeven $EBIT$ = Interest expense + [Preferred dividends/(1 − Tax rate)]	(10–4)
Growth of assets with taxes taken into account[a]	$g = b (1 - t) \left[r + (r - i) \dfrac{L}{E} \right]$	(10–5)

[a]Appendix 10A explains the development of Equations 10–2 and 10–5.

Summary

In the early phases of the life cycle, survival is the rationale for a firm, and survival demands rapid growth. Financial leverage allows firms to expand their productive capacities faster and gain experience, which lowers their costs and enhances their profits.

The growth rate of assets depends on the degree of financial leverage and the proportion of earnings retained. (The formula for determining growth rates, along with other equations introduced in the chapter, is presented again in Table 10–9.) If no earnings are retained, there will be no growth of assets no matter what degree of financial leverage is used. The maximum rate of growth is obtained when all earnings are retained and there is a high degree of financial leverage. However, a high degree of financial leverage also means a high degree of financial risk. Financial leverage is like a double-edged sword that magnifies earnings in good times and cuts them down in bad times.

Investors can create their own financial leverage by borrowing funds to buy securities. This process may increase the investor's wealth and financial risk, but it has no impact on corporate growth.

Important Terms

Break-even *EBIT*   Dividend payout ratio
Debt-to-equity ratio   Earnings per share (*EPS*)

EBIT-EPS chart

Experience

Financial leverage

Growth

Learning curve

Learning rate

Margin account

Operating return on assets

Development of Equations 10–2 and 10–5

As noted in the chapter, Equations 10–2 and 10–5 are identical except for the inclusion of an income tax factor in Equation 10–5. The explanation that follows includes the tax factor but otherwise applies equally to both equations.

Definition of Terms

A = Total assets
L = Total liabilities
E = Stockholders' equity
L/E = Debt-to-equity ratio
I = Interest payments
i = Interest rate on borrowings
$$i = \frac{I}{L}$$

PBT = Profit before taxes
t = Income tax rate
$$t = \frac{\text{Taxes (\$)}}{PBT}$$

NI = Net income or loss after taxes
$$NI = (1 - t)(PBT)$$
b = Percent of net income retained by the firm after cash dividend payment
r = Operating return on assets
$$r = \frac{PBT + I}{A}$$

Development of the Equations

1. By definition, assets equal liabilities plus stockholders' equity.

$$A = L + E$$

2. Profits can be expressed as follows.

$$PBT = rA - iL$$

3. Because $A + L = E$, profits can also be expressed in the two following ways.

$$PBT = r(L + E) - iL$$

or

$$PBT = \left[r + (r - i)\frac{L}{E} \right]E$$

4. Profits after taxes can also be expressed in two ways.

$$NI = (1 - t)(PBT)$$

or

$$NI = (1 - t)\left[r + (r - i)\frac{L}{E} \right]E$$

5. The rate of return on equity is as follows.

$$\frac{NI}{E} = (1 - t)\left[(r - i)\frac{L}{E} \right]$$

6. As long as the debt-to-equity ratio (L/E) remains constant, the company's assets, profits, and dividends will grow at the following rate.

$$g = b(1 - t)\left[r + (r - i)\frac{L}{E} \right]$$

7. Alternately, where there is no debt or tax, g may be expressed as

$$g = br$$

if b and r remain constant over time.

Questions

1. Why is growth important for survival? Use the concept of the life cycle in your answer.
2. What does a learning curve illustrate? What is meant by a 70 percent learning rate?

3. Why can the use of leverage to achieve asset expansion be in the shareholders' best interests?
4. What changes in the use of leverage and in dividend policy usually occur over the course of a firm's life cycle?
5. Under what circumstances is the growth rate in assets equal to the operating return on assets?
6. All else being equal, what happens to the growth rate in assets if a firm increases its dividend payout? Why?
7. All else being equal, what happens to the growth rate in assets if a firm decreases its debt-to-equity ratio? Why?
8. What does it mean to say that financial leverage is a double-edged sword?
9. What is illustrated in an *EBIT-EPS* chart? How can such charts be used to assist management in making capital structure decisions?
10. In calculating the level of *EBIT* at which *EPS* is 0, what adjustment must be made to allow for the impact of preferred stock adequately? Why?
11. Define the phrase *personal financial leverage*. How is personal financial leverage implemented by an investor?
12. What is meant by a 50 percent margin requirement?

Problems

1. Vitex Corporation has gathered the following data about production costs for its major product

Year	Production Volume	Unit Cost
1985	100,000 units	$10.00
1988	200,000 units	7.00
1990	400,000 units	4.90

   (a) What is the learning rate?
   (b) At this rate, what will unit costs be after output has increased to 800,000 units?

2. Astro Limited is attempting to restore its records, which were damaged in a fire. The following information has been salvaged. Based on principles of the learning curve, fill in the missing data.

Year	Production Volume	Unit Cost
1985	8 million	$8.00
1986	16 million	7.20
1993	?	5.25
1995	256 million	?

3. If a firm financed completely by equity retains all of its earnings, what growth rates will it achieve if its operating return on assets is 15 percent; 20 percent? Assume no taxes.

4. The following firms are financed completely by equity. Which can expect the highest asset growth rate? Assume no taxes.

Firm	Dividend Payout Ratio	Operating Return on Assets
A	0.0	9%
B	0.2	12
C	0.4	15
D	1.0	20

5. Martha Miller is interested in investing in firms with superior growth prospects. Assuming no taxes, rank the following firms according to their anticipated asset growth. All firms are 100 percent equity-financed.

Firm	Dividend Payout Ratio	Operating Return on Assets
Mince Motors	0.65	10%
Elton Engines	0.85	20
Oregon Oboes	0.8	8
Richardson Rafts	0.36	14

6. Compute the asset size of a firm financed completely by equity after 5 years if total assets are now $150 million, the rate if retention is 60 percent, and the operating rate of return is 15 percent. Assume no taxes and no change in the rate of return and rate of retention.

7. (a) Suppose, instead, that the firm in Problem 6 changes its rate of retention in Years 4 and 5 to 80 percent. Compute total asset size at the end of 5 years.
   (b) Suppose the rate of retention in Years 4 and 5 falls to 30 percent. Compute total asset size at the end of 5 years.

8. Bamboo Corporation, a firm financed completely by equity, wishes to reach $30 million in total assets in 4 years. Total assets are now $20.5 million. What minimum retention rate will be necessary to achieve this goal if operating return on assets is 20 percent; 15 percent; 25 percent? Assume no taxes.

9. Concord Caulk Company is currently financed completely by equity and earns a 16 percent operating return on assets. To overtake the competition, Concord would like to achieve a 30 percent growth rate next year. It can borrow at 10 percent if management chooses to use financial leverage. Assume no taxes and that the firm pays no dividends.
   (a) What debt-to-equity ratio will be necessary to achieve the desired growth rate?
   (b) What if Concord wanted both to achieve the 30 percent growth rate and to pay 50 percent of its earnings in dividends. What debt-to-equity ratio would be necessary?

10. The management of Hudson Paint has collected the following information. Assume no taxes.

Earnings after interest	$80 million
Shares of stock outstanding	10 million
Dividends per share	$ 4
Operating return on assets	11.2%
Debt	$400 million
Equity	$600 million
Interest rate on debt	8%

   (a) If none of the firm's financial policies change, what growth rate can be achieved?
   (b) Suppose dividends increase to $6 per share. What growth rate can be achieved?
   (c) Suppose, instead, that dividends remain at $4 per share but that the firm has $500 million in debt and $500 million in equity. What growth rate can be achieved?

11. The management of Hookham Horns, Inc., believes the firm is entering a new stage of the life cycle. Assume to taxes.

Earnings after interest	$200 million
Shares of stock outstanding	50 million

Dividends per share	$3
Operating return on assets	10.3%
Debt	$1200 million (1.2 billion)
Equity	$1800 million
Interest rate on debt	9%

(a) Under the current situation, what growth rate can be achieved?

(b) Suppose dividends decrease to $2 per share. What growth rate can be achieved?

(c) Suppose, instead, that dividends remain at $3 per share but that the firm has $2 billion in debt and $1 billion in equity. What growth rate can be achieved?

(d) What tradeoffs for shareholders are involved in trying to increase the growth rate by cutting the dividend or increasing the amount of debt used?

12. Kelloy Company is incorporating and its managers are considering three financing plans. The firm's tax rate is 30 percent.

	Plan 1	Plan 2	Plan 3
Stock ($10 per share)	1 million shares	800,000 shares	600,000 shares
Debt (10% interest)	$0	$2 million	$4 million

Compute earnings per share for each plan if the expected *EBIT* for Kelloy is $500,000.

13. (a) Using the information about Kelloy Company in Problem 12, compute for each plan the level of *EBIT* at which *EPS* would be zero.

(b) Calculate *EPS* for each plan if *EBIT* is expected to be $1 million; 1.5 million.

(c) Prepare an *EBIT-EPS* chart based on your findings.

(d) Which plan would you choose if *EBIT* is expected to be $100,000; $600,000; $1,200,000?

 14. Chandler Paper Company is looking at alternative financial structures. Currently it uses 25 percent debt, but its investment bankers have suggested two additional plans for management's consideration. The firm's tax rate is 40 percent.

	Current	Plan 1	Plan 2
Common			
Stock ($100 per share)	$6 million	$6 million	$6 million
Debt	$2 million (12%)	$1 million (10%)	$0
Preferred stock	$0	$1 million (12%)	$2 million (10%)

(a) Calculate *EPS* for each plan if *EBIT* is $350,000; $800,000.

(b) For each plan, calculate the level of *EBIT* at which *EPS* is 0.

(c) Prepare an *EBIT/EPS* graph.

(d) Formulate a recommendation to assist management in choosing among the plans.

15. Amherst Associates is considering two financial plans. Its tax rate is 40 percent.

	Plan 1	Plan 2
Common stock ($20 per share)	10,000 shares	8,000 shares
Debt	$800,000 (15%)	$1 million (15%)
Preferred stock	$1,000,000 (15%)	$1.2 million (15%)

(a) Compute *EPS* for each plan if *EBIT* is $600,000.

(b) Find the level of *EBIT* at which *EPS* for each plan is 0.

(c) Graphically illustrate your results.

(d) Under what circumstances would each plan be best?

16. From the library, obtain financial information from last year for a firm whose stock is traded on the New York Stock Exchange. (*Hint*: Estimate the firm's tax rate by dividing taxes paid by taxable income.)

(a) Calculate *EPS* if the firm's *EBIT* had been 20 percent greater than it actually was.

(b) Calculate *EPS* if the firm's *EBIT* had been 20 percent less than it actually was.

(c) Graph the *EBIT-EPS* relationship for the firm.

(d) Assuming no change in the firm's current financial policies, what growth rate in assets would you expect over the next year?

17. Titan Tools has recently reorganized in order to specialize in gardening equipment. Two new financing plans are under consideration. The tax rate is 30 percent.

Plan A: 100,000 shares of common stock to be sold at $4 per share; $800,000 debt at a 12% interest rate.

Plan B: 200,000 shares of common stock to be sold at $4 per share; $400,000 in loans at an 11% interest rate.

The following estimates have been prepared by the marketing department:

State of the Economy	Probability	EBIT
Poor	0.2	$ 80,000
Average	0.6	140,000
Good	0.2	200,000

(a) At the expected level of *EBIT*, what is *EPS* under the two financing plans?

(b) At what level of *EBIT* would each plan produce an *EPS* of 0.

(c) Prepare an *EBIT-EPS* chart.

(d) Based on the expected level of *EBIT*, which plan would you recommend?

(e) If the probability for a good economy was 0.9 and the probability for an average economy was only 0.05, would your recommendation change? Why or why not?

18. The three owners of a new $30 million firm are arguing about the appropriate financing plan. One prefers 100 percent equity financing, to be accomplished through the sale of 1 million shares of stock at $30 per share. A second owner advocates using debt financing, on which the interest rate would be 14 percent; if this plan is followed, 30 percent of total financing will be through borrowing. The third owner is less conservative than the others and prefers that 60 percent of total financing come from borrowing. At this level of borrowing, the interest rate would be 16 percent.

(a) If *EBIT* is expected to $3.5 million in the first year and if the tax rate is 40 percent, calculate *EPS* under the three plans.

(b) Calculate *EPS* under each plan if *EBIT* is $2 million.

(c) Prepare an *EBIT-EPS* chart.

(d) With which owner do you agree? Why?

19. Esther Miller is planning to purchase a portfolio of common stock. If she borrows in order to increase the amount of stock she can purchase, she will have to pay 10 percent interest. The expected return on the stock she is considering is 14 percent. Assuming no taxes, what rate of return can Esther expect on her equity investment if she borrows $20,000 and invests in a portfolio with a total value of $60,000 at the beginning of the year?

20. Suppose, instead, that Esther Miller (in Problem 19) invested a total of $150,000 in common stock at the beginning of the year. If the margin requirement is 50 percent, how much of her own money was Esther required to invest? What is her expected rate of return on this money?

Dividend Policy

To pay dividends or not to pay dividends? That is the question examined in this chapter. There is no simple answer, because the dividend policy of a firm depends on the level of earnings, the desires of management and shareholders, the firm's position in the life cycle, and other factors.

Earnings can be used to pay cash dividends to shareholders or they can be retained and used to increase assets or retire debts. Thus, dividend policy affects capital structure, which is the subject of this part of the book.

From the shareholders' point of view, cash dividends are the only monetary returns received from a stock until it is sold. From management's point of view, earnings that are retained are an important source of funds. As explained in Chapter 10, earnings retained are a major determinant of the growth rate of assets. Are the shareholders and the firm better off if earnings are retained or paid out as cash dividends?

265

After reading this chapter, you should know the following.

1. Why there is disagreement about dividends' relevance to stock prices.
2. How dividend policies change over the life cycle of a firm.
3. Why paying cash dividends may be a sign of weakness.
4. Why stock dividends are like stock splits—or how to divide the pie into smaller pieces.
5. What some different ways to pay cash dividends are.
6. How some companies pay cash dividends and keep the cash.
7. What four dates investors should remember.

Dividend Policies and Stock Prices

The major objective of financial management is to maximize shareholders' wealth, or the market value of the stock. Do a firm's dividend policies affect the market value of its stock? Considerable academic debate has surrounded this question. One school of thought argues that dividends should be treated as **residuals**—that is, that they should be paid only if there is money left after all worthwhile investments have been made. This suggests that dividends are irrelevant to share prices, because shareholders, recognizing that retaining earnings will enhance the value of the firm, are indifferent between receiving cash dividends and selling their shares at higher prices. The other school of thought argues that cash dividends are relevant—that they are, in fact, the primary determinants of stock prices. We will examine both these points of view.

Modigliani and Miller You may remember reading about Franco Modigliani and Merton Miller in Chapter 7. They are the leading spokesmen for the school of thought that argues that dividends are irrelevant.[1] Stock prices, they believe, are determined solely by the earning power of a firm's assets and its investment policies, not by whether the fruits of the earning power are "packaged" as retained earnings or cash dividends. If earnings are retained, shares will appreciate in value and can be sold for a capital gain. Modigliani and Miller state that, in a world of certainty, with no income taxes, investors are indifferent between receiving current cash dividends and current capital gains.

However, Modigliani and Miller recognize that we live in a world where

[1]Merton H. Miller and Franco Modigliani, "Dividend Policy, Growth, and the Valuation of Shares," *Journal of Business,* October 1961, pp. 411–433.

taxes, as well as market imperfections such as stockbrokerage fees, do exist. Consequently, investors in high income tax brackets prefer to hold stocks that provide capital gains, which are taxed at relatively low rates. Capital gains taxes were eliminated by the Tax Reform Act of 1986. Nevertheless, the underlying concepts of trading off growth for cash dividends still apply. Investors in lower income tax brackets prefer to hold stocks that pay large cash dividends. This implies that corporations tend to attract **clienteles** of investors whose desires for cash dividends or capital gains match the policies of the firm. Accordingly, widows and orphans tend to invest in safe stocks that provide the steady income of dividends, and gamblers and high-tax-bracket shareholders speculate on stocks of high-growth companies that retain their earnings.

Another cornerstone of the Modigliani–Miller theory is that any positive effect dividend payments might have on share prices are exactly offset by negative effects that result from the need to find other means of financing. When earnings are paid out as cash dividends instead of being added to the firm's equity, the firm must obtain additional financing by selling more stocks or bonds. The sale of new common stock may decrease the proportionate claims of ownership of existing shareholders. The result is that the positive effects of dividends on share prices are counterbalanced by the dilution of shareholders' claims. Similarly, it can be argued that additional debt financing will have an adverse impact on share prices.

Modigliani and Miller recognize that changes in dividend rates are often followed by changes in share prices. They attribute this fact to the **informational content** of dividends. Suppose, for example, that a firm has a longstanding policy of paying a certain dividend rate. An increase in that rate is interpreted by investors as a signal that management expects profits to be higher in the future. The stock price changes because investors believe that expectations about earnings and growth opportunities have improved, not because the dividend rate has increased.

Walter's Formula James Walter developed a formula to demonstrate that dividend policy should be determined solely by the profitability of investment opportunities.[2] According to Walter, the price of one share of stock in a company with no debt or taxes is determined by the following equation.

$$P_0 = \frac{D + \dfrac{r}{k_e}(E - D)}{k_e} \tag{11–1}$$

[2]James E. Walter, "Dividend Policies and Common Stock Prices," *Journal of Finance*, March 1956, pp. 29–41. Notation has been changed for purposes of consistency in this book.

where

P_0 = Price per share at Time 0
D = Cash dividends per share
E = Earnings per share
r = Operating return on assets
k_e = Rate of return required by shareholders

According to Walter's formula, the optimal dividend policy is as follows: No dividends should be paid as long as the firm can earn an operating return on assets that is higher than the rate of return required by investors (k_e). However, if investors require a higher rate of return than the firm can earn on its investments, all the earnings should be distributed as cash dividends. To demonstrate how this works, we'll look first at a situation in which the operating return on assets does exceed the rate of return required by shareholders. For example, suppose a firm's operating return on assets is 12 percent, the rate of return required by investors (k_e) is 10 percent, and the earnings per share are $4. When a dividend ($D$) of $2 is paid, the price of one share of stock is $44.

$$P_0 = \frac{D + \dfrac{r}{k_e}(E - D)}{k_e}$$

$$= \frac{\$2 + \dfrac{0.12}{0.10}(\$4 - \$2)}{0.10}$$

$$= \$44$$

When no dividends are paid, however, the price per share is $48.

$$P_0 = \frac{\$0 + \dfrac{0.12}{0.10}(\$4 - \$0)}{0.10}$$

$$= \$48$$

Now let's assume the operating return on assets is less than shareholders' required rate of return. For example, suppose that r is 8 percent, k_e is 10 percent, and E is $4. When a dividend of $2 is paid, the price of one share of stock is $36.

$$P_0 = \frac{\$2 + \dfrac{0.08}{0.10}(\$4 - \$2)}{0.10}$$

$$= \$36$$

However, when all the earnings are paid out as cash dividends, the price of one share of stock is $40.

$$P_0 = \frac{\$4 + \dfrac{0.08}{0.10}(\$4 - \$4)}{0.10}$$

$$= \$40$$

Walter treats cash dividends as residuals determined by the investment op-portunities of the firm. They are not the determinant of the market price of the stock. Moreover, they are considered irrelevant because investors are assumed to be indifferent between receiving current dividends and receiving current capital gains.

The Gordon Model Myron J. Gordon is the leading spokesman for the school of thought that contends that cash dividends *are* relevant to stock prices. Indeed, according to Gordon, the value of stock is determined by the discounted value of ex-pected cash dividends.[3] You should be familiar with the Gordon model from Chapters 6 and 7. According to that model, the price of one share of common stock can be determined by the following equation.

$$P_0 = \frac{D_1}{k_e - g} \qquad (11-2)$$

where

P_0 = Price per share at Time 0
D_1 = Cash dividend in Period 1
k_e = Rate of return required by shareholders
g = Growth rate of dividends

The Gordon model bases stock price on dividends because dividends are the only cash returns shareholders receive until they sell the stock. The model assumes investors prefer to receive cash dividends now rather than a promise of cash some time in the future.

We have briefly considered both schools of thought on the relevancy of dividends. Which side is correct? The answer is that the jury is still debating

[3]Myron J. Gordon, *The Investment, Financing and Valuation of the Corporation* (Homewood, Ill.: Richard D. Irwin, 1962).

the issues. Both points of view are supported by studies.[4] No matter what these and other studies conclude, we cannot ignore the fact that corporations paid more than $79 billion in cash dividends in 1985 alone, accounting for 56 percent of corporate profits after taxes. Corporate financial managers must think dividends matter, or they wouldn't be paying that amount to stock-holders.

Life Cycle

A central question in the debate concerning dividends' effect on stock prices is whether shareholders prefer dividends or are indifferent between dividends and capital gains. To obtain another perspective on this question, let's look again at the life cycle. A typical life cycle is depicted in Figure 11–1. It shows that the financial practices of business concerns, including dividend policies, change as firms mature.

As you know, during the early phases of development, firms borrow heavily and retain their earnings to finance expansion. This is a period of uncertainty, because not all firms will survive to enter the stabilization phase. Investors recognize the business and financial risks inherent in the early phases of the life cycle and demand high returns.

As the life cycle unfolds, dependence on borrowed funds diminishes and the proportion of equity financing increases. Firms not only depend more on equity financing, they also begin paying cash dividends. Over time, the dividend payments tend to increase. Investors are aware of the reduced business and financial risk and accept "average" returns. During the later phases of the life cycle, dividend payments tend to be large as long as there are profits. There is no point in retaining earnings, because the firms are sliding into extinction.

Of course, the life cycle and financial policies just described are generalizations. Many firms extend their life cycles by adding new products and acquiring other companies. (Procter & Gamble and Gulf & Western Industries are two such firms.) However, it is clear that the dividend policies of firms in the pioneering phase of the life cycle may not be the same as those in the stabilization phase. During the pioneering phase, shareholders are willing to forgo dividends for capital gains. During the latter part of the stabilization phase, shareholders know that their returns must be cash dividends, because the future growth of the firm is limited at best and nonexistent at worst.

[4]Richard R. Pettit, "Dividend Announcements, Security Performance, and Capital Market Efficiency," *Journal of Finance*, December 1972, pp. 993–1007. The opposite view is represented by Marshall Blume, "Stock Returns and Dividend Yields: Some More Evidence," *Review of Economics and Statistics*, November 1980, pp. 567–577; and R. H. Litzenberger and K. Rama-swamy, "The Effects of Dividends on Common Stock Prices: Tax Effects or Information Effects," *Journal of Finance*, May 1982, pp. 429–443.

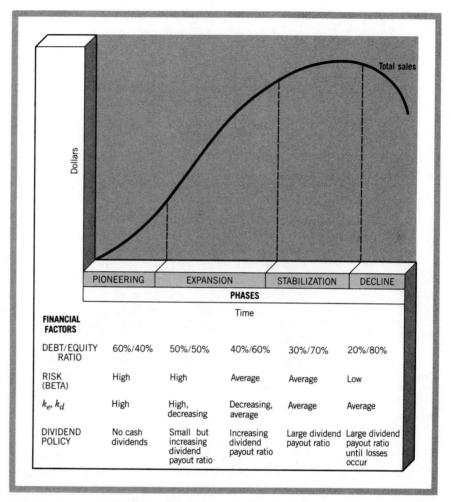

Figure 11–1   Life cycle, dividend policy, and other financial factors.

FINANCIAL FACTORS	PIONEERING	EXPANSION	STABILIZATION	DECLINE	
DEBT/EQUITY RATIO	60%/40%	50%/50%	40%/60%	30%/70%	20%/80%
RISK (BETA)	High	High	Average	Average	Low
k_e, k_d	High	High, decreasing	Decreasing, average	Average	Average
DIVIDEND POLICY	No cash dividends	Small but increasing dividend payout ratio	Increasing dividend payout ratio	Large dividend payout ratio	Large dividend payout ratio until losses occur

Other Factors Affecting Dividend Policies

So far, we have examined dividends from a theoretical point of view. However, legal and contractual obligations of business concerns also affect their cash dividend policies.

Legal Constraints   The legal aspects of dividend policy depend on the regulatory bodies that have jurisdiction over the corporation. In a world of multinational corporations, there are hundreds of regulatory bodies. Guidelines that apply to most domestic corporations are presented here.

Profits. In general, cash dividends must be paid from current earnings or from previous earnings that have been retained by the corporation and are listed on the balance sheet as retained earnings. Although most companies pay cash dividends from current earnings, it is possible to pay cash dividends that exceed current earnings. For example, a company earning $1.00 per share could pay a cash dividend of $1.50 per share by reducing its cash balance and retained earnings. One reason for paying dividends in excess of current earnings is to maintain a constant dividend when earnings decline on a temporary basis. (Constant dividends will be discussed later in this chapter.)

Protection of Capital. Most corporations are prohibited from paying cash dividends that will impair (that is, reduce the value of) their capital stock. **Capital stock** refers to the permanently invested equity capital of a corporation. In some states, the capital stock is defined as the par value of the common stock. In other states, capital stock includes capital surplus, the amount paid in excess of the par value of the stock.[5]

Suppose that the Bloch Company has total shareholders' equity of $4.3 million. The equity consists of 4 million shares of common stock, each with a par value of $1, and $300,000 in retained earnings. The company could pay cash dividends that would eliminate the $300,000 in retained earnings. However, it could not pay cash dividends that would reduce (impair) the $4 million in capital stock.

Of course, there are exceptions to the rule. One exception is the so-called **liquidating dividend**. Such dividends are paid when a firm is shrinking in size and converting its assets into cash so they may be used more effectively by the shareholders. In some states, liquidating dividends may be considered to impair capital stock. Paying this type of cash dividend may be a sign of financial weakness, suggesting the firm has nothing better to do with its money.

Insolvency. Most states prohibit corporations from paying cash dividends if they are insolvent. **Insolvent** is a legal term with two meanings. The first is that the company is unable to meet its current financial obligations and the second is that the fair value of the liabilities exceeds the value of the assets. The purpose of prohibiting cash dividend payments by insolvent firms is to protect the claims of creditors.

Excess Profits. As noted earlier, the retention of earnings may result in capital gains for shareholders, which are taxed at a lower rate than cash dividends.

---

[5]For additional information on this subject, see Paul M. Van Arsdell, *Corporate Finance, Policy, Planning, Administration* (New York: Ronald Press, 1968), Chapter 38.

Therefore, some shareholders may want a company to retain all its income. However, the Internal Revenue Code prohibits the retention of earnings in excess of the current and future needs of the corporation—that is, retention of earnings meant to help shareholders avoid paying ordinary income tax. The excess may be evidenced by large accumulations of cash and securities. Corporations that violate this prohibition are subject to an excess profits tax on their retained earnings.

Contractual Constraints Corporations enter various contractual agreements that may restrict their ability to pay cash dividends. Two examples of contractual constraints follow.

Restrictive Covenants. Bond contracts (called **indentures**) and bank loan agreements frequently contain clauses (called **restrictive covenants**) that prohibit the issuing corporation from taking certain actions. The covenants are meant to protect the lenders; for example, restrictive covenants may prohibit the corporation from issuing additional long-term debt or from paying cash dividends before a certain portion of the debt has been repaid.

Preferred Stock. Holders of preferred stock are entitled to receive their cash dividends before earnings are distributed to holders of common stock. If the corporate directors elect not to pay preferred stock dividends, none can be paid to common stock.

Noncash Dividends

Although cash is the most common type of dividend, it is only one of several types corporate directors may declare. Other types of dividends include stock dividends and stock splits, in which investors receive more shares in the company, and property dividends, in which they receive corporate assets.

Stock Dividends and Splits **Investor's Viewpoint.** From an investor's point of view, there is practically no difference between a **stock dividend** and a **stock split**. In both cases, the corporation gives the shareholder more shares of stock in the same company. Receiving either is analogous to owning a pie and cutting it into more slices. The overall size of the investor's share of the pie does not change, but the shareholder has more slices. For example, assume an investor owns one-tenth of the stock of a company that announces all shareholders will receive one additional share of stock for every share they hold. Now, the investor holds two-twentieths of the stock but is no better off than with one-tenth of it.

Some investors do not understand that after a stock dividend or split they simply have more paper representing the same proportionate share of ownership; rather, they believe their wealth has increased. One reason for the confusion is related to cash dividends. If the company continues to pay the same cash dividend per share, in addition to increasing the number of shares through a stock dividend or stock split, the investor will receive a greater monetary return on the stock. However, the investor is better off because the company has increased the cash dividends paid to common stock, not because more shares are held. To clarify this point, assume that in Year 1 a company has 100 shares of stock and pays $100 in dividends, amounting to dividends of $1 per share. In the following year, the company gives shareholders 100 additional shares of stock and increases dividends to $200. The increase permits the dividends per share to remain the same:

	Year 1	Year 2
Cash dividends	$100	$200
Number of shares	100	200
Dividends per share	$1	$1

The shareholder is better off because dividends have increased from $100 to $200, not because the number of shares has doubled.

Company's Viewpoint.   Companies that are growing rapidly generally prefer to retain earnings rather than pay them out as cash dividends to investors. In order to appease investors who want to share in the company's growth in earnings, the directors may give them more shares instead of cash. Share prices of growing companies tend to rise because earnings are increasing. The investors believe they are better off because they have more shares—not recognizing that they own the same proportion of the company.

Another reason for increasing the number of shares is to keep the price of the stock in the *popular trading range* of $30 to $60 per share. Some analysts believe that stocks in the popular trading range perform better than higher-priced stocks, because they appeal to small investors who can afford to buy 100 shares at $30 per share but cannot afford to buy 100 shares at $90 per share. Therefore, some companies use stock dividends and splits to keep their stock prices in the popular trading range. Suppose, for example, that a stock is currently selling at $90 per share and 100 shares of stock are outstanding. If the number of shares is doubled, the price of the stock will decline to $45 per share.

	Before Split	After Split
Price per share	$90	$45
Number of shares	100	200

Increasing the number of shares may have another stock market implication. It increases the *floating supply* of the stock—the average daily number of shares traded. Stocks with large floating supplies are frequently less volatile than those with *thin markets*, or small floating supplies. It is possible that a thin market will discourage *institutional investors*, financial institutions such as insurance companies, which trade large volumes of stock. Even if they find a company's stock attractive, they may not be able to invest in it if it has a thin market, because a large purchase or sale would distort the shares' price too much. Thus, increasing the number of shares may make the stock more attractive to institutional investors.

Finally, the increased number of shares may have some informational content. Some investors may believe the company is using stock dividends or splits to retain earnings and grow at a faster rate.

Technical Differences. There are some technical differences between stock dividends and stock splits. Stock dividends are usually expressed as a percentage—2 percent, 5 percent, 10 percent, and so on. For example, a shareholder who owns 100 shares when a 10 percent stock dividend is declared will receive an additional 10 shares of stock, but the proportionate share of ownership in the company will remain the same. Most stock dividends are for less than 25 percent.

When a company pays a stock dividend, it generally makes an accounting entry to decrease the retained earnings and increase the capital stock by a like amount. For example, the Nimbus Company has total equity of $500,000, consisting of 400,000 shares of $1 par value stock outstanding and $100,000 of retained earnings. If Nimbus declares a 10 percent stock dividend, the shares outstanding will increase by 40,000 to 440,000, and retained earnings will decline by $40,000 to $60,000.

Shareholders' Equity in Nimbus Company:	Before 10 percent Stock Dividend	After 10 percent Stock Dividend
Common stock (400,000 shares at $1 par value)	$400,000	$440,000
Retained Earnings	100,000	60,000
Total	$500,000	$500,000

The important point to recognize is that neither the total equity ($500,000) nor the investors' proportionate share of ownership has changed. An investor who owns 1 percent of the company (400 shares) before the stock dividend will still own 1 percent (440 shares) after the stock dividend.

Stock splits are usually expressed as 2 for 1, 3 for 1, or the like. After a 2 for 1 split, shareholders will have two shares of stock for every share previously held. When an investor is left with a fractional share, the company usually buys or sells it for the investor's convenience.

The difference between the stock dividend and the stock split is a matter of accounting entries. As shown in the previous example, when a company pays a stock dividend, it typically reduces retained earnings and increases capital stock by the same amount. When a stock is split, the dollar amount of the capital stock remains the same, but the number of shares is increased and the par value is reduced. For example, suppose the Nimbus Company had declared a 2 for 1 stock split instead of a stock dividend. The capital stock would have increased to 800,000 shares and the par value would have declined to $0.50 per share. No adjustment would have been made to retained earnings.

Shareholders' Equity in Nimbus Company	Before 2 for 1 Stock Split
Common stock (400,000 shares at $1 par value)	$400,000
Retained earnings	100,000
Total	$500,000

	After 2 for 1 Stock Split
Common stock (800,000 shares at $0.50 par value)	$400,000
Retained earnings	100,000
Total	$500,000

Reverse Splits.   One reason to split stock, you recall, is to get the price per share into the popular trading range. There are times when the price of the stock is low and may be increased by using a **reverse split**, in which the company reduces the capital stock to increase the price per share. Let's say Nimbus is selling at $8 per share and there are 800,000 shares of $0.50 par value stock outstanding. If Nimbus had a 2 for 1 reverse split, there would be 400,000 shares of $1 par value stock outstanding and the market value would increase to $16 per share. Notice that the total market value of the *firm* does not change but the market value per *share* increases as a result of the reverse split.

Shareholders' Equity in Nimbus Company	Before 2 for 1 Reverse Split	Market Value
Common stock (800,000 shares at $0.50 par value)	$400,000	At $8 per share, equals $6,400,000
Retained earnings	100,000	
Total	$500,000	

	After 2 for 1 Reverse Split	
Common stock (400,000 shares at $1 par value)	$400,000	At $16 per share, equals $6,400,000
Retained earnings	100,000	
Total	$500,000	

Property Dividends   **Property dividends** consist of assets of the corporation that are distributed to shareholders. The most common property dividend today is securities owned by the company. In 1962, for example, shareholders of E. I. du Pont de Nemours and Company were given shares of General Motors Corporation as a result of antitrust litigation. Some companies use property dividends to divest themselves of subsidiaries; this type of property dividend is commonly called a **spin-off**. During World War I, some companies distributed government savings bonds, called Liberty Bonds, as dividends. Other companies have distributed samples of liquor and cigarettes to advertise their products. Such practices are not common today.

Cash Dividends

As mentioned, **cash dividends** are the kind most commonly offered. Figure 11–2 diagrams four typical cash dividend policies, which will be illustrated with references to real companies.[6] Then other policies related to cash dividends will be briefly examined.

Constant Dividends Constant dividends stay the same size for long periods of time. Sun Chemical Corporation—a leading manufacturer of graphic arts equipment, inks, and other products—has paid constant cash dividends for long periods. During the period 1964 to 1976, for example, its earnings increased from $0.40 to $2.66 per share, but its cash dividend remained at $0.13 per share. Then Sun increased cash dividends and finally in 1981 began paying $0.48 per share, which is its current dividend.

Dividends That Change Periodically Russ Togs, Inc., a leading producer of women's and girls' clothing, provides an example of a company that makes periodic adjustments in cash dividends. Russ Togs paid $0.51 per share from 1974 to 1979; $0.59 from 1979 to 1980; and $0.67 for the next 2 years.

Some investors know when to expect such dividend increases, because many companies keep cash dividends within a range of dividend payout ratios. For example, a company may distribute between 30 percent and 50 percent of its earnings as cash dividends. Suppose the company earns $1 per share and pays a cash dividend of $0.50. The dividend payout ratio is 50 percent. If the dividend remains the same and earnings increase, the payout ratio will decline. When earnings are $1.66 per share, for example, the dividend payout ratio is 30 percent ($0.50/$1.66 = 0.30). This is the lower limit prescribed by the dividend policy; so investors will expect the company to increase its cash dividend to around $0.83 so that the payout ratio will be about 50 percent again ($0.83/$1.66 = 0.50).

Dividends That Change Cyclically Some companies respond to changing business conditions by increasing their cash dividends when earnings increase and cutting them when earnings decline. This is the pattern followed by Armco, Inc., the sixth largest U.S. steel producer. Earnings for steel producers tend to be cyclical, and Armco changes the amount of its cash dividend as earnings increase or decrease.

[6]Information on dividend policies is based on data from *Value Line Investment Survey*, a worthwhile publication readers should become familiar with. Similar information can be found in publications from Moody's Investor Service and Standard & Poor's Corporation.

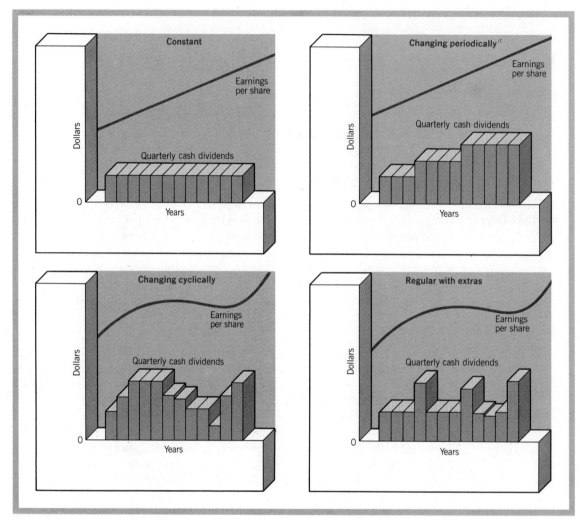

Figure 11–2   Selected cash dividend policies.

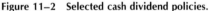

[a]The periodic changes can be increases or decreases.

Many companies try to maintain a relatively constant dividend payout ratio, which results in dividends' changing in amount from year to year. For example, a company may attempt to pay out 30 percent of earnings, regardless of how they fluctuate. Such a policy creates uncertainty for investors, because they do not know what cash dividends to expect. All other things being equal, then, it is riskier to invest in a company that follows such a policy than in one that follows a policy of paying constant dividends.

Regular Dividends with Extras   Another way to deal with cyclical earnings is to pay a regular cash dividend—that is, the dividend normally paid—plus an extra amount at the end of the year if earnings are good. General Motors has done this in the past, but the practice is not widespread.

Cash plus Stock As suggested earlier, some companies pay stock dividends or split their stock in addition to paying cash dividends. For example, Shoney's Inc., a restaurant chain located primarily in the southeastern United States, declared 4 for 3 stock splits in 1980, 1981, and 1983 and increased cash dividends in each of those years.

Dividend Reinvestment Plans One way companies can have their cake and eat it too is to offer a **dividend reinvestment plan (DRP)**. A *DRP* allows shareholders to buy newly issued shares in lieu of taking their cash dividends. The advantage to shareholders is that they need pay no stockbrokerage fees when they purchase the new issues. Some companies even offer the new shares at a discount from the market price to encourage participation in the *DRP*. However, the investors still must pay income tax on the dividends they would have received, unless the shares involved are public utility stocks. In that case, investors may exclude a certain amount of the value of the dividends they would have received from their taxable income.

The advantage of a *DRP* to the company is that it can declare large cash dividends and still retain a substantial portion of its earnings. One year, American Telephone and Telegraph Company declared cash dividends amounting to about $1 billion, but because of *DRPs* it reduced its actual payout ratio from 63.1 percent to 45.3 percent.[7] Similarly, Commonwealth Edison Company reduced its actual payout ratio from 88.1 percent to 67.4 percent. Thus, *DRPs* offer companies another source of new equity financing at a relatively low cost.

Stock Repurchases Sometimes companies repurchase their own common stock as an alternative to paying cash dividends. The effect of this policy is to reduce the number of shares outstanding and thus increase the price of the stock. As a result, investors will be able to sell their shares at a capital gain, which is taxed at a lower rate than the cash dividend they would otherwise have received.

These **stock repurchases** usually occur when a firm has an excess of funds and no profitable investment opportunities. However, companies also repurchase their own stock for other reasons. For example, a company may want the stock to offer to employees taking part in stock option plans or to acquire another company through an exchange of shares. Mortgage Trust of America announced that it would purchase shares from any shareholder with 20 shares or less in an effort to reduce the overhead of servicing small accounts. The offer to buy the shares—called a **tender offer**—was accepted by more than

[7]"Substituting Shares for Dividends," *Business Week*, August 27, 1979, p. 105.

7,000 shareholder accounts representing 54,000 shares.[8] Thus, the reader should not assume that stock repurchase is always a signal that a company's investment opportunities are limited.

Dividend Payment Procedures

The directors of a corporation are charged with the responsibility of making the formal decision to pay dividends. In the case of stock splits, their decision may be subject to shareholders' approval. Once the decision to pay a dividend has been made, four dates become important: date declared, date of record, ex-dividend date, and date payable.

The **date declared** is the date on which the directors of a company declare that a dividend is going to be paid. Such announcements are frequently reported in the financial press and elsewhere. Because dividends are usually paid on a quarterly basis, most investors know when to expect the announcement.

At the same time, the directors announce the **date of record**. Only shareholders whose names are recorded on the transfer books of the company on the date of record are entitled to receive the dividend. It generally takes four business days from the time an investor buys stock until his or her name is recorded on the company's transfer books. Therefore, a date four business days before the date of record is given to let potential buyers know if they will be eligible to receive the dividend. That date is known as the **ex-dividend date**. Investors who own the stock before the ex-dividend date are entitled to receive the dividend, because their names are on the company's books on the date of record. Those who buy the stock on or after the ex-dividend date are not entitled to the dividend, because there is not enough time to get their names on the books before the date of record. The **date payable** is the date on which the dividend is paid.

The time between the date declared and the date payable varies from company to company. The following dividend notices, adapted from the May 18, 1984, *Wall Street Journal*, illustrate various time spans:

> Del E. Webb Corporation declared its first quarterly dividend since 1980, of 5 cents, payable on July 2, 1984, to holders of record on June 1, 1984. Florida National Banks of Florida, Inc., announced a 3-for-2 stock split and a 12.5 percent increase in the quarterly dividend, bringing it to 18 cents per share (on new shares), payable June 29, 1984, to holders of record on June 12, 1984. Directors of National-Standard Company voted to pay a 10 cent quarterly dividend on July 3, 1984, to holders of record on June 14, 1984.

[8]Mortgage Trust of America, *Annual Report,* 1979, p. 4.

The ex-dividend dates do not appear in the dividend announcements, but notification that stocks have reached their ex-dividend dates can be found in the *Wall Street Journal* and other financial publications.

Summary

Considerable debate exists about the effect of cash dividends on stock prices. Modigliani and Miller argue that dividends are irrelevant and that the earning power of a firm determines stock prices, while Gordon argues that cash dividends determine stock prices. (Equations to illustrate both views are reviewed in Table 11–1.) Both camps make valid points. Examining the relationship between dividend policies and the life cycle of a firm adds another perspective to the debate. Various financial practices, including dividend policies, change over the life cycle. Thus, growth and enhanced earning power may be more important in early stages and dividends more important in later stages.

Legal and contractual obligations also affect dividend policies. Cash dividends are usually paid from current profits, although some firms pay dividends from retained earnings on a temporary basis. In general, firms are not permitted to impair their capital to pay dividends or to pay them when the firm is insolvent. In addition, contractual obligations associated with bonds and preferred stock may limit a firm's ability to pay cash dividends.

Although cash is the most common type of dividend, other types exist. They include stock dividends and stock splits, which do not increase investors' wealth, and property dividends. Stock dividends and splits may also be used in conjunction with cash dividends. Practices related to cash dividends include paying constant dividends, making periodic or cyclical changes in dividends, and paying regular dividends plus extras. In an attempt to reduce the amount of earnings paid out as cash dividends, some companies have instituted dividend reinvestment plans. Other companies have repurchased their own common stock.

Dividends are declared by the directors of the firm. The directors also establish the date of record and the date payable for the dividends. The ex-

Table 11–1
Summary of Equations

	Equations	Equation Number
Walter's formula	$P_0 = \dfrac{D + \dfrac{r}{k_e}(E - D)}{k_e}$	(11–1)
Gordon model	$P_0 = \dfrac{D_1}{k_e - g}$	(11–2)

dividend date tells investors whether they have purchased the stock far enough in advance of the date of record to receive the dividend.

Important Terms

Capital stock	Liquidating dividend
Cash dividend	Property dividend
Clientele	Residual
Date declared	Restrictive covenant
Date of record	Reverse split
Date payable	Spin-off
Dividend reinvestment plan (*DRP*)	Stock dividend
Ex-dividend date	Stock repurchase
Indenture	Stock split
Informational content	Tender offer
Insolvent	Thin market

Questions

1. Explain the concept of dividends as residuals.
2. According to Modigliani and Miller, how is dividend policy related to the idea of investor clienteles?
3. How do Modigliani and Miller explain the changes in stock prices that often accompany changes in dividends?
4. According to Walter's formula, what rule should firms follow in deciding on dividend policy? Why?
5. According to the Gordon model, what is the most important determinant in stock prices? Would Modigliani and Miller or Walter agree? Why or why not?
6. How does dividend policy change to accommodate the life cycle of the firm?
7. In general, what legal constraints are there on the payment of cash dividends?
8. What is a *liquidating dividend*?
9. How can creditors and preferred stockholders influence a firm's dividend policy?
10. What effect do stock dividends have on a shareholder's proportionate ownership in a company? What effect do they have on shareholders' wealth? Explain.
11. What significance do the terms *popular trading range* and *floating supply* have on firms' use of stock dividends?
12. In what ways do stock dividends and stock splits differ?
13. Why would a firm have a reverse split? What impact does such a move have on investors' wealth?
14. Compare the four major types of cash dividend policies.
15. Explain how a dividend reinvestment plan works. What advantages does it offer a firm and its stockholders?

16. Explain why a firm might choose to repurchase some of its shares. Is such a move a bad sign for remaining shareholders?

17. What are the four important dates in a typical dividend payment procedure? On which of these dates does the stock price change? How and why?

Problems

1. A firm has net income of $8 million and retains $5 million. With 200,000 shares outstanding, calculate the dividend per share and the payout ratio.

2. A firm earns $750,000 after taxes with 125,000 shares of common stock outstanding. Calculate dividends per share at a payout ratio of 20 pecent; 30 percent; 80 percent.

3. A firm earns $4 million in net income and has 600,000 shares outstanding. Calculate the payout ratio with dividends per share of $2.00; $3.00; $6.67.

4. The Gary Corporation's stock is now selling for 15-3/8. The firm has decided to establish a cash dividend of $1 per year, paid on a quarterly basis, with the first quarterly payment to holders of record on Friday, August 7. What date is the ex-dividend date?

5. The Wilson Corporation has announced a quarterly dividend of $0.80 to be paid to holders of record on Tuesday, May 19. What date is the ex-dividend date?

6. On January 14, Samuels Corporation announced a $1 dividend per share payable to holders of record on Wednesday, March 4. You own 40 shares of Samuels stock, purchased 10 shares at a time on January 16, February 11, February 25, and February 26. What total cash amount will you receive when the dividend is paid. Assume it is not leap year.

 7. Mansfield Dairies is using the Walter model in order to maximize the value of its stock. The firm's cost of equity capital is 14 percent and it can earn an operating return on assets of 16 percent. Earnings per share are $6.
(a) What is the market price if dividends are $4 per share?
(b) What is the market price if dividends are $2 per share?
(c) What dividend policy will maximize share price? Why?

8. Suppose, instead, that Mansfield Dairies in Problem 7 can earn an operating return on assets of 12 percent.
(a) What is the market price if dividends are $4 per share?
(b) What is the market price if dividends are $2 per share?
(c) What dividend policy will maximize share price? Why?

9. Port Henry Supply Company has a cost of equity capital of 12 percent and currently earns $2.40 per share. What dividend policy will maximize share price, according to the Walter model, if operating return on assets is 8 percent; 12 percent; 14 percent?

10. Salem China has just declared a 4 for 1 stock split. It will be cutting its cash dividend to one-quarter of the presplit amount. If you own 100 shares before the split and if cash dividends are $0.80 per share before the split, how many shares will you have after the split? If the firm does not increase its total dividends paid, will you be better off? Why or why not?

11. Suppose, instead, that the postsplit dividend per share for Salem China in Problem

10 will be one-third its presplit level. What total cash dividend will you expect to receive after the split? Will you be better of? Why or why not?

12. What stock split would result in the same number of shares outstanding as a 10 percent stock dividend; a 15 percent stock dividend?

13. Given the following information, show the impact of a 20 percent stock dividend versus a 6 for 5 stock split.

Common stock (par $10)	$1,000,000
Capital in excess of par	500,000
Retained earnings	2,000,000

14. Given the following information, show the impact of a 25 percent stock dividend versus a stock split that results in a comparable number of shares outstanding.

Common stock (par $4)	$ 8,000,000
Capital in Excess of par	5,000,000
Retained earnings	12,000,000

15. Fort Lewis Lumber earns $5.40 per share and has been paying $1.50 in dividends. If dividends increased to $1.60 per share and if a 5 percent stock dividend was paid, what total dividends would a shareholder receive if he owned 1,000 shares before the change? What would the payout ratio be after the change, assuming no immediate change in earnings?

16. Greenhunter Corporation had the following earnings pattern from 1985 to 1990

Year	EPS
1985	$2.40
1986	1.80
1987	2.80
1988	1.90
1989	2.20
1990	3.00

(a) Suppose Greenhunter followed a policy of paying 40 percent of earnings in dividends each year. Calculate dividends for each year over the period.
(b) Suppose, instead, the firm paid a regular dividend of $0.80 per share, plus 50 percent of any earnings over $2.00 per share. Calculate the yearly dividends.
(c) Which of the two policies do you think would have been better? Why?

17. Glenpool, Inc., recently had a 3 for 1 reverse stock split. Before the reverse split, its dividend per share was $1 and the price per share was $10. What was the price per share after the reverse split. If you owned 600 shares before the split and if dividends increased to $3 per share after the split, were you better off after the split? Why or why not?

18. Floyd Toy Company shows the following net worth accounts.

Common stock (par $1–2 million shares)	$2,000,000
Capital in Excess of par	3,400,000
Retained earnings	7,600,000

Show the effect of a 4 for 1 reverse split on the firm's books.

19. Fambon Scrap Iron Company has a dividend reinvestment plan. It currently pays 60 percent of earnings as cash dividends. But 40 percent of the dividends paid are reinvested by shareholders. If current earnings are $12 million, what is Fambon's actual cash payout ratio.

20. Refer to Problem 19. Suppose, instead, that Fambon's actual cash payout ratio after dividends are reinvested is 56 percent. What proportion of dividends are reinvested?

Every trade has its tools; in Part 5 we will examine the ones used for financial analysis and planning. Chapter 12 discusses break-even analysis, a technique that can be used in screening investment proposals and in financial analysis as well. Chapter 13 examines various ratios and other measures that are the standard tools of financial analysis. Anyone can calculate these measures, but it takes considerable skill and insight to *interpret* them. In that sense, financial analysis is more art than science. Financial planning is the focus of Chapter 14. This process includes preparing budgets and pro-forma financial statements and forecasting the financial needs of the firm.

Break-Even Analysis

The fleet of airliners flying domestic and international routes is aging and Boeing Company, a leading producer of commercial jet aircraft, is considering building a new model. To do so will require a more than $1 billion investment. Boeing wants to know how many airplanes must be sold for the company to break even. The term *break-even* refers to the level of sales at which revenues will equal total costs. Break-even analysis is one of several techniques that can be used to determine whether building a new jet is economically feasible. (Others include the net present value method and the internal rate of return method, discussed in Chapter 8.) Break-even analysis provides information about how many units must be sold in order for the company to break even, as well as how sensitive the break-even amount is to changes in sales prices and costs. It also provides information about the impact of investment proposals on earnings. Break-even analysis can be used as a screening device—that is, the first attempt to determine the economic feasibility of an investment proposal—as well as a tool for financial analysis. This chapter examines break-even analysis and some related topics.

After reading this chapter, you should know the following.

1. **What assumptions underlie break-even analysis.**
2. **What three methods can be used to determine the break-even quantity.**
3. **How to identify three types of leverage.**
4. **How investment proposals affect earnings.**
5. **How break-even and leverage analysis can be used in pricing decisions.**

Simplifying Assumptions

Our discussion of break-even analysis starts with certain simplifying assumptions that provide a common starting point for analyzing the relationships among prices, operating costs, and volume. Some of the simplifying assumptions are relaxed later in the chapter.

Prices The first assumption is that the selling price per unit is fixed. A simple example will help to illustrate some of the implications of this assumption. Assume that sweaters are selling for $10 apiece. As shown in Figure 12–1, if 5,000 sweaters are sold, total revenue will be $50,000. If 20,000 sweaters are sold, total revenue will be $200,000. The figure shows that total revenue increases by a constant proportion every time sales increase; therefore, total revenue appears as a straight line. This type of analysis is called **linear break-even analysis** because it is limited to straight lines. It should also be noted that break-even analysis as used here applies to a homogeneous product—sweaters in this example. However, break-even analysis can also be applied to multiproduct decisions.[1]

Fixed Operating Costs The second assumption is that fixed product costs exist and are independent of the number of units sold. Examples of **fixed costs** include the following.

Depreciation expense
Property taxes
Rent

---

[1] A break-even point expressed in terms of dollar sales rather than units sold can be determined for multiproduct firms. Such analysis generally assumes that the sales of all products increase or decrease proportionally, which may not be a valid assumption for many firms. Because this is an introductory text, the nature and limitations of multiproduct break-even models will not be covered.

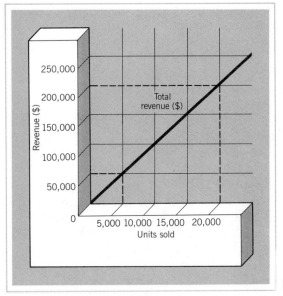

Figure 12–1 Sales revenue.

Administrative expense
Insurance expense

Fixed costs are represented by a horizontal line in Figure 12–2 because they do not change with volume. In this example, fixed costs are $50,000 no matter how many units are sold.

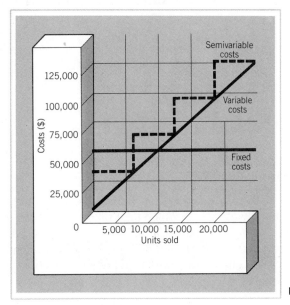

Figure 12–2 Operating costs.

Variable Operating Costs The third assumption is that variable production costs also exist and change in direct proportion to the number of units sold. **Variable costs** include the following.

Materials
Manufacturing supplies
Direct labor
Utilities
Maintenance
Sales commissions

As shown in Figure 12–2, variable costs are represented by a straight line that begins at the origin and slopes upward and to the right. When there are no sales, variable costs are zero. When 5,000 units are sold, variable costs are $25,000; and when 20,000 units are sold, variable costs are $100,000. Stated otherwise, the variable cost per unit is $5. The variable cost per unit is constant, but total variable costs increase as the number of units sold increases.

Semivariable Operating Costs Costs with the characteristics of both fixed and variable costs are called **semivariable costs**. For example, sales commissions may be fixed for a certain number of units sold and then increased for higher levels of sales. Thus, semivariable costs are represented by steps in Figure 12–2.

Throughout the rest of this chapter, for simplicity, we will consider only variable costs and fixed costs. Together, they equal total costs.

$$
\begin{array}{cccc}
\text{Total} & & \text{Variable} & \text{Fixed} \\
\text{operating costs} = & \text{operating cost per unit} & + & \text{operating cost} \\
& \text{times quantity of units sold} & & \\
\end{array}
$$

$$TC \quad = \quad VQ \quad + \quad F \qquad (12\text{–}1)$$

Determining the Break-Even Quantity

The **break-even quantity**—or the **break-even point**, as it is often called—is the quantity of sales at which total sales revenues are equal to total operating costs. At that volume of sales, there is neither a profit nor a loss; earnings before interest and taxes (*EBIT*) are zero. Two methods for determining the break-even quantity are presented here: the algebraic method and the graphic method.

Algebraic Method The algebraic method provides a convenient way to determine the break-even quantity and may also be used in further calculations. According to this method, the break-even quantity is determined by the following equation.[2]

$$BEQ = \frac{F}{P - V} \qquad (12\text{--}2)$$

where

BEQ = Break-even quantity
F = Fixed operating costs
P = Price per unit
V = Variable costs per unit

This equation tells us that the break-even quantity is equal to fixed operating costs divided by the unit price less the variable cost per unit ($P - V$). Sometimes unit price less unit variable cost ($P - V$) is called the unit **contribution margin**.

We will assume that the fixed operating cost F is $50,000, the price per unit P is $10, and the variable cost per unit V is $5. The break-even quantity is as follows.

$$BEQ = \frac{F}{P - V}$$

$$= \frac{\$50,000}{\$10 - \$5}$$

$$= \frac{\$50,000}{\$5}$$

$$= 10,000 \text{ units}$$

The break-even quantity—the quantity at which total revenue equals total

[2]At the break-even quantity, total revenue is equal to total costs.

$$(PQ) = F + (VQ)$$
$$(PQ) - (VQ) = F$$
$$Q(P - V) = F$$
$$BEQ = \frac{F}{P - V}$$

costs—is 10,000 units. If the firm sells fewer than 10,000 units, it suffers a loss. If it sells more than 10,000 units, the result is an operating profit.[3]

Graphic Method The break-even quantity can be determined by a graphic method as well. To use this method, we plot total revenue (price × quantity) and total cost (fixed

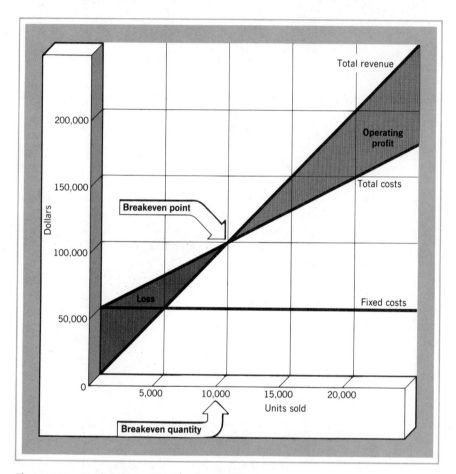

Figure 12–3   Break-even quantity in units: Graphic method.

[3]Because total revenue TR is equal to price times quantity PQ and total cost TC is equal to fixed costs plus variable costs ($F + VQ$), we can also say the following.

$$TR = TC$$
$$PQ = F + VQ$$
$$\$10Q = \$50,000 + \$5Q$$
$$\$5Q = \$50,000$$
$$Q = 10,000 \text{ units} = BEQ$$

cost + variable cost) on a graph. Figure 12–3 shows such a graph based on the assumptions already stated. Not surprisingly, it reveals that the break-even quantity is 10,000 units.

One advantage of the graphic method is that only a few calculations are needed to plot straight lines such as those depicted in Figure 12–3. Another advantage is that it is easier to make visual comparisons of charts than to evaluate figures. However, the graphic method lacks the precision of the algebraic method and it cannot be used in further calculations. Let's return to the algebraic method and examine its additional uses.

Additional Uses of the Algebraic Method

Sensitivity. The algebraic method can be used to determine how much the break-even quantity changes in response to changes in selling price or costs. As shown in Table 12–1, an increase in selling price results in a lowered break-even quantity and higher earnings before interest and taxes (*EBIT*). This, of course, assumes that the selling price increases while other factors remain constant. For example, if the selling price increases from $10 to $12 per unit and other factors remain the same, the break-even quantity declines from 10,000 to 7,143 units. Stated otherwise, a 20 percent increase in prices results in a 29 percent reduction in the break-even quantity.

$$BEQ = \frac{F}{P - V}$$

$$= \frac{\$50,000}{\$12 - \$5}$$

$$= \frac{\$50,000}{7}$$

$$= 7,143 \text{ units}$$

Reduced costs also lower the break-even quantity. Suppose that changes in technology permit the firm to lower variable costs from $5 to $4 per unit. In this case, the break-even quantity declines from 10,000 units to 8,333 units.

$$BEQ = \frac{F}{P - V}$$

$$= \frac{\$50,000}{\$10 - \$4}$$

$$= \frac{\$50,000}{\$6}$$

$$= 8,333 \text{ units}$$

Table 12–1

Effects on Break-Even Quantity of Changes in Price and Costs

	Price per Unit		Fixed Costs		Variable Costs	
	+	−	−	+	−	+
Break-even quantity	−	+	−	+	−	+
EBIT	+	−	+	−	+	−

Note: + = increase.
     − = decrease.

It follows that increases in costs and reductions in price will have the opposite effect. In any case, the algebraic method provides a convenient way to evaluate the impact of price and cost changes on the break-even quantity.

Break-Even Revenue.   Sometimes firms need to know the amount of revenue available at the break-even quantity. The **break-even revenue** is defined as the total revenue from sales available at the break-even quantity. Break-even revenue can be determined algebraically from the following equation.[4]

$$\text{Break-even revenue} = BEQ \times P \qquad (12\text{–}3)$$

where

BEQ = Break-even quantity
  P = Price per unit

Using the assumptions from previous examples, we will say that BEQ is 10,000 units and that P is $10. Accordingly, the break-even revenue is calculated as follows.

$$\text{Break-even revenue} = BEQ \times P$$

$$= 10,000 \times \$10$$

$$= \$100,000$$

Be careful not to confuse the break-even revenue with profit or *EBIT*. Recall that at the break-even quantity *EBIT* is equal to zero, whereas the break-even revenue in this example is $100,000. The difference can be demonstrated by subtracting fixed and variable costs from the break-even revenue.

[4]Break-even revenue can also be determined by the following equation.

$$\text{Break-even revenue} = \frac{F}{1 - \dfrac{V}{P}}$$

Revenue at break-even quantity	= $100,000
Less:	
Variable costs at break-even quantity (10,000 units)	− 50,000
Fixed costs	− 50,000
Equals: *EBIT*	$ 0

Nonlinear Break-Even Analysis As you recall, the previous examples assumed that revenues and costs maintain certain linear relationships. Now the assumptions that selling prices are fixed and that costs are constant for any level of production are relaxed. Relaxing these assumptions allows us to use **nonlinear break-even analysis**. We can view the world more realistically and take such things as quantity discounts and different technologies that affect costs into account.

In Figure 12–4, both revenues and total costs are nonlinear. In the top panel, total cost is nonlinear because variable costs change with the level of production. This type of pattern occurs when prices are reduced to increase sales and variable costs decline over a certain range of sales and then increase. The result is that there are two break-even quantities, a lower one and an upper one. The maximum profits are obtained when the difference between total revenue and total cost is greatest.

The lower panel of Figure 12–4 shows fixed costs increasing at certain levels of sales. Increases in fixed costs may be necessary when the company must buy additional equipment, build a new warehouse, add more delivery trucks, and incur other expenses necessary to service the higher level of sales.

Cash Break-Even Quantity The **cash break-even quantity** is basically the same as the break-even quantity already described except that only cash fixed costs are included in the break-even equation.

$$\text{Cash } BEQ = \frac{F_c}{P - V} \tag{12–4}$$

where

F_c = Cash fixed costs
P = Price per unit
V = Variable costs per unit

Cash fixed costs are always lower than regular fixed costs because they do not include noncash items such as depreciation. The result is that the cash break-even quantity is lower than the regular break-even quantity.

Cash break-even analysis assumes that all sales are made for cash, or at least that the level of accounts receivable is constant. Furthermore, both regular and cash break-even methods assume that inventory is constant. Cash

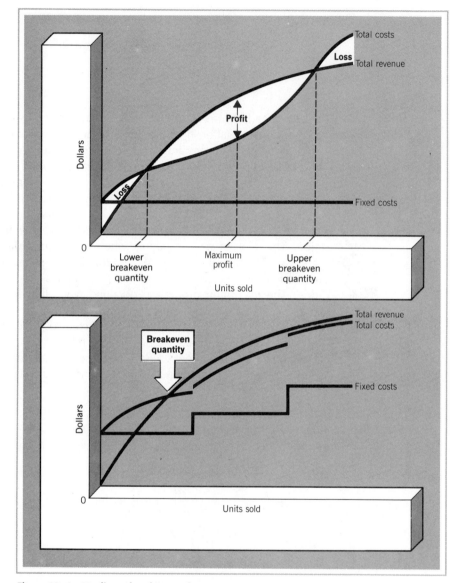

Figure 12–4   Nonlinear break-even charts.

break-even analysis is a useful tool for tying investment projects to a firm's cash budget and for determining the impact of projected sales and investments on the firm's liquidity. Unfortunately, the assumptions about constant accounts receivable and inventories tend to limit the accuracy of break-even analysis. No tool at our disposal is perfect, however, and we must use what we have.

stop

Investment Decisions and Leverage

Before deciding whether to build a new model of jet, Boeing wants to know the impact of the investment on its earnings, and break-even analysis is the starting point. A logical extension of break-even analysis involves leverage.

Total Leverage and Its Components

Total leverage is the product of operating leverage and financial leverage.

Total leverage = Operating leverage × Financial leverage

$$TL = OL \times FL \qquad (12\text{--}5)$$

As shown in Table 12–2, which depicts a simplified income statement, **operating leverage** is concerned with the relationship between sales revenues and earnings before interest and taxes (*EBIT*), while **financial leverage** is concerned with the relationship between *EBIT* and earnings per share (*EPS*). Total leverage, then, links sales revenues to earnings per share.

Operating leverage refers to the magnifying effect that changes in sales revenue can have on a firm's *EBIT* as a result of fixed costs, which were discussed earlier. If sales increase 10 percent and *EBIT* increases 100 percent, the firm is considered to be highly levered in terms of its operations. On the other hand, if earnings increase only 12 percent, the degree of operating leverage

Table 12–2
Leverage Related to Income Statement

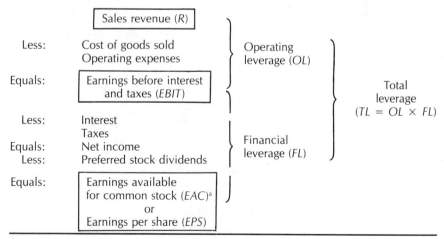

[a]Earnings available for common stock (*EAC*) is net income less preferred dividend payments and sinking fund payments (periodic payments made to retire debts). *EAC* divided by the average number of shares outstanding yields earnings per share (*EPS*).

is small. Operating leverage is important because it can be used to estimate the impact of investment decisions on earnings.

Degree of Operating Leverage The extent to which changes in sales revenues affect *EBIT* is measured by the **degree of operating leverage** (***DOL***)—the percentage change in *EBIT* that will result from a 1 percent change in sales revenue. It is determined by the following equation.[5]

$$DOL = \frac{R - (VQ)}{EBIT} \qquad (12-6)$$

where

R = Sales revenues
V = Variable costs per unit
Q = Quantity of units sold

To illustrate the use of this equation, we'll use the data presented in Table 12–3. The *DOL* for the firm described in the table is calculated as follows.

$$DOL = \frac{R - (VQ)}{EBIT}$$

$$= \frac{\$1000 - (\$10 \times 10)}{\$700}$$

$$= \frac{\$1000 - (\$100)}{\$700}$$

$$= 1.29$$

This means that for every 1 percent change in sales revenue, there will be a 1.29 percent change in *EBIT*. That is not much of an increase; this firm, because it has relatively low fixed operating costs, is considered a low-leverage firm. We will examine high-leverage firms later.

The *DOL* just computed applies only when sales revenue is $1,000. If sales

---

[5]The degree of operating leverage for a given level of revenue may also be determined by the following equation.

$$DOL = \frac{\text{Percent change in } EBIT}{\text{Percent change in sales revenue}}$$

Because the equation depends on *changes* in revenues, it can only be used to calculate the *DOL* for the base period. In contrast, Equation 12–6 can be used to calculate the *DOL* at any level of sales revenue.

Table 12–3
Data for a Low-Leverage Firm

Income and Expenses	Symbols	Amounts	Leverage Calculations	
Total revenue[a]	$R = P \times Q$	$1,000.00	$DOL = \dfrac{R - VQ}{EBIT}$	$DTL = DOL \times DFL$
Less:				$= (1.29)(1.05)$
Fixed operating costs	F	−200.00	$= \dfrac{\$1,000 - \$100}{\$700}$	$= 1.35.$
Variable costs[b]	VQ	−100.00		
Equals:			$= 1.286$	
			$\cong 1.29.$	
Earnings before interest and taxes	$EBIT$	$700.00		
Less:			$DFL = \dfrac{EBIT}{(EBIT - I) - PD/(1-t)}$	
Interest	I	−20.00		
		$680.00	$= \dfrac{\$700}{\$680 - \$10/(1 - 0.4)}$	
			$= 1.05.$	
Less:				
Taxes (40%)	t	−272.00		
Equals:				
Net income		$408.00		
Less:				
Dividends for preferred stock	PD	−10.00		
Equals				
Earnings available for common stock	EAC	$398.00		
Earnings per share (100 shares)	EPS	$3.98		

[a] P = $100 per unit; Q = 10.
[b] V = $10 per unit.

revenues change, the *DOL* changes. Suppose the quantity sold increases from 10 to 20, boosting sales revenues from $1,000 to $2,000.

Total revenue	R	$2,000
Less:		
Fixed operating cost	F	−200
Variable cost:	V	−200
Equals		
Earnings before interest and taxes	$EBIT$	$1,600

When sales revenues are $2,000, the *DOL* is as follows.

$$DOL = \frac{R - (VQ)}{EBIT}$$

$$= \frac{\$2,000 - (\$200)}{\$1,600}$$

$$= 1.125$$

Degree of Financial Leverage The concept of financial leverage was discussed in Chapter 10, where we examined its relationship to capital structure and growth. Now we examine it from a different perspective. The **degree of financial leverage (*DFL*)** measures the effect changes in *EBIT* will have on *EPS*. The *DFL* at a particular level of *EBIT* may be determined by the following equation.[6]

$$DFL = \frac{EBIT}{(EBIT - I) - PD/(1 - t)} \qquad (12\text{--}7)$$

where

I = Interest payments
PD = Dividends on preferred stock
t = Tax rate

Dividends for preferred stock are paid after income taxes: They are not deductible from income before taxes. Dividing *PD* by $(1 - t)$ puts these dividends on a pretax basis.

Again using data from Table 12–3, we can find the *DFL* for an *EBIT* of $700.

$$DFL = \frac{EBIT}{(EBIT - I) - PD/(1 - t)}$$

$$= \frac{\$700}{(\$700 - \$20) - \$10/(1 - 0.40)}$$

$$= 1.05$$

This means that a 1 percent change from the current level of *EBIT* will change *EPS* by 1.05 percent. Once again, keep in mind that this *DFL* only applies to one level of *EBIT*. If *EBIT* changes, *DFL* changes.

Degree of Total Leverage We know from Equation 12–5 that total leverage is the product of operating leverage times financial leverage. It follows that the **degree of total leverage** (**DTL**) for a given level of sales revenue is as follows.

$$DTL = \frac{R - (VQ)}{EBIT} \times \frac{EBIT}{(EBIT - I) - PD/(1 - t)}$$

$$= \frac{R - VQ}{(EBIT - I) - PD/(1 - t)} \qquad (12\text{--}8)$$

---

[6]The degree of financial leverage may also be determined by the following equation.

$$DFL = \frac{\text{Percent change in } EPS}{\text{Percent change in } EBIT}$$

Once again using data from Table 12–3, we can find *DTL* when sales revenues are $1,000.

$$DTL = \frac{R - (VQ)}{(EBIT - I) - PD/(1 - t)}$$

$$= \frac{\$1,000 - (\$100)}{(\$700 - \$20) - \$10/(1 - 0.40)}$$

$$= 1.35$$

Alternately, because we know the degrees of operating and financial leverage, we can find the degree of total leverage as follows.

$$DTL = DOL \times DFL$$

$$= (1.29)(1.05)$$

$$= 1.35$$

A 1 percent change in sales revenue (from $1,000) will result in a 1.35 percent change in earnings per share. What if sales revenues increase 100 percent? In that case, we would expect earnings per share to increase 135 percent. As shown in Table 12–4, a 100 percent increase in sales revenues (from $1,000) does produce a 135 percent increase in earnings per share for the low-leverage firm.

High Leverage versus Low Leverage The effects of higher levels of fixed expenses and other payments on the various degrees of leverage are summarized in Table 12–4. The low-leverage company is the same one we examined in the preceding example; its levels of fixed costs and payments are relatively low. The levels of fixed costs, interest payments, and dividends for preferred stock are substantially higher for the high-leverage firm. Accordingly, at a total revenue level of $1,000, the degree of operating leverage for the high-leverage firm is 4.5 and the degree of financial leverage is 3, giving a degree of total leverage of 13.5. This means that, as long as fixed costs and other payments remain constant, earnings per share will increase 13.5 percent for every 1 percent increase in sales revenue.

Recall from Chapter 10 that leverage is related to the growth rate of assets. Firms with high degrees of leverage can grow faster than similar firms with less leverage. However, as Chapter 10 illustrated, there are tradeoffs between leverage, growth, and risk.

Risk and Leverage The degrees of leverage are related to the degrees of risk a business concern faces. Operating leverage is related to business risk, which is inherent in a firm's investments and is reflected in changes in *EBIT*. If Boeing decides to

Table 12–4
Comparison of Firms with Low and High Leverage

Income and Expenses		Low-Leverage Firm		High-Leverage Firm	
		Level 1	Level 2	Level 1	Level 2
		100% increase		100% increase	
Total revenue[a]	$R = PQ$	$1000.00 ↑	$2000.00	$1000.00 ↑	$2000.00
Less:					
Fixed operating costs	F	200.00	200.00	700.00	700.00
Variable costs[b]	VQ	100.00	200.00	100.00	200.00
Equals:					
EBIT		$ 700.00 ↓	$1600.00	$ 200.00 ↓	$1100.00
		129% increase		450% increase	
DOL		1.29		4.5	
Less:					
Interest	I	20.00	20.00	100.00	100.00
		$ 680.00	$1580.00	$ 100.00	$1000.00
Taxes (40%)	t	272.00	632.00	40.00	400.00
Equals:					
Net income		$ 408.00	$ 948.00	$ 60.00	$ 600.00
Less:					
Dividends for preferred stock	PD	10.00	10.00	20.00	20.00
Equals:					
Earnings available for common stock	EAC	$ 398.00	$ 938.00	$ 40.00	$ 580.00
Earnings per-share (100 shares)	EPS	$ 3.98 ↓	$ 9.38	$ 0.40 ↓	$ 5.80
		135% increase		1350% increase	
DFL		1.05		3	
DTL		1.35		13.5	

[a]$P = 100 per unit; $Q = 10$ at Level 1 and 20 at Level 2.
[b]$V = 10 per unit.

build a new model of jet aircraft, there is no guarantee that a sufficient number can be sold for the company to break even. The high level of fixed costs necessary to build such an aircraft will create high operating leverage and the risk that the firm will not be able to cover those costs. Because Boeing also borrows large sums of money, it also uses financial leverage and thus faces greater financial risk, the risk that it might default on its debt obligations. The combination of high operating and high financial leverage can result in large changes in earnings.

To better understand the effects of total leverage, let's observe what happens to a highly leveraged firm's earnings per share when sales revenues decline. The current level of sales revenues for this high-leverage firm is $10,000. The firm has relatively high fixed operating costs ($4,000) and interest payments ($1,000). Relevant data for the firm are as follows.

Total revenue	R	$10,000.00
Fixed operating costs	F	−4,000.00
Variable costs	VQ	−1,000.00
EBIT		$5,000.00
Interest	I	−1,000.00
		$4,000.00
Taxes (40%)	t	1,600.00
Earnings available for common stock		$2,400.00
Earnings per share (500 shares)	EPS	$ 4.80

We can determine the degree of total leverage by using Equation 10–8. Because there is no preferred stock in this example, there is no need to consider preferred dividends in the equation.

$$DTL = \frac{R - VQ}{EBIT - I}$$

$$= \frac{\$10,000 - \$1,000}{\$5,000 - \$1,000}$$

$$= 2.25$$

The degree of total leverage is 2.25, which means that, at a $10,000 level of sales revenues, a 1 percent change in sales revenues will result in a 2.25 percent change in earnings per share. If sales revenues decline 20 percent, earnings per share will decline 45 percent ($0.20 \times 2.25 = 0.45$). This strong effect means that if a high-leverage company's sales materialize, its high risk is rewarded with high returns. If sales do not materialize, however, the firm may face bankruptcy.

Firms with high degrees of operating leverage and business risk tend to have a lower debt capacity than firms with low operating leverage. This means that lenders are willing to lend relatively more funds to firms with low business risk than to those with high business risk. The degree of risk depends, in part, on the variability of sales and earnings. The EBIT for electric utilities companies tends to be more stable than the EBIT for automobile manufacturers, for example; so the utilities are able to borrow more than the auto companies. Debt may account for 50 percent of the capital structure of utilities companies and 30 percent of the capital structure of automobile companies.

Life Cycle and Leverage The degrees of leverage and risk are related to the phases of the life cycle. As shown in Figure 12–5, two break-even quantities are associated with the life cycle. The lower break-even quantity is reached during the expansion phase of the cycle, when sales and profits are increasing. The upper break-even

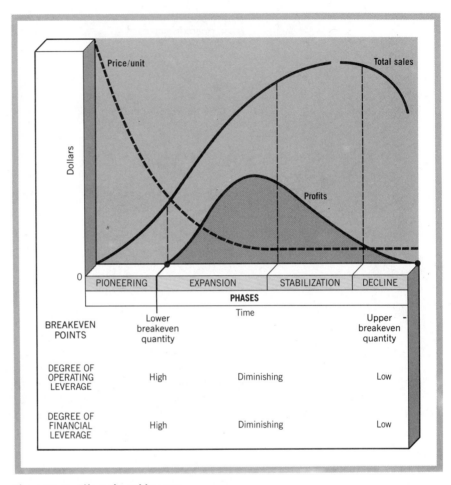

Figure 12–5   Life cycle and leverage.

quantity is reached during the declining phase, when sales have declined and profits are eroding into losses. Both operating leverage and financial leverage tend to be high during the expansion phase of the cycle and then diminish as the firm evolves.

It should be mentioned that financial managers have greater control over financial leverage than over operating leverage; that is, they can affect borrowing more easily than they can affect fixed production costs, because production technology tends to be fixed in the short run. For example, large-scale investments in plant and equipment must be made to produce steel. However, the investments may be financed by debt, equity, or any combination of the two.

Pricing Decisions[7]

Some of the techniques developed in this chapter are also useful in making pricing decisions. For example, consider the data presented in Table 12–5. Columns 1 and 2 show expected sales of a product at several prices. At $10 per unit, expected sales are 12,000 units. Total revenues, shown in Column 3, are the product of price per unit and expected sales. The data reveal that total revenue peaks at $147,000, when the price is $7 per unit. Therefore, a case could be made for selecting $7 per unit as the correct price. However, this selection ignores costs and risk, which must also be considered.

Total costs (Column 6) include variable costs and fixed costs. Notice that the fixed costs (Column 5) increase from $50,000 to $60,000 when sales reach 21,000 units. This suggests that fixed costs are fixed for only a certain range of sales. When total costs are subtracted from total revenues, the result is earnings before interest and taxes, as shown in Column 7. The largest *EBIT* ($58,000) occurs when the price is $8 per unit. This figure is also a candidate for the correct price, but risk must still be considered.

In this example, risk is measured by the degree of operating leverage (Column 11) and compared with the return on assets. (You will read more about calculating the rate of return on assets in Chapter 13.) The investment in assets necessary to accommodate the various levels of expected sales are listed in Column 9. We determine the return on these assets by dividing them into the *EBIT*. Dividing the degree of operating leverage by the return on assets gives the risk - return index listed in Column 12. This measure indicates that the best price is $9 per unit, because the risk - return index is lowest at that price.

Summary

Break-even analysis may be used as the first screen to determine the economic feasibility of investment proposals and their financial impact on earnings. Economic feasibility is determined by calculating the break-even quantity—the level of sales at which total sales revenues equal total operating costs. Two methods of calculating the break-even quantity are the algebraic method and the graphic method. Also determined algebraically is break-even revenue, the amount of revenue available at the break-even quantity. (Equations for break-even analysis, along with other equations presented in this chapter, are summarized in Table 12–6.)

[7]For additional information on this topic, see Stephen L. Hawk and Charles O. Kroncke, "The Break Even Concept: A Guide to Profitable Decision Making," *Managerial Planning*, May/June 1977, pp. 11–14, 28.

Table 12–5
Using Break-Even and Leverage Analysis in Pricing Decisions

Price per Unit P (1)	Expected Sales Q (2)	Total Revenue R = PQ (3) = (1)/(2)	Variable Costs[a] VQ (4)	Fixed Costs F (5)	Total Costs VQ + F (6) = (4) + (5)	EBIT (7) = (3) − (6)	Break-Even Quantity[b] (8)	Asset Investment (9)	Rate of Return on Assets (ROA) (10) = (7)/(9)	Degree of Operating Leverage (DOL)[c] (11)	Ratio of Risk to Return = DOL/ROA (12) = (11)/(10)
$10	12,000	$120,000	$24,000	$50,000	$ 74,000	$46,000	6,250	$300,000	15.3%	2.09	1,366
9	15,000	135,000	30,000	50,000	80,000	55,000	7,143	300,000	18.3	1.91	1,044
8	18,000	144,000	36,000	50,000	86,000	58,00	8,333	400,000	14.5	1.86	1,283
7	21,000	147,000	42,000	60,000	102,000	45,000	12,000	400,000	11.3	2.33	2,062
6	24,000	144,000	48,000	60,000	108,000	36,000	15,000	450,000	8.0	2.67	3,338
5	27,000	135,000	54,000	60,000	114,000	21,000	20,000	450,000	4.7	3.86	8,213

[a]Variable cost = $2 per unit.

[b]$BEQ = F/P - V.$

[c]$DOL = \dfrac{R - VQ}{EBIT}.$

Table 12–6
Summary of Equations

	Equation	Equation Number
Total operatory cost	$TC = VQ + F$	(12–1)
Break-even quantity	$BEQ = \dfrac{F}{P - V}$	(12–2)
Break-even revenue	Break-even revenue $= BEQ \times P$	(12–3)
Cash break-even quantity	Cash $BEQ = \dfrac{F_c}{P - V}$	(12–4)
Total leverage	$TL = OL \times FL$	(12–5)
Degree of operating leverage	$DOL = \dfrac{R - (VQ)}{EBIT}$	(12–6)
Degree of financial leverage	$DFL = \dfrac{EBIT}{(EBIT - I) - PD/(1 - t)}$	(12–7)
Degree of total leverage	$DTL = \dfrac{R - VQ}{(EBIT - I) - PD/(1 - t)}$	(12–8)

Linear break-even analysis assumes that revenues and costs maintain a linear relationship. Nonlinear break-even analysis allows us to relax this assumption and thus to view the world more realistically. Finally, cash break-even analysis gives the break-even quantity when only cash fixed costs are included.

The financial impact of investment proposals on earnings depends on the degrees of operating leverage and financial leverage. These concepts refer to the extent to which the *EBIT* and *EPS* change with changes in sales revenues. Total leverage is the product of operating leverage and financial leverage. Firms with high degrees of leverage are generally considered more risky than those with lower degrees of leverage. To some extent, the degrees of leverage are related to the phases of the life cycle of the firm.

Some of the techniques presented here can be used in pricing decisions. Determining the correct price for a product must include some consideration of risk relative to expected returns.

Important Terms

Break-even point	Financial leverage
Break-even quantity	Fixed costs
Break-even revenue	Linear break-even analysis
Cash break-even quantity	Nonlinear break-even analysis
Contribution margin	Operating leverage
Degree of financial leverage (*DFL*)	Semivariable costs
Degree of operating leverage (*DOL*)	Total leverage
Degree of total leverage (*DTL*)	Variable costs

Questions

1. What is the *break-even quantity*?
2. What assumptions underlie the calculation of the break-even quantity?
3. What is *break-even revenue*? What is *EBIT* at the level of break-even revenue?
4. What is the impact on a firm's break-even quantity of an increase in sales price per unit? An increase in variable cost per unit? A change in total fixed costs?
5. Holding the quantity sold constant, what is the impact on *EBIT* of an increase in sales price per unit? An increase in variable costs per unit? A change in total fixed costs?
6. What are some differences between linear and nonlinear break-even analysis?
7. How is cash break-even analysis different from regular break-even analysis?
8. What is the *degree of operating leverage*? Why is the concept useful for decision making?
9. What is the *degree of financial leverage*? Why is it important?
10. What is the *degree of total leverage*? What is the relationship between the degrees of total, operating, and financial leverage?
11. How do the characteristics of low-leverage firms differ from those of high-leverage firms?
12. Discuss the impact of operating and financial leverage on the riskiness of a firm. What trade-offs are involved?
13. Discuss changes in degrees of leverage that occur as a firm's life cycle progresses.
14. Explain in general how the degree of operating leverage can assist a firm in making pricing decisions.

Problems

1. Find the break-even quantity if the selling price is $5 per unit, variable costs are $3 per unit, and fixed costs are $50,000. What is the break-even quantity if fixed costs are $80,000? How much does each unit sold contribute toward covering fixed costs?
2. Find break-even revenue if the selling price is $15 per unit, variable costs are $6 per unit, and fixed costs are $200,000. What is the break-even quantity if fixed costs are $120,000?
3. Kastner Corporation produces high-quality drums that sell for $400 each. Each drum costs $225 to handcraft. Fixed expenses for the firm are $40,000.
   (a) What is the contribution margin of each drum?
   (b) What is the break-even quantity? Find it algebraically.
   (c) Find the break-even quantity through graphic analysis.
4. A textbook publisher produces paperback finance books that sell for $20 a copy. Variable costs per book are $12 and the publisher's total fixed costs are $160,000.
   (a) Calculate the break-even quantity and break-even revenue.
   (b) If inflation increases variable costs to $14 per book, but selling price is not increased, what are the new break-even quantity and break-even revenue?
5. The Mohawk Zoo has operating costs of $1 million per year. Its variable costs are $0.50 per visitor. Two million visitors are expected this year.

(a) What admission charge should be set for the zoo to break even?

(b) What admission charge should be set if variable costs increase to $0.60 per visitor?

(c) What admission charge should be set if Mohawk's fixed costs are expected to increase by 20 percent this year in addition to the increase in variable costs?

6. Operating costs can be classified as either fixed, variable, or semivariable. Classify the following into one of those three categories and explain your choices.

(a) Lease payments

(b) Wages for factory workers

(c) Salary of the financial vice-president

(d) Loan principal repayment

(e) Taxes

(f) Utilities

(g) Pension contributions for workers

(h) Marketing expenses

7. Shipley's Shirts, Inc., has started a new line of shirts. Each will sell for $30. The shirts are manufactured in a new plant that cost the firm $2 million at the beginning of this year and that is being depreciated on a straight-line basis for the next 15 years. No salvage value is expected. The variable cost per shirt is $10 and total fixed costs (including depreciation) are $500,000.

(a) Find the break-even quantity algebraically and graphically.

(b) Find the cash break-even quantity algebraically and graphically, assuming all sales on a cash basis.

8. Three competitors are vying to produce reproductions of colonial furniture. They have the following cost and price schedules.

	Firm X	Firm Y	Firm Z
Price per piece	$500	$600	$800
Variable cost per unit	200	350	600
Fixed costs	$10 million	$6 million	$4 million

(a) Calculate the break-even quantity and break-even revenue for each firm.

(b) In general, which firm faces the least operating risk? Why?

9. At sales of $20 million, calculate the degree of operating leverage for each firm in Problem 8. At that level of expected sales, which firm faces the greatest potential variability in *EBIT* if sales vary? Why?

10. The following information has been collected for NIT, Inc.

	1990	1991
Sales	$900,000	$1,500,000
Variable costs	400,000	650,000
Fixed costs	200,000	300,000
EBIT	$300,000	550,000

(a) Calculate the degree of operating leverage for NIT, Inc., for 1990 and 1991.

(b) In which year was the firm the riskiest? Why?

11. (a) Suppose the sales of NIT, Inc., (from Problem 10) increase to $1,750,000 in 1992. By what percentage would you expect *EBIT* to change as a result? What would the new level of *EBIT* be?

(b) Suppose sales decline to $1,200,000 in 1992. By what percentage would you expect *EBIT* to change? How much would the new level of *EBIT* be?

12. Manyon Routers produces a high-quality product at a price of $400 per unit.

Variable operating costs are $150 per unit and fixed operating costs are $600,000 annually.

(a) Calculate the break-even quantity for Manyon.

(b) Calculate sales revenue and *EBIT* for sales of 2,401 units; 2,500 units; 3,000 units; 10,000 units.

(c) Calculate the degree of operating leverage at each of the sales quantities in part b.

(d) In general, what happens to the degree of operating leverage as sales increase? What does this say about the riskiness of the firm as sales increase?

13. Suppose the current level of sales for Manyon Routers in Problem 12 is 3,000 units. Using the degree of operating leverage, calculate the new level of *EBIT* expected if sales increase to 3,200 units; if sales decrease to 2,700 units.

14. Bristow Corporation has $4 million of debt outstanding at 10 percent and 100,000 shares of common stock. The tax rate is 40 percent.

(a) What is the degree of financial leverage at $800,000 *EBIT*?

(b) What is the degree of financial leverage at an *EBIT* of $1.2 million?

15. Harvard Corporation's *EBIT* has increased from $150,000 to $200,000 over the past year. The firm has a $1 million loan at 12 percent and pays 20 percent of its income in taxes. There are 10,000 shares of common stock outstanding. What was the degree of financial leverage at $150,000? What is it now?

16. (a) Suppose the Harvard Corporation in Problem 15 also had $200,000 of 5 percent preferred stock outstanding during the year. Calculate the degree of financial leverage at $150,000 and $200,000 *EBIT*.

(b) Under the conditions described in part a, if *EBIT* increases from $200,000 to $300,000, by what percentage would you expect *EPS* to change? What would the new *EPS* figure be? Use the *DFL* to find your answer.

17. Austin Air, Inc., provides the following income statement for 1990.

Sales (100 aircraft)	$80,000,000
Variable costs	− 30,000,000
Fixed costs	− 25,000,000
EBIT	$25,000,000
Interest expense	− 8,000,000
Earnings before taxes	17,000,000
Taxes	− 5,100,000
Net income	$11,900,000

(a) Calculate the degree of operating leverage.

(b) Calculate the degree of financial leverage.

(c) Calculate the degree of total leverage. Show your calculation two ways.

 18. The management of Roadrunner Corporation is trying to estimate the degree of risk in its basic operations. The following information has been provided.

	1989	1990
Sales	$1,440,000	$1,728,000
Variable costs	− 400,000	− 500,000
Fixed costs	− 800,000	− 800,000
EBIT	$ 240,000	$ 428,000
Interest expense	− 60,000	− 60,000
Earnings before taxes	$ 180,000	$ 368,000
Taxes (0.4)	− 72,000	− 147,000
Preferred dividends	− 15,000	− 15,000
Earnings available to shareholders	$ 93,000	$ 206,000

There are 100,000 shares of common stock outstanding.
(a) Calculate the degree of operating leverage for each year.
(b) Calculate the degree of financial leverage for each year.
(c) Calculate the degree of total leverage for each year.

19. (a) Suppose sales forecasts for 1991 for the Roadrunner Corporation in Problem 18 indicate that sales may vary from $1.2 million to $2 million. What level of *EBIT* would you expect if sales are $1.2 million? If they are $2 million?
(b) What level of *EPS* would you expect if 1991 sales are $1.2 million? If they are $2 million?

20. (a) A firm has a degree of total leverage of 2.3. *EBIT* is $40,000 and the firm has $100,000 debt outstanding at an interest rate of 13 percent. What is the degree of operating leverage?
(b) Suppose, in addition to the information in part a, the firm has $50,000 of preferred stock outstanding at a dividend rate of 10 percent. What is the degree of operating leverage if the tax rate is 40 percent?

21. A firm has identified the following rates of return on assets and degrees of operating leverage at several possible prices per unit.

Price	ROA %	DOL
$50	12	2.70
60	14	2.25
70	15	1.90
80	18	1.80
90	13	1.95

Which sales price is preferrable? Why?

 # Financial Analysis

Complete physical examinations may include blood tests, X-rays, poking and probing by the physician, and other diagnostic procedures. Such tests are designed to provide a physician with information about the state of a person's health. Similarly, the financial health of a company may be determined by

After reading this chapter, you should know the following.

1. **How inflation distorts sales data.**
2. **How to use ratios to measure liquidity, efficiency, financial leverage, and profitability.**
3. **How to use the du Pont system of financial analysis.**
4. **Why being below average may not be bad.**
5. **How financial ratios are affected by the product life cycle and business cycles.**
6. **How financial analysis is limited.**
7. **Where to find financial information.**

use of diagnostic procedures. As in a physical examination, a variety of tests is needed to obtain a complete picture. This chapter presents diagnostic tools designed to determine the financial condition of a company. The first battery of tests consists of financial ratios. The ratios describe relationships between selected items that appear on a firm's financial statements. Financial ratios may be combined in various ways to provide different analytical perspectives.

General Observations

Perspective The purpose of financial analysis is to diagnose the current and past financial condition of a firm and to give some clues about its future condition. At this point, some general observations about financial analysis are appropriate. There is a saying that "if you don't know where you're going, it doesn't make any difference what road you take to get there." This saying is relevant here because it points to the need for deciding the objectives of a test, or what is to be measured, before deciding which diagnostic tools should be used. For example, a bank credit analyst, a securities analyst, and the financial manager of a firm have different objectives when they examine a firm's financial condition. The primary concern of bank credit analysts is whether borrowing companies can make their loan payments. They emphasize tests that measure liquidity—the ability to meet short-term financial obligations. The primary concerns of securities analysts are future earnings and dividends. These items have a major impact on stock prices, which represent shareholder wealth. In contrast, the primary concern of financial managers is the financial well-being of their companies; they are concerned with all aspects of financial analysis.

Because their perspectives are different, a bank credit analyst, a securities analyst, and a financial manager can examine the same data and have three different opinions about the financial condition of a firm. Consider the case of Northern Auto Supply Stores, which has been experiencing some difficulties. A bank credit analyst has reported to her credit supervisor that Northern will not have sufficient earnings 6 months from now to repay its loan. A securities analyst has recommended to the stockbrokerage firm's customers that they continue to hold the stock (not buy it or sell it), because work stoppages that have been depressing earnings will end soon. The financial manager of Northern is optimistic about the future, because the company is planning to sell some of its outlets to another firm, which will provide sufficient cash to repay the bank loan and eliminate some of the less profitable outlets from the chain. Therefore, Northern's dependence on borrowed funds will be reduced and its profitability increased. This example illustrates that the interpretation of information depends on what the observer is looking for. In addition, sometimes vision can be clouded by inflation and by other impediments that will be discussed later in this chapter.

Effects of Inflation Inflation distorts some data and often leads to misinterpretation of information. For example, in a recent annual report, Northern Auto Supply boasted that sales revenues increased 10 percent in each of the last four years. Management considered 10 percent good until it was pointed out that inflation increased 12 percent per year. When the sales revenues were deflated (that is, divided by an inflation index), sales growth was found to be negative. Adjusted sales in Year 4 were $88 million, compared with $100 million in Year 1.

Years		1	2	3	4
Sales (millions of dollars)		$100	$110	$121	$123
Inflation index	÷	1.00	1.12	1.25	1.40
Adjusted sales (sales/inflation index)	=	$100	$ 98	$ 97	$ 88

During this same period, the number of sales outlets increased from 10 to 13. The annual report stated that the increased number of outlets was a positive sign of growth. However, had management divided the number of outlets into adjusted sales each year, it could have been seen that adjusted sales declined from $10 million to $6.8 million per outlet.

Years	1	2	3	4
Number of outlets	10	11	12	13
Adjusted sales per outlet (millions of dollars)	$10.0	$8.9	$8.1	$6.8

The increased dollar volume of sales and number of outlets suggested that Northern Auto was growing, until inflation was taken into account. Then it was revealed that, on the average, sales expressed in constant dollars declined by 32 percent per outlet. Inflation distorted management's perception of reality.

Ratio Analysis

Now we begin the process of financial analysis. To illustrate the process, we will refer to the balance sheet and earnings statement for Best Equipment Company for 2 consecutive years (Tables 13–1 and 13–2). Data from these tables are used in calculating the financial ratios and indicators described in the remainder of this chapter. When the ratios require other data, these data are provided in the calculations. Many firms use data covering 2 years or more as a basis for their financial analysis, because some trends can be detected only over a longer time span. However, the 2-year data used here are sufficient to demonstrate some basic techniques of financial analysis.

Best Equipment Company is a medium-sized manufacturer of specialized farm equipment. It is a mature firm in a mature industry. The company sells and leases its products to farmers. Because farming is a cyclical business, sales of farm equipment change appreciably from year to year. Such fluctuations

Table 13–1
Best Equipment Company Balance Sheet

	December 31	
	1989	**1988**
	(thousands of dollars)	
Assets		
Current assets		
Cash and marketable securities	$ 1,578	$ 2,947
Accounts receivable	7,082	6,960
Inventories	34,542	38,925
Prepaid expenses	158	114
Total current assets	$43,360	$48,946
Investments and other assets		
Long-term portion of installment contracts		
receivable	$ 1,097	$ 304
Investments in unconsolidated subsidiaries	312	751
Other	705	668
Total investments and other assets	2,114	1,723
Property, plant, and equipment, at cost net of depreciation	8,513	7,627
Total assets	$53,987	$58,296
Liabilities and Shareholders' Equity		
Current liabilities		
Notes payable	$ 9,747	$13,051
Current maturities of long-term debt	1,004	1,007
Accounts payable	2,689	2,348
Customer deposits	454	230
Accrued liabilities	1,837	2,214
Accrued income taxes	1,484	1,935
Total current liabilities	$17,215	$20,785
Long-term debt, less current maturities	4,784	7,232
Other noncurrent liabilities	558	519
Total liabilities	$22,557	$28,536
Shareholders' equity[a]	31,430	29,760
Total liabilities and shareholders' equity	$53,987	$58,296

[a]Six million shares of common stock are outstanding in both years.

are part of the business risk inherent in running any firm. Business risk also includes the risks of competition, poor management, and so on. As shown in Table 13–2, sales for Best Equipment declined sharply in the most recent year; but this is due, at least in part, to depressed farm commodity prices, which have affected many agricultural firms. To some extent, the shortfall in sales was offset by increased rentals.

The financial manager of Best Equipment analyzes the company's financial condition periodically to assess its strengths and weaknesses. Then, he knows what actions are necessary to keep Best Equipment in line with its long-range plans. The first part of the analysis evaluates a wide range of financial ratios and indicators. As part of the analysis, the firm's ratios are compared with averages for the industry as a whole. The ratios are divided into four broad

Table 13–2

Best Equipment Company Statement of Earnings

	For Years Ended December 31	
	1989	1988
	(thousands of dollars)	
Revenue		
Net sales[a]	$57,546	$76,900
Rentals	7,870	4,173
Other	112	258
	$65,528	$81,331
Costs and expenses		
Cost of goods sold[b]	$47,057	$57,634
Selling, general, and administrative expenses	14,970	16,229
	62,027	73,863
Operating income	$ 3,501	$ 7,468
Other income and expenses		
Interest income	$ 548	$ 326
Interest expense	(1,421)	(1,686)
Gain	553	
Other	170	42
	$ (150)	$(1,318)
Earnings before taxes	$ 3,351	$ 6,150
Income taxes		
Current	$ 1,874	$ 1,015
Deferred	(552)	425
	$ 1,322	$ 1,440
Net income	$ 2,029	$ 4,710

[a]All sales are for credit.
[b]Credit purchases account for 75 percent of the cost of goods sold.

categories: (1) liquidity, (2) efficiency, (3) financial leverage, and (4) profitability.

The ratios, remember, are diagnostic tests. A single diagnostic test does not provide enough information about a company for its current condition to be accurately evaluated. Therefore, many tests are used to obtain a complete picture. Accordingly, a summary of 18 financial ratios is presented at the end of this section. One final caution: The ratios presented here are appropriate for manufacturing concerns and many other types of businesses. However, some lines of business and some types of analysis require special ratios not dealt with here.

Liquidity A company must survive in the short run to prosper in the long run. The following measures of liquidity assess the ability of a company to meet its short-run, or current, obligations—those due within 1 year. If a firm does not have sufficient liquidity, it may not survive the short run. That is why liquidity measures are examined first.

Net Working Capital.   As a general rule, companies pay off current obligations, or current liabilities, by reducing current assets—that is, assets that can be converted into cash on short notice. The difference between current assets and current liabilities is called **net working capital**, and it represents a cushion for creditors' loans. Although this measure is not a ratio, it is commonly included with the liquidity ratios when companies are analyzed. It is widely used by creditors and credit rating agencies as a measure of liquidity. More working capital is preferred to less—in other words, creditors like a big cushion to protect their interests. However, too much working capital can act to the detriment of the company, because it may mean management is not using the firm's funds effectively. Holding excessive nonearning assets, such as cash and accounts receivable, can hold down profits. Cash, for example, might be better employed in building up inventory or investing in fixed assets.

By using data from the balance sheet shown in Table 13–1, we can determine that Best Equipment's net working capital declined from $28,161,000 in 1988 to $26,145,000 in the following year. The decline in net working capital was expected because of the decline in sales mentioned earlier. The dollar amounts shown in this and the remaining computations are expressed in thousands of dollars, unless noted otherwise.

$$\text{Net working capital} = \text{Current assets} - \text{Current liabilities}$$

$$1989: \quad = \$43,360 - \$17,215 = \$26,145$$

$$1988: \quad = \$48,946 - \$20,785 = \$28,161 \qquad (13\text{--}1)$$

Current Ratio.   The **current ratio** is a broad measure of liquidity derived by dividing current assets by current liabilities. It is considered broad because it includes all current assets and current liabilities. Best Equipment's financial manager has determined by examining the financial statements of three competing firms that the industry average for this ratio is 2.38 times. That means current assets are 2.38 times as large as current liabilities; for every $1.00 of current liabilities, there are $2.38 of current assets. The current ratio for Best Equipment increased in the most recent year and exceeds the industry average.

$$\text{Current ratio} = \frac{\text{Current assets}}{\text{Current liabilities}}$$

$$1989: \quad = \frac{\$43,360}{\$17,215} = 2.52 \text{ times}$$

$$1988: \quad = \frac{\$48,946}{\$20,785} = 2.35 \text{ times}$$

$$\text{Industry average} = 2.38 \text{ times} \qquad (13\text{--}2)$$

The current ratio suggests that Best Equipment has sufficient funds to meet its current obligations. It may also suggest that Best is too liquid. Is the firm holding too many low-yielding assets that will adversely affect profits? At this point, we do not know the answer, so we must look further.

Acid-Test Ratio.   The **acid-test ratio** is a narrow measure of liquidity derived by dividing cash, marketable securities, and accounts receivable by current liabilities. It is considered narrow because it excludes the least liquid current assets—inventories and prepaid items—from the calculation. Best Equipment's acid-test ratio increased in 1989, and the firm's liquidity is above the industry average.

$$\text{Acid-test ratio} \quad = \frac{\text{Cash} + \text{Marketable securities} + \text{Accounts receivable}}{\text{Current liabilities}}$$

$$1989: \qquad = \frac{\$1{,}578 + \$7{,}082}{\$17{,}215} = 0.50 \text{ times}$$

$$1988: \qquad = \frac{\$2{,}947 + \$6{,}960}{\$20{,}785} = 0.48 \text{ times}$$

Industry average = 0.45 times   (13–3)

Average Collection Period.   The **average collection period** indicates the average length of time a firm waits before receiving cash for sales made on credit. All of Best Equipment's sales are made on credit; so it is important for the firm to minimize the collection period in order to be paid as soon as possible. Recall the time value of money: Funds received today are worth more than the same amount received in the future.

Two steps are required to calculate the average collection period. Step 1 involves determining the dollar amount of credit sales per day. We do this by dividing net credit sales (from Table 13–2) by 360 days. The use of 360 days to simplify calculation was developed in an era before hand-held calculators and computers, but it is still widely used by analysts. A firm can use either 360 or 365 days, as long as it is consistent in its usage. In the calculations below, notice how Best Equipment's dollar sales per day declined. Step 2 involves dividing accounts receivable by the dollar amount of credit sales per day.[1] The result is the average collection period.

[1] In other books—*The Basics of Investing* (New York: John Wiley & Sons, 1986) and *Guide to Strategic Planning* (New York: McGraw-Hill, 1980)—I argued that when a ratio is calculated from both balance sheet data, which represents one moment in time (stock), and income statement data, which represents a period of time (flow), the *averaged* data from two balance sheets should be used so that the time frames of both the numerator and the denominator of the ratio will be the same. I deviated from that method in this book in order to make all the ratios (1) consistent and (2) compatible with the du Pont method, which will be discussed later in this chapter. The averaging of balance sheet data is especially important when large differences in balance sheet levels exist.

$$\text{Average collection period} = \frac{\text{Accounts receivable}}{\text{Credit sales/day}}$$

1989: Credit sales/Day	= Net credit sales/360 days
	= $57,546/360
	= $160

$$\text{Average collection period} = \frac{\text{Accounts receivable}}{\text{Credit sales/Day}}$$

$$= \frac{\$7,082}{\$160}$$

$$= 44 \text{ days}$$

1988: Credit sales/Day	= Net credit sales/360 days
	= $76,900/360
	= $214

$$\text{Average collection period} = \frac{\text{Accounts receivable}}{\text{Credit sales/day}}$$

$$= \frac{\$6,960}{\$214}$$

$$= 33 \text{ days}$$

Industry average	= 36 days	(13–4)

You can see that Best Equipment's average collection period has increased sharply and is substantially above the industry average. This is one reason the measures of liquidity calculated earlier increased in 1989.

Aging Accounts Receivable.   Clearly, Best Equipment has become less efficient in collecting its bills. **Aging** the accounts receivable should help to clarify this situation. In aging accounts receivable, the financial manager will determine what percentage of the receivables have been outstanding for 30, 45, 60, and 90 days. Multiplying the percentage times the number of days outstanding gives the average collection period.

Accounts Receivable	Percent of Accounts Receivable	×	Days Outstanding		
$3,541	50%	×	30		=15 days
1,416	20	×	45		= 9
1,558	22	×	60		=13
567	8	×	90		= 7
$7,082	100%			Total	=44 days average collection period

The distribution of accounts receivable indicates that credit policies should be adopted to reduce the overdue accounts and to encourage customers to pay on time. Such policies are examined in Chapter 17.

Average Payment Period.   Managing current liabilities is part of managing a firm's liquidity position. The **average payment period** is one indicator of how effectively a firm manages its current liabilities. The average payment period, like the average collection period, is computed in two steps. Step 1 determines the dollar amount of credit purchases per day. Credit purchases amount to 75 percent of the cost of goods sold for Best Equipment Company. As you can see in the following calculations, Best Equipment's daily credit purchases have declined. Step 2 divides accounts payable by the dollar amount of credit purchases per day.

$$\text{Average payment period} = \frac{\text{Accounts payable}}{\text{Credit purchases/day}}$$

$$1989: \text{Credit purchases/Day} = 0.75\ (\$47,057)/360$$

$$= \$98$$

$$\text{Average payment period} = \frac{\text{Accounts payable}}{\text{Credit purchases/Day}}$$

$$= \frac{\$2,689}{\$98}$$

$$= 27 \text{ days}$$

$$1988: \text{Credit purchases/Day} = 0.75(\$57,634)/360$$

$$= \$120$$

$$\text{Average payment period} = \frac{\text{Accounts payable}}{\text{Credit purchases/Day}}$$

$$= \frac{\$2,348}{\$120}$$

$$= 20 \text{ days}$$

$$\text{Industry average} = 20 \text{ days} \qquad (13\text{–}5)$$

Although Best Equipment is buying fewer goods and services on credit, it has slowed the rate at which it pays its bills. This action temporarily increases the firm's liquidity, but it may also adversely affect profits. More will be said about stretching payments when we examine working capital in detail in Chapter 15.

Efficiency Efficiency ratios, sometimes called activity ratios, measure how effectively certain assets or liabilities are being used in the production of goods and services. The average collection and payment periods that were just calculated can be thought of as efficiency ratios. However, because they also provide information about the current financial condition of the firm, they were included in the liquidity ratios.

Inventory Turnover Ratio. We calculate the **inventory turnover ratio** by dividing the cost of goods sold by the inventory. As a general rule, the faster inventories are sold, the faster companies can realize their profits. Inventory turnover ratios vary widely from industry to industry. The inventory turnover ratio of a newspaper company should be very high (365 times per year is the maximum), whereas that of a dress shop may be relatively low (perhaps 5 times per year.) Because of the sharp decline in sales, the inventory turnover ratio for Best Equipment Company has slowed appreciably and is below the industry average.

$$\text{Inventory turnover ratio} = \frac{\text{Cost of goods sold}}{\text{Inventory}}$$

1989:
$$= \frac{\$47,057}{\$34,542} = 1.36 \text{ times}$$

1988:
$$= \frac{\$57,634}{\$38,925} = 1.48 \text{ times}$$

Industry average $= 1.53$ times $\qquad\qquad$ (13–6)

Age of Inventory. Another way to examine inventories is to determine their **age**, or the average number of days the inventory remains on hand. We accomplish this by dividing 360 days by the inventory turnover ratio. The data for Best Equipment show that the average age has increased sharply, suggesting that there may be too much inventory on hand.

$$\text{Age of inventory} = \frac{360 \text{ days}}{\text{Inventory turnover ratio}}$$

1989:
$$= \frac{360}{1.36} = 265 \text{ days}$$

1988:
$$= \frac{360}{1.48} = 243 \text{ days}$$

Industry average $= 240$ days $\qquad\qquad$ (13–7)

Although seasonal factors are not important to Best Equipment, they can make significant differences in the ratios dealing with inventories and receivables of firms that are subject to seasonal factors. Firms in the candy and greeting card industries are examples of the latter.

Asset Turnover Ratio.   The efficiency measures just described concentrate on inventories, but the **asset turnover ratio** encompasses all assets. We compute this ratio by dividing net sales by total assets. Some analysts use fixed assets instead of total assets in the denominator of the equation. The difference between the two methods can be significant, depending on the nature of the business being analyzed. (For example, banks have relatively few fixed assets, whereas automobile manufacturers have a lot of them.) One advantage of using total assets is that the measure can be used in further calculations, as you will see later in this chapter.

The asset turnover ratio for Best Equipment has slowed appreciably and is below the industry average. Best generated $1.07 in sales for every dollar of assets, while the industry average was $1.29 in sales for every dollar of assets.

$$\text{Asset turnover ratio} = \frac{\text{Net sales}}{\text{Total assets}}$$

$$1989: \quad = \frac{\$57,546}{\$53,987} = 1.07 \text{ times}$$

$$1988: \quad = \frac{\$76,900}{\$58,296} = 1.32 \text{ times}$$

$$\text{Industry average} \quad = 1.29 \text{ times} \qquad\qquad (13-8)$$

Financial Leverage   **Financial leverage**, as you recall from earlier chapters, refers to the relationship between borrowed funds (such as bonds, mortgages, and loans) and common shareholders' equity. (Some analysts consider preferred stock in the same category as bonds, because the issuing company has an obligation to make preferred dividend payments.) Companies that have a high proportion of borrowed funds are said to be highly leveraged. Leverage increases the volatility of earnings per share and the financial risk of the company. Several measures of leverage are described here.

Debt Ratio.   The **debt ratio** indicates what proportion of a firm's total assets is financed with borrowed funds. We find it by dividing total liabilities by total assets. In the case of Best Equipment, 41.78 percent of total assets were financed by borrowings in 1989, down sharply from the previous year's level and the industry average. This is a result of substantial reductions in both notes payable and long-term debt.

$$\text{Debt ratio} = \frac{\text{Total liabilities}}{\text{Total assets}}$$

$$1989: = \frac{\$22,557}{\$53,987} = 41.78\%$$

$$1988: = \frac{\$28,536}{\$58,296} = 48.95\%$$

Industry average $= 47.00\%$ \hfill (13–9)

Long-Term Debt as a Percent of Total Capital. Total capital includes both long-term debt and equity. In 1989, for example, total capital for Best Equipment was as follows.

Long-term debt	$ 4,784
Total equity	+31,430
Total capital	$ 36,214

The data for Best Equipment reveal a decline in **long-term debt as a percent of total capital**, because the amount of long-term debt was reduced. The current level is below the industry average.

$$\text{Long-term debt as percent of total capital} = \frac{\text{Long-term debt}}{\text{Total capital}}$$

$$1989: = \frac{\$4,784}{\$36,214}$$

$$= 31.21\%$$

$$1988: = \frac{\$7,232}{\$36,992}$$

$$= 19.55\%$$

Industry average $= 19.00\%$ \hfill (13–10)

The reduction in debt reduces the financial risk of the firm. Financial risk, as mentioned in earlier chapters, is that part of total corporate risk that results from borrowing funds. Part of this risk results from the possibility that the firm may not be able to repay the loans. Total risk includes both financial risk and business risk.

Times Interest Earned. By reducing the amount of debt outstanding, Best Equipment was better able to *cover* (that is, pay) its interest charges, thereby reducing its financial risk. Debt coverage is measured by dividing earnings before interest and taxes by interest expense. The resulting ratio is often called the **times interest earned ratio**, because it tells how many times interest payments are covered by earnings. Creditors prefer a high debt coverage ratio as a safety cushion. The ratio for Best Equipment declined from 1988 to 1989 and is lower than the industry average:

$$\text{Times Interest Earned} = \frac{\text{Earnings before interest and taxes}}{\text{Interest expense}}$$

1989: $= \dfrac{\$3,351 + \$1,421}{\$1,421} = 3.36 \text{ times}$

1988: $= \dfrac{\$6,150 + \$1,686}{\$1,686} = 4.65 \text{ times}$

Industry average $= 3.72$ times   (13–11)

Profitability Profits are the ultimate test of management's effectiveness. Like the other qualities discussed in this chapter, profitability can be measured in a variety of ways. All the measures described here indicate that Best Equipment was less profitable in 1989.

Earnings per Share. **Earnings per share** (*EPS*) is the statistic quoted most often when profitability is discussed. The reason for its popularity is that it is easy to understand and to relate to stock prices. You may recall that *EPS* is derived by dividing earnings available for common stock by the average number of shares outstanding. **Earnings available for common stock** is net income less preferred stock dividend payments and sinking fund payments (periodic payments made to retire debts). For Best Equipment, 6 million shares of common stock were outstanding in both years and there were no preferred dividends or sinking fund payments. The company earned $0.34 in 1989 compared with $0.79 in the previous year.

$$\text{Earnings per share} = \frac{\text{Earnings available for common stock}}{\text{Average number of shares outstanding}}$$

1989: $= \dfrac{\$2,029,000}{6,000,000} = \$0.34$

1988: $= \dfrac{\$4,710,000}{6,000,000} = \$0.79$ (13–12)

Payout Ratio. As you know, earnings can be retained by the company or paid out to shareholders in the form of cash dividends. The extent to which cash dividends are paid to common shareholders is called the **payout ratio** and is computed by dividing dividends per share by earnings per share. In 1989, Best Equipment paid a cash dividend of $0.05. None was paid in the previous year.

$$\text{Payout ratio} = \frac{\text{Cash dividends per share}}{\text{Earnings per share}}$$

1989: $= \dfrac{\$0.05}{\$0.34} = 14.71\%$

1988: $=$ No dividends paid

Industry average: $= 28.00\%$ (13–13)

Net Profit Margin. Profitability can also be measured in terms of returns on sales, assets, and equity. The **net profit margin** on sales, computed by dividing net income by net sales, is the percent of profit earned for each dollar of sales. The profit margin for Best Equipment has fallen far below the industry average.

$$\text{Net profit margin} = \frac{\text{Net income}}{\text{Net sales}}$$

1989: $= \dfrac{\$2,029}{\$57,546} = 3.52\%$

1988: $= \dfrac{\$4,710}{\$76,900} = 6.12\%$

Industry average $= 5.98\%$ (13–14)

Operating Margin. The **operating margin** measures the return on sales before expenses, such as interest payments, with taxes taken into account. Thus, it is not affected by the means of financing used to generate the sales. It is a refined version of the profit margin. We calculate the operating margin by dividing earnings from operations, or operating income, by net sales. Best Equipment's operating margin has also fallen below the industry average.

$$\text{Operating margin} = \frac{\text{Operating income}}{\text{Net sales}}$$

1989: $= \dfrac{\$3,501}{\$57,546} = 6.08\%$

1988: $= \dfrac{\$7,468}{\$76,900} = 9.71\%$

Industry average $= 8.53\%$ (13–15)

Table 13–3
Summary of Financial Indicators for Best Equipment Company

Ratio or Indicator	Formula	Results 1989	Results 1988	Industry Average 1989	Evaluation
Liquidity					
1. Net working capital	Current assets − Current liabilities	$26,145,000	$28,161,000	NA[a]	Decline expected
2. Current ratio	$\dfrac{\text{Current assets}}{\text{Current liabilities}}$	2.52 times	2.35 times	2.38 times	Good
3. Acid-test ratio	$\dfrac{\text{Cash} + \text{Marketable securities} + \text{Receivables}}{\text{Current liabilities}}$	0.50 times	0.48 times	0.45 times	Good
4. Average collection period	$\dfrac{\text{Accounts receivable}}{\text{Credit sales/Day}}$	44 days	33 days	36 days	Too high
5. Average payment period	$\dfrac{\text{Accounts payable}}{\text{Credit purchases/Day}}$	27 days	20 days	20 days	Slow pay-ing
Efficiency					
6. Inventory turnover ratio	$\dfrac{\text{Cost of goods sold}}{\text{Inventory}}$	1.36 times	1.48 times	1.53 times	Slowed appreciably
7. Age of inventory	$\dfrac{360 \text{ days}}{\text{Inventory turnover ratio}}$	265 days	243 days	240 days	Too much inventory
8. Asset turnover ratio	$\dfrac{\text{Net sales}}{\text{Total assets}}$	1.07 times	1.32 times	1.29 times	Too low

Debit Ratios

Financial Leverage

	Formula				
9. Debt ratio	Total liabilities / Total assets	41.78%	48.95%	47.00%	Low
10. Long-term debt as percent of total capital	Long-term debt / Total capital	13.21%	19.55%	19.00%	Low
11. Times interest earned	Earnings before interest and taxes / Interest expense	3.36 times	4.65 times	3.72 times	Adequate
Profitability					
12. Earnings per share	Earnings available for common stock / Average number of shares outstanding	$0.34	$0.79	NA[a]	NA[a]
13. Payout ratio	Cash dividends per share / Earnings per share	14.71%	None	28.00%	Low
14. Net profit margin	Net income / Net sales	3.52%	6.12%	5.98%	Low
15. Operating margin	Operating income / Net sales	6.08%	9.71%	8.53%	Low
16. Operating return on assets	Operating earnings before interest and taxes / Total assets	8.84%	13.44%	12.62%	Low
17. Return on assets	Net income / Total assets	3.76%	8.08%	7.71%	Very low
18. Return on equity	Net income / Shareholders' equity	6.46%	15.83%	14.56%	Very low

[a]NA = Not applicable.

Operating Return on Assets.[2]   As mentioned, returns can be expressed in terms of sales, assets, or equity. The **operating return on assets** is a broad indicator that measures productivity for shareholders, bondholders, and other creditors. It also reflects the return on total assets without any consideration of how they were financed. We compute operating return on assets by dividing operating earnings before interest and taxes by total assets. The operating return on assets for Best Equipment has fallen below the industry average.

$$\text{Operating return on assets} = \frac{\text{Operating earnings before interest and taxes}}{\text{Total assets}}$$

$$1989: \quad = \frac{\$3,351 + \$1,421}{\$53,987} = 8.84\%$$

$$1988: \quad = \frac{\$6,150 + \$1,686}{\$58,296} = 13.44\%$$

$$\text{Industry average} \quad = 12.62\% \qquad\qquad (13\text{–}16)$$

Return on Assets.   The operating return on assets can be refined to take interest and taxes into account. When this is done, we compute the ratio by dividing net income by total assets. The result reflects the impact of debt financing on profitability. It may be called the **return on assets** (*ROA*) or the **return on investment** (*ROI*), and more will be said about it later in this chapter. As we might expect, Best Equipment's return on assets fell in 1989.

$$\text{Return on assets} = \frac{\text{Net income}}{\text{Total assets}}$$

$$1989: \quad = \frac{\$2,029}{\$53,987} = 3.76\%$$

$$1988: \quad = \frac{\$4,710}{\$58,296} = 8.08\%$$

$$\text{Industry average} = 7.71\% \qquad\qquad (13\text{–}17)$$

Return on Equity.   The **return on equity** (*ROE*) measures the rate of return on the owners' investment and is calculated by dividing net income by total

---

[2]Some companies use return on net assets (*RONA*) instead of return on total assets as a measure of profitability. *Net assets* is total assets less current liabilities. Because current liabilities have little or no interest cost, they are subtracted from total assets, leaving only the total investment by holders of debt and equity. Thus, the net assets are equal to total debt and equity investment, and the return on net assets is the return on total debt and equity investments. This measure is used in multidivision companies where the parent company makes both debt and equity investments in one or more of its divisions.

shareholders' equity. Where the firm has large amounts of preferred stock outstanding or has other payments such as the principal amount on a loan to pay off, a similar ratio may be computed by dividing income available to common stock by common equity. Best Equipment has no preferred shares outstanding. Common shareholders were not happy about the company's performance in 1989.

$$\text{Return on equity} = \frac{\text{Net income}}{\text{Shareholders' equity}}$$

$$1989: \quad = \frac{\$2,029}{\$31,430} = 6.46\%$$

$$1988: \quad = \frac{\$4,710}{\$29,760} = 15.83\%$$

$$\text{Industry average} = 14.56\% \quad\quad\quad\quad (13\text{--}18)$$

Review of Indicators   Table 13–3 lists all the previously described indicators and their results for Best Equipment. The results point to a few conclusions. First, as mentioned, depressed commodity prices have contributed to a reduction in sales. Adding to the problem are excess inventories and poor collection policies for credit sales, which can be attributed to poor planning. The net result is that profitability has suffered. However, the company is still financially strong; so perhaps this is only a temporary setback.

So far, our analysis has focused on the use of ratios as diagnostic tools to evaluate a firm's financial condition. Although ratios give us some important insights, the analysis is far from complete. Other tools provide additional information. Next, you will see how the modified du Pont system looks at the same data but gives some fresh insights that were not readily apparent when ratios alone were used.

The du Pont System of Financial Analysis

At the beginning of the chapter, it was mentioned that combining ratios in various ways provides new insights into the financial condition of a firm. The modified **du Pont system of financial analysis** combines efficiency, financial leverage, and profitability ratios to give the return on assets and the return on equity. The advantage of this system is that it provides much of the same information that was derived earlier, but with fewer ratios.

Figure 13–1 is a schematic representation of the modified du Pont system. All the ratios used in the system were described earlier in this chapter; the

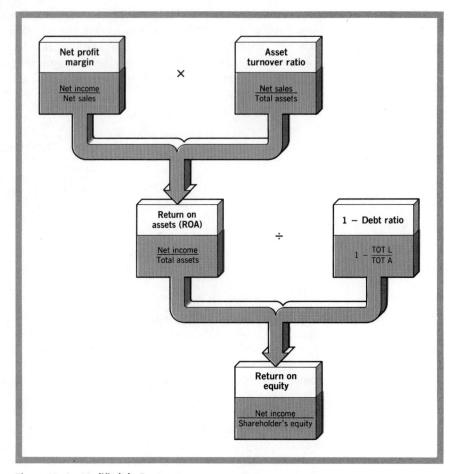

Figure 13–1   Modified du Pont system.

only new information is the unique way in which the ratios are combined. The original du Pont system was designed to determine the return on assets (*ROA*). As shown in the top part of the figure, the *ROA* can be determined by multiplying the net profit margin by the asset turnover. (This is not the method demonstrated earlier, but a widely used alternative.) The modified du Pont system includes a measure of financial leverage; when the *ROA* is divided by 1 minus the debt ratio, the resulting figure is the return on equity (*ROE*).

Figure 13–2 applies the modified du Pont system to Best Equipment. Basically, the system shows that the company's *ROA* declined as a result of lower profit margins and slower asset turnover.

An examination of the debt ratio provides a fresh insight into the return on equity. When financial leverage is taken into account, the return on equity has declined sharply. Recall that Best Equipment reduced its debt in 1989. Had the firm not reduced the debt—that is, had it maintained the same debt

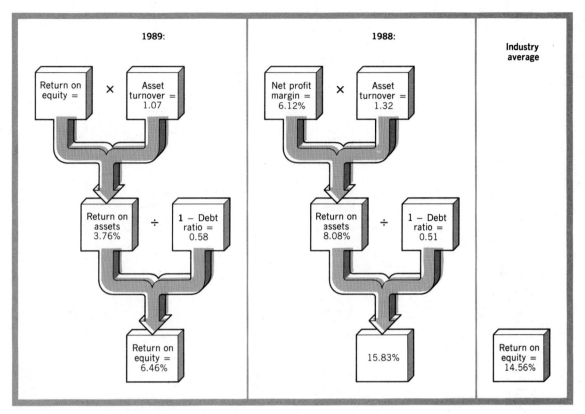

Figure 13–2   Modified du Pont system applied to Best Equipment Company.

ratio as in the previous year—the return on equity would have been 7.37 percent [−3.76/(1 − 0.4895) = 7.37%] instead of 6.46 percent. While the reduction in debt reduced the financial risk of the firm, one side effect was to reduce the return on equity. This is another example of the risk–return trade-off.

The modified du Pont system is also useful for testing the sensitivity of *ROA* and *ROE* to profit margins and asset turnovers. For example, suppose that the profit margin in 1989 had been 5 percent instead of 3.52 percent, with debt and asset turnover ratios remaining the same. The *ROA* would have been 5.35 percent and the *ROE* 9.19 percent. Stated otherwise, a 42 percent increase in the profit margin would have resulted in a 42 percent increase in the return on equity. Knowing these relationships helps the financial manager plan for the firm's growth. The following list shows other uses of the du Pont system.

Comparing different companies.
Comparing divisions within the same company.
Measuring the performance of divisions.
Serving as a basis for management rewards.
Serving as a framework for pricing decisions.

Table 13–4
Best Equipment Company Balance Sheet and Percentage of Assets[a]

	December 31			
	1989	1988	1989	1988
	(thousands of dollars)		(percent)	
Assets				
Current assets				
Cash and marketable securities	$ 1,578	$ 2,947	2.93	5.05
Accounts receivable	7,082	6,960	13.12	11.94
Inventories	34,542	38,925	63.98	66.77
Prepaid expenses	158	114	0.29	0.20
Total current assets	$43,360	$48,946	80.32	83.96
Investments and other assets				
Long-term portion of installment contracts receivable	$ 1,097	$ 304	2.03	0.52
Investments in unconsolidated subsidiaries	312	751	0.58	1.29
Other	705	668	1.31	1.15
Total investments and other assets	2,114	1,723	3.92	2.96
Property plant and equipment, at cost net of depreciation	8,513	7,627	15.76	13.08
Total assets	$53,987	$58,296	100.00	100.00
Liabilities and Shareholders' Equity				
Current liabilities				
Notes payable	$ 9,747	$13,051	18.05	22.39
Current maturities of long-term debt	1,004	1,007	1.86	1.73
Accounts payable	2,689	2,348	4.98	4.02
Customer deposits	454	230	0.84	0.39
Accrued liabilities	1,837	2,214	3.40	3.80
Accrued income taxes	1,484	1,935	2.74	3.32
Total current liabilities	$17,215	$20,785	31.88	35.65
Long-term debt, less current maturities	4,784	7,232	8.86	12.41
Other noncurrent liabilities	558	519	1.03	0.89
Total liabilities	$22,557	$28,536	41.78	48.95
Shareholders' equity[b]	31,430	29,760	58.22	51.05
Total liabilities and shareholders' equity	$53,987	$58,296	100.00	100.00

[a]Numbers may not add to totals due to rounding.
[b]Six million shares of common stock are outstanding in both years.

A careful examination of the ratios shown in Figure 13–1 reveals the following ways to improve performance.

Increase sales faster than total assets.
Reduce assets faster than sales.
Increase sales faster than expenses.
Reduce expenses proportionately more than sales.
Increase the debt ratio.

Common-Size Statement Analysis

Common-size financial statements present each item listed on the balance sheet as a percent of total assets and each item listed on the earnings statement as a percent of sales. This format facilitates the comparison of financial statements over time. Similarly, it is useful in comparing the financial statements

Table 13–5
Best Equipment Company Statement of Earnings and Percentage of Sales[a]

	For Years Ended December 31			
	1989	1988	1989	1988
	(thousands of dollars)		(percent)	
Revenue				
Net sales	$57,546	$76,900	100.00	100.00
Rentals	7,870	4,173	13.67	5.43
Other	112	258	0.20	0.33
	65,528	81,331	113.87	105.76
Costs and expenses				
Cost of goods sold	$47,057	$57,634	81.77	74.95
Selling, general, and administrative expenses	14,970	16,229	26.01	21.10
	62,027	73,863	107.78	96.05
Operating income	3,501	7,468	6.08	9.71
Other income and expenses				
Interest income	$ 548	$ 326	0.95	0.42
Interest expense	(1,421)	(1,686)	(2.47)	(2.19)
Gain	553		0.96	0.00
Other	170	42	0.29	0.06
	(150)	(1,318)	(0.26)	(1.71)
Earnings before taxes	3,351	6,150	5.82	8.00
Income taxes				
Current	$ 1,874	$ 1,015	3.26	1.32
Deferred	(552)	425	(0.96)	0.55
	1,322	1,440	2.30	1.87
Net income	$ 2,029	$ 4,710	3.52	6.12

[a]Numbers may not add to totals due to rounding.

of different companies. Financial data from large companies can be more easily compared with financial data from small companies, for example.

Tables 13–4 and 13–5 are common-size statements for Best Equipment Company. An examination of the tables reveals no surprises, because the problems of the company were mentioned earlier. However, the tables supply a different perspective that is useful to managers and analysts. For example, Best's managers may be interested in the fact that cost of goods sold did not decline in proportion to sales, and analysts may be interested in the fact that rental income became an increasingly important part of total revenue (see Table 13–5).

Limitations of Financial Analysis

You already know that the results of financial analysis depend in part on the analyst's perspective. You also know that inflation can distort the results of financial analysis. Some further limitations of financial analysis are discussed at this time to help you interpret data correctly and avoid common pitfalls.

As noted, financial data for an individual firm are frequently compared with an industry average that represents a standard for determining what is good or bad. Particular care must be taken in using such standards, for the following reasons.

1. Average means a middle value; by definition, half of the firms are "below average." The real issue is not whether a firm is above or below some average number, but how much the firm deviates from the average. For example, suppose the industry average for a particular ratio is 2:1 and a firm has a ratio of 1.8:1. The firm is below average by a small amount; so there may be no cause for concern. However, a ratio of 0.5:1 would be cause for concern.

2. A firm's financial ratios reflect its position on the product life cycle. As shown in Figure 13–3, a firm and the industry to which it belongs may be in different phases of the life cycle. In the early 1980s, for example, DeLorean was a new entrant into the mature automobile industry. The result was that the ratios for the firm differed from those for the industry. DeLorean had low liquidity ratios because it was expanding rapidly, whereas the industry average was higher. Similarly, DeLorean depended more heavily on borrowed funds (that is, financial leverage) than the industry on the average. These differences are neither good nor bad but reflect the relative positions of the firm and its industry on the life cycle. (Unfortunately, DeLorean failed, in part because it lacked sufficient funds to continue.)

3. Financial ratios may also be misinterpreted when data for the firm and the industry are measured at different phases in the business cycle. It takes

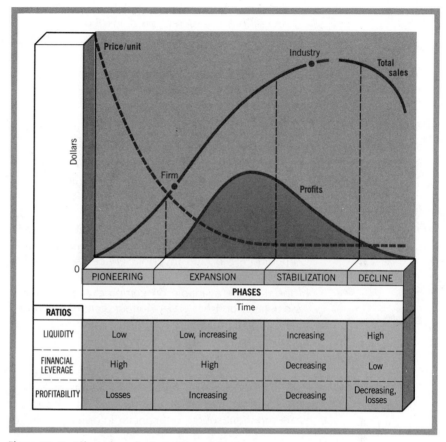

Figure 13–3   Life cycle and selected financial ratios.

time to obtain and publish industry data. Let's say that industry data were collected during the prosperity phase of the business cycle. During this phase, liquidity ratios were low and profitability was increasing. Six months later, when the data were distributed, a depression was beginning. Then, a firm might be expected to have high liquidity and decreasing profits. In this case, comparison with the industry average would be misleading, because the difference would reflect differences in the times at which measurements were taken.

4. Differences in accounting practices between firms may distort comparisons. For example, some firms use the LIFO method of inventory valuation, and others use FIFO. During periods of inflation, FIFO can result in overstatement of profits and thus in overstatement of measures of profitability. Similarly, different methods of depreciating fixed assets can affect profitability and financial ratios.

5. Finally, aggregate financial data for a firm may not accurately reflect the operations of different divisions. For example, one would expect Sears' Allstate Insurance division to behave differently from its retail sales division. Recognizing this limitation, the firm can analyze each division or business unit as though it were a separate firm.

Sources of Information

Data to be used in financial analysis are available from a wide variety of sources. A sampling of these sources follows.

Financial Services Financial service organizations publish data covering industries and individual firms. Three popular financial service organizations are Standard & Poor's Corporation, Moody's Investor Services, and Value Line Investment Survey. These services cover thousands of firms and are updated periodically. Some of the data are available on computer tapes. Another source, Robert Morris Associates, publishes *RMA Annual Statement Studies*, an excellent source of financial data organized by industry and firm size. Finally, *Dun & Bradstreet's Key Business Ratios* is also widely used.

Periodicals Periodicals containing industry and company data include *Business Week, Dun's Review, Forbes*, and *Fortune*. The *Wall Street Journal*, published daily, is an important source of financial information already cited in this book.

Government Sources The U.S. government and its agencies are sources of data on the state of the economy and various industries. Current economic data are published in *Business Conditions Digest (BCD), Economic Indicators*, and the *Survey of Current Business*. Industry data may also be found in the *Quarterly Financial Report for Manufacturing Corporations*, the *Survey of Current Business*, and the *U.S. Industrial Outlook*.

Finally, all companies whose stock is widely held must file periodic reports with the Securities and Exchange Commission (*SEC*). The annual report form, called Form 10-K, contains detailed financial information that cannot be found elsewhere. The 10-Ks and other reports can be obtained from the *SEC* or from the companies themselves.

Trade Associations Many trade publications contain financial data. "Steel Financial Analysis," for example, appears in *Iron Age*. Similarly, some banks publish financial data about particular industries. The Chase Manhattan Bank in New York publishes *Annual Financial Analysis of a Group of Petroleum Companies*.

Table 13–6

Summary of Equations

Ratio or Indicator	Equation	Equation number
Liquidity		
Net working capital	Current assets − Current liabilities	(13–1)
Current ratio	$\dfrac{\text{Current assets}}{\text{Current liabilities}}$	(13–2)
Acid-test ratio	$\dfrac{\text{Cash + Marketable securities + Receivables}}{\text{Current liabilities}}$	(13–3)
Average collection period	$\dfrac{\text{Accounts receivable}}{\text{Credit sales/Day}}$	(13–4)
Average payment period	$\dfrac{\text{Accounts payable}}{\text{Credit purchases/Day}}$	(13–5)
Efficiency		
Inventory turnover ratio	$\dfrac{\text{Cost of goods sold}}{\text{Inventory}}$	(13–6)
Age of inventory	$\dfrac{360 \text{ days}}{\text{Inventory turnover ratio}}$	(13–7)
Asset turnover ratio	$\dfrac{\text{Net sales}}{\text{Total assets}}$	(13–8)
Financial Leverage		
Debt ratio	$\dfrac{\text{Total liabilities}}{\text{Total assets}}$	(13–9)
Long-term debt as percent of total capital	$\dfrac{\text{Long-term debt}}{\text{Total capital}}$	(13–10)
Times interest earned	$\dfrac{\text{Earnings before interest and taxes}}{\text{Interest expense}}$	(13–11)
Profitability		
Earnings per share	$\dfrac{\text{Earnings available for common stock}}{\text{Average number of shares outstanding}}$	(13–12)
Payout ratio	$\dfrac{\text{Cash dividends per share}}{\text{Earnings per share}}$	(13–13)
Net profit margin	$\dfrac{\text{Net income}}{\text{Net sales}}$	(13–14)
Operating margin	$\dfrac{\text{Operating income}}{\text{Net sales}}$	(13–15)
Operating return on assets	$\dfrac{\text{Operating earnings before interest and taxes}}{\text{Total assets}}$	(13–16)
Return on assets	$\dfrac{\text{Net income}}{\text{Total assets}}$	(13–17)
Return on equity	$\dfrac{\text{Net income}}{\text{Shareholders' equity}}$	(13–18)
Modified du Pont System		
Return on assets	Net profit margin × Asset turnover ratio	
Return on equity	$\dfrac{\text{Return on assets}}{(1 - \text{Debt ratio})}$	

Summary

The purpose of financial analysis is to determine the financial condition of a company. The results depend in part on the objectives of the analyst; for example, a credit analyst and a securities analyst approach financial analysis from different perspectives. In addition, inflation may distort the results of the analysis.

Financial analysis involves examining a company's financial statements in a variety of ways. Generally, a series of financial ratios are calculated and compared with some industry average. Financial ratios and indicators are divided into four broad categories: liquidity, efficiency, financial leverage, and profitability. Liquidity ratios are concerned with the ability of a company to pay its current liabilities. Efficiency ratios measure how effectively a company uses its resources. Financial leverage ratios reflect the relationship between borrowed funds and those supplied by the owners (shareholders); these owners have a vested interest in the profitability of the firm. Table 13-6 summarizes the ratios and indicators discussed in the chapter.

The modified du Pont system of financial analysis combines several of the financial ratios and provides an alternative way of deriving the return on equity and the return on assets. This system adds valuable insights into the financial condition of a firm that may not be provided by ratio analysis alone. Common-size financial statements are useful in detecting changes in the financial condition of a firm and in comparing different firms.

In performing financial analysis, it is important to remember that company and industry averages may differ for a variety of reasons. For example, the firm and the industry may be located at different points on the product life cycle, or measurements for the firm and for the industry may have been taken during different phases of a business cycle.

Important Terms

Acid-test ratio
Age (of inventory)
Aging (of accounts)
Asset turnover ratio
Average collection period
Average payment period
Common-size financial statements
Current ratio
Debt ratio
du Pont system of financial analysis
Earnings available for common stock
Earnings per share (*EPS*)
Financial leverage
Inventory turnover ratio
Long-term debt as percent of total capital
Net profit margin
Net working capital
Operating margin

Operating return on assets   Return on equity (*ROE*)
Payout ratio   Return on investment (*ROI*)
Return on assets (*ROA*)   Times interest earned ratio

Questions

1. What is the general purpose of financial analysis? Within that general purpose, what different specific objectives might an analyst have?
2. Why should an analyst be cautious in interpreting data that has not been adjusted for inflation?
3. What are liquidity ratios intended to measure?
4. Compare and contrast several measures of liquidity. Which measure is best for which purpose? Why?
5. How can an aging schedule for accounts receivable assist in analyzing the liquidity of a firm?
6. What are efficiency ratios intended to measure?
7. Identify several measures of financial leverage. How do they differ from one another?
8. Discuss several ways of measuring profitability. What is the purpose of each measure?
9. What is the modified du Pont system of financial analysis? What does it accomplish that simple ratio analysis does not?
10. Suppose a firm's return on assets and return on equity are lower than the industry averages. What are some possible causes, and how might these problems be addressed? (*Hint*: Think about insights from the modified du Pont system.)
11. What are common-size financial statements? How can they be used?
12. How do business cycles affect the interpretation of financial ratios, especially in situations where a firm is compared with an industry average?
13. How does a firm's stage in the life cycle affect interpretation of its ratios in comparison with industry averages?
14. When firms are compared, how do accounting policies affect interpretation of financial ratios?
15. Identify several sources of information about industry average. Is being below average always bad? Why or why not?

Problems

1. Over the last 4 years, the annual sales of Cramer Corporation have been $50,000, $52,000, $59,000, and $67,000. Management is pleased with the $17,000 increase over this period. If the inflation index over the 4 years has been 1.15, 1.21, 1.37, and 1.56, is management's pleasure justified?

   For Problems 2 through 7, use the following data for Tenkiller Corporation and related industry averages.

Balance Sheet
Tenkiller Corporation
December 31, 1990

Assets

Current assets:

Cash	$ 40,000
Marketable securities	30,000
Accounts receivable	100,000
Inventory	80,000
Total current assets	$250,000
Gross fixed assets	$500,000
Less:accumulated depreciation	150,000
Net fixed assets	$350,000
Other assets	$ 50,000
Total assets	$650,000

Liabilities and net worth

Current liabilities

Accrued liabilities	$ 20,000
Notes payable	100,000
Accounts payable	80,000
Total current liabilities	$200,000
Long-term debt	$100,000

Net worth (equity):

Preferred stock (1,000 shares)	50,000
Common stock (10,000 shares)	100,000
Paid-in capital	50,000
Retained earnings	150,000
Total net worth	$350,000
Total liabilities and net worth	$650,000

Income Statement
Tenkiller Corporation
December 31, 1990

Net sales:

Cash		$ 750,000
Credit		1,500,000
Total sales		$2,250,000
Less: Cost of goods sold		1,450,000
Gross profit		$ 800,000
Less: Operating expenses:		
Selling expenses	200,000	
Administrative expenses	140,000	
Depreciation	80,000	
Total operating expenses		420,000
Operating income (*EBIT*)		$ 380,000
Less: Interest expense		30,000
Profit before taxes		$ 350,000
Less: Taxes		150,000
Profit after taxes (net income)		$ 200,000
Less: Preferred dividends		10,000
Earnings available to common stock		190,000

Additional information: Common stock dividends were $80,000.
Credit purchases are 80% of cost of goods sold.

Industry Averages, 1990

Current ratio	2.50
Acid-test ratio	1.00
Average collection period (days)	36
Average payment period (days)	42
Inventory turnover (times)	25
Total asset turnover (times)	3.75
Fixed asset turnover (times)	7.20
Debt ratio	.40
Long-term debt to total capital	.20
Times interest earned	15
Earnings per share	$10
Dividends per share	$ 4
Net profit margin	.07
Operating profit margin	.15
Return on assets	.26
Return on common equity	.44

2. Analyze the liquidity position of Tenkiller in 1990. Include all relevant measures of liquidity. Compare Tenkiller with the industry and recommend changes for the firm if you believe any are necessary.

3. Analyze the efficiency of Tenkiller. Include all relevant measures. Compare the firm with the industry and recommend necessary changes.

4. Analyze Tenkiller's use of financial leverage compared with the industry's. Are changes necessary to make Tenkiller compare more favorably with the industry? Why or why not? What trade-offs for Tenkiller's stockholders are involved in these changes?

5. Analyze the profitability of Tenkiller and compare it with the industry average. Include all relevant ratios. Is Tenkiller doing better than, worse than, or the same as the industry? Explain.

6. Using the modified du Pont system, analyze the profitability of Tenkiller. Identify the firm's strengths and weaknesses. Recommend any changes that follow from your analysis. For this purpose, consider the preferred stock of the firm as debt.

7. From a creditor's point of view, how well is Tenkiller doing? From a shareholder's point of view? From management's point of view? Explain the basis of your answers.

For Problems 8 through 11, use the data provided for Monroe Machines, Inc., and related industry averages.

Balance Sheet
Monroe Machines, Inc.
December 31, 1990

Assets
Current assets:

Cash	$ 250,000
Marketable securities	50,000
Accounts receivable	1,200,000
Inventory	2,000,000
Total current assets	$ 3,500,000

Balance Sheet (*Continued*)

Gross fixed assets	$ 3,800,000
Less: Accumulated depreciation	1,500,000
Net fixed assets	$ 2,300,000
Other assets	$ 200,000
Total assets	$ 6,000,000
Liabilities and net worth	
Current liabilities	
Accrued liabilities	$ 400,000
Notes payable	900,000
Accounts payable	600,000
Total current liabilities	$ 1,900,000
Long-term debt	$ 1,000,000
Net worth (equity):	
Common stock (100,000 shares)	1,000,000
Paid-in capital	100,000
Retained earnings	2,000,000
Total net worth	$ 3,100,000
Total liabilities and net worth	$ 6,000,000

Income Statement
Monroe Machines, Inc.
December 31, 1990

Net sales:		
Cash		$ 1,500,000
Credit		9,000,000
Total sales		$10,500,000
Less: Cost of goods sold		6,200,000
Gross profit		$ 4,300,000
Less: Operating expenses:		
Selling expenses	800,000	
Administrative expenses	900,000	
Depreciation	300,000	
Total operating expenses		2,000,000
Operating income (*EBIT*)	—	$ 2,300,000
Less: Interest expense		200,000
Profit before taxes		$ 2,100,000
Less: Taxes		840,000
Profit after taxes (net income)		$ 1,260,000

Additional Information: Common stock dividends were $200,000.
All purchases are on credit.

Industry Averages and Historical Data

	Industry 1990	Monroe 1988	Monroe 1989	
Liquidity				
Current ratio	2.25	2.24	2.01	1.84
Acid-Test ratio	0.99	1.05	0.95	.79
Average collection period (days)	35	35	40	.48
Average payment period (days)	35	30	32	.35
Efficiency Inventory turnover (times)	5	4.60	4	3.1
Total asset turnover (times)	1.90	2.20	2.00	1.75
Fixed asset turnover (times)	5.50	5.20	4.80	4.57
Debit Ratio Debt ratio	0.45	0.57	0.53	.48
Long-term debt to total capital	0.32	0.40	0.33	.32
Times interest earned	11	9.40 *good*	10.50	11.5
Profitability Earnings per share	$5.00	$8.40	$10.00	12.60
Dividends per share	$1.50	$1.50	$ 1.80	2.00
Net profit margin	0.10	0.09	0.09	.12
Operating profit margin	0.18	0.26	0.24	.22
Return on assets	0.19	0.20	0.18	.21
Return on common equity	0.35	0.47	0.38	.41

 8. Consider whether, as a bank loan officer, you would be willing to offer Monroe $2 million in additional short-term loans in 1991. Use all relevant ratios and analyze the firm on the basis of trends in its own performance as well as in comparison with other firms.

 9. Comment on the efficiency of Monroe, both in relation to its own history and in comparison with other firms. Use all relevant ratios and explain your analysis fully.

10. As a shareholder, how would you assess the current and recent performance of Monroe? Use all relevant ratios and explain your analysis. Use trends as well as industry average data.

11. As the financial manager for Monroe, determine where you should place most of your efforts in the future. Use all relevant ratios and explain your recommendations by referring to trend and industry average data. The modified du Pont system should be a useful tool in performing this analysis.

12. Jason Limited, Inc., has current assets of $1.6 million, of which $0.8 million is inventory. Current liabilities are $1 million. Calculate the effects on the current and acid-test ratios of each of the following transactions.

(a) The firm sells $200,000 of inventory and uses the proceeds to pay off current liabilities.

(b) The firm sells $200,000 of marketable securities and uses the proceeds to pay off current liabilities.

(c) The firm collects $200,000 in accounts receivable and deposits the proceeds in its cash account.

(d) The firm sells $200,000 of new common stock and uses the proceeds to pay off current liabilities.

(e) The firm sells $200,000 of long-term debt. It uses $100,00 of the proceeds to pay off current liabilities and $100,000 to increase the cash account.

13.. Quick Corporation had sales last year of $5.2 million, 27 percent of which were for cash. Calculate Quick's average accounts receivable balance if the average collection period was 40 days.

14. Pressy Printing has just purchased a novelty T-shirt firm with fixed assets of $200,000. The previous owner has told Pressy to expect a fixed asset turnover of 6, a total asset turnover of 4, and a net profit margin of 6 percent. What level of sales and net profit can Pressy expect to receive from the division? What are the current assets of the division?

15. Linblad, Inc., has sales of $1 million, total assets of $500,000, an operating margin of 20 percent, and interest payments of $50,000. The tax rate is 40 percent. Calculate its times interest earned and return on assets ratios.

16. Roger Corporation has a return on assets ratio of 13 percent and a profit margin of 6 percent in 1989.
    (a) What is the firm's total asset turnover ratio?
    (b) If the debt ratio is 0.4, what is the firm's return on equity?

17. Doug's Donut Shoppe has a return on equity of 36 percent in 1990.
    (a) What is Doug's return on assets if the debt ratio is 0.35?
    (b) What is the net profit margin if total asset turnover is 6?
    (c) What are total dollar sales if dollar profits are $150,000?

18. The manager of a small corporation has lost last year's financial statements and can find only bits and pieces of the records. Reconstruct the balance sheet given the following information and partial balance sheet. Assume a 360-day year.

Current ratio	2.0
Acid-test ratio	1.0
Total asset turnover	2.5
Credit sales	0.8 of total sales
Debt ratio	0.4
Average collection period	36 days

Assets

Current assets:	
Cash	$
Marketable securities	100,000
Accounts receivable	
Inventory	
Total current assets	$_____
Gross fixed assets	$400,000
Less: Accumulated depreciation	100,000
Net fixed assets	$
Other assets	$200,000
Total assets	$_____

Liabilities and net worth

Current liabilities	
Notes payable	$ 80,000
Accounts payable	
Total current liabilities	$_____
Long-term debt	$100,000
Net worth (equity):	
Common stock	200,000
Paid-in capital	200,000
Retained earnings	300,000
Total net worth	$_____
Total liabilities and net worth	$_____

19. The firm in Problem 18 has just found additional information. Help management reconstruct the income statement for last year.

Inventory turnover	15	times
Operating margin	0.2	
Times interest earned	5	
Return on equity	0.367	
Sales	_____	
Less: Cost of goods sold	_____	
Operating income (*EBIT*)	_____	
Less: Interest	_____	
Earnings before taxes	_____	
Taxes	_____	
Net income	_____	

20. Tuba City Iron Corporation has offered you a job as a financial analyst. Unfortunately, the firm's last balance sheet was lost and your first task is to reconstruct it from the information below. Assume a 360-day year.

Cost of goods sold	$3,000,000
Net working capital	$400,000
Inventory turnover	6 times
Average collection period	60 days
Average payment period	90 days
Asset turnover	2.5 times
Common stock	50,000 shares at $10 par
Preferred stock	1,000 shares at $100 par

Assets

Current assets:	
Cash and marketable securities	150,000
Accounts receivable	750,000
Inventory	
Total current assets	$ _____
Gross fixed assets	$ _____
Less: Accumulated depreciation	200,000
Net fixed assets	$ _____
Total assets	$ _____

Liabilities and net worth

Current liabilities	
Accrued liabilities	$250,000
Accounts payable	
Total current liabilities	$ _____
Net worth (equity):	
Preferred stock	_____
Common stock	_____
Retained earnings	_____
Total net worth	$ _____
Total liabilities and net worth	$ _____

14 Financial Planning and Forecasting

Chapter 13 quoted the saying "if you don't know where you're going, it doesn't make any difference what road you take to get there." **Financial planning** helps management take the right road by providing forecasts of future income and expenses. As a rule, the forecasts take the form of cash budgets and other financial statements. This chapter covers some of the fundamentals of financial

After reading this chapter, you should know the following.

1. **How funds flow through a company.**
2. **What items are classified as sources and uses of funds.**
3. **How funds flow statements are constructed and used.**
4. **How cash budgets are constructed and used.**
5. **What is involved in the percentage of sales method of forecasting.**
6. **How external financial needs are determined.**
7. **How the graphic method, regression analysis, and simulations aid in long-term forecasting.**

planning, including the preparation of cash budgets and several forecasting techniques.

Comments on Planning

Financial planning is part of the corporate planning process. As a rule, planning contributes to higher profits, improved decision making, and fewer mistakes. Planning involves making decisions today that will affect the future of a company. However, the future is a moving target; planning improves the aim, but does not guarantee its accuracy.

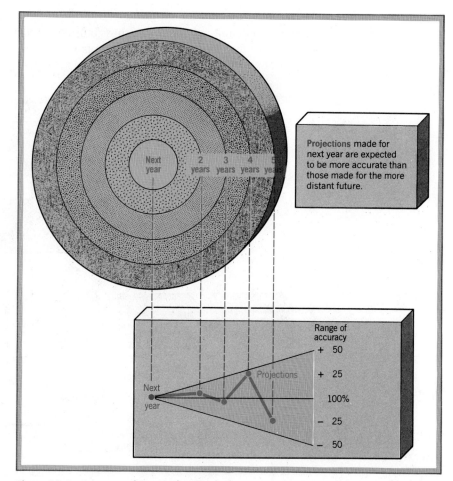

Figure 14–1 Accuracy of 5-year planning cycle.

Because the future is uncertain, plans made today should not be expected to work precisely. Plans should be amended to reflect changes in the company's environment that may occur next week or a year from now. This continuous updating means that short-term plans and budgets are more accurate than long-term plans and budgets. Figure 14–1 depicts a 5-year plan as a series of expanding circles. The greatest accuracy is in the smallest circle, which represents the next year. Accuracy diminishes as additional years are added. Thus, there is danger in adhering to plans made in the past that do not fit the conditions existing today. Plans must be adapted to help management cope with a changing world; they are not rules carved in granite that must be followed unquestioningly.

How Funds Flow

Financial planning may affect a firm's future financial structure as well as its sources and uses of funds. In order to plan, we must understand how funds flow through a company.

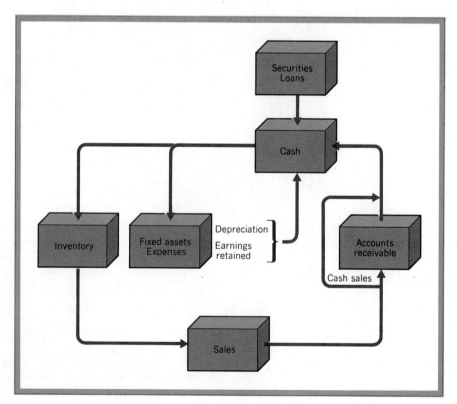

Figure 14–2   Funds flow cycle.

Funds Flow Cycle Figure 14–2 shows a simplified, static version of a funds flow cycle. It is simplified because not all the sources and uses of funds are shown; it is static because it does not take time into account. (We will focus on the effect of time on flows of funds after we examine the funds flow cycle.)

The **funds flow cycle** is sometimes referred to as a **working capital cycle**. However, the word *funds* is more appropriate because it encompasses a wider range than *working capital*. **Funds** include cash as well as other sources of value such as tax credits and depreciation.

The flow of funds is depicted in Figure 14–2 as a continuous stream circulating through a firm. Cash and other funds are used to acquire fixed assets and inventory. The fixed assets are depreciated and the depreciation shields operating income from income taxes with expenses that do not require cash outlays. Therefore, depreciation is considered a source of funds.

Inventory is sold for cash or credit. The credit sales give rise to accounts receivable, which are ultimately collected and added to the firm's cash. Cash is also used to pay ongoing expenses. The difference between sales revenues and expenses is profit. Some of the profit is paid to shareholders in the form of cash dividends and the remainder is retained as a source of funds. The earnings that have been retained may not be sufficient to support the firm's growth. Consequently, the firm will have to use external sources, such as selling securities or making loans, to acquire additional funds.

Timing of Funds The purchase of fixed assets and inventory, the sale of inventory, and the
Flow collection of accounts receivable do not occur simultaneously. To follow the sequence of events, we'll enter the funds flow cycle at the point at which inventory is acquired. Table 14–1 shows four transaction categories and four time periods. In the first period, inventory is acquired (indicated by a +, for increase) and financed by accounts payable. In the second period, the inventory is sold (indicated by a −, for decrease) for credit, which increases accounts receivable. The accounts receivable are collected in the third period, adding to the firm's cash. Finally, the cash is used to pay the accounts payable incurred in the first period.

This example demonstrates the sequential nature of the flow of funds through a company. Understanding such sequences is essential in budgeting, which will be discussed later in the chapter. This example also provides an introduction to the sources and uses of funds.

Sources and Uses Collectively, all **sources and uses of funds** make up the **funds flow statement**;
of Funds this statement is a formalized way to examine the flow of funds through a company. Preparing a funds flow statement involves classifying the changes in balance sheet items that occur between two dates into the categories shown in Table 14–2—sources and uses. Before examining the funds flow statement, let's look more closely at these classifications.

Table 14–1

Flow of Funds

Transaction Categories	Period			
	1	2	3	4
Cash	0	0	+	−
Accounts receivable	0	+	−	0
Inventory	+	−	0	0
Accounts payable	+	0	0	−

Note: + = increase; − = decrease; 0 = unchanged.

The transactions presented in connection with Table 14–1 are classified here as sources or uses of funds. In the first period, the source of funds was an increase in liabilities (accounts payable) and the use of funds was an increase in an asset (inventory). By definition, the sources of funds must equal the uses of funds. In the second period, the sale of inventory was the source of funds, an increase in accounts receivable was the use, and so on, outlined as follows.

Period	Sources	Uses
1	Increase liabilities (accounts payable)	Increase assets (inventory)
2	Decrease assets (inventory)	Increase assets (accounts receivable)
3	Decrease assets (accounts receivable)	Increase assets (cash)
4	Decrease assets (cash)	Decrease liabilities (accounts payable)

Funds Flow Statements　Like ratio analysis and the du Pont system, funds flow statements provide a perspective on a firm's financial condition. To illustrate this perspective, consider the case of Lumber Supply Company, whose balance sheets covering three years are presented in Table 14–3.

Table 14–2

Sources and Uses of Funds

Sources	Uses
Increase liabilities	Decrease liabilities
Increase equity 　Includes sale of stock and earnings 　retained	Decrease equity 　Includes repurchase of stock and 　payment of cash dividends
Decrease current assets	Increase current assets
Decrease fixed assets before 　depreciation	Increase fixed assets
Depreciation	

Table 14–3
Balance Sheet for Lumber Supply Company

	December 31		
	1993	**1992**	**1991**
Assets			
Current assets:			
Cash	$ 70,450	$ 41,242	$ 58,430
Certificate of deposit	0	37,000	19,000
Notes and accounts receivable			
Trade	2,378,630	1,328,968	1,225,758
Other	27,500	7,000	7,000
Inventories	2,608,791	1,890,327	1,648,189
Prepaid expenses	9,437	9,030	8,432
Total current assets	5,094,808	3,313,567	2,966,809
Fixed assets:			
Plant and equipment	467,900	376,526	356,130
Other	207,839	147,674	139,855
Total fixed assets	675,739	524,200	495,985
Less:			
Accumulated depreciation	386,736	337,467	310,948
Total net fixed assets	289,003	186,733	185,037
Total assets	$5,383,811	$3,500,300	$3,151,846
Liabilities and Shareholders' Equity			
Current liabilities:			
Notes payable	$ 497,643	$ 179,630	$ 197,483
Accounts payable	2,638,737	1,385,390	1,227,439
Accrued liabilities	112,164	94,101	90,921
Total current liabilities	3,248,544	1,659,121	1,515,843
Long-term debt	47,665	53,840	56,557
Total liabilities	3,296,209	1,712,961	1,572,400
Shareholders' equity:			
10,000 shares of common stock at par value	250,000	250,000	250,000
Retained earnings	1,837,602	1,537,339	1,329,446
Total shareholders' equity	2,087,602	1,787,339	1,579,446
Total liabilities and shareholders' equity	$5,383,811	$3,500,300	$3,151,846

The first step in preparing a funds flow statement is to calculate the change in each of the balance sheet items, noting whether it is an increase or a decrease. For example, from Table 14–3 we can determine that in 1993 certificates of deposit declined $37,000 and inventory increased $718,464. The next step is to determine whether the changes are sources or uses of funds; then, they are arranged into a format such as that shown in Table 14–4.

The sources of funds are grouped into three major categories: internal operations, changes in liabilities (referring to the right side of the balance sheet), and decreases in assets. Sources from internal operations include changes in retained earnings. Depreciation is also considered an internal source of funds.

Table 14–4
Funds Flow Statement for Lumber Supply Company

	1993		1992	
Sources of funds:				
Internal operations:				
Change in equity (retained earnings)	$ 300,263	15%	$207,893	50%
Depreciation	49,269	2	26,519	6
Total	349,532	17	234,412	56
Increases in liabilities:				
Accounts payable	1,253,347	63	157,951	39
Accrued expenses	18,063	1	3,180	1
Notes payable	318,013	17	0	0
Decreases in assets:				
Cash	0	0	17,188	4
Certificates of deposit	37,000	2	0	0
Total sources of funds	$1,975,955	100%	$412,731	100%
Uses of funds:				
Increases in assets:				
Cash	$ 29,208	1%	$ 0	0%
Certificates of deposit	0	0	18,000	4
Notes and accounts receivable—net	1,049,662	54	103,210	25
Inventory	718,464	36	242,138	59
Prepaid expenses	407	0	598	0
Other	20,500	1	0	0
Fixed assets	151,539	8	28,215	7
Decreases in liabilities:				
Notes payable	0	0	17,853	4
Long-term debt	6,175	0	2,717	1
Total uses of funds	$1,975,955	100%	$412,731	100%

Increases in liabilities and decreases in assets are self-explanatory. Uses of funds are grouped into increases in assets and decreases in liabilities, which are also self-explanatory.

The funds flow statement shows that the total sources and uses of funds in 1993 amounted to $1,975,955, compared with $412,731 in the previous year. Because this difference is so great, it is particularly useful to express each item as a percentage of the total sources and uses of funds. This puts the balance sheets on a relative basis, which facilitates comparisons.

The data reveal substantial differences in financing patterns between the periods. In 1992, for example, increased equity and accounts payable accounted for 89 percent of the total funds raised by Lumber Supply Company. Most of the funds were used to build inventory (59 percent) and accounts receivable (25 percent). Keep in mind the sequence of financial transactions presented earlier. Inventory was sold, giving rise to increased accounts receivable. Accordingly, in 1993, the increase in accounts receivable was the major use of funds (54 percent), followed by further increases in inventory (36 percent). The higher levels of inventory indicate that the company expects sales to rise. This time, however, the expansion of assets is being financed primarily by short-term loans from creditors in the form of accounts payable (63 percent). Extending this analysis to cover additional years, either in the future or in the past, would make it possible to track the financial policies of a firm over time and to determine the firm's needs for funds. In addition, funds flow statements enable the user to determine if short-term needs are being financed with short-term funds and long-term needs with long-term funds.

Forecasting Financial Needs

Although most financial managers have 20/20 hindsight, none can see what tomorrow holds in store. Certain techniques have been developed to help them anticipate the firm's financial needs. The cash budget is one such technique, and the percentage of sales method is another. However, both techniques depend heavily on the accuracy of a sales forecast. If the sales forecast is wrong, it does not matter which technique is used to determine the financial needs of the firm—the projections will be wrong!

Cash Budgets Cash budgets are useful in financial planning because they highlight a firm's liquidity position. **Cash budgets** show the amount and timing of revenues and expenses over various periods of time. Weekly and monthly cash budgets are commonly used tools in the ongoing operations of many business concerns. Cash budgets focus on the future, in contrast to funds flow statements, which analyze the past—that is, where the firm got funds and where they went. Nevertheless, understanding the "where got–where go" concept is essential in preparing a cash budget.

The accuracy of a cash budget depends on the accuracy of the sales forecast, as noted, and on the accuracy of the assumptions used in developing the budget. If the sales forecast is inaccurate, revenues will be misstated. Similarly, expenses will be misstated if assumptions about the volume of credit sales, wages, and other expenses are not correct. The result will be a poor forecast of cash needs. Thus, cash budgets, like other tools we have examined, have their limitations. The major limitation is our inability to know with absolute certainty what the future holds. To some extent, this limitation is overcome by forecasting techniques and other methods that take uncertainty into account, such as the simulations discussed later in this chapter.

Assumptions. The first step in preparing a cash budget is to make a detailed list of assumptions concerning cash receipts and disbursements for the budget period. The assumptions used to prepare a budget for Lumber Supply Company for January through March 1994 are listed in Table 14–5.

Table 14–5
Assumptions for Cash Budget, January–March 1994

I. Sales will increase at a rate of 15% per month over the next 3 months. Sales in December 1993 were $14,991,341.

II. Credit sales comprise 85% of the total sales volume; the remaining are cash sales.

III. Of the credit sales, 90% are collected in the month incurred; the remaining 10% are collected in the following month.

IV. On January 1, the firm borrowed $100,000 from the bank to buy equipment. The principal will be repaid in equal installments of $20,000 over the next 5 months. Interest payments are $883, $667, and $500 during the January–March period.

V. No fixed assets will be sold during the 3-month period.

VI. Purchases may be figured at 50% of expected monthly sales.

VII. Of the purchases, 90% are on credit; the remaining 10% are cash purchases.

VIII. Of the credit purchases, 95% are paid for in the month incurred, and the remaining 5% are paid in the following month.

IX. Selling and general and administrative expenses remain at approximately 12.6% of total sales.

X. Projected wage figures of $5.1 million, $5.8 million, and $6.75 million were obtained from consultation with all departments concerning predicted personnel levels.

XI. Other manufacturing expenses include heat, light, water, and power.

XII. Tax payments are expected to remain at the $200,000 level through the next 2 months and increase to approximately $225,000 during the following month.

XIII. A cash balance of $90,000 will be maintained.

The first assumption is that sales will increase 15 percent per month over the next 3 months. This reflects a seasonal upswing in the business as well as major new commercial real estate developments in the area. Basically, the company has extrapolated the growth of sales over the past few years and made a simple forecast that sales would grow at the same rate in the future. Other methods of forecasting will be presented later in this chapter.

The second assumption is that credit sales will account for 85 percent of the total sales volume, and the third assumption concerns the rate at which the credit sales will be collected. The remaining assumptions concern a bank loan, purchases, and other items that affect cash inflows and outflows.

Schedule of Receipts.   The second step in preparing a cash budget is to develop a **schedule of receipts** based on the budget assumptions. The schedule of receipts for Lumber Supply Company is presented in Table 14–6. For your convenience, the number of the assumption used to derive each item in the table is listed. Lumber Supply Company expects total sales to reach $17,240,042 in January 1994. Of that amount, the company expects 85 percent to be credit sales ($14,654,036). According to the assumptions, 90 percent of the credit sales are collected in the month in which they originate ($13,188,632 for January 1994), and the remainder in the following month;

Table 14–6
Schedule of Receipts

	Assumption (from Table 14–5)	January 1994	February 1994	March 1994
1. Total sales	I	$17,240,042	$19,826,048	$22,799,956
2. Credit sales	II	14,654,036	16,852,141	19,379,962
3. Accounts receivable:				
4. Collected in month incurred	III	13,188,632	15,166,927	17,441,966
5. Collected in month following sale	III	1,274,264	1,465,404	1,685,214
6. Total receipts from receivables		14,462,896	16,632,331	19,127,180
7. Cash sales	II	2,586,006	2,973,907	3,419,993
8. Total cash receipts from sales (lines 6–7)		$17,048,902	$19,606,238	$22,547,173

10 percent of the December 1993 credit sales should therefore be collected in January 1994. Total sales in December 1993 amounted to $14,991,341; so the amount collected in January 1994 is $1,274,264 ($14,991,341 × 0.85 × 0.10 = $1,274,264). Thus, total receipts from credit sales are forecast to be $14,462,896 in January. This amount is added to cash sales, giving total cash receipts from sales of $17,048,902. The process is repeated for each of the following months.

Schedule of Disbursements.   The third step is to develop a **schedule of cash disbursements**. As shown in Table 14–7, Lumber Supply Company plans total purchases amounting to $8,620,021 for January 1994. This amount is based

Table 14–7
Schedule of Disbursements

	Assumption (from Table 14–5)	January 1994	February 1994	March 1994
1. Total purchases	VI	$ 8,620,021	$ 9,913,024	$11,399,978
2. Credit purchases	VII	7,758,019	8,921,722	10,259,980
3. Cash payment for credit purchases in month incurred	VIII	7,370,118	8,475,636	9,746,981
4. Cash payment for credit purchases in previous month	VIII	337,305	387,901	446,086
5. Cash purchases	VII	862,002	991,302	1,139,998
6. Selling, general and administrative expenses	IX	2,172,245	2,498,082	2,872,795
7. Wages	X	5,100,000	5,800,000	6,750,000
8. Other manufacturing expenses	XI	900,000	1,250,000	1,475,000
9. Income taxes	XII	200,000	200,000	225,000
10. Interest	IV	833	667	500
11. Principal payments on loans	IV	20,000	20,000	20,000
Total cash disbursements (lines 3–11)		$16,962,503	$19,623,588	$22,676,360

on the assumption that purchases are 50 percent of sales. The company has also assumed that 90 percent of the purchases ($7,758,019) will be made on credit. The remaining items used in the calculations are also based on the budget assumptions. By now, it should be clear that errors or changes in the assumptions can have a major impact on total cash disbursements, which are shown on the bottom line of the table.

Schedule of Cash Balances.   The final step in the preparation of a cash budget is to subtract total cash disbursements from total cash receipts; this gives the net change in cash, or **schedule of cash balances**, shown in Table 14–8. For example, in January 1994, the net change in cash was $86,399. This amount is added to the cash balance at the beginning of the year ($70,450, from the balance sheet shown in Table 14–3) resulting in a $156,849 cash balance at the end of the year. The firm's desired cash level is $90,000. Accordingly, there is a cash surplus of $66,849 on hand at the end of the month. As shown in Table 14–8, there are also cash surpluses in the following month. But the firm must borrow $79,688 in March.

The figures showing cash surpluses or deficits highlight the usefulness of a cash budget. It is used primarily to help management plan for financial needs. In doing so, the cash budget serves an additional purpose. It acts as a standard of behavior against which the firm's or manager's performance can be measured. Deviations from that standard must be explained and corrective action taken.

Finally, it should be noted that the cash budget may take on a degree of importance that causes it to become an end in itself. Budgets, like plans, are not supposed to be numbers carved in granite; they should be flexible tools. Financial managers can emphasize flexibility by testing the sensitivity of the budget to changes in revenues and disbursements. For example, they may make three forecasts of revenues: optimistic, pessimistic, and something between the two. This procedure may disclose that, for example, if revenues fall short of optimistic projections, additional borrowing may be required.

Table 14–8
Summary of Net Cash Flows and Balances (Schedule of Cash Balances)

	Reference	January 1994	February 1994	March 1994
Total cash receipts from sales	Table 14–6	$17,048,902	$19,606,238	$22,547,173
Total cash disbursements	Table 14–7	16,962,503	19,623,588	22,676,360
Net change in cash		86,399	(17,350)	(129,187)
Cumulative cash (cash at beginning + or − net change in cash)	Table 14–3	70,450	156,849	139,499
		156,849	139,499	10,312
Less: Desired cash level	Table 14–5, VIII	90,000	90,000	90,000
Surplus cash		66,849	49,499	0
Additional cash needed		$ 0	$ 0	$ 79,688

Percentage of Sales Method   The **percentage of sales method** of developing *pro forma* (projected) financial statements is a forecasting technique based on the assumption that a constant relationship exists between sales and selected balance sheet and income statement items that relate to operations. (Extraordinary income is not considered here.) For example, a firm may assume that in order to sell $100 worth of goods annually, it must have $20 worth of inventory on hand. The inventory is turned over five times each year. If projections indicate that sales will increase to $200, it follows that the firm should have $40 in inventory. The ratio of inventory to sales is 20 percent in both periods.

Advantages.   The major advantages of the percentage of sales method are that it provides management with short-term *pro forma* financial statements and with requirements for external financing. The examples that follow demonstrate that this method is also relatively easy to use. (In order to use the percentage of sales method properly, however, the analyst must be thoroughly conversant with the firm to which it is being applied.)

Disadvantages.   The percentage of sales method also involves disadvantages. If the assumptions regarding stable financial relationships are not correct, policy actions may result that are not in the best interest of the firm. For example, assume that a firm's inventory-to-sales ratio is 20 percent, as described earlier,

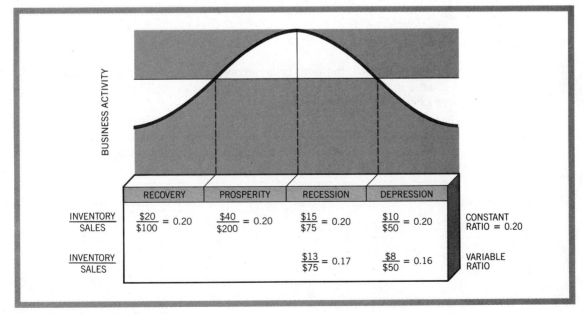

Figure 14–3   Inventory/sales ratio.

and that the economy is in transition from prosperity to recession. As shown in Figure 14–3, the firm expects a decline in inventories in direct proportion to the projected level of sales during the recession and depression. However, the financial manager may decide that inventory should be further reduced in both periods, because sales forecasts for the firm are often too optimistic. In this case, the financial manager would prefer a variable ratio of inventory to sales. If one relationship on the balance sheet is changed, all the others are affected, thereby rendering the percentage of sales method ineffective.

Furthermore, it can be shown that relationships between sales and assets are different for business concerns in the expansion phase of the life cycle than for business concerns in the stabilization phase. Thus, constant ratios are not appropriate for long time spans.

Finally, the percentage of sales method assumes that a linear relationship exists between inventory and sales. The following equation describes this straight line.

$$I = a + bS \qquad (14–1)$$

where

I = Inventory
S = Sales
a and b = Constant intercept and slope of line

The ratio of inventory to sales is calculated as follows.

$$\frac{I}{S} = \frac{a + bS}{S} = \frac{a}{S} + b \qquad (14–2)$$

Unless a is zero, the ratio of inventory to sales will not be constant. If a is greater than zero, the ratio will decline as sales increase and the percentage of sales method will give incorrect results.

The following example using Equation 14–1 illustrates the point. If the intercept term a is zero and sales increase from \$100 to \$200, the inventory-to-sales ratio, I/S, remains unchanged. However, if the intercept term is, for example, 5, the inventory-to-sales ratio declines when sales increase.

		Sales	
		$100.00	$200.00
$I = a + bS$			
If $a = 0$			
$I = 0 + 0.2S$			
	$I =$	20.00	40.00
	$I/S =$	0.20	0.20
If $a = 5$			
$I = 5 + 0.2S$			
	$I =$	25.00	45.00
	$I/S =$	0.25	0.225

More will be said about linear equations when regression analysis is explained later in this chapter.

In spite of its shortcomings, the percentage of sales method is a useful technique for evaluating short-term financial needs.

Pro Forma Income Statement Projected sales are used in connection with the percentage of sales method to develop a pro forma income statement and a pro forma balance sheet. (These can be thought of as pro forma common-size statements.) The **pro forma income statement** is developed first so that the retained earnings that will appear on the balance sheet can be estimated.

As an illustration, consider the pro forma income statement for Lumber Supply Company shown in Table 14–9. Column 1 is the income statement for the base year, 1993. All the items in the income statement are expressed as a percentage of net sales in the base year. Thus, Column 2 lists each of the items in Column 1 as a percentage of sales in 1993. This column could be called a **percent income statement**. Such statements, like the financial ratios described in Chapter 13, are widely used tools for analyzing the financial behavior of firms. In this case, we are using percentage of sales as the basis for making a pro forma statement.

The two largest amounts that appear in the percent income statement relate to cost of goods sold and general and administrative expenses. The net **profit margin** is also derived from this statement; net income is 2 percent of sales. Because the company pays no cash dividends, all the net income is retained and will be added to retained earnings on the pro forma balance sheet.

Table 14–9
Pro Forma Statement of Income for Lumber Supply Company

	For Year Ended 1993 (1)	Percent of Sales in 1993 (2)	For Year Ended 1994— Pro Forma (3)
Revenue:			
Net sales	$14,991,341	100.0%	$17,240,042
Other income	21,683	0.1	17,240
	15,013,024		17,257,282
Costs and expenses:			
Cost of goods sold	11,467,243	76.5	13,188,632
General and administrative expenses	3,059,573	20.4	3,516,969
	14,526,816		16,705,601
Earnings from operations	486,208	3.2	551,681
Interest expense	37,303	0.2	34,480
Earnings before taxes	448,905		517,201
Income taxes	148,642	1.0	172,400
Net income	$ 300,263	2.0	$ 344,801

The final step in constructing the pro forma income statement is to multiply the percentages listed in Column 2 by the expected sales ($17,240,042) listed in Column 3, which gives the pro forma income statement for 1994.

Pro Forma Balance Sheet The **pro forma balance sheet** shows the approximate composition of projected assets and liabilities as well as the amount of external funds that must be raised to support the growth in sales. We will project the balance sheet of Lumber Supply Company for 1 year, again using the percentage of sales method.

Remember that the percentage of sales method assumes that selected balance sheet items related to operations vary directly with sales. These are called responsive items. Examples of **responsive assets** and **responsive liabilities** include cash, accounts receivable, inventories, net fixed assets, accounts payable, and accrued liabilities. Net fixed assets are used because it is assumed that the funds generated from depreciation are used to replace assets. Items such as long-term debt and common stock are not usually responsive in the short run. Retained earnings are not directly responsive; this special case will be explained later.

The difference between the responsive assets and the responsive liabilities and retained earnings is the amount of external funds required. For example, assume that responsive assets are $100, responsive liabilities are $60, and the amount of earnings retained is $5. In this case, $35 in external funds will be required.

Responsive assets	$100
Less: Responsive liabilities	−60
Less: Earnings retained	− 5
Equals: External funds required	$35

This projection rests on a principle already mentioned: Sources and uses of funds must be equal. This principle is true for both past and future sources and uses of funds.

Against this background, we construct and interpret Lumber Supply Company's pro forma balance sheet for 1994 in the following manner.

Step 1. The first step is to express the responsive balance sheet items as a percentage of sales for the base year. As shown in Table 14–10, 1993 is the base year, and sales in that year were $14,991,341. Percentages of sales for responsive items are listed in Column 2. Balance sheet items that are not responsive, such as long-term debt, are followed by NA (not applicable).

The percentages listed in Column 2 and the memo at the bottom of the balance sheet indicate that for every $1 increase in sales, assets will increase $0.358. These figures represent the *gross financial needs of the firm associated with increased sales.* They will be partially financed by an $0.183 increase in responsive liabilities. The increased responsive liabilities are called **sponta-**

Table 14–10
Pro Forma Balance Sheet for 1994 for Lumber Supply Company

	December 1993 Balance Sheet from Table 14–3 (1)	Percent of 1993 Sales of $14,991,341 (2)	December 1994 Pro Forma Balance Sheet Based on $17,240,042 Sales (3)
Assets			
Cash	$ 70,450	0.5%	$ 86,200
Accounts receivable	2,406,130	16.0	2,758,407
Inventories	2,608,791	17.4	2,999,767
Prepaid expenses	9,437	NA	9,437
Net fixed assets	289,003	1.9	327,561
Total assets	$5,383,811	35.8%	$6,181,372
Liabilities and Shareholders' Equity			
Notes payable	$ 497,643	NA	$ 497,643
Accounts payable	2,638,737	17.6%	3,034,247
Accrued liabilities	112,164	0.7	120,680
Long-term debt	47,665	NA	47,665
Total liabilities	$3,296,209	18.3%	$3,700,235
Common stock	250,000	NA	250,000
Retained earnings	1,837,602	NA	2,182,403
Total liabilities and shareholders' equity	$5,383,811		
Total funds available			$6,132,638
Additional *external* funds required for balancing			48,734 $6,181,372
Memo:			
Responsive assets as percent of sales		35.8%	
Less: Responsive liabilities as percent of sales		18.3	
Equals: Percent of each dollar of additional sales that must be financed		17.5%	

Note: NA = Not applicable.

neous liabilities, because they increase automatically; for example, accounts payable automatically increase when inventories increase.

The difference between gross financial needs and spontaneous liabilities ($0.175) represents the *net financial needs of the firm associated with increased sales*. These needs must be financed, either internally or externally. In this example, 0.175 of the $2,248,701 increase in sales ($393,523) is the net amount to be financed. Step 3 explains the amount that will be financed internally in connection with retained earnings. The amount that will be financed externally is explained in Steps 3 and 4.

Step 2. Next, the percentages listed in Column 2 are multiplied by expected sales in 1994 ($17,240,042), resulting in some of the figures listed in Column 3. With the exception of retained earnings and the additional external funds required, the remaining figures listed in Column 3 are the same as those followed by NA in Column 1. This procedure develops most of the numbers required to construct the pro forma balance sheet and determine external funding requirements.

Step 3. Retained earnings are increased by the amount of net income retained by the company. We find the amount retained in the pro forma income statement (Table 14–9). Recall that Lumber Supply Company has a 2 percent profit margin, which means that net income is 2 percent of sales, or $344,801 for 1994. Because the company pays no cash dividends, it retains all the net income. Thus, $344,801 is added to retained earnings from 1993, resulting in the $2,182,403 amount listed in Column 3.

The change in retained earnings can be expressed as follows.

$$\Delta RE = mbS_2 \qquad (14-3)$$

where

ΔRE = Change in retained earnings
m = Profit margin
b = **Retention rate,** or percentage of net income retained by the firm[1]
S_2 = Expected sales in second period

Stated otherwise, mS_2 is net income for the period and mbS_2 is retained earnings. The change in retained earnings is $344,801 ($0.02 \times 1 \times \$17,240,042 =$ $344,801).

Subtracting the amount of funds generated internally ($344,801) from the total amount to be financed ($393,523, from Step 1), yields the amount that must be financed externally ($48,722).

Step 4. Finally, each side of the pro forma balance sheet is totaled. The assets for 1994 add to $6,181,372 and the liabilities and equity add to $6,132,683. The difference, $48,734, is (1) a balancing figure that equates the two sides of the balance sheet and (2) the amount of funds that must be financed externally. Rounding accounts for the slight difference between this amount and the amount of external financing calculated in Step 3.

Column 3 is the pro forma balance sheet for 1994. The final composition of the balance sheet may change, depending on how Lumber Supply Company actually finances the $48,734.

---

[1] The retention rate, b, should not be confused with the constant b used in Equations 14–1 and 14–2.

Shortcut Method for Determining Additional External Funds Required It is not necessary to construct an entire balance sheet to determine the amount of additional external funds required to support sales. We can determine the amount by solving the following equation.

Additional   Responsive   Responsive   Increase in
external = increase in − increase in − retained
funds   assets   liabilities   earnings
required

$$= \sum \frac{RA}{S} (\Delta S) - \sum \frac{RL}{S} (\Delta S) - \Delta RE \tag{14–4}$$

where

Σ = Sum

Δ = Change

$\sum \frac{RA}{S}$ = Sum of responsive assets in the base year divided by sales in the base year. The ratio of responsive assets to sales in 1993 is 35.8 percent (see Table 14–10).

ΔS = Change in sales between the base year and the year to be projected. In the example, the change is \$2,248,701.

$\sum \frac{RL}{S}$ = Sum of responsive liabilities in the base year divided by sales in the base year. In this example, the ratio is 18.3 percent.

ΔRE = Change in retained earnings between the base year and the year that is being projected ($\Delta RE = mbS_2$). As noted, the change is \$344,801.

Using the figures above and Equation 14–4, we can find the additional external funds required.

$$0.358(\$2,248,701) - 0.183(\$2,248,701) - \$344,801 = \$48,722$$

Suppose Lumber Supply Company's financial manager wanted to know how much financing would be required if sales increased by \$5,000,000 instead of \$2,248,701. Recall from the memo in Table 14–10 that the net financial needs of the firm associated with increased sales are \$0.175 per dollar of increased sales. Thus, the net additional financing required to support the \$5,000,000 increase in sales is \$875,000 (0.175 × \$5,000,000 = \$875,000). The amount of additional external funds required in this case can be determined by use of Equation 14–4.

$$0.358(\$5,000,000) - 0.183(\$5,000,000) - \$399,827 = \$475,173$$

Recall that the addition to retained earnings is mb^S_2. In this example, S_2 is the base year's sales plus \$5,000,000, which amounts to \$19,991,341. Accordingly, the addition to retained earnings is \$399,827 (0.02 ×

$19,991,341 = $399,827). After performing this series of calculations, the financial manager knows that if sales increase $5,000,000, an additional $875,000 financing will be required, of which $475,173 will have to be raised externally through stock sales or borrowings.

A word of caution is in order here. Small rounding errors can make appreciable differences in the numbers generated. If 0.357 had been used instead of 0.358 for the ratio of responsive assets to sales in the example above, the result would have been $5,000 less! Great care must be taken in the development and interpretation of the data.

Long-Range Forecasting Techniques

The percentage of sales technique is useful for projecting short-term financial needs, but it has definite limitations for projecting long-term needs. As mentioned, the assumption about a constant relationship between sales and balance sheet and income statement items does not hold up over long time spans. Profit margins, operating capacities, and other factors that change limit its usefulness. Therefore, it is necessary to become familiar with tools that are more reliable—although still imperfect—for longer time spans.

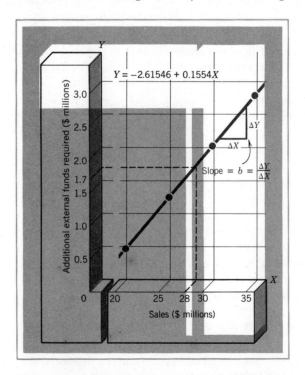

Figure 14–4   Relationship between sales and additional external funds required.

Graphic Method One simple method of forecasting involves plotting the relationship between sales and, for example, additional external funds required on a graph and drawing a line connecting the points. Figure 14–4 depicts such a line based on the following figures, calculated from the equations just described.

Estimated Sales (millions)	External Funds (millions)
$19.9	$0.47
24.9	1.26
29.9	2.04
34.9	2.80

This method is useful because it is easy to employ and it allows the user to visualize the amount of external funds required for any level of sales. For example, if sales are expected to be $28 million, a glance at the graph shows that an additional $1.7 million of external funds will be required to support that level. The $1.7 million is a rough approximation. Greater accuracy can be obtained by using linear regression analysis.

Linear Regression Analysis **Linear regression** is a statistical technique used to determine the straight line that comes closest to all the data points. Historical data are used to determine the straight line used to make predictions. The straight line is represented by the following equation.

$$Y = a + bX \qquad (14–5)$$

where

Y = Vertical axis
a = Intercept when the value of X is 0
b = Slope of the line (slope = $\Delta Y / \Delta X$)
X = Horizontal axis

The astute reader will recognize that Equation 14–5 is basically the same as Equation 14–1, which was used in connection with inventory and sales. In this case, we use the linear equation to predict the amount of additional external funds required for a given level of sales. In other words, it allows us to predict data points along the line with a reasonable degree of accuracy.

All the terms except the intercept (a) are shown in Figure 14–4. There, the regression equation for predicting additional external funds required is as follows.

$$Y = -2.61546 + 0.1554X$$

The method for calculating this equation and the limitations of the technique are explained in textbooks dealing with statistical analysis. Computer programs that perform linear regression analysis are available at many universities, from private data-processing companies, on personal computers, and on some hand-held calculators.

The equation is used in the following manner. Suppose we wanted to know the amount of additional funds required if sales were $28 million. We already found by using the graphic method that approximately $1.7 million would be required. By applying the equation, we can find the exact amount.

$$Y = -2.61546 + 0.1554 \ (\$28)$$
$$= 2.61546 + 4.3512$$
$$= \$1.7357$$

Do not be lulled into a false sense of security because $1,735,700 appears to be more accurate than $1,700,000. Keep in mind that if the sales forecast is inaccurate, the results of linear regression analysis will also be inaccurate. Equally important, the linear regression analysis takes only one variable—sales—into account in estimating external funding requirements. In reality, other factors—such as profit margins, capacity, and expected economic conditions—affect the amount of additional external funds required. These factors may be included in more complex forms of multiple regression or in a simulation.

Another word of caution is in order. It is important to test the fit of the regression line. Two statistical tests used to accomplish this are the *coefficient of determination* and the *standard error of the estimate*. They measure the extent to which variations in the dependent variable (for example, additional external funds required) are explained by variations in the independent variables (for example, sales, profit margins, and so on), as well as the standard deviation of errors about the regression line. These tests are described in textbooks dealing with statistical analysis.

Finally, regression analysis can be used in connection with inventories. Recall that Equations 14–1 and 14–2 are linear equations dealing with inventories and inventory-to-sales ratios. Regression techniques can be used to forecast the levels of inventories.

Simulation   In a **simulation**, we construct a model to represent reality and then use the model to draw conclusions about a real-life problem. (You may recall that such a model was described in Chapter 9.) A simulation model can be constructed to determine the amount of additional external funds that will be required to support sales, for example, 3 years from now. As shown in Figure 14–5, the basic input data for the model include information about sales, costs and expenses, cash dividends, and plant capacity.

Data concerning each of these items are expressed in terms of a probability distribution instead of a single number. The probability distribution for sales, for example, shows that $25 million is the most likely sales level. However, sales may be as low as $20 million or as high as $30 million. These ranges are based on management estimates. Similar estimates are made for the remaining input data.

Once all the estimates have been made, the information is processed in a computer using various equations that take the probability distributions into account and calculate the additional external funds required. The output data also take the form of a probability distribution. The simulation results in Figure 14–5 indicate that $1.3 million is the most likely level of additional funds required; but the values could be as low as $1.1 million or as high as $1.4 million.

Simulations are powerful tools for answering "what if" questions: What happens to the amount of external funds required if sales are $20.0 million, if costs increase 13 percent, if a cash dividend of $0.20 is paid, if the plant is

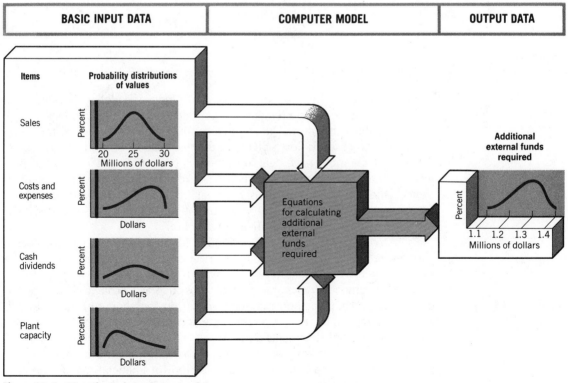

Figure 14–5   Hypothetical simulation model.

Table 14–11
Summary of Equations

	Equation	Equation Number
Straight line (in connection with inventory and sales)	$I = a + bS$	(14–1)
Inventory-to-sales ratio	$\dfrac{I}{S} = \dfrac{a}{S} + b$	(14–2)
Change in retained earnings	$\Delta RE = mbS_2$	(14–3)
Additional external funds required	Additional external funds required $= \sum \dfrac{RA}{S}(\Delta S) - \sum \dfrac{RL}{S}(\Delta S) - \Delta RE$	(14–4)
Straight line (for linear regression)	$Y = a + bX$	(14–5)

operating at 65 percent of capacity? The simulation provides a range of answers to such questions and indicates which answers are most likely.

Summary

Financial planning includes projecting the timing and dollar amounts of a firm's future financial requirements. To plan, it is necessary to understand how funds flow through a firm. The continuous funds flow cycle can be traced by use of a series of funds flow statements that list the sources and uses of funds.

Several techniques have been developed to help firms make financial projections. One, the cash budget, is a basic tool of financial management. It projects the timing and amount of cash balances. The usefulness of cash budgets and other planning tools depends on the accuracy of sales forecasts and the other assumptions used in their construction.

The percentage of sales method, another forecasting technique, assumes a constant relationship between sales and selected balance sheet and income statement items that relate to operations. It is used in constructing pro forma financial statements. In general, relationships such as the one assumed by the percentage of sales method may be constant in the short run, but they are likely to change in the long run. Thus, the accuracy of the percentage of sales pro forma financial statements diminishes for periods in the distant future.

Several techniques have been developed to help firms make financial projections. One, the cash budget, is a basic tool of financial management. It projects the timing and amount of cash balances. The usefulness of cash budgets and other planning tools depends on the accuracy of sales forecasts and the other assumptions used in their construction.

Important Terms

Cash budget	Responsive assets and liabilities
Financial planning	Retention rate
Funds	Schedule of cash balances
Funds flow cycle	Schedule of disbursements
Funds flow statement	Schedule of receipts
Linear regression	Simulation
Percent income statement	Sources of funds
Percentage of sales method	Spontaneous liabilities
Pro forma balance sheet	Uses of funds
Pro forma income statement	Working capital cycle
Profit margin	

Questions

1. Why is financial planning important to a firm? What major limitation do planners face? What steps can be taken to lessen the impact of this limitation?
2. Describe in general terms the flow of funds through a business.
3. In what way can depreciation be considered a source of funds?
4. What are the major categories of funds sources?
5. What are the major categories of funds uses?
6. What information is provided by statement of sources and uses of funds?
7. What is the purpose of a cash budget? What perspective does a cash budget provide that is not provided in a statement of sources and uses of funds?
8. On what data does the accuracy of a cash budget most depend? Why?
9. Explain the major steps necessary to prepare a cash budget.
10. What is the percentage of sales forecasting method? Explain its advantages and disadvantages.
11. Explain how to construct a pro forma income statement using a percentage of sales basis.
12. Distinguish between responsive and unresponsive balance sheet items. How does this distinction affect the preparation of pro forma balance sheets?
13. In preparing a pro forma balance sheet, how can a planner estimate the change in retained earnings?
14. Explain two ways of determining the amount of external financing needed during a planning period. Are these methods consistent? Why or why not?
15. Explain in general the use of regression analysis as a forecasting technique. What are its limitations?

16. How can simulation assist in financial planning? How does simulation differ from the percentage of sales and regression methods of forecasting?

Problems

1. Classify the changes in the following balance sheet items as either sources or uses of funds.

(a) Cash	− $ 10
(b) Notes payable	+ 15
(c) Depreciation	+ 100
(d) Other assets	− 20
(e) Accrued liabilities	+ 5
(f) Marketable securities	+ 20
(g) Accounts receivable	+ 30
(h) Long-Term debt	− 15
(i) Inventory	− 15
(j) Gross fixed assets	+ 140
(k) Accounts payable	− 20
(l) Retained earnings	+ 40

2. Management has made available the balance sheets for Acme Health Clubs, Inc., for year-end 1988 and year-end 1989.

Acme Health Clubs
December 31, 1988 and 1989

Assets	1988	1989
Current assets:		
Cash	$ 40,000	$ 30,000
Marketable securities	80,000	60,000
Accounts receivable	100,000	140,000
Inventory	20,000	50,000
Total current assets	$240,000	$280,000
Gross fixed assets	$500,000	$650,000
Less accumulated depreciation	80,000	180,000
Net fixed assets	$420,000	$470,000
Other assets	$ 30,000	$ 30,000
Total assets	$690,000	$780,000

Liabilities and net worth		
Current liabilities		
Accrued liabilities	$ 20,000	$ 30,000
Notes payable	100,000	120,000
Accounts payable	40,000	40,000
Total current liabilities	$160,000	$190,000
Long-term debt	$200,000	$200,000
New worth (equity):		
Common stock (10,000 shares)	100,000	100,000
Paid-in capital	50,000	50,000
Retained earnings	180,000	240,000
Total net worth	$330,000	$390,000
Total liabilities and net worth	$690,000	$780,000

(a) Prepare a sources and uses funds statement for 1989. Express your statement in both dollars and percentages.

(b) Based on your statement, analyze the financing decisions made during the year. Consider such things as reliance on external financing, use of short-term versus long-term sources of funds, and so on.

3. (a) Williams Snow Removal, Inc., had a good year in 1990 because of extremely heavy snowfall from January through March. Prepare a sources and uses of funds statement for the firm, using 1989 and 1990 balance sheet information. Indicate both dollar and percentage changes.

Williams Snow Removal
December 31, 1989 and 1990

Assets	1989	1990
Current assets:		
Cash	$ 50,000	$ 20,000
Marketable securities	90,000	110,000
Accounts receivable	200,000	350,000
Inventory	10,000	20,000
Total current assets	$350,000	$ 500,000
Gross fixed assets	$800,000	$1,020,000
Less: Accumulated depreciation	200,000	300,000
Net fixed assets	$600,000	$ 720,000
Other assets	$ 30,000	$ 10,000
Total assets	$980,000	$1,230,000
Liabilities and net worth		
Current liabilities		
Accrued liabilities	$ 20,000	$ 50,000
Notes payable	250,000	150,000
Accounts payable	40,000	40,000
Total current liabilities	$310,000	$ 240,000
Long-term debt	$200,000	$ 150,000
Net worth (equity):		
Common stock (10,000 shares)	100,000	150,000
Paid-in capital	50,000	100,000
Retained earnings	320,000	590,000
Total net worth	$470,000	$ 840,000
Total liabilities and net worth	$980,000	$1,230,000

(b) Analyze the financial decisions made by management during the year based on your statement.

4. The following balance sheet changes for Formica Exterminators have been identified during 1989: increase in cash, $500,000; decrease in inventory, $300,000; decrease in accounts payable, $450,000; increase in long-term debt, $100,000. Assuming no other balance sheet changes accurred during the year, what was the change in retained earnings?

Use the following sales forecasts to answer Problems 5 through 8.

Nirvana Corporation is forecasting cash receipts for the next several months. Expected sales for the period are as follows.

June	July	August	September	October	November	December
$50,000	$40,000	$60,000	$80,000	$60,000	$80,000	$100,000

5. Assume that 40 percent of each month's sales are on a cash basis and 30 percent of the total are collected in each of the 2 months following the sale. Prepare a schedule of cash receipts for September through December.

6. Assume instead that 20 percent of each month's sales are for cash, 50 percent of the total are collected in the next month, 20 percent 2 months after the sale, and 10 percent 3 months after. Prepare a schedule of cash receipts for September through December.

7. The following purchasing policies are in effect for Nirvana: Purchases are 80 percent of each month's sales and they occur in the month of the sale; 10 percent of purchases are for cash, 50 percent are paid the next month, and 40 percent are paid 2 months later. Prepare a schedule of purchase payments for September through December.

8. Suppose that instead of the policies described in Problem 7, purchases are 90 percent of forecast sales and they occur in the month before the sale; 50 percent of purchases are paid for in cash and 25 percent are paid for in each of the next 2 months. Prepare a schedule of purchase payments for August through November. Use the following information for Moore, Inc., for Problems 9 through 11.

	November	December	January	February
Purchases	$150,000	$150,000	$120,000	$130,000
Sales	200,000	250,000	150,000	220,000
	March	April	May	June
Purchases	$160,000	$140,000	$140,000	$120,000
Sales	280,000	300,000	260,000	240,000

20 percent of purchases are paid for in cash in the month of purchase and 40 percent are paid in each of the next 2 months. Payroll is 10 percent of sales and is paid in the month of the sale. Operating expenses are 20 percent of the following month's sales. Interest payments of $20,000 will be made in both January and April.

9. Prepare a schedule of disbursements for Moore, Inc., for the months January through May.

10. Suppose, in addition to the information above, Moore's management tells you that 30 percent of sales are made for cash and that the remaining amount is collected at a rate of 35 percent in each of the 2 months following the sale. In February, a machine will be sold for an expected cash inflow of $15,000. Prepare a schedule of cash inflows for Moore for January through May.

11. Using the schedules you developed in Problems 9 and 10, prepare a schedule of cash balances for January through May. Assume the beginning cash balance in January is $30,000 and that figure is the desired cash balance at the end of each month. When will additional cash be needed? When are cash surpluses forecast?

12. Todds Corporation has been asked by its banker to provide a cash budget for January through June. Use the following information to do so.

	December	January	February	March
Sales	$200,000	180,000	120,000	140,000
	April	May	June	July
Sales	140,000	160,000	180,000	220,000

Sales are 40 percent cash, with 60 percent collected in the next month.
Purchases are 70 percent of sales. They occur in the month of the sale. Sixty percent are in cash, and 40 percent are paid in the next month.

Payroll expenditures each month are 5 percent of the next month's sales and cash overhead expenses are 8 percent of the next month's sales.

Cash operating expenses are 15 percent of the current month's sales.

Depreciation of $10,000 per month is estimated.

A new machine will be bought for cash in April for $10,000.

Interest payments of $20,000 will be paid in March and in June.

Tax payments of $40,000 each will be made in January and April.

The beginning cash balance in January is $50,000.

The minimum required cash balance is $25,000.

13. (a) Prepare a pro forma income statement for the Boyce Ski Company using the percentage of sales method, given last year's income statement and a forecast for a sales increase of 20 percent during 1991. Assume no change in common or preferred dividends.

Income Statement

Boyce Ski Company
December 31, 1990

Net sales:		
Cash		$ 200,000
Credit		1,000,000
Total Sales		$1,200,000
Less: Cost of goods sold		800,000
Gross profit		$ 400,000
Less: Operating expenses:		
Selling expenses	72,000	
Administrative expenses	106,000	
Depreciation	40,000	
Total operating expenses		218,000
Operating income (*EBIT*)		$ 182,000
Less: Interest expense		18,000
Profit before taxes		$ 164,000
Less: Taxes		73,000
Profit after taxes (net income)		$ 91,000
Less: Preferred dividends		10,000
Earnings available to common stock		81,000

Additional information: Common stock dividends were $21,000.

(b) How much will be added to retained earnings in 1991?

14. Lakewood, Inc., has made its 1989 income statement available to a potential creditor. The creditor has asked your help in estimating the firm's income for 1990. Project a pro forma income statement for the firm using the percentage of sales method. Sales are expected to increase to $200,000. Assume to change in the firm's dividend policy.

Income Statement

Lakewood, Inc.
December 31, 1989

Net sales:	
Cash	$120,000
Credit	8,000
Total sales	$128,000

Income Statement (*Continued*)

Less: Cost of goods sold		80,000
Gross profit		$ 48,000
Less: Operating expenses:		
Selling expenses	4,000	
Administrative expenses	12,000	
Depreciation	10,000	
Total operating expenses		26,000
Operating income (*EBIT*)		$ 22,000
Less: Interest expense		2,000
Profit before taxes		$ 20,000
Less: Taxes		3,400
Profit after taxes (net income)		$ 16,600

Additional information: No common stock dividends were paid in 1989.

15. Speculator Corporation is preparing a business plan that will include pro forma statements. Given the following information for 1988, prepare a pro forma income statement. Assume that preferred stock dividends will remain unchanged and that common stock dividends will increase by $0.10 per share in 1989. Sales are estimated to be $1.5 million and there are 10 thousand shares of common stock outstanding.

Income Statement

Speculator Corporation
December 31, 1988

Net sales:		
Cash		$ 400,000
Credit		800,000
Total sales		$1,200,000
Less: Cost of goods sold		1,000,000
Gross profit		$ 200,000
Less: Operating expenses:		
Selling expenses	40,000	
Administrative expenses	20,000	
Depreciation	40,000	
Total operating expenses		100,000
Operating income (*EBIT*)		$ 100,000
Less: Interest expense		8,000
Profit before taxes		$ 92,000
Less: Taxes		36,000
Profit after taxes		$ 56,000
Less: Preferred dividends		6,000
Earnings available to common stock		50,000

Additional information: Common stock dividends were $10,000 in 1988.

16. Aardvark Imports projects a sales expansion of $18 million for 1991, up from its level of $80 million in 1990. Based on a percent of sales analysis, the firm requires asset increases totaling 28 percent of anticipated sales increases. Spontaneous liabilities will increase by 17 percent of the sales increase. The firm anticipates a net profit margin of 3 percent and a dividend payout ratio of 40 percent. Estimate Aardvark's need for external funds in 1991.

17. Suppose, instead, that Aardvark Imports (Problem 16) pays no dividends and that its profit margin is 5 percent. Estimate the firm's need for external funds in 1991.
18. Return to the 1989 balance sheet for Acme Health Clubs first presented in Problem 2. Assume that 1989 sales were $1.5 million and that a 15 percent increase is anticipated in 1990. Also assume "other assets" are not responsive to sales increases. Using the percent of sales method, prepare a pro forma balance sheet for Acme for 1990. The firm's estimated profit margin is 5 percent, and 60 percent of 1990's profits will be paid in dividends.
19. Return to the 1990 balance sheet for Williams Snow Removal first presented in Problem 3. Suppose 1990 sales were $2,750,000 and a 10 percent increase in sales is anticipated in 1991. Prepare a pro forma balance sheet for Williams in 1991. Net profit margin is anticipated to be 4 percent, and 85 percent of earnings for the year will be retained.
20. Anderson Awnings has estimated that external funds required next year will be $49,000. Spontaneous liabilities are about 18 percent of sales, the firm's profit margin is 2 percent, and all earnings are retained in the business. If sales next year are expected to increase by $2,250,000 over their current level of $15,000,000, by how much (in dollars) are assets expected to increase in response?

6

Working
Capital
Management

In many respects, Part 6 is the most important part of the
book because working capital management makes up such a
large proportion of financial managers' work. The firm's working capital includes cash, short-term securities, accounts receivable, and inventories. Chapter 15 provides an overview of working capital policy, and Chapters 16 through 18 examine the components of working capital in detail.

Working Capital Policy

Many financial managers spend much of their time dealing with working capital problems. Moreover, working capital accounts for more than half of the assets of many firms. Equally important, business concerns must have working capital to grow. What is working capital?

After reading this chapter, you should know the following.

1. What *working capital* means.
2. How working capital and working capital management differ.
3. How industry requirements, life cycles, and business cycles affect the levels of working capital.
4. What *hedging* means and how it is related to risk.
5. How the expectations theory of interest rates and yield curves are used.
6. How interest rates and financing strategies are related.

Definitions

Every profession has its own jargon and financial management is no exception. The following terms are commonly used in connection with working capital and its management.

Working Capital   **Working capital** is the dollar amount of a firm's current assets, including cash and short-term investments, accounts receivable, and inventories. These assets are considered **liquid** because they can be converted to cash within one year. The dollar amount of current assets changes over time because of seasonal variations in sales and changing business conditions. Therefore, the amount of working capital held by a firm is not constant.

We can divide working capital into two categories: permanent and temporary. **Permanent working capital** is the dollar amount of working capital that persists over time regardless of fluctuations in sales. For example, Sweet Tooth, a candy store located in a large shopping center, maintains $8,000 in inventory to satisfy the normal pedestrian flow of traffic. However, on Valentine's Day and other holidays, the inventory must be trebled to satisfy demand. The $8,000 level of inventory is part of the permanent working capital. The additions to inventory made for the holidays are part of the temporary working capital. In other words, **temporary working capital** is the additional assets required to meet variations in sales above the permanent level.

Working Capital Management   **Working capital management** involves not only the management of current assets but also the management of current liabilities and the relationship between the two. In practice, a distinction is usually made between the investment decisions concerning current assets and the financing decisions concerning working capital. To some extent, this separation exists because models have been developed to help determine the optimal quantities of assets, such as inventories, that firms should hold. Several optimization models are presented in later chapters. This chapter focuses on some of the relationships between current assets and current liabilities. As we will see, the manner in which working capital is financed has a marked effect on risk and profits. Specific methods of financing are examined in Part 7 of the book.

Net Working Capital   **Net working capital** is the difference between current assets and current liabilities. As you may recall from Chapter 13, it is used as a financial indicator in conjunction with other indicators (for example, the current ratio) to gauge the liquidity of business concerns. An adequate amount of net working capital is considered desirable, because it suggests that a firm has ample assets to meet its short-term obligations. But too much working capital can hurt profits.

The optimal amount depends on the needs of the firm and varies over the course of the life cycle and business cycle.

Keep in mind that some current assets, such as inventory, may not be very liquid. In the fall of 1979, for example, Chrysler Corporation had a $700 million inventory of 80,000 unsold vehicles. Most of them were large, gas-guzzling cars that were produced when buyers wanted small, energy-saving cars. The large unsold inventory constituted a major working capital problem for Chrysler. The company needed additional working capital of $500 million in 1979 and the same amount in the following year to relieve financial pressures.[1] It took Chrysler several years to resolve its manufacturing and inventory problems.

Level of Working Capital

The plight of Chrysler Corporation highlights the importance of working capital. A firm must have sufficient working capital to survive. The alternatives are not pleasant. Bankruptcy is one alternative; being acquired on unfavorable terms is another. Each firm must decide how to balance the amount of working capital it holds against the risk of failure. The level of working capital a firm chooses to hold depends in part on the requirements of its industry, its position on the life cycle, and current business conditions.

Industry Levels The amount of working capital held, measured by the ratio of working capital (current assets) to total assets, varies widely among industries. As shown in Table 15–1, the average ratio for all manufacturing concerns is 49.2 percent.

Table 15–1
Current Assets as a Percentage of
Total Assets for Selected Industries

Industry	Average Percentages
Manufacturing	49.2%
Aircraft	66.8
Industrial Chemicals	33.2
Mining	19.2
Retail Trade	50.9[a]
Wholesale Trade	65.0

Source Excerpted from Federal Trade Commission, *Quarterly Financial Report for Manufacturing, Mining and Trade Corporations,* 3rd quarter, 1983.

[a]Estimate from previous quarter.

[1]"Can Chrysler be Saved?" *Newsweek,* August 13, 1979, pp. 52–58.

Keep in mind that half the firms are above the average number and the other half are below it. For example, the ratio for aircraft manufacturers is 66.8 percent, whereas the ratio for industrial chemicals manufacturers is 33.2 percent. These variations indicate that the level of working capital is determined in part by industry factors. The ratio of working capital to total assets for aircraft manufacturers is high because of the long production process required to build complex aircraft. Aircraft manufacturers hold large inventories of aircraft that are in the process of being built. Similarly, wholesalers maintain large inventories to supply retail outlets. The large inventories account for the high ratios of working capital to total assets. In contrast, the ratio for mines is only 19.2

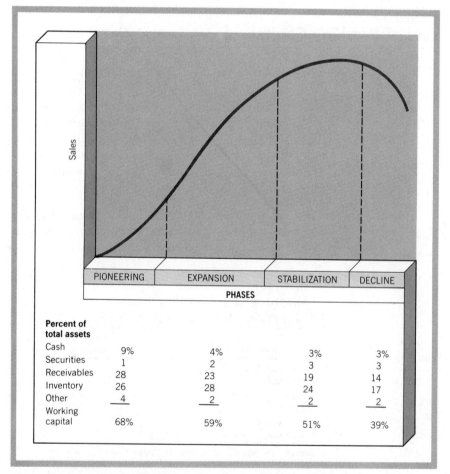

Figure 15–1   Selected financial ratios over the life cycle for a hypothetical manufacturing concern.
Source: Data adapted from the Federal Trade Commission's *Quarterly Financial Report for Manufacturing, Minning and Trade Corporations.*

percent, because mines generally maintain small inventories of their basic products.

Life Cycle   The level of working capital for individual firms is also influenced by their location on the life cycle. Figure 15–1 shows the life cycle for a hypothetical manufacturing concern and the ratios of current assets expressed as a percent of total assets. Examination of the ratios reveals that the level of working capital is highest during the early phases of the life cycle and diminishes as the firm matures. In the pioneering phase of development, the firm is small and holds a relatively large proportion of its assets in cash and accounts receivable. As the firm increases in size and maturity, the proportions held in cash and receivables decline sharply, while funds invested in short-term securities increase. Inventories reach their peak proportion during the expansion phase and then taper off. The point is that the proportion and composition of working capital change significantly over the life cycle of a firm.

Business Cycle   Changing business conditions also influence the level of working capital. Figure 15–2 shows the changes in working capital that should occur during the four phases of a business cycle. In general, firms should increase their working capital when business activity is expanding and reduce it when business activity declines. This is more easily said than done. Recall that Chrysler had an inventory of 80,000 unsold vehicles in 1979, when the economy was sliding into a recession. Reduced prices and rebates to dealers helped to reduce the unwanted inventory, but it remained too large and the firm suffered.

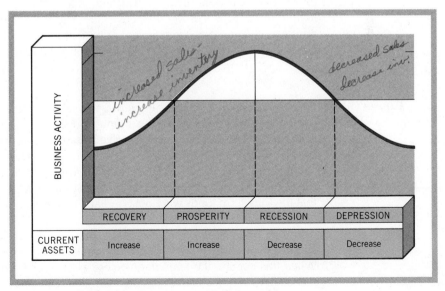

Figure 15-2   Changes in current assets and business cycles.

Hedging

As noted at the beginning of this chapter, working capital management involves the management of both current assets and current liabilities. The foregoing discussion centered on working capital—that is, current assets. Now we are going to deal with the financing of working capital.

The term **hedging** as used here means matching expected cash inflows from assets with outflows from their respective sources of financing. (The term is also used in connection with commodities transactions, which are described in Chapters 16 and 18.) For purposes of illustration, three types of financial hedging are discussed: perfect, conservative, and aggressive. Figure 15–3 graphically depicts these hedging methods.

Perfect Hedge   The **perfect hedge** consists of financing temporary current assets with short-term sources of funds and fixed assets and permanent current assets with long-term sources of funds. As shown in the top panel of Figure 15–3, current assets are classified as either temporary current assets, which change with sales, or permanent current assets, which persist over time.

The basic strategy of the perfect hedge is to *match* expected inflows and outflows of funds. This method is considered sound financing, because inflows of funds from the sale of assets are being used to repay the loans that financed the assets' acquisition. For example, the Sweet Tooth candy store borrowed $16,000 for 45 days from its bank to finance the additional inventory it needed for Mother's Day. Shortly after the holiday, Sweet Tooth repaid the short-term loan from the proceeds of the candy sales. The risk Sweet Tooth incurred was minimal, because management was confident that the additional candy would be sold and that the loan could be repaid in 45 days or less.

Conservative Hedge   In the **conservative hedge**, all fixed assets, all permanent current assets, and some temporary current assets are financed with long-term sources of funds. This method is considered conservative because the firm finances only a small portion of its temporary current assets with short-term funds. The major advantage of conservative hedging is that during periods of credit restraint the firm already has most of the funds it needs to finance its activities. It is hoped that the long-term funds were obtained at a time when their cost was favorable to the firm.

In the middle panel of Figure 15–3, long-term sources of funds exceed the amount needed to finance the temporary current assets on two occasions. When this occurs, the temporary excess assets may be invested in short-term marketable securities. If the returns on short-term securities are lower than those on operating assets, profits may be adversely affected.

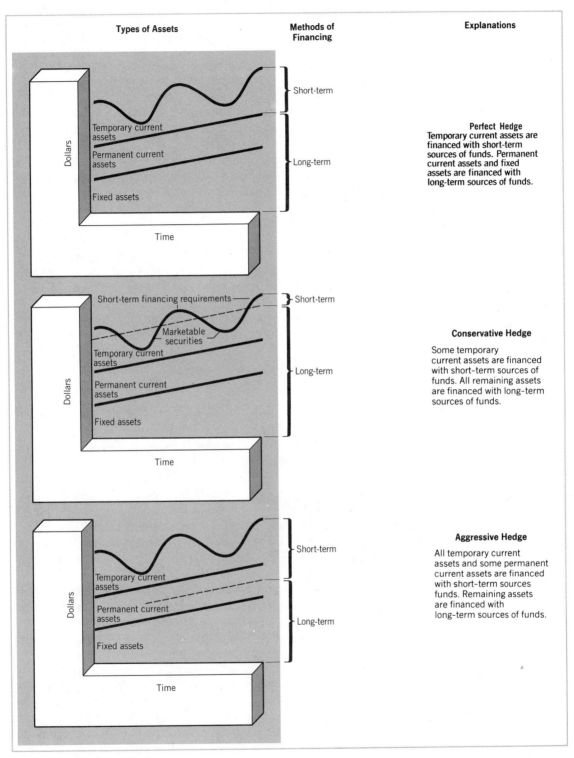

Figure 15-3   Hedging positions.

Aggressive Hedge In the **aggressive hedge**, all temporary current assets and some permanent assets are financed with short-term sources of funds. The remaining assets are financed with long-term sources of funds.

The case of Surfside Mortgage Company illustrates why aggressive financing may be dangerous. Throughout most of our economic history, short-term interest rates have been lower than long-term interest rates. Therefore, it has cost less to borrow short-term funds than to borrow long-term funds. (The relationship between interest rates and time will be discussed again later in this chapter.) In June 1980, the manager of Surfside Mortgage Company could borrow short-term funds from commercial banks at 9 percent interest. The mortgage company used these funds to make long-term construction loans to builders and mortgage loans to home buyers at an average yield of 11 percent. This strategy was profitable while Surfside's borrowing costs were low and its lending rates were high. However, there was upward pressure on interest rates in late 1980, and they reached record levels in 1981; the *prime rate* (the base rate on corporate loans) at commercial banks was 15.3 percent. During this period, the cost of Surfside's borrowed short-term funds—now 15.3 percent—exceeded the returns of 11.0 percent. Because the manager was unable to reduce the firm's short-term debts or meet the interest payments, Surfside Mortgage Company went bankrupt.

Hedging, Profits, and Risk Many business concerns use aggressive hedging successfully. They recognize that it increases their risk, but it also increases their profits. To examine the effects of hedging on profits, let's consider the conservative and aggressive methods further.

Table 15–2 shows that Foxfire Company has $200 million in total assets. Current assets account for $100 million of that total. The assets could be financed either conservatively or aggressively. Under the conservative method, short-term credit might provide $25 million and long-term debt, $125 million. Under the aggressive method, short-term credit might provide $100 million and long-term debt, $50 million. Equity under both these conditions would be $50 million.

The impact of the difference in the mix of short-term and long-term debt is reflected in Foxfire's net income—$19.95 million when conservative financing is used, compared with $22.2 million when aggressive financing is used. Differences in interest cost account for most of the difference in income. The cost of short-term credit is 7 percent, whereas the cost of long-term debt is 12 percent. Because the aggressive financing method makes extensive use of short-term credit, it produces lower costs and higher profits.

The impact of the two financing methods is also reflected in financial indicators. The conservative financing method results in a strong current ratio, $75 million in net working capital, and a 39.9 percent return on equity. In contrast, the current ratio for the aggressive financing method reveals that current assets are just equal to current liabilities; there is no net working capital, but the return on equity is 44.4 percent.

Table 15–2
Effects of Conservative and Aggressive Financing for the Foxfire Company (millions of dollars)

Assets	Current assets	$100.00	
	Fixed assets	100.00	
	Total assets	$200.00	

		Conservative	Aggressive
Financing	Short-term credit (at 7%)	$ 25.00	$100.00
	Long-term debt (at 12%)	125.00	50.00
	Equity	50.00	50.00
	Total liabilities and equity	$200.00	$200.00
Income and expenses	Earnings before interest and taxes	$ 50.00	$ 50.00
	Less:		
	Interest	−16.75	−13.00
	Taxes (40%)	−13.30	−14.80
	Net income	$19.95	$22.20
Financial indicators	Current ratio	4.0×	1.0×
	Net working capital	$ 75.00	$ 0
	Rate of return on equity	$\frac{\$19.95}{\$50.00} = 39.9\%$	$\frac{\$22.20}{\$50.00} = 44.4\%$

This example demonstrates the trade-off between risk and return associated with different methods of financing. Firms should keep this trade-off in mind when they change their financing patterns in response to changing business conditions. For example, aggressive hedging should be used when firms are expanding their working capital during the recovery and prosperity phases of a business cycle. The increased profitability resulting from the aggressive financing provides a competitive edge over more conservatively financed firms. However, aggressively financed firms must be on guard for the turning points in business cycles so they can revert to a conservative financing posture. If management is wary and acts in time, it can accomplish this by reducing short-term debt.

Interest Rates and Financing Strategies

Clearly, interest rates play an important part in financing decisions. The current level of interest rates is determined by the supply of and the demand for funds. This, in turn, reflects the beliefs of both borrowers and lenders about the future course of interest rates. For example, suppose a banker wants to earn 8 percent interest, in real terms, on a loan. The **real rate of interest** is the market rate of interest less the inflation rate. If the banker believes that the rate of inflation will be 5 percent, she will charge 13 percent interest (8 percent + 5 percent = 13 percent). If she believes the rate of inflation will be 10 percent, she will charge 18 percent interest.

Business cycles also affect the course of interest rates. In general, market rates of interest rise and fall with business activity. When business activity increases, business concerns borrow funds to finance inventories they hope to sell in the future, as well as other current assets, and they borrow to acquire new plants and equipment. Conversely, when business activity declines, they borrow less as they try to liquidate excess inventories.

To some extent, the changing levels of interest rates can be explained by expectations theory and predicted by yield curves. The shape of yield curves can help firms determine future financing strategies, as you will see.

Expectations Theory

Expectations theory explains the relationships between interest rates and the maturity of a security in terms of expectations. According to the theory, borrowers and lenders forecast the course of short-term interest rates. Their expectations about future short-term rates form the basis for predictions of long-term rates.

In theory, long-term interest rates are the geometric average of intervening future short-term rates. A simplified example will clarify this point. Assume that the *current rate* on a 1-year security is 6 percent, and the *expected rate* next year on a 1-year security is 8 percent. If the current rate on a 2-year security is around 7 percent, the market is in equilibrium, because an investor who wants to hold a security for 2 years can invest either in two 1-year securities that will provide an average return of 7 percent ($\sqrt{(1.06)(1.08)}$ − 1 = 1.0699 − 1 = 7%) or in one 2-year security at 7 percent.

If the 2-year security yielded more than 7 percent, investors would prefer holding it to holding two 1-year securities. The investors are assumed to be wealth maximizers, so they would sell the 1-year securities and buy the 2-year securities until the yields on both were equal. Because investors are supposed to be able to predict future short-term interest rates accurately and because long-term interest rates are an average of short-term rates, the yields for all securities of a given maturity with similar risk should be equal.

Yield Curves

A **yield curve**, which is also called the **term structure of interest rates**, graphically shows the relationship between interest rates and the maturity of a security. The normal pattern of a yield curve shows that interest rates on short-term securities are lower than those on long-term securities, as mentioned earlier and as depicted in Figure 15–4.

The **normal yield curve** is upward sloping for two principal reasons. First, there is more risk in holding long-term securities than in holding short-term securities. This is because we can predict what business conditions will be for the next, say, 90 days with greater accuracy than we can predict what they will be 20 years from now. Because investors want to be compensated for the

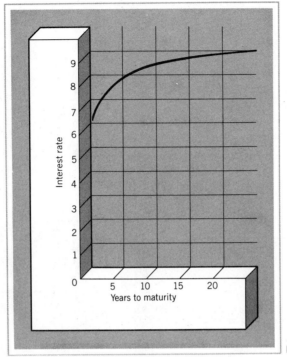

Figure 15–4 Normal yield curve.

additional risk, interest rates are generally higher on long-term securities than on short-term securities. The second reason is that investors want to be compensated for having funds tied up for long periods. Therefore, they want higher yields on long-term securities than on short-term securities.[2] Collectively, these factors contribute to the normal yield curve's upward slope.

Strategies Yield curves can be useful to financial managers. According to expectations theory, a yield curve that slopes upward *by more than the normal amount,* such as the **upward-sloping yield curve** shown in the top panel of Figure 15–5, indicates that long-term interest rates are expected to rise. Knowing this, financial managers whose firms need funds should borrow now to avoid higher borrowing costs in the future.

If current short-term and long-term interest rates are equal, the result is a **flat yield curve**. Flat curves do not last long, because interest rates change constantly. If the financial manager has other information from an economic forecast indicating that interest rates may rise, now may be the time to borrow long-term funds, because the cost of borrowing short-term and long-term are the same. On the other hand, if the forecast indicates that interest rates may

[2]There is an inverse relationship between the market price of outstanding debt securities and current rates of interest. Saying that investors are willing to accept low yields on short-term securities and high yields on long-term securities is another way of saying that they will pay high prices for short-term securities and low prices for long-term securities.

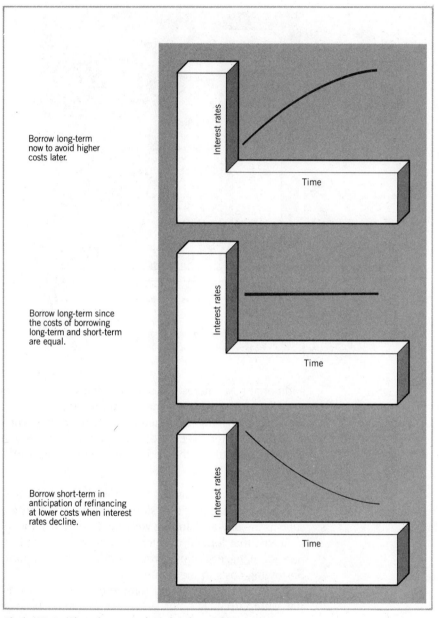

Borrow long-term now to avoid higher costs later.

Borrow long-term since the costs of borrowing long-term and short-term are equal.

Borrow short-term in anticipation of refinancing at lower costs when interest rates decline.

Figure 15–5   Financing strategies related to yield curves.

decline, borrowing long-term funds should be delayed until rates fall. (Of course, neither the expectations theory nor the economic forecast is a precise tool; but financial managers must use the tools available to help them decide the amount and the terms of loans.)

If current short-term interest rates are higher than long-term rates, the result is a **downward-sloping yield curve**. According to the theory, long-term interest rates will decline. Armed with this knowledge, financial managers should borrow short-term funds now in the expectation of refinancing their loans at a lower cost when long-term interest rates fall.

Figure 15–6 shows the levels of long- and short-term interest rates since the early 1900s. Through most of the period shown, short-term rates were lower than long-term rates. During these periods, yield curves were upward sloping.

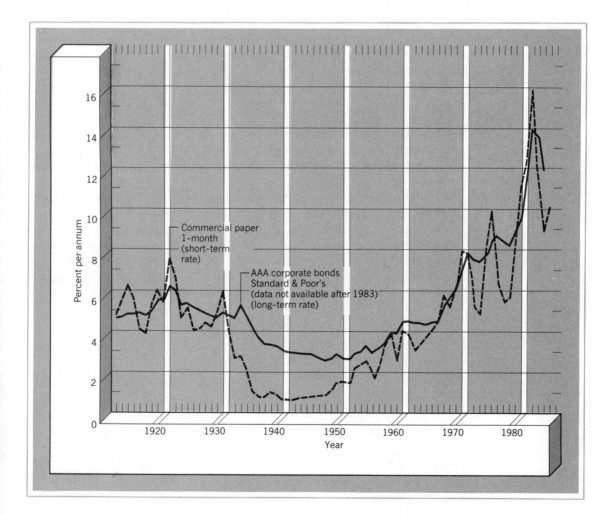

At other times, short-term rates exceeded long-term rates, giving rise to downward-sloping yield curves. Notice that the periods of downward-sloping yield curves were generally followed by lower long-term interest rates, at least for short periods. Nevertheless, since the 1940s, the general level of long-term rates has increased to reach record levels. Equally important, in recent years, the swings in short-term rates have been larger and have occurred more frequently than in earlier periods. This pattern of rapid change makes it difficult to manage working capital effectively. It also makes understanding the risks associated with aggressive hedging especially important.

Summary

Working capital includes a firm's current assets, but working capital management extends to the financing of those assets. The level of working capital a firm holds depends on many factors. Three important determinants are industry requirements, which are dictated by the nature of the business; the firm's position on the life cycle; and business conditions. In general, levels of working capital are higher for firms in the early phases of the life cycle and during expansions in business activity.

Working capital can be financed in a variety of ways. One way involves a perfect hedge, in which the maturity of assets and the funds used to finance them are equal. Alternately, firms may use a conservative hedge, which favors long-term financing, or an aggressive hedge, which favors short-term financing. Each hedging method affects profits in a different way. Aggressive hedging produces the greatest profits, but it also carries the greatest risk.

The degree to which firms use conservative or aggressive financing may be influenced by their outlook on future business conditions and by the shape of yield curves, which show the relationship between interest rates and the maturity of a security. Recent wide swings in the levels of interest rates suggest that a firm's financing strategies must be flexible so it can profit from change.

Important Terms

Aggressive hedge

Conservative hedge

Downward-sloping yield curve

Expectations theory

Flat yield curve

Hedging

Liquid assets

Net working capital

Normal yield curve

Perfect hedge

Permanent working capital

Real rate of interest

Temporary working capital

Term structure of interest rates

Upward-sloping yield curve

Working capital

Working capital management

Yield curve

Questions

1. Define *working capital* and *net working capital*. Why is the distinction between the terms important?
2. Distinguish between *permanent* and *temporary* current assets.
3. Explain the effects of the product life cycle and industry classification on working capital requirements.
4. What role do business cycles play in the level of working capital held by businesses?
5. Define *hedging* in the context of working capital policy.
6. Define a *perfect hedge,* a *conservative hedge,* and an *aggressive hedge.*
7. Explain the relationship between hedging, profitability, and risk.
8. What is the real rate of interest?
9. How are market interest rates influenced by expected inflation?
10. What is the expectations theory of interest rates?
11. What is a yield curve? What is its usual pattern? Why?
12. According to the expectations theory, what explanation can be given for an upward-sloping yield curve? A flat curve? A downward-sloping curve?
13. How can financial managers use forecasts based on the term structure of interest rates to assist in financing decisions?

Problems

1. Consider the balance sheet for Burgess Barbecue, Inc.

Burgess Barbecue
December 31, 1990

Assets
Current assets:

Cash	$ 50,000
Accounts receivable	100,000
Inventory	50,000
Total current assets	$200,000
Net fixed assets	$100,000
Total assets	$300,000

Liabilities and net worth
Current liabilities

Accrued liabilities	$ 40,000
Accounts payable	10,000
Total current liabilities	$ 50,000
Net worth (equity):	
Common stock	100,000
Retained earnings	150,000
Total net worth	$250,000
Total liabilities and net worth	$300,000

(a) How much working capital and net working capital does Burgess have?

(b) Suppose the level of temporary current assets is $50,000. Characterize the hedging policy of Burgess's management. Explain. Do the same for a level of temporary current assets of $25,000; $100,000.

2. Review the following balance sheet for Woffard Corporation.

Woffard Corporation
December 31, 1990

Assets
Current assets:

Cash	$ 10,000
Accounts receivable	20,000
Inventory	$100,000
Total current assets	$130,000
Net fixed assets	$500,000
Total assets	$630,000

Liabilities and net worth
Current liabilities

Accrued liabilities	$ 5,000
Notes payable	10,000
Accounts payable	80,000
Total current liabilities	$ 95,000
Long-term debt	$100,000
Net worth (equity):	
Common stock	100,000
Paid-in capital	135,000
Retained earnings	200,000
Total net worth	$435,000
Total liabilities and net worth	$630,000

(a) Calculate the working capital and net working capital position of Woffard.
(b) Calculate the current and acid-test ratios for the firm. How liquid is the firm, based on your answers to parts a and b.
(c) How conservative or aggressive is the overall working capital policy? Explain.
(d) Suppose Woffard's long-term debt is maturing. What factors should be considered by management in determining whether it should be replaced by a new long-term loan or whether short-term financing should be obtained instead?

3. Select three firms in the airline industry and obtain balance sheet information for them from the same year. Analyze their working capital and net working capital positions. Rank them according to relative liquidity. Which firm would you say has a riskier working capital policy? Why?

4. Select three firms from three different industries and obtain balance sheet information for them from the same year. Explain any differences you find in their working capital policies. Consider the impact of industry membership, life cycle, and phase of the business cycle.

5. Ben's Pizzas, Inc., is a new chain opening in Arizona. Management is concerned with the effect of changing interest rates on the financial health of the business. Current short-term rates average about 10 percent, while long-term rates are generally about 15 percent. Ben's will initially need to finance $500,000 of fixed assets and $500,000 of current assets. Trade credit (accounts payable) will be used to finance $100,000 of current assets and owners will be contributing $100,000 in equity. All remaining funds must come from debt financing. *EBIT* is expected to be $200,000 in the first year and the applicable tax rate is 30 percent.

Two financing plans are being considered to supplement funds from accounts payable and owners' equity.

Plan 1: All current assets will be financed with short-term debt; fixed assets will be financed with long-term debt.

Plan 2: The only short-term credit to be used is trade credit; all other financing will be long-term.

Calculate net income, the current ratio, and return on equity for both plans. Explain the trade-offs involved in choosing one plan over another.

6. Suppose, instead, that average short-term rates for Ben's Pizzas in Problem 5 were 20 percent. Calculate net income, the current ratio, and *ROE* under the two plans described in that problem. Which plan is preferable? Why?

7. Herbert Printing has established all financial plans for the coming year except its working capital policy. Current rates on notes payable are 7.5 percent, and long-term rates are averaging 12 percent. Herbert must finance $800,000 of fixed assets and $400,000 of current assets. Permanent current assets total $250,000. Accounts payable (trade credit) can be used to finance $150,000 of current assets, and net worth is $300,000, but additional financing must come from other sources. *EBIT* is expected to be $500,000, and Herbert's tax rate is 40 percent.

Two financing plans are being considered.

Plan X: All current assets and $200,000 of fixed assets will be financed with notes payable.

Plan Y: Short-term financing will be used for temporary current assets only, and long-term financing for remaining needs.

Calculate net income, the current ratio, and return on equity for each plan. Explain the trade-offs involved in choosing one plan over another. Under what circumstances would you recommend each plan?

8. JWF, Inc., must find financing for $200,000 in fixed plant and equipment and $800,000 in current assets, of which $300,000 are permanent current assets.

(a) Management plans to finance the fixed assets and one-half of the permanent current assets with long-term financing at 12 percent. Short-term financing costs 9 percent. JWF is in the 40 percent tax bracket and expected *EBIT* on these assets is $400,000. Calculate net income under this plan.

(b) An alternate plan would finance all fixed assets, all permanent current assets, and one-half the temporary current assets with long-term financing. Calculate net income under this plan.

(c) Compare the relative riskiness of the two plans.

9. Following is the balance sheet of the Meeds Corporation.

Meeds Corporation
December 31, 1991

Assets

Current assets:

Cash	$ 2,000,000
Marketable securities	3,000,000
Accounts receivable	10,000,000
Inventory	5,000,000
Total current assets	$20,000,000
Net fixed assets	$50,000,000
Total assets	$70,000,000

Liabilities and net worth

Current liabilities

Accrued liabilities	$ 1,000,000
Notes payable	5,000,000
Accounts payable	4,000,000
Total current liabilities	$10,000,000
Long-term debt	$20,000,000
Net worth (equity):	
Common stock	10,000,000
Retained earnings	30,000,000
Total liabilities and net worth	$70,000,000

(a) How much net working capital does Meeds have? Calculate the current and the acid-test ratios.

(b) If Meeds refinances notes payable with long-term financing, what will be the effect on net working capital, the current ratio, and acid-test ratio?

(c) Under normal term structure conditions (i.e., a normal yield curve), what changes might you expect in the firm's net income if the refinancing occurs? Why? (No calculations are required.)

10. The Bamboo Import Company had the following balance sheet last year.

Bamboo Imports
December 31, 1989

Assets

Current assets:

Cash	$ 120,000
Marketable securities	80,000
Accounts receivable	600,000
Inventory	1,500,000
Total current assets	$2,300,000
Net fixed assets	$4,000,000
Total assets	$6,300,000

Liabilities and net worth

Current liabilities

Accrued liabilities	$ 100,000
Notes payable	400,000
Accounts payable	800,000
Total current liabilities	$1,300,000
Long-term debt	$2,500,000
Net worth (equity):	
Common stock	500,000
Paid-in capital	1,200,000
Retained earnings	800,000
Total net worth	$2,500,000
Total liabilities and net worth	$6,300,000

(a) Calculate net working capital, the current ratio, and the acid-test ratio for Bamboo. Suggest ways in which Bamboo could reduce the riskiness of its working capital policy.

(b) Calculate what net working capital, the current ratio, and the acid-test ratio will be if Bamboo pays off notes payable with the proceeds of a long-term debt issue.

(c) Under normal term structure conditions, what changes might you expect in the firm's net income if the refinancing occurs? Why? What changes would you expect in net income if the existing term structure was downward-sloping? (No calculations are necessary.)

11. The following relationships are currently observed to exist in the financial markets.

Maturity of Security (years)	Interest Rate (%)
1	6.0
2	6.5
3	8.0
5	9.0
10	10.0
20	10.2

Plot the yield curve that results from these relationships. Based on the expectations theory, in what direction do you expect short-term interest rates to move? Why?

12. Find the "Treasury Issues" column in a recent *Wall Street Journal*. Select about 10 security issues from the column and plot their maturity against their yield. Be sure to choose some securities with very short maturities as well as some with maturities in excess of 10 years. What is the shape of the resulting yield curve? If the expectations theory is correct, what is your forecast for short-term rates in the future? Use the expectations theory as the bais for your answers to Problems 13 through 17.

13. If the current rate on a 1-year security is 8 percent and the expected rate 1 year from now on a 1-year security is 12 percent, what is the current rate on a 2-year security?

14. If the current rate on a 1-year security is 8 percent and the current rate on a 2-year security is 7 percent, what is the expected rate on a 1-year security 1 year from now?

15. If 1-year rates of return for the next 2 years are expected to be 15 percent and 12 percent what average rate of return would you expect over the 2-year period?

16. The current market rate for a 1-year security is 14 percent and for a 2-year security, 16 percent. What is the expected 1-year rate 1 year from now?

17. The current 2-year rate on a government security is 12 percent. What is the current 1-year rate on a government security if the forecasted rate on a 1-year security 1 year from now is 14 percent?

16 Cash and Short-Term Securities

Current asset management;

+ Inventory Control
trade credit + retail credit

You may remember from earlier discussions that cash and marketable short-term securities are a business concern's most liquid assets. **Cash** consists of coin, currency, and demand deposits; and **short-term marketable securities** are those that mature within 1 year. These assets provide the liquidity needed to meet financial obligations that are not perfectly synchronized with expected cash inflows. If business concerns do not have sufficient liquidity to meet financial obligations, they may become technically insolvent and be forced into bankruptcy. On the other hand, excess liquidity, while safer, adversely affects profitability because cash is a nonearning asset and it is assumed the firm can earn more on other assets than on short-term securities. Accordingly, liquidity management offers yet another example of the trade-off between risk and return. This chapter examines liquidity management.

After reading this chapter, you should know the following.

1. **Why business concerns maintain liquid assets.**
2. **Why cash cycles should be as short as possible.**
3. **How to collect cash faster.**
4. **How to slow down the payment of bills.**
5. **How to use two models that deal with the size of cash balances and transfers of cash to and from securities portfolios.**
6. **What advantages and disadvantages are offered by short-term securities.**
7. **How business concerns use hedging in managing cash and short-term investments.**

Liquidity Preference

John Maynard Keynes's classic work *The General Theory of Employment, Interest, and Money* contributed to a revolution in economic thought and the foundation of Keynesian economics. Of interest here is the fact that some aspects of his work are concerned with the management of liquidity. Keynes asked why a preference for liquidity exists, and answered his question in the following manner:

> We can usefully employ the ancient distinction between the use of money for the transaction of current business and its use as a store of wealth. As regards the first of these two uses, it is obvious that up to a point it is worthwhile to sacrifice a certain amount of interest for the convenience of liquidity. But, given that the rate of interest is never negative, why should anyone prefer to hold his wealth in a form which yields little or no interest to holding it in a form which yields interest?[1]

Keynes goes on to answer the question by stating that "the existence of *uncertainty* as to the future of the rate of interest, i.e., as to the complex of rates of interest for varying maturities which will rule at future dates," is a major consideration in holding cash.[2] In addition, Keynes states that "different people will estimate the prospects differently and anyone who differs from the predominant opinion expressed in market quotations may have good reason for keeping liquid resources in order to profit, if he is right."[3] Thus, uncertainty

[1] John Maynard Keynes, *The General Theory of Employment, Interest, and Money* (New York: Harcourt, Brace and Company, 1936), p. 168.

[2] Ibid.

[3] Ibid., p. 169.

about interest rates and investors' psychology are important determinants of the amount of liquid assets an investor holds.

In summary, we can say that, in Keynes's view, liquidity preference depends on (1) a transaction motive, (2) a precautionary motive, and (3) a speculative motive. A fourth motive not mentioned by Keynes is the requirement for a compensating balance.

Transaction Motive Business concerns require a certain amount of cash to carry out their daily transactions; this cash is held because of the **transaction motive**. The amount of cash required depends on the nature of the business. Grocery stores, for example, transact most of their business for cash. In contrast, automobile dealerships transact most of their sales for credit.

The amount of cash held also depends on the regularity of receipts and disbursements. Business concerns that have highly predictable inflows and outflows of funds can hold relatively less cash than firms whose cash flows are irregular. For example, the cash inflows of life insurance companies are highly predictable, and they hold less than 1 percent of their assets in the form of cash. In contrast, cash flows for aircraft manufacturers are subject to wide variations; they keep about 8 percent of their assets in the form of cash.

Precautionary Motive The **precautionary motive** is also related to the nature and level of business activity. Precautionary balances are set aside because cash inflows and outflows are not synchronized. For example, precautionary balances may be used to meet some expenses when an unanticipated decline in sales revenues occurs.

Speculative Motive According to Keynes, the object of the **speculative motive** is "securing a profit from knowing better than the market what the future will bring forth."[4] As the name implies, speculation is at the heart of this motive. Some firms hold practically no speculative balances, whereas others hold large speculative balances because they are aggressively seeking acquisitions or good buying opportunities for the commodities they use in their operations. For example, Modern Office Furniture Company took advantage of a recent dip in the price of steel to purchase 5 tons. Although this is three times the firm's normal inventory of steel, the company's economist was predicting higher steel prices and the possibility of an extended labor strike. The company could take advantage of the lower price to hoard steel because it had a speculative balance for that purpose. Speculative balances are sensitive to interest rate changes and are usually held in the form of interest-bearing securities.

[4]Ibid., p. 170.

Compensating Balance Requirement The **compensating balance**, as mentioned, is not associated with Keynesian theory but with commercial banks that require borrowers to leave a portion of their borrowed funds on deposit. Banks may require that 10 percent or more of the amount of a loan be left on deposit. There are two reasons for requiring a compensating balance: (1) It raises the effective interest rate for the bank, and (2) it provides the bank with funds to make additional loans. From the firm's point of view, it can be used as a bargaining tool to lower the cost of borrowing.

Cash Management ommit

The goal of cash management is to maintain the minimum cash balance that will provide the firm with sufficient liquidity to meet its financial obligations and to enhance its profitability without exposing it to undue risk. Two general approaches may be used to achieve this goal. As shown in Figure 16–1, one approach views cash as a financial asset. The objective of this approach is to minimize the cost of the cash cycle, which will be explained next. The second approach views cash as if it were a physical asset and uses inventory control models to determine the appropriate cash levels. These models, which will be examined later in this chapter, also provide information about buying and selling marketable securities.

Cash Cycle The cash cycle reflects the average number of days a firm's cash is invested in inventory and accounts receivable (which we will assume produce no cash

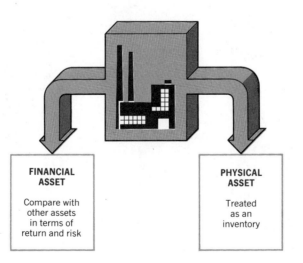

FINANCIAL ASSET

Compare with other assets in terms of return and risk

PHYSICAL ASSET

Treated as an inventory

until payments for credit sales are received). For reasons that will soon be explained, it is in the firm's best interest to keep the cash cycle as short as possible. To illustrate how that might be accomplished, we will consider the case of Fixim Company, which provides emergency repair service on large X-ray machines.

The operating cycle and the cash cycle for Fixim Company are shown in Figure 16–2. The **cash cycle**, which is part of the operating cycle, is defined as the average age of the inventory plus the average age of accounts receivable, less the average age of accounts payable. The methods used to compute the average age of these assets were explained in Chapter 13.

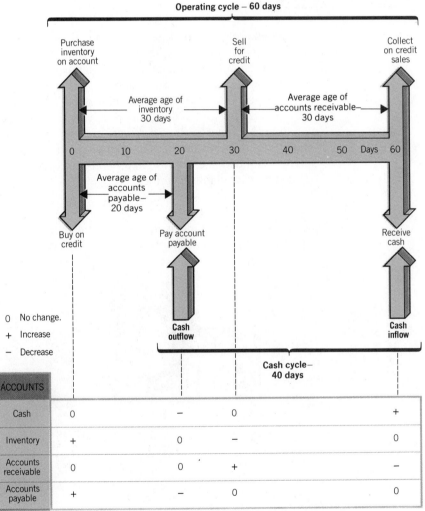

The **operating cycle** begins when Fixim Company purchases inventory on account on Day 0. Because the firm has purchased the items on credit, its accounts payable increase. Twenty days later, Fixim Company pays the bill and reduces its accounts payable and cash accounts. On Day 30, the inventory is sold for credit, resulting in a reduction in inventory and an increase in accounts receivable. The end of the operating cycle occurs when credit sales are paid on the 60th day, which reduces the accounts receivable and increases cash. Figure 16–2 shows that, on the average, cash outflows occur on Day 20 and inflows on Day 60, resulting in a cash cycle of 40 days (60 days − 20 days = 40 days).

Cash Turnover. A cash cycle of 40 days means that Fixim Company turns over its average cash balance nine times per year. In other words, the **cash turnover** is calculated as follows.

$$\text{Cash turnover} = \frac{360 \text{ days}}{\text{Cash cycle}}$$

$$= \frac{360}{40}$$

$$= 9 \text{ times} \qquad (16\text{–}1)$$

As mentioned, the cash cycle should be kept as short as possible. A short cash cycle means a high cash turnover, which is desirable because it reduces a firm's average cash balance and the cost of holding those funds. The Fixim Company, for example, has total annual outlays of $2 million. The **average cash balance** ($222,222) is determined by dividing total annual outlays by the cash turnover.

$$\text{Average cash balance} = \frac{\text{Total annual outlays}}{\text{Cash turnover}}$$

$$= \frac{\$2,000,000}{9}$$

$$= \$222,222 \qquad (16\text{–}2)$$

Assume that Fixim has an opportunity cost of 10 percent, which means that the firm can invest its funds elsewhere and receive a 10 percent return. Because cash is a nonearning asset, the cost of maintaining the average cash balance of $222,222 is $22,222 ($222,222 × 0.10 = $22,222). If the firm keeps its cash balance as low as possible, it can invest in short-term securities to obtain both liquidity and income.

Strategies.   Three basic strategies can be used to reduce the length of cash cycles, which, in turn, results in lower costs and higher earnings. The use of these or any other strategies depends on their benefits and costs. In other words, marginal benefits must be compared with marginal costs. The strategies are as follows.

1.   *Collect accounts receivable as soon as possible*. However, great care must be taken not to use collection techniques that may have adverse effects, such as alienating new or existing credit customers.
2.   *Delay paying the accounts payable as long as possible without adversely affecting the company's credit rating, while still taking advantage of cash discounts on purchased goods*. (Cash discounts are used by those who sell on credit to encourage buyers to pay their bills early. More will be said about them in the next chapter.)
3.   *Increase inventory turnover, either by increasing sales or by reducing the amount of inventory held*. One problem that may result from reducing inventory too far is loss of sales when items customers want to buy are unavailable.

   We can see the effect of shortening the cash cycle by looking more closely at one of these strategies—increasing the average age of accounts payable. Assume that the average age of accounts payable for Fixim Company has been increased from 20 days to 30 days. Now the cash outflow occurs on Day 30. Because there is no change in the average age of inventory or accounts receivable, the cash inflow still occurs on Day 60. Therefore, the cash cycle has been reduced from 40 days to 30 days. The cash turnover has increased to 12 times per year (360/30 = 12) and the average cash balance has been reduced to $166,667 ($2,000,000/12 = $166,667). The opportunity cost of holding this amount of cash is $16,667 ($166,667 × 0.10 = $16,667). By using this or any strategy that reduced the cash cycle by 10 days, Fixim could reduce its average cash balance from $222,222 to $166,667, reduce its opportunity cost from $22,222 to $16,667, and earn an additional $5,555 ($22,222 − $16,667 = $5,555).

Methods of Collection

Techniques have been developed to help firms reduce their average cash balances and manage their cash more efficiently. The techniques are used to accelerate the receipt of cash or to slow its disbursement—the first two strategies just described. This section examines methods used to accelerate the receipt of cash.

Taking Advantage of Float **Float**, which is associated with the collection of funds from credit sales, is the time delay between the moment of disbursement of funds by a buyer and the use of those funds by the seller. The delay is caused by mail time, processing time, and the time it takes collection items to clear the banking system. Thus, float may also be defined as the dollar difference between the bank balance and the book balance for cash. Keep in mind that float is a double-edged sword: It can work for a firm or against it, depending on whether the firm is paying or receiving the funds.

Mail Float.   Although the mail must go through, it is not always clear how long that process will take. The time required for a letter to go by mail from one city to another can range from a day to a week or more.

Processing Float.   Many firms do not deposit checks as soon as they are received. For one reason or another, checks may be allowed to accumulate for several days before they are deposited. This is particularly true for firms with branch offices that send checks to the main office for processing.

Clearing Float.   Many banks will not give full credit for checks that have been deposited until they have been cleared through the commercial banking system. **Clearing** includes the processing of the check and the collection of the funds. Credit may be deferred for several days or longer, depending on the check's origin. For example, a check deposited in New York and drawn on a Chicago bank may be credited the following day. But several weeks may elapse before a check drawn on a bank located in South America is fully credited. Therefore, the amount of deposits shown on the company's books may differ from the amount the company has available for use at its bank.

The expression "time costs money" applies to float. Assume that a company is expecting to receive $50,000 that is delayed 15 days. If the opportunity cost of the funds is 10 percent, the late payment costs the firm $208.33, computed as follows.

$$\text{Cost of float} = \text{Amount} \times \text{Opportunity cost} \times \frac{\text{Days late}}{360 \text{ days}}$$

$$= \$50{,}000 \times 0.10 \times \frac{15}{360}$$

$$= \$208.33 \tag{16-3}$$

Lockbox Collection Systems Lockbox collection systems are widely used to reduce mail and processing float. A **lockbox** is a post office box. Firms such as major oil companies receive checks from all over the country, rent post office boxes in strategic locations, and have the checks sent to the post office box closest to the sender. Arrangements are made with commercial banks to collect the funds from the post office boxes at specified intervals. During slow periods, the mail may be picked up only once a day, whereas during peak periods it may be picked up hourly. The banks process and deposit the checks and notify the company the same day as to the amount of funds that have been received.

The case of Moonlite Auto, a dealer in used automobile parts, demonstrates the usefulness of a lockbox system. Moonlite Auto is located in Atlanta. As shown in Table 16–1, one-fourth of its business is done in Atlanta, half is done in New York, and the remainder is done in Los Angeles. The firm has a daily sales volume of $1 million, and all its sales are for credit. Average collection times range from 2 to 5 days. Total float, which is obtained by multiplying the daily sales volume by the average collection time, amounts to $3,750,000.

If Moonlite Auto uses two lockboxes—one in New York and the other in Los Angeles—it can reduce total float to $2 million, as the table shows. If Moonlite's opportunity cost is 10 percent, it will save $175,000 annually ($3,750,000 − $2,000,000 × 0.10 = $175,000), less the cost of the lockbox service, which varies.

Moonlite Auto uses a *wholesale* lockbox. Wholesale lockboxes are usually used by wholesale firms and characterized by a low volume of high-dollar-value transactions. As mentioned, the objective of using the lockbox is to reduce float. There are also *retail* lockboxes, used by large retail outlets, such as department stores, and characterized by a high volume of low-dollar-value transactions. In addition to reducing float, retail lockboxes can be used in the processing of accounts receivable; this is called an **automated remittance process**. At a cost of 8 to 10 cents per item, this service may permit a retail firm to reduce its collection costs.

Table 16–1
Lockbox Analysis for Moonlite Auto

Location	Daily Sales Volume (1)	Average Collection Time in Atlanta (days) (2)	Float (3) = (1) × (2)
No Lockboxes			
Atlanta	$ 250,000	2	$ 500,000
New York	500,000	4	2,000,000
Los Angeles	250,000	5	1,250,000
	$1,000,000		$3,750,000
Two Lockboxes			
Atlanta	$ 250,000	2	$ 500,000
New York	500,000	2	1,000,000
Los Angeles	250,000	2	500,000
	$1,000,000		$2,000,000

Concentration Banking   The lockbox system is one method of accelerating the collection of funds by using regional collection centers. **Concentration banking** is a variant of the regional collection approach. Many business concerns that have sales outlets throughout the country collect cash from their outlets' sales and deposit these funds in regional concentration banks. This pooling of funds facilitates efficient working capital management. Several vehicles are used to transfer funds from local banks to concentration banks. They include wire transfer, depository transfer checks, electronic funds transfer systems, and couriers.

Wire Transfer.   Funds can be transferred between commercial banks with almost no delay by use of **wire transfer**. The Federal Reserve Wire System, often called the Fed Wire, is the major wire transfer system. Although the system may be used only by banks that are members of the Federal Reserve System, nonmember banks may have their correspondent banks transfer funds for them. (Correspondent banks are those that provide services, such as check clearing, for other banks.) The advantage of the Fed Wire is its speed, which provides instant availability of credit. The Western Union Bank Wire provides a private alternative to the Federal Reserve's wire system. However, fewer banks subscribe to the Western Union Bank Wire, which limits its usefulness.

Depository Transfer Checks.   A **depository transfer check** is drawn on a local bank and made payable to a concentration bank for the account of a specified business concern. The advantage of a depository check is that it costs about 10 cents, compared with about $7 to send a wire transfer and $4 to receive one. The disadvantage is that it must pass through the normal clearing process, and that takes time. Consequently, the funds are not available for immediate use.

Electronic Funds Transfer System.   The Federal Reserve System and private banking organizations are developing a nationwide **electronic funds transfer system** (**EFTS**) designed to reduce the volume of paper checks by making increased use of computer technology. The idea is to make funds transfers by using electronic debits and credits instead of mailing paper checks. Some parts of the *EFTS* are already in operation and are speeding the clearing of funds. As the system evolves, business concerns will have their own terminals that tie into the *EFTS* and permit them to make deposits and receive credits instantaneously.

Already, many firms use **automated clearing houses** (**ACHs**) a part of the *EFTS* in which debits and credits are electronically transferred between financial institutions. *ACHs* allow businesses to transfer funds quickly (in about a day) and at low cost (about $1 per item), while eliminating mail float and the problems of clearing checks. In addition, items can be *value dated*, or paid on a predetermined date, through an *ACH*. For example, suppose a firm in New York wanted to pay a bill on the 18th of the month to a firm in El Paso, Texas. The item could be sent through an *ACH* with the proviso that it be credited to an El Paso bank on that date. The funds would then be immediately available to the El Paso bank's customer.

Preauthorized payments are another aspect of *EFTS*. For example, customers of a telephone company or a life insurance company may give written authorization to withdraw funds from their checking accounts to pay their utility bill or life insurance premium. The obvious advantage of this system is the instant access to customers' funds. Some business concerns make use of **preauthorized checks** drawn on customers' demand deposit accounts. Both systems result in improved cash balances for the receiving firms.

Couriers. Many business concerns use personal **couriers** to transfer large sums of money. For example, assume that a company in New York must make a $3 million payment to a firm in Los Angeles. If the average mail time is 6 days and the opportunity cost is 10 percent, the cost of the mail float is $5,000.00, or $833.33 per day.

$$\$3,000,000 \times 0.10 \times \frac{6}{360} = \$5000$$

$$\$5000 \div 6 \text{ days} = \$833.33$$

If for some reason a wire transfer cannot be used to make the payment, the receiving firm would be better off paying a courier to make a 1-day pickup and delivery of the funds. Of course, the firm making the payment would prefer to mail the check and retain the funds in its account as long as possible.

Methods of Disbursement   *ommit*

While the preceding section focused on methods for accelerating the receipt of cash, this section deals with methods for slowing disbursements. The combination of fast collections and slow payments enhances the availability of funds. There are risks to be considered, too. Firms that meet their financial obligations too slowly may hurt their credit standings.

Drafts A **draft**, or **bill of exchange**, is an unconditional order in writing signed by the *drawer* (the one who orders payment) requiring the *drawee* (the one ordered to pay) to pay on demand or at some determinable time in the future a definite sum of money to a *payee* (the one to whom payment must be made).

The most common form of draft is a bank check. For example, Joe Doe (the drawer) writes a check ordering First National Bank (the drawee) to pay the Flakey Department Store (the payee) $125 on demand.

The **payable-through draft**, another type of bill of exchange, is used by some business concerns to slow disbursements. In this case, the drawer and the drawee are the same party. In other words, payable-through drafts are orders drawn on a business by itself and payable through a bank; that is, the bank will present the draft to the drawer for payment. Any delays in presenting the drafts for collection provide the issuing company with additional time to use its funds. Another advantage of payable-through drafts is that funds to cover the drafts need not be deposited until the drafts are presented. Therefore, the firm can maintain smaller deposits at the bank.

Controlled Disbursing As noted, float is a double-edged sword. While firms receiving payments would like to eliminate float, firms sending payments would like to take advantage of it. Some business concerns make disbursements from strategically located banks to maximize clearing time and float; this is called **controlled disbursing**. For example, a firm that has national operations but is headquartered in Denver may write checks against its account at a bank in Tacoma, Washington. The checks may also be mailed from remote locations, which adds time to the mail float. However, firms with only regional or local operations may not be able to use remote disbursing. The Federal Reserve System, which wants to eliminate float, is attempting to use its influence to stop this practice.

Timing of Payments Some business concerns time their payments so that checks arrive on Friday. For example, many firms send paychecks with this intention. Paychecks received on Friday are often not cashed and cleared until the following week, giving the issuing firm several additional days of float. To some extent, the increasing use of *EFTS* and direct payroll deposit will eliminate the advantage of paying salaries on Friday.

Zero-Balance Accounts Many companies with multiple divisions maintain numerous bank accounts so that each division can make disbursements for operating and other expenses. One technique to minimize the cash balances held in the various banks uses **zero-balance accounts**. The name stems from the fact that the accounts are managed so that they have a zero balance most of the time.

A zero-balance account system consists of various divisional checking accounts and a corporate checking account, all located at the same concentration bank. When deposits are made in a divisional account, the funds are transferred immediately into the corporate account, and the balance in the division's account is reduced to zero. When a division makes disbursements, the corporation instructs the bank to transfer a sufficient amount of funds from the corporate account into the division's account to cover the checks presented for payment.

The major advantage of a zero-balance account system is that it allows the corporation to maintain control over cash outflows while allowing the divisions to maintain autonomy in making disbursements. Equally important, this method reduces excess cash balances.

Inventory Models

As noted earlier in this chapter, some models used for the management of inventories may be applied to the management of cash and marketable securities.[5] The decisions covered by the models deal with the size and timing of transfers between cash and marketable securities. The two models presented here are cost-balancing models. That means they attempt to minimize the cost of holding cash instead of marketable securities against the cost of converting marketable securities into cash.

A firm *must* know its liquidity requirements before it can employ cash management models. In other words, the firm must determine, by using cash budgets or some other means, that it wants a certain amount of liquidity. Then, and only then, can it consider using models that help determine the levels of cash and marketable securities it should hold. Because many firms do not plan their liquidity needs in advance and do not have the expertise to work with the models described here, the use of the models is less widespread than the methods of cash management already discussed.

It should be noted that marketing or technical considerations may be more important to some firms than the optimization of liquidity or inventory positions. For example, Ellwood Fabricators, producers of metal parts used in the construction industry, recently stocked up on sheet metal far out of proportion to its normal inventory. To do so, it reduced its liquidity to dangerously low levels. However, Ellwood was willing to take this action because it expected a steel strike that would prevent it from obtaining the raw materials necessary to carry on its business.

Economic Order Quantity Firms require an inventory of cash, just as they require inventories of raw materials. The objective of the first model we will examine is to determine the optimal average amount that must be transferred from a firm's marketable securities portfolio into its cash account so that it can meet its demand for cash over time. That amount is called the **economic order quantity**, or **EOQ**.

[5]The first use of inventory models for cash management is attributable to William J. Baumol, "The Transactions Demand for Cash: An Inventory Theoretic Approach," *Quarterly Journal of Economics,* November 1952, pp. 545–556.

Assumptions. It has been said that a model is only as good as the assumptions on which it is based. If the assumptions are not valid, the results obtained by using the model may not be meaningful. Therefore, it is important to examine the assumptions underlying the *EOQ* model.

1. *Certainty*. The first assumption is that certainty exists—that is, that the financial manager has precise knowledge as to what the cash balance will be over time.
2. *Steady demand for cash*. The second assumption is that the firm's use of cash will be steady over time. Figure 16–3 depicts the use pattern connected with the *EOQ* model. The letter *Q* denotes the total amount of cash that has been ordered and that is available for disbursement at the beginning of the period. Cash is used in constant amounts until the cash balance is depleted, at which time additional cash is added to the account. The process of adding and withdrawing cash is repeated over time, resulting in a saw-toothed pattern.
3. *Instantaneous transfer of funds from the securities portfolio into the cash account*. When the cash account has been depleted, it is replenished through sale of marketable securities and transfer of the resulting funds into the cash account. It is assumed that this transfer occurs instantaneously.
4. *Fixed cost per transaction*. It is further assumed that the cost of transactions is fixed, regardless of size. The cost referred to here includes the costs of making the transactions, such as telephone expenses and commissions, as well as administrative costs, safekeeping costs, and so on.

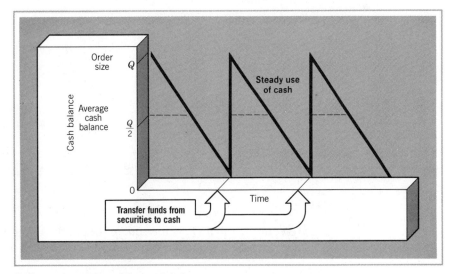

Figure 16–3 *EOQ* model of cash balances.

Costs. The total cost of holding cash is equal to the ordering cost plus the opportunity cost of giving up interest income. Accordingly, total cost may be expressed as follows.

$$
\begin{array}{ll}
\text{Total cost of} \\
\text{holding cash}
\end{array}
=
\begin{array}{l}
\text{Ordering} \\
\text{cost}
\end{array}
+
\begin{array}{l}
\text{Opportunity} \\
\text{cost}
\end{array}
$$

$$
= B\left(\frac{T}{Q}\right) + i\left(\frac{Q}{2}\right) \tag{16--4}
$$

where

B = Fixed cost per order of converting marketable securities into cash
Q = Amount of marketable securities to be converted into cash per order
T = Total demand for cash during a given period
i = Interest rate on marketable securities, which remains constant over the period being considered

The first term in the equation deals with the ordering cost of converting marketable securities into cash. It is derived by multiplying the fixed cost (B) by the number of transactions that occur during a period (T/Q). As shown in Figure 16--4, total ordering costs decline as the amount of marketable securities to be converted into cash increases.

The second term represents the opportunity cost of holding cash. The opportunity cost is equal to the interest rate on short-term marketable securities (i) times the average cash balance ($Q/2$). This cost increases as the amount of marketable securities to be converted into cash increases. The objective of the *EOQ* model is to balance the ordering cost and the opportunity cost so that the total cost is minimized.

Q^* in Figure 16--4 represents the level of Q that minimizes total cost; it is the economic order quantity. We find Q^* by solving the following equation.[6]

$$
Q^* = \sqrt{\frac{2BT}{i}} \tag{16--5}
$$

or

$$
Q^* = \sqrt{\frac{2\ (\text{Conversion cost}) \times \text{Total demand for cash}}{\text{Interest rate}}}
$$

We could say that Q^* is the square root of the dollar volume of transactions. If the volume of transactions quadrupled, Q^* would only double in size. If the

[6]The derivation of the *EOQ* model is explained in more detail in Chapter 18.

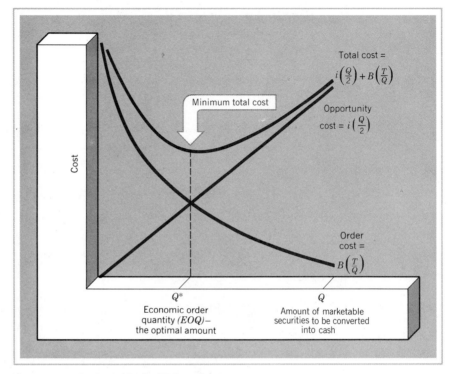

Figure 16–4 Costs used in the *EOQ* model.

dollar volume of transactions increased a hundredfold, Q* would increase 10 times. This suggests that there are some economies of scale in cash management that should be taken into account.

Equation 16–5 also shows that Q* is inversely related to the interest rate on short-term marketable securities (*i*). Although the impact is diminished because of the square root, higher levels of interest contribute to smaller economic order quantities.

Equation 16–5 is used in the following manner. Assume that the Fixim Company knows that its total demand for cash next month will be $300,000 and that the fixed cost per order of converting marketable securities into cash is $100. The annual interest rate on short-term marketable securities is 9 percent. Because we are interested in a 1-month period, the interest rate we use in the equation is as follows.

$$\frac{0.09}{12 \text{ months}} = 0.0075$$

By inserting these numbers into Equation 16–5, we can determine the economic order quantity, or the optimal amount of marketable securities to convert into cash.

$$Q* = \sqrt{\frac{2\ (\$100 \times \$300,000)}{0.0075}} = \$89,442.72$$

We can find out how many times securities will have to be converted into cash during any period by dividing the total demand for cash by $Q*$.

$$\text{Number of orders per period} = \frac{T}{Q*} \qquad (16\text{--}6)$$

The Fixim Company will have to transfer securities into cash about three times ($\$300,000.00/\$89,442.72 = 3.4$ times) per month.

Limitations.   The *EOQ* model has some weaknesses that limit its usefulness. First, the model assumes that certainty exists; but in fact, financial managers operate in a world of uncertainty. Nevertheless, some financial managers have considerable knowledge about their firms' expected cash balances for relatively short periods in the future. Second, withdrawals of cash may not be steady over time, as they are assumed to be. These shortcomings are addressed in the Miller–Orr model.

Miller–Orr Model   The **Miller–Orr model** establishes control limits for managing cash balances in conjunction with a portfolio of short-term securities.[7] In contrast to the *EOQ* model, the Miller–Orr model assumes uncertainty and random fluctuation in cash balances.

Figure 16–5 depicts the random behavior of daily cash balances, which are equally likely to increase or decrease. As long as the cash balance remains within the bounds of the upper and lower limits, no transactions occur. If cash balances reach the upper limit (H) the financial manager buys enough securities to reduce the cash balance to the return point (Z). If cash balances reach the lower limit, the financial manager sells enough securities to increase the cash balance to the return point. The model determines the values of Z and H that minimize the cost of transferring funds and the opportunity cost of holding idle cash. Management sets the lower limit (L).

[7]Merton H. Miller and Daniel Orr, "A Model of Demand for Money by Firms," *Quarterly Journal of Economics,* August 1966, pp. 413–435; "The Demand for Money by Firms: Extension of Analytic Results," *Journal of Finance,* December 1968, pp. 735–759.

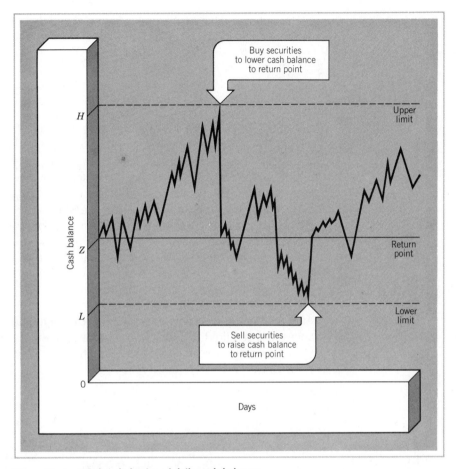

Figure 16–5   Random behavior of daily cash balances.

The optimal level of the return point (Z) may be determined by use of the following equation.[8]

$$Z = \sqrt[3]{\frac{3B\sigma^2}{4i*}} + L \qquad (16\text{–}7)$$

where

B = Fixed cost per order of converting marketable securities into cash or cash into marketable securities

$i*$ = *Daily* interest rate on short-term marketable securities

σ = Standard deviation (a measure of volatility) of daily cash balances

L = Lower limit

[8]The Miller–Orr model has been modified here to include a lower limit (L). When L is zero, the model gives the same results as the original version.

The optimal value of the upper limit (*H*) and the average cash balance are determined as follows.

$$H = 3Z - 2L \tag{16-8}$$

$$\text{Average cash balance} = \frac{4Z - L}{3} \tag{16-9}$$

An examination of these equations reveals that the return point (*Z*) varies directly with the fixed costs of making transactions (*B*) and the volatility of cash balances (s). The consequence of increasing transaction costs and volatility is an increase in the dollar difference between *Z* and the upper limit. However, the effect is diminished because of the cube root.

An example will illustrate the use of the Miller–Orr model. Assume that the standard deviation (s) of daily cash balances for Bravo Company is $500. **Standard deviation**, a statistical concept we have used before in connection with risk, may be used to measure the extent to which cash balances fluctuate. Further assume that the fixed cost per order is $50 and the annual interest rate is 10 percent. Because the equation requires a daily interest rate, we must divide the annual rate by 360 days, thereby obtaining a daily rate of 0.00028. After examining the company's cash needs, including the compensating balances it is required to hold, Bravo's management has set the lower limit at $2,000. Using these numbers and Equation 16–7, we can find the optimal value of *Z*.

$$Z = \sqrt[3]{\frac{3B\sigma^2}{4i}} + L$$

$$= \sqrt[3]{\frac{3 \times \$50 \times (\$500)^2}{4 \times 0.00028}} + \$2,000$$

$$= \$3,223 + \$2,000$$

$$= \$5,223$$

Once we have determined the value of *Z*, we can find the values of *H* and the average cash balance by using Equations 16–8 and 16–9.

$$H = 3Z - 2L$$

$$= (3 \times 5223) - 2(2,000)$$

$$= \$11,669$$

$$\text{Average cash balance} = \frac{4Z - L}{3}$$

$$= \frac{(4 \times 5,223) - 2,000}{3}$$

$$= \$6,297$$

The values for Z, H, and the average cash balance are shown along with the daily cash balances in Figure 16–6. As you can see, when the cash balance reaches the upper limit, the financial manager buys $6,446 to reduce the cash balance from $11,669 to $5,223. Conversely, when the cash balance reaches the lower limit, the financial manager sells $3,223 to increase the cash balance from $2,000 to $5,223. Although the daily cash balance follows a random pattern, the financial manager knows that, on the average, the cash balance will be $6,297.

If for some reason the cash balance fluctuated more, causing the standard deviation to increase from $500 to $1,000, the optimum value of Z would increase from $5,223 to $7,116. As noted, taking the cube root dampens the effect of increased volatility or costs. Nevertheless, the effect suggests that some economies of scale may be gained by concentration of cash balances.

Miller and Orr tested their model by comparing it against the actual transactions of the Union Tank Car Company. The results were impressive: Had

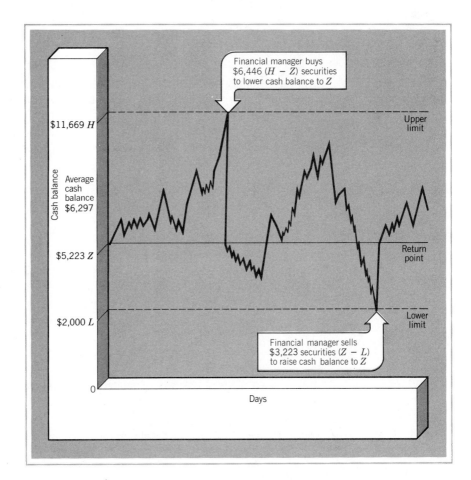

the model been used, the average daily cash balance would have been reduced by about 40 percent, and about one-third fewer transactions would have been required.[9]

Effect of Business Cycles   Inventory models focus on the size and timing of transfers between cash and marketable securities. A basic assumption underlying these models is that the pattern of cash flows will not change dramatically. However, changing business conditions can alter the pattern of cash flows and so must be taken into account. For example, suppose that following a long period of prosperity, economic indicators signal that a recession may be coming. This means that sales will decrease; so the firm can reduce its average cash balances by, say, 15 percent in the next quarter and by more in the following quarter. The inventory models can be recomputed to take the expected parameters into account.

Short-Term Marketable Securities

Inventory models are concerned with transferring cash into short-term marketable securities, and vice versa. Short-term marketable securities are considered "near-cash" because they can be converted into cash on short notice at low cost with little risk of loss. Equally important, they provide income for many business concerns. This section examines advantages, disadvantages, and types of short-term marketable securities.

Advantages   Advantages of investing in short-term marketable securities involve maturity, safety, marketability, and income.

Maturity.   By definition, short-term securities mature in 1 year or less. They include long-term bonds that will mature within the year as well as securities originally issued with a maturity of less than 1 year. Investors can buy outstanding securities that mature in 1 day, 10 days, 69 days, or almost any number of days they wish.

Safety.   Two types of risk are associated with dealing in securities: price risk and default risk. **Price risk** refers to adverse price movements, which in most

[9]Merton H. Miller and Daniel Orr, "Mathematical Models for Financial Management," in *Management of Working Capital,* ed. Keith V. Smith (St. Paul, Minn.: West Publishing Company, 1974), pp. 67–76.

cases means price declines. Short-term securities are less subject to large price changes than long-term securities; hence, they are safer. **Default risk**, as you may recall, is the risk that an issuing organization will be unable to pay its obligations.

Many of the securities traded by business concerns are issued by the U.S. Treasury or other government-related organizations. Obligations of the Treasury, remember, are considered free of default risk; and the risk associated with the obligations of other government agencies is considered small. The difference in degrees of risk is reflected in the securities' yields. If a Treasury issue yields 9 percent, for example, an issue of another government agency may yield 9.2 percent. These differences, although they seem small, become significant when billions of dollars are involved.

To a limited degree, the riskiness of many securities can be determined by the ratings issued by financial service organizations such as Moody's Investor Service. For example, the ratings on commercial paper, a type of short-term debt, range from highest quality to high quality and are identified by Moody's in the following manner.

Prime-1: Highest quality.
Prime-2: Higher quality.
Prime-3: High quality.

Marketability.   Most securities can be bought and sold through securities dealers in a matter of minutes. You may recall from Chapter 4 that the major securities dealers include banks, investment bankers, and stockbrokerage firms. The following list shows some of the largest dealers in Treasury securities.

Aubrey G. Lanston & Company
Bankers Trust Company
Bank of America
Blyth Eastman Paine Webber
Chase Manhattan Bank
Chemical Bank New York Trust Company
Continental Illinois National Bank
First Boston Corporation
First National Bank of Chicago
First National City Bank
Harris Trust and Savings Bank
John Nuveen & Company, Inc.
Merrill Lynch Pierce Fenner & Smith
Morgan Guaranty Trust Company
Salomon Brothers
United California Bank

Prices and yields on government and other securities are listed daily in the *Wall Street Journal* and other periodicals. In addition, the *Journal* carries articles about the economic outlook and interest rates that are pertinent to the management of a securities portfolio.

Income.   The income earned on short-term marketable securities depends on the interest they pay. As shown in Figure 16–7, wide swings have characterized interest rate levels in recent years. Interest on 3-month Treasury bills ranged from about 4 percent to more than 16 percent over the period depicted, for example. The daily income earned on $1 million invested in Treasury bills is $444 at 16 percent, compared with $110 at 4 percent. At the end of 1985, IBM held $4.73 billion in marketable securities. The average interest rate on 3-month Treasury bills was 7.07 percent. Therefore, IBM might have earned about $900,000 per day from its securities.

Chapter 15 (Figure 15–1) showed that securities as a percentage of total assets vary over the life cycle. Business concerns in the pioneering stage may

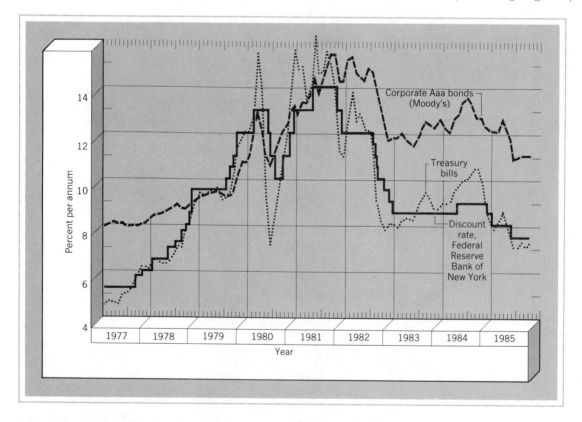

Figure 16–7   Interest rates and bond yields, 1977 through mid–1985.
Source: Council of Economic Advisors, *Economic Indicators* (Washington, D.C.: Government Printing Office, October 1985).

have about 1 percent of their assets invested in securities; for those in the stabilization phase, the figure may be about 3 percent. If a firm in the stabilization phase has $50 million in total assets, then, about $1.5 million will be invested in securities. A market rate of interest of 10 percent produces daily interest income of $278 per million; in this case, the firm will earn $150,120 ($1,500,000 [×] $278 [×] 360 days = $150,120) on its short-term investments over the course of a year.

Finally, we should consider the effect of taxes on the income earned from securities. The income from some securities issued by state and local government organizations is exempt from federal income tax and sometimes from state tax as well. This encourages investors to provide state and local governments with funds. Income earned on other investments is subject to federal income tax. Therefore, holding excess taxable investments reduces shareholders' wealth because of double taxation, the situation in which tax is paid on the income from the investments and on the dividends from the corporation.

Disadvantages The major disadvantages of dealing in short-term securities are (1) the amount of knowledge required to do so and (2) the large minimum denomination of some short-term securities—$100,000 or more. However, these disadvantages have been overcome by the development of money market funds, which will be described in the next subsection.

Types of Securities Several types of securities are widely used as short-term investments. Space does not permit a complete description, but a brief discussion of each follows. More will be said about several of these types of securities in later chapters.

Banker's Acceptances. **Banker's acceptances** are associated with foreign and domestic trade. A firm writes a draft to pay for specific merchandise it has ordered. When the firm's bank formally acknowledges the obligation to pay the draft in writing, the word *accepted* is stamped on its face. That means the bank unconditionally guarantees that it will pay the face amount of the obligation at its maturity. Acceptances may be bought and sold and are considered high-quality securities because they are backed by the credit of the bank.

Commercial Paper. **Commercial paper** refers to short-term promissory notes of leading industrial companies, finance companies, and bank holding companies.

Eurodollars. Short-term deposits denominated in dollars and placed in banks outside the United States are called **Eurodollars**. They generally carry interest rates higher than those available on bank deposits in the United States.

Negotiable Certificates of Deposit. Negotiable certificates of deposit (*CDs*) are marketable receipts for funds deposited in a bank for a specified period at a specified rate. Negotiable *CDs* have denominations of $100,000 or more.

Repurchase Agreements. **Repurchase agreements**, commonly called *RPs* or *repos*, are short-term loans made to government securities dealers. The lender, perhaps a large corporation, buys securities from a dealer at a low price with the agreement to sell them back at a higher price; the difference between the prices represents an interest charge. These short-term loans may have a stated maturity; or they may have no maturity date, in which case the loan may be terminated by either the borrower or the lender.

U.S. Treasury and Federal Agency Securities. U.S. government obligations include bills, notes, and bonds issued by the Treasury. Bills may have a maturity of up to a year but generally have maturities of 3 to 6 months; notes have maturities up to 7 years, and bonds are longer term. Other government-sponsored corporations and agencies also issue marketable securities. Leading sponsored corporations include the Federal National Mortgage Association (known as Fannie Mae), Federal Land Banks, Federal Intermediate Credit Banks, Banks for Cooperatives, and Federal Home Loan Banks. Other government-related issuers include the Federal Financing Bank and the Export–Import Bank of the United States (Ex–Im Bank). The Federal Financing Bank was established in 1973 to consolidate and reduce the cost of borrowing by a large number of federal agencies and other organizations whose obligations are guaranteed by the Treasury.

Tax-Exempt Securities. States, municipalities, and other political subdivisions (such as school districts) frequently issue short-term tax and bond anticipation notes. They issue these securities in anticipation of collecting taxes, receiving federal or state aid, or selling bonds to repay the borrowed funds. The interest income on the securities is exempt from federal income tax and in some cases from state income taxes; hence they are sometimes called **tax-exempts**.

Money Market Funds

Money market funds are investment companies (mutual funds) that pool the monies of investors to buy short-term obligations such as those just described. As mentioned, many short-term securities sell in denominations of $100,000 or more, which inhibits some investors. However, money market funds are available in much smaller increments; for example, the initial investment may be $2,000 and additional investments, $100 or more. Investors pay no commission when they buy shares in money market funds; the funds' managers take a small percentage of the total assets under management as compensation for their services.

Some money market funds allow investors to withdraw funds by writing checks against their current holdings. A company that invested in such a fund could eliminate the need for separate cash and securities holdings. Many banks offer accounts called *sweep accounts* to provide the same service.

The Interest Rate Futures Market

Remember that investing in marketable securities involves price risk and default risk. Price risk results from the fact that future interest rates cannot be predicted with precision. Several techniques have been developed to reduce the price risk of investing in marketable securities. Hedging is one such technique. One type of hedging was described in the preceding chapter; another type is described here. Hedging was originally used to reduce the risk of price fluctuations in grains and other commodities. Now grain-trading techniques are being used in the securities markets.

The process of hedging requires the existence of **standardized contracts** for a commodity and of a cash market and a futures market. An investor may obtain a contract for 5,000 bushels of corn or for Treasury securities with a face value at maturity of $100,000, for example. In the **cash market**, commodity dealers buy and sell commodities for immediate delivery. In the **futures market**, contracts for the future delivery of the commodity are traded. For simplicity, we will assume that a price change in the cash market is matched by an equal price change in the futures market and we will ignore transaction costs.

Hedging is taking equal (referring to the size of the contract) but opposite positions in the cash market and the futures market. For example, suppose a farmer owns 5,000 bushels of corn but does not want to sell it for 90 days. The current price of corn is $2.50 per bushel and the farmer wants to protect himself against a drop in that price. He can hedge by selling a 90 day contract for 5,000 bushels of corn in the futures market at, say, $2.60 per bushel. If the price declines $0.10 in the cash market over the next 90 days, the farmer will experience a "paper" loss when he sells his corn at the end of that time, because he could have sold it at a higher price earlier. However, we are assuming the price also drops $0.10 in the futures market; so the farmer can cover his position by buying corn at $2.50 per bushel, creating a $0.10 profit that exactly offsets his $0.10 loss in the cash market.

Hedging in the securities markets works similarly. Suppose a financial manager was advised on March 1 that his firm would receive $1 million from the sale of an asset on June 1. At the beginning of March, interest rates on marketable securities were high, but the manager believed they would decline over the next few months. He wanted to take advantage of the current high yield, even though he would not get the $1 million until June. Accordingly, he hedged by using U.S. Treasury bond futures contracts.

These contracts had a face value of $100,000 at maturity, an interest rate

Table 16–2
Hedge of Long-Term U.S. Treasury Bond Futures[a,b]

Cash Market	Futures Market
March 1	**March 1**
Manager wants to lock in yield of 7.82% on 20-year, 8.00% U.S. Treasury bonds at 101-24.	Manager buys 10 September long-term U.S. Treasury bond futures contracts at 100-00 (8.00% interest rate)
June 1	**June 1**
Manager buys $1 million of 20-year, 8.00% U.S. Treasury bonds at 103-00 (7.70% yield to maturity) *Opportunity loss*: $12,500 (40/32 percent of $1 million)[c]	Manager sells 10 September bond futures contracts at 101-08 (7.88% yield to maturity) Gain: $12,500 (40[c] × $31.25 × 10)

[a]The illustration does not include commissions and fees.
[b]For additional details, see *An Introduction to the Interest Rate Futures Market*, Chicago Board of Trade, 1983.
[c]103-00 − 101-24 = 40/32; 101-08 − 100-00 = 40/32.

of 8 percent, and 15 years or more to maturity. Prices for such contracts are quoted as a percentage of face value. For example, a price of 100-00 means 100 percent of the face value. The digits to the right of the hyphen are 32nds, each worth $31.25 per $100,000 contract. Thus, 98-12 translates into $98,375.

The basic elements of the hedge are presented in Table 16–2. On March 1, the current yield to maturity on Treasury bonds was 7.82 percent and they were selling at 101-24. Remember that the manager did not own any of these bonds. To hedge, he bought 10 September futures contracts at 100-00 to yield 8 percent.

As time passed, interest rates declined in both the cash and the futures market. Recall that when market rates of interest fall, the price of outstanding bonds and contracts goes up. By June 1, the yield in the cash market had declined to 7.70 percent and the price was 103-00. The manager bought the bonds at the higher price, incurring an opportunity loss of $12,500 because he had to pay a higher price than he would have paid in March. However, the price of the futures contracts increased by a like amount and he sold them at a $12,500 profit. Thus, his gain in the futures market offset his loss in the cash market—a perfect hedge.

Summary

Business concerns hold liquid assets such as cash and short-term marketable securities to meet needs associated with daily transactions, to serve as a precaution against unanticipated expenses, and to provide the means to speculate on future price movements. In addition, businesses may be required to hold certain liquid assets as compensating balances against bank loans.

Because cash is a nonearning asset, business concerns attempt to shorten their cash cycles by using techniques that speed up the collection process, by using disbursement techniques that slow down cash payments, and by increasing inventory turnover. Collection techniques reduce float through the use of lockboxes, concentration banking, and other methods of transmitting payment, such as wire transfer and electronic funds transfer. Methods of slowing disbursement include the use of drafts, controlled disbursing, timing of payments, and zero-balance accounts.

Inventory models provide another approach to cash management. Such models can be used only after a firm has determined its liquidity needs. The economic order quantity model and Miller–Orr model are concerned with minimizing the cost of transfers between cash and securities portfolios. The models also deal with the timing of transfers between cash and marketable securities. Equations related to inventory models and to other topics in this chapter are reviewed in Table 16–3.

Short-term marketable securities, considered near-cash items, offer four distinct advantages: Their maturity is short-term; they are relatively safe; they are marketable; and they provide income. Many types of short-term securities and money market funds may be used as liquid assets. Some commonly used short-

Table 16–3
Summary of Equations

	Equation	Equation Number
Cash turnover	Cash turnover $= \dfrac{360 \text{ days}}{\text{Cash cycle}}$	(16–1)
Average cash balance	Average cash balance $= \dfrac{\text{Total annual outlays}}{\text{Cash turnover}}$	(16–2)
Cost of float	Cost of float $=$ Amount $\times$ Opportunity cost $\times \dfrac{\text{Days late}}{360 \text{ days}}$	(16–3)
Total cost of holding cash	Total cost of holding cash $= B\left(\dfrac{T}{Q}\right) + i\left(\dfrac{Q}{2}\right)$	(16–4)
Economic order quantity	$Q^* = \sqrt{\dfrac{2BT}{i}}$	(16–5)
Number of orders per period	Number of orders per period $= \dfrac{T}{Q^*}$	(16–6)
Z (Miller–Orr model)	$Z = \sqrt[3]{\dfrac{3B\sigma^2}{4_i{}^*}} + L$	(16–7)
H (Miller–Orr model)	$H = 3Z - 2L$	(16–8)
Average cash balance (Miller–Orr model)	Average cash balance $= \dfrac{4Z - L}{3}$	(16–9)

term securities are banker's acceptances, commercial paper, certificates of deposit, and U.S. Treasury and federal agency securities.

The level of interest on short-term and other investments has varied dramatically in recent years. Accordingly, investors have developed techniques for reducing the risk of price fluctuations on securities. One way to reduce risk is to hedge securities investments.

Important Terms

Automated clearing house (*ACH*)
Automated remittance process
Average cash balance
Banker's acceptance
Bill of exchange
Cash
Cash cycle
Cash market
Cash turnover
Clearing
Commercial paper
Compensating balance
Concentration banking
Controlled disbursing
Courier
Default risk
Depository transfer check
Draft
Economic order quantity (*EOQ*)
Electronic funds transfer system (*EFTS*)
Eurodollar

Float
Futures market
Hedging
Lockbox
Miller–Orr model
Money market fund
Negotiable certificate of deposit (*CD*)
Operating cycle
Payable-through draft
Preauthorized check
Precautionary motive
Price risk
Repurchase agreement
Short-term marketable security
Speculative motive
Standard deviation
Standardized contract
Tax-exempt
Transaction motive
Wire transfer
Zero-balance account

Questions

1. In general, what risk–return trade-off is involved in the management of a firm's most liquid assets?
2. Explain three motives for holding cash as developed by the economist John Maynard Keynes in his discussion of liquidity preference. What additional motive exists for a corporation's holding cash?
3. What is the major goal of the corporate cash manager? What general cash management approaches are available to the cash manager to achieve these goals?

4. Define the term *cash cycle* and distinguish between it and the *operating cycle*. How is the cash cycle used by the financial manager to analyze the cash needs of the firm?

5. How can the cash manager attempt to reduce the length of cash cycles?

6. Explain why cash managers must use careful judgment in speeding up the collection of receivables and slowing down disbursements.

7. Define the term *float*. Differentiate between mail float, processing float, and clearing float. Why does the cash manager try to reduce float when collecting accounts receivable?

8. What is a lockbox? Distinguish between wholesale and retail lockboxes. How are lockboxes used to decrease float?

9. Describe concentration banking and its use in reducing float. How are depository transfer checks used in concentration banking?

10. What is Fed Wire?

11. In what ways can electronic funds transfer systems be used in corporate cash management?

12. Many firms pay bills by using payable-through drafts rather than checks. What benefit do these firms receive?

13. Why would a firm in Boca Raton, Florida, write checks against an account in a bank in Missoula, Montana?

14. Define a zero-balance system of accounts. Explain the effect of these accounts on cash management.

15. Identify the objective of the economic order quantity (*EOQ*) model for cash management. What assumptions underlie the model?

16. According to the *EOQ* cash management model, there are economies of scale involved in managing cash. Explain.

17. How does the Miller–Orr model differ from the *EOQ* cash management model?

18. Discuss three advantages of short-term marketable securities.

19. Identify two disadvantages of investing in short-term securities. How can these disadvantages be overcome?

20. Define the following terms: *commercial paper, banker's acceptances, Eurodollars, certificates of deposit, repurchase agreements, Treasury securities,* and *federal agency securities.*

21. Describe interest rate futures contracts in general. How can they be used to hedge investments in short-term securities?

22. How might a firm's cash management policies vary with the life cycle? With the business cycle?

Problems

Assume a 360-day year in all problems.

1. Northern Fan Company is trying to improve its cash management. Over the past year, accounts receivable have averaged 80 days' sales, and inventories have averaged 60 days. Northern has paid its creditors, on the average, 25 days after receiving the bill. The firm expects to spend $18 million during the next year on materials and supplies.

(a) Compute the cash cycle.

(b) Compute the cash turnover.

(c) Compute the average cash balance needed for operations.

(d) What is the dollar cost of tying up funds if Northern's opportunity rate is 20 percent?

2. BFD Corporation has an inventory turnover ratio of 15, an accounts receivable turnover ratio of 12, and an accounts payable turnover ratio of 20. Yearly expenditures are $400 million and are spread evenly throughout the year.

(a) Compute the cash cycle.

(b) Compute the cash turnover.

(c) Compute the cost of the cash cycle if the opportunity cost is 12 percent.

3. Rose Tea Company presently estimates average accounts receivable at 55 days, inventory at 40 days, and accounts payable at 30 days. After careful analysis, management has decided to reduce accounts receivable by 10 days and inventory by 5 days, while lengthening its payment period by 10 days.

(a) Calculate the change in the cash cycle that will occur if the new policies are implemented.

(b) If the opportunity cost for the firm is 22 percent and if yearly expenditures are $30 million, what annual savings will result from the changes.

4. Cagley Imports currently has an average accounts receivable balance of 90 days, an average inventory of 75 days, and average accounts payable of 40 days. Cagley's purchases total $150 million per year. Which of the following cash management plans is most effective if the opportunity cost is 18 percent?

Plan	Increase or Decrease in Average Age of			Annual Administrative Cost of Plan
	Receivables	Inventory	Payables	
1	− 5 days	− 5 days	+ 5 days	$ 500,000
2	−10 days	− 8 days	+10 days	1,200,000
3	−20 days	−15 days	+15 days	3,000,000

5. Bleck Corporation writes checks totaling an average of $20,000 per day on a local bank. They clear in an average of 5 days. If Bleck's opportunity costs are 10 percent, how much is earned from using the float over a period of 1 year?

6. Skylark Company of Virginia writes an average of $2 million in checks per day on its local bank. The average time to clear is 4 days. Management is considering moving the firm's checking accounts to Nevada, estimating that the clearing time will increase to 8 days. If the opportunity cost of holding cash is 15 percent, how much will Skylark's annual savings be if it moves its accounts to Nevada.

7. Public Service Company is interested in speeding up collection of receivables. Currently all bills are mailed from company headquarters in Rapid City, South Dakota, to customers throughout the state. Management estimates that mail float averages 5 days, processing float averages 2 days, and clearing float averages 2 days. The firm's local bank has suggested a lockbox system to reduce mail float to 2 days and processing float to zero, although clearing float would not change.

Currently, Public Service receives $800,000 per day in payments and has an opportunity cost of 13 percent. If the bank charges an annual fee of $150,000 for managing the lockbox system, should the company go to the new system? If so, what will the dollar amount of annual savings be?

8. Gold Oil Company operates nationwide. On the average, it receives $12 million

per day in receivables from customers, all of which are deposited in a bank near the home office. The bank has suggested a national lockbox system to reduce processing float by 1 day, mail float by 2 days, and clearing float by an average of 3 days. To compensate participating banks, Gold Oil would have to deposit non-interest-earning balances at each bank. Total compensating balances would be $10 million. Should the lockbox system be set up?

9. The city of Yuma, Arizona, currently expects federal payments totaling $1 million. The check can be mailed or it can be picked up in person by a courier. Mail float is 4 days and the city's opportunity cost is 7 percent. Should a courier be sent to Washington to get the check? The cost of the service is $800 and a total of one day's travel time is involved.

10. Alice's Restaurant has a weekly payroll of $100,000 paid on Friday evenings at closing. The bookkeeper has observed the following pattern by which the checks are cashed by employees.

Day Cashed	Percentage of Total Payroll
Saturday	30
Monday	40
Tuesday	20
Wednesday	10

If Alice currently deposits enough funds each Friday to allow all checks to clear, how much can she save annually by altering deposits according to the pattern by which checks are cleared? The opportunity cost is 10 percent.

11. Tisdale Tile Company has a payroll of $80,000 per week. Checks are cashed, on the average, 3 days after they are issued. The firm is considering direct deposit. If the firm can earn 15 percent on its funds, how much in annual before-tax earnings will Tisdale lose with the direct deposit system? Tisdale now deposits cash in its accounts to cover payroll checks as they are cashed.

12. Cammack Company keeps a $200,000 average checking account balance. Its bank has offered a zero-balance system at an annual cost of $15,000. If the opportunity cost of holding cash is 12 percent, should Cammack go to the zero-balance system?

13. Halonen Hospital Supply Company is attempting to determine the most economical cash balance to service its $2.6 million annual cash needs. The firm can earn 15 percent on marketable securities, and every transfer to cash from securities costs $400.
(a) Find the economic order quantity for a transfer from marketable securities to cash.
(b) What average cash balance will result?
(c) How many transfers per year will be necessary?
(d) What will the total annual cost of such a cash management system be?

14. Suppose market interest rates fall and Halonen Hospital Supply (Problem 13) reestimates its opportunity cost at 10 percent. Rework Problem 13 under the changed condition. Explain why your answers change as they do.

15. Rupp Shoe Company presently keeps an average cash balance of $50,000. Each transfer between cash and securities costs $250. Securities now earn 12 percent per year and the firm has estimated its total annual need for cash at $1.8 million. Is the current average cash balance optimal? If not, what average cash balance should be held?

16. Warren Marina's owner is interested in improving management of the firm's cash

and is focusing on the Miller–Orr model. The cost of converting marketable securities to cash is $20 and the standard deviation of daily cash balances is $1,500. The lowest acceptable balance is $10,000. The firm can earn 14 percent on short-term investments. Calculate the appropriate upper limit for the firm's checking account balance. What is the return point after transactions between cash and securities? What average balance will be held?

17. (a) Suppose the opportunity cost for Warren Marina in Problem 16 falls to 8 percent. Recalculate the upper and average balances and the return point. Explain why your answers are different from those in Problem 16.

(b) Suppose that instead of a decrease in opportunity costs, Warren Marina's management discovers an error in the standard deviation of daily cash balances. If the correct figure is $2,000, what are the upper and average checking account balances. What is the new return point? Explain why your answers differ from the ones in Problem 16.

18. A firm can purchase and sell $100,000 of marketable securities, yielding 14 percent, for a total transaction cost of $1,200. Should they be purchased if the total holding period is 10 days; 30 days; 60 days; 90 days; 120 days?

19. Describe the transactions necessary to lock in (make sure of receiving) a return currently available on a cash inflow that will not be received for 90 days. Rates are expected to fall in the interim.

20. A firm is planning to issue $25 million in bonds in 6 months. Rates are expected to rise during the period. How can the current interest rate be locked in?

17 Credit and Accounts Receivable

read

A headline in the *Wall Street Journal* read "Dunners' Delight: More Firms Pay Bills Slowly, Spurring Boom in Collectors' Business."[1] The article explained how Alcan Aluminum Corporation received a $44,000 order from a regular customer, shipped the goods, and expected to be paid in the usual manner. Payment, however, was not forthcoming. After trying unsuccessfully to collect the funds, Alcan turned the account over to a collection agency. The agency had better results; the customer agreed to make a small downpayment and pay the remainder plus interest in 12 monthly installments. The customer's excuse was that, because sales had declined and it had already borrowed as much as it could, it didn't have the money to pay Alcan's bill.

This incident supports the old maxim that a sale is not complete until the money is collected. Credit sales are reflected in accounts receivable until they are collected. Accounts receivable, along with some other aspects of credit, are the subject of this chapter.

---

[1] "Dunners' Delight: More Firms Pay Bills Slowly, Spurring Boom in Collectors' Business," *Wall Street Journal,* July 31, 1979, p. 1.

After reading this chapter, you should know the following.

1. How to define public, private, trade, and consumer credit.
2. Why credit is important.
3. What trade-offs firms must make with regard to credit.
4. What credit policies involve.
5. What the five Cs of credit include.
6. How credit terms affect profits.
7. Why credit extension and collections must be controlled.
8. Why business firms extend credit to consumers.
9. Why an 18 percent annual percentage rate may mean different things to different companies.

Credit

The use of credit is widespread in the U.S. economy and takes many different forms. **Public credit** includes borrowing by federal, state, and local governments. **Private credit** includes borrowing by business concerns and individuals. This chapter focuses on two types of private credit—trade credit and consumer credit—from the issuer's point of view.

Trade credit is credit extended by a nonfinancial business concern to another business concern for the purchase of goods and services. It is recorded as an **account receivable** on the balance sheet of the seller and an **account payable** on the balance sheet of the buyer. Because we are interested in the issuer's point of view, most of the chapter concerns the management of accounts receivable. Chapter 19 looks at trade credit from the buyer's perspective.

Consumer credit is credit extended to an individual to buy goods and services such as automobiles, insurance, vacations, and so on. It should not be confused with **real estate credit**, which is used for the acquisition and improvement of real estate.

Importance of Accounts Receivable The crucial role of accounts receivable in the working capital cycle is suggested in Figure 17–1. The figure shows that sales result in either immediate cash to the firm or accounts receivable. When the accounts receivable are collected, they too will provide cash. However, the story about Alcan Aluminum makes it clear that collecting accounts receivable should not be taken for granted. When firms are unable to collect the accounts receivable, shortfalls of funds to invest in inventory may result. Without sufficient inventory, the firm cannot make sales and it is in trouble.

How much trade credit business concerns give varies widely from industry

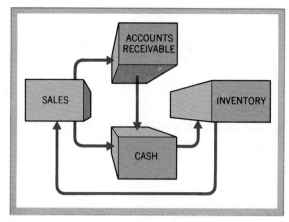

Figure 17–1 Working capital cycle.

to industry. Table 17–1 shows accounts receivable as a percentage of total assets for selected industries. The average percentage for manufacturing industries is 15.7 percent. Percentages for specific types of manufacturers range from 8.4 percent for tobacco manufacturers to 23.4 percent for manufacturers of fabricated metals.

Equally important, accounts receivable as a percentage of total assets vary over the life cycle. Chapter 15 (Figure 15–1) showed that accounts receivable might range from 28 percent of assets in the pioneering phase to 14 percent in the declining phase. Accordingly, the 15.7 percent average for manufacturing firms and the other numbers shown in Table 17–1 must be interpreted with caution. Recognizing their limitations, it is still interesting to note that the percentages range from a low of 7.6 percent for mining companies to a high of 25.1 percent for the wholesale trade. The high percentage of accounts receivable for wholesalers suggests that they finance a large portion of their customers' assets.

Table 17–1

Accounts Receivable, Percentage of Total Assets in Selected Industries

Industries	Percentage
Manufacturing	15.7%
Fabricated metals	23.4
Tobacco manufacturing	8.4
Mining	7.6
Retail trade	15.1
Wholesale trade	25.1

Source Federal Trade Commission, *Quarterly Financial Report for Manufacturing, Mining, and Trade Corporations,* 2nd quarter, 1985.

Table 17–2
Credit Decisions and Trade-offs

Decisions	Trade-offs
1. Level and risk of accounts receivable	Credit sales versus profits
2. Form of assets	
Grant credit	Inventory versus accounts receivable
Collect credit	Cash versus accounts receivable

Credit Policies

Credit policies are management guidelines concerning the extension of trade credit and the management of accounts receivable. Credit policies influence the level of sales, profits, and the form of assets. The long-run objective of credit policies is to increase shareholders' wealth. In the short run, however, credit policies may focus on maximizing sales, increasing collections, or something else.

Credit policies can be thought of as involving two decisions, one dealing with the level of receivables and the other with the composition of assets. First, what level of accounts receivable and what risks are acceptable? As outlined in Table 17–2, this decision involves a trade-off between increased credit sales and profits. Extending more credit to boost sales may adversely affect profits if the sales result in bad debt losses. On the other hand, overly restrictive credit policies may result in lost sales and forgone profits.

The second decision concerns the form of assets. As noted in Chapter 15, working capital consists of current assets that may be readily transformed into cash, inventories, or accounts receivable. Therefore, granting credit can be thought of as a trade-off between holding inventory and holding accounts receivable. Similarly, collecting on credit sales can be thought of as a trade-off between holding cash and holding accounts receivable. Managers who set the goals of credit policies should determine the mix of these assets that will maximize sales and profits, minimize expenses, keep bad debt losses at a reasonable level, and maximize shareholders' wealth. If these goals are incompatible, maximizing shareholders' wealth should come first.

As shown in Table 17–3, the dollar volume of accounts receivable outstanding depends on the dollar volume of credit sales and the rate at which they

Table 17–3
Credit Policy Variables

Accounts receivable	{	Credit sales	{	Standards Terms Collection policy Economy Control	{	Credit period discounts
		Collection rate				

are collected. These factors, in turn, depend on (1) the standards set for extending credit, (2) the terms of trade, (3) collection policies, (4) the level of economic activity, and (5) the degree of control used to monitor credit. These variables are explained next.

Credit Standards **Credit standards**, the criteria used to grant credit, determine the maximum risk a firm is willing to take in extending credit. By lowering credit standards, the firm can increase credit sales and accounts receivable. However, collection costs and bad debt losses may increase by a greater amount. Therefore, as mentioned, management must use sound judgment in developing credit standards.

Credit standards include the so-called **five Cs** of credit.

1. Character (personal characteristics and attitudes about paying debts)
2. Capacity (ability to pay)
3. Capital (financial condition)
4. Collateral (pledged assets)
5. Conditions (economic conditions)

Another factor that affects credit standards involves industrial capacity.

Character.   The word *character* may be defined as a combination of qualities that distinguishes one person or group from another. Used as a credit standard, *character*, like *reputation*, refers to the borrower's honesty, responsibility, integrity, and consistency. These characteristics are evidenced in a variety of ways. For example, police and legal actions and complaints to the Better Business Bureau are clues to a person's or a company's honesty. Similarly, records of past paying behavior give insights about some other characteristics. When all the information is combined, it should indicate the borrower's willingness to pay.

Capacity.   Capacity relates to borrowers' ability to pay their financial obligations. The ability to pay is determined by current and expected income, existing debts, and ongoing operating expenses. This type of information is revealed in current and pro forma financial statements. Other important clues about capacity come from an understanding of the borrower's business. For example, suppose a domestic shoe factory wants to buy specialized machinery on credit. The manufacturer of the specialized equipment knows that low-priced imported shoes are sweeping the market and that the shoe manufacturer is going to have to pay higher labor costs following current contract negotiations. Although the shoe factory has a strong financial statement for the current period, higher labor costs and intense competition threaten the firm's viability.

Accordingly, the machinery manufacturer may decide against extending credit.

Capital.   Equity capital represents the dollar amount of assets, less liabilities, that can be liquidated for the payment of debt if all other means of collection fail. It is a safety cushion for creditors. (However, there may be a considerable difference between the book values of assets and their liquidation values.) Capital also relates to the financial condition of the borrower.

Collateral.   Collateral is assets pledged for security in a credit transaction. For example, a business concern that buys an office building typically pledges the building as collateral against the loan. Lenders prefer collateral that is tangible, durable, and easily identifiable, such as an office building. Accordingly, collateral such as fresh flowers or fresh food products is less desirable.

Conditions.   Conditions include economic and other factors beyond the firm's control that may affect its ability to pay debts. Increased foreign competition such as that faced by the shoe factory belongs in this category. Similarly, changes in tax laws, regulations, markets, and weather may be relevant to some firms.

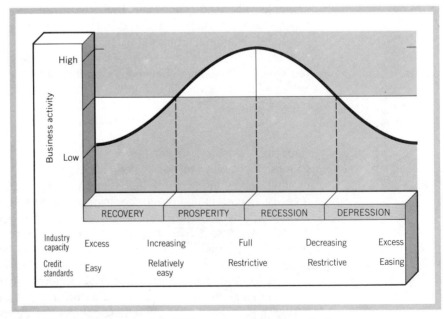

Figure 17–2   Business cycles, industrial capacity, and credit standards.

Industrial Capacity. The lending firm's industrial capacity is another criterion used in granting credit and establishing credit standards. If a business concern is in the recovery phase of the business cycle and has excess capacity, it may ease credit standards in an effort to increase sales and plant utilization. In contrast, if the business concern foresees a recession, it may apply rigid credit standards, denying credit to weak firms that may not withstand severe economic conditions. The phases of the business cycle related to industrial capacity and credit standards are depicted in Figure 17–2.

Credit Information. Information about customers' character, capacity, capital, and collateral comes from a variety of sources. First, many business concerns that extend trade credit require their customers to provide them with periodic financial statements. The lenders can monitor the financial statements and the payments made by the customers to determine how much credit will be extended in the future.

Business concerns also make extensive use of **mercantile credit agencies**, which collect and disseminate credit information about potential customers for a fee. Dun & Bradstreet, Inc., is the largest and oldest general mercantile agency (*general* because of the broad scope of its coverage). There are also specialized mercantile agencies, such as the Lyon Furniture Mercantile Agency, which specializes in reporting on credit risks in the furniture and home furnishings business, and Alfred M. Best Company, which deals with insurance companies. In addition, local credit bureaus throughout the nation use an interchange system to share information about local and distant customers.

Table 17–4 shows a credit report from Dun & Bradstreet for a hypothetical company, Rettinger Paint Corporation. Credit reports provide information about a company's financial condition, banking relationships, history, and operations. For example, the "Payments Reported" section reveals that Rettinger Paint's high credit was $30,000, that it still owes $17,000, and that it takes trade discounts. (Trade discounts, offered by sellers to customers who pay their bills by a certain date, are discussed later in the chapter.) Such information is used by credit analysts in their evaluation of the firm.

Dun & Bradstreet publishes a reference book that provides an index to more than 2.5 million business concerns in the United States and Canada. It lists the names of companies, their line of business, estimates of their financial strength (i.e., net worth), credit appraisals, and other information. The estimation of financial strength and the credit appraisal are indicated by the letters and numbers shown in the key to ratings in Table 17–4. Rettinger Paint Corporation has a CC2 rating, indicating that it has an estimated financial strength of $75,000 to $124,999 and a good credit rating.

Sequence of Analysis. Lenders use credit reports to gain information that will permit them to decide whether to grant credit. The decisions whether to grant

Table 17–4

A Credit Report

CONSOLIDATED REPORT		{FULL REVISION}

```
DUNS:  06-647-3261              DATE PRINTED                SUMMARY
RETTINGER PAINT CORP.           AUG 13, 197-         RATING      CC2

727 WHITMAN WAY                 WHOL PAINTS &        STARTED     1950
BENSON, MI  48232               VARNISHES            PAYMENTS    DISC-PPT
     TEL 313 961-0720                                SALES     $ 424,612
                                SIC NO.              WORTH     $ 101,867
CARL RETTINGER, PRES.           51 98                EMPLOYS     5
                                                     HISTORY     CLEAR
                                                     CONDITION   GOOD
                                                     TREND       STEADY


SPECIAL EVENTS   Business burglarized July 3 but $18,000 loss is fully insured.

PAYMENTS  {Amounts may be rounded to nearest figure in prescribed ranges}
REPORTED  PAYING      HIGH        NOW       PAST      SELLING       LAST SALE
          RECORD      CREDIT      OWES      DUE       TERMS         WITHIN
07/7-     Disc        30000       17000     -0-       2 10 30       1-2 mos.
          Disc        27000       14000     -0-       1 10 30       2-3 mos.
          Disc-Ppt    12000       4400      200       2 10 30       1 mo.
          Ppt         9000        8000      -0-       30            1 mo.
06/7-     Disc        16000       7500      -0-       2 10 30       2-3 mos.
05/7-     Disc        9000        3800      -0-       2 10 30       1 mo.
          Ppt         1500        -0-       -0-       30            1-2 mos.


FINANCE
06/22/7-       Fiscal statement dated May 31, 197-:
          Cash            $  20,623     Accts Payable        $  47,246
          Accts Rec          55,777     Owing Bank              34,000
          Merchandise        92,103     Notes Pay {Trucks}       7,020
                          ---------                           ---------
          Current           168,503     Current                 88,266
          Fixts. & Equip.    13,630     Common Stock            35,000
          Trucks              8,000     Earned Surplus          66,867
                          ---------                           ---------
          Total Assets      190,133     Total                  190,133
          SALES {Yr}: $424,612.  Net profit $17,105.  Fire ins. mdse $95,000;
       equipt $20,000.  Mo. rent: $3500.  Prepared by Steige Co., CPAs, Detroit, MI.
                            --0--
               06/22/7- Lawson defined monthly payments: $3000 to bank, $400 on notes.
       Admitted collections slow but losses insignificant.  Said inventory will drop
       to $60,000 by December.  Expects 5% sales increase this year.
PUBLIC FILINGS
03/25/7-       March 17, 197- financing statement A741170 named subject as debtor and
       NCR Corp., Dayton, O. as secured party.  Collateral: equipment.
05/28/7-       May 21, 197- suit for $200 entered by Henry Assoc., Atlanta, Ga. Docket
       A27519.  Involves merchandise which Lawson says was defective.
BANKING
06/25/7-       Account, long maintained, carries average balances low to moderate five
       figures.  Unsecured loans to moderate five extended and now open.
HISTORY
06/22/7-  CARL RETTINGER, PRES.            JOHN J. LAWSON, V PRES.
          DIRECTORS:  The Officers
               Incorporated Michigan February 2, 1950.  Authorized capital 3500 shares,
       no par common.  Paid in capital $35,000, officers sharing equally.
               RETTINGER, born 1920, married.  Employed by E-Z Paints, Detroit 12 yrs,
       five as manager until starting subject early 1950.
               LAWSON, born 1925, married.  Obtained accounting degree 1946 and then
       employed by Union Carbide, Chicago until joining Rettinger at inception.
OPERATION
06/22/7-       Wholesales paints and varnishes {85%}, wallpaper and supplies.  500
       local accounts include retailers {75%} and contractors.  Terms: 2 10 30.  Peak
       season spring thru summer.  EMPLOYEES: Officers active with three others.
       LOCATION: Rents 7500 sq ft. one-story block structure, good repair.
```

Table 17–4 (*Continued*)

Dun & Bradstreet
Key to Ratings

ESTIMATED FINANCIAL STRENGTH			COMPOSITE CREDIT APPRAISAL			
			HIGH	GOOD	FAIR	LIMITED
5A	$50,000,000	and over	1	2	3	4
4A	$10,000,000 to	$49,999,999	1	2	3	4
3A	1,000,000 to	9,999,999	1	2	3	4
2A	750,000 to	999,999	1	2	3	4
1A	500,000 to	749,999	1	2	3	4
BA	300,000 to	499,999	1	2	3	4
BB	200,000 to	299,999	1	2	3	4
CB	125,000 to	199,999	1	2	3	4
CC	75,000 to	124,999	1	2	3	4
DC	50,000 to	74,999	1	2	3	4
DD	35,000 to	49,999	1	2	3	4
EE	20,000 to	34,999	1	2	3	4
FF	10,000 to	19,999	1	2	3	4
GG	5,000 to	9,999	1	2	3	4
HH	Up to	4,999	1	2	3	4

credit and how much credit to grant can be described in terms of the decision tree shown in Figure 17–3. Here, if all five Cs of credit are strong, suggesting low risk, the lender will extend its maximum credit. If the character, capacity, and collateral are strong, but the capital and conditions are not, substantially less credit will be extended, and so on.

The sequence of analysis presented in the figure illustrates only one way in which credit information may be organized. Some firms use different techniques and place their emphasis on other factors. Recently, for example, a visiting professor applied for a credit card from a major international oil company. The application form contained a number of routine questions dealing with length of residence, employment, and so on. The oil company used a computerized model to evaluate the forms. The model was based on a study of the company's accounts that associated certain characteristics with cardholders who were bad credit risks. This information was assimilated and built into a "credit scoring" model that evaluated the application forms. The professor's application was rejected because he had just moved, he lived in a rented apartment, and—since he was only temporarily working at the university—his length of employment was less than 1 month. These factors were more important to the oil company than the ones previously described. (The professor wrote to the oil company and explained what he thought of the credit scoring system. Two weeks later, a letter of apology and a credit card were in the mail.)

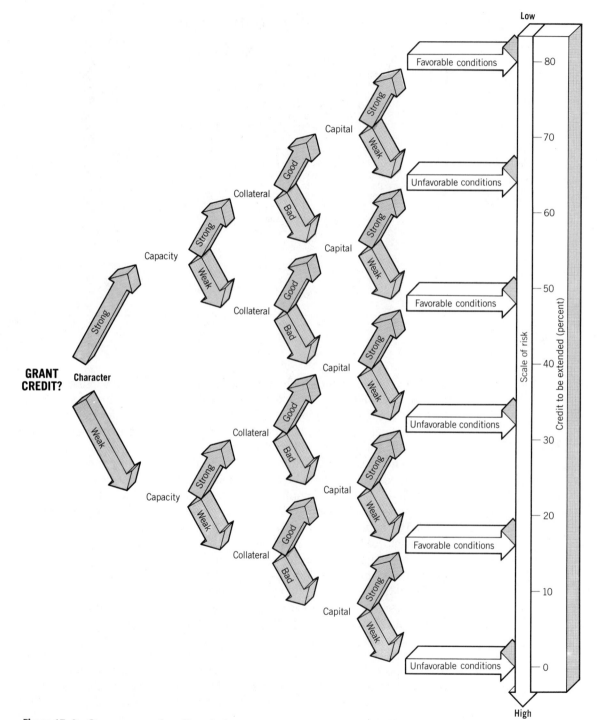

Figure 17–3 One sequence of credit analysis.

Credit Terms **Credit terms** set the period of time for which credit is granted and the amount of trade discounts. Some typical credit terms include the following.

EOM, or end of month. Goods invoiced before the 25th of the month are payable or subject to discount up to the 10th of the following month.

2/10/n30. A discount of 2 percent from the purchase price is allowed if the invoice is paid within 10 days of the invoice date, or the full (net) amount is due in 30 days.

2/10/60X. A discount of 2 percent from the purchase price is given if the invoice is paid within 10 days of the invoice date, but an additional 60 days' credit is extended. In other words, a discount of 2 percent is allowed if the invoice is paid by the 70th day.

Net 30. Payment is due within 30 days of the invoice date.

10th and 25th of each month. Purchases made between the 1st and 15th of the month are due on the 25th and purchases made after the 15th are due on the 10th of the following month.

Credit terms vary widely from industry to industry and product to product. The terms of some companies are "cash," whereas others may extend credit for 6 months or longer. For example, credit terms for menswear include net 30 for suits, 3/10,*EOM* for underwear, and 2/10/n30 for shirts.

Credit Terms and Elasticity. As mentioned earlier, companies can ease their credit terms to increase their sales. Increasing a discount from, say, 2 percent to 3 percent has the same effect as cutting the product's price for those who buy on credit. For example, suppose a customer wants to buy a drill press for $100,000. If the customer gets a 2 percent discount, the price is $98,000. If the discount is 3 percent, the price is $97,000.

The extent to which sales will increase as a result of the price cut depends on the elasticity of demand for the product. **Price elasticity** is the responsiveness of the demand for a product to a change in price. If the price of suits is reduced 15 percent and the demand increases 20 percent, the demand for suits is elastic. If the price of toothpicks is reduced 15 percent and demand increases 5 percent, the demand for that product is inelastic. In general, a firm should increase a discount, which has the same effect as reducing the price, only if it increases sales enough to increase revenues. However, firms may also use this strategy for other reasons, such as matching competition and gaining market share.

Credit Terms and Profit. Changing credit terms affects profits. To illustrate, we'll compare the impact of three terms—cash, net 30, and 2/10/n30—on profits. Gross profit is defined for this example as gross revenues less the cost of goods sold and the cost of accounts receivable.

$$\text{Gross profit} = \text{Gross revenue} - \begin{array}{c}\text{Cost of goods}\\\text{sold}\end{array} - \begin{array}{c}\text{Cost of}\\\text{accounts receivable}\end{array}$$

$$P = Sn \qquad\qquad - Cn \qquad\qquad - ARc \qquad\qquad (17\text{--}1)$$

where

P = Gross profit
S = Selling price per unit
n = Number of units sold
C = Cost of goods sold per unit
ARc = Cost of accounts receivable

Cash.   To examine the impact of cash transactions on profit, assume that the selling price per unit (S) is \$50, the cost per unit (C) is \$25, and the number of units sold (n) is 1,000. Since we are analyzing cash transactions, there are no accounts receivable. Using these assumptions and Equation 17–1, we can find the profit from the cash transactions.

$$P = Sn \qquad\quad - Cn \qquad\quad - ARc$$
$$= \$50(1,000) - \$25(1,000) - \$0$$
$$= \$25,000$$

Net 30.   For terms other than cash, the cost of financing accounts receivable for the period during which they are outstanding must be taken into account. The costs of accounts receivable include the cost of the funds or capital tied up in receivables (k) and the collection cost per unit (CC).

$$ARc = Cnk + CCn \qquad\qquad (17\text{--}2)$$

where

ARc = Cost of accounts receivable
Cn = Cost of goods sold
k = Cost of capital for the period used (days/360)
CC = Collection cost per unit
n = Number of units

If the cost of capital is 15 percent, the collection cost per unit is $1, and the credit period is 30 days, the cost of accounts receivable is as follows.[2]

$$ARc = Cnk \qquad\qquad\qquad\qquad\qquad + CCn$$

$$= \$25(1,000)(0.15 \times 30\ days/360\ days) + \$1(1,000)$$

$$= (\$25,000)(0.0125) \qquad\qquad\qquad + \$1,000$$

$$= \$1,313$$

Using $1,313 as the cost of accounts receivable in Equation 17–1 produces the following gross profit figure.

$$P = Sn \qquad\quad - Cn \qquad - ARc$$

$$= \$50,000 - \$25,000 - \$1,313$$

$$= \$23,687$$

2/10/n30. When a trade discount is given, the selling cost per unit must be adjusted. Adjusted revenue ($S'n$) is determined as follows.

$$S'n = (1 - d)Sn \qquad\qquad\qquad (17\text{–}3)$$

where

S' = Adjusted selling price per unit
S = Selling price per unit
d = Percentage rate of discount
n = Number of units sold

If the discount is 2 percent, $S'n$ is $49,000.

$$S'n = (1 - d)Sn$$

$$= (1 - 0.02)\$50 \times 1,000$$

$$= \$49,000$$

The cost of accounts receivable when the credit period is 10 days is $1,104.

$$ARc = Cnk \qquad\qquad\qquad\qquad\qquad + CCn$$

$$= \$25(1,000)(0.15 \times 10\ days/360\ days) + \$1(1,000)$$

$$= \$1,104$$

---

[2]Because none of the $50,000 revenue is collected for 30 days, we could include the opportunity cost of those funds (i.e., the cost of not being able to use them) as part of the collection cost. The opportunity cost would be $625 [$50,000 revenue (15% cost of capital) (1/12 year) = $625].

Substituting the adjusted selling price ($S'n$) for Sn in Equation 17–1, we can find the profit when the credit terms are 2/10/n30.

$$P = S'n \quad\quad - Cn \quad\quad - ARc$$

$$= \$49{,}000 - \$25{,}000 - \$1{,}104$$

$$= \$22{,}896$$

This example reveals that altering credit terms from cash reduces profit if the level of sales remains unchanged.

Credit Terms	Profit
Cash	$25,000
Net 30	$23,687
2/10/n30	$22,896

If demand for the product is elastic, the increased volume of sales will add profit and may offset the added costs of extending credit. However, as Figure 17–4 shows, the costs of credit may increase over time, producing increasingly adverse effects on profit.

Collection Policies The story of Alcan Aluminum at the beginning of this chapter demonstrated the difficulties one company had in collecting accounts receivable. As shown in Figure 17–4, the costs of collecting increase as time passes and methods of collection are intensified.

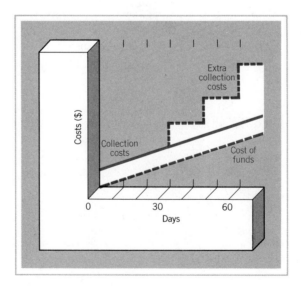

Figure 17–4   Costs of credit.

Collection policies and the techniques used to collect delinquent accounts affect profitability. As a rule, the more quickly accounts receivable are converted to cash, the greater the profits. However, if collection policies are too harsh, some potential customers may deal elsewhere. Financial managers must balance sales, profits, and the composition of assets when they establish collection policies. The following points must also be considered.

Delinquent accounts become increasingly difficult and costly to collect as time passes.

Sales to slow-paying customers are inhibited by slow collections.

The reputation for stringent credit policies discourages some customers from becoming delinquent.

Delinquent receivables add to the volume of working capital that must be financed.

Methods of Collection. Collection becomes a problem when customers do not pay for their goods or services according to the terms of trade. Therefore, the collection policy should be designed to make payment as easy and convenient as possible. For example, **preauthorized drafts**, mentioned in Chapter 16, are used by some utility companies for collecting their receivables. Such a company may be authorized by its customers to withdraw funds from their accounts to pay utility bills when they are due. Some business concerns use preauthorized drafts for the payment of trade credit. This technique reduces collection expenses, gives credit standing to the customer, and permits the customer to take trade discounts. As a safeguard against misuse of preauthorized drafts, some firms allow them to be cancelled or adjusted within 15 days after they have been received.

Reminders that accounts are overdue take a variety of forms. After a grace period, a company may send letters to customers reminding them that their accounts are overdue. The first letter is a "gentle" reminder. As time passes, the letters take a firmer tone. Some companies prefer to use telephone calls instead of letters. Others use their salespersons to nudge slow-paying customers. (Salespersons prefer selling to collecting, but they know that credit will not be extended to their customers whose bills remain unpaid.)

Collection letters are generally stronger than reminders. They range from an invoice with "payment overdue" or some similar comment stamped across its face to an announcement that the account is being turned over to a collection agency.

Collection agencies specialize in collecting overdue accounts for a fee. Their methods also include letters, phone calls, personal visits, and telegrams. Many collection agencies retain attorneys who specialize in collection and make their living from credit collection lawsuits.

Penalties for late payment are becoming a popular method of inducing debtors to pay on time. A creditor may add a penalty charge of 1 1/2 percent per month (18 percent per year) or more on balances more than 30 days old.

Level of Economic Activity   Current and expected levels of economic activity affect the extension and collection of credit. As mentioned earlier, credit standards should be relatively easy during the recovery and prosperity phases of the business cycle to encourage sales and growth (see Figure 17–2). During the recession and depression phases, credit standards should be restrictive. However, during these periods collections are most difficult; customers' revenues are falling, so they attempt to stretch their payments as long as possible. Therefore, collection efforts must also vary according to the phase of the business cycle.

Credit Control   Finally, we will examine controls on credit extension and collection. For convenience, controls are placed in two categories: external and internal.

External Controls.   External controls on credit extension set limits on how much credit will be granted to particular customers. (This is somewhat different from credit standards, discussed earlier, which are used to evaluate prospective credit customers.) As a rule, credit limits are determined by a customer's needs and ability to pay.

For example, assume a firm expects a customer to buy $200,000 worth of goods at retail prices on credit this year. To set the customer's credit limit, the firm may first determine the minimum turnover of the customer's account payable. The normal terms of trade are 2/10/n30 and the maximum duration of credit is 40 days; accordingly, the minimum turnover of the customer's account payable (the firm's account receivable) is nine times.

$$\text{Minimum turnover of customer's account payable} = \frac{360 \text{ days}}{40 \text{ days}} = 9$$

The firm can use this figure in the following equation to determine the customer's credit limit.

$$\text{Credit limit} = \frac{\text{Expected sales to customer} \left(\begin{array}{c} \text{Cost of goods} \\ \text{sold as percent} \\ \text{of total sales} \end{array} \right)}{\text{Minimum turnover of customer's account payable}} \qquad (17\text{–}4)$$

The firm's cost of goods sold is 85 percent of the retail price; so the cost of the goods sold to the customer is $170,000. Dividing this amount by the minimum turnover rate yields the credit limit, $18,889.

$$\text{Credit limit} = \frac{\$200,000 \ (0.85)}{9}$$

$$= \$18,889$$

Equation 17–4 does not take into account the customer's current payables or the rate at which they are paid. Suppose that, at present, this customer's outstanding account payable totals $12,500. A credit history reveals that the customer usually pays every 30 days, resulting in an actual turnover rate of 12 (360 days/30 days = 12), instead of 9. If the current amount owed is typical, the customer uses only $150,000 worth of credit annually ($12,500 × 12 = $150,000), although the firm is willing to extend credit worth $170,000.

Equation 17–4 can be modified to take this additional information into account. The resulting equation identifies the additional credit that should be extended when both needs and ability to pay are considered. The additional credit for this customer is $2,222, calculated as follows.

$$\text{Additional credit} = \frac{\text{Expected sales to customer}\left(\begin{array}{c}\text{Cost of goods}\\\text{sold as percent}\\\text{of total sales}\end{array}\right) - \left(\begin{array}{c}\text{Accounts payable} \times\\\text{Rate of turnover of payables}\end{array}\right)}{\begin{array}{c}\text{Minimum turnover rate}\\\text{of customer's account payable}\end{array}}$$

$$= \frac{\$200,000\ (0.85) - (\$12,500 \times 12)}{9}$$

$$= \frac{\$20,000}{9}$$

$$= \$2,222 \qquad\qquad (17\text{–}5)$$

The amount of a firm's receivables is related directly to its collection policies. Dun & Bradstreet recommends that the collection period should be no more than one-third greater than the net selling terms.[3] If the selling terms for a particular business are net 30 days, for example, the collection period should not exceed 40 days. The collection period may be determined by the following equation.

$$CP = D + D/3 \qquad\qquad (17\text{–}6)$$

where

CP = Collection period
D = Number of days credit extended in credit terms

For companies that normally sell goods or services on an installment basis, the average collection period for all the firm's receivables should be no more than one-third greater than one-half the average selling terms. This period can

[3]*How to Control Accounts Receivable for Greater Profit,* 4th ed. (New York: Dun & Bradstreet, 1972), p. 22.

be determined for any period of installment credit by use of the following equation.

$$CP = 2m/3 \tag{17-7}$$

where

CP = Collection period
m = Number of months for which installment credit is granted

A firm whose average selling terms call for 24 months of equal installment payments should have an average collection period of 16 months, determined as follows.

$$CP = 2m/3$$
$$= (2 \times 24 \text{ months})/3$$
$$= 16 \text{ months}$$

In practice, collection periods may vary with the strategies that have been established for various phases of the business cycle. Keep in mind that extending the collection period has the same impact on profits as extending credit terms.

Internal Controls. Internal controls concentrate on the aggregate amount of credit extended by the firm. To determine how much credit, in the aggregate, should be extended, firms use ratios such as those described in Chapter 13. For example, the **average collection period** measures how long a firm must wait before receiving cash for sales made on credit. It also measures the average age of accounts receivable. You may recall from Chapter 13 that the average collection period is determined as follows.

$$\text{Average collection period} = \frac{\text{Accounts receivable}}{\text{Net credit sales}} \times 360 \text{ days} \tag{17-8}$$

The **turnover of accounts receivable** is another measure used to monitor credit. In general, turnover ratios are considered efficiency ratios, because they measure the extent to which particular assets are used during the year. We calculate the turnover of accounts receivable by dividing annual credit sales by accounts receivable.[4]

$$\text{Turnover of accounts receivable} = \frac{\text{Annual credit sales}}{\text{Accounts receivable}} \tag{17-9}$$

[4]Some analysts use *average* accounts receivable in the numerator of Equation 17–8 and the denominator of Equation 17–9. For a discussion of this point, see footnote 1 in Chapter 13.

In interpreting whether a turnover rate is good or bad, analysts use the same rules they would use in interpreting other ratios. Careful consideration must be given to the life cycle, the business cycle, the firm's financial strategies, and the type of business involved. For example, the ratios may be 75 for retail vending machine operators and 18 for tobacco-leaf wholesalers, because of differences in their business practices.

The ratio of bad debts to credit sales indicates the "quality" of the accounts receivable. Obviously, bad debts are not desirable. Nevertheless, firms that extend credit must expect some. The absence of bad debts or an extremely low number of bad debts suggests that credit policies may be too restrictive. This is not an optimal strategy because it results in lost sales and forgone income.

Consumer Credit—A Growing Business

The preceding section examined various aspects of trade credit. Now, the focus shifts to an examination of consumer installment credit extended by nonfinancial business concerns. These business concerns include such giants as General Motors, General Electric, Exxon, and Sears, as well as thousands of other firms that provide consumers with installment credit to buy goods and services. Some major companies have their own "captive" finance companies; for example, General Motors has the General Motors Acceptance Corporation, and Ford has Ford Credit. Consumer installment credit extended by all lenders increased from $210.7 billion in 1976 to $550.7 billion in January 1986. The largest growth was attributable to retailers, which include automobile dealers.

Regulation One major difference between trade credit and consumer installment credit involves their regulatory environments. Trade credit is relatively free from government regulation, whereas consumer credit is replete with it. Laws regulating consumer credit include the following.

Truth in Lending Act (1968)
Fair Credit Reporting Act (1970)
Fair Credit Billing Act (1974)
Equal Credit Opportunity Act (1974)
Consumer Leasing Act (1976)
Fair Debt Collection Practices Act (1978)

Responsibility for enforcing the laws is shared by the following federal agencies, among others.

Federal Trade Commission
Comptroller of the Currency
Federal Reserve System

Federal Deposit Insurance Corporation
Federal Home Loan Bank Board
National Credit Union Administration
Interstate Commerce Commission
Civil Aeronautics Board
Secretary of Agriculture

These lists suggest how heavily consumer credit is regulated. However, nonfinancial business concerns are less heavily regulated than financial intermediaries such as commercial banks; so nonfinancial businesses have a competitive advantage. For example, a commercial bank may be limited to opening branch offices in the same county, state, or geographic region. In contrast, General Motors, Sears, and Exxon can do business anyplace in the world. Similarly, the sources of funds for financial institutions are regulated, whereas the sources of funds for nonfinancial business concerns are largely free of regulation. Thus, nonfinancial businesses have greater flexibility in raising funds to lend to consumers.

Rationale Nonfinancial business concerns extend installment credit to consumers because it helps them sell their goods and services. Automobile manufacturers make it easy for consumers to buy $18,000 cars by enticing them with small downpayments and modest monthly payments over a period of 3 years or longer. Similarly, retail outlets provide customers with plastic credit cards so they can "buy now and pay later."

Many nonfinancial business concerns encourage credit buying because they make greater profits from financing consumer credit than from selling their goods and services. That is why many gasoline companies stuff their monthly bills with advertisements for automobile supplies, clothing, appliances, and vacations. They earn interest when they sell these items on installment credit. To some extent, the profitability of such practices depends on how credit charges are calculated.

The "Real Cost" of Credit Credit cards are widely used for extending open-end consumer loans. In an **open-end loan**, the amount of the loan depends on the amount of goods and services purchased. Credit cards permit consumers to make purchases up to some specified limit, such as $1,000. The resulting open-end consumer loan accrues interest until it is repaid. If the consumer pays the monthly bill within a specified period of time, no interest is charged on the loan. Loans repaid over a longer period accrue interest on the unpaid balance.

The Truth in Lending Act requires that consumers buying on credit be advised of the exact amount of finance charges (the dollar amount charged) and the applicable **annual percentage rate**, or **APR** (the interest rate charged). The purpose of providing consumers with this information is to help them make intelligent decisions when shopping for credit.

The *APR* can be computed in several ways, and the method used affects the "real cost" of borrowed funds to the consumer. In other words, business concerns that offer consumer credit can alter their revenues by altering the way they compute interest charges. The following examples illustrate how an 18 percent *APR* can result in different finance charges, depending on the method of calculation used.[5] The calculations are based on the following transactions.

On June 5, Jeremy receives a statement for the billing period ending May 31. A total of $100.00 is due. There is no finance charge if the balance is paid by June 30. On June 1, he made a purchase amounting to $100.00 that will appear on the next monthly statement. On June 15, he makes a $20.00 payment on the loan.

Adjusted Balance Method. When the adjusted balance method is used, the finance charge is applied against the amount that has been billed, less any payments made before the end of the current billing period. In our example, the amount billed is $100.00 and the payment is $20.00, resulting in a balance of $80.00. The interest rate of 1 1/2 percent per month (18 percent per year) is multiplied by the $80.00 balance to give a finance charge of $1.20.

Average Daily Balance Method Excluding Current Transactions. Firms that use this method base the finance charge on the average daily balance outstanding over the current 30-day period, excluding current transactions. The average daily balance is $90.00 ($100.00 for 15 days and $80.00 for 15 days) and the finance charge is $1.35 ($90.00 × 1 1/2% = $1.35).

Previous Balance Method. With the previous balance method, the charge is applied against the original amount billed and no consideration is given for the $20.00 payment. Here, the finance charge amounts to $1.50 ($100.00 × 1 1/2% = $1.50).

Average Daily Balance Method Including Current Transactions. When this method is used, the finance charge is based on the average daily balance outstanding during the current 30-day period, including current transactions. The average balance is $200.00 for the first 15 days ($100.00 from May and $100.00 purchased on June 1) and $180.00 for the last 15 days ($200.00 less the $20.00 payment); the average balance for the entire period is $190.00. The finance charge amounts to $2.85 ($190.00 × 1 1/2% = $2.85).

[5]This example is based on data presented at the U.S. Congress, Senate, Committee on Banking, Subcommittee on Housing and Urban Affairs, *Consumers' Guide to Banking*, 94th Cong. 2nd sess., April 1976, pp. 15–18.

Table 17–5
Summary of Equations

	Equation	Equation Number
Gross profit	$P = Sn - Cn - ARc$	(17–1)
Cost of accounts receivable	$ARc = Cnk + CCn$	(17–2)
Adjusted selling cost per unit	$S'n = (1 - d)Sn$	(17–3)
Maximum Credit limit	$\text{Credit limit} = \dfrac{\text{Expected sales to customer}\left(\begin{array}{c}\text{Cost of goods}\\ \text{as percent of}\\ \text{total sales}\end{array}\right)}{\begin{array}{c}\text{Minimum turnover of}\\ \text{customer's account payable}\end{array}}$	(17–4)
Additional credit	$\text{Additional credit} = \dfrac{\text{Expected sales to customer}\left(\begin{array}{c}\text{Cost of goods}\\ \text{sold as percent}\\ \text{of total sales}\end{array}\right) - \left(\begin{array}{c}\text{Accounts payable} \times \text{Rate of}\\ \text{turnover of payables}\end{array}\right)}{\begin{array}{c}\text{Minimum turnover rate of customer's}\\ \text{account payable}\end{array}}$	(17–5)
Collection period	$CP = D + D/3$	(17–6)
Collection period (installment credit)	$CP = 2m/3$	(17–7)
Average collection period	$\text{Average collection period} = \dfrac{\text{Accounts receivable}}{\text{Net credit sales}} \times 360 \text{ days}$	(17–8)
Turnover of accounts receivable	$\text{Turnover of accounts receivable} = \dfrac{\text{Annual credit sales}}{\text{Accounts receivable}}$	(17–9)

In review, the use of different methods for determining the unpaid balance produces finance charges on the same transactions, based on the same *APR*, that range from a low of $1.20 to a high of $2.85.

Summary

It is said that Queen Isabella hocked her crown jewels to finance Columbus's explorations. If that is so, then America was founded on credit. Types of credit in common use today include trade credit and consumer credit.

Trade credit, as reflected in accounts receivable, plays a pivotal role in the working capital cycle. Because of its strategic importance, business concerns must have established credit policies to manage it. The major variables included in a credit policy include (1) credit standards (the five Cs of credit), (2) credit terms (discounts and duration), (3) collection policies, (4) strategies that take into account the phase of the life cycle and the business cycle, and (5) controls on credit. Equations relating to credit are summarized in Table 17–5.

In general, an easing of credit standards, credit terms, and collection policies contributes to increased sales; but it also increases expenses, such as the cost of financing accounts receivable, collection expenses, and bad debt losses. Consequently, a trade-off must be made between increased sales and returns.

Many nonfinancial business concerns extend consumer installment credit because it helps them sell their goods and services and because it is profitable in itself. The consumer installment credit industry is highly regulated, although nonfinancial businesses enjoy more flexibility in this regard than financial intermediaries. By using different methods of calculation, businesses that extend consumer credit can change finance charges on the same transactions with the same quoted interest rate by more than 100 percent!

Important Terms

Accounts payable
Accounts receivable
Annual percentage rate (*APR*)
Average collection period
Collection agency
Collection letter
Collection policy
Consumer credit
Credit policy
Credit standards
Credit terms
Five Cs

Mercantile credit agency
Open-end loan
Penalty
Preauthorized draft
Price elasticity
Private credit
Public credit
Real estate credit
Reminder
Trade credit
Turnover of accounts receivable

Questions

1. How do public, private, consumer, and trade credit differ?
2. Explain how a firm that makes a profit by selling an excellent product on credit can become insolvent.
3. Describe how the financial manager may change the firm's credit standards over a business cycle; over the firm's life cycle.
4. What general types of decisions are involved in the establishment of a credit policy?
5. Define each of the five Cs of credit.
6. What type of information is provided by a mercantile credit agency? How is this information used?
7. Explain the following terms: *EOM, 2/10/n30, 2/10/50X,* and *net 30.*
8. Explain how a financial manager can use credit terms to increase sales. How can the manager determine if the change has benefitted the firm?
9. What factors determine the cost of accounts receivable?
10. Why is it important to have an established collection policy?
11. What methods are available to expedite the payment of overdue accounts receivable?
12. Describe the internal and external controls of accounts receivable available to the financial manager.
13. Define the term *annual percentage rate (APR).* Will a 12 percent *APR* always cost a consumer the same dollar amount? Why or why not?
14. What effect has inflation had on accounts receivable management?

Problems

1. Skidmore Shirt Company plans to sell 430,000 shirts during the next year at an average price of $26 per shirt. The average cost of producing a shirt is $18. The collection cost if credit is extended is $0.50 per unit, and the cost of capital for the firm is 12 percent.
   (a) What will Skidmore's gross profit be if all sales are cash?
   (b) What will Skidmore's gross profit be if all sales are net 30?
   (c) What will Skidmore's gross profit be if all sales are 2/10/n30 and the discount is taken by all customers?
2. Shamrock Corporation is setting credit policy but is unsure of the costs associated with increasing sales by easing credit terms. Currently all sales are cash. Shamrock estimates that credit will have a fixed cost of $2 per unit. The cost of the product per unit is $70; selling price is $110 per unit; the cost of capital is 14 percent. Given the following information, determine the best credit policy for Shamrock. Assume that if credit is offered, all customers will use it.

Terms:	Cash	Net 30	2/10/n30
Expected unit sales:	72,000	80,000	92,000

3. A firm extends credit on a 2/15/n 45 basis. Sales are 150,000 units at $37 per unit, and unit cost is $22. Collection costs average $0.80 per unit, and the firm has a 15 percent cost of capital.

(a) What is the cost of accounts receivable if no customers take the discount.

(b) What is the cost of accounts receivable if the discount is taken by all customers.

4. Use the credit terms described in Problem 3, but assume the discount is taken on only half of total sales. Compute the cost of accounts receivable.

5. Gunn Imports specializes in importing sandals from India. The firm can buy as many pairs as needed at $2 per pair. Gunn sells the sandals to retailers nationwide and is trying to determine credit terms that will maximize profit. The price of the product is $4 to retailers. Gunn's cost of capital is 18 percent. Determine the best credit terms from among those below if credit costs are $0.25 per pair. Assume that all customers take the cash discount when offered.

Terms:	Cash	Net 20	3/10/n20
Expected sales (pairs):	440,000	650,000	720,000

6. Sawtooth Steel Company sells products on net 30 terms. Credit sales are $224 million and are evenly distributed throughout the year. Cost of goods sold is 60 percent of sales price, and Sawtooth has average accounts receivable of $21 million.

(a) Calculate the average collection period.

(b) If Sawtooth has a cost of capital equal to 10 percent and a 0.2 percent collection cost, what is the total cost of accounts receivable over a 1-year period?

7. Gemstone, Inc., is contemplating changing its credit terms from 4/15/n90 to 5/30/n120. The firm has credit sales of $8.6 million per year, and cost of goods sold averages 45 percent of sales price. Gemstone expects the new policy to increase credit sales 20 percent, while having no effect on cash sales.Collection costs are 0.3 percent of credit sales, and Gemstone has a cost of capital of 16 percent. The firm expects the new policy to change accounts receivable from $1.5 million to $1.8 million.

(a) Calculate credit sales per day under both plans.

(b) Calculate accounts receivable turnover under both plans.

(c) Calculate profits for both plans assuming the discount is taken on half of sales and the other half remains on the books until the end of the credit period.

8. Suppose instead that Gemstone, Inc., in Problem 7 expects all customers to take the discount no matter which credit terms are offered. In addition, if the new plan is implemented, collection costs will rise to 0.4 percent of credit sales. Which credit terms are expected to be more profitable under these conditions?

9. Bailey Chemical Company has established trade credit controls for its customers. Normal credit terms are 2/10/n30, and the maximum credit extended is 50 days. Cost of goods sold averages 75 percent of the selling price, and sales to Wertz Company are expected to be $680,000 this year.

(a) Calculate the minimum turnover in accounts receivable for Bailey.

(b) Calculate the maximum line of credit that should be extended to Wertz.

10. A firm has established credit controls of 3/20/n90 but usually extends credit to 115 days. Cost of goods sold averages 82 percent of retail price. What maximum line of credit should be extended to the following customs?

Customer	Expected Purchases (millions)
A	$1.2
B	2.6
C	.8
D	4.7

11. Vathe, Inc., is trying to determine the maximum credit a major creditor will extend. Vathe purchases goods on a net 30 basis and usually pays in 30 days, although management is aware that other customers do not pay for 45 days. Current purchases average $360,000 annually, and the supplier's cost of goods sold is 80 percent of sales. Vathe's average payables balance with this supplier is now $20,400. Based on other customers' 45-day payment periods, how much additional credit could be extended to Vathe?

12. Suppose that other customers of Vathe's supplier in Problem 11 delay payment for 60 days without incurring any penalty. How much additional credit should Vathe ask for?

13. Based on Dun and Bradstreet's formula for credit sales, calculate the recommended credit period for the following credit terms.

Net 30
2/10/n30
4/20/n90

14. Using Dun and Bradstreet's formula for credit sales, calculate the recommended credit period for the following credit terms.

Net 60
2/15/net 45
5/10/net 120

15. Based on Dun and Bradstreet's formula for installment sales, compute the recommended collection period for the sales terms below.

12 months
30 months
60 months

16. Using Dun and Bradstreet's formula for installment sales, compute the recommended collection period for the sales terms below.

18 months
24 months
120 months

17. Sluggo Corporation has credit sales of $740,000 per year with net 30 terms. The average collection period is 35 days.
    (a) Compute the average accounts receivable balance.
    (b) Compute the receivables turnover.

18. Now suppose the Sluggo Corporation in Problem 17 offers credit terms of 2/10/n30. Half the sales volume takes the discount; all others pay in 40 days. Calculate the new receivables balance and the average collection period.

19. Jan Keene holds a credit card issued by a major retailer on which the APR is 18

percent per year. On March 31, she receives a bill for $250. On April 1, Jan charges merchandise worth $500; the charge will appear on her next bill. On April 20, she pays $150 to the store.

What will her monthly finance charge be if the retailer uses the adjusted balance method; the average daily balance method excluding current transactions; the previous balance method.

20. Suppose instead that Jan Keene in Problem 19 receives a March 31 bill for $500. On April 10, Jan charges merchandise worth $500; on April 20, she pays $350. What will her finance charges be if the retailer uses the adjusted balance method; the average daily balance method including current transactions; the previous balance method?

Inventories

We'll start this chapter with a riddle.

> Most businesses have some of it, but too much is as bad as too little, and the right amount never stays the same; moreover, it can change in physical form.

The answer, of course, is inventory. The riddle suggests some of the difficulties firms encounter in managing the least liquid of the current assets. These and other problems of inventory management are presented in this chapter.

After reading this chapter, you should know the following.

1. **How to identify three types of inventories.**
2. **How cycles affect inventory investment.**
3. **How to use the economic order quantity model.**
4. **When it is worthwhile to take quantity discounts.**
5. **When to reorder inventory.**
6. **How hedging is used in relation to inventories.**

Types of Inventory

A dictionary defines **inventory** as all goods and materials in stock. This definition is a good starting point because it provides a general idea of what an inventory is—namely, goods and materials. However, there are different types of inventories, and it is convenient to classify them as raw materials, work in process, and finished goods.

Raw Materials The term **raw materials** generally refers to items such as chemicals, steel, oil, paint, nuts and bolts, and other things used in the productive processes of the firm, other than the plant and equipment. The amount of materials a firm holds depends on frequency of use, sources of supply, lead time, physical characteristics, cost, and technical considerations.

Frequency of Use. It makes sense that firms keep frequently used items in stock, while waiting to obtain those only occasionally used until they are needed.

Sources of Supply. If the company has good sources of supply and can obtain goods and materials on short notice, it may not need to hold large inventories of those items. However, if the source may be interrupted because of, say, a labor dispute or foul weather, the firm may wish to maintain a safety stock of some items. **Safety stock** is an extra amount of inventory held to meet contingencies such as a shortfall of supplies.

Lead Time. **Lead time** is the number of days necessary to reorder and receive inventory. The level of inventory investment can be reduced if management knows far enough in advance when particular goods or materials will be needed in the productive process. It does not make sense to stock materials today that will not be used until 6 months from now—unless they may not be available then or the cost will be appreciably higher.

Physical Characteristics. An inventory of fresh flowers may deteriorate and become worthless if it is not sold soon; an inventory of crushed rock is impervious to time and weather. Thus, durability, size, and other physical characteristics must be taken into account by inventory managers.

Cost.   Much of this chapter is devoted to explaining how to minimize costs associated with inventories. The costs we will examine are total costs, holding costs, and order costs. These costs relate not just to raw material inventories but to inventories of all types.

Technical Considerations.   Sometimes technical considerations are more important than inventory costs. For example, Agrico is a major producer of fertilizers. Some of its products contain corrosive chemicals that would damage its equipment if the production process were stopped for long periods of time. Therefore, Agrico keeps its production facilities working all the time, because holding surplus inventory costs less than replacing equipment.

Work in Process   The level of inventory investment in **work in process**—that is, raw materials in the process of being converted into a finished good—depends to a great degree on the production process. For example, it may take several years to build an aircraft carrier but only a few hours to print a newspaper. Thus, one would expect the work-in-process inventory to be larger for a shipbuilding firm than for a newspaper publisher.

The technology plays an important role in the productive processes of many firms. By automating and using preassembled parts and technological innovations, business concerns have been able to cut their production time and maintain smaller work-in-process inventories.

The work-in-process inventory is the least liquid of the three categories of inventory. A business concern in financial distress could sell its raw materials and finished goods, but selling half-finished goods would be very difficult.

Finished Goods   **Finished goods**—items ready to be sold—are supposed to be the most liquid type of inventory, but this is not always the case. The assumption here is that a demand exists for the finished goods. But consumers are fickle and their tastes for products change over time. For example, a large stock of E. T. dolls was desirable in 1983, when they were a popular consumer item, but a few years later it was almost difficult to give them away. The lesson to be learned here is that demand is one of the primary determinants of how much finished goods inventory should be held. Other determinants include the production process and the size of safety stocks.

The financial manager can change credit policies to encourage demand for finished goods. In the preceding chapter, we looked at how credit policies affect the trade-off between the amount of inventory held and accounts receivable.

Investment in Inventory

Determinants of Investment in Inventory The chapters that dealt with working capital explained that the extent to which business concerns invest in cash and accounts receivable depends on their position in the life cycle, their industry, and business conditions. The same holds true for inventory. In general, business concerns in the early phases of the life cycle hold more inventory relative to assets than those in the later phases of the life cycle (see Chapter 15, Figure 15–1).

Investments in inventory also vary widely from industry to industry. As shown in Table 18–1, the average inventory investment for all manufacturing firms is 17.5 percent of total assets. However, inventory investment ranges from 6.3 percent for petroleum manufacturers to 19 percent for tobacco manufacturers. Similarly, the ratio for mining is 3.1 percent, compared with 29.6 for retail trade.

The level of investment in inventories for each phase of the business cycle depends in part on management decisions. As shown in Figure 18–1, the level of sales generally conforms with the level of business activity. Therefore, one strategy for managing inventories is to increase or decrease inventories as sales rise or fall. This strategy results in a constant **inventory-to-sales ratio**; for example, inventory may be managed to remain at 170 percent of sales.

For a variety of reasons, it may not be feasible to change inventory as sales change or in the amounts necessary to maintain a constant ratio. Consequently, the inventory-to-sales ratio may vary over the course of a business cycle. For example, notice in Figure 18–1 that the inventory-to-sales ratio for manufacturing companies was 1.4 during the peak of a business cycle in November 1973 and 1.64 at the trough of that cycle. In general, the inventory-to-sales ratio is low at cyclical peaks, because sales increase more than inventory; the reverse is true at the trough.

Table 18–1
Inventory as a Percentage of Total Assets in Selected Industries

Industries	Percentage
Manufacturing	17.5%
Tobacco	19.0
Petroleum	6.3
Mining	3.1
Retail trade	29.6
Wholesale trade	25.7

Source Federal Trade Commission, *Quarterly Report for Manufacturing, Mining and Trade Corporations,* 2nd quarter, 1985.

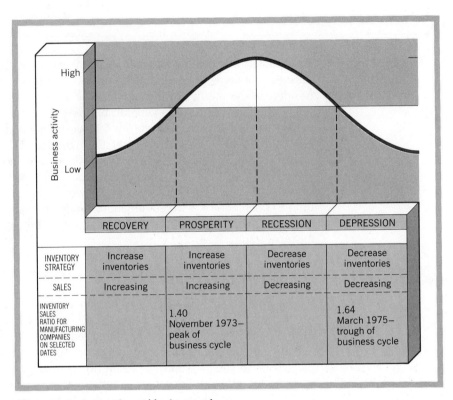

Figure 18–1   Inventories and business cycles.

Lowering Investment in Inventory Managing inventories means keeping the total investment in inventory at the lowest level that will enhance the long-run profitability of the firm and shareholders' wealth. To illustrate lowering investment in inventory, we'll use the Apex Company. The cost of goods sold for Apex Company is $5 million and the inventory turnover ratio is 10 times per year. We use these figures to find the firm's average investment in inventory, as follows.[1]

$$\text{Average investment in inventory} = \frac{\text{Cost of goods sold}}{\text{Inventory turnover ratio}}$$

$$= \frac{\$5,000,000}{10}$$

$$= \$500,000 \qquad (18\text{--}1)$$

[1] Conversely, if we knew the cost of goods sold and the average investment in inventory, we could find the inventory turnover ratio by using the following equation.

$$\text{Inventory turnover ratio} = \frac{\text{Cost of goods sold}}{\text{Average investment in inventory}} \qquad (18\text{--}2)$$

Table 18–2

Effect of Change in Turnover Rate on Investment in Inventory

Inventory Turnover Ratio (1)	Average Investment in Inventory (2)	Cost of Funds (3)	Annual Cost (4 = 2 × 3)
10	$\dfrac{\$5,000,000}{10} = \$500,000$	0.15	$75,000
20	$\dfrac{\$5,000,000}{20} = \$250,000$	0.15	$37,500

If the company's cost of funds is 15 percent, the cost of holding that inventory is $75,000, determined as follows.

$$
\begin{aligned}
\text{Annual cost} &= \text{Average investment} \times \text{Cost of funds} \\
\text{of inventory} &\quad\ \ \text{in inventory} \\
&= \$500,000 \qquad\qquad\ \times 0.15 \\
&= \$75,000
\end{aligned}
\tag{18–3}
$$

One way to lower this cost is to increase the inventory turnover ratio. If this ratio increased from 10 to 20 times per year, for example, the cost would decline to $37,500, as shown in Table 18–2.

Alternately, Apex could hold a smaller inventory for the same level of sales to reduce its costs. However, some other costs must be considered here. If the inventory is too small, the company might not have a sufficient number of products to sell to customers. In that case, the customers might buy from the competition. So the real cost of not having enough inventory is the potential loss of customers.

ABC Method of Inventory Control

The preceding discussion focused on reducing the total cost of holding inventories. Before examining the components of total cost and techniques for minimizing them, let's consider the distribution of inventory investment shown in Figure 18–2. The figure shows that 40 percent of the *items* in inventory account for 88 percent of the total *investment* in inventory. The remaining 60 percent of the items in inventory account for only 12 percent of the investment in inventory.

Firms that use the **ABC method** of inventory control divide their inventories into three categories—A, B, and C—based on the amount of investment in

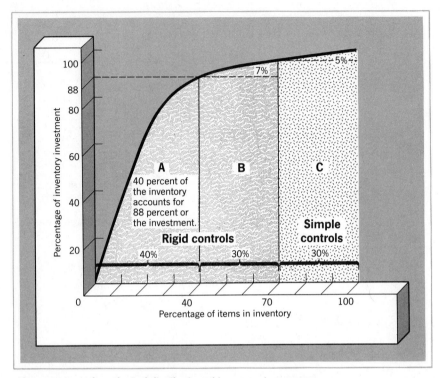

Figure 18–2   A hypothetical distribution of inventory investment.

each category. The A category includes items that call for the largest dollar investment. For example, an automobile dealership has its largest investment in new and used cars. Because of their cost, it makes sense to impose more rigid controls on the amount of investment in them. Although spare parts (category B) account for only 7 percent of the investment (and 30 percent of the items), they are crucial to the operation of the dealership. Therefore, rigid controls are imposed on spare parts, too. However, lubricants such as oil and grease (category C) do not require rigid controls. One widely used method of imposing control involves use of the economic order quantity model.

Economic Order Quantity

Objective   The objective of the **economic order quantity** (EOQ) model is to determine the quantity of inventory that minimizes the firm's total cost of inventory management. As you may recall, the EOQ model was used in Chapter 16 in connection with cash management. The model assumes that certainty exists,

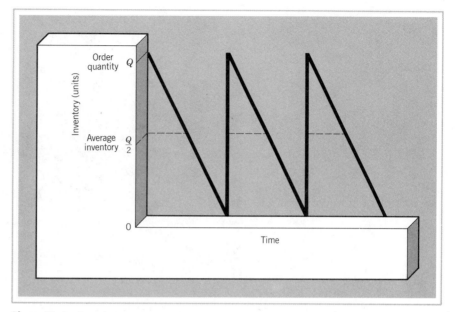

Figure 18–3 Inventory usage.

which means that the financial manager knows precisely what the demand for a particular product will be over time. Moreover, it assumes that inventory is depleted at a steady rate until it reaches a specified level; then it is replenished and the process starts again. The result is a saw-toothed pattern of inventory usage such as the one shown in Figure 18–3. Firms that have multiple products have to develop *EOQ* models for each item they wish to control.

Table 18–3
Inventory Costs for Sierra Hi-Fi

Assumptions:

F (fixed cost per order)	= $20
H (holding cost)	= $25
S (number of units used per period)	= 1,000

Quantities Q (1)	Ordering Cost $F(S/Q)$ (2)	Holding Cost $H(Q/2)$ (3)	Total Cost $F(S/Q) + H(Q/2)$ (4 = 2 + 3)
10	$2,000	$ 125	$ 2,125
20	1,000	250	1,250
30	667	375	1,042
40	500	500	1,000
50	400	625	1,025
100	200	1,250	1,450
500	40	6,250	6,290
1,000	20	12,500	12,520

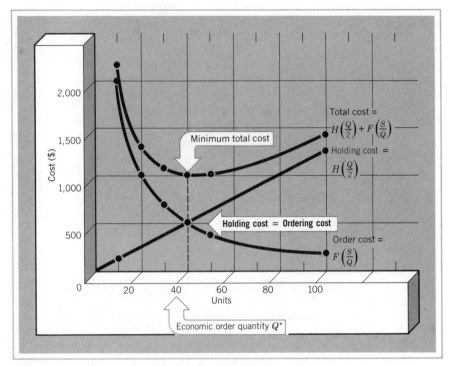

Figure 18–4   Inventory costs (based on Table 18–3).

Costs The *EOQ* model divides total costs into order costs and holding costs. The concepts of total cost, order cost, and holding cost are best explained in the context of a simple example. Sierra Hi-Fi Company has decided to expand its line of business to include a new brand of amplifiers. To determine how many it should order, Sierra will use the *EOQ* model and organize its information in the format shown in Table 18–3, plotting that information on a graph such as the one shown in Figure 18–4.

Order Cost.   The first step Sierra should take is to determine its **order cost**. The term *order* refers to the purchase or production of materials or goods for inventory. Thus, the *EOQ* model can be used for raw materials, work-in-process, or finished goods inventories. The model assumes that there is a fixed cost for placing each order, regardless of the amount ordered. This fixed cost includes clerical costs, costs of receiving and checking the materials and goods, and so on. The order cost is defined as follows.

$$\text{Order cost} = F\,(S/Q) \qquad\qquad (18\text{–}4)$$

where

F = Fixed cost per order
S = Number of units of inventory used per period (demand)
Q = Quantity of units ordered
S/Q = Number of orders per period

The financial manager of Sierra Hi-Fi knows that the fixed cost per order is $20 and that 1,000 units will be sold each year. Column 1 in Table 18–3 lists various quantities of amplifiers that may be purchased. If the firm orders 10, the cost for that order, determined by the use of Equation 18–4, is $2,000.

$$\text{Order cost} = F\,(S/Q)$$

$$= \$20\,(1{,}000/10)$$

$$= \$2{,}000$$

Order costs associated with other order quantities are listed in Column 2 of the table. When these costs are plotted in Figure 18–4, it becomes apparent that, as the quantity of amplifiers ordered increases, order costs decline sharply at first and then at a more gradual rate.

Holding Cost. The second step is to determine the **holding cost**, which includes the costs of storage, handling, funds, taxes, insurance, and deterioration or shrinkage. These costs are also assumed to be constant per unit of inventory. In the EOQ, the holding cost is expressed as follows.

$$\text{Holding cost} = H\,(Q/2) \tag{18–5}$$

where

H = Constant holding cost per unit
Q = Quantity of units ordered
$Q/2$ = Average inventory

Sierra's constant holding cost per unit (H) is $25. This amount is multiplied by the average inventory ($Q/2$) to give the figures listed in Column 3 of Table 18–3. Plotting these values in Figure 18–4 reveals that holding costs increase linearly as the number of amplifiers per order increases.

Total Cost. **Total cost** is the sum of order cost and holding cost.

$$\text{Total cost} = \text{Order cost} + \text{Holding cost}$$

$$= F\,(S/Q) \quad + (Q/2) \tag{18–6}$$

The total cost, which is listed in Column 4 of the table and plotted on the graph, declines sharply and then increases gradually with increases in order quantity. The lowest point on the total cost curve is directly above 40 units; this is the economic order quantity (Q*). Stated otherwise, 40 amplifiers is the order quantity that minimizes total cost.

Notice that total costs are minimized at the point at which order cost equals holding cost. Knowing this, we can arrange an equation so that order cost is equal to holding cost and solve for Q*, the economic order quantity. First set order cost equal to holding cost.

$$\text{Order cost} = \text{Holding cost}$$

$$F(S/Q) = H(Q/2)$$

Multiply both sides by Q.

$$FS = \frac{HQ^2}{2}$$

Then multiply both sides by 2.

$$2\,FS = HQ^2$$

Divide both sides by H.

$$\frac{2\,FS}{H} = Q^2$$

Finally, take the square root of both sides.[2]

$$\sqrt{\frac{2\,FS}{H}} = Q^* \qquad\qquad (18\text{--}7)$$

[2]The same equation can be derived by differentiating the total cost equation (Equation 18–6) with respect to Q, setting the derivative equal to zero, and solving for Q*. The result is identical to Equation 18–7.

$$\frac{dT}{dQ} = \frac{H}{2} - \frac{FS}{Q^2} = 0$$

$$HQ^2 - 2FS = 0$$

$$Q^2 = \frac{2FS}{H}$$

$$Q^* = \sqrt{\frac{2FS}{H}}$$

Stated otherwise:

$$Q^* = \sqrt{\frac{2 \text{ (Order cost)(Number of units used per period)}}{\text{Holding cost per unit}}}$$

Using Equation 18–7 is more convenient for solving *EOQ* problems than preparing a lengthy table such as the one used earlier. For example, Sierra Hi-Fi can make the same assumptions as used in Table 18–3 and find its *EOQ* as follows.

$$Q^* = \sqrt{\frac{2FS}{H}}$$

$$= \sqrt{\frac{2 \times \$20 \times 1,000}{\$25}}$$

$$= \sqrt{1,600}$$

$$= 40 \text{ amplifiers}$$

Sensitivity. The *EOQ* is also useful in testing the sensitivity of Q^* to changes in demand, holding cost, or order cost. For example, assume that Sierra Hi-Fi expects demand to double next year to 2,000 amplifiers. If that happens, the economic order quantity will be as follows.

$$Q^* = \sqrt{\frac{2FS}{H}}$$

$$= \sqrt{\frac{2 \times \$20 \times 2,000}{\$25}}$$

$$= \sqrt{3,200}$$

$$= 56.6 \text{ (57) amplifiers}$$

Although demand increases by 100 percent, the economic order quantity only increases by about 43 percent ($57 - 40 = 17/40 = 42.5\%$). (Taking the square root dampens the growth in demand.)

Interestingly, if holding cost per unit doubles from $25 to $50 at the same time demand doubles to 2,000, the economic order quantity remains at 40.

$$Q^* = \sqrt{\frac{2FS}{H}}$$

$$= \sqrt{\frac{2 \times \$20 \times 2,000}{\$50}}$$

$$= \sqrt{1,600}$$

$$= 40 \text{ amplifiers}$$

Quantity Discounts Quantity discounts are frequently given for large purchase orders. Therefore, the financial manager must decide whether the firm is better off ordering the economic order quantity or buying some larger amount and taking advantage of the quantity discount. The basic procedure for making this determination consists of comparing the marginal (i.e., additional) cost of holding more inventory with the savings from the discount. If the savings exceed the cost of holding the additional inventory, the firm should take advantage of the discount. On the other hand, if the holding costs exceed the benefits from the discount, the firm should order the economic order quantity.

To examine this process, we'll assume that the manufacturer of Sierra Hi-Fi's new brand of amplifiers is offering a $2 discount per unit for orders of 100 amplifiers or more. Should Sierra take advantage of the quantity discount and order 100 amplifiers instead of 40? We will use the following assumptions in answering this question.

Q' (new order quantity associated with discount price) = 100 amplifiers.
Q^* (economic order quantity associated with regular price) = 40 amplifiers.
H (holding cost per unit) = $25.
F (fixed cost per order) = $20.
S (number of units used per period, or demand) = 1,000 amplifiers.

The first step in answering this question is to determine the marginal cost of holding the larger quantity of inventory. The **marginal holding cost** is defined as the constant holding cost per unit times the average difference between the order quantity associated with the discount and the economic order quantity.

$$\text{Marginal holding cost} = H \frac{(Q' - Q^*)}{2} \qquad (18-8)$$

Ordering 100 amplifiers instead of 40 would involve a marginal holding cost of $750, as determined by the use of Equation 18–8.

$$\text{Marginal holding cost} = H \frac{(Q' - Q^*)}{2}$$

$$= \$25 \frac{(100 - 40)}{2}$$

$$= \$750$$

The second step is to determine the savings in order cost. These savings are equal to the difference between the order cost for the economic order quantity and the order cost associated with the new quantity.

$$\text{Savings in order cost} = F(S/Q^*) - F(S/Q') \qquad (18–9)$$

The saving in order cost for Sierra Hi-Fi is $300, calculated as follows.

$$\text{Savings in order cost} = F(S/Q^*) - F(S/Q')$$

$$= \$20(1,000/40) - \$20(1,000/100)$$

$$= \$500 - \$200$$

$$= \$300$$

Next, the net increase in costs is compared with the saving in order costs. The marginal cost of holding the extra inventory is $750 and the saving is $300; so buying the additional inventory to take advantage of the saving would cost Sierra $450. However, the saving from the quantity discount amounts to $2,000, which is determined by multiplying the discount ($2) by the demand (1,000 units). Therefore, the firm should buy the amplifiers in lots of 100 units.

Reordering Sierra Hi-Fi has decided to order in lots of 100 amplifiers, which we will now treat as if it were the *EOQ*. The firm will keep an additional 10 amplifiers on hand as a safety stock. (The costs associated with these 10 amplifiers are not covered by the following calculations.) As shown in Figure 18–5, the firm's maximum inventory will be 110 units. The firm must now make some calculations associated with reordering.

Number of Orders. We can determine how many times per year Sierra must order the new amplifiers by dividing the number of units used per period by the economic order quantity. Because 1,000 amplifiers will be used per period and amplifiers are ordered in lots of 100, Sierra must order amplifiers 10 times per year.

$$\text{Number of orders per year} = \frac{S}{EOQ}$$

$$= \frac{1,000}{100}$$

$$= 10 \text{ times} \qquad (18\text{--}10)$$

Inventory Period.   The **inventory period** is the approximate number of days required to exhaust the quantity of inventory ordered. We find it by dividing 360 days by the number of orders. The inventory period for Sierra Hi-Fi is 36 days.

$$\text{Inventory period} = \frac{360 \text{ days}}{\text{Number of orders}}$$

$$= \frac{360}{10}$$

$$= 36 \text{ days} \qquad (18\text{--}11)$$

The 36-day inventory period is depicted on the horizontal axis of Figure 18–5.

Daily Usage Rate.   To determine the **daily usage rate**, we divide the economic order quantity by the inventory period. Sierra Hi-Fi uses (i.e., sells) about three amplifiers per day.

$$\text{Daily usage rate} = \frac{EOQ}{\text{Inventory period}}$$

$$= \frac{100}{36}$$

$$= 2.78, \text{ or approximately 3 amplifiers per day} \qquad (18\text{--}12)$$

The daily usage rate is depicted in Figure 18–5 by the sloped line that descends from the maximum inventory of 110 amplifiers to the minimum inventory of 10 on Day 36.

Lead Time.   You may recall from the beginning of this chapter that the time needed to reorder is called the lead time. The financial manager of Sierra Hi-Fi knows that it takes 2 days to reorder and receive amplifiers.

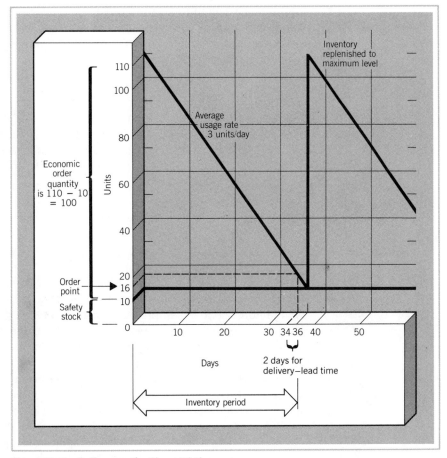

Figure 18–5   Daily usage for Sierra Hi-Fi.

Reorder Point.   We use the lead time and the daily usage rate to determine the **reorder point**; when the inventory falls to this point, the firm must reorder. To find the reorder point, we multiply the lead time by the daily usage rate, less any amplifiers in transit, plus the safety stock, if any. If there are no amplifiers in transit, Sierra's financial manager should reorder amplifiers when 16 are left in inventory.

$$\text{Reorder point} = \text{Lead time (days)} \times \text{Daily usage rate}$$
$$- \text{Goods in transit} + \text{Safety stock}$$
$$= 2 \times 3 - 0 + 10$$
$$= 16 \qquad\qquad (18\text{–}13)$$

As shown in Figure 18–5, the reorder point occurs on day 34 of the inventory period. If the amplifiers are received two days later, the inventory will be restocked up to the maximum level of 110, and the saw-toothed pattern will start over again.

Safety Stock.   If for some reason the amplifiers do not arrive on time, Sierra Hi-Fi has a safety stock of 10 units. This hedge against delayed shipments or unexpected demand allows the company to reduce the risk of losing sales and customers because of stock outages. Sierra Hi-Fi has to balance that risk against the cost of holding the extra inventory. Remember that costs associated with safety stock are not part of the *EOQ* calculations.

Hedging

The concept of hedging in the futures market was mentioned in connection with the interest rate futures market in Chapter 16. **Hedging** is buying and selling futures contracts to protect against a potential loss from adverse price changes in commodities. Commodities traded in the futures market include financial instruments and currencies, grains and oil seeds, livestock and meat, food and fiber, metals, and wood.

The prices of commodities tend to fluctuate because of changes in supply and demand, creating problems for those who manage inventories. For example, consider the case of Mal-Pan Bakery, a producer of breakfast foods. Mal-Pan receives an order on April 1 to deliver 5,000 bushels of processed oats on June 1 to a food store. Mal-Pan agrees on a price of $2 per bushel, which is based on the current price in the cash market. However, the oats will not be purchased for processing until 1 week before the delivery date in June. If the cash market price increases before the oats are purchased, Mal-Pan may lose money.

To protect against this possible loss, the financial manager turns to the futures market (as you recall, it is separate from the cash market). The financial manager buys a futures contract for 5,000 bushels of July oats, which are selling at $1.95 a bushel. As the weeks pass, the price of oats increases. One week before the delivery date, Mal-Pan buys 5,000 bushels in the cash market at $2.05 and experiences a "paper" loss of 5 cents per bushel—the difference between the contract price and the price at which the oats are actually purchased.

At the same time, however, the financial manager sells the futures contract for July oats for $2 per bushel, resulting in a gain of 5 cents per bushel. The gain from trading the futures contract exactly offsets the paper loss on the cash market transaction, so that Mal-Pan is perfectly hedged—it has lost no money in waiting to buy the commodity. Table 18–4 summarizes these transactions.

Table 18–4
Mal-Pan's Hedging Transactions

Cash Market	Futures Market
April 1	**April 1**
Sells 5,000 bushels of oats at $2.00 per bushel for delivery in processed form in June.	Buys contract for 5,000 bushels of July oats at $1.95 per bushel.
June 1	**June 1**
Buys 5,000 bushels of oats at $2.05 per bushel	Sells contract for 5,000 bushels of July oats at $2.00 per bushel.
"Paper" loss = $0.05 per bushel	Gain = $0.05 per bushel
Net gain or loss = 0	

By hedging, Mal-Pan transferred the risk of buying inventory at higher prices to speculators in the commodities markets. If the firm had not hedged, it would have lost 5 cents per bushel. In actual market situations, commissions, taxes, and unanticipated price changes may affect profits or losses in hedging transactions.

Summary

Inventory includes all goods and materials in stock and is divided into three categories: raw materials, work in process, and finished goods. Materials include various items used in the productive processes of the firm. Work in process, the intermediate stage between raw materials and finished goods, includes items being built or made; and finished goods are items ready for sale.

The extent to which business concerns invest in inventory depends on their position in the life cycle, the nature of their business, and conditions related to the business cycle. In general, managing inventory means keeping the total investment at the lowest level that will enhance long-run profitability and shareholders' wealth.

Some firms use the *ABC* method to determine what parts of inventory should be most rigidly controlled. To control inventory investment, a firm may use the economic order quantity model, which determines the quantity of inventory that minimizes total costs. Total costs include order costs and holding costs. Once costs are known, the firm can evaluate the desirability of taking quantity discounts and can determine when to reorder. Equations relevant to inventory are summarized in Table 18–5.

Hedging can help inventory managers protect their firms against potential losses from fluctuations in commodity prices.

Table 18–5
Summary of Equations

	Equation	Equation Number
Average investment in inventory	Average investment in inventory $= \dfrac{\text{Cost of goods sold}}{\text{Inventory turnover ratio}}$	(18–1)
Inventory turnover ratio	Inventory turnover ratio $= \dfrac{\text{Cost of goods sold}}{\text{Average inventory}}$	(18–2)
Annual cost of inventory	Annual cost of inventory = Average investment in inventory × Cost of funds	(18–3)
Order cost	Order cost $= F(S/Q)$	(18–4)
Holding cost	Holding cost $= H(Q/2)$	(18–5)
Total cost	Total cost $= F(S/Q) + H(Q/2)$	(18–6)
Economic order quantity (EOQ)	$Q^* = \sqrt{\dfrac{2FS}{H}}$	(18–7)
Marginal holding cost	Marginal holding cost $= H\dfrac{(Q' - Q^*)}{2}$	(18–8)
Savings in order cost	Savings in order cost $= F(S/Q^*) - F(S/Q')$	(18–9)
Number of orders per year	Number of orders per year $= \dfrac{\text{Demand } S}{EOQ}$	(18–10)
Inventory period	Inventory period $= \dfrac{360 \text{ days}}{\text{Number of Orders}}$	(18–11)
Daily usage rate	Daily usage rate $= \dfrac{EOQ}{\text{Inventory period}}$	(18–12)
Reorder point	Reorder point = Lead time (days) × Daily usage rate − Goods in transit + Safety stock	(18–13)

Important Terms

ABC method
Daily usage rate
Economic order quantity (EOQ)
Finished goods
Hedging
Holding cost
Inventory
Inventory period
Inventory-sales ratio

Lead time
Marginal holding cost
Order cost
Raw materials
Reorder point
Safety stock
Total cost
Work in process

Questions

1. Define three inventory classifications.
2. What factors determine the quantity of raw materials held in stock?
3. Which class of inventory is most liquid? Least liquid? Explain.

4. How are receivables policy and inventory management related?
5. How and why does the stock of inventory vary with the firm's life cycle?
6. How can the financial manager use business cycle analysis to improve the management of inventories?
7. What trade-offs are involved in lowering investment in inventory?
8. Explain the term *ABC* system. How can this system improve inventory control?
9. What is the purpose of the *EOQ* model?
10. In general terms, explain how the *EOQ* varies with increases in demand; holding costs; ordering cost.
11. What process should be used to determine whether quantity discounts should be taken?
12. What factors determine the reorder point?
13. What is the purpose of safety stock? Explain the trade-off between having large versus small safety stocks.
14. How can hedging be used in inventory management?

Problems

1. Compute the average investment in inventory in the following situations.
   (a) Sales, $2.6 million; cost of goods sold, 74 percent of sales; inventory turnover, 12.
   (b) Sales, $12.2 million; cost of goods sold, 82 percent of sales; average age of inventory, 12 days.
   (c) Cost of goods sold, $1.4 million; average age of inventory, 42 days.
2. Yale Corporation has sales of $7.3 million, and inventory averages 16 percent of sales. Cost of goods sold is 63 percent of sales, and the cost of capital is 12 percent.
   (a) What is the value of the inventory?
   (b) What is inventory turnover?
   (c) What is the cost of carrying inventory on an annual basis?
3. Clarkson Ice Company is refurbishing its equipment and will be able to reduce current inventory of $800,000 by 25 percent. What is the savings to Clarkson if the minimum required return on investment is 18 percent?
4. The cost of goods sold for Colby Cheese Company is 64 percent of sales. Sales are $1,075,000. Its inventory turnover is 8 and its cost of capital is 14 percent.
   (a) Calculate average inventory.
   (b) Calculate the annual cost of investment in inventory.
   (c) How much would be saved if inventory turnover increased to 12?
5. RPI Technology has improved its production process and is able to reduce inventory by $200,000. The change will cost $25,000 per year in additional maintenance of equipment. If the cost of capital is 16 percent, what is the profit or loss from inventory reduction?
6. Hobart Corporation has two proposals to decrease average inventory from its present level of $840,000. Hobart has a cost of capital of 10 percent. Which proposal, if either, should be chosen?

   Proposal A: Annual cost of change, $12,000; inventory level, $730,000.
   Proposal B: Annual cost of change, $18,000; inventory level, $690,000.

7. St. Lawrence Lumber has decided to use the *ABC* system of inventory control. Inventory consists of the following.

Item	Units in Stock	Cost per Unit
1	124	$ 8.75
2	438	10.20
3	16	580.00
4	1,500	22.00
5	640	2.25
6	97	87.50
7	2,640	1.40

The following criteria have been established: Group A, greater than 10 percent of total inventory value; Group B, greater than 3 percent and less than 10 percent; Group C, less than 3 percent.
Classify each item.

8. Simmons Hardware is planning to use the *ABC* system of inventory control. The following items are in stock.

Item	Units in Stock	Cost per Unit
Q	27	$ 68.10
R	3	2,540.00
S	3,480	3.60
T	1,430	5.30
U	1,832	16.60
V	860	59.90
W	52	32.00

Classification rules are: Group A, greater than 20 percent of total inventory value; Group B, greater than 5 percent and less than 20 percent; Group C, less than 5 percent.
Classify each item.

9. Niagara Water Company must know the holding costs and ordering costs of the following items. Provide the information for them

Item	H	F	S	Q
1	$26	$15	$1,000	$100
2	18	10	840	60
3	12	30	150	30
4	40	12	1,500	500

10. Canus Dog Biscuits use 150,000 units of beef stock at an even rate each year. The cost of carrying a unit of stock is $0.40 and ordering costs are $90 per order.
   (a) Calculate ordering, holding, and total costs for ordering 1,000, 3,000, 5,000 7,000, 9,000, and 11,000 units at a time.
   (b) Graph your results on cost/quantity axes.

11. Using the data from Problem 10, compute the *EOQ*. Compare this answer with the one indicated on your graph.

12. SJF Corporation is in the process of developing an inventory system. The following information has been collected: annual usage, 420,000; holding costs, $1.20 per unit; ordering costs, $180 per order.
   (a) What is the *EOQ*?
   (b) How would the *EOQ* change if annual usage were 800,000? 200,000?

13. Potsdam Music Museum buys a special solvent to restore antique musical instruments. Currently, Potsdam orders 80 gallons per order based on an *EOQ* analysis. The solvent company has offered savings of $1 per gallon 500-gallon lots are purchased. If Potsdam uses 800 gallons per year, should the quantity discount be taken? Storage costs are $5 per gallon and ordering costs are $20 per order.

14. Everett Supply orders 850,000 units of an item annually in lots indicated by the *EOQ* model. The item is bulky and costs $80 per unit to store. Ordering costs are $300 per order. A discount of $5 per unit has just been offered if Everett will order 10,000 units at a time. Should the discount be taken?

15. PBS Power uses 100,000 barrels of oil per day and carries a safety stock of 700,000 barrels. Tankers in the Gulf of Mexico can replenish the firm's supply within 4 days. What is the reorder point?

16. Canton Cotton Mills uses 1.2 million bales of cotton annually and receives 120,000 bales at a time. Its preferred safety stock is 60,000 bales, and it takes 10 days to receive an order. What is the daily usage rate? The reorder point?

17. Isometric Equipment uses 72,000 units of inventory per year. Order costs are $150 per order and carrying costs are $12 per unit.
(a) What is the *EOQ*?
(b) What is the average inventory?
(c) What would be the effect of a decrease in order costs? Of a decrease in holding costs?

18. Dayco Industries orders 14.4 million tons of corn each year. Carrying costs are $0.20 per ton and each order costs $60 to process. Safety stock is kept at 1 million tons, and an 8-day lead time is necessary.
(a) What is the *EOQ*?
(b) What is the average inventory?
(c) What is the reorder point?

19. Suppose Dayco Industries in Problem 18 increased its safety stock to 2 million tons. Compute the new *EOQ*, average inventory, and reorder point.

20. Pensky Fuel Oil Company is concerned about the possibility of rising fuel oil prices by the end of the year. In July, it signed contracts to sell fuel oil at $1.10 for December delivery. What transaction is necessary in the futures markets to hedge against the risk of increased oil prices between July and December?

Sources of Funds

Part 7 focuses on how business concerns obtain funds from
external sources. Its five chapters cover short-term and intermediate-term sources of funds, leasing, bonds, stocks,
and convertible securities. Within these chapters, you will learn,
among other things, how business concerns deal with banks,
how they use other companies' assets without buying them, why
some unsecured bonds are financially stronger than some secured bonds, and how options (puts and calls) are used.

Short-Term and Intermediate-Term Sources of Funds

Sources of funds are classified by their original maturity as short-term, intermediate-term, or long-term. Original maturity is the maturity of a financial obligation at the time it is issued. For example, suppose a company issues a security with an original maturity of 5 years. After 2 years have passed, 3 years remain on the security's original maturity. Short-term sources of funds have original maturities of 1 year or less. Intermediate-term sources of funds have maturities of up to about 7 years. Long-term sources of funds have maturities beyond 8 years.

This chapter is about short-term and intermediate-term sources of funds. It explains how business concerns obtain a substantial portion of the funds they need to operate. Short-term and intermediate-term financing is used by firms of every size throughout the life cycle.

After reading this chapter, you should know the following.

1. **What advantages and disadvantages are associated with short- and intermediate-term sources of funds.**
2. **How employees and government provide funds at very low cost.**
3. **How credit lines and revolving credits are used.**
4. **How companies borrow without collateral.**
5. **Why companies sell accounts receivable.**
6. **How inventory is used as collateral.**
7. **Why companies get others to guarantee their loans.**

Short-Term versus Long-Term Financing

Hedging   **Hedging** has already been discussed in connection with working capital policy. Hedging also means matching expected cash inflows from assets with the assets' source of financing. Chapter 15 described three types of hedging positions—perfect, conservative, and aggressive—and these are shown again in Figure 19–1. The figure reveals that the extent to which short-term financing is used depends on what strategy the financial manager selects. It also highlights the flexibility of short-term financing. (For the moment, we'll ignore intermediate-term funds to focus on the two extremes of long- and short-term financing.)

Advantages of Short-Term Sources of Funds   **Flexibility.**   Flexibility in altering financial strategies is one advantage of short-term financing. Suppose interest rates on borrowed funds are high but are expected to decline within the next 3 months. The financial manager may use an aggressive hedge, borrowing short-term funds to finance temporary and some permanent current assets. If predictions are correct and interest rates decline, most of the current assets can be refinanced at lower interest rates with long-term sources of funds, and the firm will have moved to a conservative hedge.

Cost.   Under normal credit market conditions, the cost of borrowing short-term funds (as well as intermediate-term funds) is less than the cost of borrowing long-term funds.[1] This is because of the time value of money and because the lender assumes less risk in lending for a short time than in lending for a long time. For example, the cost of funds may be 10 percent for 180 days, 11

---

[1]Under abnormal credit market conditions, such as prevailed in early 1980, short-term interest rates may exceed long-term interest rates. Such periods usually do not last long. See Figure 16–7, which shows interest rate movements in recent years.

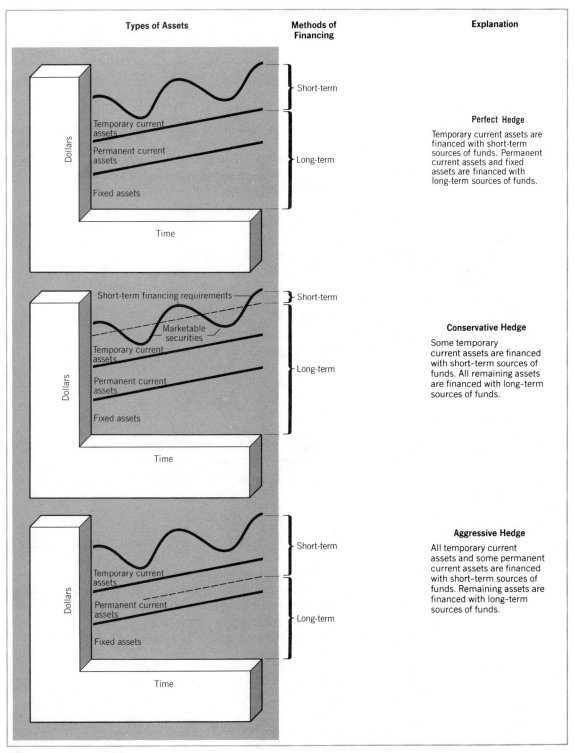

Figure 19–1   Hedging positions.

485

percent for 2 years, and 12 percent for 10 years. Some short-term sources of funds may involve little or no cost. More will be said about these later in this chapter.

Control.   A final advantage of using short-term funds is that management loses little control. Suppliers of short-term funds generally do not impose **restrictive covenants** (prohibitions against certain actions, such as allowing working capital to fall below a certain level), nor do they demand a voice in management.

Disadvantages of Short-Term Sources of Funds

Administrative Cost.   By definition, short-term sources of funds mature frequently. Renewing them involves relatively high administrative costs.

Changes in Cost of Funds.   The fact that short-term sources of funds mature frequently can be a disadvantage if the cost of funds goes up when the loan is renewed. Conversely, of course, it can be an advantage if the cost of funds goes down.

Credit Restraint.   During periods of credit restraint in the economy, lenders may not be willing to extend as much credit as the firm desires. Therefore, risk is involved in depending too heavily on short-term sources of funds. This is why many firms use a conservative hedge during periods of economic uncertainty. Then they can be sure they will have funds when they need them.

Spontaneous Sources of Credit

Spontaneous sources of credit arise from the normal operations of business concerns. For example, many businesses buy supplies but do not pay for them for 30 days. Similarly, their employees may work every business day but be paid only once each month. Such practices give rise to accounts payable—as trade credit—and accrued wages.

Trade Credit   As mentioned, **trade credit** refers to accounts payable that arise from the purchase of goods and services. The accounts payable on the balance sheet of the firm that purchases the goods and services appear as accounts receivable on the supplier's balance sheets. Chapter 17 explained how firms use credit terms and discounts to enhance their profits. Now we examine how firms use trade credit as short-term financing.

Trade credit is a means of financing short-term assets because it allows business concerns to get goods and services now and pay for them later. For example, on April 2, Mike's Body Shop purchases $8,000 worth of parts. The terms of trade are 2/10/n30—a 2 percent discount will be given if the invoice is paid within 10 days; otherwise, the full amount will be due within 30 days. Mike can take advantage of the discount and save $160 (0.02 × $8,000 = $160) if he pays the bill within 10 days, or he can wait and pay the entire amount in 30 days. The parts supplier is financing Mike's inventory until the invoice is paid. The cost of financing under the supplier's terms of trade is negligible, amounting to the cost of the paperwork necessary to pay the bills. However, if Mike waits 30 days or longer to pay the bill, he incurs other costs, which are calculated in the following manner.

Cost of Credit. The annual cost of *not* taking trade discounts can be computed by use of the following equation.

$$\text{Annual cost of not taking discount} = \frac{\text{Discount}}{1 - \text{Discount}} \times \frac{360 \text{ days}}{\text{Number of days' credit} - \text{Discount period}} \quad (19\text{--}1)$$

Applying this equation to terms of 2/10/n30, we find the annual cost to be 36.74 percent.

$$\text{Annual cost of not taking discount} = \frac{0.02}{1 - 0.02} \times \frac{360}{30 \text{ days} - 10 \text{ days}}$$

$$= 0.0204 \times 18$$

$$= 36.72\%$$

Equation 19–1 is also useful for evaluating the costs of credit for various periods of time. Suppose Mike decides not to pay the supplier for 45 days. In this case, the cost is 20.99 percent.

$$\text{Annual cost of not taking discount} = \frac{0.02}{1 - 0.02} \times \frac{360 \text{ days}}{45 \text{ days} - 10 \text{ days}}$$

$$= 20.99\%$$

If Mike waits 60 days to pay the invoice, the cost drops to 14.69 percent.

$$\text{Annual cost of not taking discount} = \frac{0.02}{1 - 0.02} \times \frac{360 \text{ days}}{60 \text{ days} - 10 \text{ days}}$$

$$= 14.69\%$$

Interest costs decline as the number of days' credit increases. Therefore, in some instances, it may be desirable to stretch payables as far as possible. However, firms that are "slow payers" may lose their credit ratings, suffer poorer service, or be forced to pay *COD* (cash on delivery).

Accruals **Accruals** are spontaneously generated funds a company can use at little or no cost. The most common accruals involve wages and taxes. Accrued wages represent salaries that have been earned by employees but have not been paid by the company. The level of accrued wages depends, in part, on the length of the payment period. A company that pays salaries once a month builds a greater amount of accrued wages than a firm that pays wages weekly. Similarly, by paying salaries on Friday afternoon, a company can take advantage of float over the weekend and maintain the accruals for several extra days.

The level of accrued taxes depends on the type of tax involved. Federal income tax payments must be made on a quarterly basis, but the payment of property taxes and sales taxes varies according to state law. In some states, property taxes are paid annually or semiannually, whereas sales taxes are paid monthly.

Other expenses besides wages and taxes are accrued in the ordinary course of business—utility bills and interest payments on loans, for example. Moreover, some business concerns act as self-insurers for certain types of claims and build accruals in accordance with actuarial evaluations. One such business is the Pittston Company, a diversified firm with primary interests in coal mining, which insured itself against claims for Black Lung disease (Pneumonocconiosis).

Business concerns have relatively little control over the level of accrued expenses, because wages and taxes must be paid on time. Nevertheless, it is important to recognize that unpaid wages and taxes payable provide an important source of short-term, low-cost funds.

Loans

Loans are the principal sources of short- and intermediate-term funds for businesses. Business concerns borrow from commercial banks, finance companies, the Small Business Administration, and other types of lenders. As mentioned, the loans are generally classified according to original maturity. **Short-term loans** have an original maturity of less than 1 year, and **intermediate-term loans** have maturities between 1 year and 7 years.

Short-Term Loans Table 19–1 gives some insights into certain characteristics of short-term loans. The table shows some results of a survey on short-term commercial and industrial loans made by banks during one 5-day period.

Table 19–1

Survey of Terms of Bank Lending Made during November 4–8, 1985
Short-Term Commercial and Industrial Loans (Other than Construction
and Land Development)

Characteristics	Amount (thousands of dollars)	Average size (thousands of dollars)	Average Maturity (days)	Average Interest Rate	Percent Made under Commitments
Total under one year	$52,408,698	$ 98	76	10.18%	58.5%
—Fixed rate					
by size ($1,000)	26,328,470	$ 124	34	9.69	56.7
1-24	1,233,951	8	99	12.61	19.0
50-99	936,831	63	110	11.76	15.5
100-499	2,100,140	169	87	11.32	37.4
500-999	498,206	680	30	10.11	27.3
1000 +	20,824,773	6,603	18	9.16	64.6
— Floating rate					
By size ($1,000)	26,080,228	81	134	10.67	60.3
1-24	1,712,591	9	128	11.59	55.1
25-49	1,828,727	34	135	11.45	46.7
50-99	2,403,748	65	128	11.16	55.3
100-499	7,463,212	183	119	10.85	54.7
500-999	3,702,715	618	200	10.65	56.0
1,000 +	8,969,234	2,981	122	10.07	71.8

Source U.S. Federal Reserve Statistical Release, December 31, 1985.

The dollar volume of the loans was divided fairly evenly between loans made under fixed interest rates and loans made under variable (floating) interest rates. However, the use of floating rates tended to increase with the size of the loan.

The largest dollar volume involved large loans ($1 million or more) made under fixed rates. These loans had an average size of $6.6 million and an average maturity of 18 days. Many such transactions are 1-day loans to large corporations that finance part of their operations with commercial paper. When redemptions of commercial paper exceed sales, corporations may finance this difference by borrowing from banks until new commercial paper can be sold. The fixed-rate, 1-day loans are repriced every day; so in effect, they are like floating-rate loans.

Although not shown in the table, other surveys reveal that large loans account for about 3 percent of the *number* of loans made. In contrast, small loans (loans under $24,000) account for the largest number of loans but for only a small portion of the dollar amount lent.

The table also shows that, on the average, interest rates on fixed-rate loans tend to decline with the size of the loan. In other words, interest costs tend to be less for large loans than for small ones. One reason is the maturity of the loans. (For simplicity, we'll assume that the default risk is the same for all of the loans.) The table shows that the small loans tend to have longer maturities than the large ones. Thus, it is not surprising that the small, longer-term loans tend to have higher interest rates than the large, shorter-term loans.

Another reason for the difference in interest rates has to do with administrative costs. It is costlier to administer a large number of small loans than a few large ones. The large one-day loans mentioned earlier are treated more like securities than loans.

Loan Commitments.   **Loan commitments** are agreements between bankers and their customers that cover certain conditions under which funds may be borrowed. Table 19–1 shows that the use of loan commitments tends to increase with the size of the loan. Loan commitments take a variety of forms, including credit lines and revolving credits.

Credit Lines.   **Credit lines** permit customers to borrow up to predetermined amounts any time within a specified period, usually a year. The credit line is the maximum dollar amount the customer may borrow. Loan documents specify the actual terms and conditions of the loan. Such loans are generally used to finance working capital and repaid when the inventories or accounts receivable are liquidated.

Revolving Credits.   **Revolving credits** are formalized and binding agreements between bankers (or other types of lenders) and their customers that specify the amount of a loan, the payment schedule, restrictive covenants, interest cost, and other terms and conditions. Most revolving credits cover more than 1 year; thus, where they are concerned, the distinction between short-term and intermediate-term loans may be blurred. Revolving credits are frequently used in conjunction with term loans, explained later.

The borrower generally pays a fee to the lender for the privilege of having credit available at the agreed-on terms and conditions over time. Consider the case of Center Chemicals. When interest rates were 10 percent, the company's financial manager, believing they would go higher, decided to make a commitment with a lender that would give Center the ability to borrow up to $200 million during the next 3 years. The company paid a fee of 1 percent of the total amount, or $2 million, for the commitment. Within a year, market interest rates had soared to 16 percent. The company took advantage of the commitment and borrowed the entire amount at 10 percent. Although the $2 million fee seemed expensive at the time the commitment was made, the commitment enabled the company to reduce its borrowing cost from $32 million (0.16 × $200 million = $32 million) to $20 million (0.10 × $200 million = $20 million). Had interest rates declined instead of increased, of course, the outcome would have been less favorable to Center Chemicals. This is one of the financing risks every financial manager must face at one time or another.

Intermediate-Term Loans   Intermediate-term commercial and industrial loans, or **term loans**, as they are commonly called, share some characteristics with short-term loans. A few large customers account for the majority of the total dollar volume of such loans, and the number of small loans is large. The average maturity is about 4 years for the large loans and 3 years for the small ones. In addition, the average interest rate, percent of loans with floating rates, and percent made under commitments generally increase with the size of the loan. However, it should be mentioned that interest rates charged on term loans are frequently lower than those charged on short-term loans, because of lower administrative costs.

Because, as suggested earlier, the distinction between intermediate-term and short-term loans may not always be clear, it is useful to classify loans according to the security behind them. The rest of the chapter will describe various types of unsecured and secured loans of short and intermediate term.

Unsecured Borrowing

The use of collateral to provide security for business loans is widespread. From the lender's point of view, collateral reduces risk because it can be sold if the loan goes into default. In addition, the existence of collateral provides the lender with some degree of control over the borrower. From the borrower's point of view, collateral may make the difference between obtaining a loan and being denied it. However, some types of loans do not require collateral. These are unsecured loans.

Unsecured Loans Many short-term loans and some loans of longer term are not secured by collateral, for several reasons. First, the borrower may have sufficient financial strength so that the lender does not require collateral. Second, for many small, short-term loans, the administrative costs of obtaining a security interest are not worth the costs. This is particularly true when the lender is familiar with the borrower's business practices.

Commercial Paper **Commercial paper**, you may recall, refers to unsecured promissory notes issued by the most creditworthy companies to borrow funds on a short-term basis. About three-fourths of commercial paper is issued by finance companies, bank holding companies, and other financial organizations. The remainder is issued by nonfinancial companies. For most commercial paper, maturity is 6 months or less, although maturities can range up to 1 year.

Commercial paper may be sold to dealers who then sell it to investors, or it may be directly placed with investors by the issuer.[2] The investors are banks, insurance companies, and other types of financial intermediaries and business

---

[2]Data on the dollar volume of commercial paper issues are published monthly in the *Federal Reserve Bulletin*.

concerns. About four-fifths of commercial paper is directly placed. By selling directly to investors, issuers reduce their costs.

The advantages of commercial paper include relatively low interest costs, flexibility of financing periods, and lack of costs and restrictions associated with bank loans (collateral, compensating balances, and so on). The interest cost of commercial paper is lower than the prime rate. For example, in April 1986, the prime rate was 9 percent and the 3-month commercial paper rate was 7.59 percent.

Small business concerns and large business concerns without sufficient financial strength are excluded from the commercial paper market. Nevertheless, occasionally a weak company does issue commercial paper. For example, Penn-Central had commercial paper outstanding when it declared that it was in serious financial trouble—and eventually declared bankruptcy. Moreover, the commercial paper had a high credit rating. In this case, the market was not efficient.

Banker's Acceptances   You may recall from Chapter 16 that banker's acceptances are used in connection with foreign and domestic trade. For example, suppose a U.S. importer buys tires from an Italian manufacturing concern. The importer agrees to pay for the tires 45 days after they have been delivered. The means of payment is a **time draft**, which is similar to a predated check. From the importer's point of view, the amount due the Italian manufacturer is an account payable (as spontaneous credit) that must be paid in 45 days. From the Italian manufacturer's point of view, the amount to be received from the U.S. firm is an account receivable.

The Italian manufacturer can send the receivable—the time draft—to the U.S. importer's bank and have it "accepted." That means the bank assumes responsibility for payment of the draft and will collect the funds from the importer when the draft becomes due. The accepted draft, called a **banker's acceptance**, is a negotiable instrument that can be traded in the securities markets. Therefore, the Italian manufacturer can sell the banker's acceptance and collect the funds before 45 days have expired. However, the banker's acceptance is sold at a discount to compensate the investor who buys it. The investor will not receive the full value until it matures; the difference between the discounted price and the face value at maturity is the return. Interest rates on banker's acceptances are sometimes slightly lower than those on commercial paper. In February 1986, the average 3-month commercial paper rate was 7.76 percent, and the average 3-month banker's acceptance rate was 7.58 percent.

Secured Borrowing

As mentioned earlier, the use of collateral for business loans is widespread. Virtually any asset can be used as collateral if the lender is willing to accept it. For example, airplanes, computers, machinery, and real estate are frequently used as collateral for term loans. Accounts receivable and inventories are commonly used as collateral for short-term loans and in some instances for longer-term loans.

Pledging Accounts Receivable

Pledging accounts receivable is using accounts receivable as collateral for a loan. Some firms pledge their receivables on a seasonal basis, others on a continuing basis, adding new receivables as the old ones are retired. Before accepting receivables as collateral, the lender evaluates the credit ratings of the firms owing them and the age of the accounts. Accounts from firms with weak credit ratings and substantially overdue accounts may not be acceptable as collateral.

The amount of the loan is less than the full face value of the accounts receivable pledged as collateral. What percentage the lender is willing to advance depends on the size, number, and quality of the receivables. Most lenders prefer to advance funds on a few receivables from well-established companies that do not customarily return the merchandise they have purchased. Under these conditions, the loan may amount to 80 percent or more of the face value of the accounts receivable. However, if there are many receivables from lesser-quality companies that have histories of being delinquent in their payables, the lender may advance only 40 percent of the face value.

The cost of pledging accounts receivable can be relatively high, for several reasons. First, some companies that pledge accounts receivable have weak credit ratings, and lenders charge them relatively high interest rates because of the risk inherent in lending them money. Second, the lender may impose a service charge to cover administrative costs involved in managing the receivables. These costs involve collecting the receivables from customers. On the other hand, the collection services provided by the lender may enable the borrower to reduce its collection costs.

Notification. Customers of the borrowing firm may or may not be told that their accounts have been pledged as collateral for a loan. If the loan is made on a notification basis, customers are advised that their accounts have been pledged, and they make subsequent payments directly to the lender. If the lender has advanced 80 percent on the receivables, then 80 percent of each payment is used to reduce the borrower's loan and the remainder is credited to the borrower's checking account. The advantage of this method to the lender is control over the payments. The disadvantage is the relatively high administrative cost.

If the loan is made on a nonnotification basis, the borrower's customers do not know their accounts have been pledged, and they continue to pay the borrower in the usual manner. The borrower is supposed to repay the lender as payments are received. Nonnotification reduces the lender's administrative expense, but its success depends on the honesty of the borrower. To discourage late payments and to prevent fraud, the lender conducts periodic audits of the borrower's accounts.

Factoring **Factoring** involves the sale of accounts receivable by manufacturing concerns and other types of businesses to a *factor*, a financial institution such as a commercial bank or a finance company. Here, instead of offering a lender a claim against accounts receivable, the firm sells them outright. The use of factoring is widespread in the textile and furniture industries, and it is used to a lesser degree in other industries, such as shoe manufacturing and floor-covering manufacturing.

Procedure. The factor selects the accounts receivable it is willing to buy from a manufacturer. Factors prefer to buy accounts that are not overdue and that are from high-quality firms. Consider the case of W. T. Grant, which was one of the nation's leading retail chains. In 1975, W. T. Grant, in severe financial trouble, wanted manufacturers to supply it with merchandise and credit for the Christmas season. However, factors said they would not be willing to buy Grant's accounts receivable from the manufacturers. The manufacturers did not provide the merchandise or the credit and W. T. Grant went into bankruptcy soon after. The granting of credit would have prolonged the life of the firm; however, it would not have cured the basic problems that ultimately caused its demise.

Nonrecourse. Factors generally buy accounts receivable on a **nonrecourse** basis. That means the factor accepts the credit risk for the accounts it purchases. If the accounts cannot be collected, the factor takes the loss. This is why factors carefully select the accounts receivable they will buy.

Notification. As with pledging, notification means that customers are advised of the transfer of their accounts receivable. All customers affected are told their accounts have been sold and are instructed to make payments directly to the factor. Some customers find it objectionable to pay a factor instead of a manufacturer. If something is wrong with the merchandise, they may withhold payment from the manufacturer until the problem is resolved; they do not have the same leverage when making payments to the factor.

Advances. Although the manufacturer sells the accounts receivable to a factor, it receives only 80 or 90 percent of the funds immediately. The factor keeps the remaining 10 to 20 percent as a reserve against merchandise returns and other claims by customers. Thus, the factor advances the manufacturer funds until the accounts receivable are collected or until some predetermined date.

Costs. The costs of factoring include (1) a commission to cover the lender's handling of the accounts receivable and the credit risk the lender takes and (2) an interest charge on advances. Factoring commissions range from 1 to 3 percent of the total face value of the accounts receivable. The monthly interest charge on the advances may amount to 2 or 3 percent of the amount advanced. For example, assume a manufacturer sells $100,000 in accounts receivable to a factor. The factoring commission is 3 percent of the face value of the accounts; the interest charge on the amount advanced is 2 percent per month; and the factor holds in reserve 10 percent of the accounts' face value. As shown in the following table, the manufacturer will receive $85,260 now. The $10,000 held in reserve will be paid at a later date:

Face value of accounts receivable	$100,000
Reserve held by factor (10%)	10,000
Commission (3%)	3,000
Funds that may be advanced	87,000
Less monthly interest charge (2%)	1,740
Funds available to manufacturer	$ 85,260

This example illustrates some of the advantages and disadvantages of factoring. The principal advantage is that the sale of accounts receivable provides a flexible source of financing. A certain percentage of the total face value of the receivables is available immediately. There are no compensating balances and no restrictive covenants. However, the costs associated with factoring may be relatively high—in the example, the commission cost is 3 percent and the cost of the advances 24 percent per year, without the compounding of the 2 percent per month taken into account. (The manufacturer's collection costs and credit risk may be reduced, which offsets some of these costs.) Another disadvantage is that many factors will only deal with seasoned companies whose cash flows are steady. Thus, some growing companies are excluded from factoring. Finally, a stigma may be associated with factoring: Some view it as a sign of financial weakness. However, others view it as a perfectly acceptable means of financing.

Inventory Used as Collateral Inventory is widely used as collateral against loans. The physical characteristics of the inventory determine its desirability as collateral. Clearly, lenders prefer inventory that is durable, easily identified, and marketable. Inventory that may spoil, such as fresh strawberries, is not as desirable as car parts. It is also easier for lenders to maintain control over inventories that are durable and identifiable than over perishable, homogeneous inventories such as salad oil. The great salad oil scandal of 1963 will illustrate the point.[3] Anthony DeAngelis and his Allied Crude Vegetable Oil Refining Corporation used 161 million pounds of salad oil as collateral for loans. The oil was supposed to be stored in huge tanks in Bayonne, New Jersey. However, the tanks contained only several million pounds of salad oil; the rest had been secretly removed. As a result of this fraud, lenders lost about $150 million. This expensive lesson made them keenly aware of the pitfalls of lending against inventory that is difficult to monitor. Equally important, it underscored the importance of knowing the character of the borrower. Honest firms had been borrowing against similar collateral for years but had not defrauded lenders.

Lenders attempt to maintain control over inventories in several ways. The first three methods discussed here—floating lien, trust receipt, and chattel mortgage—permit the borrower to maintain possession of the inventory. The last two methods—terminal warehouse and field warehouse—place control of the inventory in the hands of a third party.

Floating Lien.   A **lien** is a claim on another's property as security against a loan. A **floating lien**, or **continuous lien**, can be used to cover all of a firm's inventory—raw materials through finished goods, or a wide variety of finished goods. The assignment may also include inventory acquired after the loan agreement has been made.

The floating lien gives borrowers two advantages. First, it enables the borrower to pledge its entire inventory as collateral (and thus receive more money), although part of the inventory may be work in process or hundreds of items in a retail store. Second, the borrower can sell the finished inventory in the ordinary course of business, because the lien does not follow each item. The borrower is expected to repay the loan when a sufficient dollar volume of the items have been sold.

A disadvantage of this arrangement is that lenders may only lend 50 or 60 percent of the value of the inventory, because they cannot clearly identify particular items. From the lender's point of view, a disadvantage involves wide variations in the value of inventories. A lender forced to liquidate an inventory might be able to sell, say, shirts and ties at book value but might be able to sell some work in process only at scrap value. Therefore, in reality, a floating lien may add little to a lender's security.

Trust Receipt.   **Trust receipts** are widely used in the financing of automobiles, trucks, airplanes, and consumer durable goods such as washing machines. Here, the lender holds title to the inventory and the borrowing firm assumes the role of trustee for the goods in its possession. When the inventory is sold,

[3]For details on this story, see Norman C. Miller, *The Great Salad Oil Swindle* (Baltimore: Penguin Books, 1965).

the borrower repays the lender, who then releases the lien and the title to the property. This method of financing, commonly called **floor planning**, is illustrated by the following example. Nissan sells 10 new cars to a dealer, who finances them through a local bank. The bank pays Nissan, retains the title to the cars, and permits the dealer to display and sell them under a trust receipt security agreement. When the dealer sells a car, the bank is paid with the proceeds from the sale and releases the lien against the car.

Trust receipts provide greater security for lenders than floating liens, but the method is not foolproof. For example, some unscrupulous borrowers may attempt to use titles from wrecked vehicles as collateral. This is why most lenders make physical audits of the inventory on a periodic basis.

Chattel Mortgage. A **chattel mortgage** gives the lender a lien on tangible personal property. The property must be clearly identified by a serial number or some other means. Then the lien can be registered with the appropriate government authorities. This legal arrangement is most widely used for inventories that contain a small number of items with high dollar values. Frequently, automobiles that are "floor planned" have chattel mortgages. When they are sold, the appropriate government authority must be notified to release the lender's claims and provide a clear title.

Warehouse Receipts. Control and security for the lender are greatest when the inventory is held in a **terminal warehouse**. Under this arrangement, the goods are stored in a bonded public warehouse and the receipt for the goods is held by the lender. Inventory can be released only when the proper receipt is presented at the warehouse. Warehouse receipts may be negotiable or nonnegotiable. Negotiable warehouse receipts are commonly used to finance inventories of commodities, such as wheat, that are traded actively. Most lenders prefer to use nonnegotiable receipts, which gives them greater control.

Sometimes the borrower and the lender agree to establish a **field warehouse** on the borrower's premises. A certain area designated as the field warehouse is segregated by a fence or some other security arrangement to contain the inventory. Here, the borrower gains the advantage of having the inventory in a convenient location. Whether a terminal warehouse or a field warehouse is used, the borrower must pay a fee for storage and for guarding of the inventory.

The security of the inventory depends on the warehouse providing the service. Although a warehouse provides greater security for lenders than floating liens or trust receipts, opportunities for fraud still exist. (The salad oil from the great salad oil scandal was stored by American Express Field Warehousing Company, for example.) Because some risk is involved, lenders may offer only up to about 85 percent of the book value of the inventory even when it is stored under these conditions.

Endorsements   Lenders can improve their security in a loan by having a third party guarantee the payments, thus making an **endorsement**. The third party may be an individual, a company, or a government agency. For example, a parent company may guarantee a loan made by a subsidiary. Without the guarantee, the subsidiary might not be able to borrow the funds. Similarly, the Small Business Administration and other government agencies often guarantee all or part of certain loans. Where the guarantor is not a government agency, the quality of the guarantee depends on the guarantor's financial strength.

Summary

Hedging—matching the maturity of assets with the maturity of liabilities—is sound financial practice. Therefore, short-term assets, such as working capital, are frequently financed from short-term sources of funds and longer-term assets are financed from longer-term sources of funds. How firms utilize short-term, intermediate-term, and long-term funds to finance their assets affects their profitability. The impact on profits was examined in Chapter 15; this chapter focuses on sources of short-term and intermediate-term funds.

Spontaneous credit is an important source of short-term funds. It arises from the daily operations of business concerns when they buy goods and services and pay for them later. Trade credit and accruals are the two major sources of spontaneous credit.

Loans are the principal sources of short-term and intermediate-term funds. Because the distinction between short-term and intermediate-term may sometimes be blurred, it is convenient to classify loans according to the security behind them. Some loans are not secured by assets, because of the financial strength of the borrower. For example, commercial paper is backed by the credit standing of the issuing corporation and by the faith the lender places in the corporation. Banker's acceptances are backed by a bank's guarantee.

Other loans are secured by assets. When accounts receivable are used as collateral, the firm may pledge them or sell them to a factor. Inventories are frequently used as collateral; in this case, lenders must decide how to maintain control over them. Loans may also be guaranteed by the endorsement of a third party.

Important Terms

Accrual	Credit line
Banker's acceptance	Endorsement
Chattel mortgage	Factoring
Commercial paper	Field warehouse

Floating (continuous) lien
Floor planning
Hedging
Intermediate-term loan
Lien
Loan commitment
Nonrecourse
Pledging (of accounts receivable)
Restrictive covenant

Revolving credit
Short-term loan
Spontaneous source of credit
Term loan
Terminal warehouse
Time draft
Trade credit
Trust receipt

Questions

1. Explain how short-term, intermediate-term, and long-term loans differ.
2. What are the advantages and disadvantages of short-term loans?
3. What are the lowest-cost forms of short-term financing? Why?
4. When does trade credit represent a low-cost source of credit? When does it not?
5. What is a loan commitment? Contrast two different forms of commitments.
6. Why are many short-term loans made on an unsecured basis?
7. What is commercial paper? What are the advantages of this form of financing?
8. Explain in general the process by which banker's acceptances are created.
9. Some firms pledge accounts receivable as security for loans. Explain this method of financing.
10. What is factoring? What costs are associated with factoring? What benefits?
11. Identify three methods of inventory financing that allow the borrower to maintain control of the collateral. How do these methods differ from one another?
12. Identify two methods of inventory financing that take collateral out of the borrower's control. How do they differ from one another?

Problems

1. Compute the annual cost of not taking the discount on terms of 3/15/n45 and paying on the 45th day. Recompute the cost assuming payment is not made until the 75th day.
2. A firm can obtain terms of 1/10/n30 from a supplier or can finance the purchase with a bank loan at 15 percent. Which alternative is cheaper? What if the firm stretches its payables to 40 days?
3. A firm receives terms of 3/10/n40. What is the annual cost of trade credit if the firm:
   (a) takes the discount.
   (b) pays in 40 days.
   (c) pays in 80 days.
4. Determine what the annual cost of the following credit terms will be if the discount is not taken.

(a) 1/15/n40
(b) 3/10/n60
(c) 2/5/n20
(d) Net 30

5. A firm sells $500,000 of receivables to a factor. The factor holds 15 percent in reserve, charges a 3 percent commission, and charges 2 percent per month on funds advanced. Collection on the accounts is expected in 30 days. After all costs are considered, how much will the firm receive on the agreement?

6. Recalculate the amount of funds the firm in Problem 5 will receive if it sells $750,000 of receivables to the factor, the factor holds 10 percent in reserve, and payment on the accounts is not expected for 60 days. Other terms remain the same.

7. Adams Advertising Agency sells all services on credit, then factors receivables to obtain cash. A factor has agreed to buy $2 million of Adams's receivables with 20 percent held in reserve, a 3 percent monthly interest rate on funds advanced, and a 2.5 percent commission. Funds are advanced 1 month before collection. If Adams needs $1.5 million in cash, will the factoring agreement provide it?

 **Leasing**

Leasing is becoming an increasingly popular source of *asset-based financing*—that is, financing for tangible long-term assets. Recently, for example, Hughes Communications Services, Inc., a subsidiary of Hughes Aircraft, built four communications satellites valued at more than $350 million. Hughes sold the four satellites to a group of investors, led by J. P. Morgan Interfunding, Citicorp Industrial Credit, Inc., and Security Pacific and Bankers Trust, and then leased the satellites back. In a subsequent transaction, Hughes contracted with the U.S. Navy to use the satellites to provide communications services.

Island Creek Coal Sales, a subsidiary of Occidental Petroleum, provides another example of leasing. For many years, Island Creek Coal left the responsibility of supplying hopper cars for carrying coal to the railroads. Frequently, however, Island Creek Coal found that not enough hopper cars were available when they were needed. To solve this problem, the company leased a fleet of 100 hopper cars. The fleet did not add a maintenance burden, because mechanical services and repairs were included in the term of the lease.

Leasing is also used to finance airplanes, computers, ships, typewriters, and virtually any other type of tangible asset. Although the examples above concern large companies, leasing can be used by firms of any size at any point in the life cycle.

501

After reading this chapter, you should know the following.

1. **How operating leases and financial leases differ.**
2. **How companies sell assets and still use them.**
3. **What is involved in leveraged leasing.**
4. **What advantages and disadvantages are involved in leasing.**
5. **How to compare the cost of leasing with the cost of borrowing.**

Types of Leases

A **lease** is a contract that enables a user—the **lessee**—to secure the use of a tangible asset over a specified time by making periodic payments to the owner—the **lessor**. The contract also specifies the details of the payments, the disposition of income tax benefits, provisions for maintenance, renewal options, and other clauses. Lease contracts display infinite variety, because frequently leases are written to suit the specific needs of the lessor and lessee. Nevertheless, it is convenient to place leases into two broad categories: operating leases and financial leases. Each category has its own characteristics.

Operating Leases   **Operating leases**, sometimes called **service leases**, are short-term leases used to finance equipment such as computers, railroad cars, or tankers. The term of an operating lease generally covers only a fraction of the economic life of the asset. Stated otherwise, the asset is not fully amortized over the term of the lease. Thus, an oil company can lease a tanker that has an economic life of 25 years for a 6-month period. The lessor hopes to make subsequent leases over the remaining life of the tanker.

Operating leases generally contain a provision for service and maintenance. Island Creek Coal's lease of 100 hopper cars was an operating lease, and it contained a maintenance feature. Many companies that use computers, office copying equipment, word processors, and other machines do not have the ability or desire to maintain them. Therefore, the maintenance feature is an advantage to the lessee. It is an advantage to the lessor as well, because it gives the lessor some control over the physical condition of the leased equipment—an important consideration if the asset will be sold at some time in the future.

Finally, operating leases frequently contain a cancellation clause that permits the lessee or the lessor to break the lease. To protect the lessor, a minimum period of time (or number of payments) typically must pass before the lease can be canceled.

Financial Leases **Financial leases** are sometimes called **capital leases**. The word *capital* suggests a capital asset, and financial leases are usually used in financing capital, or long-term, assets. A financial lease is similar to a bond in that it represents a noncancelable financial obligation. At the end of the lease period, the lessee may have the option to purchase the asset.

As a rule, financial leases are **full payout net leases**. This means that the cost of the asset and the return to the lessor are amortized over the term of the lease. The word *net* means that the lessee is responsible for maintenance, service, taxes, insurance, and other expenses that arise in connection with the use of the asset.

Sale and Leaseback. A **sale and leaseback** is a special type of financial lease. When Hughes Communications Services built four communications satellites, sold them to a group of investors, and then leased them back, it engaged in a sale and leaseback transaction. The sale and leaseback arrangement is more commonly used for real estate. Suppose a firm that owns land and a building needs additional working capital to support its growth. The firm can sell the land and building to an investor and simultaneously enter into a lease agreement to use the property. The proceeds from the sale provide working capital and the firm still has the use of the land and the building.

Leveraged Lease. The **leveraged lease** is another special type of financial lease used in connection with large transactions. It involves at least three parties: a lessee, a lessor (the equity participant), and a long-term lender (the debt participant). Here, the lessor arranges a transaction wherein a long-term lender provides most of the funds to acquire the asset to be leased. The lessor may provide only 10 percent of the funds, with the remaining 90 percent provided by the lender on a nonrecourse basis. The lender is repaid from the lease payments and generally also holds some security on the loan, such as a lien on the leased asset.

Although the lessor provides only 10 percent of the loan, it receives 100 percent of the tax benefits, which include an investment tax credit and depreciation of the asset. Under the Tax Reform Act of 1986, the investment tax credit was generally repealed. However, it may be reinstated in the future. Accordingly, we will continue to include tax credits as a benefit. The effect of the deductions is to create tax losses in the early years of the lease, which the lessor uses to offset other taxable income. As a result, the lessor's capital is returned rapidly, and the lessor is frequently willing to charge the lessee an effective interest rate lower than the rate for a nonleveraged (or *direct*) lease.

The lessee gains the greatest advantage when it could not take advantage of tax credit or accelerated depreciation if it purchased the asset outright. Here, the lessee trades tax benefits it would lose anyway for a lower interest rate on the lease. The following example illustrates such a situation. In 1971, the government of Chile expropriated the Anaconda Company's mines there. The result of that misfortune was a $356.3 million tax write-off for Anaconda that could be carried forward for 10 years. That same year, Congress approved a 7 percent investment tax credit. Because Anaconda's tax liabilities would be low for 10 years, it could not take full advantage of the tax credit or depreciation on new investments. However, Anaconda wanted to build a $138 million mill near Sebree, Kentucky.

U.S. Leasing International arranged a leveraged lease to finance the mill. A group of equity participants (Chrysler Financial and six banks) invested about $38 million, and several debt participants (Prudential, Metropolitan, and Aetna Life) invested a total of $72 million. Anaconda financed $28 million on its own. For Anaconda, the lease payments would amount to about $74 million less than it would have paid had it financed the project by selling bonds.

Identifying True Leases

The tax advantages of leasing exist only if the contract is a **true financial lease**—that is, one that qualifies as a lease under the Internal Revenue Code so that the lessee can claim all lease payments as tax deductions and the lessor can claim the investment tax credits and depreciation. Lessees must be careful to distinguish between a true lease and an installment loan. Installment loans are similar to leases, but only the interest portion of installment loan payments is tax deductible.

One often needs a tax lawyer to determine what constitutes a true financial lease. The definition and exceptions to definitions of a true financial lease have been modified under the Economic Recovery Tax Act of 1981 and the Tax Equity and Fiscal Responsibility Act of 1982. To simplify matters, we will assume that a true financial lease involves assets that qualify as *ACRS* (accelerated cost recovery system) recovery property, as described in Chapter 3. In addition, a true lease has economic substance independent of the tax benefits and the lessee may be permitted to buy the leased asset when the lease expires at a price of 10 percent or more of the original cost. This definition of a financial lease is adequate for our purposes, but it is not complete.

Advantages of Leasing

Tax Advantages. The discussion of leveraged leasing pointed out some of the tax advantages of leasing. The lessor benefits from investment tax credits and depreciation. In the case of a leveraged lease, some of these benefits may be passed on to the lessee in the form of lower lease payments. The lessee can also deduct lease payments as an expense.

Leases that include land provide the lessee with another tax advantage. Land is a nondepreciable asset; companies that own land are allowed no income tax deduction for using it. However, if the land is leased, the lease payment is a deductible expense.

Avoidance of Obsolescence. Short-term cancelable leases permit the lessee to use new equipment while avoiding some problems associated with technological change and obsolescence. For example, assume a firm wants a new computer now, but has heard rumors that a superior computer will be on the market within 2 years. Instead of buying the computer, the firm can lease it for 2 years and then evaluate new products at the end of that time.

In cases such as this, the lessor takes the risk associated with obsolescence. This risk is passed on to the lessee in the form of higher lease payments. In addition, when the lease contains a provision making it noncancelable for a certain period, the lessor tries to recover as much of the investment as possible during the noncancelable portion of the contract.

Flexibility. Lease financing may require little or no downpayment from the lessee. In addition, the lessee does not have to maintain a compensating balance, which might be the case if the financing involved a term loan. Nor does the lease include restrictive covenants, as term loans or bond indentures might.

Finally, lease financing may be available when other sources of financing cannot be obtained. This is particularly true for small business concerns that do not have sufficient financial strength to borrow from banks or sell bonds. Many lessors will deal with small business concerns because the lessors retain title to the leased asset and thus have a superior claim to other creditors. In addition, during periods of credit restraint, some firms that could not borrow from banks to finance the purchase of assets are able to lease those same assets from leasing companies.

Off-Balance-Sheet Financing. For many years, vendors of equipment promoted leasing as a means of financing that would not appear on the balance sheet as a financial obligation. Because lease arrangements did not show up on the balance sheet, it appeared to unsophisticated investors or analysts that the company had less debt than was really the case.

Beginning in November 1976, the Financial Accounting Standards Board (*FASB*) required that financial lease obligations be reflected on the lessee's balance sheet.[1] Subsequent *FASB* statements, interpretations, and technical bulletins provide a rich body of literature on details of accounting for financial leases and presenting them in financial statements. Today, firms are required to reveal capital leases under fixed assets and to show the present value of future lease payments as a debt. The typical entries for a financial, or capital, lease are shown in Table 20–1.

Fixed Payments. Lease financing provides for payments of a fixed dollar amount. If, instead of leasing an asset, a company bought it and financed it with a bank loan, the interest charges on that loan might change when the

---

[1]Financial Accounting Standards Board, Statement No. 13.

Table 20–1
Balance Sheet Entries for Financial (Capital) Leases

Assets		Liabilities	
Current:		Current:	
Fixed:		Current portion of capital	
Buildings and equipment		lease obligations	xxx
under capital leases, less		Long term:	
accumulated amortization	xxx	Capital lease obligations, less	
		current portion	xxx
		Shareholders' equity	
Total	___	Total	___

bank's cost of funds changed. As a result, the dollar amount of the loan payments might vary.

Disadvantages of Leasing

Residual Value.   During a period of inflation, the market value of real assets may appreciate by more than was anticipated at the making of a lease agreement. For example, a firm that leases a warehouse instead of buying it may find at the conclusion of the lease term that the warehouse has quadrupled in value. By leasing, the firm has incurred an opportunity cost; if it had bought the warehouse, it could now sell it at four times its earlier value. The firm may have the option to purchase the warehouse now—but at the inflated value.

High Cost.   In some cases, the cost of leasing exceeds the cost of buying an asset and financing it by some other means. The cost of leasing and the cost of term loans will be compared later in this chapter.

Other Factors.   "Lost Lease, Must Move" describes a situation that can happen. When it does, the move can disrupt a business or even destroy it if the business depends on a particular location. For example, a college bookstore forced to move off campus will probably lose a large portion of its income.

Another problem is that a lessee may find it difficult to borrow funds to improve leased property, because the lender may not be able to obtain a security interest in the improvements.

Cost of Leasing versus Cost of Borrowing

In theory, businesses should separate investment decisions (decisions about whether to acquire assets) from financing decisions (decisions about how to finance assets). In practice, the distinction between investment and financing decisions becomes blurred when leasing is involved, because the financing is tied to the acquisition of a specific asset. Confusion arises because the cost and benefits of leasing may be analyzed in two ways. First, leasing can be considered an alternative means of financing and its costs compared with the costs of a term loan or a bond issue. Second, it can be considered in the context of a capital budgeting problem, where the objective is to determine the difference between the net present value of leasing and the net present value of buying.

To avoid confusion, we'll assume the first approach is used if the company knows the asset should be acquired. In this case, the problem is to determine how the asset can be financed at the lowest cost. The second approach is used when the company does not know whether to acquire the asset and when the acquisition may be tied to a leasing transaction. The $138 million Anaconda mill in Kentucky is one example of a project for which the net present value approach is useful. Frequently, such large transactions involve a leveraged lease. Analyzing this type of transaction becomes very complex and is beyond the scope of this book. Therefore, we will focus on the first approach, examining some of the issues and practices involved in evaluating the cost of leasing versus the cost of buying with funds borrowed from a bank.

For example, Hard Rock Mining Company has decided to acquire a new drilling machine. According to the vendor, the machine is made of a maintenance-free space age metal. It costs $1,000,000 and the company expects to use it for at least 5 years. At the end of that time, the machine will have no salvage value; but Hard Rock usually keeps old drills for use in case new ones break down.

Hard Rock must finance about $1,000,000. It can borrow the money by obtaining a 5-year term loan at 8 percent interest from a bank. Alternately, it can lease the machine for the same period. The financial manager of Hard Rock Mining Company has analyzed proposals from two leasing companies and a bank to determine the lowest-cost method of financing. For simplicity, we will assume that both leasing companies, like the bank, charge 8 percent. Both leasing companies and the bank are willing to provide financing; but the financial manager has found subtle, yet costly, differences in their proposals.

Evaluating the Cost of Leasing One leasing company and the bank will accept payments at the end of each of the 5 years. Because the payments represent an annuity, we can determine the amount of each payment by dividing the total cost by the interest factor for the present value of an annuity.

$$R^E = \frac{A}{PVAIF_{i,n}}$$
(20–1)

where

R^E = Periodic payments at ends of periods
A = Total cost
$PVAIF_{i,n}$ = Interest factor for present value of an annuity of i percent for n years

With an interest rate of 8 percent and five periods, the payments amount to $250,457 each, determined as follows.

$$R^E = \frac{A}{PVAIF_{8\%,\ 5\ \text{years}}}$$

$$= \frac{\$1,000,000}{3.9927}$$

$$= \$250,457$$

For convenience, we'll round the figure to $250,000.

The other leasing company's annual payments are lower, but it wants the first year's payment in advance and the remaining payments at the beginnings of Years 1 through 4. (Many leasing companies require payments in advance.) The equation to determine the annual payment in this case is as follows.

$$R^B = \frac{A}{1 + PVAIF_{i,n-1}} \qquad (20\text{--}2)$$

where

R^B = Periodic payments at beginnings of periods

Substituting the relevant numbers into the equation yields the annual payment figure of $231,906.

$$R^B = \frac{A}{1 + PVAIF_{8\%,\ 4\ \text{years}}}$$

$$= \frac{\$1,000,000}{4.3121}$$

$$= \$231,906$$

For convenience, again, we'll round the figure to $232,000.

The difference between Equation 20–1 and Equation 20–2 is in the denominator. In Equation 20–1, the denominator is $PVIF_{i,n}$. In Equation 20–2, the denominator is $1 + PVAIF_{i,n-1}$; here, the first term (1) represents the payment made at the beginning of the year. The subscript $n - 1$ indicates that the interest factor used should cover only the four remaining payments of the 5-year lease.

At first glance, annual lease payments of $232,000 appear preferable to payments of $250,000. However, after taking taxes and the time value of money into account, the financial manager has discovered that the firm will actually save money if it makes five $250,000 payments. The information presented in Table 20–2 was used to make that determination.

The first line in Table 20–2 contains data that pertain to the lease for which all payments are made at the end of the year. Recall that each payment amounts to about $250,000. Lease payments are tax deductible in the year in which they apply. (As you will see, however, the year in which a payment applies is not necessarily the year in which it is made.) Hard Rock Mining Company is in the 40 percent income tax bracket, so its after-tax cost is $150,000, or 60 percent of the lease payment.

$$\text{After-tax cost of leasing} = \text{Lease payment} (1 - \text{Tax rate})$$

$$= \$250,000 (1 - 0.4)$$

$$= \$150,000 \qquad (20-3)$$

There is considerable debate as to what discount rate should be used to determine the present value of the after-tax cash flows. If the lease is being evaluated as part of a financing decision, the appropriate rate might be the firm's after-tax cost of debt (k_d), which was explained in Chapter 7. If the lease is being evaluated as an investment decision, the appropriate rate might be the firm's target cost of capital. Usually, both rates result in the same conclusion with respect to financing decisions. Because the data presented in Table 20–2 deal with a financing decision, the after-tax costs are discounted

Table 20–2
Cost of Two Leases (thousands of dollars)[a]

Timing of Payments	Years	Lease Payment (at 8%) (1)	After-Tax Cost (40% tax bracket) (1) × (1 − 0.4) (2)	Present Value of Expenditures (6% discount rate) $PV_{6\%,\,n} \times (2)$ (3)		
1. All payments at year end	1–5	$250	$150	$PVAIF_{6\%,\,5\text{ years}} = 4.2123 \times (2) =$		$632
2. First payment in advance; remaining payments at beginnings of Years 1–4	0	$232	$232[b]	$PVAIF_{6\%,\,0\text{ years}} = 1.0000 \times (2) =$		$232
	1–4	$232	$139	$PVAIF_{6\%,\,4\text{ years}} = 3.4651 \times (2) =$		$482
	5	0	−$ 93[c]	$PVIF_{6\%,\,5\text{ years}} = 0.7473 \times (2) =$		−$ 69
						$645

[a]Rounded to nearest thousand.
[b]No tax deduction in Year 0; after-tax cost is same as payment.
[c]Year 4 payment is tax-deductible in Year 5 ($232 × 0.4 = $92.8 ≅ $93).

by Hard Rock's after-tax cost of debt, which is 6 percent. Thus, the present value of the cash flows from the first lease proposal is $632,000. Do not confuse the after-tax cost of debt with the 8 percent cost of the lease under consideration.

The remaining three lines of the table deal with the other lease proposal. Here, the first payment of $232,000 is made at the end of Year 0. Because the lease payment applies to the first year, however, it is tax deductible *not* in Year 0 but in Year 1. Similarly, the payment made in the first year does not apply until the second year, and so on. The present value of the $93,000 tax deduction in Year 5 is subtracted from the present value of the other cash flows. This tax saving compensates for the lack of tax benefit in Year 0, when the first payment was made. The sum of the present values of the cash flows is about $645,000.

Comparing the present values in Table 20–2 shows that the lessor that requires lease payments of $250,000 offers the proposal with the lower present value. The reason the present value is lower relates to the timing of the payments; payments made at year end are more favorable to the lessee than payments made in advance. Remember that the present values relate to cash *expenditures*, so Hard Rock prefers a lower present value to a higher one. In other words, it wishes to spend as little as possible for financing.

Evaluating Term Loans As mentioned, a commercial bank is willing to make a 5-year term loan at a fixed interest rate of 8 percent. The annual amortization payments are made at the end of each year and amount to $250,457 each, as determined by use of Equation 20–1.

$$R^E = \frac{A}{PVAIF_{i,n}}$$

$$= \frac{A}{PVAIF_{8\%,\ 5\ years}}$$

$$= \frac{\$1,000,000}{3.9927}$$

$$= \$250,457$$

Once again, we will round this amount to $250,000.

Table 20–3 shows the repayment schedule for the term loan. The interest on the loan is based on the declining balance. During the first year, the balance is $1 million and the 8 percent interest amounts to $80,000. This means that $80,000 of the $250,000 loan payment is applied to interest and the remaining $170,000 is used to amortize the loan. Subtracting the $170,000 amortization from the original $1 million loan balance yields the remaining

Table 20–3
Loan Repayment Schedule (thousands of dollars)[a]

Year End	Loan Payments (1)	Interest 0.08 × Previous Balance (2)	Amortization (1) − (2) (3)	Balance at End of Year Previous Balance − (3) (4)
0				$1,000
1	$ 250	$ 80	$ 170	830
2	250	66	184	646
3	250	52	198	448
4	250	36	214	230
5	250	20	230	0
	$1,250	$250	$1,000	$ 0

[a]Figures are rounded to the nearest thousand dollar.

balance, $830,000. In the second year, interest is about $66,000 (0.08 × $830,000 = $66,400) and the remainder of the $250,000 payment goes toward amortizing the loan. The process continues until the loan is paid off at the end of Year 5.

An examination of the loan repayment schedule reveals that interest accounts for a larger proportion of the loan payment in the first few years than in later years, because the interest is based on a declining balance. Thus, a relatively small part of the loan is amortized in the first few years. This is important if the firm is considering early prepayment of the loan. First, in the early years of the loan a large loan balance is still outstanding. Second, the lender may charge a penalty for early prepayment of the loan balance. Such penalties are frequently based on a percentage of the interest due.[2]

Cost and Depreciation.   Determining the present value of loan payments is similar to determining the present value of lease payments. The relevant cash flows are discounted by the firm's after-tax cost of debt—in this case, 6 percent. However, the method of depreciation used also affects the cost of purchasing the equipment.

Table 20–4 shows how much Hard Rock will pay for a $1 million term loan if it uses straight-line depreciation. Because this is a loan and not a lease, the annual payment is not tax deductible. However, the interest payments and

[2]The **Rule of 78s** is commonly used to calculate the interest rate penalty charged when installment and other types of loans are paid off before they are due. Suppose that a firm borrows $1,000, to be repaid in 12 monthly installments. The annual finance charge is $100 (10%). To determine the amount of interest collected on early prepayments, add all the whole numbers between 1 and 12 (1 + 2 + ⋯ + 12 = 78). The sum is 78. If the loan is repaid after one month, the lender will collect 12/78 of the finance charge (12/78) = $15.38). If the loan is repaid after two months, the lender will collect 23/78 of the finance charge (12/78 + 11/78 = 23/78 = $29.49). After three months, the lender collects $42.31 (12/78 + 11/78 + 10/78 = 33/78 = $42.31). Using this method, the lender collects most of the interest even if the loan is paid off early. The sum for loans with other maturities is calculated in the same manner.

Table 20–4

Cost of a Term Loan with Straight-Line Depreciation (thousands of dollars)[a]

Year End	Loan Payments (1)	Interest[b] (2)	Depreciation[c] (Straight-Line) (3)	Tax Savings (2 + 3)(0.4) (4)	After-Tax Cash Flows (1) − (4) (5)	$PVIF_{6\%,\,n}$	(5) × $PV_{6\%,\,n}$ (6)
1	$250	$80	$100	$ 72	$178	0.943	$168
2	250	66	200	106	144	0.890	128
3	250	52	200	101	149	0.840	125
4	250	36	200	94	156	0.791	124
5	250	20	200	88	162	0.747	121
6			100	40	− 40	0.705	− 28
							$638

Note Tax rate = 0.4.

[a] Rounded to the nearest thousand.

[b] From Table 20–3.

[c] The half-year convention rule for depreciation applies.

the depreciation of the drilling machine are tax-deductible. Therefore, we determine the after-tax cost by subtracting these tax savings from the loan payment. Then, we subtract the after-tax cost from the loan payment to find the relevant cash flow. When the cash flows are discounted at 6 percent, the cost of the term loan is about $638,000.

Table 20–5 shows the cost of the term loan if Hard Rock uses the ACRS. This accelerated method depreciates a somewhat larger proportion of the asset's value in the early years than straight-line depreciation. This is important because present value assigns a greater weight to the first few years than to more distant years. The net result is that the cost of the term loan when the accelerated method is used is $623,000—$15,000 less than the cost under straight-line depreciation.

Comparing Costs After evaluating the two leasing proposals and the term loan, the financial manager of Hard Rock Mining Company has concluded that the term loan is the lowest-cost method of financing the drilling machine. As you can see in the following table, the costs range from a high of $645,000 for one of the leases to a low of $623,000 for the term loan when ACRS is used.

Source of Financing	Present Value of Costs
Leases:	
Payments at ends of periods	$632,000
Payments at beginnings of periods	$645,000
Term loan:	
Straight-line depreciation	$638,000
ACRS	$623,000

Table 20–5
Cost of a Term Loan with *ACRS* (thousands of dollars)[a]

Year End	Loan Payments (1)	Interest[b] (2)	Depreciation (ACRS) (3)	Tax Savings (2 + 3)(0.4) (4)	After-Tax Cash Flows (1) − (4) (5)	$PVIF_{6\%,\,n}$	(5) × $PV_{6\%,\,n}$ (6)
1	$250	$80	$200	$112	$138	0.943	$130
2	250	66	320	154	96	0.890	85
3	250	52	192	98	152	0.840	128
4	250	36	115	60	190	0.792	150
5	250	20	115	54	196	0.747	146
6			58	23	− 23	0.705	− 16
							$623

[a]Rounded to the nearest thousand.
[b]From Table 20–3.

It should be noted that cost may not be the only consideration in a decision whether to lease or buy. Other factors, such as service contracts, cancellation options, availability, flexibility, and so on, must also be taken into account. If the cost of leasing and the cost of alternative methods of financing are about equal, other advantages and disadvantages will be the deciding factors.

Summary

In general, leasing is a mechanism by which a firm can use an asset without owning it. Types of leases include operating leases and financial leases. Financial leasing involves tax benefits, but only if the lease involved is a true financial lease. Equations related to leasing are reviewed in Table 20–6.

Leasing creates other benefits, such as flexibility and the avoidance of ob-

Table 20–6
Summary of Equations

	Equation	Equation Number
Lease payment (end of period)	$R^E = \dfrac{A}{PVAIF_{i,n}}$	(20–1)
Lease payment (first payment at beginning period)	$R^B = \dfrac{A}{1 + PVAIF_{i,n\,-1}}$	(20–2)
After-tax cost of leasing	After-tax cost of leasing = Lease payment (1 − Tax rate)	(20–3)

solescence. Disadvantages include possible opportunity costs related to rising market values, as well as high costs and other problems.

Once the decision has been made to acquire an asset, the financing decision becomes important. Should the asset be financed with a lease or a term loan? The process of comparing the financing costs of these methods of funding consists of discounting the relevant cash flows from leasing and discounting the term loan by the firm's after-tax cost of debt. Then, the alternative that provides the lowest cost may be selected.

Important Terms

Capital lease	Leveraged lease
Financial lease	Operating lease
Full payout net lease	Rule of 78s
Lease	Sale and leaseback
Lessee	Service lease
Lessor	True financial lease

Questions

1. What is an operating lease? Compare the provisions of an operating lease with those of a financial lease.
2. Which kind of lease contract is best for lessees if they are not sure of continued need for an asset? Why?
3. What kind of lease is best for lessors who want some physical control over the leased asset? Why?
4. Describe the role of each of the three participants in a leveraged lease. What are the benefits to the lessee?
5. Why is it important to identify whether or not a lease is a true financial lease?
6. What flexibility does lease financing give the lessee that other financing terms might not provide?
7. Explain the disadvantages of leasing assets rather than purchasing them.
8. Why is separating the investment and financing decision in a lease analysis more difficult than in other types of analysis?
9. All else being equal, why are beginning-of-year lease payments less desirable for lessees than end-of-year payments?
10. Compare the tax deductions available to a firm from purchasing an asset with those from leasing the same asset.
11. Why do interest charges account for a larger proportion of installment loan payments in early periods than in later periods? How does this affect the cost of financing an asset through a term loan?
12. On what financial basis should the decision to lease rather than purchase an asset be made?

Problems

1. Acme Leasing has purchased a road grader for lease to the city of Bloomington. The cost of the grader is $450,000 and its expected life is 10 years. Acme requires a 10 percent rate of return on all leases. What lease payments will it charge if they are to be made on a beginning-of-year basis? What payments will be charged if they are made on an end-of-year basis?

2. Elbert Leasing has acquired a new fleet of limousines to be leased to firms that provide their executives with a car and driver. Each limo costs $50,000 and will be leased for a period of 3 years. If Elbert requires a 12 percent rate of return on lease agreements, what beginning-of-year payments will it charge? What end-of-year payments?

3. Gains Drilling Company has leased a truck-mounted drilling rig for a 5-year period. Annual lease payments are $160,000 at the beginning of each year. What are the after-tax cash flows required for Gains? Gains is in the 30 percent tax bracket.

4. Suppose the lease payments for Gains Drilling Company in Problem 3 are to be made at the end of each of the 5 years. What after-tax cash flows are required of Gains?

5. What are the after-tax cash flows associated with each of the following leases? Assume a 40 percent tax bracket.
   (a) Annual payment, $40,000; length, 3 years; beginning-of-year payments
   (b) Annual payment $180,000; length, 10 years; end-of-year payments
   (c) Annual payment $95,000; length, 6 years; beginning-of-year payments

6. Brie Cheese Company is borrowing $45,000 on a term loan agreement from the Mole City Bank. The loan is to be paid over a 10-year period at an interest rate of 10 percent annually. What end-of-year annual payments are required? What will the loan balance be after the first payment?

7. Suppose that Brie Cheese Company in Problem 6 repays the $45,000 over an 8-year period. What end-of-year annual payments are required? What dollar amount of interest charges will be owed the second year?

8. Sam's Sandwich Shop borrowed $10,000 from the bank 4 months ago on an installment basis. The interest rate was 9 percent and the maturity of the loan was 12 months. Sam is now able to repay the full balance after only 4 payments. According to the Rule of 78s, how much interest will the bank collect?

9. Beaumont Bowl Corporation is interested in leasing a small computer. Management has decided on an eighth-generation model made by a reputable manufacturer, and two leasing companies have submitted proposals for 7 year leases. Proposal A requires $80,000 at the beginning of each year; Proposal B requires $92,000 at the end of each year. Beaumont is in the 30 percent tax bracket and uses an 8 percent discount rate for decisions of this type. Which lease has the lowest cost?

10. Elmer Electronics is evaluating two leases for new equipment. One requires beginning-of-year payments of $84,000 and the other calls for end-of-year payments of $90,000. Both leases are for 20 years. If Elmer is in the 40 percent tax bracket and the discount rate is 10 percent, which lease is most advantageous to Elmer?

11. Catonic Seltzer Company has recently negotiated a 5-year, 12 percent loan for $150,000 from a local bank. The proceeds will be used to purchase a new machine to produce carbonated water, on which straight-line depreciation will be taken.

There is no salvage value anticipated and the equipment has a 5-year life. Catonic is in the 40 percent tax bracket and the discount rate is 8 percent. Calculate the after-tax cost of purchasing the machine with the term loan.

12. Suppose instead that Catonic Seltzer Company in Problem 11 can lease the same equipment for five beginning-of-year lease payments of $50,000 each. Is the lease or the purchase a better method of financing the machine?

13. Dillard's Delivery is considering the purchase of a new truck for $64,000. The truck has a 3-year life. No salvage value is anticipated and straight-line depreciation is used. Northrup National Bank has offered a term loan with end-of-year payments at a 14 percent rate. The truck could also be leased for three beginning-of-year payments of $24,000. Dillard's is in the 35 percent tax bracket and uses a 9 percent discount rate for decisions of this type. Which alternative should be selected?

14. Bellview Bicycle is analyzing a lease-versus-purchase decision for new manufacturing equipment costing $1.4 million with a depreciable life of 10 years. The firm can borrow from Cascade National Bank at a cost of 10 percent per year with repayments in 10 equal end-of-year installments; it uses straight-line depreciation and is in the 30 percent tax bracket.

As an alternative, Bellview can lease the equipment for $225,000 per year, payable at the beginning of each of the next 10 years. Which financing plan should be chosen if the discount rate is 7 percent?

Bonds

The major types of corporate debt are bank loans and bonds. This chapter focuses on corporate bonds, which are basically long-term IOUs sold by businesses to investors. They provide an important source of funds during the expansion and stabilization phases of the life cycle. In general, they are sold by medium-sized and large companies to finance plant and equipment. Small firms are frequently excluded from this method of financing.

After reading this chapter, you should know the following.

1. What types of collateral are used as security for bonds.
2. Why some bonds that have no collateral security may be better than some that do have security.
3. Why some bonds have their interest payments guaranteed and why others may not pay interest.
4. How bonds are retired.
5. How some investors retain the security of a bond while sharing in the growth of the company.
6. How the refunding of a bond issue is accomplished.
7. How bond ratings affect interest costs.

Overview

Corporate business concerns borrow billions of dollars every year. The amounts they borrow vary from year to year, depending on the condition of the economy and the financial markets. For example, nonfinancial corporate borrowings ranged from $54 billion during the 1982 recession to $110 billion in 1984 when the economy was expanding. While the composition of business borrowings also varies widely, bonds and bank loans are the principal sources of funds. Other important sources include mortgage loans, commercial paper, finance company loans, and U.S. government loans.

Table 21–1 shows the gross proceeds of new corporate bond issues in 1984. The top part of the table reveals that most of the bonds were **publicly offered**

Table 21–1
Gross Proceeds of New Corporate Bond Issues
in 1984 (billions of dollars)

	Amount	Percent
Type of Offering		
Public	$ 73.4	66.9%
Private	36.3	33.1
	$109.7	100.0%
Industry Group		
Manufacturing	24.6	22.4%
Commercial and miscellaneous	13.7	12.5
Transportation	4.7	4.3
Public Utility	10.7	9.8
Communication	3.0	2.7
Real estate and financial	53.0	48.3
	$109.7	100.0%

Source   Board of Governors of the Federal Reserve System

(that is, sold to the public). The remainder were **privately placed** with financial institutions such as life insurance companies, pension plans, and state and local government retirement plans.

The lower part of the table shows the major industry groups that issued bonds in 1984. Real estate and financial corporations, followed by manufacturing corporations, were the largest issuers during the period shown. Although the proportions may vary from year to year, these groups usually account for most bond offerings.

Types of Bonds

One way to classify corporate bonds relates to the type of security or collateral backing them. Security is provided by liens against assets of the borrowing corporation. Bondholders, like other lenders, like to think their interests are protected by holding a lien on the borrower's assets. Although this is true in a legal sense, from a practical point of view, their best protection is the earning power of the issuing corporation. That is why many bonds issued today are unsecured.

The specific terms of each bond (interest rates, maturity, security, and so on) are described in the **indenture**, or bond contract. The indenture also describes **covenants**, or limitations placed on the issuer.

Debentures **Debentures** are bonds backed by the general credit of the issuing corporation without specific liens against particular assets. These bonds are widely used by well-established companies that have high credit ratings. Although debentures are the weakest form of bond in terms of security, a debenture from a strong corporation may be a better investment than a bond secured by the assets of a weak corporation that cannot meet its financial obligations. Nevertheless, because debentures are backed only by the general credit of the issuer, they generally carry slightly higher interest rates than issues of similar quality backed by specific assets. For example, if a company issues a debenture and a mortgage bond at the same time, the debenture's interest rate will be slightly higher. However, the interest rate on the debenture of a strong company may be lower than the interest rate on a bond backed by the assets of a weak company. The reason, of course, relates to the lender's risk.

Mortgage Bonds Bonds secured by liens on real estate are known as **mortgage bonds**. Those secured by the first mortgage are called **first-mortgage bonds**. Similarly, **second-mortgage bonds** are backed by the second mortgage, and so on.

Claims based on second and subsequent mortgages are subordinated to claims based on the first mortgage. Bonds backed by such collateral are called **general mortgage bonds** or **consolidated mortgage bonds**. (Changing the name of, say, a fifth-mortgage bond to a consolidated mortgage bond makes some investors happy. Perhaps they do not understand the terminology, or perhaps the security associated with the specific mortgage is not important to them.)

Mortgage bonds that prohibit other mortgage liens against the property used as collateral are called **closed-end mortgage bonds**. Bonds without that restrictive covenant are called **open-end mortgage bonds**.

Collateral Trust Bonds

Collateral trust bonds are secured by stocks and bonds owned by the issuing corporation. The securities are deposited with a trustee, such as a bank, for the benefit of the bondholders. Corporations frequently use their own bonds as collateral. When collateral trust bonds are secured by mortgage bonds, they have the same lien as a mortgage bond. This enhances the collateral trust bonds' value.

Equipment Obligations

The equipment obligation is a method of financing used to acquire *rolling stock*, such as railroad cars or airliners. The obligation is secured by the rolling stock and the general credit of the issuing corporation. The most widely used form of equipment obligation involves a lease arrangement called the **Philadelphia Plan**. Under this arrangement, certificates known as **equipment trust certificates** are sold to investors to pay for part of the equipment. A large advance payment by the borrower covers the remainder. The borrower then makes lease payments to a trustee for the benefit of the certificate holders. The lease generally runs about 15 years. Usually, earnings generated by the rolling stock are sufficient to pay off the obligation at a rate faster than that at which the equipment is depreciated. Investors generally consider equipment trust certificates to be high-grade investments.

Industrial Revenue Bonds

Some state and local governments induce companies to move to their communities by providing them low-cost lease payments on plants and other facilities. These facilities are financed by the sale of **industrial revenue bonds, or private activity bonds,** which are secured in principal and interest by the industrial user. To accomplish the financing, the government body sells bonds to supply plant and equipment. These, in turn, are leased to the company for a period of 10 to 15 years. At the end of that period, the company can buy the plant and equipment.

State and local governments may use similar methods to finance corporate expenditures on environmental improvements by means of **pollution-control bonds**. For example, the state of Ohio sold $17.5 million in environmental improvement revenue bonds to finance emission control systems for United States Steel Corporation at its Lorain, Ohio, facility.[1]

An advantage of financing with industrial revenue–type bonds was that bonds sold by state and local government before August 15, 1986 were **tax exempt**, which meant that investors who bought them paid no federal income tax on the interest they supplied. Tax-exempt bonds are usually bought by banks and wealthy investors who want tax-free income. These bonds carry lower interest rates than taxable issues. The lower interest rates are reflected in lower lease payments for the lessee.

Under the Tax Reform Act of 1986, private activity bonds are not tax exempt, except for certain issues used for airports, docks, waste disposal facilities, and so on.

Special Types of Bonds

Several special types of bonds have been created to meet the needs of corporations. They are variants of the basic types of bonds just discussed.

Junk Bonds **Junk bonds**, as their name implies, are not considered high-quality investments. These bonds are used in connection with mergers and takeovers. For example, a prospective buyer may sell junk bonds to raise money to acquire a firm, planning to sell parts of the firm to pay off the bonds if the takeover attempt succeeds.

Guaranteed Bonds **Guaranteed bonds** develop from mergers, from consolidations, and from financing subsidiaries. Basically, one corporation guarantees the financial obligations of another. The guarantee applies to interest, principal, or both. The terms of the guarantee are usually stated on the face or the back of the bond, in which case the bond is referred to as **stamped** or **endorsed**. Bonds guaranteed by two or more corporations are called **joint bonds**. The value of the guarantee depends on the financial strength of the corporations involved.

Guaranteed bonds are not the same as **assumed bonds**, which are obligations issued by one company that have been taken over, or assumed, by another company.

Income Bonds Several types of hybrid bonds developed out of the reorganizations of railroads and other types of businesses. The hybrid bonds were exchanged for other

[1]Ohio Air Quality Development Authority, State of Ohio, 6–12 Percent Floating Rate Environmental Improvement Revenue Bonds, 1980 Series B (United States Steel Corporation Project), Due 2010.

bonds or stocks held by investors in railroads that could not meet their financial obligations. Suppose, for example, that investors hold a bond secured by the railroad track between two small towns. If the railroad defaults on the bond, the investors will have to rip up the track and try to sell it to recover their investment. Obviously, this is not a workable solution in most cases.

The railroad may offer to exchange **income bonds** (sometimes called **adjustment bonds**) for the bonds held by the investors. The income bonds will pay interest only if income is earned by the corporation—that is, the payment of interest is secured by the corporation's income. The interest payments are generally *cumulative*, which means that they accumulate until there is sufficient income for them to be paid. The corporation gains an advantage in that it does not have to make interest payments until it earns sufficient income. From the investor's point of view, the promise of some income is better than no income at all.

Participating Bonds   A **participating bond** not only bears a fixed rate of interest but also offers a profit-sharing feature. In other words, the bondholder is entitled to participate in earnings along with shareholders to the extent described in the bond's indenture. Participating bonds are not common in the United States, but they are used in Europe. In the United States, they are usually used by companies that want to attract bond investors by offering an extra inducement. Because investors expect to earn more than the interest paid on the bond, they may be willing to accept an interest rate lower than what they would demand from a straight bond with no special feature.

Bonds with Warrants   Some bonds include **warrants**, which give the bondholder the right to purchase common stock at some specified price. The price is usually higher than the market price of the stock at the time the bond is issued. Most warrants are *detachable*, which means they can be detached from the bonds and traded separately. Such bonds are generally issued by companies that require an extra inducement to attract investors. As mentioned, such inducements reduce interest costs. However, the increased number of shares outstanding may result in diluted earnings (lower earnings per share), which may be more costly in the long run.

Zero-Coupon Bonds   A **zero-coupon bond** does not make periodic interest payments; the interest is built into the price of the bond. The bonds are sold at a deep discount (a price far below the face value) and the investors receive the full face value of the bond (usually $1,000) when it matures. The market price of a zero-coupon bond may be determined by the following equation.

$$P_0 = \frac{F}{(1 + k_{db})^n} \qquad (21-1)$$

where

P_0 = Market value at time zero
F = Face value of the bond, payable at maturity
k_{db} = Rate of return required by bondholders
n = Number of periods

To illustrate the use of this equation, let's assume a company wants to issue a zero-coupon bond with 15 years to maturity and bondholders require a 10 percent rate of return. Using Equation 21–1, we find the bond's price to be $239.39, a deep discount.

$$P_0 = \frac{F}{PVIF_{10\%,\ 15\ years}}$$

$$= \frac{\$1,000}{4.1773}$$

$$= \$239.39$$

Recently, J. C. Penney issued a zero-coupon bond priced at $247.50 and Archer–Daniels–Midland issued one at $262.50. The yields on the bonds are 13.91 percent and 14.11 percent, respectively. Both bonds mature in 1992.

Zero-coupon debt securities are widely used, especially for short-term issues. For example, U.S. Treasury bills are sold at a discount and are redeemable at face value. Commercial paper, bank certificates of deposit, and savings bonds are additional examples.

Bond Retirement Features

Businesses retire bonds by using one or more of eight principal methods: (1) paying a lump sum at maturity, (2) converting to stock, (3) calling, (4) retiring serially, (5) using a sinking fund, (6) purchasing on the open market, (7) defeasing, and (8) swapping for stock. The first method is self-explanatory; the others are described here.

Conversion is the only method of retirement in which the bondholder decides to retire the bonds rather than the issuing corporation. The business frequently obtains funds to pay off bonds at retirement by selling new bonds to replace the old ones. The new bonds are commonly called **refunding bonds**. Refunding will be discussed later in the chapter.

Convertible Bonds Conversion provisions offer bondholders the opportunity to share in the growth of a company by converting their bonds into a specified number of shares of common stock at a specified price. For example, a bond with a $1,000 par value may be convertible into common stock at $50 per share. That means the bondholder can exchange each **convertible bond** into 20 shares of common stock ($1,000/$50 = 20).

If the market value of the stock increases from $50 to $60 per share, the bondholder can still convert each bond to 20 shares of stock; so the bond is now worth $1,200 ($60 × 20 = $1,200). However, a decrease in the stock's price below the conversion price of $50 per share does not cause the bond's value to fall. If the market price of the stock falls below $50, the bond sells at its true bond value, which depends on the market rate of interest and may be above or below face value.[2] Investors who buy convertible bonds can therefore benefit from increases in the value of the company's stock and still have the security of a bond if stock prices fall. Convertible bonds are discussed in more detail in Chapter 23.

Companies frequently force conversion by calling their bonds (repurchasing them before maturity) when their stock's price is above the conversion price. One reason for forcing conversion is to obtain additional equity capital. Another is to reduce the debt ratio.

Because convertible bonds are attractive to investors seeking both growth and safety, they generally carry lower coupon interest rates than nonconvertible bonds issued by the same corporation.

Callable Bonds Corporations frequently reserve the right to call in their bond issues before maturity at a small premium above the par value. The price at which the bonds are redeemable is the **call price**. This price may be, for example, 105, or 105 percent of the bond's par value. The call provision is used for the following reasons.

1. *To avoid high interest rates over prolonged periods.* Suppose a bond is issued when market rates of interest are 17 percent; 2 years later, market rates are 10 percent. If the company could call the issue and replace it with one at 10 percent, it could save a substantial amount of money. However, investors who buy bonds at high rates like their high returns. Therefore, they may require a **call protection** feature on the bonds. This clause in the indenture states that the company cannot call the bonds for a certain period of time—usually 3 to 5 years or longer.
2. *To eliminate bond issues with clauses unfavorable to the company in the indenture.* For example, the indenture may prohibit the company from issuing any additional bonds until this issue is paid off.
3. *To force holders of convertible bonds to convert when it is in the company's interest that they do so.* If the stock is selling above the conversion price, the company may want to call the bonds to reduce its debt ratio.
4. *To satisfy sinking fund requirements.* Sinking funds are described later.

[2]Convertible bond values also reflect the value of an implicit call option. Call options are explained in Appendix 23A.

The size of the premium a company must pay when it calls its bond issues depends on when the bond is called. For example, if the bond has been outstanding for 5 years, the premium might be 1.75 percent of the principal amount. Bonds called in later years will have progressively smaller premiums. When companies call bonds, they use serial numbers drawn by lot to determine what bonds will be called.

Serial Bonds The bonds in a **serial bond** issue mature at different dates instead of maturing at the same time. Thus, investors are offered a variety of maturities to meet their needs. Serial bonds are more common in real estate and equipment financing than in industrial financing, because the rental income from real estate is considered more stable than earnings from industrial concerns.

Serial maturities are also advantageous when the collateral depreciates over time. In the case of equipment trust certificates, you may recall, the bonds are retired faster than the equipment depreciates.

Sinking Funds A **sinking fund** provides for the periodic retirement of a certain portion of a bond issue through payments made by the corporation. Ordinarily, the payment is made to the trustee of the issue, usually a bank, which may let payments accumulate or may retire the bonds periodically by purchasing them in the open market or calling them. As long as the bonds may be bought in the open market at or below the call price, the company will use this method. However, when the market price is above the call price, it is advantageous to retire the bonds by exercising the call provision.

Under some circumstances, a sinking fund is necessary for the protection of the bondholder—for example, when the collateral consists of a wasting asset such as a coal mine. Bonds backed by mining properties frequently have a sinking fund based on the tonnage mined.

Sinking Fund Payments. The amount of funds a firm must pay periodically for the sinking fund can be determined by use of the following equation, which was developed in Chapter 5 in connection with one type of annuity.[3]

$$SF_a = AMT \frac{1}{FVAIF_{i,n}} \tag{21-2}$$

where

$$SF_a = \text{Sinking fund payment}$$
$$AMT = \text{Payment due at end of bond life}$$
$$i = \text{Interest rate earned per period}$$
$$n = \text{Number of periods}$$

[3]An alternate equation is the following.

$$SF_a = AMT \frac{i}{(1 + i)^n - 1}$$

By way of illustration, assume that a corporation needs $30 million in 15 years to pay off a bond. One requirement of the bond is that sinking fund payments be made at the end of each year to retire the issue when it matures. The accumulated payments in the sinking fund will be invested in U.S. Treasury securities. If the company can earn 12 percent after taxes on the sinking fund investments, the annual payment is $804,727.

$$SF_a = AMT \frac{1}{FVAIF_{12\%, \ 15 \ yrs}}$$

$$= \$30,000,000 \left(\frac{1}{37.280}\right)$$

$$= \$30,000,000 \ (0.0268)$$

$$= \$804,727$$

Open-Market Purchases Record interest rate levels of recent years have caused some bonds to sell at deep discounts. Because an inverse relationship exists between market interest rates and the prices of outstanding bonds, when interest rates go up, the market price of outstanding bonds declines. For example, suppose that 5 years ago a company issued a $1,000.00 bond paying 8 percent interest and maturing in 25 years. Today, interest rates are 12 percent and the market value of the bond is $699.10. Under these circumstances, the company might be tempted to buy the bonds in the open market at $699.10 today instead of paying $1,000.00 when the bonds mature, thereby saving around $300.00 per bond. However, the $300.00 gain from the early extinguishment of the debt is taxed at ordinary income tax rates. In addition, many companies prefer to retain the low-cost debt when current interest rates are high.

Defeasance **Defeasance** is an accounting term that refers to the extinguishment of debt.[4] The general idea behind defeasance is to retire old debt by depositing U.S. Treasury securities with a trustee empowered to pay out the interest and principal on the outstanding bonds as required by the indenture. This relieves the borrower of the responsibility for making the payments.

To illustrate how defeasance works, consider the Daytona Company. The company has outstanding a $50 million issue of 6 percent bonds that cannot be called for 5 years and then only on payment of a 3 percent call premium. To defease the outstanding bond issue, the company must set aside in an irrevocable trust a sufficient amount of U.S. Treasury securities to cover both principal and interest of the outstanding bonds when they become due. The securities in the trust can be funded by surplus cash or by the sale of new

---

[4]For additional details, see Financial Accounting Standards Board (*FASB*) 76.

securities. Treasury securities now yield 11 percent. The present value of the $50 million, 6 percent bond issue (until the call date in 5 years), discounted at 11 percent, is calculated as follows.

Principal	$29,672,566
Call premium	890,177
Interest (semiannual)	11,306,439
	$41,869,182

Daytona plans to sell a new bond issue to fund the Treasury securities it must hold. The company will sell a 5-year, 12 percent bond issue for $42 million. For simplicity, we'll ignore the flotation costs of the new bond. As shown on the balance sheet in Table 21–2, after defeasance this new debt will have replaced the old debt. The difference between the book value of the old debt ($50 million) and the present value of that debt (about $41.9 million, as shown before) is the gain from the defeasance. Assuming the company retains all its profit and is in the 50 percent income tax bracket, half the gain will go to retained earnings and the remainder to deferred income taxes.

The company will, of course, disclose to shareholders what it has done. However, the irrevocable trust does not appear on the balance sheet, although the balance sheet is substantially altered. The alterations affect the company's debt ratios, coverage ratios, and returns on assets and equity.

Daytona Company has total revenues of $300 million. Its net income is $10 million before defeasance and will be $14 million after defeasance. Its profit margin (i.e., net income/total revenue) will increase from 3.3 percent ($10/300 = 3.3) to 4.7 percent ($14/300 = 4.7). In addition, the return on assets (i.e., net income/total assets) will increase from 5 percent to 7 percent and the return on equity (i.e., net income/total equity) will increase from 10 percent to 13.5 percent.

Daytona will also reduce its financing costs by refinancing the $50 million,

Table 21–2
Daytona Company Balance Sheet
before and after Defeasance

(millions of dollars)		
	Before	**After**
Assets		
Cash	$100	$100
Fixed assets	100	100
	$200	$200
Liabilities and shareholders' equity		
Current liabilities	$ 50	$ 50
Deferred taxes		4
Long-term debt, 6%	50	
Long-term debt, 12%		42
Equity	100	104
	$200	$200

6 percent bond with a $42 million, 12 percent bond. The total after-tax cost, ignoring the time value of money, is $59 million for the old bond and $54.6 million for the new one—a saving of $4.4 million in financing costs.

	Old Bond Issue	New Bond Issue
Amount	$50,000,000	$42,000,000
Annual interest rate	×0.06	×0.12
Annual interest charge	$ 3,000,000	$ 5,040,000
Time period (5 years)	× 5	× 5
Call premium	$15,000,000	$25,200,000
for old bond	$ 3,000,000	
	$18,000,000	
Tax rate	0.50	0.50
Tax expense	$ 9,000,000	$12,600,000
Cost to retire bond	$50,000,000	$42,000,000
Total cost	$59,000,000	$54,600,000

Finally, it should be noted that Daytona's cost of capital will increase after defeasance because of the increased use of higher-cost debt.

Debt–Equity Swaps Bonds are recorded at face value on corporate balance sheets without regard for their market price. As a result of the general increase in the level of interest rates in recent decades, the market prices of some bonds are less than the values shown on corporate books. This difference between the book value of bonds and their market value has presented a profitable opportunity for some brokers, who buy bonds at a discount and trade them back to companies for stock. The brokers, in turn, sell the stock. The companies' balance sheets show less debt and more equity with much the same consequences as defeasance.

Debt–equity swaps do not relate only to bonds; they can also be used to deal in foreign financial markets, where *exchange rates*—the rates at which currencies can be exchanged for other currencies—often vary. For example, Vulcan Aggregates bought a British firm for $40 million and financed it with a $35 million loan from a British bank. At the time, the British pound sterling was worth $2.60 (that is, it took $2.60 U.S. dollars to buy 1 pound sterling), and both the British company and the British loan were valued on Vulcan's books in pounds. When the exchange rate dropped to $1.50, Vulcan sold stock to raise funds to buy pounds at the $1.50 exchange rate and pay off the old loan at the $2.60 exchange rate. The point is, when the market value of a liability is less than the value shown on the company's balance sheet, the opportunity for a debt–equity swap exists.

Bond Refunding

Refunding is retiring one bond issue and replacing it with another. This is accomplished by calling the old bond issue and selling a new one. Companies refund bonds for several reasons. The most common is that market interest

Table 21–3
Sportline Bond Issues

	Old Bond	New Bond
Face amount	$50,000,000	$50,000,000
Interest rate	12%	10%
Remaining maturity	20 years	20 years
Unamortized flotation cost	$800,000	$1,000,000
Call price	105% of face value	105% of face value
Tax rate—40%		
Overlap period—2 months		

rates have fallen and high-interest-rate bonds can be replaced with lower-interest-rate bonds. Another reason is to eliminate obnoxious restrictive covenants.

A bond refunding can be analyzed as a capital budgeting problem. The objective of the analysis is to determine the net present value (NPV) of the refunding operation.

$$\text{Net present value} = \begin{pmatrix} \text{Annual savings (present} \\ \text{value of an annuity} \\ \text{for the remaining life} \\ \text{of the bond)} \end{pmatrix} - \text{Investment outlay}$$

$$NPV = \text{Annual savings } (PVAIF_{i,n}) - \text{Investment outlay}$$
$$(21\text{–}3)$$

Here, the receipts are the savings that result from lower interest payments for the remaining life of the bond. The investment outlay takes into account the repurchase of the old bond and the sale of the new one. The whole process is complicated by some income tax factors that will be explained later. Nevertheless, if the NPV is positive, the firm should refund the bond issue.

To illustrate this approach to evaluating refunding decisions, suppose that 5 years ago Sportline Industries issued $50 million in debentures. The bond had a 12 percent coupon interest rate and a maturity of 25 years. It was callable at 105, which means that bondholders would receive a 5 percent premium above the par value if the bond was called. The flotation cost of the bond was $1 million. As a rule, the flotation cost is amortized over the life of the bond; here, it amounted to $40,000 per year ($1,000,000/25 years = $40,000/year). Today, 20 years remain to maturity, so the unamortized flotation cost is $800,000 (20/25 × $1,000,000 = $800,000).

Since the old bond's issuance, interest rates have declined. Today, the financial manager of Sportline Industries is considering refunding the old bond with a similar issue, but at a lower interest rate—10 percent. The relevant data are listed in Table 21–3.

Savings Recall that the first element of the NPV equation involves annual savings. The financial manager of Sportline began her analysis by calculating the annual

Table 21–4
Annual Savings for Sportline

	Old Bonds		New Bonds	
Before-tax interest		$6,000,000		$5,000,000
Tax-deductible expenses:				
Interest	$6,000,000		$5,000,000	
Amortized flotation costs[a]	40,000		50,000	
Total	$6,040,000		$5,050,000	
Less:				
Tax savings = 40% × total	$2,416,000	−2,416,000	$2,020,000	−2,020,000
After-tax interest		$3,584,000		$2,980,000
Savings:				
Old bond after-tax interest =	$ 3,584,000			
Less: New bond after-tax interest =	−2,980,000			
	$ 604,000			

[a]$800,000/20 years = $40,000/year; $1,000,000/20 years = $50,000/year.

savings that would result if the new bond was issued. The reduction in costs constitutes savings to Sportline. The details of the calculations are shown in Table 21–4.

You can see that tax considerations play an important part in the calculations. The tax-deductible costs associated with the bond issues are the annual interest payments and the amortized flotation cost. Because Sportline is in the 40 percent income tax bracket, its tax saving amounts to 40 percent of the total tax-deductible expense. For the new bond issue, the total tax-deductible expense is $5,050,000 and the tax saving is $2,020,000 (0.4 × $5,050,000 = $2,020,000). The tax saving is deducted from the before-tax interest payment to give the after-tax interest cost of $2,980,000. The same process is applied to the old bond. The final savings figure is the difference between the after-tax interest costs of the two bond issues, which amounts to $604,000 for the next 20 years. We will discount these savings to determine their present value after determining the investment outlay.

Table 21–5
Investment Outlay before Taxes for Sportline

Old bonds (outflow)	
Repayment of old bonds	$50,000,000
Call premium	2,500,000
Accrued interest[a]	1,000,000
Total	$53,500,000
Less:	
New bonds (inflow)	
Net proceeds[b]	−49,000,000
Equals: Before-tax investment outlay	$ 4,500,000

[a](2/12) × 0.12 × $50,000,000 = $1,000,000.
[b]Gross proceeds less flotation cost of $1 million.

Investment Outlay The second part of the *NPV* equation is the investment outlay. Table 21–5 shows Sportline's investment outlay before taxes. The outflow of funds associated with the old bonds consists of three items: (1) the $50 million to retire the old issue, (2) the $2.5 million call premium (0.05 × $50,000,000 = $2,500,000), and $1 million in accrued interest.

Accrued interest is interest that must be paid on the old bonds during the **overlap period**—the time between the issuance of the new bonds and the retirement of the old ones. The overlap period, which is generally 1 or 2 months, allows the issuing company some flexibility in the timing of the new bond issue. In this example, we'll assume the overlap period is 2 months. The amount of accrued interest is $1 million, determined by multiplying 2 months (2/12) by 12 percent by $50 million. The total outlay for the old bonds is $53.5 million, as shown in the table.

The flotation cost for the new $50 million bond issue is $1 million; so the net proceeds to Sportline are $49 million. Subtracting the net proceeds from the outlays for the old bonds yields the before-tax investment outlay, $4.5 million.

The call premium is tax deductible in the year in which it is paid. In addition, the accrued interest and the unamortized flotation costs are tax deductible. As shown in Table 21–6, these expenses amount to $4.3 million. Since Sportline is in the 40 percent income tax bracket, the after-tax investment outlay is $2,780,000.

Net Present Value To find the net present value of the refunding operation, we must first discount the annual savings by the appropriate interest rate and then subtract the investment outlay. There is considerable debate about what interest rate is appropriate, and a full discussion of the issue is beyond the scope of this text.[5] Several interest rates may be used: the firm's cost of capital, the before-tax cost of the new bond, and the after-tax cost of the new bond.

We can reject the firm's cost of capital, because from the firm's point of

Table 21–6
Investment Outlay after Taxes for Sportline

Before-tax investment outlay		$4,500,000
Tax-deductible expenses:		
Call premium	$2,500,000	
Accrued interest	1,000,000	
Unamortized flotation cost	800,000	
Total	$4,300,000	
Less: Tax savings of 40% × Total from column 2		−1,720,000
Equals: After-tax investment outlay		$2,780,000

[5]Ahron R. Ofer and Robert A. Taggart, Jr., "Bond Refunding: A Clarifying Analysis," *Journal of Finance*, March 1977, pp. 21–30.

view, bond refunding is different from other types of investments. Using the before-tax cost of debt would be equivalent to refunding the old bond with an equity issue instead of a bond issue. Because the old bond issue is being refunded with a new bond issue, the appropriate discount rate is the after-tax interest rate on the new issue. This rate best reflects the firm's opportunity cost. The rate is determined by multiplying the before-tax interest rate by 1 minus the tax rate. The interest rate on the new bond issue is 10 percent, and the tax rate is 40 percent, so the after-tax interest rate is 6 percent $[0.10 \times (1 - 0.40) = 0.06]$.

Because the annual savings will occur over a 20-year period, we determine the present value of the savings by multiplying the savings by the interest factor for the present value of a 20-year annuity (11.4699). After subtracting the investment outlay from the discounted savings, we find the net present value to be $4,147,820.

$$NPV = \text{Annual savings } (PVAIF_{6\%,\ 20\ years}) - \text{Investment outlay}$$

$$= \$604,000\ (11.4699) - \$2,780,000$$

$$= \$4,147,820$$

The Cost of Bonds

Interest Rates The discussion of refunding made it clear that interest expense is the largest cost associated with bonds. Individual companies have no control over market interest rates, which fluctuate from year to year. As shown in Figure 21–1, since the 1940s interest rates have irregularly moved higher, reaching record levels in the later 1970s and early 1980s. The sharp increases in interest rates were followed by abrupt declines. These respites from advancing interest rates offered unique opportunities to refund old bonds and issue new ones.

An examination of Figure 21–1 reveals that the yields on Moody's Baa-rated bonds are higher than those on Aaa-rated bonds. Moreover, the difference between them, called the *spread*, is not constant. These ratings and the yields that may be associated with them will be examined later in this chapter.

Variable Rates The high levels and wide swings in interest rates in recent years have made some investors wary of buying long-term fixed-interest-rate bonds and other debt instruments such as mortgages. They do not want to hold long-term fixed-interest-rate debt instruments when interest rates are rising, because the market value of outstanding bonds and mortgages will decline. Since the general pattern of interest rates has been to rise, many companies are issuing bonds with variable interest rates and, in some cases, variable principal amounts to make the bonds more attractive to investors.

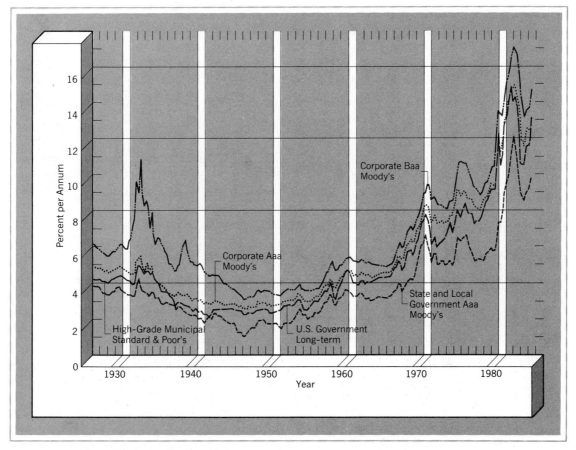

Figure 21–1   Historical long-term bond yields.

Several selected variable-rate and indexed bonds are listed in Table 21–7. Notice that the interest rate on the Petro-Lewis bond can range from 13 percent to 15.5 percent. The changes in the interest rates paid on the bond are based on changes in crude oil prices. In contrast, the changes in the interest rates paid on the U.S. Steel and New Orleans Home Mortgage Authority bonds are based on the interest rates of Treasury securities. Note that upper and lower limits apply to the rates that can be paid on these three bond issues. However, the Gulf Oil bond has only a lower limit, and the General Motors Acceptance bond has no limits. Finally, Sunshine Mines issued a bond whose principal amount is indexed to the market price of silver. Several oil companies are considering issuing bonds in which the principal amount is indexed to the price of crude oil. Although not shown in the table, many mortgages issued today have variable interest rates.

Table 21–7
Variable-Rate and Indexed Corporate Debt

Conditions of Variability	Selected Issues	Terms
Upper and lower limit on interest rate	Petro-Lewis 13.00%, 2000	13.00%–15.50%, interest rate based on crude oil prices
	U.S. Steel 9.00, 2010	6.00%–12.00%, interest rate based on Treasury bill rate (pollution-control bond)
	Floating Rate Environmental Protection Revenue Bonds, 1980 Series B	
	New Orleans Home Mortgage Authority Floating Rate	7.00%–13.00%, interest rate based on combination of Treasury bill (13 week) and bond (30 year) rates
	Sincle Family Mortgage Revenue Bonds, 1980 Series A	
Lower limit only on interest rate	Gulf Oil 9.55%, 2009	Minimum 8.375%; otherwise, 0.35% above 30-year constant maturity Treasury bonds
No upper or lower limit on interest rate	General Motors Acceptance Corp. 13.45%, 1990	107.2% of Treasury bill rate
Indexed principal	Sunshine Mines 8.50%, 1995	Each $1,000 of face amount payable at maturity or redemption at greater of $1,000 or market price of 50 ounces of silver

Bond Ratings Two principal services—Moody's and Standard & Poor's—assign letter ratings to indicate the quality of bonds. Their rating scales are shown in Table 21–8. Moody's Aaa and Standard and Poor's AAA are the highest ratings. Bonds with such ratings are referred to as **gilt edge**; they carry the smallest degree of investment risk, and their interest and principal are protected by substantial financial strength. Moody's Aa-rated and Standard & Poor's AA-rated bonds are not backed by the same degree of financial strength as the highest-rated bonds, but they still represent prime-quality investments. A-rated bonds are backed by still less financial strength and are susceptible to adverse economic

Table 21–8
Bond Ratings

Quality	Moody's	Standard & Poor's
Prime or investment grade	Aaa	AAA
	Aa	AA
	A	A
Medium grade	Baa	BBB
	Ba	BB
	B	B
Lowest grade	Caa	CCC
	Ca	CC
	C	C
		D

conditions. Bonds with ratings from Baa or BBB to B range in quality from medium grade to speculative. The junk bonds mentioned earlier have ratings of Baa/BBB or lower. Bonds with Caa or CCC ratings or worse are the lowest-quality bonds.

Some corporate bonds are not assigned ratings; the absence of ratings may or may not reflect the quality of the bond. For example, one rating service does not rate corporate bond issues under $600,000. Therefore, it may not rate some high-quality bonds issued by small companies.

Bond ratings are important because, as a proxy for risk, they affect the interest rates that companies pay on the bonds they issue. Better-quality bonds carry lower interest rates than lower-quality bonds. As shown in Table 21–9, substantial differences among the yields reflect the different ratings. For example, on the average, a Baa bond had an interest rate of 14.19 percent in 1984, whereas an Aaa-rated bond had an interest rate of 12.71 percent.

Under these circumstances, a company that improved its security rating from Baa to A could save 0.45 percent—45 **basis points**—in interest expense. That does not appear to be much until it is applied to a typical bond issue. Suppose, for example, that Sportline could reduce the interest cost on its new bond by 45 basis points. The interest cost of the $50 million bond issue would be reduced $225,000 per year before taxes. The present value of that amount over 20 years is $2,580,728 (0.0045 × $50,000,000 × 11.4699 = $2,580,728).

Bond ratings can indeed change over the life of the bond as the financial condition of the issuer changes. Changing the quality of the bond once it has been issued does not change the interest rate on the bond. However, it does affect the investment quality of the bond, and this, in turn, influences the type of investors who will buy it in the secondary market. Some pension plans and trust funds, for example, are prohibited from buying bonds with a rating lower than A. Furthermore, in making their investment decisions, investors will now apply a discount rate appropriate for the bond's revised rating to the cash flows for the bond. Changes in a company's bond ratings also affect the interest cost of new bonds the company issues.

Most companies recognize the advantage of having a high bond rating and strive to improve their financial condition. For example, TRW, a manufacturer

Table 21–9
Average Corporate Bond Yields for Seasoned Issues in 1984

Moody's Ratings	Yield	Basis Points
Aaa	12.71	
Aa	13.31	
A	13.74	148
Baa	14.19	45

Source Board of Governors of the Federal Reserve System.

of aerospace equipment and other high-technology products, had a capital structure with a 40/60 debt-to-equity ratio as an upper limit on debt. Keeping this ratio below the upper limit was one factor that helped the company maintain an A rating on its debt securities. The rating agencies also consider debt coverage ratios, financial leverage, and other factors when assigning ratings.

Summary

Bonds are a major source of debt financing for corporations. Corporate bonds finance plant and equipment, typically during the expansion and stabilization phases of the life cycle. The bonds are often classified according to the type of security behind them. Except for debentures, which are backed by the credit of the issuing corporation, bonds are backed by tangible assets or securities. Mortgage bonds, for example, are backed by real estate; collateral trust bonds by securities; and equipment obligations by equipment.

Some special types of bonds, called guaranteed bonds, are backed by the financial strength of another corporation. Junk bonds, income bonds, participating bonds, bonds with warrants, and zero-coupon bonds are other bonds with special features.

Bonds are retired in eight ways. Conversion is the only method of retirement that takes place at the option of the investor. Other methods are paying off the bonds at maturity, calling the bonds, retiring them serially, using sinking funds, purchasing bonds on the open market, defeasing the bonds, or instituting a debt–equity swap.

Bond refunding is widely used to "roll over" corporate debt, particularly when interest rates have fallen. The analysis of a refunding is treated like a capital budgeting problem. The objective is to determine the net present value of the savings less the investment outlay. The discount rate used is the after-tax cost of the new bond issue. The equation used to determine NPV, along with other equations used in this chapter, is reviewed in Table 21–10.

Interest expense is the largest cost associated with bonds. Generally rising

Table 21–10
Summary of Equations

	Equation	Equation Number
Price of zero-coupon bond	$P_0 = \dfrac{F}{PVIF_{k_{db},n}}$	(21–1)
Sinking fund payment	$SF_i = AMT\,\dfrac{1}{FVAIF_{i,n}}$	(21–2)
Bond refunding	$NPV = $ Annual savings $(PVAIF_{i,n})$ − Investment outlay	(21–3)

interest rates have caused many corporations to issue bonds whose interest rates vary over time. Several services rate bonds to indicate their quality. These ratings affect the interest rates corporations must pay on their debt securities.

Important Terms

Adjustment bonds	Industrial revenue bond
Assumed bond	Joint bond
Basis point	Junk bond
Call price	Mortgage bond
Call protection	Open-end mortgage bond
Closed-end mortgage bond	Overlap period
Collateral trust bond	Participating bond
Consolidated mortgage bond	Philadelphia Plan
Convertible bond	Pollution-control bond
Covenants	Private activity bond
Debenture	Privately placed bond issue
Debt–equity swap	Publicly offered bond issue
Defeasance	Refunding
Endorsed bond	Refunding bond
Equipment trust certificate	Second-mortgage bond
First-mortgage bond	Serial bond
General mortgage bond	Sinking fund
Guaranteed bond	Stamped bond
Gilt edge bond	Tax-exempt bond
Income bond	Warrant
Indenture	Zero-coupon bond

Questions

1. Why do secured bonds protect investors' interests in a legal sense but not necessarily in an economic sense?
2. What are debentures? What type of firms issue them?
3. Why do mortgage bonds usually carry a lower interest rate than debentures of the same issuer?
4. Distinguish between a first mortgage bond and a general or consolidated mortgage bond.
5. Distinguish between closed-end and open-end mortgage bonds.
6. What are collateral trust bonds?
7. Explain how equipment certificates work from the borrower's and lender's points of view.

8. What are junk bonds and why are they usually issued?
9. Distinguish between a guaranteed bond and an assumed bond.
10. Explain the features of an income or adjustment bond.
11. What is participating bond? How does it differ from a bond with a warrant?
12. What is a zero-coupon bond? Why are these bonds sold at a deep discount?
13. What bond retirement method is under the control of the investor? Explain.
14. What general factors determine the value of a convertible bond?
15. Identify at least three circumstances in which bonds may be called.
16. What are serial bonds?
17. What is the purpose of a sinking fund?
18. What are the advantages and disadvantages of retiring debt through open-market purchases?
19. Explain in general the process of defeasance. What is its purpose? What are its financial consequences?
20. Under what circumstances would a debt–equity swap be feasible?
21. What is the objective of bond refunding? What information is required to determine whether or not a bond issue should be refunded?
22. Why have fixed-rate bonds been unattractive to some investors in recent years?
23. In general, what types of bonds are rated AA or higher? What types are rated Baa or lower? Why are these ratings important?

Problems

1. A $1,000 face value bond is convertible into 40 shares of stock. If the market value of the bond is now $1,600, what is the current market value of the firm's stock?
2. Suppose the market value of the bond in Problem 1 is now $1,500 and the market price of the firm's stock is $50 per share. Into how many shares can the bond be converted?
3. Hill Billiards Company has just issued a 14 percent bond with a par value of $68 million and a 20-year maturity. What annual sinking fund payments are required if the firm can earn 12 percent on its investments? If it can earn 9 percent?
4. HBO Corporation has an established sinking fund into which it pays $1.8 million per year and on which it earns 10 percent. If the bond with which the sinking fund is associated has a 15-year maturity, what is the total par value of the issue? What is its total par value if the bond issue has a 10-year maturity?
5. Dunne Dance Studios has a 20-year, $46 million bond issue outstanding. Compute the annual sinking fund payment necessary to retire the bond if the sinking fund earns 6 percent; 10 percent; 14 percent.
6. The market requires a 10 percent return on the bonds of Desmond Corporation. What is the current market price of a zero-coupon bond with a $1,000 par value and a maturity of 10 years; 15 years; 5 years?
7. Elmo Corporation is considering issuing zero-coupon bonds with a 20-year maturity. At what price will the bonds sell if the market requires a rate of return of 8 percent; 12 percent; 6 percent?

8. If a firm's zero-coupon bonds are selling at $600 with 6 years to maturity, approximate the market's required return on these bonds. Assume $1,000 par. What if the bonds have 8 years to maturity?

9. Compute the after-tax cost of calling each of the following bond issues immediately. Assume the firm is in the 40 percent tax bracket and all bonds have a par value of $1,000.

Bond	Size of Issue	Call Price
A	$40 million	115
B	10 million	106
C	25 million	108

10. Compute the after-tax cost of calling each of the following bond issues immediately. Assume the firm is in the 30 percent tax bracket and all bonds have a par value of $1,000.

Bond	Size of Issue	Call Premium (%)
X	60,000 bonds	3
Y	85,000 bonds	5
Z	20,000 bonds	1.5

11. The management of Walter Washing Machines, Inc., has noted that the firm's bonds are selling below par and is considering purchasing some of them on the open market to retire the debt at a savings. The firm is in the 30 percent tax bracket. Each bond has a par value of $1,000. What additional taxes must be paid this year if the bonds are selling at $735 and 40,000 of them are outstanding?

12. Return to the Daytona Company defeasance example in the chapter. Suppose that the firm plans to sell new bonds with a coupon rate of 10 percent and a principal value of $44 million. By how much will its total financing costs be reduced? Assume the total cost of the old bonds remains the same.

13. Return to the Daytona Company defeasance example in the chapter. Suppose that the market value of the old debt is $44 million. Assuming that a new issue of bonds for $44 million will be made, how will the firm's new balance sheet look after defeasance? If net income is expected to be $14 million after defeasance, what will return on assets and return on equity be?

14. The following bonds are to be refunded. Calculate the interest overlap for a firm in the 40 percent tax bracket. Assume a 360-day year.

Bond	Size of Issue	Coupon Rate (%)	Overlap Period (days)
A	$10 million	11.0	30
B	18 million	10.5	120
C	26 million	14.0	90

15. Ignoring flotation costs, calculate the annual after-tax savings for each bond refunding situation below.

Size of Issue	Old Coupon Rate (%)	New Coupon Rate (%)	Years to Maturity	Tax Rate (%)
$27 million	16	10	18	30
14 million	15.5	9	12	40
75 million	14	8	25	35

16. Calculate the before- and after-tax investment outlay for each refunding situation below. Assume a 40 percent tax bracket.

Size of Issue	Call Premium	Unamortized Flotation	Net Proceeds from New Issue	Overlapping Interest
$ 25 million	$2 million	$0.3 million	$ 24.6 million	$0.4 million
76 million	5%	0.7 million	75.0 million	1.2 million
115 million	$6.5 million	1.0 million	112.0 million	1.0 million

For problems 17 through 20, round discount rates, if necessary, to the nearest whole percent. Assume a 360-day year.

17. The Ford Fabric Company is considering refunding a bond issue of $30 million it issued 5 years ago. The firm is in the 40 percent tax bracket and has collected the following data.

Old bond: Face value, $1,000
   Coupon rate, 16%
   Original maturity, 25 years
   Flotation costs at time of issue, $1 million
   Call price, 112
New bond: Face value, $1,000
   Coupon rate, 10%
   Original maturity, 20 years
   Flotation costs at time of issue, $0.75 million
   Size of issue, $30 million
   Overlap period, 45 days

Should the refunding be undertaken?

18. Fogerty, Inc., had to issue long-term debt 5 years ago and is now considering refunding, since interest rates have fallen. If the firm is in the 40 percent tax bracket, should the refunding be pursued?

Old bond: Face value, $1,000
   Coupon rate, 15%
   Original maturity, 15 years
   Flotation costs at time of issue, $450,000
   Size of issue, $24 million
   Call price, 109
New bond: Face value, $1,000
   Coupon rate, 13%
   Original maturity, 10 years
   Flotation costs at time of issue, $800,000
   Size of issue, $24 million
   Overlap period, 60 days

19. Weeks Electronics is analyzing the option to refund a bond issue made 5 years ago. If the firm is in the 30 percent tax bracket, what decision should be made?

Old bond: Face value, $1,000
   Coupon rate, 13.25%
   Original maturity, 30 years

Flotation costs at time of issue, $2.4 million
Size of issue, $80 million
Call premium 6%
New bond: Face value, $1,000
Coupon rate, 11%
Original maturity, 25 years
Flotation costs at time of issue, $2 million
Size of issue, $80 million
Overlap period, 30 days

20. Cole Corporation must decide whether to refund a $10 million bond issue made 3 years ago and replace it with an issue of identical size. The firm is in the 30 percent tax bracket and has collected the following data. Should the issue be refunded?

Old bond: Face value, $1,000
Coupon rate, 12%
Original maturity, 18 years
Flotation costs at time of issue, $120,000
Call price, $1,080
New bond: Face value, $1,000
Coupon rate, 9%
Original maturity, 15 years
Flotation costs at time of issue, $200,000
Overlap period, 60 days

 **Stocks**

There are more than 42 million individual shareholders in the United States and they hold about three-fourths of the market value of all outstanding stock. The remainder is held by financial institutions such as casualty insurance companies and pension plan administrators. These individuals and institutions provide business concerns with long-term equity capital. This chapter examines the nature of equity capital—of stocks.

After reading this chapter, you should know the following.

1. **What shareholders can and cannot do as owners.**
2. **How a few shareholders can magnify their voting power to elect corporate directors.**
3. **Why rights have value.**
4. **What tax benefits are associated with stock.**
5. **What preferred stock is and why it is like a bond.**

Shareholders' Equity

Balance sheets are divided into three parts: assets, liabilities, and shareholders' equity. Assets are what the firm owns or controls, liabilities are what it owes, and **shareholders' equity** is the difference between them. It is the shareholders' claim on the book value of the company's assets. A typical shareholders' equity section of a balance sheet includes the following entries.

Preferred stock (80,000 shares, $25 par value)	$ 2,000,000
Common stock (10 million shares, $1 par value)	10,000,000
Retained earnings	4,000,000
Total shareholders' equity	$16,000,000

The figures shown on the balance sheet are accounting entries that do not necessarily represent the market value of the shares. The preceding accounting entries indicate that shareholders invested $2 million in the firm's preferred stock and $10 million in its common stock. In addition, the firm retained $4 million in past earnings that also belong to the shareholders. That does not mean the shareholders can withdraw the $4 million retained earnings from the firm's cash account. The funds that were retained are invested in various assets, including cash.

Chapter 7 explained the difference between the book value and the market value of stock. Par value is different from either of these, as will be explained later in the chapter. In this example, the book value of the shareholders' equity is $16 million, as shown in the preceding table. The market value may be quite different—for example, $3 million for the preferred stock and $19 million for the common, giving a total market value of $22 million for shareholders' equity. Investors who own shares in the company are interested in further enhancing the market value of their shares. However, their ability to do so is limited by their influence over the firm's financial and investment policies.

Common Stock

Common stock represents ownership in a corporation. The word **ownership** implies that someone has possession or control of something. I own my car; therefore, I can drive it whenever and wherever I want. I also own stock in American Airlines and General Motors. However, I cannot walk into the cockpit of an American airliner and tell the pilot to fly the jet to San Diego instead of Chicago. Nor can I call General Motors and demand that it redesign the trunks of Cadillacs because I do not like the design. I do not even get a discount when I fly American or buy a General Motors car. So what does one get for being a shareholder?

Ownership Obviously, owning shares in a corporation is not the same as owning a car. Shareholders' ownership is represented by a **stock certificate**—a piece of paper that shows the name of the company, the name of the owner of the shares, the number of shares owned, the name of the registrar, and the par value of the stock. On the back of the stock certificate is a form that must be completed when the holder decides to transfer ownership of the shares.

Some investors who buy and sell stock frequently do not even get a stock certificate. They prefer not to have their shares registered in their names, in part because it may take a month or longer to have a stock certificate registered in the name of the owner. Stocks bought on margin (credit) must be left with the stockbroker. In addition, when stock held by an investor is sold, the certificate must be properly endorsed (signed) and delivered to the seller's stockbrocker. To avoid some of the paperwork, shares are commonly registered in **street name** and held by the brokerage firm in the customer's account. That means the stock is registered in the name of the stockbrokerage firm or some other nominee so the stock certificate can be transferred easily from one party to another.

Par Value   All stock is issued with a par value, or some nominal value. The **par value**, or **nominal value**, of the stock is found on the face of the stock certificate and in the corporate charter. One purpose of the par value is to determine what proportionate share of ownership each share represents. The total par value represents the amount of capital subscribed by the stockholders. Suppose the total par value for all the common stock of a firm is $10 million and each share has a par value of $1. Then, each share represents one-tenth of a millionth ownership in the company.

If the shares are sold to the original stockholders for less than the par value, the owners of the shares may be liable for an assessment of the difference in the event of insolvency. If the shares are sold to the original stockholders for an amount equal to or greater than the par value, the stock certificates are designated fully paid and nonassessable. Excess funds are recorded in the equity part of the balance sheet in a capital surplus account or some other account with a similar title.

Taxes are another factor affecting par value. Some states charge excise taxes and franchise fees based on the par value of the stock. Such laws encourage the issuance of stocks with low par values.

Finally, be careful not to confuse par value with book value. Par value is a legal concept, while book value is an accounting concept. Par value is declared by the corporation, whereas book value is determined by dividing the number of common shares outstanding into the shareholders' equity less the value of any preferred stock. The book value per share of the common stock used in the earlier example is $1.40, determined as follows.

Total shareholders' equity		$16,000,000
Less: Preferred stock		2,000,000
		$14,000,000
Divided by 10 million shares	÷	10,000,000
Book value per share	=	$1.40

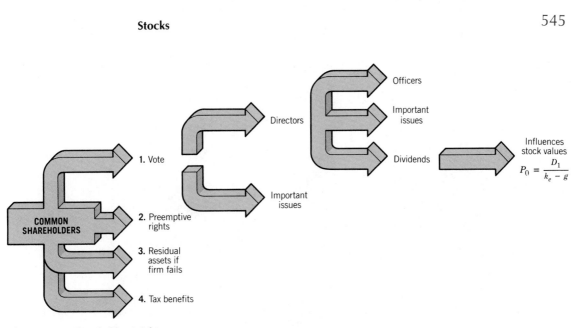

Figure 22–1   Shareholders' rights.

Shareholders' Figure 22–1 illustrates some of the rights generally available to holders of
Rights common stock. Each of the four items shown in the table is discussed here.

Voting Rights.   First, shareholders have the right to elect the board of directors
of the corporation and to vote on other important issues at the annual meeting.

Directors.   The **board of directors** is responsible for hiring the officers that
run the company on a daily basis and for establishing the basic operating
guidelines for the company. Equally important, it controls the firm's dividend
policy. By determining the dividend payout ratio and the growth rate of dividends, the directors influence the growth rate of the company and the value
of the stock. You may recall that firms that have high earnings and retain them
tend to grow faster than firms that have large dividend payout ratios.

Annual Meeting.   Generally, stockholders are given the opportunity to vote
once a year at the corporation's **annual meeting**, which is usually held at the
corporate headquarters or some other convenient location. In years past, many
corporations held their meetings at obscure places and on holidays in order
to keep stockholders away. Stockholders were—and still are—viewed as a
necessary evil by some managers.

   Many stockholders are unable or unwilling to attend the annual meeting.
Accordingly, many corporations are required by their bylaws or by stock exchange rules to send their stockholders a **proxy statement** along with the
notification of the annual meeting. A proxy is a power of attorney that assigns
the owner's right to vote on particular issues to another person or persons.
Such a statement is shown in Figure 22–2.

   Apathy toward attending annual meetings or even signing proxy statements

IBM
International Business Machines Corporation
Armonk, New York 10504

Proxy Solicited by the Board of Directors
for the Annual Meeting of Stockholders
April 30, 1984

Punched in this card is the proxy number used for machine sorting and counting of votes.

Shares: Account No.:

John F. Akers, John R. Opel. and Paul J. Rizzo or any of them with power of substitution are hereby appointed Proxies of the undersigned to vote all stock of International Business Machines Corporation owned by the undersigned at the Annual Meeting of Stockholders to be held in the Los Angeles Convention Center, Los Angeles, California, at 10:00 a.m., on Monday, April 30, 1984, or any adjournment thereof, upon such business as may properly come before the meeting, including the items on the reverse side of this card as set forth in the Notice of Meeting and the Proxy Statement.

MR BENTON E GUP
UNIVERSITY AL 35486

(Shares cannot be voted unless this proxy card is signed and returned, or other specific arrangements are made to have the shares represented at the meeting.)

IBM
Proxy No.

X66 326
00000
111111
2222 2
333 33
444444
555555
6 66
77777
888888
999999

IBM's directors recommend a vote for the proposals numbered 1 through 3 and against the stockholder proposals numbered 4 through 7 and SHARES WILL BE SO VOTED UNLESS OTHERWISE INDICATED:

1. FOR ☐ NOT FOR ☐ election of directors

J. F. Akers, S. D. Bechtel, Jr., G. B. Beitzel, H. Brown, J. E. Burke, F. T. Cary, W. T. Coleman, Jr., P. R. Harris, C. A. Hills, A. Houghton, Jr., N. Katzenbach, R. W. Lyman, J. G. Maisonrouge, W. H. Moore, J. R. Munro, J. R. Opel, D. P. Phypers, P. J. Rizzo, W. W. Scranton, I. S. Shapiro, C. R. Vance
except vote withheld from nominee(s) listed below:

_____

2. FOR ☐ AGAINST ☐ ABSTAIN ☐
ratifying auditors appointment

3. FOR ☐ AGAINST ☐ ABSTAIN ☐
amending stock option plans

4. FOR ☐ AGAINST ☐ ABSTAIN ☐
stockholder proposal on board service (page 19)

5. FOR ☐ AGAINST ☐ ABSTAIN ☐
stockholder proposal on corporate contributions (page 20)

6. FOR ☐ AGAINST ☐ ABSTAIN ☐
stockholder proposal on use of computers (page 22)

7. FOR ☐ AGAINST ☐ ABSTAIN ☐
stockholder proposal on tax burden (page 24)

X _____

PLEASE SIGN HERE AND RETURN PROMPTLY
Dated: , 1984

☐ Please send me a ticket for the Los Angeles meeting

Figure 22–2   Proxy Statement.

is widespread among shareholders. The shareholders of one large corporation were recently asked by the company's president what they thought of educating shareholders about their rights and about important issues facing the company. The response to the question was, in effect, "We don't know and we don't care. We only want the stock price to go up and dividends to increase." As a result of such attitudes, managers may act in their own interest rather than in the interest of the owners.

To understand more clearly what transpires at an annual meeting, consider the basic format of the 1980 annual meeting of Exxon Corporation—which was held at the Civic Opera House in Chicago, although the company is headquartered in New York City.[1]

The first order of business was the election of directors. Nineteen people had been nominated by the firm to fill directorships. Nine of the nominees were current or retired Exxon officials. If elected, they would be *inside directors*, because they work or have worked for the firm. The 10 remaining nominees—who would become *outside directors*—included two college professors, a university president, and the presidents of several major corporations. Some firms stagger the terms of their directors so all do not come up for a vote at the same time, but that is not the case with Exxon.

The second item on the agenda was the ratification of appointment of independent public accountants. Next came some shareholders' resolutions. One shareholder wanted to place a limit on corporate donations. (In 1979, the company had donated $38 million for charitable purposes out of $5 billion operating revenues.) Another shareholder wanted to divide Exxon into two separate entities because "it is too large for its own good and for the survival of the American free enterprise system." Other shareholders' resolutions concerned reporting on pricing, diversification, and lobbying; restricting South African activities; limiting nuclear power investments; and cumulative voting (discussed later).

No additional business was included in the agenda. It is interesting to observe that Exxon had 438 million shares of stock outstanding and that only about 12 million shares, or 2.7 percent of the total, had voted the previous year.

Voting Restrictions.   Not all holders of common stock have the right to vote. Some corporations issue Class A and Class B common stocks. Generally, one class has voting rights and the other has either limited voting rights or none at all. An unusual example is Resorts International (listed on the American Stock Exchange), whose Class B common stock has full voting rights (one vote for each share) and whose Class A common stock does not have full voting rights (1/100 vote for each share). In the more typical situation, Class A stock has voting rights and Class B stock does not.

Ordinary and Cumulative Voting.   Typically, stockholders are entitled to cast one vote per share for each vacancy on the board of directors. This is known as **ordinary** or **straight voting**. Under this method, a group of investors controlling the majority of the votes could elect all the directors, and minority owners outside the controlling group would be excluded from representation on the board of directors. An alternative method, **cumulative voting**, gives increased weight to minority owners' votes.

The following illustrations will clarify the difference between ordinary and cumulative voting. Suppose a company has 1,000 shares of stock outstanding and five directors are to be elected. One shareholder group controls 800

---

[1]Exxon Corporation, Notice of Annual Meeting, May 15, 1980, and Proxy Statement.

shares, leaving 200 for the minority group. Under ordinary voting, minority shareholders can cast 200 votes for each vacancy, while majority shareholders can cast 800 votes for each vacancy and can thus elect all five directors.

Under cumulative voting, as under ordinary voting, the minority shareholders are entitled to cast a total of 1,000 votes (200 shares × 5 vacancies = 1,000 votes); and the majority shareholders, a total of 4,000 votes (800 shares × 5 vacancies = 4,000 votes). However, the votes need not be divided among all the vacancies. Minority shareholders can cast all 1,000 votes for one directorship vacancy and thus obtain one seat on the board. There is no way the majority stockholders can combine their votes to capture all the vacancies. This can be determined by use of the following equation.

$$R = \frac{s \times d}{D + 1} + 1 \tag{22-1}$$

where

R = Number of shares required to elect specified number of board members (d)
s = Number of voting shares
d = Specified number of vacancies
D = Total number of directors to be elected

Suppose we want to find out how many shares the minority stockholders described earlier would need to elect one director. We can use Equation 22–1 and the preceding information, setting d at 1 because we want to know how many votes are needed to fill one vacancy. The number of shares required to elect one director is 168.

$$R = \frac{1,000 \times 1}{5 + 1} + 1$$

$$= 167.66$$

$$\simeq 168$$

As already noted, less than 3 percent of the Exxon shareholders voted at a recent annual meeting. A minority group might have been able to gain a seat on the board if there had been cumulative voting at that meeting. Suppose that 19 directors were to be elected and that the minority shareholders wanted to gain one seat. If 12 million shares were voted, the minority would have needed only 600,001 shares (1.3 percent of the total number of shares outstanding) to obtain one seat on the board of directors, calculated as follows.

$$R = \frac{12,000,000 + 1}{19 + 1} + 1$$

$$= 600,001 \text{ shares}$$

Under ordinary voting, they would have needed more than 6 million shares to obtain a seat.

You may remember that cumulative voting was the subject of a resolution at the Exxon annual meeting described earlier. Exxon's board of directors recommended that shareholders vote against instituting cumulative voting. They argued that some groups of shareholders might be inclined to act on Exxon's business in their own behalf rather than for the benefit of all shareholders.

Preemptive Rights.   The second shareholders' right listed in Figure 22–1 is the **preemptive right**. Shareholders have a common-law right to maintain their proportionate, or **pro rata**, share of ownership when a company raises new capital by selling common stock. That means a company issuing new stock may first give its shareholders the right to buy new shares in proportion to the number they already hold. This is called a **rights offering**.

We should note that not all states recognize preemptive rights and some have waived provisions for them in corporate charters. In addition, preemptive rights usually do not apply when the company sells **treasury stock** (outstanding stock that the company buys back), when new stock is issued to purchase another company, or when new stock is used for employee stock options.

Procedure for Rights Offering.   Preemptive rights (or simply **rights**) are given to the shareholders in a document called a warrant. This warrant should not be confused with warrants that are long-term option contracts to buy stock. Recall from the preceding chapter that some bonds are sold with detachable warrants, which are used to make the bonds of relatively weak companies more attractive to investors.

Stockholders are generally given one right for each share held. Rights have value because they are option contracts to buy stock at a stated price within a given period of time. The stated price—that is, the price at which the holder of rights can buy the stock—is called the **subscription price** and should be lower than the stock's current market price. The shareholder who receives rights has three courses of action: exercise them, sell them, or let them expire. Because rights have value, most shareholders exercise them or sell them. More will be said about the trading of rights in Chapter 23.

Value of Rights.   The following example illustrates the theoretical value of one right when it is attached to the stock. Assume that a corporation's stock is selling for $40 per share and shareholders are given rights to buy new shares at $35 each (the subscription price). Nine rights are required to buy one new share at $35. The theoretical value of one of these rights is $0.50, determined by the use of the following equation.

$$V_1 = \frac{P_0 - S}{N + 1}$$

$$= \frac{\$40 - \$35}{10}$$

$$= \$0.50 \hspace{3cm} (22\text{--}2)$$

where

V_1 = Theoretical value of one right when the stock is cum rights
P_0 = Market price of a share of stock
S = Subscription price of one share
N = Number of rights necessary to buy one share of new stock.

Chapter 23 will examine the value of rights more closely.

Success in Issuing Rights. A successful rights offering depends on several factors. First, the subscription price must be sufficiently lower than the market price to make the issue attractive to investors. In the example above, the *spread* (or difference) between the market price and the subscription price was $5 ($40 − $35 = $5). Second, because the company has no control over the market price of the stock, the maturity of the rights offering must be relatively short so that the market price does not fall below the subscription price during the period when rights are being offered. The maturity is usually 1 month or less. Finally, the company should use a standby underwriter to guarantee the success of the offering. This underwriter will exercise all the rights not subscribed by investors, thereby providing the company with the funds it needs.

Dividend Reinvestment Plans. Dividend reinvestment plans and stock purchase plans are other options available to some shareholders. Many companies are offering holders of their common and preferred stock the opportunity to buy additional shares without paying brokerage fees. Philadelphia Electric Company, for example, permits shareholders to reinvest their dividends and make cash investments up to $5,000 per quarter in new shares of common stock on the dividend payment date. This policy permits companies to pay cash dividends yet retain a large portion of those dividends. In addition, it provides new equity funds from the new shares purchased. Since no underwriters' fees are involved, the cost of the funds is lower than it would have been otherwise.

Residual Claims. Common shareholders can vote, they have preemptive rights, and they are the **residual claimants** if the company fails. That means they are entitled to all that remains after all prior claims have been satisfied. In regard to this shareholder right, it might be noted that, where security is concerned, common stock is the most risky type of corporate investment. It is not backed by specific assets that can be attached to the investment if the company fails. Furthermore, the market price of the shares can fluctuate widely. However, common stock offers the greatest opportunities for rewards in dividends and capital appreciation.

Tax Benefits. Finally, common shareholders gain certain tax benefits. The Internal Revenue Code includes tax provisions designed to promote the growth of equity capital.

Dividend Exclusion. Shareholders can exclude from federal income taxes up to $100 of dividends received from qualifying domestic corporations. This **dividend exclusion** means that if an investor received $500 in cash dividends from IBM, $100 of that amount would be excluded from federal income tax, although income tax would be paid on the remaining $400. People who file joint income tax returns can exclude up to $200 of dividends ($100 each).

The dividend exclusion, though small, was designed to encourage widespread participation by investors in the corporate equity market. This, of course, facilitates equity financing by increasing the number of investors.

Preferred Stock

Preferred stock is a hybrid security. It has some characteristics of both corporate bonds and common stock. Like bonds, preferred stocks have a stated rate of return on the par value, but they do not have the collateral associated with many types of bonds. In this respect, they are similar to debentures. Like common stock, they represent ownership in a corporation, but the preferred stockholders generally do not benefit from increased earnings or participate in management to the same extent as the owners of common stock. On the other hand, as the term *preferred* implies, the holders of preferred shares take precedence over the holders of common stock as to (1) dividends and (2) assets in the event the company is liquidated.

Par Value Many preferred stocks have a par value of $100. Some have par values of $50 or some other amount and others have no par value. Par values are important because dividends are expressed as a percentage of the par value. For example, Niagara Mohawk Power Corporation has a 7.72 percent preferred stock outstanding; the dividend of this stock is 7.72 percent of the stock's $100 par value, or $7.72. Preferred stocks with no par value express dividends in dollar amounts. Par value may also affect the priority accorded to preferred stockholders if the company is liquidated. In such cases, preferred stocks with high par values may rank ahead of those with low par values.

Dividends Dividends on preferred stock are paid from net income after taxes have been deducted. Because this is so, it is more costly for corporations to pay dividends on preferred stock than to pay interest on bonds, which is tax deductible.

Cumulative Preferred. If the board of directors declares a cash dividend, preferred shareholders must be paid before common shareholders. If the board decides not to pay a cash dividend when the preferred dividend is due, the stock is said to be in **arrears**.

Many preferred stocks have what is called a cumulative clause. For this **cumulative preferred** stock, unpaid dividends accumulate for future payment. The dividends in arrears must be paid before holders of common stock can receive dividends. If the arrearages become too large, however, preferred stockholders may lose the dividends, or the company may negotiate with them for payment of a reduced amount.

Considerable risk is involved in investing in noncumulative preferred stock. Holders of such stock have no claim on earnings if no cash dividends are declared. Even if the company earns the money, it is not obliged to pay preferred dividends if the funds are necessary for improvements.

Participating Preferred. Some preferred stocks participate in the earnings of the company in addition to earning their stated dividends. Holders of these **participating preferred** stocks may share equally with the common stockholders after the usual preferred dividends have been paid. The participating clause makes preferred stock a much more attractive investment. In fact, the best combination from the investor's point of view is to own a cumulative, participating preferred that is convertible into common stock. Such a security is similar to a convertible debenture.

Tax Exemption. Corporate investors can deduct 80 percent of the dividends they receive on certain preferred stocks from their taxable incomes. As a result of this tax advantage, many new preferred stock issues are sold to corporate investors. Some corporate investors trade preferred stocks to capture as many as eight or more partially tax exempt dividends per year. This cash management strategy is called *preferred dividend rolls*.[2]

Assets It has already been stated that, in the event a company is liquidated, holders of preferred stock have priority over holders of common stock in asset distribution. More specifically, this is true when the preferred stock includes an **asset preference** provision. The preference must clearly state the priority accorded to the various par values and dividend arrearages. In the absence of an asset preference provision, preferred stockholders may be no better off than

---

[2]Michael D. Joehnk, Oswald D. Bowlin, and J. William Petty, "Preferred Dividend Rolls: A Viable Strategy for Corporate Money Managers?" *Financial Management*, Summer 1980, pp. 78–87.

common stockholders. In any case, before any assets can be distributed to the owners of the company, fixed-claim creditors must be paid. Finally, the asset preference does not apply in mergers or consolidations unless stated in the agreement.

Voting Preferred stockholders frequently have the same voting rights as common stockholders. However, in some cases, preferred stockholders can only vote under special circumstances. For example, if dividends reach a certain level of arrearages, preferred stockholders may be able to elect a specified number of directors to reflect their interests. Accordingly, holders of IC Industries' $3.50 cumulative convertible second preferred, series 1, have one and one-half votes per share in the event of default on six quarterly dividends. The preferred shareholders are then entitled to elect two directors. In contrast, holders of IC Industries' 8 3/4 percent, series A, first preferred have one-tenth of one vote per share.

Redemption Provisions **Call Features.** The resemblance of preferred stocks to bonds has already been mentioned. Another feature that makes the two similar is that most preferred stocks have **call provisions**. The issuing company may call the stock to force conversion or to eliminate the issue for some other reason.

Because stockholders may be inconvenienced by having their shares called, they receive a premium above the par value. Call premiums are sometimes quite high. General Motors $4 preferred, callable at $120, and Southeastern Public Service 4.15 percent preferred, callable at $116.50, offer examples of high call premiums. In general, call premiums tend to be relatively small and to diminish over time.

Preferred stocks are frequently called to meet sinking fund provisions. The **sinking fund** provision, you may recall, requires the periodic retirement of a security issue through payments made by the issuing corporation. For preferred stock, the sinking fund provision ordinarily requires redemption of a certain number of preferred shares for a dollar amount based on net income after payment of preferred dividends. Philadelphia Electric Power Company has a sinking fund provision of 8,000 shares per year for its 7 percent preferred stock. The shares are purchased on the open market.

Conversion. Conversion is another method of retiring preferred stocks, but in this case the decision is made by the stockholder rather than the company. The conversion privilege gives investors the right to exchange **convertible preferred** stock for common stock at a predetermined price or ratio. For example, each share of Kaiser Aluminum and Chemical Corporation's 4 1/8 percent cumulative convertible preferred is convertible into 1.6826 shares of common stock at $59.43 per share.

Table 22–1
Summary of Equations

	Equation	Equation Number
Number of shares necessary to elect directors under cumulative voting	$R = \dfrac{s \times d}{D + 1} + 1$	(22–1)
Value of one right attached to stock	$V_1 = \dfrac{P_0 - S}{N + 1}$	(22–2)

Summary

Common and preferred stockholders are the owners of corporations. On balance sheets, the book value of their claim is shown as shareholders' equity.

Common stock gives holders ownership in the corporation, represented by a stock certificate. Common stock is assigned a par value, which is different from the book value and the market value.

As owners, common stockholders have the right to elect directors and vote on certain important issues, usually at the firm's annual meeting. Cumulative voting offers advantages to minority shareholders. (Equations related to cumulative voting and other topics in this chapter are summarized in Table 22–1.) In some cases, common shareholders have preemptive rights to maintain their proportionate share of ownership when new stock is issued to the public. These rights can be traded. Common stockholders also are the residual claimants if the company is liquidated. Finally, they gain some tax advantages.

Preferred stockholders enjoy a preference over common stockholders in the payment of dividends and in the distribution of assets if the company is liquidated. Most preferred stock carries a par value, and preferred stock pays dividends, which may be cumulative. Some preferred stock allows holders to participate in earnings and to gain tax advantages. Preferred stock often also carries voting rights.

Preferred stock has some characteristics that make it more like a debt security than an equity security. Those characteristics include a financial obligation on the company's part to pay dividends, call features, sinking fund provisions, and convertible features.

Important Terms

Annual meeting   Common stock
Arrears   Convertible preferred
Asset preference   Cumulative preferred
Board of directors   Cumulative voting
Call provision   Dividend exclusion

Nominal value
Ordinary voting
Ownership
Par value
Participating preferred
Preemptive right
Preferred stock
Pro rata share
Proxy statement
Residual claimant

Right
Rights offering
Shareholders' equity
Sinking fund
Stock certificate
Straight voting
Street name
Subscription price
Treasury stock

Questions

1. Illustrate a typical equity section of a balance sheet and explain each account.
2. What is the par value of a share of common stock? How does it compare with the stock's book value? Its market value? What purposes does the par value serve?
3. Why is some stock registered in street name?
4. Describe the functions of a corporate director.
5. What is a proxy? When are proxies used?
6. What is the difference between inside and outside directors?
7. What is treasury stock?
8. What is a stock right? Why do firms issue them? What are the characteristics of successful rights offerings?
9. What are some advantages in offering shareholders dividend reinvestment plans?
10. Why are stockholders considered residual claimants?
11. What is cumulative preferred stock? Participating preferred?
12. Why do corporations often buy the preferred stock of other corporations?
13. What are preferred dividend rolls?
14. Identify some similarities between bonds and preferred stock. Between common and preferred stock.
15. Identify three methods of retiring a preferred stock issue.

Problems

1. Jimco Carburetors has the following balance sheet entries

Preferred stock ($50 par)	$500,000
Common stock ($1 par)	100,000
Paid-in capital in excess of par	400,000
Retained earnings	700,000

The market price of Jimco preferred is $36 and the market value of the firm's common stock is $23.
(a) Calculate the book value per share for Jimco's common stock.
(b) Calculate the total market value for Jimco's preferred and common stock-holders.

2. Eden Cosmetics shows the following accounts for stockholder's equity.

Preferred stock ($100 par)	$1,800,000
Common stock ($2 par)	800,000
Paid-in capital in excess of par	2,000,000
Retained earnings	6,000,000

Calculate book value per share for common shareholders.

3. Tight Corporation plans to elect nine directors this year. There are 8.5 million shares of stock outstanding. Minority stockholders want to elect two directors.
(a) How many shares do they need if ordinary voting is in effect?
(b) How many shares do they need if cumulative voting is in effect?

4. Two groups of shareholders are waging a battle for control of Tidwell Tools. The firm has issued 12.2 million shares. The terms of seven directors are expiring, so new elections must be held. Cumulative voting is in effect and the shareholder group that controls the election will control policies for the next several years.
(a) How many shares are necessary to elect four of the new directors?
(b) How many shares are necessary to elect six of the new directors?

5. Suppose Tidwell Tools in Problem 4 has issued 15 million shares and that five directors are to be elected. How many shares must one shareholder group hold if it wishes to elect three new directors?

6. What is the theoretical value of a right if the stock is selling with rights at $27.50, the subscription price is $22, and eight rights are needed to buy one share?

7. Skymore Seaplanes is planning to issue 2 million shares through a rights offering. It will take five rights to buy one share. If the market price of Skymore with rights is $20 per share and the subscription price is $15, what is the value of one right?

8. Boxer Sports Company has a dividend reinvestment plan. The firm pays an annual dividend of $6 per share, and its stock has an average market price of $80 per share. There are 6 million shares outstanding. How many new shares will Boxer issue through its reinvestment plan if stockholders owning 40 percent of the stock participate?

9. The market price of Boxer Sports' stock in Problem 10 has just increased to $100 because of the favorable reception given to the firm's new basketball shoe. If shareholders owning 75 percent of the firm's stock decide to participate in the reinvestment plan, how many new shares will be issued?

10. Garbo Corporation has an issue of 8.8 percent preferred stock outstanding. What is the dividend in dollars if the market price is $110 per share and the par value is $100 per share?

11. Zero Corporation has purchased 20 percent of a $50 million preferred stock issue from the Delta Corporation. The stock pays an 8 percent dividend and sells for a market price of $120 on a par value of $100. What dollar amount of Zero's dividend income will be sheltered from taxes?

Convertibles, Warrants, and Rights

Convertible bonds and convertible preferred stocks are hybrid securities. At times they have some characteristics of fixed income securities such as bonds and at other times they have some characteristics of stocks. Investors like convertible securities because they offer the opportunity to invest in relatively safe income-bearing securities with the capital gains potential of common stock. Issuing corporations like convertibles because they provide long-term capital that might not be available on satisfactory terms from straight debt or preferred stock. The ability to convert securities from debt to equity also permits firms to restructure their capitalizations.

Warrants and rights are also convertible securities. Warrants are long-term call options to buy common stock, and rights are short-term call options to buy common stock. You may remember that a **call option** allows the holder of the security to convert that security into a specified number of shares of common stock at a predetermined price on or before a certain date. As you will see, convertible bonds and convertible preferred stocks also contain call options to buy stock.

After reading this chapter and appendix, you should know the following.

1. How convertible bonds and preferred stocks are used.
2. Why companies like convertibles.
3. How investors can "have their cake and eat it too" by using convertibles.
4. How warrants are used.
5. Why warrants and rights are good for speculation.
6. How to calculate the value of rights.
7. What option features are included in convertibles, warrants, and rights.
8. How puts and calls are traded.

Convertible Bonds and Preferreds

A convertible security can be exchanged for another security, usually common stock of the issuing corporation. Two types of convertible securities are debenture bonds and preferred stock. The former are generally called **convertible bonds**; the latter, **convertible preferreds**. Table 23–1 contains a partial listing of major companies that have issued convertible bonds and preferreds. An examination of the listing reveals the diversity of the firms that use convertibles, suggesting that their use is widespread.

Characteristics of Convertibles Some basic terms must be defined before the mechanics of convertibles can be described. The following discussion concentrates on convertible bonds, but convertible preferreds have many of the same characteristics.

Table 23–1

Selected Companies with Convertible Securities

Convertible Bonds	Convertible Preferreds
Aluminum Company of America	Aetna Life & Casualty
American Hospital Supply	American Home Product
Bank New York, Inc.	Bendix Corp.
Citicorp	Cluett Peabody & Co., Inc.
Commonwealth Edison	Commonwealth Edison
W. R. Grace and Co.	Gould, Inc.
Hilton Hotels Corp.	Household Finance
Lockheed Corp.	Litton Industries, Inc.
McGraw–Hill, Inc.	McGraw–Hill, Inc.
Occidental Petroleum	Owens–Illinois, Inc.
Trans World Corp. (TWA)	Trans World Corp. (TWA)
Xerox	Zale Corp.

Conversion Price. The **conversion price** is the dollar amount exchangeable for one share of common stock and the **conversion rate** expresses this dollar amount as a proportion of the bond's face value. Recall that most bonds have a face value of $1,000; for them, a conversion price of $50 per share is equivalent to a conversion rate of 20. The relationship between conversion rates and prices is shown in the following equation.

$$\frac{\text{Face value of bond}}{\text{Conversion price}} = \text{Conversion rate} \qquad (23-1)$$

This equation was used to generate the following table of conversion rates for bonds with a face value of $1,000.

Conversion Price	Conversion Rate
$100	10
50	20
25	40
10	100

Sometimes the conversion rate and the conversion price change over time. For example, a $1,000 bond may have a conversion price of $25 for the first 5 years, $30 for the next 5 years, and $40 for its remaining life. Conversion prices are also adjusted to take into account stock splits or dividends that occur during the life of the bond. For example, if the stock were split two for one, the conversion price would be halved.

Conversion Value. The **conversion value** is the current market value of the number of shares into which the security can be converted. Suppose a bond with a face value of $1,000 has a conversion rate of 40 and the stock into which it is convertible has a current market price of $30 per share. We can find the conversion value by multiplying the conversion rate by the current price of a share of stock.

$$\text{Conversion rate} \times \text{Current stock price} = \text{Conversion value}$$
$$R \times S \qquad\qquad\qquad = CV \qquad (23-2)$$

In this example, the conversion value of the bond is $1,200 (40 × $30 = $1,200).

The conversion value determined above is the **theoretical value** of the bond.[1] (In Chapter 6 this was called the intrinsic value, but the term *theoretical value* is more commonly used in connection with convertibles.) The actual **market price** of the bond may or may not be the same as the theoretical value. When the market price and the theoretical value are the same, the convertible

---

[1] The implicit value of a call option is also included here. Call options are discussed in the appendix to this chapter.

is selling at **parity**. If the market price exceeds the conversion value, the bond is selling at a premium, or above parity. Conversely, a convertible bond selling for less than the conversion value is selling at a discount.

Conversion Premium or Discount.   Unfortunately, the terminology used in finance is confusing at times, and this is one of those times. The terms *premium* and *discount* have two meanings with respect to bonds. One meaning, which you have encountered in earlier chapters, refers to the relationship between the market price and the face value of the bond; for example, a bond with a face value of $1,000 and a market price of $1,400 is selling at a premium. If the market price is $600, the bond is selling at a deep discount.

As just noted, the terms are also used in connection with convertible bonds that are selling above or below parity. In this case, we will use the term **conversion premium** or **conversion discount** to distinguish the two usages of the terms.

To illustrate the calculation of a conversion premium or discount, we'll consider a bond with a current market price of $1,100 and a conversion rate of 40.[2] The current market price of the stock into which the bond is convertible is $26 per share. Using Equation 23–2, we can determine the conversion value of the bond, $1,040.

$$R \times S = CV$$

$$40 \times \$26 = \$1,040$$

We find the conversion premium or discount by dividing the difference between the market price of the bond and the conversion value by the conversion value. In this example, the conversion premium is 5.77 percent.

$$P^* = \frac{P_B - CV}{CV}$$

$$= \frac{\$1,100 - \$1,040}{\$1,040}$$

$$= 5.77\% \tag{23–3}$$

where

P^* = Conversion premium or discount based on market value
P_B = Current market price of the bond

So far, the conversion premium or discount has been based on market value.

---

[2]Bond prices are quoted without accumulated interest, but the buyer must pay the current market price plus accumulated interest from the date of the last interest payment.

Another method of determining conversion premiums or discounts uses the **investment value**—that is, the price at which the bond would sell if it had no conversion feature. Such values are estimated by investment advisory services such as Moody's. Let's assume that the bond used in the preceding example has an investment value of $950. Using this method, we would find the conversion premium or discount by dividing the difference between the conversion value of the bond and the investment value by the investment value.

$$P^{**} = \frac{CV - I}{I}$$

$$= \frac{\$1,040 - \$950}{\$950}$$

$$= 9.47\% \qquad\qquad (23\text{--}4)$$

where

P^{**} = Conversion premium or discount based on investment value
I = Investment value

The relationships among investment value, market price, and premium are depicted in Figure 23–1. The figure shows that—as we determined earlier—if the stock sells at $26 per share, the conversion value is $1,040. At this point, the market price of the bond is $1,100. The difference between the market price and the conversion value is the conversion premium based on market price (P^* = 5.77 percent). The difference between the conversion value and the investment value is the conversion premium based on investment value (P^{**} = 9.47 percent).

Figure 23–1 also indicates that when the market value of the stock falls to $15 per share, the conversion value of the bond is $600. Nevertheless, the bond may still sell at a premium over both the conversion value and the investment value (this amount is about $950 in the figure). The reason is that investors are willing to pay for the conversion feature of the bond. Although the stock is selling at $15 per share today, tomorrow its price may be appreciably higher. The conversion feature can be thought of as a long-term call option on the stock. Consequently, the premium paid for the bond is similar to the premium paid to buy a call option. More will be said about options later in the chapter.

Notice that the two conversion premiums are shown in Figure 23–1 as dollar amounts—the difference between the market price of the bond and the conversion value, and the difference between the conversion value and the investment value. Conversion premiums (or discounts) can be expressed as dollar amounts or percentages. The shaded area to the left of the line representing conversion values is the dollar equivalent of P^*; the shaded area to the right of the line is the dollar equivalent of P^{**}.

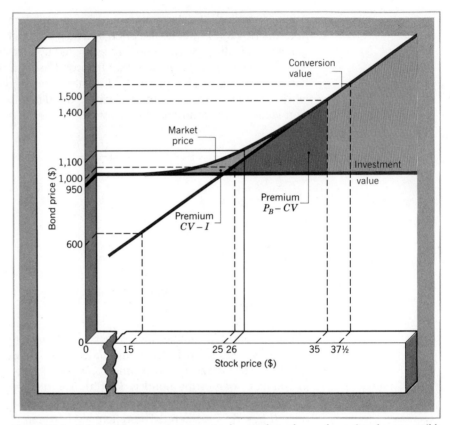

Figure 23–1   Relationship among investment value, market value, and premium for convertible bonds.

An examination of the shaded area to the left of the line representing conversion value shows that the conversion premium between the market price and the conversion value diminishes as the stock price increases. When the stock price is $35 per share, there is no premium over the theoretical value of the bond. The market price and the conversion price are the same. However, the premium between the market price of the bond and its investment value becomes larger as the stock price increases. Higher stock prices and bond prices imply greater risk for investors who are interested in the investment value of the bond (because it is selling above its investment value) but greater returns for those who bought the bonds for capital gains.

A Theory of Convertibles   Because convertible bonds have some characteristics of a bond and some characteristics of a common stock, the valuation model for convertible bonds contains some elements of the bond and stock valuation models developed in Chapter 6.

The market value of a straight (nonconvertible) bond with annual interest payments can be determined by use of the following equation.[3]

$$P_B = \sum_{t=1}^{n} \left[\frac{I}{(1 + k_{db})^t} \right] + \frac{F}{(1 + k_{db})^n} \qquad (23-5)$$

where

P_B = Current market price of bond (price at Time 0)
I = Annual interest payment
F = Face value of bond at maturity
n = Number of years to maturity
t = Time (1 to n)
k_{db} = Current market rate of interest on newly issued straight (nonconvertible) bonds with similar characteristics

If the bonds are converted, they will not be held until maturity. Equation 23-5 can be modified as follows to take conversion into account.[4]

$$P_B = \sum_{t=1}^{N} \left[\frac{I}{(1 + k_c)^t} \right] + \frac{CV}{(1 + k_c)^N} \qquad (23-6)$$

where

CV = Conversion value of the bond
k_c = Expected rate of return on convertible bonds ($k_c \geq$ interest rate on the convertible)
N = Number of years until conversion ($N \leq n$)

From the preceding discussion, you know that the conversion value of a bond is related to the price of the stock into which it is convertible. Increases in stock prices over time can be expressed by the following equation.

$$P_t = P_S (1 + g)^t \qquad (23-7)$$

where

P_t = Market price of stock at end of period
P_S = Current market price of a share of stock
g = Expected rate of growth of stock price

[3]This equation is the same as Equation 6-2; as explained in Chapter 6, the equation can also be stated as follows.

$$P_B = I(PVAIF_{i,n}) + F(PVIF_{i,n})$$

[4]As for Equation 23-5, we can use an alternate form for Equation 23-6.

$$P_B = I(PVAIF_{i,n}) + CV(PVIF_{i,n})$$

The conversion value is equal to the expected stock price times the conversion rate (i.e., the number of shares received upon conversion). The conversion value can be stated as follows.

$$CV = P_t R \qquad\qquad (23–8)$$

where

CV = Conversion price
P_t = Market price of stock at end of Period t
R = Conversion rate

For example, suppose a bond has a conversion rate of 40 shares (which is the same as a conversion price of $25 per share) and the current market price of the stock is $26 per share. The price of the stock is expected to increase 10 percent a year for 5 years. The market price of the stock at the end of 5 years is found by use of Equation 23–7:

$$P_t = P_S (1 + g)^t$$

$$= \$26 (1.10)^5$$

$$= \$41.87$$

The result is used in Equation 23–8 to determine the conversion value of the bond in 5 years.

$$CV = P_t R$$

$$= \$41.87 (40)$$

$$= \$1,674.80$$

$$\approx \$1,675$$

Now assume that the bond pays $90 annual interest and that investors expect an 8 percent return on their investment. Using Equation 23–6 in the alternate form given in footnote 4, we find that the bond has a market price of about $1,500.

$$P_B = I (PVAIF_{8\%,\ 5\ years}) + CV (PVIF_{8\%,\ 5\ years})$$

$$= \$90 (3.9927) + \$1,675 (0.68058)$$

$$= \$1,499.31$$

$$\approx \$1,500$$

The prices of the stock and bond, as well as the conversion premiums, were shown in Figure 23–1.

Reasons for Issuing Convertibles Once a company decides to borrow long-term funds, it must weigh the advantages and disadvantages of the various debt instruments. Some advantages and disadvantages of issuing convertible bonds are listed in Table 23–2 and discussed here.

Financing Strategy. Figure 23–2 depicts the life cycle of a typical business concern and suggests how the debt-to-equity ratio may change as the firm matures. Firms in the pioneering and expansion phases of the life cycle tend to have high debt-to-equity ratios because they borrow heavily to support their growth. Part of their debt issues may include convertibles. As firms mature, they tend to decrease debt relative to equity. They accomplish this in several ways. They can retire existing bond issues, sell stock, and retain earnings. Alternatively, they can force conversion of convertible bonds, resulting in reduced debt and increased equity. Of course, many mature companies have convertible and other types of debt issues outstanding.

Issuing convertible bonds is a form of deferred common stock financing, because the issuer and investors generally assume that the bonds will be converted before maturity. In order to assure that the conversion takes place, the conversion terms (i.e., conversion rate and price) must be set so that they can be attained; otherwise, investors will not buy the bonds. However, that does not mean investors will convert as soon as their bonds are selling at a conversion premium. All other things being equal, investors may see no reason to convert or sell the bonds as long as they believe the bonds will appreciate in value.

As a further inducement, most bonds contain a **call provision**. If the market price of the bonds becomes sufficiently high and the timing is right from the issuer's point of view, the company can force investors to convert by exercising the call provision. Suppose, for example, that the bond described in the preceding example is called at 104 ($1,040) when its market price is $1,500. Investors will convert their bonds into stock rather than turn the bonds back to the company for $1,040 and lose $460 per bond ($1,500 − $1,040 = $460).

Table 23–2

Advantages and Disadvantages of Convertible Bonds

		Advantages	Disadvantages
Corporation	{	Deferred equity financing Timing of issue Lower interest cost	Might be able to sell stock at a premium price
Investor	{	Safety of bond and growth potential of stock Higher return than common stock	Overhanging issue Dilution of equity

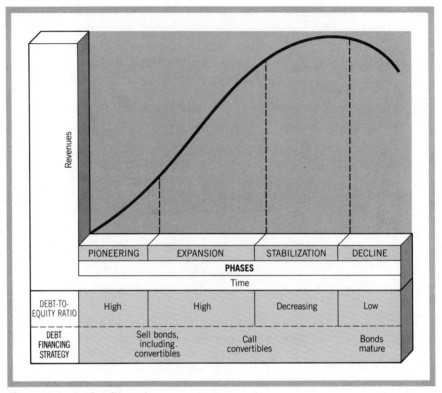

Figure 23–2   Product life cycle.

Timing.   Convertible bonds may be issued when market conditions are not right for issuing common stock, even if the company would prefer a common stock issue. Wide swings in stock market prices in recent years have made the timing of new issues very important. During a period of declining stock prices, companies may turn to convertibles or straight bonds.

Lower Interest Cost.   Short-term cost is also an important consideration when firms decide among financing alternatives. Generally speaking, coupon rates on convertible bonds are lower than those on comparable nonconvertible bonds. This is so because the convertible feature acts as an incentive to investors, who view it as a low-cost call option. Consequently, they are willing to accept a slight reduction in interest payments. The interest cost on a straight debenture may be 13 percent, for example, whereas the interest cost on a convertible issued by the same company may be 12.5 percent.

One-half percentage point doesn't sound like much, but let's put it in the proper context. On a $100 million bond issue, one-half percentage point represents a $500,000 interest payment each year. If the bond has a maturity of 20 years, the one-half percentage point will save the company $10 million in interest payments. Because many convertible bonds are called before maturity, the actual savings on interest costs may be somewhat less, albeit substantial.

Attractiveness to Investors.   Investors like convertible bonds because they combine the safety of a bond with the growth potential of a common stock. If stock prices fall, the bond will sell at its investment value or at a premium above that value. If stock prices rise, the bond will sell at a premium or at its conversion value (see Figure 23–1). In general, convertible bonds allow investors to "have their cake and eat it too."

In addition, the interest payments on newly issued convertible bonds are generally larger than the cash dividends on common stock paid by the issuing corporation. Therefore, investors get a higher dollar return with less risk.

Disadvantages of Convertibles   Convertibles have disadvantages, too. Some of them are discussed here.

Possibility of Selling Stock at a Premium.   Sometimes new issues are considered "hot stocks" by investors, and the company is better off selling new stock at a premium than selling convertible bonds. In 1980, for example, Genentech, a company engaged in biological engineering, issued common stock at $35 per share that soared to $89 per share the same day. Genentech stock was issued at 40 times revenues (not earnings), which is a high premium, reflecting investors' speculative interest in the stock. It is not likely that the company could have sold bonds at such a high premium.

Overhanging Issue.   The potential conversion of bonds to stock creates an **overhanging issue** in the stock market. That is, there is a possibility that the supply of stock traded in the market will increase as a result of conversion. As any student of finance knows, an increase in the number of shares outstanding (supply) without a commensurate increase in the demand for those shares will result in lower stock prices. Accordingly, it is widely believed that potential conversion exerts some downward pressure on the issuer's stock prices, particularly when the bond is in a price range in which it can be converted.

Dilution of Equity.   Another disadvantage of convertibles is that their conversion into common stock results in some dilution of earnings and equity. That is, the same amount of earnings and assets must be spread over a larger number of shares.

Convertible Although the discussion so far has focused on convertible bonds, there is a
Preferreds great deal of financing activity in convertible preferred stocks. Convertible
preferreds are frequently used to give investors both income and the potential
of capital gains. Eighty-five percent of the income from the preferred stock's
dividends is exempt from federal income tax.

As with bonds, the issuers of preferred stock force conversion when it is to
their advantage to do so. This reduces their fixed dividend payments, may
eliminate some restrictive covenants attached to their issues of preferred stock,
and increases the common stock of their firms. In late 1983, United Technologies sent a redemption notice to the holders of its $3.875 convertible pre-
ferred stock, offering them a call premium over the face value of the stock.
Almost all the preferred stock was converted into common stock before the
redemption date. United Technologies also purchased some shares of the
$3.875 convertible preferred on the open market.

Warrants

A **warrant** is a call option to buy a stated number of shares of stock at a
specified price (the **exercise price**), on or before a predetermined date. Warrants often come attached to bonds or preferred stocks but are usually detachable, which means they can be traded on their own investment worth. Most
warrants have a life of 5 or 10 years, but some are perpetual. The **perpetual
warrant** has no expiration date. Tri-Continental Corporation has perpetual
warrants that entitle the holder to buy 4.12 shares of the company's common
stock at $5.46 per share. In contrast, warrants of the Charter Company expire
in 1988. They entitle the holder to purchase one share of stock at $10 per
share until the expiration date.

The holder of a warrant can buy the stock of the issuing corporation by
paying cash or, in some cases, by surrendering bonds (usually at face value)
in lieu of cash. Companies to which bonds can be surrendered in lieu of cash
include the Charter Company, Fugua Industries, Loews Corporation, and Trans
World Corporation.

Value of Warrants The theoretical value of a warrant can be determined by use of the following
equation.

$$\begin{array}{l} \text{Value} \\ \text{of Warrant} \end{array} = \left(\begin{array}{l} \text{Market price of} \\ \text{stock} \end{array} - \begin{array}{l} \text{Exercise} \\ \text{price} \end{array} \right) \times \begin{array}{l} \text{Number of shares} \\ \text{that can be purchased} \\ \text{with each warrant} \end{array} \quad (23\text{--}9)$$

To illustrate the use of this equation, we'll examine Tri-Continental Corporation warrants. Recall that each warrant entitles the holder to 4.12 shares of Tri-Continental common stock at $5.46 per share. If the stock is selling at $20 per share, each warrant is worth $59.90.

$$\text{Value} = (\$20.00 - \$5.46) \times 4.12 = \$59.90$$

This equation only applies when the market price of the stock is greater than the exercise price. When the market price is less than the exercise price, the warrant may still sell for a few cents. If the stock has any growth potential, that is a small price to pay for a long-term call option. Therefore, like convertible bonds, warrants may sell at a premium above their investment value.

Speculative Appeal of Warrants
Warrants have great speculative appeal. A $500 investment in RKO warrants in 1942 would have been worth $104,000 in 1946! But glittering opportunities may prove to be fool's gold. A $500 investment in Atlantic Richfield Oil warrants in 1969 would have been worth $15.87 3 years later.

The reason for the speculative appeal lies in the leverage warrants provide. For example, what if the price of Tri-Continental Corporation's common stock doubled (increased 100 percent) from the current $20 price. In this case, the warrant would increase in value from $59.90 to $142.30, or by 138 percent, calculated as follows.

$$\text{Value} = (\$40.00 - \$5.46) \times 4.12 = \$142.30$$

Leverage, remember, is a double-edged sword. If the price of Tri-Continental stock fell from $20 per share to $10 per share (a decrease of 50 percent), the value of the warrants would fall from $59.90 to $18.70—a reduction of 68.8 percent.

Reason for Issuing Warrants
Companies issue warrants as a sweetener—a means to make a bond or preferred stock issue more attractive to investors. Sweeteners are used by companies of all sizes and degrees of financial strength. For example, American Telephone and Telegraph Company (AT&T) raised $1.6 billion in 1970 by selling bonds with warrants attached. This sweetener was designed to attract equity investors to the issue.

Investors are willing to accept somewhat lower interest rates for securities sold with warrants attached. As noted in the discussion of convertible bonds, a small reduction in interest cost can save the issuing company millions of dollars over the life of the bond.

Rights

Companies may offer new stock issues to their existing shareholders instead of offering them to the public, primarily to allow existing shareholders to maintain their proportionate shares of ownership in the corporation. As explained in Chapter 22, shareholders are said to have **preemptive rights** to purchase their **pro rata share** of new stock issues. Although the concept of preemptive rights is currently being questioned in the courts, so-called **privileged subscriptions**, or **rights offerings**, are commonplace.

Normally, stockholders receive one right for each share of stock they own. The issuing company informs its stockholders how many rights are required to buy a new share at a specified **subscription price**. The subscription price must be lower than the current market price to induce shareholders to take advantage of the rights offering. In essence, as mentioned, a right is like a short-term option.

As noted in Chapter 22, three courses of action are open to shareholders who receive rights: (1) exercise the rights and subscribe to the stock (2) sell the rights, or (3) let the rights expire. Because the rights have monetary value, most shareholders exercise them or sell them. Keep in mind that shareholders who sell their rights are reducing their share of ownership in the company, as they would if they sold some of the stock they held.

Rights can be bought and sold from the date the offering is announced until they expire, which is usually 2 or 3 weeks after the **date of record**—the date by which stockholders must have their names on the company's books to receive distributions. Between the announcement date and the date of record, the stock is traded **cum rights**, or with rights attached. After the date of record, the stock sells **ex-rights**, or without rights, and the rights trade separately.

Until the rights are mailed to the shareholders, they are traded on a *when-issued (W.I.)* basis. Trading W.I. usually begins the day the stock goes ex-rights and can last from several days to several weeks. As soon as the rights are mailed to stockholders, trading on a *regular way* basis begins.

Value of Rights **Cum Rights.** When a stock sells cum rights, the theoretical value of one of these rights is determined by the use of the following equation.

$$V_1 = \frac{P_0 - S}{N + 1} \tag{23-10}$$

where

V_1 = Value of one right when the stock is cum rights
P_0 = Market price of a share of stock
S = Subscription price of one share
N = Number of rights necessary to buy one share of new stock

For purposes of illustration, we'll examine Brush Company's rights offering. The company's stock is selling at $40 per share, and four rights are required to buy a new share at the subscription price of $38. When the rights are still attached to the stock, each has a theoretical value of $0.40, as determined by use of Equation 23–10.

$$V_1 = \frac{P_0 - S}{N + 1} = \frac{\$40 - \$38}{4 + 1} = \$0.40$$

Rights, like warrants, are highly leveraged. For example, if the stock price increased 10 percent, to $44 per share, the value of the rights would increase 300 percent, to $1.20.

$$V_1 = \frac{P_0 - S}{N + 1} = \frac{\$44 - \$38}{4 + 1} = \$1.20$$

If the stock's market price fell below the subscription price to $37 per share, theoretically the rights would have no value. Investors would buy the stock at the current market price ($37) instead of buying it at the higher subscription price ($38). In reality, as with warrants, the rights might still sell for a few cents each. This premium is attributable to speculators who think the stock will increase in value before the rights expire. Since the market price is below the subscription price, investors will not subscribe the new issue. This is why some companies use standby underwriters, as mentioned in Chapter 22.

Ex-Rights. When the stock sells ex-rights, the market price of a share of stock should decline by an amount equal to the value of one right. In other words, the market value of a share of stock selling ex-rights is equal to the value cum rights less the value of a right. Therefore, when a stock is selling ex-rights, the theoretical value of one right can be determined as follows.

$$V_2 = \frac{P_0 - V_1 - S}{N}$$

$$= \frac{(\$40 - \$0.40 - \$38)}{4}$$

$$= \$0.40 \qquad\qquad (23\text{–}11)$$

where

V_2 = Value of one right when the stock is ex-rights

In other words, V_1 should equal V_2.

Summary

Convertible securities include bonds, preferred stock, warrants, and rights. Convertible bonds and preferreds can be converted into common stock during a specified period before the bonds mature. The conversion rate and the price per share at which the common stock may be acquired are also specified. (Equations related to conversion, with other equations from this chapter, appear in Table 23–3.) Investors frequently pay a conversion premium to buy convertible bonds. The premium may be based on the bond's market value or its investment value. In effect, the premium is the price paid for a call option on the stock. The valuation model for a convertible bond is similar to that for a straight bond, but it takes into account the price of the stock into which the bond can be converted.

Investors like convertible bonds because they combine the safety of a bond with the growth potential of common stock. For the issuing company, con-

Table 23–3
Summary of Equations

	Equations		Equation Number
Conversion rate	Conversion rate $= \dfrac{\text{Face value of bond}}{\text{Conversion price}}$		(23–1)
Conversion value	$CV = R \times S$		(23–2)
Conversion premium based on market value	$P^* = \dfrac{P_B - CV}{CV}$		(23–3)
Conversion premium based on investment value	$P^{**} = \dfrac{CV - I}{I}$		(23–4)
Market price of bond	$P_B = \displaystyle\sum_{t=1}^{n} \dfrac{I}{(1 + k_{db})^t} + \dfrac{F}{(1 + k_{db})^n}$		(23–5)
Market price of bond taking conversion into account	$P_B = \displaystyle\sum_{t=1}^{n} \dfrac{I}{(1 + k_c)^t} + \dfrac{CV}{(1 + k_c)^N}$		(23–6)
Stock price at end of period t	$P_t = P_S (1 + g)^t$		(23–7)
Conversion value	$CV = P_i R$		(23–8)
Value of Warrant	Value of warrant $= \left(\begin{matrix} \text{Market price} \\ \text{of stock} \end{matrix} - \begin{matrix} \text{Exercise} \\ \text{Price} \end{matrix} \right) \times$	Number of shares that can be purchased with each warrant	(23–9)
Value of right, cum rights	$V_1 = \dfrac{P_0 - S}{N + 1}$		(23–10)
Value of right ex rights	$V_2 = \dfrac{P_0 - V_1 - S}{N}$		(23–11)

vertible financing is a form of deferred equity financing that can be used when the timing may not be optimal for a stock issue. Moreover, interest rates on convertibles are typically lower than interest rates on straight bond issues. On the negative side, new stock issues may be more likely to bring a premium price. Further, the possibility of conversion associated with convertibles creates an overhanging issue, and actual conversion dilutes shareholders' equity and earnings.

Warrants and rights also act as call options on common stock. Warrants are generally attached to other securities as sweeteners, but they can be traded separately. The value of a warrant is determined by the relationship of the stock's market value to the stock price set by the warrant. Because of the way they are valued, warrants are highly leveraged and have great speculative appeal.

Rights are like short-term warrants. They are call options given to existing shareholders that allow them to maintain their proportionate shares of ownership and earnings. Like warrants, rights can be traded separately and are highly leveraged.

One effect of convertibles, warrants, and rights is to increase the number of common shares outstanding. In the case of convertibles and warrants, the increase in number of shares dilutes the earnings for existing shareholders.

Important Terms

Call option	Investment value
Call provision	Market price
Conversion discount	Overhanging issue
Conversion premium	Parity
Conversion price	Perpetual warrant
Conversion rate	Preemptive rights
Conversion value	Privileged subscription
Convertible bond	Pro rata share
Convertible preferred	Rights
Cum rights	Rights offering
Date of record	Subscription price
Exercise price	Theoretical value
Ex-rights	Warrant

Options

The word **option** has been used extensively in this chapter. Convertible securities, warrants, and rights all contain call options to buy stock. Options have a long history, usually associated with speculation. For example, Aristotle in his *Politics* criticized Thales' use of options. Thales was a man of modest means who gained control of the olive presses of Miletus. He believed that the next olive harvest would be a big one and thus secured options for the use of the presses at harvest time. His forecast proved to be correct and he rented the presses at a substantial profit. More recently, options have been associated with such well-known speculators as Commodore Vanderbilt, Daniel Drew, and Jay Gould. Today, options are traded on several stock exchanges.

In spite of their speculative appeal, the use of options did not become widespread until organized trading began in 1973 on the Chicago Board Options Exchange (CBOE). At about that time, both public and academic interest in options increased. The public became interested in options because they are a unique vehicle for both investment and speculation. Academic interest increased when Fischer Black and Myron Scholes published their seminal paper explaining the value of an option.[1] Although a discussion of the Black–Scholes model is beyond the scope of this book, the following explanation of options may induce some readers to explore their model.

Basic Terms

Two basic types of options are used to buy and sell stocks: calls and puts. A **call option** is a contract to buy a specified number of shares of stock at a predetermined price on or before a stated date. For example, we'll assume an investor can buy a call option on 100 shares of Clover Company at $40 per share for 95 days. This contract gives the holder the right to buy 100 shares of Clover company at $40 per share any time between the time she buys the option and 95 days from then.

A **put option** is a contract to sell a specified number of shares of stock at a

---

[1]Fischer Black and Myron Scholes, "The Pricing of Options and Corporate Liabilities," *Journal of Political Economy,* May–June 1973, pp. 637–654.

predetermined price on or before a certain date. The discussion to follow will focus on call options, but remember that the only difference between a put and a call is that a call is an option to buy and a put is an option to sell.

Most options specify a price close to the market price of the stock. Thus, if the stock is selling for about $40 per share, the **contract price** or **striking price** of the option is also $40 per share.

A **premium** is a fee the option buyer pays to the option seller. The amount of the premium, or the value of the option, is determined by supply and demand for the option; the price, volatility, and riskiness of the underlying security; and the maturity of the option. Suppose the buyer of the Clover call option pays $400 for it. This amount goes to the seller of the option and to the brokers that act as intermediaries. As a rule, premiums amount to between 10 and 15 percent of the market value of the underlying security.

Options traded on the CBOE and other exchanges have standardized expiration dates and striking prices that facilitate continuous trading activity in many options.

If the option is exercised, the holder of the option receives the value of all dividends and rights distributed during the contract period. For example, let's say that during the contract period Clover Company declares a $0.50 per share dividend and then goes ex-dividend. If the option is exercised, the option holder is entitled to the cash dividend. However, if the option is exercised after the stock goes ex-dividend, the option holder is not entitled to the dividend.

Buying Call Options for Speculation

For the past 3 weeks, the financial press has been reporting that the Clover Company is trying to acquire another company. If Clover does acquire the other company, it will triple its assets. On the basis of the news stories, Clover's stock price has risen $20 in the past few weeks. It is currently selling at $40 per share.

In this situation, a speculator has two courses of action. The first is to buy, say, 100 shares of stock for $4,000. In this case, there is $4,000 *at risk*—$4,000 that can be lost. If the stock price goes up to $50 per share, the speculator can sell the stock and realize a $1,000 profit, or a 25 percent return on the funds at risk.

The second course of action is to buy a 95-day call option at $40 per share for $400. If the stock price increases to $50 per share, the value of the option will increase to about $1,000 and the speculator who bought the option can exercise it or sell it. If the speculator exercises the option, she buys stock for $4,000 and immediately sells it at the current market price for $5,000. The gross profit (ignoring commissions and taxes) is $600 ($5,000 − $4,000 −

$400 = $600). In this case, the speculator has $400 (the cost of the option) at risk. Selling the stock immediately prevents the $4,000 paid for the stock from being placed at risk. The same results can be obtained if the speculator sells the option for $1,000, realizing a $600 gross profit on a $400 investment ($1,000 − $400 = $600). The three strategies are summarized in the following table.

Course of Action	Gross Profit	Percent Return on Funds at Risk
1. Buy and sell stock	$1,000	25% ($4,000 at risk)
2a. Buy call option, exercise it, and sell stock	$ 600	150% ($ 400 at risk)
2b. Buy and sell call option	$ 600	150% ($ 400 at risk)

By buying a call option, the speculator has accomplished the following.

1. Reduced maximum loss in case of a decline in stock price to $400, the cost of the option.
2. Controlled 100 shares of Clover Company stock for 95 days by investing $400 instead of $4,000.
3. Gained financial leverage. A small investment of $400 has tied up $4,000 of someone else's money for 95 days. Moreover, the potential profits amount to a 150 percent return on investment in 95 days or less.

Selling Call Options

Investors sell, or *write*, call options to make money. However, the option seller, or *writer*, must give up the opportunity to make large gains in a stock for the opportunity to make continuous smaller gains. The option writer is like a banker making loans to business concerns. The business concerns use the borrowed funds to make large profits and the banker is satisfied to get back the funds that were lent, plus interest.

In the preceding examples, the buyer of the 95-day call option on Clover Company paid a $400 premium. Let's ignore the brokerage commissions and say that the entire premium went to the writer who sold the option to that buyer. Further assume that the option writer bought 100 shares of Clover Company stock to write the option. Although the option writer can borrow 50 percent of the funds necessary to buy the stock, he still has $4,000 at risk. Therefore, the option writer's return on invested funds is greater than the return on funds at risk if the option is exercised or expires above the contract (striking) price. The return on the funds at risk is 11.1 percent and the return on the invested funds is twice that amount, as shown in the following table.

Rate of return on funds at risk

Buy 100 shares at $40	$4,000
Less premium	− 400
Total cash involvement	$3,600
Percent return	$400/$3,600 = 11.1%

Rate of return on invested funds

Buy 100 shares at $40	$4,000
	− 400
	$3,600
Less borrowed funds	− 1,800
Total cash investment	$1,800
Return on invested funds	$400/$1,800 = 22.2%

If the option writer can repeat this performance over and over, his annual return on funds at risk will be more than 40 percent. When commissions and taxes are taken into account, the annual return is substantially lower. Nevertheless, the possible returns induce many investors to write options.

The option writer gets to keep the premium no matter what happens to the stock. The two best things that can happen to the option writer are to have the stock called before the option expires so that the funds can be used to write more options, or to have the option expire just below the striking price so that another call can be written on the same stock. The worst thing that can happen is to have the stock decline in price. If it falls too far and the writer does not sell it, a loss will result.

Some option writers write *naked* call options; that is, they do not buy the stock when they sell call options. Others are naked on some and covered on others. They do this to increase their returns, particularly if the stock price declines. However, naked options also add a significant degree of risk to the investment because, if the stock does increase in price, writers have to buy the shares at a higher price to cover their options.

Important Terms

Call option	Premium
Contract price	Put option
Option	Striking price

Questions

1. What general benefits do convertible bonds and preferred stock offer investors? What general benefits do they offer firms?
2. Define *conversion price, conversion value, conversion rate,* and *investment value.*
3. What does it mean to say that a convertible bond is selling at parity?

4. Why might investors pay $1,000 for a convertible bond when the conversion value is $840?

5. Distinguish between two types of conversion premiums.

6. How does the valuation of a convertible bond differ from the valuation of a straight bond?

7. Why are call features on convertibles useful to financial managers?

8. Explain the term *overhanging issue*. What problem may underlie such an issue?

9. Identify some disadvantages of convertible bond financing.

10. Define *stock warrants*. What are detachable and perpetual warrants?

11. What gives warrants speculative appeal to investors?

12. What are some benefits of warrants to issuing corporations?

13. Briefly explain the process of a rights offering.

14. Why might both rights and warrants have positive market values when the current stock price is below the subscription or exercise price?

Problems

1. Calculate the conversion rate for each of the following securities:
(a) $1,000 face value bond convertible into common stock at $40 per share.
(b) $1,000 face value bond convertible into common stock at $33.33 per share.
(c) $50 par value preferred convertible into common stock at $40 per share.
(d) $100 par value preferred convertible into common stock at $32 per share.

2. Find the conversion price for each of the following issues:
(a) $1,000 face value bond convertible into 23 shares of common stock.
(b) $80 par value preferred with a conversion rate of 6.
(c) $1,000 face value bond with a conversion rate of 40 for 5 years, 30 for years 6 through 10, and 20 thereafter.

3. Troy Pump Company has a convertible bond outstanding with a current market price of $930. The conversion rate is 23 and the current price of the stock is $35 per share. What is the conversion premium?

4. Calculate the conversion premium for the following bonds.

Bond	Market Price of Bond	Conversion Rate	Market Price of Stock
a	$1,120	9	$135
b	980	32	29
c	620	17	15

5. Scranton Chemicals issued a convertible bond 5 years ago with a face value of $1,000, a 9 percent coupon, and a conversion rate of 25. Its investment value is $795. The firm's common stock is currently selling at $38 per share. Calculate the conversion premium based on investment value.

6. Calculate the conversion premiums based on investment value for each of the following bonds.

Bond	Investment Value	Conversion Value
v	$860	$1,100
w	840	840
x	720	510

7. White Corporation issued a convertible bond 10 years ago when its common stock sold for $12 per share. The price has grown at a rate of 6 percent annually since the date of issue.
   (a) Compute the current stock price.
   (b) Compute the conversion value if the conversion rate is 75.

 8. Hemlock Brewery is planning a convertible bond issue. The bond will have a 9.5 percent annual interest rate and a conversion rate of 40 on a face value of $1,000. The current price of common stock is $20 per share and a growth rate of 8 percent per year is forecast. The bonds are expected to be converted in 4 years. Calculate the current market value of the bond. Investors require an 11 percent rate of return on convertible bonds of similar risk.

9. Briggs Shoe Company has just issued a 20-year, 11 percent coupon, $1,000 face value convertible bond. The firm expects growth in its stock price, now at $30, of 10 percent per year. The conversion rate on the bond is 28. What will investors pay for the bond if their required rate of return is 14 percent and the bonds are expected to be converted in 3 years?

10. Mike Howard is considering the purchase of a convertible bond with a 9 percent coupon, a $1,000 face value, and a conversion rate of 50. The current market price of the stock is $14, and Mike expects a 12 percent annual growth rate. He requires a 15 percent return on his investment and plans to convert the bond when its conversion value reaches $1,225. How much should he pay for the bond?

11. Truroad Tire Company is analyzing the market's expected reaction to the following two bond issues.

	Bond A	Bond B
Coupon rate	11%	8%
Conversion rate	23	28.85
Maturity	20 years	20 years
Face value	$1,000	$1,000

The firm's stock price, currently $25, is expected to grow at 12 percent annually. Conversion is expected in 4 years, regardless of which bond is issued, and investors require in a 14 percent rate of return. Which bond will sell at the higher price?

12. Thunder Corporation has issued perpetual warrants that allow the investor to buy 3.4 shares of common stock at $12 per share for each warrant held. Calculate the theoretical value of a warrant if the stock price is now $10; $15; $20.

13. Dogpatch Recreation has warrants outstanding with a market price of $5 per warrant. Each warrant permits the purchase of one share of Dogpatch stock for $17 per share. The stock is now selling for $20 per share. Calculate the theoretical value of a warrant. Compare this value with the market price and offer an explanation for the difference, if any.

14. Investors have a choice of purchasing the common stock of Isotope Genetics or of buying Isotope's warrants. The market price of the stock is $54 per share. The warrants, which allow the holder to purchase two shares of stock at $50 per share, currently sell for $20. Calculate the percentage loss or gain on both the warrant and the stock in the following situations:
    (a) Common stock increases to $70 per share, warrants to $45.
    (b) Common stock increases to $100 per share, warrants to $102.
    (c) Common stock decreases to $40 per share, warrants to $8.
    (d) Common stock decreases to $10 per share, warrants to $0.50.

15. Panama Corporation wishes to raise $13 million by issuing common stock through a rights offering. There are now 10 million shares outstanding. The current market price of the stock is $32 per share and the subscription price is $26. How many new shares will be issued? If one right per current share is issued, how many rights will it take to purchase one share?

16. Calculate the value of one right under the following situations.

P_0	S	N
$40	$36	7
73	68	8
62	58	12
27	24	6

17. Lana Lamar owns 1,200 shares of Hollywood Highlights, a firm that purchases the rights to old movies. The firm recently offered stockholders the right to purchase new shares at $16 per share. The market price at the time was $21, but it has since risen to $25. Stockholders need four rights to purchase one share at the $16 price. What is the total dollar value of Ms. Lamar's holding if she purchases 100 additional shares of Hollywood Highlights and sells her remaining rights as soon as the stock goes ex-rights?

18. Great Lakes Coal's common stock is selling for $73 per share. The company is considering the issuance of rights, permitting shareholders to purchase one additional share of stock at $67.50 for each six rights held. What is the theoretical value of a right if the stock price increases to $76 per share?

Problems 19 and 20 are based on material in the appendix to this chapter.

19. Illini Welding is rumored to be a takeover target. Its stock is now selling at $20 per share. An option writer has offered to sell you a call option on Illini stock. The option will entitle you to purchase 400 shares at $20 per share, will cost you $900, and will expire in 90 days. As an alternative, you can buy 400 shares of stock and skip the call. Assuming the stock price rises to $30 per share and the option value to $1,500, calculate your percentage return on funds at risk in situations a through d below.

(a) You buy the stock now, then sell it after it rises to $30.

(b) You buy the call now, then exercise it and sell the stock after it rises to $30 per share.

(c) You buy the call now and sell it after the stock rises to $30.

(d) You buy the stock and its price falls to $15.

(e) What is the maximum loss you could sustain from buying the call?

20. Suppose you are the option writer in the situation described in Problem 19. What is the rate of return on your funds at risk? What is your rate of return on invested funds if you borrow 40 percent of the money to purchase the stock at the time the option is written?

Special Topics

Part 8 deals with two topics of special interest in today's business world. One involves mergers. Lots of big firms buy little firms, and in some cases little firms buy big firms, as though they were playing Monopoly. Chapter 24 explains some of the rules of this game. Chapter 25 is about international finance, a subject that is becoming increasingly important. Why? To answer that question just look around at all the foreign-made cars, television sets, shoes, and other products we use every day.

24 External Growth and Contraction

I was having lunch with a crafty banker who was telling how his organization had grown from one bank with $3 million on deposit to 22 banks with $1.5 billion on deposit. Someone at the table asked him what factors he considered important when he bought his first banks. The banker smiled and said, "You can't get ahead of the next man if you follow in his tracks." He wanted to be different. He went on to explain that he wanted a bank in every major market in the state and in the minor markets too. He wanted to be the dominant factor in each market. The fastest way to achieve that goal was to buy existing banks. This kind of entrepreneurial spirit—a desire for wealth, power, or whatever—is behind many mergers and acquisitions. Mergers provide some firms with a vehicle for rapid growth and others with a vehicle for survival.

After reading this chapter, you should know the following.

1. **How mergers and the life cycle are related.**
2. **Why mergers take place.**
3. **How to identify various types of business combinations.**
4. **How to evaluate merger terms.**
5. **What tactics are used to effect and to guard against unfriendly mergers.**
6. **How mergers are accounted for.**

A White Knight[1]

The management of Pullman Inc., a company that makes railway cars and various other products, believed the company was going to be the target of a takeover attempt. To guard against an unfriendly takeover, management wanted to find a **white knight**—a merger partner of its own choosing. The chairman of Pullman consulted First Boston Corporation, a leading investment banking firm that had been working with Pullman for 15 years, and asked for help.

The team of specialists in First Boston's mergers and acquisitions department narrowed a list of potential merger candidates down to 65 companies that had the technical expertise and financial ability to consummate the deal. Each of the prospective partners was consulted to determine its interest. Interested firms were provided data about Pullman—the greater the interest, the more data.

A few weeks after the search process began, there was some unusually heavy trading activity in Pullman's stock. Shortly thereafter, J. Ray McDermott & Company, a builder of offshore oil rigs, made a **tender offer** for Pullman stock—that is, an offer to buy a certain number of shares at a fixed price on or before a certain date. A tender offer signals a takeover attempt. The company offered $28 per share for 2 million shares of Pullman stock—a low bid, since the market price of the stock was $27 at that time. McDermott's low bid reflected its belief that Pullman would have difficulty attracting a white knight, because the firm had been experiencing various problems. In this belief, McDermott was mistaken.

One of First Boston's candidates, Wheelabrator-Frye (an engineering firm), expressed interest in Pullman. First Boston and Wheelabrator developed strat-

---

[1]This section is based on Bob Tamarkin, "A Crazy Kid from Newark," *Forbes*, September 29, 1980, pp. 42–43; and "Wheelabrator's Edge in the Fight for Pullman," *Business Week*, September 22, 1980, pp. 35–36.

egies for the next moves in the merger game. Wheelabrator offered $43 per share for 2 to 4 million shares and a call option at the market price for an additional 1.8 million shares. In addition, an option was included that would allow Wheelabrator to buy Pullman's construction division for $200 million if the merger fell through. The construction division was the part of Pullman that McDermott wanted most.

The battle lines were drawn. McDermott moved with a $43.50 bid for stock, $0.50 more than the Wheelabrator bid. Wheelabrator counterattacked with a bid of $52.50 per share. Then McDermott increased the ante to $54 per share for 5.4 million shares and $39 per share for additional shares.

In addition to the bidding war, legal battles raged in the courts. Pullman filed a lawsuit to block McDermott's offer by alleging violations of securities laws. Among other things, Pullman charged McDermott with "tawdry maneuvering" that "flagrantly mistreated" minority shareholders. This lawsuit was dropped, but Pullman was also pressing an antitrust lawsuit against McDermott.

By this time Wheelabrator had already purchased 49 percent of the stock at $52.50 or less. Speculators were afraid of the McDermott offer because of the lawsuits and the possibility that McDermott might withdraw the offer, leaving them holding Pullman stock. So Wheelabrator won the battle for Pullman. But the story doesn't end there.

Wheelabrator did not really want all of Pullman; it wanted the construction division. Therefore, Wheelabrator planned to **spin off** some of Pullman's assets by giving shares to stockholders. Wheelabrator shareholders would receive half the shares of the new Pullman Transportation Company (PTC) and Wheelabrator would own the other half. The shareholders of PTC would be given the option to buy the Trailmobile division (trucks), Pullman Leasing Company, and Pullman Finance Company from Wheelabrator. Thus, the white knight saved Pullman from McDermott but then dismembered Pullman. Was Pullman better off with the white knight?

Reasons for Mergers

The story of Pullman and its white knight presents mergers in a dramatic light. However, the primary reasons for mergers generally involve the everyday concerns of businesses. Theories of why firms merge may be divided into four broad areas: managerialism, market power, taxes, and efficiency.[2]

The idea behind *managerialism* is that managers acquire other firms so they can receive larger rewards—the bigger the firms they control, the more they get paid. However, it has been shown that management compensation is more closely related to profitability than to sales.

[2]J. Fred Weston and Kwang S. Chung, "Some Aspects of Merger Theory," *Journal of the Midwest Finance Association*, 1983, pp. 1–33.

Another reason suggested for mergers is that they will result in *increased market power*, although what market power means is not altogether clear. Presumably, if the merged firms are in the same industry (for example, if they are food stores), the reduction in the number of competing firms leads to increased concentration of sellers.

Taxes are a frequently suggested reason for buying or selling firms. One reason for acquiring firms is to expand depreciable assets, because increased depreciation expenses mean lower taxes. Inheritance tax considerations also play an important role in the sale of many small, privately owned firms.

The *efficiency* theories of mergers encompass a number of categories, some of which are examined in the remainder of this section. Collectively, efficiency motives for mergers appear to be more important for large mergers than managerialism, market power, or taxes. Little, however, is known about the mergers of small companies.

Life Cycle Considerations From previous discussions, you know that the expansion phase of the life cycle for an industry is characterized by increasing total sales and revenues and declining unit prices (see Figure 24–1). Many companies enter the industry during the expansion phase in hopes of making large profits. However, high

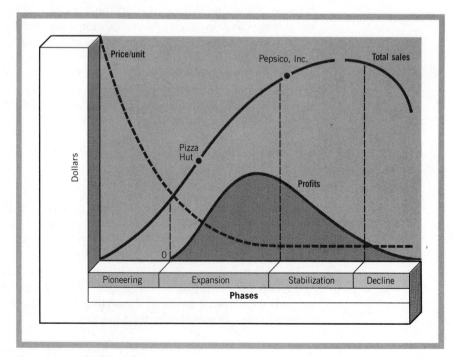

Figure 24–1   The life cycle.

startup costs and declining unit prices make it impossible for some to survive on their own. Some of these companies go out of business. Others are acquired by firms that have the financial strength to support the weaker firms' remaining in the market. The idea is to permit the weak company to produce enough so that the acquiring company benefits from the weak company's learning curves. Recall from Chapter 10 that learning curves are based on production experience and are used to cut costs. By reducing costs sufficiently, in spite of declining revenues, the company can make a profit.

Another aspect of the life cycle involves the growth potential of a company. Consider the case of Pepsico, Inc., the world's second largest producer of soft drinks. Pepsico, a successful firm, can be expected to grow at a more moderate rate in the future than it has in the past, as suggested in Figure 24–1. One way to accelerate growth is to acquire growing companies. Thus, Pepsico acquired Pizza Hut, one of the nation's leading fast-food franchisers. Pizza Hut's sales and profits were expanding rapidly at the time of acquisition; it was clearly a growing company. Pepsico hoped the addition of Pizza Hut would contribute significantly to its profits. Unfortunately, not all mergers work out for the best. Pizza Hut's performance was mediocre for several years following the acquisition.

Diversification.   The concept of **diversification** can be examined in the context of the life cycle. Think of a firm as a portfolio of individual (subsidiary) companies. In order for the firm to survive, it must have some growing companies to replace those in the declining phase of the life cycle. Similarly, it needs companies in the stabilization phase to provide funds for the growing companies. The financial manager's job is to determine the proper mix of companies in various phases of the life cycle. In some cases, new companies should be added to the portfolio, and in other cases, existing companies should be sold.

Esmark, Inc., provides a good example of a portfolio adjustment made by a diversified holding company. Esmark owned Swift & Company (meats), Playtex (undergarments), and other investments. In the early 1980s, Esmark's management sold Vickers Energy Company (petroleum), a profitable company with good growth prospects, for $1.1 billion. Esmark used some of the funds to reduce its long-term debt, some to provide working capital, and the remainder to expand its other diverse activities.

Tenneco is another example of a diversified company. It controls the following eight businesses

Tenneco Oil—oil drilling and exploration.
Tenneco Gas Transmission—natural gas pipelines.
Newport News Shipbuilding—liquid natural gas (LNG) carriers and other ships.
J. I. Case—tractors and construction equipment.

Tenneco Automotive—exhaust systems, Monroe Auto Equipment.
Packaging Corporation of America—corrugated boxes.
Tenneco Chemicals—additives for paints, vinyl plastics.
Tenneco West—Sun Giant raisins and other foods.

An examination of the eight components reveals logical connections between some of them. The oil, pipelines, and chemicals seem to fit together. This gives rise to possible *synergy*; that is, the components may have a greater impact when combined than they can have individually. Examination also reveals that some of the businesses have little in common—raisins and Monroe Auto Equipment, for example. Thus, Tenneco may be considered a conglomerate, a combination of essentially unrelated firms. Esmark is also a conglomerate. More will be said about this subject later in the chapter.

Viewing diversification in a portfolio context involves another aspect. The returns from the various assets in the portfolio may result in less volatile earnings for the firm as a whole. This, in turn, can affect credit ratings and the cost of capital. Investors, of course, can achieve diversification on their own by investing in assets whose returns are not perfectly positively correlated. Therefore, conglomerates may not do anything for investors that, with sufficient funds, they could not do for themselves.

Limited Financial Resources   Limited financial resources are a chronic problem for small companies. While a conglomerate may not be able to generate all the funds a newly acquired company wants, it frequently can arrange for the company to borrow more easily from a commercial bank or other type of lender because of the conglomerate's size and earnings base. It is not surprising that borrowing usually occurs at banks where other affiliates of the conglomerate maintain large deposits.

On the other hand, many large companies also have borrowing problems, particularly high-technology companies that need a great deal of capital. To obtain funds to sustain their operations, such companies may try to acquire firms that will provide either a substantial cash flow or access to external funds. For example, Control Data acquired Commercial Credit.

Management Talent   Management is another limited resource. Growth requires management talent in addition to capital resources. In theory, conglomerate mergers provide management with expertise in many areas, such as engineering, marketing, labor relations, and so on. The entrepreneur who started a small business may be a good chemist but a poor accountant or salesperson. Presumably, the conglomerate will take over management and other technical functions to allow the entrepreneur to specialize in areas where she or he is most proficient.

New Markets   A merger can open new markets. A large electronics company, for example, may acquire a small printing shop. The electronics company can use the printing company for its own work and can also market the acquired services to its customers. Therefore, it is possible that the conglomerate's printing costs can be reduced while the printing division's sales are increased. It follows that mergers may encourage entry into new fields or expansion in existing fields.

New Product Lines Special circumstances in some industries lend themselves to merger activity. For example, the computer industry faces growing customer demand to buy full product lines from a single source rather than components from many manufacturers. Customers want both hardware and software from the same firm. This situation contributes to the growth of multiproduct firms in this important industry.

Undervalued Assets Sometimes it costs less to acquire an undervalued company than to create assets afresh. Such was the case in various oil company mergers in 1981, when stock prices of oil companies were depressed. In August, Du Pont acquired Conoco Oil. In October, Mobil made an offer to buy the shares of Marathon; Mobil had decided it would be cheaper to buy Marathon and obtain its existing oil reserves than to spend huge sums and take large risks exploring for new reserves. U.S. Steel also wanted Marathon, as part of a diversification plan. Mobil lost the battle for Marathon. Other large mergers involving oil companies included Texaco's purchase of Getty Oil Company and Socal's purchase of Gulf Oil.

Liquidity Several of the rationales for mergers already discussed have focused on the acquiring company's point of view. The acquired company's point of view is equally interesting. For example, many small companies were formed during the Depression and after World War II. Their owners are now approaching retirement age and seeking marketability and liquidity for their estates. Many of these owners have attained an acceptable level of material comfort and have little desire for change and the rigors of competition. Selling out is one way to satisfy their needs.

Timing The time may be right for a merger. Some companies, realizing that current success may not last long, sell out before business declines. Such companies must decide in advance on strategies with regard to debt, sales, and so on, to make the company "look good" and obtain a high price.

Acquisition, Divestiture, and Shareholders Some used car dealers buy cars at a low price, fix them up, and then sell them for a profit. Every now and then they make a bad deal and have to take a loss to get rid of the car. Other dealers specialize in one type of car for a few years and then change, for one reason or another. Some corporate giants buy companies and sell (or divest) them in much the same way. Esmark, mentioned earlier, was one such giant. Some of Esmark's major acquisitions and divestitures are listed in the following table.

Acquisitions	Divestitures
Norton Simon	Swift Independent Packing
International Playtex	Swift's soybean milling, broiler chicken, and oil refinery edible businesses
Danskin	Vickers Petroleum
Doric Corporation	GSI & Globe Life Insurance
Jhirmack	Canadian food operations

This list is not complete, but it does help illustrate one large company's practice of buying and selling other companies. In 1984, Esmark itself was bought by Beatrice Foods Company.

What does all this buying and selling do for shareholders? A recent study reported that voluntary divestitures, or selling of acquired companies, benefited shareholders—and the stronger the financial position of the seller, the more shareholders benefited.[3]

Types of Combinations

So far, the term *merger* has been used in a general way to describe the combination of two or more firms; and we will continue to use it in this way. However, important differences exist among the various types of business combinations.

Merger A **merger** is the combination of two or more companies with only one company surviving. For example, Pizza Hut merged into Pepsico, and Pepsico is the surviving company in terms of stock ownership. Pizza Hut is an operating division of Pepsico; it retains the Pizza Hut name only to enhance its marketability.

Consolidation A **consolidation** occurs when two or more companies combine to form a new company and the original companies cease to exist. The Pennsylvania Railroad and the New York Central Railroad combined to form the PennCentral Railroad. Similarly, North Central Airlines and Southern Airways combined to form

[3]Douglas Hearth and Janis K. Zaima, "Voluntary Corporate Divestitures and Value," *Financial Management*, Spring 1984, pp. 10–16.

Republic Airlines. Republic was then acquired by Northwest Airlines. In these examples, all operations, assets, and liabilities became the responsibility of the new corporate entities; the old companies no longer exist.

Types of Mergers and Consolidations The Federal Trade Commission (FTC), which oversees merger activity in the United States, classifies mergers and consolidations according to the economic relationship between the acquired and acquiring firm. The two economic classifications the commission uses are horizontal merger and vertical merger.

Horizontal Mergers. A merger is **horizontal** when the companies involved produce identical or closely related products in the same geographic area. A bank acquiring another bank in the same geographic area is an example of a horizontal merger.

Vertical Mergers. A merger is **vertical** when the companies involved had a potential buyer-seller relationship prior to the merger. A steel company acquiring a coal company is an example of a vertical merger, because steel companies purchase coal.

Conglomerate Mergers A **conglomerate merger** involves the combination of essentially unrelated firms. The word *conglomerate* has negative connotations for some investors and companies—a result of the speculation and empire building by conglomerates in the late 1960s. Some conglomerates bought companies indiscriminately in order to grow rapidly. Some of the mergers did not work out and the organizations failed. Other conglomerate firms were luckier and are still around; but they do not like to be called conglomerates.

In spite of the fact that it is not a popular term with companies, *conglomerate* is the official designation used by the Federal Trade Commission. Gulf & Western Industries, for example, is a conglomerate with interest in machine tools (E. W. Bliss), paper products (Brown Company), motion pictures (Paramount), financial services (Associated Corporation), automotive parts (A.P.S.), cigars (Consolidated Cigars), menswear (Kayser–Roth), sugar, and natural resources.

The Federal Trade Commission classifies conglomerate mergers as product extension, market extension, or other. The first two categories are somewhat similar to the horizontal mergers described earlier, but they apply to conglomerate mergers.

Product Extension. A conglomerate merger is considered **product extension** when the companies are functionally related in production or distribution but sell products that do not compete with one another. A soap manufacturer acquiring a bleach manufacturer is one example of a product extension.

Market Extension.   **Market extension** occurs when the merging companies manufacture the same products but sell them in different geographic markets. A shoe store in New York acquiring a shoe store in Los Angeles is an example of market extension.

Other Conglomerate Mergers.   The final category is a catchall for mergers that do not qualify as product extensions or market extensions. The acquisitions of Gulf & Western Industries fit this category. Those of Tenneco, described earlier, might also fit.

Holding Companies   A **holding company** is one that acquires **controlling interest** in the voting shares of one or more companies. The amount of stock that must be held to gain control varies from company to company. It may be possible to control some companies with 5 percent of the voting stock, whereas for others 51 percent may be required. Holding companies are common in banking, insurance, utilities, and some other industries. A bank holding company may own banks, leasing companies, finance companies, credit life insurance companies, mortgage banking companies, and other types of businesses related to banking and finance.

Equity Earnings.   Each of the companies controlled by the holding company is an independent entity. The holding company is not liable for these companies' debts or transgressions, but it does benefit from their earnings.

Under an Accounting Principles Board (APB) ruling, a company owning between 20 percent and 50 percent of another company's shares is required to report the earnings of that company in an amount equal to the proportion owned. The company earning the income must also show all the income it earns. That means the earnings are reported twice, once by the company that earned them and once by the holding company. The following example will clarify this point.

Suppose a holding company owns 100 shares of Luray Industries. Last year, Luray earned $10 per share and paid a $4 cash dividend. The holding company received $400. However, it was required to report $1,000 income (100 shares $\times$ $10 earnings = $1,000). The extra $600, called **equity earnings**, was not real income, although it belonged to the holding company. It was reinvested by Luray. Meanwhile, Luray also reported all of its earnings.

Although equity earnings are not available for the shareholders of the holding company, they do have a favorable impact on the holding company's measures of success—profit margins, returns on equity, and share prices.

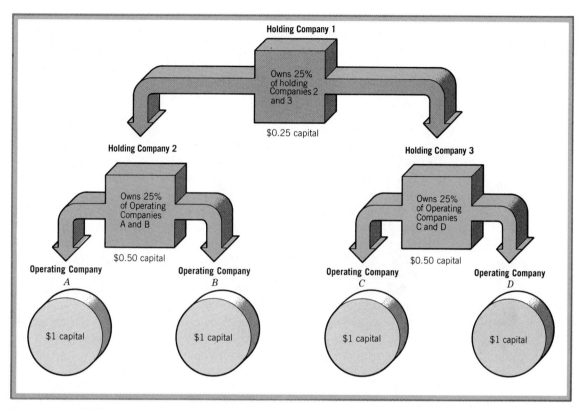

Figure 24–2 Holding company leverage.

Leverage. Another advantage of holding companies is that the parent company can control the assets and earnings of many operating companies with a relatively modest investment. For example, as shown in Figure 24–2, Holding Company 1 owns 25 percent of the stock of Holding Companies 2 and 3, which, in turn, own 25 percent of four operating companies—A, B, C, and D. For every dollar of equity capital invested in each of the four operating companies, Holding Company 1 has only invested $0.25 ($4.00 × 0.25 × 0.25 = $0.25). Stated otherwise, Holding Company 1 can control $4.00 in the capital of the operating companies with only a $0.25 equity investment. By reducing the percentage invested, the holding company increases the amount of leverage. However, as you know, leverage magnifies both increases and decreases in earnings.

Double Taxation. **Double taxation** is a disadvantage of holding companies. If the holding company owns 80 percent or more of the subsidiary's voting stock, dividends received by the holding company are accounted for in a consolidated return and are not taxed. However, if the holding company owns less than 80 percent of the subsidiary's voting stock, it pays tax on 20 percent of the income it receives from the subsidiary. The shareholders of the holding company are taxed again on the dividends they receive. Thus, the dividend income from the subsidiary is taxed twice if the holding company pays a cash dividend.

Joint Ventures

A **joint venture** is a new organization formed by two or more companies (or other types of organizations) to conduct some form of business activity. When large organizations are interested in a certain activity but unwilling or unable to take it on by themselves, a joint venture may be the answer. For example, two or more oil companies may form a joint venture to explore high-cost, high-risk geologic structures for oil. Ashland Oil, Inc., Texaco, Inc., Shell Oil Company, Murphy Oil Corporation, and Marathon Oil Company formed such a joint venture, called Loop, Inc. Similarly, some major utilities in New York formed a joint venture called Empire State Power Resources, Inc., to share power and other resources.[4]

Another common use of the joint venture involves domestic corporations with foreign businesses or governments as partners. Many governments demand a share of the profits of foreign businesses operated in their countries, and being a partner in the business is their method of control. Thus, the Egyptian government and Coca-Cola Company formed a joint venture named Ramses Agriculture Company; and the government of Jamaica and Kaiser Aluminum & Chemical Corporation formed Kaiser Jamaica Bauxite Company. Sometimes the foreign interests are represented by individual companies. For example, Hitachi Ltd. and General Electric formed two joint ventures, General Television of America, Inc., and High Voltage Breakers, Inc.

Leveraged Buyouts[5]

In a **leveraged buyout**, a company buys another company or a division of another company by using large amounts of borrowed funds. Sometimes leveraged buyouts are used to "go private"; that is, a few shareholders buy out a large number of public shareholders and then operate as a closely held, private company.

The borrowed funds used to finance the buyout are repaid in various ways. After the purchase, the book value of the buyer's assets is increased, providing

---

[4]The utilities are Central Hudson Gas and Electric Corp., Consolidated Edison of New York, Long Island Lighting Co., Niagara Mohawk Power Corp., Rochester Gas and Electric Corp., New York State Electric and Gas Corp., and Orange and Rockland Utilities, Inc.

[5]For additional information, see Allan Sloan, "Luring Banks Overboard?" *Forbes,* April 9, 1984, pp. 39–43; Steve Kichen and Leslie Pittel, "Selling High," *Forbes,* May 21, 1984, pp. 248–249.

greater depreciation and lower taxes. Some of the funds that would have been used to pay income taxes are used instead to service the borrowed funds. The interest expense on the borrowed funds is also deductible from taxable income. Therefore, income tax subsidies, in the form of lower tax payments because of depreciation and interest expense, help to finance leveraged buyouts. In other cases, the buyer may sell part of the acquired company to repay part of the debt.

To make leveraged buyouts work, the company to be purchased should have the following characteristics:

A low debt ratio.
A high times interest earned ratio.
Low requirements for future capital expenditures.
Steady cash flows.
A low price/earnings ratio. (More will be said about this ratio later in the chapter.)
A good spread between the cost of borrowed funds and the earnings yield (the reciprocal of the price/earnings ratio).

Let's examine the last characteristic more closely. Suppose a company will pay 10 percent interest on borrowed funds to buy another company with a price/earnings ratio of 8. This ratio is equivalent to an earnings yield of 12.5 percent. (As noted, the earnings yield is the reciprocal of the price/earnings ratio. Thus, 1 divided by the price/earnings ratio is the earnings yield.) Since this earnings yield is higher than the interest on the borrowed funds, the buyout may be a good idea if the other conditions are met. However, paying 13 percent interest to buy a company with a price/earnings ratio of 14 (producing an earnings yield of 7.1 percent) would not work, unless part of the company's assets were sold to repay the debt or securities were sold in a public offering to inject new capital. As for the other criteria, they fit mature companies in manufacturing, distribution, and retailing more than growing companies in, say, high-technology industries.

The availability of money is another essential ingredient in leveraged buyouts, as well as other types of mergers. Banks have been willing to lend billions of dollars to finance mergers. For example, Texaco established a $9 billion line of credit with a consortium of 14 foreign and 35 domestic banks so that it could buy Getty Oil Company. Banks lent Socal $14 billion when it bought Gulf Oil.

Evaluating Mergers

At the beginning of Chapter 8, it was noted that Eaton Corporation paid $350 million to acquire Cutler–Hammer, Inc., and that Northwest Industries, Inc., paid $205 million to acquire Coca-Cola Bottling Company of Los Angeles.

Both acquiring companies used capital budgeting techniques to help them determine what prices to pay. Once the price has been determined, the terms of exchange must be considered. In other words, what combination of cash and securities will the acquiring company give to buy the assets of or controlling stock in the firm to be acquired?

Merger Terms Table 24–1 shows a variety of merger terms that stockholders of acquired companies have received in selected mergers. The terms include cash, cash plus common stock, common stock plus preferred stock, and debt securities. These terms have various implications.

Taxes. The composition of the merger terms affects income taxes for investors in the acquired company and for the acquiring company. An exchange made for voting stock of the acquiring company is generally considered a **tax-free exchange**. The voting stock is usually common stock or convertible preferred stock. Convertible preferred offers investors a higher dividend yield than common stock, but it must be noncallable for at least 5 years to qualify in a tax-free exchange.

In contrast, exchanges for cash or nonvoting securities, such as bonds, are taxable for the stockholders of the acquired firm. Because some sellers want cash and are willing to pay the tax and others do not, companies may offer sellers a choice of merger terms. For example, Reynolds (R. J.) Industries offered shareholders of Del Monte Corp. the option of $48.50 in cash or one share of $2.12 convertible preferred for each share of their stock.

Depreciation is another consideration. If the exchange is taxable, as previ-

Table 24–1
Selected Mergers and Terms

Acquired Company	Acquiring Company	Stockholders of Acquired Company Received per Common Share
Aristar, Inc.	Gamble–Skogmo, Inc.	$10 principal amount, 10% senior sinking fund debentures due in 1989
Carrier Corp.	United Technologies Corp.	1 share $2.55 convertible preferred
Cyprus Mines Corp.	Standard Oil Co. (Indiana)	0.519 shares capital stock
Del Monte Corp.	Reynolds (R. J.) Industries, Inc.	Option of $48.50 cash or 1 share $2.12 convertible preferred
Falcon Seaboard, Inc.	Diamond Shamrock Corp.	1.65 shares common stock
Gardner–Denver Co.	Cooper Industries	0.333 shares common stock and 0.5 shares $2.90 preferred
Green Giant Co.	Pillsbury Co.	0.8324 shares common stock
Skil Corporation	Emerson Electric Co.	0.895 shares common stock
Western Publishing Co., Inc.	Mattel, Inc.	Option of $28.35 cash or 1.134 shares $2.50 Series A preferred

Source Information from New York Stock Exchange, *Fact Book 1980.*

ously described, depreciation of the acquired firm's assets is based on the price paid for the firm. Suppose, for example, that a firm is acquired for $20 million, but its assets have a book value of $17 million. The acquiring firm will use $20 million as the depreciation base. On the other hand, if the exchange is nontaxable, the assets will have a depreciation basis of $17 million, the same basis used by the selling firm. Some acquiring firms favor taxable exchanges because they provide greater depreciation, increased cash flow, and lower taxable income.

Liability. An acquiring company can buy stock or assets of the acquired company. We have just looked at the tax implications of the exchange; liability is another element that should be considered. If the acquired company is dissolved, liabilities and other claims against it must be satisfied before shareholders can receive dividends or assets. In contrast, the purchase of physical assets does not carry with it the liabilities of the acquired company.

Market Value Exchange Ratio The value of the terms of a proposed merger to the shareholders of the firm to be acquired can be measured by the **market value exchange ratio**, which is calculated as follows.

$$\text{Market value exchange ratio} = \frac{\text{Market value of benefits offered to seller}}{\text{Market value of seller's stock}} \quad (24\text{--}1)$$

The ratio compares what the shareholders are being offered with what they have. If the ratio is greater than 1, they are being offered more than they have. If the ratio is less than 1, they will be worse off if they accept the merger terms. As a rule, acquiring firms pay a premium to shareholders to make acquisition attractive.

To illustrate the use of the market value exchange ratio, consider the following situation. The acquiring company is offering the prospective seller a choice between the following exchanges for each share of common stock.

1. $2 cash and 0.4 shares of common stock valued at $50 per share, or
2. 0.375 shares of common stock valued at $50 per share and 0.25 shares of preferred stock valued at $30 per share.

The seller's stock currently sells for $20 per share. For simplicity, we will ignore the tax effects of the exchange, as well as cash dividends. The ratio focuses on the immediate value of the exchange. Using the market value exchange ratio, we can determine that the seller is better off with the second offer, which gives the larger premium.

$$\text{Offer \#1:} \quad \frac{\$2 + 0.4\,(\$50)}{\$20} = 1.1$$

$$\text{Offer \#2:} \quad \frac{0.375\,(\$50) + 0.25\,(\$30)}{\$20} = 1.3$$

Price/Earnings Ratio   Price/earnings (P/E) ratios are important in mergers. One reason is that the P/E ratio is one of the most widely used methods of determining the value of common stock. Perhaps the major reason for its popularity is that it is easy to calculate and convenient to use. We determine it by dividing the market price of the stock by its earnings per share. Newspapers and some investment services use a firm's most recent annual earnings to calculate the P/E ratios used in their publications. A better approach, however, is to use a firm's expected earnings, if such figures are available. If a stock is selling at $60 per share and its earnings are $3, the P/E ratio is 20. Stated otherwise, investors are paying 20 times earnings to buy shares of that company. It is easier to think about 20 times earnings than about equations and discounting. Nevertheless, the P/E ratio embodies some of the theoretical considerations of the dividend valuation model, although they are generally not made explicit. The P/E ratio may be related to the dividend valuation model as follows.[6]

$$P/E = \frac{1 - b}{k_e - g} \tag{24-2}$$

where

b = Proportion of earnings retained by the firm after cash dividends have been paid

k_e = Rate of return required by equity investor

g = Growth rate of dividends

If b is 0.50, k is 0.20, and g is 0.10, the P/E ratio is 5, determined as follows.

$$P/E = \frac{1 - 0.50}{0.20 - 0.10}$$

$$= 5$$

---

[6]An alternate form more similar to the dividend valuation model as stated in Equation 6–7 is as follows.

$$P_0 = \frac{D_1}{k_e - g}$$

$$\frac{P_0}{E_1} = \frac{D_1/E_1}{k_e - g}$$

Here, $D_1/E_1 = 1 - b$.

If the growth rate were 15 percent, the *P/E* ratio would be 10. Similarly, a growth rate of dividends of 18 percent would produce a *P/E* ratio of 25. In general, a high *P/E* ratio implies that investors expect substantial growth.

If a firm retains all its earnings $(1 - b = 0)$, the equation cannot be used. However, it may be expected that the firm will pay dividends at some time in the future. When the retention rate (b) is 100 percent over a finite period in the future, an adaptation of Equation 6–8 can be used to determine the theoretical *P/E* ratio. (See Table 6–3, the Summary of Equations for Chapter 6.)

As noted earlier, the *P/E* ratio is used in mergers to determine the value of common stock. A more important reason for considering *P/E* ratios in mergers involves assessing the mergers' effect on the combined earnings of the merged firms. To illustrate, we'll examine the financial data presented in Tables 24–2 and 24–3.

Table 24–2 shows that an acquiring firm's stock earns $5 per share and has a *P/E* ratio of 12, which means that the market price of the stock is $60 per share. Three situations are shown for the firm to be acquired (the seller): a higher *P/E* ratio, the same *P/E* ratio, and a lower *P/E* ratio than the acquiring firm (the buyer). As shown, if the seller's *P/E* ratio is 16, the total equity of the seller's firm is $9.6 million. If the seller's *P/E* ratio is 12, the equity is worth $7.2 million; and if the *P/E* ratio is 8, total equity is worth $4.8 million.

Now let's assume the buyer plans to pay the seller the full price of the equity by exchanging shares of common stock (here, the market value exchange ratio is 1). As shown in Table 24–3, if the seller has a higher *P/E* ratio than the buyer, the buyer will have to give the seller 160,000 shares of stock. This is determined by dividing the total value of the seller's equity by the market price of the buyer's stock ($9.6 million/$60 = 160,000).

Notice that the combined earnings of both companies ($1,000,000 + $600,000 = $1,600,000) and the increased number of total shares outstanding (200,000 + 160,000 = 360,000) result in lower earnings per share (*EPS*) for the buyer. Before the merger the buyer's *EPS* was $5 (see Table 24–2), but after the merger the combined *EPS* is $4.44. If the stock price of the merged company is $60 per share, the initial *P/E* ratio of the combined companies will be higher, at 13.5, than the buyer's original *P/E* ratio of 12. When the seller and the buyer have the same *P/E* ratio, earnings per share will stay the

Table 24–2
Selected Financial Data before Merger

	Acquiring Firm (Buyer)	Firm to be Acquired (Seller)		
		Higher *P/E*	Same *P/E*	Lower *P/E*
Earnings	$1,000,000	$600,000	$600,000	$600,000
Number of shares	200,000	300,000	300,000	300,000
EPS	$ 5	$ 2	$ 2	$ 2
P/E ratio	12	16	12	8
Market value per share	$ 60	$ 32	$ 24	$ 16
Total equity	$ 12 million	$ 9.6 million	$ 7.2 million	$ 4.8 million

Table 24–3
Selected Financial Data after Merger

	Higher P/E (16)	Same P/E (12)	Lower P/E (8)
Cost at market value	$9,600,000	$7,200,000	$4,800,000
Addition to buyer's capital shares[a]			
$\dfrac{\text{Market value of seller's stock}}{\text{Buyer's price per share}}$	$\dfrac{\$9,600,000}{\$60} = 160,000$ shares	$\dfrac{\$7,200,000}{\$60} = 120,000$ shares	$\dfrac{\$4,800,000}{\$60} = 80,000$ shares
Combined earnings	$1,600,000	$1,600,000	$1,600,000
Number of shares after merger	360,000	320,000	280,000
EPS of combined company	$4.44	$5.00	$5.71
Initial P/E ratio of combined company	$\dfrac{\$60}{\$4.44} = 13.5$	$\dfrac{\$60}{\$5.00} = 12.0$	$\dfrac{\$60}{\$5.71} = 10.5$

[a]The market value exchange ratio is 1.0.

$$\frac{\text{Market value offered seller}}{\text{Market value of seller's stock}} = \frac{\$60/\text{share} \times 160,000 \text{ shares}}{\$9,600,000} = \frac{\$9,600,000}{\$9,600,000} = 1.0$$

Table 24–4
**The Initial Effect of *P/E* Ratios on Earnings
per Share of the Combined Companies**

Buyer's *P/E*		Seller's *P/E*	Earnings per Share of Buyer
Buyer	>	Seller	Increased
Buyer	=	Seller	Same
Buyer	<	Seller	Decreased

same and the initial *P/E* ratio after the merger will also remain as before. If the seller's *P/E* ratio is lower than the buyer's, the combined earnings per share will increase to $5.71 and the initial combined *P/E* ratio will be lower, at 10.5. The initial effect after a merger of the buyer's and seller's price/earnings ratios on the combined companies' earnings per share is summarized in Table 24–4.

The word *initial* is important here, because the initial earnings are only a starting point for the combined companies. The important thing is how the combined companies will perform in the long run. Figure 24–3 illustrates this point. Without the merger, expected earnings will increase over the years. With the merger, in spite of an initial dilution in earnings, the combined earnings potential is greater over the long run than without the merger.

Offensive and Defensive Merger Tactics

As suggested at the beginning of the chapter, not all mergers are friendly. In fact, many are hostile; and that is why a variety of offensive and defensive

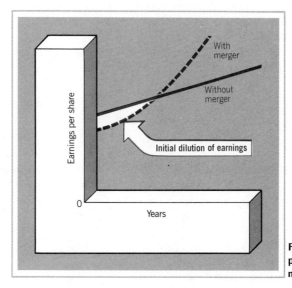

Figure 24–3 Expected earnings per share with and without merger.

merger tactics have been developed to make it easier to take over a firm or to avoid being taken over. Several of the principal tactics in each category are presented here.

The Offense   Remember that J. Ray McDermott & Company began its takeover attempt of Pullman Inc. with a tender offer. This is the offensive tool most widely used when the target company is likely to oppose the acquisition. In a tender offer, the acquiring company offers to buy from shareholders of the target company a certain number of shares of stock for cash or some combination of cash and securities.

The method's major advantage is speed; the offer can be made by announcements in major newspapers and there isn't much time for unprepared target companies to respond. This is what T. Boone Pickens (of Mesa Petroleum) did when he tried to take over giant Gulf Oil. After obtaining 10 percent of Gulf's stock on the open market, he made a tender offer at $65 per share for 21 percent of the company's outstanding shares. Gulf's management was not prepared for the assault. Other firms joined in the melee with bids as high as $87 per share. Socal (Standard Oil of California) was the winner at $80 per share. Don't feel sorry for Pickens; he made $760 million profit on his $1 billion investment in Gulf shares.[7]

Buying shares of the target company's stock before making a formal offer, as T. Boone Pickens did when he acquired 10 percent of Gulf's stock on the open market, is another common offensive strategy. Rupert Murdoch, an Australian entrepreneur, made such pre-offer purchases during an attempt to take over Warner Communications, Inc. He acquired 7 percent of the company's outstanding shares for $100 million before announcing his intention to buy 49.9 percent of the shares. Warner was able to buy Murdoch's stock for $180 million, giving him an $80 million gross profit for not getting the company he wanted.

Here are T. Boone Pickens's gross profits on several pre-offer purchases; he acquired none of the companies:[8]

General American Oil—$43.6 million.
Supron Energy—$32.5 million.
Cities Service—$44.2 million.
Superior Oil—$31.6 million.

In these huge merger attempts, even the losers were winners. However, although such mergers are the ones we read about in headlines, most mergers and acquisitions involve small companies and substantially smaller dollar amounts.

[7]"Why Gulf Lost Its Fight for Life," *Business Week*, March 19, 1984, pp. 76–84.

[8]Peter Nulty, "Boone Pickens, Company Hunter," *Fortune*, December 26, 1983, p. 57.

The Defense It is sometimes said that the best defense is a good offense. One offensive tactic to defend against takeovers involves changing corporate charters and bylaws to make unwanted takeovers difficult. Such changes focus on keeping purchasers of large blocks of stock from exercising too much voting power. The following list cites several common changes.

Staggering the terms of the corporate directors so that only a few are elected in any year.

Abolishing cumulative voting.

Requiring that a supermajority (such as 80 percent) of shareholders approve mergers, sale of certain assts, and some other transactions.

Enacting provisions protecting existing officers and directors from removal from office. (These are known as **golden parachutes**.)

Finding white knights is another defense. White knights, recall, are merger partners of the target companies' own choosing. Gulf Oil, for example, brought in Socal to fight T. Boone Pickens. This strategy may not always be a good one in the long run, however; remember that Pullman's white knight dismembered the company.

The following are other defensive strategies.

Repurchasing shares to reduce the number outstanding and retain as much control as possible.

Arranging defensive mergers.

Negotiating contracts with labor unions, banks, and so on to require renegotiation of contracts or accelerated payment of debts in the case of a substantial change in management or ownership.

Accounting for Mergers

The method used to account for mergers affects the value of assets and earnings of the merged firms. The purchase method and the pooling of interests method are considered here.

Purchase Method According to Accounting Principles Board (APB) Opinion 16, the **purchase method** treats a business combination as the acquisition of one company by another. The buyer records the cost of the acquired assets at their fair market value. If the fair market value of the assets exceeds the value shown on the seller's books, the difference is recorded as goodwill. The buyer accounts for the increase in the assets' total value by increasing the value of the equity account. The following example will clarify the point.

Table 24–5
Accounting for Mergers (millions of dollars)[a]

	Balance Sheet Entries before Merger		Balance Sheet Entries after Merger	
	Buyer	Seller	Purchase Method	Pooling of Interests Method
Net tangible assets	$30	$10	$41	$40
Goodwill	0	0	1	0
Total	$30	$10	$42	$40
Liabilities	$25	$ 9	$34	$34
Equity	5	1	8	6
Total	$30	$10	$42	$40

[a]Merger terms: 1. The buyer exchanged stock valued at $3 million, a $2 million premium over the book value of the seller's equity.
2. The fair market value of the seller's net tangible assets was $11 million, a $1 million increase over book value.
3. The difference between the premium paid for the equity ($2 million) and the increase in value of the seller's assets ($1 million) is goodwill ($1 million) under the purchase method.

Table 24–5 shows entries from the balance sheets of a buyer and seller before and after a merger. According to the terms of the merger, the buyer exchanged stock valued at $3 million—a $2 million premium over the value of the equity shown on the seller's balance sheet. Accounting rules require that a $2 million increase on the right side of the balance sheet be matched by an equivalent increase on the left side. The $2 million on the left side is allocated as follows: The fair market value of the seller's assets is $11 million, although the amount shown on the books is $10 million. Therefore, there is a $1 million increase in the value of the assets. The remaining $1 million is recorded as goodwill. After the merger, the combined balance sheet shows net tangible assets of $41 million ($30 million + $11 million = $41 million) and goodwill of $1 million for a total of $42 million. Because the liabilities assumed by the buyer do not change, the value of the equity account increases by $2 million to make the balance sheet balance. Accordingly, the value of the equity after the merger is $8 million ($5 million + $1 million on seller's books + $2 million premium paid over book value for seller's stock = $8 million). The total value of the liabilities and equity is $42 million.

The allocation of the premium paid over the book value of the stock between net tangible assets and goodwill has important tax implications. The increased value of the net tangible assets is depreciable for both income tax purposes and for reporting to shareholders. The increase in goodwill is not deductible for income tax purposes but can be amortized for reporting to shareholders. It follows that the increased depreciation resulting from the increased value of the assets results in lower taxable income but increased cash flow.

Pooling of Interests Method According to APB Opinion 16, the pooling of interests method treats a business combination as the uniting of equity interests of two or more companies through the exchange of stock. Both ownership interests continue, the former basis of accounting is retained, and the merger is recorded by combining the balance sheets of the two companies. As shown in Table 24–5, if the merger described earlier had been accounted for on a pooling of interests basis, the combined balance sheet would show $40 million in total assets ($30 million + $10 million = $40 million). The premium for the stock that was exchanged is not shown; hence there is no goodwill.

Again, the value of the tangible assets is less when the pooling of interest method is used than when the purchase method is used—$40 million under pooling and $41 million under the purchase method. Thus, reported earnings are higher under the pooling method because less depreciation can be deducted.

Income Another difference between the two methods of accounting for mergers concerns reporting income. Under the purchase method, income is recorded from the date of the merger. That is, income that was earned before the merger is not recorded on the combined books. In contrast, under the pooling method, income for both companies for all prior periods is combined and restated as income of the combined corporation. Thus, under the pooling method, the acquiring company can restate its historical earnings to include the earnings of the newly acquired company.

Restrictions Accountants have specified conditions under which pooling of interests can be used. The following list cites several of the major restrictions.

1. The merger must have been accomplished through the exchange of stock and not primarily through use of cash, other assets, or liabilities.
2. The stock exchanged in the merger must have the same powers as the majority of the acquiring company's outstanding voting common stock.
3. The combining companies must have been autonomous for at least 2 years before the merger was initiated.
4. Each of the companies must be independent of other combining companies.
5. The combined corporation must not plan to dispose of its assets within 2 years after the combination occurs, except for transactions that would occur in the ordinary course of business.
6. No agreements can be made that will have the effect of negating the exchange of equity that occurred. In other words, no preferential loans to prior stockholders are allowed.

Summary

Mergers have assumed an important role in today's business world. Theories of why firms merge concern managerialism, market power, taxes, and efficiency. Of these, efficiency appears most important for large mergers.

We can classify several reasons for mergers under the efficiency motive. One involves the life cycle; diversifying by acquiring firms in different phases of the life cycle gives the acquiring company several benefits. Expanding limited financial resources, gaining new management talent, expanding into new markets and product lines, acquiring undervalued assets, taking advantage of timing, and (for the acquired firm) gaining liquidity are other reasons for mergers.

Technically, the term *merger* does not apply to all business combinations (although it is often used in this general way). Types of business combinations, besides merger, include consolidation, conglomerate merger, combination under a holding company, and joint ventures. Acquisition of other companies is often accomplished through leveraged buyouts, in which large amounts of borrowed funds are used.

The terms of a merger are important to both the acquiring company and its target. Merger terms may include the exchange of cash and/or securities. An exchange of voting stock is generally considered a tax-free exchange, whereas exchanges involving cash or nonvoting securities are considered taxable.

The market value exchange ratio is one method to evaluate merger terms; it compares the value of shareholders' stock with the value of what they would receive from the acquiring company. The companies' *P/E* ratios are also important, especially in measuring the effects of the merger on earnings. Market value exchange and *P/E* ratios are reviewed in Table 24–6.

Since not all mergers are friendly, tactics have been developed both to acquire firms and to guard against acquisition. Tender offers and pre-offer purchases are common offensive strategies; defensive tactics include changing corporate charters and bylaws and finding white knights.

Finally, the choice of an accounting procedure affects the value and earnings of the combined firm. Two procedures are the purchase method, which treats

Table 24–6
Summary of Equations

	Equation	Equation Number
Market value exchange ratio	Market value exchange ratio $= \dfrac{\text{Market value of benefits offered to seller}}{\text{Market value of seller's stock}}$	(24–1)
P/E ratio related to dividend valuation model	$P/E = \dfrac{1 - b}{k_e - g}$	(24–2)

the merger as the acquisition of one firm by another, and the pooling of interests method, which treats the merger as a union of equity ownership.

Important Terms

Conglomerate merger
Consolidation
Controlling interest
Diversification
Double taxation
Equity earnings
Golden parachute
Holding company
Horizontal merger
Joint venture
Leveraged buyout
Market extension

Market value exchange ratio
Merger
Pooling of interests method
Price/earnings *P/E* ratio
Product extension
Purchase method
Spin off
Tax-free exchange
Tender offer
Vertical merger
White knight

Questions

1. What is a white knight?
2. Briefly explain the general reasons for mergers.
3. How does the firm's life cycle affect the possibilities of merger? During what phase are firms often acquired? During what phase do companies acquire other firms?
4. Define *synergy*. How is it related to mergers?
5. Why is viewing a firm as a diversified portfolio a useful concept in understanding motivations for mergers?
6. Why might small firms encourage their own takeover?
7. How does a merger differ from a consolidation?
8. The Federal Trade Commission classifies mergers as horizontal, vertical, or conglomerate. Differentiate among these kinds of mergers.
9. Identify and describe the advantages and disadvantages of holding companies.
10. What are joint ventures? Why are they used?
11. What is a leveraged buyout? What kinds of companies are good candidates for leveraged buyouts?
12. Describe differences between a tax-free exchange and a taxable exchange in a merger. How does each type of exchange affect depreciation expense?
13. Explain what the market value exchange ratio is.
14. Should merger decisions be based on *EPS* in the next period? Why or why not?
15. How are tender offers used in mergers?
16. Identify several defensive tactics against mergers.
17. Identify necessary conditions for the pooling method to be used in accounting for mergers.

Problems

1. Beaver Lake Corporation owns 40 percent of Eureka Log Homes. Last year, Beaver Lake reported earnings of $6.50 per share and Eureka paid dividends of $2.50 per share. There are 10,000 shares of Beaver Lake stock outstanding, and the firm owns 10,000 shares in Eureka. Compute earnings per share for Beaver Lake exclusive of its holdings in Eureka. Eureka had a 40 percent dividend payout ratio.

2. Acme Appliance is a subsidiary of Paramount, Inc. Last year, Acme paid dividends to Paramount totaling $8 million and Paramount reported total earnings of $20 million. Paramount owns 50 percent of Acme's stock. If Acme follows a 60 percent dividend payout ratio, what were Paramount's earnings from other sources?

3. Pyramid Corporation is a holding company owning 20 percent of four other companies, each of which own 25 percent of four other firms. How much capital does Pyramid control for every $1 invested?

4. Ponzi Instruments owns 45 percent of three firms, each of which owns 30 percent of two other firms. How much capital does Ponzi control for every $100 invested? If each of the six firms at the bottom of the pyramid earns $2 million, how much in earnings will Ponzi report before taxes?

5. Firm A is considering the acquisition of Firm B. The market price of Firm B's common stock is $40 per share and Firm A has developed two alternative offers for it: (1) two shares of Firm A common stock, now selling at $30 per share, for one share of Firm B; and (2) a $100 face value 20-year bond with a coupon at the current market rate. Calculate the after-tax compensation of each alternative if the average stockholder in Firm B is in the 30 percent tax bracket.

6. Walnut Creek Cement plans to acquire Forest Creek Gypsum. The financial vice-president of Walnut Creek is trying to decide whether to offer a taxable or a tax-free exchange. A taxable exchange will cost Walnut Creek $5 million more, but will allow $1 million more cash flow from depreciation. The additional cash flow will last 10 years and Walnut Creek expects a 12 percent return on its investments. Should the taxable exchange be considered?

7. Vista Exploration is interested in acquiring Terra Cotta Resources, a firm which has been faltering in recent years but which Vista believes has potential. Vista has gathered the following information on Terra Cotta.

Cash	$ 8,000	Accounts payable	$ 45,000
Accounts receivable	34,000	Notes payable	40,000
Inventory	21,000	Long-term debt	40,000
Net fixed assets	222,000	Equity	160,000

Number of shares outstanding: 20,000
Price per share: $2.50

   Which of the following offers is the best deal for Vista: $4 per share for Terra Cotta's stock or the purchase of Terra Cotta's assets at market value. The firm's fixed assets are estimated to be worth only $0.60 on the dollar, and the current assets are worth $0.85 on the dollar. What other factors might affect the decision?

8. Siesta Motels and Sleepwell Lodges are competing with one another for the acquisition of a motel chain, Sandman Inns. Siesta's stock price is $22 per share, Sleepwell's is $13, and Sandman's is $34.

(a) What is the market exchange ratio if Siesta offers two shares of its stock for every one of Sandman's?

(b) What is the market value exchange ratio if Sleepwell offers 3.5 shares of its stock for every one of Sandman's?

(c) What other factors would influence Sandman's choice of merger partners?

9. Given the following information, estimate the price range in which bargaining would occur if Firm A desired to acquire Firm T.

	Firm A	Firm T
Earnings	$8,000,000	$3,000,000
EPS	$1.60	$1.50
Market price	$24	$13.50

(a) What is the absolute minimum offer T would accept?

(b) Suppose A wished EPS to remain at $1.60 after the merger. What is the maximum offer it would make?

(c) What would the market value exchange ratio be if A offered 0.625 share for every share of Firm T? Is this within the range suggested by your answers to a and b?

10. The Moss Bottle Company is negotiating with Carr Glass Corporation. The following data have been collected on the two potential merger partners.

	Moss	Carr
Earnings	$12,500,000	$7,200,000
EPS	$4	$1.80
Market price	$32	$22.50

(a) Calculate the postmerger EPS for the combined firm assuming the exchange ratio is 0.75 share of Moss for every share of Carr stock.

(b) Suppose postmerger EPS was $3. What market value exchange ratio would have been offered?

 11. A local manufacturing firm has asked you to compute the effect of a possible merger on the firm's earnings per share. The following information has been offered.

	Buyer	Seller
Earnings	$28 million	$8 million
Number of shares	5.6 million	2.6 million

Compute the market value exchange ratio and the postmerger EPS of the combined firm assuming the market price of the buyer's stock is $60 per share, one share of the buyer's stock is exchanged for each share of the seller's stock, and the seller's P/E ratio is 10; the seller's P/E is 14.

12. The Golden Record Company is a mature firm with stable earnings and low growth prospects. It is interested in acquiring Target, a smaller company that has contracts with today's hottest recording stars. The following information has been collected.

	Golden	Target
Earnings	$11,400,000	$4,800,000
Growth rate	4%	12%
Market price	$32	$16
Number of shares	4.6 million	1.5 million

(a) Calculate expected *EPS* for each firm for the next 5 years assuming there is no merger.

(b) Suppose Golden offers a market value exchange ratio of 1.4 for Target's stock. What *EPS* would be projected for the combined firm for each of the 5 years after the merger? Assume a postmerger growth rate of 6 percent.

13. Durable Floor Coverings plans to acquire Tough Turf, a manufacturer of indoor–outdoor carpeting. Durable's financial manager has collected the necessary data to assist the board of directors in determining whether to make an offer.

	Durable	Tough Turf
Earnings per share	$5.20	$3.80
Growth rate	5%	10%
Market price	$34.50	$21
Number of shares	9.4 million	2.8 million

(a) Calculate Durable's *EPS* for 5 years without a merger.

(b) Calculate post merger *EPS* for 5 years assuming that 0.75 shares of Durable's stock are offered for each share of Tough Turf and that post merger growth will be 6 percent per year.

(c) Graph your results for parts a and b. Based on the graph, do you believe the merger is a good long-run decision?

14. Cameron Coal has received merger offers from several potential acquirers, including Chouteau Oil. Chouteau's offer was based on the following information.

	Chouteau	Cameron
Earnings per share	$5.9	$3.80
Growth rate	11%	3%
Market price	$40	$29
Number of shares	15 million	10 million

(a) Calculate expected *EPS* for each firm for the next 5 years.

(b) Calculate the market value exchange ratio if Chouteau offers a 1-for-1 swap of stock.

(c) Calculate *EPS* for the combined firm for the next 5 years, assuming the offer in part b is accepted. Assume a postmerger growth of 9 percent.

(d) Graph the results. Is the merger expected to benefit both groups of shareholders?

15. MCP is merging with ERA. The following are both companies premerger balance sheets (in millions).

MCP Corporation		
Current assets		
Cash		$ 42
Marketable securities		28
Accounts receivable		120
Inventories		80
Total current assets		$270
Gross fixed assets	$350	
Depreciation	120	
Net fixed assets		$230
Other assets		50
Total assets		$550

Balance Sheet (*Continued*)

Current liabilities	
Accrued expenses	$ 10
Notes payable	60
Accounts payable	110
Total current liabilities	$180
Long-term debt	$100
Net worth	
Common stock	40
Paid-in capital	80
Retained earnings	150
Total net worth	$270
Total liabilities and net worth	$550

ERA Corporation

Current assets		
Cash		$ 18
Marketable securities		12
Accounts receivable		48
Inventories		60
Total current assets		$138
Gross fixed assets	$ 80	
Depreciation	15	
Net fixed assets		$ 65
Other assets		17
Total assets		$220
Current liabilities		
Accrued expenses		$ 5
Notes payable		25
Accounts payable		42
Total current liabilities		$ 72
Long-term debt		$ 50
Net worth		
Common stock		30
Paid-in capital		20
Retained earnings		48
Total net worth		$ 98
Total liabilities and net worth		$220

Present the postmerger balance sheet of the combined firm, using both the purchase and pooling methods of accounting. Assume the MCP Corporation exchanges stock worth $110 million for ERA's common equity and that the market value of ERA's assets is $225 million. Use the simplified format shown in Table 24–5 of this chapter.

16. DePalma Hardware is considering a merger with Deadbolt Lock Corporation. Suppose DePalma offers $75 million in exchange for the common equity of Deadbolt. Assume that Deadbolt's accounts receivable and inventory are worth only 90 percent of their book value but that fixed assets have a market value $22 million over book value. Prepare a postmerger balance sheet for the combined firm under both the pooling and purchase methods of accounting, using the simplified format shown in Table 24–5 of the chapter.

DePalma Hardware

(in millions)

Current assets		
Cash		$ 12
Marketable securities		15
Accounts receivable		37
Inventories		32
Total current assets		$ 96
Gross fixed assets	$312	
Depreciation	154	
Net fixed assets		$158
Other assets		17
Total assets		$271
Current liabilities		
Accrued expenses		$ 7
Notes payable		21
Accounts payable		45
Total current liabilities		$ 73
Long-term debt		$ 40
Net worth		
Common stock		38
Paid-in capital		36
Retained earnings		84
Total net worth		$158 .
Total liabilities and net worth		$271

Deadbolt Lock

(in millions)

Current assets		
Cash		$ 4
Marketable securities		6
Accounts receivable		30
Inventories		50
Total current assets		$ 90
Gross fixed assets	$120	
Depreciation	84	
Net fixed assets		$ 36
Other assets		12
Total assets		$138
Current liabilities		
Accrued expenses		$ 3
Notes payable		5
Accounts payable		60
Total current liabilities		$ 68
Long-term debt		$ 20
Net worth		
Common stock		10
Paid-in capital		14
Retained earnings		26
Total net worth		50
Total liabilities and net worth		$138

25 International Business Finance

What could be more American than a cowboy hat and a Chevrolet? Well, the cowboy hat I bought in Houston, Texas, was made in Korea and the Sprint and Spectrum models of Chevrolet are made by Suzuki Motor Company and Isuzu Motors, Ltd., respectively—both of Japan and both partially owned by General Motors.

Chapter 24, which dealt with mergers, mentioned that Texaco bought Getty Oil Company. To help finance that deal and to raise additional funds, Texaco sold $1.5 billion in **Eurobonds**, which are bonds sold outside the borrower's country and denominated in any one of a variety of currencies. IBM, Sears, and other major U.S. corporations borrow overseas, too.

What does all this mean? Simply that there is an international dimension to financial management, resulting from the fact that business concerns throughout the world deal with each other on a regular basis. This chapter explores the various aspects of international business finance. Avoiding many technical

Professor Hany Shawky, State University of New York at Albany, was primarily responsible for the writing of this chapter in the first edition. The second edition retains much of the earlier version.

details, it takes a broad view of foreign exchange markets, international trade, and the financial management of multinational corporations.

After reading this chapter, you should know the following.

1. **What happens in the foreign exchange market.**
2. **What determines foreign exchange rates.**
3. **How spot and forward currency exchange rates differ.**
4. **How international trade differs from domestic trade.**
5. **How multinational corporations usually evolve.**
6. **What benefits and risks are involved in doing business overseas.**
7. **How overseas investments are evaluated.**
8. **How foreign operations are financed.**
9. **How to compute the cost of capital for a multinational firm.**

International Finance

The most distinguishing feature of an international financial transaction is that it involves more than one currency. For example, when a U.S. firm sells goods to a British firm, the U.S. firm wants to be paid in dollars and the British firm expects to pay in pounds. For such a transaction to take place, a rate of exchange between the two currencies must be established. This occurs in a foreign exchange market, which provides a systematic mechanism by which such transactions can be easily consummated.

Foreign Exchange Market   The **foreign exchange market** is the market in which currencies are bought and sold. The demand for and supply of each currency determine its value. This value, in turn, is the basis for exchange rates among currencies.

The foreign exchange market is much like the over-the-counter market for securities. Participants include individual dealers and banks throughout the world linked together by various means of communication, including satellites. The major participants, or *market makers*, are a dozen large commercial banks concentrated in major money centers such as New York and London. These banks operate in the foreign exchange market at two levels. At the *retail level* they deal with their clients—corporations, exporters, importers, and so on. At the *wholesale level* they maintain an interbank market; that is, they maintain inventories of various foreign currencies. The other participants in the foreign exchange market are the central banks of various countries. These institutions sometimes intervene to keep the value of their currencies in a desired range and to smooth fluctuations within this range.

Foreign Exchange Rates **Foreign exchange rates** have already been mentioned; they are simply the rates at which one country's currency are exchanged for another's. An exchange rate may be stated in terms of either currency. For U.S. businesses, the **indirect exchange rate** uses one U.S. dollar as the base amount and the **direct exchange rate** uses one unit of the relevant foreign currency. The exchange rate between the U.S. dollar and the United Kingdom (U.K.) pound sterling may be stated in either of the following ways.

Indirect rate: 1 U.S. dollar = 0.7231 U.K. pounds

Direct rate: 1 U.K. pound = 1.3829 U.S. dollars

Each of these rates is the reciprocal of the other; therefore, when rates change, they move in opposite directions. If the indirect rate rises, for example, the direct rate falls.

Indirect rate: 1 U.S. dollar = 0.8333 U.K. pounds

Direct rate: 1 U.K. pound = 1.20   U.S. dollars

This simple but important relationship will be discussed again in connection with the effect of exchange rates on trade.

Indirect foreign exchange rates for the major world currencies are listed in Table 25–1. By reading Line 4, you can observe the effects of rampant inflation in Brazil. In 1982, $1 was worth 179.22 cruzeiros; in November 1985, $1 was worth 8,913.95 cruzeiros! (In terms of the direct rate, in November 1985 each cruzeiro was worth $0.00011; 1/8,913.95 = 0.00011.) More will be said about inflation later in the chapter. In contrast, Line 16 reveals that the value of the Japanese yen was relatively stable over the period shown.

Figure 25–1 shows the direct exchange rates and the effective exchange rate index for selected currencies. The **effective exchange rate index** shows how much the external value of a country's currency has moved relative to 17 other major currencies.[1] Except for the Japanese yen, the value of the other foreign currencies shown in the figure has declined. Why exchange rates change is the issue examined next.

Factors Determining Exchange Rates As mentioned earlier, the forces of supply and demand determine the value of a given currency at a given time. This, in turn, determines its value relative to every other currency. Under the current **floating exchange rate system**, currency values are allowed to fluctuate freely against each other until equilibrium is reached. Before March 1973, curency values were set by each country's central bank and were not allowed to fluctuate. This system was

[1]Details of this index can be found in Federal Reserve Bank of St. Louis, *International Economic Conditions.*

Table 25-1
Foreign Exchange Rates (currency units per dollar)

Country/currency	1982	1983	1984	1985 June	July	Aug.	Sept.	Oct.	Nov.
1 Australia/dollar¹	101.65	90.14	87.937	66.51	69.95	70.70	68.96	70.25	67.74
2 Austria/schilling	17.060	17.968	20.005	21.532	20.446	19.632	19.949	18.569	18.236
3 Belgium/franc	45.780	51.121	57.749	61.719	58.626	56.543	57.395	53.618	52.474
4 Brazil/cruzeiro	179.22	573.27	1841.50	5786.00	6236.19	6714.00	7453.33	8203.57	8913.95
5 Canada/dollar	1.2344	1.2325	1.2953	1.3676	1.3526	1.3575	1.3703	1.3667	1.3765
6 China, P.R./yuan	1.8978	1.9809	2.3308	2.8693	2.8809	2.9093	2.9722	3.0782	3.2086
7 Denmark/krone	8.3443	9.1483	10.354	10.9962	10.456	10.1459	10.2906	9.5880	9.3918
8 Finland/markka	4.8086	5.5636	6.0007	6.3660	6.0798	5.9464	6.0140	5.6836	5.5709
9 France/franc	6.5793	7.6203	8.7355	9.3414	8.8513	8.5323	8.6599	8.0641	7.9095
10 Germany/deutsche mark	2.428	2.5539	2.8454	3.0636	2.9083	2.7937	2.8381	2.6446	2.5954
11 Greece/drachma	66.872	87.895	112.73	136.00	131.75	131.75	136.74	145.74	153.037
12 Hong Kong/dollar	6.0697	7.2569	7.8188	7.7698	7.7527	7.7906	7.8043	7.7908	7.8042
13 India/rupee	9.4846	10.1040	11.348	12.441	12.031	11.898	12.126	12.033	12.1010
14 Ireland/poundª	142.05	124.81	108.64	102.19	107.79	111.43	109.55	117.00	119.19
15 Italy/lira	1354.00	1519.30	1756.10	1953.92	1900.33	1873.51	1903.42	1785.43	1753.72
16 Japan/yen	249.06	237.55	237.45	248.84	241.14	237.46	236.53	214.68	204.07
17 Malaysia/ringgit	2.3395	2.3204	2.3448	2.4685	2.4696	2.4644	2.4841	2.4529	2.4341
18 Netherlands/guilder	2.6719	2.8543	3.2083	3.4535	3.2732	3.1429	3.1921	2.9819	2.9230
19 New Zealand/dollar¹	75.101	66.790	57.837	45.949	49.826	53.564	53.285	56.931	57.230
20 Norway/krone	6.4567	7.3012	8.1596	8.8255	8.4438	8.2487	8.3337	7.9099	7.8076
21 Portugal/escudo	80.101	111.610	147.70	176.15	169.77	167.34	172.5	164.59	162.963
22 Singapore/dollar	2.1406	2.1136	2.1325	2.2291	2.2109	2.2191	2.2268	2.1387	2.1084
23 South Africa/rand¹	92.297	89.85	69.534	50.54	51.07	43.07	39.49	38.38	37.57
24 South Korea/won	731.93	776.04	807.91	875.00	876.46	885.09	847.46	894.49	893.35
25 Spain/peseta	110.09	143.500	160.78	173.43	167.97	164.49	168.91	161.712	159.658
26 Sri Lanka/rupee	20.756	23.510	25.428	27.433	27.327	27.377	27.430	27.421	27.449
27 Sweden/krona	6.2838	7.6717	8.2706	8.8565	8.4703	8.3106	8.3907	7.9557	7.8127
28 Switzerland/franc	2.0327	2.1006	2.3500	2.5721	2.4060	2.2962	2.3749	2.1692	2.1306
29 Taiwan/dollar	n.a.	n.a.	39.633	39.857	40.136	40.501	40.465	40.195	39.981
30 Thailand/baht	23.014	22.991	23.582	27.433	27.053	26.889	27.050	26.569	26.315
31 United Kingdom/poundª	174.80	151.59	133.66	128.08	138.07	138.40	136.42	142.15	143.96
MEMO									
32 United States/dollarᵇ	116.57	125.34	138.19	147.71	140.94	137.55	139.14	130.71	128.08

ªValue in U.S. cents.

ᵇIndex of weighted-average exchange value of U.S. dollar against currencies of other G-10 countries plus Switzerland. March 1973 = 100. Weights are 1972–76 global trade of each of the 10 countries. Series revised as of August 1978. For description and back data, see "Index of the Weighted-Average Exchange Value of the U.S. Dollar: Revision" on p. 700 of the August 1978 BULLETIN.

Note. Averages of certified noon buying rates in New York for cable transfers.

Data in this table also appear in the Board's G.5 (405) release. For address, see inside front cover.

Source *Federal Reserve Bulletin*, February 1986.

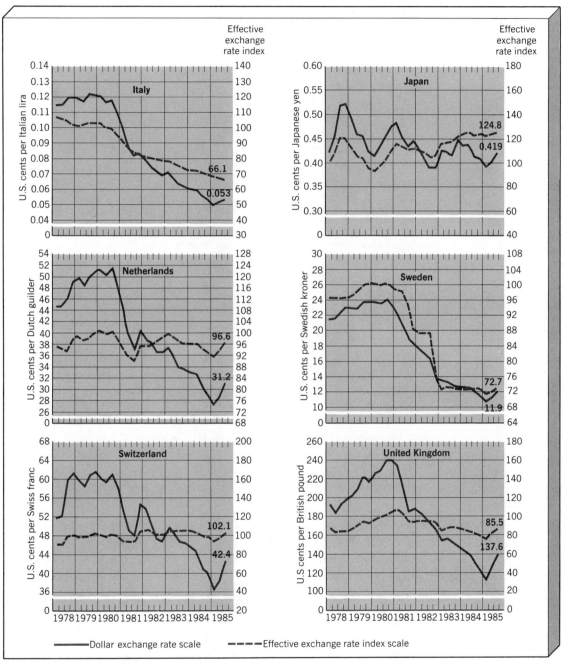

Figure 25–1 Movements in exchange rates.

Note: Latest data plotted: third quarter, 1985.
Source: Federal Reserve Bank of St. Louis.

called the **fixed exchange rate system**. Factors such as inflation, interest rates, and government policies affect exchange rates.

Inflation.   The perils of inflation extend beyond national boundaries. An economy experiencing a high rate of inflation relative to other economies quickly experiences a decline in the value of its currency. There are three important reasons for this relationship.

First, the higher prices of products relative to those in other economies make the products less competitive in world markets. This results in fewer exports and more imports. Once products become less attractive, there is less demand for the currency of that economy, which translates into lower value for it relative to other currencies.

The second reason results from the direction of investment flows among economies. Investors are more likely to invest their money where inflation rates are low because the value of their investment will not deteriorate as fast. This process also results in less demand for the currency and a lower value for it relative to other currencies.

The third reason is psychological. There is usually less confidence in an economy where inflation is rampant. On the international scene, this lack of confidence in the performance of an economy translates into less confidence in its currency. Investors are likely to liquidate their holdings in that currency and the result is an increase in supply and a reduction in demand. This lack of confidence usually results in an even lower value for the currency than is warranted.

During the late 1970s and early 1980s, the United States experienced the worst inflationary period in its history. The effect on the dollar's value compared with the values of 17 major currencies is shown in Figure 25–2. As you can see, the effective exchange rate index for the United States decreased in the late 1970s and then began to increase in the early 1980s, inversely following the path of inflation.

Interest Rates.   Although the level of interest rates in the economy is not independent of inflation, it is often a more visible and direct determinant of currency exchange rates. If interest rates are higher in one country than another, all other things being equal, investors will place their funds where interest rates are higher. As investors flock to invest in the country where interest rates are higher, the demand for that country's currency increases, causing the currency's value to increase relative to other currencies' values. This process continues until the difference in interest rates is exactly offset by the difference in the exchange rates. The process is described by the **theory of interest rate parity**; more will be said about it later.

Government Policies.   Governments frequently intervene in the currency exchange markets to help bring the value of their currencies to a desired level.

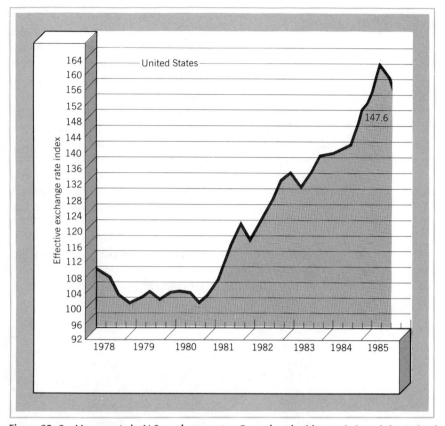

Figure 25–2 Movements in U.S. exchange rates. Reproduced with permission of the Federal Reserve Bank of St. Louis.

While this intervention is generally undesirable and usually short-lived, it nevertheless occurs, often with immediate results. All a government has to do to temporarily improve the value of its currency is to buy its own currency and, at the same time, reduce its holdings in other major currencies. This process reduces the supply of its own currency and increases the supply of the other currencies, leading to an artificial improvement in the value of its currency in relation to others.

Other government policies usually enacted for domestic reasons may also have a significant impact on the foreign exchange market. These include policies related to the level of interest rates and restrictions on free trade, such as tariffs, quotas, and stringent controls on foreign exchange transactions.

Exchange Rates and Trade

Exchange rates affect international trade. A brief description of this effect follows; later in the chapter, strategies to deal with the effect of exchange rates on trade are discussed.

Figure 25–3 shows the dollar price of United Kingdom (U.K.) pounds on the vertical axis and the volume of U.K. imports to and exports from the United States on the horizontal axis. If people in the United States want to buy goods from the United Kingdom, a demand is created for pounds to pay for them. Suppose the initial direct exchange rate for the pound is $1.40 (Point A on Figure 25–3); because people in the United States want to import more U.K. goods, they demand more pounds. At the same time, demand in the United Kingdom for U.S. goods remains stable. The increased demand for pounds causes a shift in the demand curve from DD to D_1D_1. The increase of imports relative to exports is followed by a shortage in the amount of pounds on foreign exchange markets available for purchase with dollars. This shortage forces the dollar exchange rate from $1.40 (Point B) to $1.60 (Point C). As the exchange rate increases, the quantity of pounds demanded declines from Point B to Point C.

At Point C, people in the United Kingdom find that U.S. goods and services are a better buy than before, because they can get more for their money. Recall the reciprocal relationship between direct and indirect exchange rates: The higher the dollar price of pounds, the lower the pound price of dollars. One pound, which only bought $1.40 worth of U.S. goods before, now buys

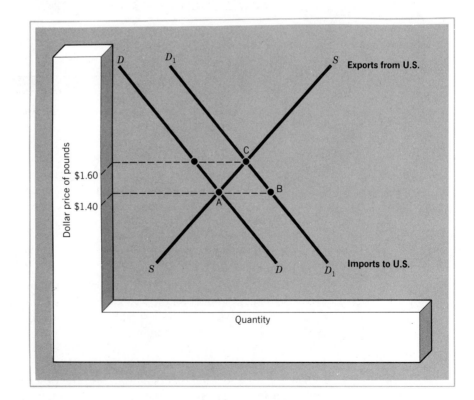

$1.60 worth; therefore, U.S. exports to England increase until equilibrium is established at Point C.

Spot and Forward Rates The foreign exchange market, like the commodities markets, has spot rates and forward rates. The **spot rate** of exchange between two currencies is the daily rate used to exchange currencies being bought and sold for immediate delivery. The **forward rate** of exchange is a rate agreed on today to exchange two specific currencies at some time in the future. Forward exchange rates are usually quoted for periods of 1, 3, or 6 months. Forward rates may be greater than the spot rate (*premium*) or less than the spot rate (*discount*).

For example, consider the prices in U.S. dollars of the West German mark and the U.K. pound on April 1, 1986, as listed in Table 25–2. The spot quotations give the exchange rates on that day for immediate delivery. Thus, on that day a bank's foreign exchange trader could buy marks for immediate delivery at $0.4264 per mark.

Forward contracts were also made on April 1 for delivery 1, 3, or 6 months later. For instance, purchasing a futures contract to exchange 1,000 pounds for dollars 3 months from April 1, 1986, assured the purchaser that 1,000 pounds could be exchanged for $1,457.30 (1,000 × 1.4573 = 1,457.30) at that time regardless of the spot rate in effect.

Forward rates are often expressed in terms of a percent-per-annum premium or discount, which is calculated as follows.

$$\frac{\text{Forward rate} - \text{Spot rate}}{\text{Spot rate}} \times \frac{12}{\text{Number of months forward}} \times 100$$

$$= \begin{array}{l}\text{Forward percent-per-annum} \\ \text{premium or discount}\end{array} \qquad (25\text{--}1)$$

By applying this equation to the 3-month forward rate for the West German mark given in the table, we find that the mark quote yields the following premium.

$$\frac{0.4294 - 0.4264}{0.4264} \times \frac{12}{3} \times 100 = 2.81$$

Table 25–2
Selected Spot and Forward Exchange Rates, April 1, 1986

	West German Mark	U.K. Pound
Spot	$0.4264	$1.4715
One-month (30-day) forward	0.4274	1.4660
Three-month (90-day) forward	0.4294	1.4573
Six-month (180-day) forward	0.4320	1.4485

A similar application shows that the 3-month forward U.K. pound was selling at a discount of −3.86 percent per annum on April 1, 1986.

The premiums or discounts may be used to evaluate the prices of securities. The theory of interest rate parity, mentioned earlier, states that the difference in national interest rates for securities of equal risk and maturity should be equal but opposite in sign to the forward exchange rate discount or premium for the foreign currency. For example, the theory implies that the 3-month Treasury bill rate in the United States should be 0.70 percent lower than those in West Germany. This is determined by dividing the 2.81 percent annual premium for the West German mark, previously calculated, by 4 (2.81/4 = 1.70), because 3-month Treasury bills mature in one-quarter of a year.

International Trade

International trade is the movement of goods across national boundaries. A country is likely to export products when it has a competitive advantage in the form of either superior technology or lower production costs. The United States, for instance, although it has lost its competitive advantage for many products, still maintains a technological advantage in the fields of computers and airplanes. Japan, on the other hand, has captured a competitive edge for a wide range of products, such as steel products, television sets, and automobiles, largely because of lower production costs.

A country that exports more than it imports experiences a positive trade balance. A deficit in a country's trade balance indicates that it imports more than it exports, and that is likely to cause the value of its currency to decline in relation to other currencies. A deficit in a country's trade balance can usually be traced to one or more factors, such as inflation, lack of productivity, or heavy dependence on foreign material or natural resources.

In noncommunist countries, almost all trade is consummated through private industry. Nearly all of the largest 1,000 U.S. industrial firms engage in some form of exporting. They may export either to a foreign importer or to their own affiliates overseas.

Importing and exporting differ from typical domestic exchanges of goods because of three important factors: (1) two currencies are involved, which creates a foreign exchange risk; (2) the parties to international trade often have limited or no knowledge of each other and thus a more systematic mechanism of assuring the performance of each party is needed; and (3) during shipping, which can take several months, neither the seller nor the buyer has access to the goods, yet someone must be financing them.

Protection against Foreign Exchange Risk   Whenever foreign exchange is to be received in the future because of a trade transaction on an open account, the risk exists that the relative value of the currencies will change in the intervening time. One of the most commonly used methods to protect against such risk is to cover the transaction in the forward exchange markets. The following example demonstrates this process.

Suppose you have decided to import a German car that costs 40,000 marks. We'll assume the rates that apply now are the same as the ones in Table 25–2. As shown in the table, the current price of your car is equivalent to $17,056 (40,000 × 0.4264 = 17,056). The German dealer bills you in marks with payment due within 6 months. You could avoid exchange rate risk by paying $17,056 today. However, that would mean you could not take advantage of credit available to you and the benefit of investing the $17,056 for 6 more months. On the other hand, you could wait for 6 months to pay for the car. In 6 months, you would have to buy 40,000 marks on the spot market, and if the exchange rate had risen to, say, 0.4500 by then, the 40,000 marks would cost you $18,000.

Instead of these two extreme positions, you could protect yourself against foreign exchange risk by covering your transaction in the forward exchange market in this way. You could purchase a 6-month forward contract for 40,000 marks at an exchange rate of 0.4320. This contract guarantees that, at the end of the 6 months, you will be able to obtain 40,000 marks to purchase your car at a fixed cost of $17,280 regardless of what the exchange rate is at that time. The net effect of this transaction is that you have eliminated the uncertainty associated with future changes in currency exchange rates by paying a certain price now. It is important to note that, if after 6 months, the spot rate for the mark remains at 0.4264 or decreases, you would have been better off not to undertake such a strategy. As in other financing decisions, you place your bets and take your chances.

The costs of protection against foreign exchange risks must always be carefully weighed against the potential benefits. The transaction costs of buying forward contracts are not trivial, especially if the desired protection involves a longer period of time or a volatile currency. Regular traders may be wise not to seek such protection because, in the long run, their gains and losses should cancel each other out. This is especially true for large export–import firms that continually deal in many currencies.

Futures Options. The International Money Market (*IMM*), which is part of the Chicago Mercantile Exchange, provides a market for put and call options on foreign exchange. Puts and calls were discussed in the appendix to Chapter 23. **Puts**, you may recall, are contracts to sell a specified number of shares of stock—or a specified amount of currency—at a predetermined price (the **striking price**) on or before a certain date. **Calls** are contracts to buy. The contracts on the *IMM* expire on the third Wednesdays of March, June, September, and December.

Suppose contracts for 125,000 West German marks are being traded. The contracts, which expire in June and September, are expressed in cents per mark, as shown in Table 25–3. Thus, at a striking price of 41 ($0.41 per mark),

Table 25–3
Examples of Call Options on West German Mark

Striking Price	Option Price (cents per mark)	
	June Expiration	September Expiration
41	2.22	2.77
42	1.55	2.13
43	1.02	1.59
44	0.65	1.19
45	0.39	0.85

a call option expiring in June costs 2.22 cents per mark and one expiring in September costs 2.77 cents per mark. Because the contracts specify 125,000 marks, it would not be practical for a person buying a car for 40,000 marks to use options to protect against exchange rate fluctuations. However, many import contracts involve larger dollar amounts and for them the use of options is worthwhile.

Suppose an importer buys precision equipment for 750,000 marks, with payment due in September. The importer can (1) do nothing and hope the price of marks drops, (2) buy forward contracts on marks, or (3) buy call contracts. Each choice has advantages and disadvantages.

Let's say the importer buys six call options (750,000/125,000 = 6) expiring in September at a striking price of 43. The options cost the importer 1.59 cents per mark (plus a brokerage fee). If the price of marks increases to, say, 46 by September, the importer can either sell the options on the *IMM* or exercise them to obtain marks at 43 cents each. If, on the other hand, the price of marks declines, the importer loses the cost of the contract (1.59 cents per mark).

Protection against Nonperformance   Limitations on how much international trading partners know about each other, differences in business practices among countries, and possible communication difficulties add more uncertainty to international transactions. To protect against nonperformance by any party, several ways of documenting transactions have evolved over many centuries and have become standard practice in the trade. They are the letter of credit, the draft, and the bill of lading. These three documents, plus some additional papers of lesser importance, are designed to protect one party of an international transaction against nonperformance by the other. Specifically, they designate the rights and responsibilities of each party at every step of the transaction.

Letter of Credit.   A **letter of credit** is an instrument issued by a bank at the request of an importer, in which the bank promises to pay a beneficiary upon presentation of documents specified in the letter of credit. These documents usually include: (1) a signed commercial invoice certifying that the goods are in accordance with the purchase order, (2) a special customs invoice, (3) packaging lists, (4) insurance documents, and (5) a bill of lading to the order of the shipper.

IRREVOCABLE
DOCUMENTARY
LETTER OF CREDIT

AmSouth Bank N.A.
1900 5TH AVENUE NORTH, BIRMINGHAM, ALABAMA 35203
TELEX: 596150   CABLE ADDRESS: AMSOUBKBHM

Taiwan Manufacturing Company
No. 17 Chang Chen Road
Taipei, Taiwan

Advised by AIRMAIL/CABLE through:

Bank of Taiwan
P. O. Box 1000
Taipei, Taiwan

WE ESTABLISH OUR IRREVOCABLE LETTER OF CREDIT NUMBER IC- 4000   DATED January 16, 1983 IN YOUR FAVOR

AT THE REQUEST OF The First Bank of Elmore, P. O. Box 200, Elmore, Kansas, U.S.A. 35000

AND FOR THE ACCOUNT OF U.S.A. Importing Company, Inc., 1907 Main Street, Birmingham, Alabama
U.S.A. 35000
UP TO THE AGGREGATE SUM OF Twenty thousand and no/100 U.S. Dollars ($20,000.00 U.S.)

AVAILABLE BY YOUR DRAFT (S) AT   SIGHT DRAWN ON AmSouth Bank N.A., Birmingham, Alabama

AND ACCOMPANIED BY THE FOLLOWING DOCUMENTS:

Commercial invoices and 4 copies.
Special U.S. Customs invoice and one copy.
Packing list in duplicate.
Insurance policy or certificate in negotiable form covering marine and war risks
  for 110% of CIF value of the goods.
GSP form A in duplicate.
Full set of negotiable clean, "On board" ocean bills of lading made out to order of
  AmSouth Bank N.A., Birmingham, Alabama marked "Notify" Mitchell Customs Broker,
  P. O. Box 100, Mobile, Alabama 36100 and "Notify" U.S.A. Importing Company, Inc.,
  1907 Main Street, Birmingham, Alabama, U.S.A. 35000 and marked "Freight Prepaid".
Container shipments are required.
Latest shipment date on first 5,000 buttons is March 1, 1983; and on remaining
  5,000 buttons is April 1, 1983.
All bank charges other than those of issuing bank are for account of beneficiary.

EVIDENCING SHIPMENT OF   10,000 buttons as per Purchase Order No. 1001 and Sales Confirmation
No. S-5005

FROM   Taiwan   TO C.I.F. Mobile, Alabama

LATEST SHIPMENT DATE IS (See above) (Two only PARTIAL SHIPMENTS ARE   PERMITTED.)
TRANSHIPMENT IS Not PERMITTED.   INSURANCE IS TO BE EFFECTED BY Sellers
LATEST NEGOTIATION DATE OF THIS LETTER OF CREDIT IS April 15, 1983
DRAFTS DRAWN AND NEGOTIATED UNDER THIS LETTER OF CREDIT MUST BE ENDORSED HEREON AND MUST BEAR THE CLAUSE:
"DRAWN UNDER THE AMSOUTH BANK, N.A. LETTER OF CREDIT NUMBER   IC-4000   DATED 1/16/83
WE HEREBY ENGAGE WITH BONA FIDE HOLDERS THAT DRAFTS DRAWN STRICTLY IN COMPLIANCE WITH THE TERMS OF THIS CREDIT
AND AMENDMENTS SHALL MEET WITH DUE HONOR UPON PRESENTATION. THIS CREDIT IS SUBJECT TO THE UNIFORM CUSTOMS AND
PRACTICE FOR DOCUMENTARY CREDITS (1974 REVISION), INTERNATIONAL CHAMBER OF COMMERCE PUBLICATION NUMBER 290.

(SAMPLE - NOT NEGOTIABLE)
Authorized Signature

WHEN OPENED BY CABLE, THIS CREDIT IS ONLY AVAILABLE IF
ATTACHED TO OUR CORRESPONDENT'S ADVICE OF CABLED
CREDIT, THE TWO CONSTITUTING EVIDENCE OF THE OUTSTAND-
ING AMOUNT OF THIS CREDIT.

Authorized Signature

FORM 400-03-2

Figure 25–4 An import letter of credit. Reproduced with permission of the AmSouth Bank, Birmingham, Alabama.

From the exporter's viewpoint, the letter of credit substitutes the creditworthiness of the bank for that of the importer; thus, it becomes a financial contract between the issuing bank and the designated beneficiary.

Figure 25–4 shows an import letter of credit spelling out the terms under which $20,000 will be paid to a Taiwan firm for the sale of buttons to a domestic importer. The bank's role is to make payment when all the conditions of the letter of credit have been met. The bank is not responsible for the quality of the merchandise.

Draft.   The **draft** is the instrument used in international trade to effect payment. A draft is written by an importer (buyer) ordering its agent (a bank) to pay a specified amount at a specified time to an exporter (seller). As explained in earlier chapters, the exporter can have the draft "accepted" by the importer's bank, which makes it a **banker's acceptance**. Banker's acceptances are bought and sold in the money market. Thus, the exporter can sell the banker's acceptance and collect most of the funds due before the draft matures.

Bill of Lading.   A **bill of lading** is issued to a shipper by the common carrier transporting the merchandise. It performs three important functions. As a *receipt* it indicates that the carrier has received the goods described on the face of the document. As a *contract* it spells out the obligation of the carrier to provide transportation for a specific price. As a *document of title* it can be used to obtain payment or a written promise of payment before the merchandise is released to the possession of the consignee.

Other Documents.   Other documents used in international commerce include insurance documents, commercial invoices (which describe the merchandise and the shipping conditions), consular invoices, and certificates of analysis.

Financing International Trade   The most common source of international trade financing is commercial banks. Once the three main supporting documents previously described have been agreed on, banks are usually willing to finance goods in transit, even though transit may take several months. The financing of goods in transit by banks is in many ways similar to inventory and receivables loans. The goods, inventory, or receivables serve as the collateral for the loan.

If exporters wish to receive immediate payment, they may borrow from their bank against a fixed percentage of the drafts outstanding. The bank's willingness to lend will depend on the credit history of the exporter's clients. Similarly, importers may arrange to finance their imports through a local bank. The bank will usually lend against the import draft with a loan agreement that uses the goods as collateral. For this case, the creditworthiness of the importer is the most important basis for obtaining credit.

In addition to commercial banks, most industrialized countries have special financial institutions for the sole purpose of facilitating and stimulating international trade. The most important of these institutions in the United States are the Export–Import Bank, the Overseas Private Investment Corporation (OPIC), and the Private Export Funding Corporation (PEFCO).

Ex–Im Bank. The Export–Import, or Ex–Im, Bank, established in 1934, is an independent agency of the U.S. government. To facilitate the financing of U.S. exports, the bank has a program to support commercial banks and another to provide direct lending opportunities for foreign importers. To support commercial banks that finance exports, the bank guarantees repayment of some export obligations acquired by U.S. banks from U.S. exporters. Its direct lending program is designed to lend dollars to borrowers outside the United States for the purchase of U.S. goods and services.

Overseas Private Investment Corporation. The Overseas Private Investment Corporation (OPIC) is a government-owned entity with two major functions. The first is to provide insurance for U.S. private investments in less-developed countries against political risk. The second is to help U.S. businesses finance projects through an investment guarantee program. OPIC provides insurance coverage for three types of political risk: inconvertibility (where one currency cannot be exchanged for another), expropriation (where the host country confiscates the property of the foreign subsidiary), and war or revolution. Political risk is discussed later in this chapter.

Private Export Funding Corporation. The Private Export Funding Corporation (PEFCO) is a private corporation established in 1970 to provide U.S.-dollar loans to foreign importers to finance purchases of U.S. manufactured goods. PEFCO's stockholders include large U.S. commercial banks and manufacturing companies. Through use of private capital, it supplements the financing already available through the Ex–Im Bank and other lending institutions. PEFCO's loans are unconditionally guaranteed by the Ex–Im Bank.

The Multinational Corporation

A firm is defined as a **multinational corporation (MNC)** if it has facilities in more than one country. In a sense, a multinational firm perceives the whole world as its place of business, whatever its country of origin. It can invest anywhere in the world and can raise funds on the international market. The list of *MNCs* includes the major industrial giants, the major oil companies, and the major banks, as well as many smaller firms. And the list grows as an increasing number of domestic and foreign firms share common ownership and embark on joint ventures that take advantage of each participant's unique advantages. General Motors' partial ownership of Isuzu Motors Ltd. in a venture to produce Spectrum model Chevrolets is one example.

The advantages an *MNC* derives from international diversification and its ability to exploit investment and market opportunities on a global basis are not without costs. As we will see, the cost of doing business on a global level introduces a multitude of complicating factors in almost every aspect of the business.

Benefits of Investing Overseas

Most U. S. firms start their international experience by exporting their finished goods. Once they find a steady demand for their products, they set up sales offices overseas. Then, to reduce transportation costs and various import fees on finished products, they establish an assembly plant in a foreign country to service the surrounding market. The final step in this evolutionary process is to establish a subsidiary in that country that will actually produce the product and act as an independent entity. At this stage, the firm has committed a sizable investment and is in that country to stay.

Many motives have led U.S. firms to establish subsidiaries abroad. The following are among the most significant.

To tap new foreign markets while avoiding the high cost of transporting goods.
To avoid foreign tariffs against U.S. products.
To reduce production costs through the use of cheaper labor.
To transfer U.S. know-how and managerial talents to subsidiaries abroad.
To gain favorable tax treatment.
To develop a better rapport with the country involved as a result of producing the product locally rather than exporting it.

Risks of Investing Overseas

Before a multinational firm commits resources to an investment project abroad, it has to consider a multitude of risks unique to overseas investments. These risks can be grouped into three main categories: financial, political, and environmental.

Financial Risk.   **Financial risk** variables involve the economic conditions in the host country. In addition, a host country might impose some financial restrictions on foreign-owned firms; for example, it might restrict remittances to the parent company. Such factors may significantly influence the profitability and the desirability of foreign investment. Financial risk variables that should be considered before investment in a foreign country include the following.

Currency stability.
Currency convertibility.
Local ownership requirements.
Remittance restrictions on dividends, management fees, and royalties.
Availability of local financing.
Restrictions on trade flow.
Inflation rates.
Price controls.
Taxation rates.

Political Risk. **Political risk** involves the host country's political environment and the fact that it might influence the subsidiary's financial and operating performance. At the extreme, a host country may expropriate a foreign-owned subsidiary. The MNC may or may not receive compensation from the host country after this occurs. Recent examples of expropriation took place in Chile, Peru, Bolivia, and Libya; most of the U.S. firms involved were in mining and oil industries.

A less drastic but perhaps more prevalent form of political risk involves intervention by the host country's government in the affairs of foreign-owned firms. For instance, a host country may require the use of local nationals in top management positions. Additional taxes might also be imposed on foreign-owned firms. Sometimes the intervention takes the form of a joint venture.

The following list represents some of the variables an MNC should consider in assessing the political risk of a specific country.

Stability of the government.
Quality of the host government's economic management.
Changes in government policy.
Host country's attitude toward foreign investment.
Host country's relationship with other nations.
Host country's attitude toward assignment of foreign nationals.
Extent of private versus state-controlled sectors of the economy.
Fairness and honesty of administrative procedures.

These factors are by no means the only ones to be considered. Furthermore, the importance of factors may differ for different businesses. Extractive industries (such as oil and mining) are usually more sensitive to political interference than high-technology industries, for example.

To protect against political risk, U.S. firms invariably buy insurance for overseas investment. As mentioned, the Overseas Private Investment Corporation provides specific insurance policies for political risk. This insurance, however, does not substitute for careful assessment of each country's political risks.

Environmental Risk.   **Environmental risk** is the risk inherent in doing business in a foreign environment. The following is a list of environmental factors firms should consider.

Availability of local managers.
National policies discriminating against foreign firms.
Patent and trademark laws.
Influence and attitude of labor unions.
Freedom to hire and fire locals.
Bureaucratic red tape.
Local environment's support of noncitizens.
Social and cultural factors.
Socioeconomic infrastructure.

Financial Management of the Multinational Firm   The financial and operating goal of an MNC, like that of any other firm, is to maximize the wealth of its shareholders. This goal is achieved through the simple principle of investing in projects with an expected rate of return higher than the firm's cost of capital. Although the goals and principles are the same as those for a domestic firm, implementing these objectives in an international environment is considerably more complicated.

In making an investment decision, an MNC should incorporate all the added risks—financial, political, and environmental—inherent in investing abroad. The capital budgeting decision is considerably more detailed and involves many more variables than the domestic capital budgeting decisions discussed in earlier chapters.

As an MNC can invest anywhere in the world, so can it raise funds anywhere in the world. To finance a specific project, an MNC can raise funds within the host country, through another subsidiary in another country, or through the parent country. Theoretically, an MNC should raise funds wherever they are least costly and utilize them wherever they can produce the highest rate of return.

Capital Budgeting.   The theoretical framework used for an overseas investment decision is essentially the same as that for a domestic one. Once the appropriate annual cash flows have been estimated, the net present value (*NPV*) approach will determine whether the project should be accepted or rejected. In determining the appropriate cash flows, however, the firm must consider a number of complicating factors unique to international investment, described as follows.

Parent versus Subsidiary Cash Flow. From whose perspective should the cash flows be considered? The project's cash flows are typically quite different from the cash flows the parent company can expect to receive from the project. This is due to many factors. Adjustments for certain taxes, foreign exchange rates, inflation rates, and the possibility of exchange controls can all significantly affect cash flow figures.

It is quite possible that a project will yield a positive *NPV* from the subsidiary's perspective but a negative *NPV* from the parent's viewpoint. The important question, then, is whose perspective should be considered. From a theoretical standpoint, the answer is clear: The cash flows should be those of the parent. A project's value to a firm is only what it contributes to the firm's overall cash flow. A project's relevant cash flows, then, are those that can eventually be remitted to the parent and realized by the firm's shareholders in the form of dividends or capital appreciation.

From a practical standpoint, however, many *MNCs* evaluate investment projects from both points of view. The idea is that examining the cash flows from the subsidiary's perspective can serve as a preliminary screening. Once the project has passed this first step, its cash flows are examined from the parent's viewpoint. But it is important to keep in mind that the second test overrides the first if a conflict exists between the two.

Foreign Tax Considerations. Tax laws vary considerably among countries. The effective tax burden on remitted funds and on reinvested funds can have a significant bearing on the size as well as the pattern of expected cash flows. Again, it is the after-tax contribution a project (or subsidiary) makes to the parent's cash flows that is relevant in the capital budgeting process.

Exchange Rates and Inflation. Some countries experience annual inflation rates of 50 and 60 percent and more. Expecting a 20 percent return in an environment with 50 percent inflation makes little sense. One way to deal with the effects of inflation in different economies is to adjust the cash flows from a given project upward to account for the difference in inflation rates between the host country and the United States. For instance, if the U.S. inflation rate is 5 percent and the host country's is 30 percent, the annual cash flows should be adjusted upward by 25 percent every year these rates are expected to continue.

A better approach than adjusting for inflation is to adjust for the expected changes in the foreign exchange rates between the two currencies. As explained earlier, a country experiencing a 30 percent inflation rate will almost certainly experience a decline in the value of its currency relative to other currencies. Specifically, a country with a 30 percent inflation rate is likely to experience a 25 percent devaluation in the value of its currency relative to the value of the currency of a country with a 5 percent rate of inflation. The idea that the difference in national inflation rates is directly reflected in the currency exchange rates is known as the **theory of purchasing power parity**.

Cash flows should be adjusted either for changes in the exchange rates or for the difference in the inflation rate between the two countries, but not for both.

Adjusting the project's cash flows to account for expected changes in exchange rates requires the use of some econometric model to forecast the direction in which an economy is going. Fortunately, several models are available that can be used to assess the strength of a currency over time. The procedure then is to adjust the expected annual cash flows according to the expected changes in exchange rates.

Blocked Funds.　For various economic reasons, countries frequently impose currency control restrictions. The effect of these controls is usually to limit the free flow of funds to and from the country. A subsidiary operating in such a country will be unable to send back funds to the parent company for a specific period or perhaps indefinitely; in other words, the funds are blocked. The occurrence of such controls during the life of a project is likely to affect the size and timing of expected cash flows to the parent. A careful analysis assessing the possibility that such controls will be instituted in a given country is necessary in evaluating overseas capital budgeting projects.

Discount Rate.　Determining the appropriate rate to use in discounting the adjusted cash flows is perhaps the most critical issue in capital budgeting for overseas projects. Theoretically, the appropriate discount rate is the firm's weighted average cost of capital. For an *MNC*, however, should the cost of capital for the subsidiary alone be used as the discount rate? Should the weighted average cost of capital for the parent be used? Or should the firm use some combination of the two?

As you will see, the appropriate discount rate is the worldwide weighted average cost of capital for the *MNC*. Having an appropriate discount rate, however, does not solve all problems. How to adjust that rate for political risk, environmental risk, and the advantages of international diversification are only some of the issues that continue to present problems for the multinational executive.

Cost of Capital　The basic principles of computing an *MNC*'s weighted average cost of capital are the same as those discussed in earlier chapters for the domestic firm. The distinguishing feature is that an *MNC* is not restricted to raising its funds in one national market. To capture the opportunity cost of raising funds worldwide, an *MNC* uses as the appropriate cost of capital its **worldwide weighted average cost of capital (WWACC)**. Once the firm has calculated the component cost of each source of funds and determined its proportion in the firm's capital structure, it computes the *WWACC* in the same way a domestic firm calculates the *WACC*.

Cost of Equity. Few if any *MNCs* resort to equity financing through their overseas subsidiaries or through foreign markets. Virtually all the equity financing raised by U.S.-based *MNCs* is raised through U.S. capital markets. As a result, the cost of equity for a U.S.-based *MNC* can be determined by use of the Gordon model (see Chapter 6).

It is important to recognize that, while the cost of equity computation for an *MNC* is similar to that for a domestic firm, the resulting numbers incorporate a great deal of information based on the firm's international activity. For instance, the *WWACC* for an *MNC* generally incorporates the level and extent of the firm's international diversification. Increased international diversification tends to reduce the firm's overall risk exposure to any one economy.

On the other hand, the cost of capital for a firm reflects the riskiness of its assets. Overseas projects are generally riskier than domestic investments; this tends to increase the firm's overall riskiness and result in a higher *WWACC*. Whether the increased riskiness of overseas projects outweighs the benefits of international diversification is an empirical question to which we have no answer. It is safe to suggest, however, that the two forces tend to cancel each other out, resulting in a small net effect on the firm's *WWACC*.

Cost of Debt. Many *MNCs* use foreign sources of long-term debt, as when a foreign subsidiary finances its investment projects through local borrowing. This may be advantageous in several ways. First, using local funds reduces the subsidiary's exposure to foreign exchange risk. Second, local sources of funds may be less expensive than others. Third, a subsidiary can establish better relations in the host country by using local sources of funds. Finally, in some instances special local financing (either through a government or through an international organization) is attached to a specific investment.

Another important source of financing for *MNCs* is the Eurodollar market. **Eurodollars** are simply U.S. dollars deposited in banks outside the United States, mostly in Europe. The Eurodollar market is a network of large European banks and branches of large U.S. banks in major European money centers. At present, short-term and long-term loans are available for qualified customers. Eurodollar loans are generally available to large, well-established firms as well as to countries. Rates are based on the creditworthiness of the borrower.

Regardless of the source or place of the funds' origin, an *MNC*'s cost of debt is a composit of all its worldwide borrowing. This cost of debt therefore includes two important components: foreign debt and local debt.

As an illustration, assume that an *MNC* maintains a 40 percent debt-to-total-assets ratio, with one-fourth of its total debt obtained from foreign sources. The firm's cost of equity capital based on the Gordon valuation model is 18 percent. Its after-tax yield to maturity is 6 percent for local debt and 5 percent for foreign debt. The *WWACC* is calculated as follows. The *WWACC* for this *MNC* is 13.1 percent; this is the figure the firm should use as its discount rate in evaluating capital budgeting projects.

Item	Percentage of Total (1)	Percent Cost of Component (2)	Weighted Average (1) × (2)
Foreign debt	0.10	0.05[a]	0.0050
U.S. debt	0.30	0.06	0.0180
Equity	0.60	0.18	0.1080
	1.00		0.1310

[a]Includes foreign exchange gains or losses.

Working Capital Management The management of cash, receivables, and inventory is clearly more complicated for the multinational firm than for the domestic firm. With subsidiaries in many countries, an MNC is usually faced with the difficult task of synchronizing the flow of funds worldwide so that it can minimize any idle funds in any one place and take advantage of the tax rates, exchange rates, and interest rates in various countries. Most MNCs establish a centralized operation to handle cash requirements. They do this by pooling cash in a central place and then funneling it to subsidiaries as needed. The central place is usually in a country with a major money center, sophisticated communication and transfer systems, and a stable currency.

The management of receivables is usually handled in a similar fashion. Although not all MNCs use a centralized decision-making system, the trend is in this direction. Inventory management follows the same principles as in domestic firms. A basic difference, however, is the fact that inventory is usually in transit longer. In addition, MNCs tend to allow for higher levels of inventory, especially for essential raw materials, to avoid the possibility of falling short of inventory if a given country decides to impose import restrictions.

Finally, the management of working capital for a multinational firm is complicated by fluctuations in exchange rates. As figures are translated to the home or reporting currency, foreign exchange gains and losses are likely. An important task of the MNC's financial manager is to compare the potential losses caused by exchange rate changes to the cost of avoiding those losses.

Summary

The foreign exchange market is where currencies are bought and sold. The supply and demand for each currency determine its relative value. Foreign exchange rates are the rates at which currencies are exchanged for others. These rates are affected by a number of factors, including inflation, interest rates, and government policies.

Unlike the spot exchange rate, which is simply the current rate for immediate delivery, the forward exchange rate is an agreed on rate at which one currency can be exchanged for another several months in the future. Futures contracts are often used to reduce foreign exchange risks in international trade as well as to reduce foreign exchange losses for a multinational firm. Put and call options on foreign exchange are also available.

International trade involves three important differences from domestic trade: foreign exchange risk, the risk of nonperformance by one of the parties, and the risk associated with transporting the goods. Various means of dealing with each of these risks has been developed.

Direct foreign investment by U.S.-based multinational corporations has increased substantially. Among the various motives for going overseas are: to open new markets, to avoid transportation costs, and to take advantage of cheaper labor in some parts of the world. The risks of doing business overseas can be grouped into three important categories: financial risk, political risk, and environmental risk.

The capital budgeting process for the multinational firm is similar to that for its domestic counterpart but considerably more complicated. Not only political risk but also such factors as foreign exchange rates, foreign tax rates, possible price controls, and currency controls in the host country must be systematically incorporated into the decision process.

The multinational corporation can raise funds worldwide. While this is probably a significant advantage for these firms, their financing options become numerous and complicated. When the cost of capital for multinational corporations is computed, the worldwide weighted average cost of capital must be used to reflect the cost of raising funds internationally.

Important Terms

Banker's acceptance	Foreign exchange rate
Bill of lading	Forward rate
Call	Indirect exchange rate
Direct exchange rate	Letter of credit
Draft	Multinational corporation (*MNC*)
Effective exchange rate index	Political risk
Environmental risk	Put
Eurobonds	Spot rate
Eurodollars	Striking price
Financial risk	Theory of interest rate parity
Fixed exchange rate system	Theory of purchasing power parity
Floating exchange rate system	Worldwide weighted average cost of
Foreign exchange market	capital (*WWACC*)

Questions

1. Briefly explain how a foreign exchange market works, including the role of major participants.
2. Distinguish between direct and indirect exchange rates. How are the two related?
3. What is an effective exchange rate index?
4. Distinguish between a floating and fixed exchange rate system.
5. How does inflation affect the value of a country's currency? Why?
6. What is the theory of interest rate parity?
7. How can the actions of governments affect foreign exchange markets?
8. What is a spot rate in the currency markets? What does it mean to say that a forward rate is at a premium compared with the spot rate? At a discount?
9. What is a trade deficit?
10. Explain, in general, how importing and exporting differ from domestic exchanges of goods.
11. Explain how a forward contract protects against exchange rate risk. What disadvantages are associated with forward contracts.
12. What do call options on currency entitle their holders to do? Put options?
13. What is a letter of credit? Why is it used in international trade?
14. What is a draft? What is the relationship between a draft and a banker's acceptance?
15. What is a bill of lading?
16. What role do commercial banks play in the financing of international trade?
17. What are the purposes of the Export–Import Bank?
18. What are the functions of the Overseas Private Investment Corporation? The Private Export Funding Corporation?
19. Define *multinational corporation*. Identify several benefits of being a multinational.
20. Name some important financial risks faced by multinationals.
21. What is political risk? What are some of its sources?
22. What is environmental risk? What are some of its sources?
23. How does capital budgeting for multinationals differ from capital budgeting for domestic firms? How are these two types of budgeting alike?
24. What is the theory of purchasing power parity? What are its implications for multinational capital budgeting?
25. What is the appropriate cost of capital for multinational firms? Why?
26. How is the cost of equity affected by international investments?
27. What advantages can local borrowing provide for multinationals? How does local borrowing affect the cost of capital?
28. What is the Eurodollar market?
29. In what ways is working capital management more complicated for multinationals than for domestic firms? How do firms address these complications?

Problems

1. Using Table 25–1 in the text, calculate how many U.S. dollars could have been obtained in June 1985 from the exchange of:
   (a) 1,000 Chinese yuans.
   (b) 1,000 Canadian dollars.

(c) 1,000 Spanish pesetas.

(d) 1,000 Swedish krona.

(c) 1,000 Italian lira.

2. Using Table 25–1 in the text, calculate how many units of each foreign currency below could have been obtained in 1984 from the exchange of $1,000 American dollars.

(a) Austrian schillings

(b) Italian lira

(c) Indian rupees

(d) Japanese yen

(e) Portugese escudos

3. In1983, Bob went on a five-country, 14-day tour of Europe. He left the United States with $600. Based on the following itinerary, calculate how much (in dollars) he had left when he arrived back at Washington National Airport. Use Table 25–1.

(a) London, spent 70 pounds

(b) Paris, spent 1000 francs

(c) Munich, spent 400 marks

(d) Geneva, spent 200 francs

(e) Rome, spent 150,000 lira

4. Suppose the direct exchange rate between dollars and U.K. pounds is $1.80 when the demand for British goods in the U.S. begins to decline. Illustrate and explain the equilibrium effect of this change on the exchange rate and on the demand for U.S. goods.

5. Using the *Wall Street Journal* or another source, find recent spot and forward currency exchange rates for dollars and French francs; for dollars and Japanese yen. Calculate the premium or discount on francs for 90-day delivery; on yen for 30-day delivery.

6. Suppose German marks and Australian dollars are quoted in the spot and forward markets as follows.

	German Marks	Australian Dollars
Spot	0.6039	1.2541
30-day forward	0.6107	1.2511
90-day forward	0.6132	1.2493
180-day forward	0.6180	1.2475

Calculate the premium or discount on 6-month forward contracts in each currency; on 1-month forward contracts.

7. Return to the exchange rates in Table 25–2. Assuming they are in effect now, how many dollars would you pay for stereo equipment costing 4,000 marks if the transaction were for cash today? How much would the equipment cost in dollars if you arranged to pay in 90 days and purchased a 90-day forward contract for marks? (Ignore transactions costs.) When would you choose one approach over the other?

8. Suppose the Spanish peseta has the following spot and forward exchange rates.

Spot	1.6109
30-day forward	1.6098
90-day forward	1.6042
180-day forward	1.6006

Calculate the premium or discount on forward contracts for each maturity.

9. Based on the data in Problem 8 and using the theory of interest rate parity, estimate the difference in interest rates on 1-, 3-, and 6-month securities issued by the governments of the United States and Spain.

10. Return to the call options described in Table 25–3. Explain the possible financial consequences of buying June call options at a striking price of 44. Assume the options are purchased in January to protect against currency fluctuations on imports costing 1,250,000 marks payable in June and that the current exchange rate between marks and dollars is $0.44.

11. Podwright Exports' Malaysian division has purchased industrial equipment locally and must make a payment of 5 million ringgits in 90 days. The spot exchange rate for ringgits is 0.5132. The 3-month forward rate is 0.5049.
    (a) What is the cost at the current spot rate?
    (b) What is the cost at the 3-month forward rate?
    (c) If the ringgit will be worth 5 percent less at the end of 3 months, how much would Podwright lose by buying a forward contract today?

12. An international cash manager is responsible for the investment of $8 million cash for 6 months and observes that the yield on 6-month securities of the Mexican government is 8 percent higher than the yield on U.S. Treasury bills. If the spot peso rate is 4.5672, what 6-month forward rate for pesos will create interest rate parity?

13. Herb's TV has ordered 500 Japanese sets. They cost 5,000 yen apiece, due in 90 days. The current spot rate for yen is 0.1453 and the 3-month forward rate is 0.1547. At what annual rate must Herb invest funds to make paying now and paying later equally desirable alternatives? Assume the forward rate is a good predictor of the spot rate in 3 months.

14. Flintco Steel is purchasing iron ore from Canada for 200 million Canadian dollars, due in 1 month. The current spot rate for Canadian dollars is 83.8562 and the 30-day forward rate is 83.9461. Cash is now invested at 16 percent. Which is best: payment now or investment for 30 days and payment at the forward rate in 30 days? Assume the forward rate is a good predictor of next month's spot rate.

15. Calculate the worldwide cost of capital for Hi-Lie Corporation, given the following information.

Dividend per share	$5
Market price of stock	$60
Growth rate	8.0%
After-tax cost of foreign debt	7.5%
After-tax cost of U.S. debt	8.4%

Capital structure: 50 percent equity; 20 percent domestic debt; 30 percent foreign debt

16. Calculate the worldwide cost of capital for Hobart Hotels, given the following information.

Dividend per share	$4
Market price of stock	$30
Growth rate	12.0%
After-tax cost of Eurobonds	7.0%
After-tax cost of U.S. debt	9.0%

Capital structure: 60 percent equity; 25 percent domestic debt; 15 percent Eurobonds.

Glossary

This glossary defines many terms commonly used in financial management and in the business world in general. Italicized words within definitions are defined elsewhere in the glossary.

ABC method A method of inventory control that categorizes *inventory* items according to the amount of *funds* invested in them. Those involving the greatest investment are the most highly controlled.

accelerated cost recovery system (ACRS) A method of recovering cost established by the Economic Recovery Tax Act of 1981 to simplify *depreciation* and encourage investment in capital.

Accounting Principles Board (APB) A body that specifies acceptable accounting procedures.

accounts payable *Trade credit* recorded on the balance sheet of the buyer.

accounts receivable *Trade credit* recorded on the balance sheet of the seller.

accrual Spontaneous source of funds available to a firm at little or no cost. The most common accruals are for wages and taxes.

accrual accounting A system of accounting in which expenses are recognized when a cost is incurred in the creation of revenue, not when a disbursement is made, and in which revenue is recognized at the time services are performed or goods are delivered, not when cash is received.

acid-test ratio A narrow measure of *liquidity*; derived by dividing cash, marketable securities, and *accounts receivable* by current liabilities; sometimes called the "quick ratio."

add-on interest Interest charge added to the amount borrowed to determine the total amount due.

adjustment bond See *income bond*.

after-tax cash flow In *capital budgeting*, the expected net returns from an investment project. One measure of cash flow is net income plus *depreciation*.

after-tax cost of debt *Before-tax cost of debt* times (1 − *marginal tax rate*).

agency costs Costs incurred by one party (e.g., stockholders) in monitoring the behavior of another (e.g., managers) when the behavior is not readily observable.

aggressive hedge In *working capital management*, financing all temporary current assets and some permanent assets with short-term sources of funds and remaining assets with long-term sources of funds. See also *conservative hedge*, *perfect hedge*.

aging of accounts receivable Process by which a business concern determines the percentage of receivables outstanding for various periods.

alpha The excess return expected on a security if the return on a market *portfolio* is zero.

analysis In the context of this book, the process of monitoring the financial performance of a company.

annual cleanup A requirement in some loan agreements that short-term working capital loans be repaid in full once a year for a specified period of time, such as 30 days.

annual meeting A yearly meeting at which shareholders vote for corporate directors and on other matters.

annual percentage rate (*APR*) The amount of interest charged on the unpaid balance of a consumer loan. It is calculated by various methods, which may give different results.

annuity A series of periodic payments, such as lease payments and interest payments on *bonds*, usually made in equal amounts for a specified period of time. See also *annuity due, ordinary annuity*.

annuity due An *annuity* in which payment is made at the beginning of each period. See also *ordinary annuity*.

arbitrage pricing theory (APT) A theory of asset pricing that allows for consideration of a number of risk factors, such as unanticipated changes in *inflation*, industrial production, certain *bond* yields, and certain interest rates. In contrast, the *capital asset pricing model* considers only one risk factor, that is represented by *beta*.

arrears Condition of a *preferred stock* when the company fails to pay the preferred stock *dividend*.

articles of incorporation Legal instrument filed with an appropriate state agency for the purpose of creating a *corporation*.

asked price Price at which an investor can buy a security. See also *bid price, spread*.

asset-based financing Financing secured by tangible long-term assets such as real estate or equipment.

asset depreciation range (ADR) One of several depreciation classes for assets based on the asset's useful life; associated with the *accelerated cost recovery system*.

asset preference Provision that gives preferred shareholders priority over common shareholders in the distribution of assets if a firm is dissolved.

asset turnover ratio A measure of efficiency; calculated by dividing net sales by total assets, or in some cases by fixed assets.

assumed bond *Bond* issued by one company that has been taken over by another company and has become an obligation of the latter.

auction basis See *stock exchange*.

automated clearing house (ACH) A part of the *electronic funds transfer system* in which debits and credits are electronically transferred between financial institutions.

automated remittance process Retail *lockbox collection system* used in the processing of *accounts receivable*.

average cash balance Total annual outlays divided by *cash turnover*.

average collection period The average length of time a firm must wait before receiving cash for sales made on credit; calculated by dividing *accounts receivable* by credit sales per day.

average payment period The average length of time a

firm takes to pay for credit purchases; calculated by dividing *accounts payable* by credit purchases per day.

average portfolio beta Weighted average *beta* for a *portfolio*.

average rate of return A *capital budgeting technique* that compares average net income to average investment.

average tax rate The tax rate paid on total income as distinct from the *marginal tax rate* paid on additional income.

balloon payment A large payment due at the end of a loan period.

banker's acceptance Negotiable security used in connection with trade. A buyer writes a *draft* to pay for specific merchandise. When the buyer's bank acknowledges the obligation to pay the draft, the word "accepted" is stamped on its face.

bankruptcy A legal procedure under which a business is liquidated or reorganized.

basis point One-hundredth of a percentage point (0.01); used in quoting *bond* and other prices.

before-tax cost of debt Interest rate on borrowed funds.

best efforts A type of *underwriting* in which *investment bankers* attempt to sell a new security issue but do not buy it from the issuer.

beta (beta coefficient) An index of the volatility in the return on an asset relative to the volatility in the returns on a market *portfolio* of assets; a measure of *systematic risk*.

bid price Price at which an investor can sell a security. See also *asked price, spread*.

bill of exchange See *draft*.

bill of lading Document issued to a shipper of goods by the common carrier transporting the goods; it may function as a receipt, a contract, and a document of title.

block of stock A quantity of 10,000 shares or more.

board of directors A group of individuals responsible for running a *corporation* (through officers, which they hire), for establishing the corporation's operating guidelines, and for setting dividend policy. They are elected by the *shareholders*.

bond A long-term debt instrument. The specific features of the bond, including call features, *collateral*, *restrictive covenants*, and so on, are written in the bond's *indenture*.

bond ratings Ratings of some *bonds* according to investment quality by agencies such as Moody's and Standard & Poor's.

book value (1) The original cost of an asset less its accumulated *depreciation*. (2) For a stock, the assets per dollar or share of common shareholders' *equity*.

bracket creep A process by which taxpayers move into higher income tax brackets because of *inflation* rather than increases in real income.

break-even analysis A method for analyzing the relationships among prices, operating costs, and sales volume. Linear break-even analysis assumes that revenues and costs maintain certain linear relationships. Nonlinear break-even analysis relaxes those assumptions and enables the analyst to take into account such things as quantity discounts.

break-even point See *break-even quantity*.

break-even quantity The level of sales at which revenues equal total costs; also called the "break-even point."

break-even revenue The total revenue from sales available at the *break-even quantity*.

broker See *stockbroker*.

business cycle A cycle comprising alternating periods of economic expansion and contraction.

business failure Situation in which a business has ceased to operate as a result of *bankruptcy* or has voluntarily withdrawn from the market leaving unpaid financial obligations.

business plan A plan that explains the nature, goals, and intended future actions of a company; presented to lenders with requests to borrow funds.

business risk Risk inherent in a business, such as the risk that competition will cause a decline in sales; evidenced by variability of earnings before interest and taxes. See also *financial risk, total risk*.

call option A contract to buy a specified number of shares of stock or commodities at a predetermined price on or before a certain date.

call price Price at which a callable security is redeemable.

call protection For *bonds*, a feature that prohibits the issuing corporation from calling a bond for a certain number of years.

call provision Provision that allows a corporation to retire a *bond* before maturity or redeem *preferred stock*.

capital asset pricing model (CAPM) A model that relates *systematic risk* to the return on assets such as *common stocks*. It postulates that the required rate of return on the asset is equal to the *risk-free rate of return* plus a *risk premium*. See also *security market line*.

capital budgeting Evaluating long-term investment proposals, usually for plant and equipment.

capital budgeting techniques Methods used to evaluate the desirability of long-term investment proposals. They include *average rate of return, internal rate of return, net present value, payback period*, and *profitability index*.

capital gain (loss) Gain (loss) created out of the sale of certain assets that have useful lives of more than six months and that are not normally bought or sold in the ordinary course of business. The gain (loss) is short term if the asset is held for less than six months and long term if it is held for six months or longer. The Tax Reform Act of 1986 repealed special tax rates for capital gains, although capital losses are deductible under certain conditions.

capital investment Investment in goods used in production.

capital lease See *financial lease*.

capital market Market in which long-term debt and *equity* securities are traded; includes financial institutions, government, business concerns, and individual investors who buy and sell stocks and *bonds*. See also *primary securities market, secondary securities market*.

capital rationing Situation in which the amount of *funds* available for investment is limited.

capital stock The *equity* capital of a corporation.

capital structure The permanent long-term financing of a business concern represented by long-term debt, *preferred stock, common stock*, and retained earnings. *Financial leases* may also be included.

capitalization rate See *discount rate*.

captive finance company A finance company owned by a nonfinancial business.

cash A balance-sheet item that may include coin, currency, and certain bank deposits.

cash break-even quantity *Break-even quantity* that includes only cash *fixed costs* rather than total fixed costs.

cash budget Budget that shows the amount and timing of revenues and expenses over various periods.

cash cow A company that has more funds than it needs to finance continued operations.

cash cycle Average amount of time that a firm's cash is tied up in *inventory* and receivables; calculated as average age of inventory plus average age of *accounts receivable*, less average age of *accounts payable*.

cash dividend Cash return paid by a corporation to shareholders.

cash flow Income less receipts; a common proxy for cash flow is net income plus *depreciation*.

cash management Management aimed at maintaining the minimum cash balance that provides the firm with sufficient *liquidity* to meet its financial obligations and enhance its profitability without exposing it to undue risk.

cash market Market in which commodities are bought and sold for immediate delivery; also called "spot market." See also *futures market*.

cash turnover The number of *cash cycles* per year.

CD See *negotiable certificate of deposit*.

Celler–Kefauver Act An antitrust law enacted in 1950; strengthened Section 7 of the *Clayton Antitrust Act*.

certificate of incorporation Authority granted by the state to conduct business as a *corporation*.

chattel mortgage A mortgage that gives a lender a *lien* on tangible personal property; commonly used in connection with *floor planning*.

circular flow of money Process by which business concerns pay individuals, who, in turn, use the funds to buy goods and services from the business concerns.

Clayton Antitrust Act An antitrust law enacted in 1914; supplemented the *Sherman Act*. A key provision is Section 7, which forbids a corporation to acquire stock of another corporation when the effect might be to substantially lessen competition or restrain trade.

clearing The processing of a check and the collection of the funds.

closed-end mortgage bond *Mortgage bond* that prohibits the placing of other mortgage *liens* against the property used as *collateral*.

coefficient of variation (CV) A relative measure of risk, often used in comparing projects of different sizes.

collateral An asset used to secure a loan.

collateral trust bond *Bond* secured by stock and bonds owned by the issuing corporation.

collection policies Policies related to the collection of *accounts receivable*; methods of collection may include reminders, collection letters, collection agencies, and penalties for late payment.

commercial paper Unsecured short-term promissory notes of leading industrial, finance, and bank holding companies.

common stock Voting stock that represents ownership of a *corporation*. The common stockholder is the last to receive assets if the firm is liquidated but benefits from growth through appreciation of share prices and increased *cash dividends*.

common-size financial statement Financial statement in which each item is shown as a percentage of sales.

compensating balance The amount a commercial bank requires a borrower to leave on deposit.

compound interest Interest computed on the accumulated interest as well as the original principal amount.

compounding Process by which the *future value* of a principal amount and interest is found; assumes interest is earned at a specified rate over time. The inverse is *discounting*.

concentration banking A system used by business concerns with deposits and funds throughout the country. The funds are handled by a few banks, each responsible for a different geographic area.

conglomerate merger A *merger* of essentially unrelated firms. Conglomerate mergers are classified by the Federal Trade Commission as *product extension* or *market extension*.

conservative hedge In *working capital management*, financing all fixed assets, all permanent current assets, and some temporary current assets with long-term sources of funds. See also *aggressive hedge, perfect hedge*.

consol *Perpetuity* issued by the British during the Napoleonic wars.

consolidated mortgage bond See *mortgage bond*.

consolidation A combination of two or more companies to form a new company; the original companies cease to exist.

consumer credit Credit extended to individuals, not including real estate credit.

continuous market For securities, a market with five attributes: frequent sales, narrow *spread*, minimum price changes, prompt execution, and *liquidity*.

continuous probability distribution *Probability distribution* that shows all possible outcomes and their probabilities of occurring.

contract price See *striking price*.

controlled disbursing Making disbursements from banks strategically located to maximize *clearing time* and *float*.

conversion discount See *parity*.

conversion premium See *parity*.

conversion price For *convertible securities*, the dollar amount exchangeable for one share of *common stock*. For example, if a $1,000 *bond* can be exchanged for 20 shares of common stock (the *conversion rate*), its conversion price is $50.

conversion rate The number of shares of common stock for which a *convertible security* can be exchanged.

conversion value The current *market value* of the number of shares into which a *convertible security* may be converted; determined by multiplying the *conversion rate* by the current market price of the stock. It is a theoretical value that may differ from the current market price of the convertible security itself.

convertible securities *Bonds* and *preferred stocks* that can be converted or exchanged for another type of security, typically *common stock* of the issuing corporation.

corporate bond calendar The dollar volume of new corporate *bonds* to be issued in coming months.

corporate charter A corporation's *articles of incorporation* and *certificate of incorporation* along with its bylaws and a statement of its powers.

corporation A legal organization chartered by the state to conduct business; an artificial being existing only in the eyes of the law.

cost of capital (1) The minimum rate of return that a firm must earn on its assets to satisfy its investors. (2) The rate of return on assets at which the market value of the firm will remain unchanged. The cost of capital is applicable only to new funds being raised by the firm; hence, it is sometimes called the "marginal" or "incremental cost of capital." See also *weighted average cost of capital*.

covenant See *restrictive covenant*.

credit line Loan that permits borrower to borrow up to a specified limit at any time within a specified period, usually one year.

credit policy Management policy concerning the extension of *trade credit* and the management of *accounts receivable*.

credit standards The criteria that a firm uses to grant credit. These include the five C's of credit: character, capacity, capital, *collateral*, and conditions.

credit terms The period of time for which credit is granted and the amount of *trade discounts*.

cumulative preferred *Preferred stock* on which unpaid *dividends* accumulate for future payment.

cumulative voting A system of voting that entitles *shareholders* to have as many votes for each share held as there are directors to be elected. This method makes it easier for minority shareholders to gain representation on the *board of directors* of a *corporation*. See also *ordinary voting*.

current ratio A broad measure of *liquidity* derived by dividing current assets by current liabilities.

current yield The dollar return (*dividend* or coupon) divided by the current market price of a security.

d

daily usage rate Rate of inventory usage; determined by dividing the *economic order quantity* by the *inventory period*.

date declared The date on which the directors of a company declare that a *dividend* or *right* is going to be paid.

date of record The date by which stockholders' names must be on the company's books to receive a declared *dividend*. It takes four business days from the time stock is bought until the buyer's name is properly recorded on the company's books. See also *ex-dividend date*.

date payable Date on which a *dividend* or *right* is paid.

dealer See *stockbroker*.

debenture A corporate *bond* backed only by faith in and credit of the issuing corporation.

debt ratio A ratio that indicates what proportion of a firm's total assets is financed with borrowed funds; calculated by dividing total liabilities by total assets.

debt–equity swap Procedure by which *bonds* or other debt are replaced by stock. The opportunity for a debt–equity swap exists when the *market value* of the debt is less than the value shown on the company's balance sheet.

debt-to-equity ratio The proportion of debt to *equity* in a firm's financial structure.

declining phase Fourth and final phase of the *life cycle*, characterized by decreasing sales and falling profits that ultimately turn into losses.

deep discount For a debt security, a market price far below *face value*.

default risk For securities, the risk that the issuing organization will be unable to pay its obligations.

defeasance (1) In accounting, the extinguishment of debt. (2) In real estate, the revoking of a deed.

degree of financial leverage (*DFL*) The percentage change in *earnings per share* that will result from a 1 percent change in earnings before interest and taxes.

degree of operating leverage (*DOL*) The percentage change in earnings before interest and taxes that will result from a 1 percent change in sales revenue.

degree of total leverage (*DTL*) The product of *degree of financial leverage* and *degree of operating leverage*.

depository transfer check A check drawn on a local bank and made payable to a *concentration bank* for the account of a specified business concern.

depreciation A variety of accounting methods used to allocate the initial cost of an asset, over its useful life. Accelerated methods show a large amount of depreciation during the early life of the asset; the straight-line method distributes depreciation evenly over the asset's life. See also *accelerated cost recovery system*.

differential cash flow In *capital budgeting*, the *cash flow* of a particular investment proposal with cash flows from other assets or proposals taken into account; also called "incremental cash flow."

direct exchange rate *Exchange rate* stated in terms of the foreign currency.

discount See *forward rate, par value, parity, trade discount*.

discount broker Stockbrokerage firm that handles securities transactions for its clients at relatively low commission rates because it does not provide research and other costly services.

discount rate Interest rate used in various calculations, such as those to find the *present value* of a stream of income; also called the "capitalization rate."

discounting Finding the *present value* of dollars that will be received in the future; the inverse of *compounding*.

discrete probability distribution *Probability distribution* in which only a finite number of possible outcomes and their probabilities of occurring are shown.

diversification Combining in a *portfolio* assets whose returns are not perfectly positively correlated and thereby eliminating some or all *unsystematic risk*.

dividend Return paid by a *corporation* to *shareholders*; may take the form of cash, stock, or tangible property.

dividend payout ratio The *cash dividend* per share expressed as a percentage of *earnings per share*.

dividend reinvestment plan (DRP) Plan through which some companies allow shareholders to buy additional shares of newly issued stock instead of taking *cash dividends*.

double taxation Taxation of earnings when they are reported by the corporation and again after they have been paid to shareholders as dividends.

downward-sloping yield curve *Yield curve* depicting the situation in which short-term interest rates are higher than long-term interest rates. See also *flat yield curve, normal yield curve, upward-sloping yield curve*.

draft An unconditional order in writing signed by the drawer requiring the drawee to pay on demand or at some determinable time in the future a definite sum of money to the payee. A check is one common form of draft.

du Pont system of financial analysis A method used to determine the *return on equity* based on various combinations of assets. It also reveals information about efficiency, *financial leverage*, and profitability.

e

earnings available for common stock Net income less *preferred stock dividend* payments and *sinking fund* payments.

earnings per share (*EPS*) A popular measure of profitability derived by dividing net income by the average number of shares outstanding.

EBIT–EPS chart Graphic representation of the relationship of earnings before interest and taxes to *earnings per share*.

economic concentration The share of assets, sales, or deposits held by the largest firms in an industry or market.

economic order quantity (*EOQ*) A model used for *inventory* and *cash management*. It may be used to determine the quantity of inventory that minimizes a firm's total cost of inventory management or the average amount that must be transferred from a firm's securities *portfolio* into *cash* so that the firm can meet its demands for cash over time.

efficient capital market A *capital market* characterized by a large number of investors with access to all relevant information, which they act on to maximize profit. Thus, the market price of securities fully reflects all available information. A weak form, a semistrong form, and a strong form of the efficient-market hypothesis have been postulated, with the weak form assuming that securities prices are randomly determined and the strong form assuming that market prices accurately reflect all current information.

electronic funds transfer system (EFTS) The transfer of funds using computer technology; includes credit cards, direct deposit payroll systems, *automated clearing houses*, and so on.

endorsed bond See *guaranteed bond*.

endorsement Guarantee of loan payments by a third party.

environmental risk The risk inherent in doing business in a foreign environment.

equipment trust certificate Obligation used in the financing of rolling stock such as railroad cars through a lease arrangement called the Philadelphia Plan. The certificates are sold to investors to pay for part of the equipment, and the borrower makes lease payments to a trustee for the benefit of the certificate holders.

equity The residual value of a business after the liabilities have been discharged; it represents ownership. The equity, or net worth, portion of the balance sheet includes *capital stock, preferred stock*, retained earnings, and certain other reserves or surplus accounts.

equity earnings Earnings reported by *holding companies* under certain conditions. A company that owns between 20 and 50 percent of another company's shares must report the earnings of that company in the proportion owned, although the earnings need not be distributed.

Eurobonds *Bonds* sold outside the borrower's country and denominated in any of a variety of currencies.

Eurodollars Short-term deposits in dollar denominations placed in banks outside the United States. They generally carry higher rates of interest than domestic deposits.

ex ante returns Returns that investors expect to earn in the future.

ex post returns Historical returns.

exchange rate Price of one currency relative to another.

ex-dividend date Date on which buyers of stock are no longer eligible to receive the latest declared *dividend*; four business days prior to *date of record*.

exercise price Price at which a *warrant* allows the holder to buy stock.

expansion phase Second phase of the *life cycle*, characterized by increasing competition, declining prices, and rising profits.

expansion proposal Investment proposal expected to add substantially to revenues.

expectations theory A theory that explains the relationship between interest rates and the maturity of a security in terms of expectations about future interest rates.

expected cash flow The most likely *cash flow*; the weighted average cash flow.

experience Accumulated volume of production. See also *learning curve*.

ex-rights Condition of a stock selling without *rights* attached.

face amount or value See *par value.*

factoring Sale of *accounts receivable* to a bank or finance company; the financial institution is called the factor.

federal funds rate The interest rate that banks charge on excess reserves lent to other banks on a short-term basis. See also *LIBOR.*

field warehouse Secured area on a borrower's premises in which inventory used as *collateral* is stored.

financial asset Asset such as cash, securities, and receivables, as opposed to a *real asset.*

financial intermediary The modern term for financial institution. It encompasses banks, insurance companies, savings and loan associations, and other institutions that facilitate the flow of funds in the credit markets.

financial lease *Lease* used in connection with financing long-term assets. It generally amortizes the entire cost of the asset over the life of the lease and is not cancelable. To be a true financial lease, it must be recognized as one under the Internal Revenue Code. Also called a "capital lease."

financial leverage The relationship between borrowed funds and shareholders' *equity.* Firms that have a high proportion of debt to equity are said to be highly leveraged; this increases the volatility of earnings and the *financial risk* of the firm.

financial management Management aimed at making optimal use of a firm's financial resources for the purpose of maximizing the owners' wealth.

financial risk The risk that a firm might not be able to meet its financial obligations. In international business, financial risk variables refer to economic conditions in the host country.

financing decision Decision that involves raising funds for the firm.

finished goods inventory *Inventory* that includes items ready to be sold.

first-mortgage bond See *mortgage bond.*

fiscal policy Government policies relating to spending and taxing.

five C's See *credit standards.*

fixed cost Cost not affected by sales volume, such as *depreciation* expense, property taxes, and rent. See also *semivariable cost, variable cost.*

fixed exchange rate system *Exchange rate* system in effect before March 1973, in which currency values were set by each country's central bank and were not allowed to fluctuate. See also *floating exchange rate system.*

flat yield curve *Yield curve* depicting the situation in which current short-term and long-term interest rates are equal. See also *downward-sloping yield curve, normal yield curve, upward-sloping yield curve.*

float The time delay between the moment of disbursement of funds by a buyer and the collection of those funds by the seller; caused by mail time, processing time, and clearing and collection time.

floating exchange rate system *Exchange rate* system currently in effect, in which currency values are allowed to fluctuate freely against one another. See also *fixed exchange rate system.*

floating lien A continuous *lien* that can be used to cover a firm's *inventory* when it is being used as *collateral* for a loan.

floating supply For a stock, the average daily number of shares traded.

floor planning A method of financing in which title for *inventory,* such as automobiles, is held by the lender, and the borrower assumes the role of trustee for the goods. When they are sold, the loan is repaid and the lender releases title to the property.

flotation cost Difference between buying and selling price of a securities issue; includes legal fees and other expenses.

foreign exchange market Market in which currencies of various nations are bought and sold. The participants are mainly dealers and banks linked together by communication systems.

foreign exchange rate See *exchange rate.*

forward rate A rate of exchange agreed on today to exchange specific currencies for future delivery. Forward rates can be greater than the *spot rate* (premium) or less than the spot rate (discount).

franchise An agreement between a franchisor and a franchisee granting the right to use the franchisor's name, equipment, and other processes in a certain geographic area, generally for a fee and a share of the revenue.

full payout net lease *Lease* in which the cost of the asset and the return to the lessor are amortized over the term of the lease. Most *financial leases* are full payout net leases.

funds Cash and other sources of value (such as *depreciation*) that arise from inside and outside the firm.

funds flow cycle The flow of *funds* through the firm; sometimes called the "working capital cycle." See also *funds flow statement*.

funds flow statement A formalized statement of the *funds flow cycle*; incorporates all sources and uses of *funds*.

future value The value at some future date based on the *compounding* process, which assumes interest is earned at a specified rate over time.

future value interest factor Multiplier used in *compounding*; a table of future value interest factors is presented in Appendix A.

futures market Market in which contracts for the future delivery of a commodity are traded. See also *cash market, hedging, interest rate futures market*.

general mortgage bond See *mortgage bond*.

general partnership *Partnership* in which each partner's liability is unlimited.

gilt edge bond See *bond ratings*.

going concern A business whose operations are expected to continue.

golden parachute Provision to protect existing officers and directors of a corporation from removal from office, often involving the payment of a large sum of money on dismissal.

Gordon model A model developed by Myron Gordon, used to determine the theoretical value of a stock by discounting expected dividends by the rate of return required by investors.

gross profit margin The difference between net sales and the cost of goods sold expressed as a percentage of net sales.

guaranteed bond *Bond* guaranteed by a corporation other than the issuing corporation; develops from *mergers, consolidations*, and financing of subsidiaries. The terms of the guarantee are usually

stated on the bond, in which case the bond is referred to as "stamped" or "endorsed."

half-year convention Accounting convention according to which only one-half of the first year's *depreciation* on an asset is taken in the first year, no matter when the asset is acquired during that year.

hedging (1) In connection with *working capital management*, the matching of expected cash inflows from assets with the outflows from their respective sources of financing. (2) Taking equal but opposite positions in the *cash market* and the *futures market* to prevent loss due to price fluctuations.

holding company A company that holds stock in one or more other companies. The degree of control exercised by the holding company depends on the amount of stock held, but a relatively small investment can yield substantial control.

holding cost In the *Economic Order Quantity (EOQ)* model, inventory costs for storage, handling, funds, taxes, insurance, and deterioration or shrinkage. Holding cost plus *order cost* equals total cost.

holding period yield The *dividend* yield plus the percentage change in capital value of a stock during a given period. Because negative yields can cause difficulties in some mathematical calculations, the value 1 can be added to the holding period yield to form a substitute, the "holding period return." Both sums measure return on investment.

horizontal merger A *merger* of firms in the same line of business.

hurdle rate The minimum rate of return that will be accepted on an investment proposal.

income bond A hybrid *bond* on which interest is paid only if it is earned, and interest payments accumulate until there is sufficient income to pay them.

incremental cash flow See *differential cash flow*.

indenture The contract portion of a *bond*, which specifies all terms and obligations of the debtor.

independent proposals Investment proposals whose selection does not affect the selection of other proposals. See also *mutually exclusive proposals*.

indirect exchange rate *Exchange rate* stated in terms of the domestic currency. For U.S. businesses, the indirect exchange rate uses one U.S. dollar as the base amount.

industrial revenue bond *Bond* sold by a government body to finance a plant or other facilities for a business concern; the facilities are leased to the industrial user.

inflation Erosion of the purchasing power of a currency, resulting in price increases.

insolvent (1) Condition of a company unable to meet its current financial obligations. (2) Condition of a company when the fair value of its liabilities exceeds the *market value* of its assets; this may not mean that the company cannot meet its current financial obligations.

interest rate futures market *Futures market* organized to trade in financial contracts on various government securities, currencies, and *commercial paper*.

intermediate-term loan Loan with an original maturity of between one and seven years.

internal rate of return (*IRR*) The rate of interest that equates the *present value* of expected *cash flows* to the investment outlay; sometimes referred to as the DCF/ROR (discounted cash flow rate of return).

intrayear period Period less than one year.

intrinsic value See *investment value*.

inventory All goods and materials in stock. Inventory may be categorized as *raw materials*, *work in process*, and *finished goods*.

inventory period The approximate number of days required to exhaust the quantity of *inventory ordered*.

inventory turnover ratio A ratio that measures the number of times an *inventory* is turned over (sold) each year; calculated by dividing cost of goods sold by inventory.

inventory-to-sales ratio Proportion of *inventory* to sales; one method of inventory management involves maintaining a constant inventory-to-sales ratio.

investment banker Intermediary between business concerns that need capital and investors who have funds to invest; investment bankers under-

write security issues and provide other services for the issuing company and its investors.

investment company A *financial intermediary* that pools the funds of investors and invests them in securities such as stocks and *bonds*. See also *money market funds*.

investment decision Decision that involves the allocation of resources among various types of assets.

investment opportunity schedule (IOS) A listing of investment proposals according to their expected returns.

investment outlay The dollar amount spent on an investment proposal, taking into account cash outlays, changes in *working capital*, *investment tax credit*, taxes, *depreciation*, disposition of an old asset, if applicable, and other factors.

investment tax credit (ITC) *Tax credit* given by the government to induce business concerns to invest in capital equipment. The Tax Reform Act of 1986 repealed the ITC for new investments. For investments made before 1986, the ITC will be phased out in stages.

investment value (1) The theoretical or intrinsic value of an asset (i.e., what an analyst believes it to be worth). The investment value may differ from the *market value*. (2) The theoretical price at which a convertible bond would sell if it had no conversion feature; the present value of the coupon payments and principal amount discounted by the current market rate of interest for an equivalent bond.

j

joint bond *Bond* guaranteed by two or more corporations. See also *guaranteed bond*.

joint venture An agreement between business concerns to enter into partnership for a specific project.

junk bond Low-quality *bond* used in connection with *mergers* and takeovers.

l

lead time The number of days necessary to reorder and receive *inventory*.

learning curve A graphic representation of the learning rate, which relates production costs to *experience*. Firms that have the greatest experience tend to have the lowest production costs.

learning rate See *learning curve*.

lease A contract that enables a lessee to secure the use of tangible property for a specified period by making payments to the owner (lessor).

lessee, lessor See *lease*.

letter of credit An instrument issued by a bank that promises to pay a beneficiary upon presentation of certain documents and under certain conditions; widely used in international trade.

leverage See *financial leverage, operating leverage, total leverage*.

leveraged buyout A buyout in which the buyer borrows funds to buy the stock of a company and then uses the resources of that company to repay the loan.

leveraged lease A *financial lease* used to finance large transactions. It involves a lessor, a lessee, and a long-term lender that supplies some of the capital to acquire the asset to be leased. The lessor may provide a relatively small percentage of the funds to acquire the asset but may obtain 100 percent of the tax benefits.

LIBOR The London Interbank offering rate; the interest rate charged between banks for short-term funds in the *Eurodollar* market; analogous to the *federal funds rate*.

lien Creditor's right to claim debtor's property being used as security or *collateral* for a loan.

life cycle A series of four phases—*pioneering, expansion, stabilization,* and *decline*—through which products, companies, and industries pass.

limited liability An advantage of the corporate form of business organization; owners are liable only for the amount invested in the business concern.

limited partnership *Partnership* in which at least one partner has *unlimited liability* but other partners have *limited liability*. Limited partners are not active in the management of the firm.

line of credit An agreement that allows a firm to borrow under certain conditions up to a specified limit from a bank or some other lender.

linear break-even analysis See *break-even analysis*.

linear regression analysis A statistical technique that determines the best linear unbiased estimate, or the straight line that comes closest to all the data points.

liquid asset Asset that can be converted to cash within one year.

liquidating dividend *Dividend* paid when a firm is shrinking in size and converting its assets into *cash* for the benefit of the *shareholders*.

liquidity (1) The ability of a firm to meet its current financial obligations. (2) The ability of investors to sell assets on short notice with little or no loss from the assets' current *market value*.

loan commitment Arrangement between bankers and their customers that allows for borrowing under certain conditions. Prospective borrowers generally pay a fee for having the bank reserve funds for their use. Sometimes a *compensating balance* is required.

lockbox collection system A system used to reduce mail *float* by collecting payments at strategically located post office boxes (lockboxes) throughout the country.

mandatory proposal An investment proposal required for the continued operation of the firm.

margin account An account used to buy securities on credit from brokers and banks.

marginal cost of capital Incremental *cost of capital*; the cost of the next *funds* to be raised.

marginal holding cost In reference to inventory, the constant *holding cost* per unit times the average difference between the order quantity associated with a quantity discount and the *economic order quantity*.

marginal tax rate The income tax rate paid on additional income, as distinct from the *average tax rate* paid on total income.

market extension *Conglomerate merger* involving companies that manufacture the same product in different markets.

market value For securities, the price investors are willing to pay in the securities markets. The market value of a *going concern* is equal to the market value of its debt plus the market value of its *equity*.

market value exchange ratio A ratio used to evaluate the terms of a proposed *merger*; it compares what is offered to the seller with the *market value* of the seller's stock.

maximization of shareholder wealth Maximization of the firm's total value; the appropriate objective of all financial decision making.

member firm A stockbrokerage firm that has the right to trade in an organized *stock exchange*, such as the *New York Stock Exchange*.

mercantile credit agency Business concern that collects and disseminates credit information about potential customers for a fee.

merger The combination of two or more firms in which only one firm survives and retains its identity.

Miller–Orr model A model that establishes certain limits for managing cash balances in conjunction with a *portfolio* of short-term securities. The model assumes that cash balances can fluctuate in a random fashion.

Modigliani and Miller Franco Modigliani and Merton Miller, authors whose works have made major contributions to the analysis of valuation and dividend policy.

monetary policy The Federal Reserve System's handling of the money supply.

money market Market in which short-term securities, such as Treasury bills, *commercial paper*, and so on, are traded. Participants include financial institutions, business concerns, governments, and individual investors.

money market funds Funds created by *investment companies* to pool the monies of investors and invest in short-term financial obligations. The funds provide relatively high yields, and *drafts* can be written against current holdings.

mortgage bond A corporate *bond* backed by a mortgage on specific real estate. A first-mortgage bond is backed by the first mortgage on that real estate. A second-mortgage bond is backed by the second mortgage. A general mortgage bond (or *consolidated mortgage bond*) is backed by any subsequent mortgages on that same real estate.

multinational corporation (MNC) A firm that has production facilities in more than one country.

mutually exclusive proposals Investment proposals that involve "either–or" situations. For example, a firm can build a factory or an office building on a parcel of land, but not both. See also *independent proposals*.

national market system A nationwide computer-based system, still developing, that will provide price and volume data related to securities trading and reduce the importance of stock exchanges.

negotiable certificate of deposit (CD) Negotiable instrument representing funds deposited in a financial institution for a specified period at a specified interest rate. Negotiable CD's have denominations of $100,000 or more.

negotiated basis See *over-the-counter market*.

net present value (*NPV*) The *present value* of *expected cash flows* discounted at the *cost of capital*, less the *investment outlay*.

net profit margin The percentage of profit earned for each dollar of sales; calculated by dividing net income by net sales.

net working capital The difference between current assets and current liabilities.

net worth See *equity*.

New York Stock Exchange (NYSE) The largest organized securities exchange in the United States. About 1500 companies have their securities traded on the NYSE.

nominal value See *par value*.

nonlinear break-even analysis See *break-even analysis*.

nonprofit corporation A *corporation* that does not have profit as a goal. Public nonprofit corporations are created by a public authority to perform governmental functions. Private nonprofit corporations are usually established to pursue religious, charitable, educational, or social goals.

nonrecourse Not involving a right to demand payment. For example, *factors* generally buy *accounts receivable* on a nonrecourse basis; if an account cannot be collected, the factor cannot demand payment from the company that sold the account.

normal yield curve *Yield curve* depicting the situation in which current long-term interest rates are somewhat higher than short-term rates, resulting in a positive slope. See also *downward-sloping yield curve*, *flat yield curve*, *upward-sloping yield curve*.

open-end loan Credit in which the amount loaned can vary. Credit cards are widely used for extending such loans.

open-end mortgage bond *Mortgage bond* that does not prohibit the placing of other mortgage *liens* against the property used as *collateral*.

operating cycle A cycle that begins with the purchase of *inventory* and ends with the collection of receipts from goods sold.

operating lease Short-term *lease* used to finance assets such as computers and trucks; sometimes called a service lease. The asset is not fully amortized over the life of the lease, and frequently the leases are cancellable.

operating leverage The magnifying effect that changes in sales can have on earnings as a result of certain fixed expenses. See also *financial leverage, total leverage*.

operating margin A measure of return on sales; calculated by dividing earnings from operations (operating income) by net sales.

operating return on assets A broad measure of productivity; calculated by dividing earnings before interest and taxes by total assets.

opportunity cost The rate of return a firm must forgo when it selects one use of funds over another.

option See *call option, put option*.

order cost In the *Economic Order Quantity (EOQ)* model, the cost of buying or producing materials or goods for *inventory*. Order cost plus *holding cost* equals total cost.

ordinary annuity *Annuity* in which the periodic payments and interest payments are made at the end of each payment interval, and the term of the annuity is specified. See also *annuity due*.

ordinary voting A system that entitles *shareholders* to one vote for each share held when voting for directors of a corporation and on other issues; also called "straight voting." See also *cumulative voting*.

overhanging issue Potential increase in the supply of stock traded in the market, caused by conversion of *convertible securities*, liquidation of large blocks, and so on.

overlap period In bond refunding, the time between issuance of the new *bond* and retirement of the old one.

over-the-counter market Market in which securities not traded in *stock exchanges* are said to be traded. Prices are negotiated rather than determined on an auction basis, as they are in a *stock exchange*.

overvalued Condition of an asset whose *market value* is greater than its *investment value*.

par value For a *bond*, the value stated in the *indenture*, typically $1,000; also called "face amount" or "face value." If the market price of the bond is higher than the par value, the bond is selling at a premium. If the market price is lower than the par value, the bond is selling at a discount. *Common* and *preferred stocks* also have par values or nominal values stated on the face of the stock certificate. Generally, these values have little to do with the *market value* of the stock, although the par value of a preferred stock may be important in the case of liquidation.

parity A state of equality. When a *convertible bond* is selling for its *conversion value*, it is selling at parity. If the market price exceeds the conversion value, it is selling at a premium. If it is selling below its conversion value, it is selling at a discount. See also *theory of purchasing power parity*.

participating bond *Bond* that bears a fixed rate of interest and also offers a profit-sharing feature.

participating preferred *Preferred stock* that provides stated *dividends* but also shares in the earnings of the corporation.

partnership An unincorporated business owned by more than one person.

payable-through draft Order drawn on a corporation by itself and payable through a bank; used to slow disbursements.

payback period The number of years required to return an *investment outlay*.

payout ratio The percentage of earnings paid to *common shareholders* in the form of cash *dividends*.

percent income statement Income statement in which items are stated as a percentage of sales.

percentage of sales method A method of developing

pro forma financial statements based on the assumption that a constant relationship exists between sales and selected balance sheet and income statement items that relate to operations.

perfect hedge In *working capital management*, financing temporary current assets with short-term sources of funds, and financing fixed assets and permanent current assets with long-term sources of funds. See also *conservative hedge, aggressive hedge*.

perfect negative correlation A statistical term describing a condition in which series of data change in exactly opposite manners.

perfect positive correlation A statistical term describing a condition in which series of data change in exactly the same manner.

permanent working capital The dollar amount of *working capital* that persists over time regardless of fluctuations in sales. See also *temporary working capital*.

perpetual warrant *Warrant* with no expiration date.

perpetuity Annuity that never ends.

Philadelphia Plan See *equipment trust certificate*.

pioneering phase First phase of the *life cycle*, in which a new product is introduced by a limited number of firms; characterized by high costs, low volume, and high market price.

planning Deciding on goals; evaluating alternatives; taking a course of action, and reviewing the process.

pledging Assigning assets such as certificates of deposit (*CD's*) or *accounts receivable* as *collateral* for a loan.

point In stock quotations, $1. Prices are quoted in fractions of a point; thus, 1/8 is $0.125.

political risk The risk faced by a *multinational corporation* related to the host country's political environment and the fact that it might influence the corporation's financial and operating performance.

pollution-control bond *Tax-exempt bond* used to finance corporate expenditures for environmental improvements.

pooling of interests method According to APB 16 (*Accounting Principles Board*), a method of accounting for *mergers* that treats a business combination as the uniting of *equity* interests of two or more companies by the exchange of stock. See also *purchase method*.

portfolio A combination of assets; for example, all stocks listed on the *New York Stock Exchange* comprise a portfolio.

portfolio theory A method of asset selection that considers the combined risk of all assets held by the firm.

preauthorized check or draft Agreement by which funds are transferred from a customer's account to a creditor's account at the creditor's request.

precautionary motive According to John Maynard Keynes, one of three reasons to hold liquid assets. The precautionary motive relates to the need to meet expenses not perfectly synchronized with income. See also *speculative motive, transaction motive*.

preemptive rights See *rights*.

preferred stock Stock representing one class of ownership in a *corporation*. Preferred stock generally has fixed *dividends* and may include other features. Preferred shareholders receive preference over *common shareholders* in the distribution of assets following liquidation.

preliminary prospectus A *prospectus* issued in advance of a securities offering; also called a "red herring" because some of the statements on the front page are printed in red ink to warn investors that the prospectus is incomplete.

premium See *forward rate, par value, parity*.

present value The current value of dollars that will be received in the future; determined by *discounting*.

present value interest factor Multiplier used in *discounting*; a table of present value interest factors is presented in Appendix C.

price elasticity The responsiveness of the demand for a product to a change in price.

price risk A risk associated with dealing in securities. It is the risk of adverse price movements.

price/earnings (*P/E*) ratio A ratio determined by dividing the market price of a stock by its earnings. It is an indicator of investors' expectations about a company's growth; a high ratio suggests high expectations.

primary securities market Market in which newly issued securities are sold to investors by *investment bankers*. The securities can be sold by *private placement* with financial institutions, such as insurance companies, or by a public offering.

prime rate The base interest rate that banks use to

determine the rate they will charge corporate borrowers.

principal amount The original amount of a loan, deposit, or the like, on which interest is paid.

private credit Borrowing by business concerns and individuals.

private placement See *primary securities market*.

privileged subscription *Rights* offering.

pro forma Projected. Pro forma financial statements are projections of financial statements of future periods.

pro rata share Proportionate share. Shareholders have a common-law right, not recognized in all states, to maintain their proportionate share of ownership when a corporation sells new securities. See also *rights*.

probability distribution A distribution of the probabilities associated with certain outcomes. See also *continuous probability distribution, discrete probability distribution*.

product extension *Conglomerate merger* involving companies that are functionally related but that do not compete.

product life cycle See *life cycle*.

profit margin A measure of profitability derived by dividing net income by net sales. It is the percent of profit earned for each dollar of sales.

profitability index (*PI*) A benefit/cost ratio used in *capital budgeting*. It is the value of the *expected cash flows*, discounted at the *cost of capital*, divided by the *investment outlay*.

property dividend Assets of the corporation distributed to shareholders; most commonly, property dividends are securities of other companies. See also *spin-off*.

prospectus Legal document required by the Securities and Exchange Commission for certain new securities issues. It is supposed to provide prospective investors with enough information so that they can make an intelligent decision about buying the security.

proxy Substitute. For example, the *beta coefficient* is a commonly used proxy for *systematic risk*.

proxy statement A power of attorney given by one stockholder to another to vote in the former's behalf.

public credit Borrowing by federal, state, and local governments.

public offering See *primary securities market*.

purchase method A method of accounting for *mergers* that treats a business combination as an acquisition of one company by another. See also *pooling of interests method*.

put option A contract to sell a specified number of shares of stock or a commodity at a predetermined price on or before a certain date.

q

quick ratio See *acid-test ratio*.

r

random walk A process determined by chance. Stock prices are said to follow a random walk by theorists who believe that stock prices in previous periods cannot be used to predict stock prices in future periods. Random walk is the statistical description of Brownian motion.

raw materials inventory *Inventory* that includes items used in the productive processes of the firm, not including plant and equipment.

real asset An asset such as *inventory* or plant and equipment, as opposed to a *financial asset*.

real rate of interest The market rate of interest less the *inflation* rate.

red herring See *preliminary prospectus*.

refunding bond New *bond* issued to pay off an existing bond issue at retirement.

reinvestment rate The interest rate at which *funds* are reinvested in *compounding* and *discounting* calculations.

reinvestment rate assumption The assumption that *funds* are reinvested at a certain rate in *compounding* and *discounting* calculations.

rejuvenation In terms of the *life cycle*, a process by which new demand is created for a product that has been in decline.

reorder point Point at which inventory is reordered; determined by multiplying the *lead time* by the *daily usage rate*, less *inventory* in transit, plus *safety stock*.

replacement chain A method of comparing *mutually exclusive investment proposals* with substantially different lifetimes. It assumes that they will be duplicated in all respects until their lives are of equal length.

replacement proposal An investment proposal that involves the replacement of existing equipment.

repurchase agreement (RP, repo) Short-term loan in which a corporation sells securities to dealers and agrees to buy the securities back at a different price, the difference representing an interest charge, which will provide earnings to the lender.

residual claimant One entitled to all that remains after prior claims have been satisfied. Shareholders are the residual claimants when corporations are liquidated.

responsive assets and liabilities In the *percentage of sales method* of developing *pro forma* financial statements, the items that vary directly with sales.

restrictive covenant Clause in many loans and long-term bond contracts that prohibits the debtor from taking certain actions. Covenants are meant to protect the creditor.

retention rate Percentage of net income retained by the firm.

return The net gain or loss on an investment.

return on assets (*ROA*) Net income divided by assets.

return on equity (*ROE*) Net income divided by equity.

return on investment (*ROI*) A general term that may apply to *return on assets* or *return on equity*, depending on whose investment is being considered.

reverse split A *stock split* used to decrease the number of shares outstanding. After a two-to-one reverse split a stockholder would hold one share for every two shares held before.

revolving credit Credit involving formalized and binding agreements between bankers and customers specifying the amounts of the loans, payment schedules, restrictions, and so on. ''Revolvers'' generally enable customers to borrow over the course of one year or longer.

rights In effect, short-term *call options* to buy a certain number of shares at a set price; frequently offered to shareholders by a corporation selling additional common stock so that they can maintain their *pro rata share* of ownership. The rights have a *market value* and can be traded.

risk The probability that actual returns will deviate from expected returns. The *standard deviation* is one commonly used measure of deviation from expected returns.

risk premium Used in connection with the *capital asset pricing model*, the risk premium is *beta* times the difference between the expected rate of return on the market and the *risk-free rate of return*.

risk-free rate of return Generally considered to be the return on a default-free U.S. government (Treasury) security.

Robinson–Patman Act An antitrust law enacted in 1936; it made certain types of price discrimination illegal.

rule of 72 A rule stating that the length of time required to double the original principal amount can be determined by dividing the compound growth rate into 72. For example, a business growing at 10 percent per year will double in size in about 7.2 years.

rule of 78s A rule commonly used to calculate interest rate penalties when installment loans are prepaid. It reveals that most of the interest will be collected even when a loan is paid off early.

safety stock Extra *inventory* held to meet contingencies such as a shortfall of supplies.

sale and leaseback A procedure by which a firm sells an asset and retains use of it through a *financial lease*.

secondary distribution The sale of a large *block of stock* at a reduced price.

secondary securities market The market in which investors who bought newly issued securities in the *primary securities market* can sell them to other investors. The secondary market provides *liquidity* for investors.

security market line (*SML*) A graphic representation of the relationship between the expected rate of return on an asset and its *systematic risk* as measured by beta. See also *capital asset pricing model*.

semistrong form of efficient market hypothesis See *efficient market hypothesis*.

semivariable cost Cost that shares some characteristics of both *fixed cost* and *variable cost*; for example, sales commissions may be fixed for a certain number of units sold and then increased at a certain number of sales.

serial bond issue Bond issue in which *bonds* mature at different dates.

service lease See *operating lease*.

shareholder One who owns a share in a *corporation* through ownership of *common* or *preferred stock*.

shareholders' equity See *equity*.

shelf registration A procedure that allows a firm to register a new security issue with the Securities and Exchange Commission and then hold it for sale at any time within the next two years.

Sherman Antitrust Act A principal antitrust law enacted in 1890; designed to protect trade and commerce against restraint and monopoly.

short sale Selling a borrowed security at a high price in anticipation of buying it back at a lower price. The borrowed stock is returned after the repurchase.

short-term loan Loan with an original maturity of less than one year.

short-term marketable security Marketable security that matures within one year.

simulation A model constructed to represent reality, on which conclusions about real-life problems can be based.

sinking fund A fund that provides for the periodic retirement of certain portions of a bond issue through periodic payments made by the corporation. Ordinarily, payment is made to a trustee, who can purchase the *bonds*, *call* them, or let the funds accumulate.

Small Business Administration A government agency that provides financial and management assistance and other services to small business concerns.

sole proprietorship An unincorporated business owned by one person.

speculative motive According to John Maynard Keynes, one of three reasons to hold liquid assets. The speculative motive relates to the desire to take advantage of unexpected opportunities. See also *precautionary motive*, *transaction motive*.

spin-off A *property dividend* used by a corporation to divest itself of subsidiaries.

spontaneous source of credit Source of credit (liabilities) that arises out of the ordinary course of business, including *accounts payable*, accrued wages, and accrued taxes. The *funds* represented by spontaneous sources of credit are generally available at little or no cost to the firm.

spot rate The current cash price for immediate delivery; applies to both commodities market and *currency exchange*.

spread (1) Difference between prices; for example, the difference between the price at which an investor can sell a security (bid price) and the price at which an investor can buy a security (asked price). (2) The difference between the yields of *bonds* with different degrees of risk.

stabilization phase Third phase of the *life cycle*, characterized by slowed increase in sales and decline in prices and profits.

stamped bond See *guaranteed bond*.

standard deviation A statistical tool that measures dispersion; used as a proxy for *risk*.

standby underwriting A form of *underwriting* in which a company planning a *rights* offering employs an *investment banker* to stand by to purchase rights not exercised by investors.

stockbroker Component of the *secondary securities market*. Stockbrokerage firms act as brokers and dealers. As brokers, they are agents for their customers, and as dealers they trade for their own accounts.

stock certificate Document that represents a *shareholder's* ownership interest in a *corporation*. It shows the name of the company, the name of the owner of the shares, the number of shares owned, the name of the registrar, and the *par value* of the stock.

stock dividend *Dividend* paid in shares of stock, stated as a percentage of shares held. When the company issues the additional shares, the increase in capital stock is offset by a reduction in retained earnings. The *pro rata share* of ownership is not affected. See also *stock split*.

stock exchange Physical place where *member firms* buy and sell securities. Transactions take place on an auction basis; that is, stocks are sold to the highest bidder. The major stock exchange in the United States is the *New York Stock Exchange*. See also *over-the-counter market*.

stock repurchase Process by which a corporation buys back its own stock; the effect is to reduce the number of shares outstanding and increase the price of the stock.

stock split An action by the *board of directors* to increase the number of shares outstanding. Most splits are two-for-one; stockholders receive one additional share for each share held and their *pro* *rata share* of ownership remains the same. Stock splits are similar to *stock dividends* but involve no accounting adjustment to retained earnings.

straddle A combination of a *put option* and a *call option*.

straight voting See *ordinary voting*.

street name Refers to a method of stock registration; the stock is registered in the name of the stock-brokerage firm or some other nominee rather than the owner's name to facilitate transfer.

striking price With reference to options, the specified price at which a commodity or security can be bought or sold on or before a specified date. Also called "contract price."

strong form of efficient market hypothesis See *efficient market hypothesis*.

Subchapter S A section of the Internal Revenue Code that permits certain small business concerns to combine some advantages of *corporations* and *partnerships*. The avoidance of *double taxation* is the principal advantage.

subscription price In a *rights* offering, the price at which the holder of rights can buy new shares. It should be lower than the stock's current market price.

syndicate A type of *joint venture* in which several *investment bankers* join to purchase securities from the issuing corporation and resell them to investors.

systematic risk Risk that is common to all assets and that cannot be eliminated by diversification; *beta* is a *proxy* for systematic risk.

t

target value Value set as a goal. In *weighted average cost of capital* calculations, target value weights are based on the *capital structure* the firm wishes to maintain as it raises new funds.

tax cost For a depreciable assets, original cost less accumulated *depreciation*.

tax credit A deduction from tax liability.

tax-exempt security Security issued by state or local government; the interest is exempt from federal income tax.

tax-free exchange Exchange in which shareholders of a corporation being acquired receive shares of voting stock in the acquiring corporation and pay no taxes on the shares.

temporary working capital *Working capital* required to meet variations in sales above the level of *permanent working capital*.

tender offer A time-limited offer to buy stock from shareholders at a predetermined price, generally limited to a certain total number of shares. It is commonly used by companies that wish to acquire the stock of other companies.

terminal warehouse A bonded public warehouse.

term loan Commercial or industrial loan from commercial bank, commonly used for plant and equipment, *working capital*, or debt repayment. Term loans generally have a maturity of five years or less.

term structure of interest rates See *yield curve*.

theoretical value See *investment value*.

theory of interest rate parity The theory that the difference in interest rates between two countries is exactly offset by the difference in their currency exchange rates.

theory of purchasing power parity The theory that the difference in the national *inflation* rates of two countries is directly reflected in their currency exchange rates.

thin market Condition of a stock with a small *floating supply*.

time draft An order to pay a specified amount at a specified date in the future; similar to a predated check.

time value of money The principle that money received in the present is worth more than the same amount received in the future.

times interest earned ratio A ratio that measures debt coverage; calculated by dividing earnings before interest and taxes by interest expense.

total cost In the *Economic Order Quantity* (*EOQ*) model, the sum of *holding cost* and *order cost* of *inventory*.

total leverage The product of *operating leverage* and *financial leverage*.

total risk *Systematic risk* plus *unsystematic risk*. It can be measured as the deviations from the expected return on an asset.

trade credit *Accounts payable* arising from the purchase of goods or services from another business concern; an important source of low-cost short-term financing.

trade discount A percentage reduction in the amount due when *accounts payable* are paid by a certain date.

transaction motive According to John Maynard Keynes, one of three reasons for holding liquid assets. The transaction motive relates to the need for cash to carry out daily business transactions. See also *precautionary motive, speculative motive*.

treasury stock Formerly outstanding stock that the corporation has repurchased.

true financial lease See *financial lease*.

trust receipt Instrument used in connection with *floor planning*.

turnover of accounts receivable Measure used to monitor credit; calculated by dividing annual credit sales by *accounts receivable*.

undervalued Condition of an asset whose *investment value* is greater than its *market value*.

underwriting Process in which *investment bankers* buy a security issue from a company attempting to raise funds and sell the issue to investors.

unlimited liability A disadvantage of some forms of business organization; the owner's (or owners') personal wealth may be used to satisfy claims against the business concern.

unsystematic risk Risk that is unique to a particular asset and that can therefore be eliminated by diversification in a *portfolio*.

upward-sloping yield curve *Yield* curve that slopes upward by more than the normal amount; it indicates that long-term interest rates are expected to rise. See also *downward-sloping yield curve, flat yield curve, normal yield curve*.

variable cost Cost that changes in direct proportion to the number of units sold. See also *fixed cost, semivariable cost*.

variance A statistical measure of dispersion.

venture capital company Private business concern that uses its sources of capital (not including government funds) to finance other business concerns.

vertical merger A *merger* that can affect the acquiring company's production or distribution process; for example, a steel producer's acquisition of an iron mine and a steel distributorship.

Walter's formula Formula developed by James Walter to demonstrate that dividend policy should be determined solely by the profitability of investment opportunities.

warehouse receipt Receipt for *inventory* used as *collateral* and held in a *terminal warehouse* or a *field warehouse*.

warrant A *call option* to buy a stated number of shares of stock at a specified price on or before a predetermined date. Most warrants have an original maturity of five years or longer.

weak form of efficient market hypothesis See *efficient capital market*.

weighted average cost of capital (WACC) The *cost of capital* that takes into account the proportions and costs of debt, *preferred stock*, and *equity*. The weights can be based on *book value, market value*, or *target value*.

when issued (W.I.) A condition under which securities may be traded before they are actually issued. For example, when a stock goes *ex-rights*, trading in the *rights* will occur on a W.I. basis until the rights are mailed to the stockholders. Then they will be traded the "regular way."

white knight A *merger* partner of a company's own choosing; generally obtained to keep some unwanted suitor away.

wire transfer Transfer of funds between organizations by use of the Federal Reserve Wire System or the Western Union Bank Wire.

working capital The dollar amount of a firm's current assets.

working capital cycle See *funds flow cycle*.

working capital management The management of current assets, current liabilities, and the relationship between them.

work-in-process inventory *Inventory* that includes raw materials in the process of being converted into finished goods.

worldwide weighted average cost of capital (WWACC) The *weighted average cost of capital* for multinational firms, which takes into account their global sources of funds and risks.

y

yield curve A graphic representation of the relationship between interest rates and the maturity of a security; also called the term structure of interest rates. A configuration of yield curves can be used to estimate the future course of interest rates. See also *downward-sloping yield curve, flat yield curve, normal yield curve, upward-sloping yield curves.*

yield to maturity The average return on a debt security if kept until maturity, taking into account the income provided by interest payments as well as *capital gains* or *losses.*

z

Z A statistic used to relate the *standard deviation* to the area under a normal curve.

zero-balance account System comprising various divisional checking accounts and a corporate checking account, all located at the same *concentration bank*. Divisional accounts are managed to maintain a zero balance most of the time.

zero-coupon bond *Bond* issued at a *deep discount* and making no periodic interest payment. The difference between the issue price and the *face value* provides a return to the holder at maturity.

APPENDIX A Future Value of One Dollar:
$$FV_n = PV_0 (1 + i)^n$$

where $(1 + i)^n = FVIF_{i,n}$ and is shown in the following table.

n	1%	2%	3%	4%	5%	6%	7%	8%	9%	10%
1	1.0100	1.0200	1.0300	1.0400	1.0500	1.0600	1.0700	1.0800	1.0900	1.1000
2	1.0201	1.0404	1.0609	1.0816	1.1025	1.1236	1.1449	1.1664	1.1881	1.2100
3	1.0303	1.0612	1.0927	1.1249	1.1576	1.1910	1.2250	1.2597	1.2950	1.3310
4	1.0406	1.0824	1.1255	1.1699	1.2155	1.2625	1.3108	1.3605	1.4116	1.4641
5	1.0510	1.1041	1.1593	1.2167	1.2763	1.3382	1.4026	1.4693	1.5386	1.6105
6	1.0615	1.1261	1.1941	1.2653	1.3401	1.4185	1.5007	1.5869	1.6771	1.7716
7	1.0721	1.1487	1.2299	1.3159	1.4071	1.5036	1.6058	1.7138	1.8280	1.9487
8	1.0829	1.1717	1.2668	1.3686	1.4775	1.5939	1.7182	1.8509	1.9926	2.1436
9	1.0937	1.1951	1.3048	1.4233	1.5513	1.6895	1.8385	1.9990	2.1719	2.3580
10	1.1046	1.2190	1.3439	1.4802	1.6289	1.7909	1.9672	2.1589	2.3674	2.5937
11	1.1157	1.2434	1.3842	1.5395	1.7103	1.8983	2.1049	2.3316	2.5804	2.8531
12	1.1268	1.2682	1.4258	1.6010	1.7959	2.0122	2.2522	2.5182	2.8127	3.1384
13	1.1381	1.2936	1.4685	1.6651	1.8857	2.1329	2.4098	2.7196	3.0658	3.4523
14	1.1495	1.3195	1.5126	1.7317	1.9799	2.2609	2.5785	2.9372	3.3417	3.7975
15	1.1610	1.3459	1.5580	1.8009	2.0789	2.3966	2.7590	3.1722	3.6425	4.1773
16	1.1726	1.3728	1.6047	1.8730	2.1829	2.5404	2.9522	3.4259	3.9703	4.5950
17	1.1843	1.4002	1.6529	1.9479	2.2920	2.6928	3.1588	3.7000	4.3276	5.0545
18	1.1962	1.4283	1.7024	2.0258	2.4066	2.8543	3.3799	3.9960	4.7171	5.5599
19	1.2081	1.4568	1.7535	2.1069	2.5270	3.0256	3.6165	4.3157	5.1417	6.1159
20	1.2202	1.4860	1.8061	2.1911	2.6533	3.2071	3.8697	4.6610	5.6044	6.7275
21	1.2324	1.5157	1.8603	2.2788	2.7860	3.3996	4.1406	5.0338	6.1088	7.4003
22	1.2447	1.5460	1.9161	2.3699	2.9253	3.6035	4.4304	5.4365	6.6586	8.1403
23	1.2572	1.5769	1.9736	2.4647	3.0715	3.8198	4.7405	5.8714	7.2579	8.9543
24	1.2697	1.6084	2.0328	2.5633	3.2251	4.0489	5.0724	6.3412	7.9111	9.8497
25	1.2824	1.6406	2.0937	2.6658	3.3864	4.2919	5.4274	6.8485	8.6231	10.835

Example   The future value of $1.00 compounded at 10 percent for 10 years is $2.59 ($1.00 × 2.5937 = $2.59).

n	11%	12%	13%	14%	15%	16%	17%	18%	19%	20%
1	1.1100	1.1200	1.1300	1.1400	1.1500	1.1600	1.1700	1.1800	1.1900	1.2000
2	1.2321	1.2544	1.2769	1.2996	1.3225	1.3456	1.3689	1.3924	1.4161	1.4400
3	1.3676	1.4049	1.4429	1.4815	1.5209	1.5609	1.6016	1.6430	1.6852	1.7280
4	1.5181	1.5735	1.6305	1.6890	1.7490	1.8106	1.8739	1.9388	2.0053	2.0736
5	1.6851	1.7623	1.8424	1.9254	2.0114	2.1003	2.1925	2.2878	2.3864	2.4883
6	1.8704	1.9738	2.0820	2.1950	2.3131	2.4364	2.5652	2.6996	2.8398	2.9860
7	2.0762	2.2107	2.3526	2.5023	2.6600	2.8262	3.0012	3.1855	3.3793	3.5832
8	2.3045	2.4760	2.6584	2.8526	3.0590	3.2784	3.5115	3.7589	4.0214	4.2998
9	2.5580	2.7731	3.0040	3.2520	3.5179	3.8030	4.1084	4.4355	4.7855	5.1598
10	2.8394	3.1059	3.3946	3.7072	4.0456	4.4114	4.8068	5.2338	5.6947	6.1917
11	3.1518	3.4786	3.8359	4.2262	4.6524	5.1173	5.6240	6.1759	6.7767	7.4301
12	3.4985	3.8960	4.3345	4.8179	5.3503	5.9360	6.5801	7.2876	8.0642	8.9161
13	3.8833	4.3635	4.8980	5.4924	6.1528	6.8858	7.6987	8.5994	9.5965	10.699
14	4.3104	4.8871	5.5348	6.2616	7.0757	7.9875	9.0075	10.147	11.420	12.839
15	4.7846	5.4736	6.2543	7.1379	8.1371	9.2655	10.539	11.974	13.590	15.407
16	5.3109	6.1304	7.0673	8.1373	9.3576	10.748	12.330	14.129	16.172	18.488
17	5.8951	6.8660	7.9861	9.2765	10.761	12.468	14.427	16.672	19.244	22.186
18	6.5436	7.6900	9.0243	10.575	12.376	14.463	16.879	19.673	22.901	26.623
19	7.2633	8.6128	10.107	12.056	14.232	16.777	19.748	23.214	27.252	31.948
20	8.0623	9.6463	11.523	13.744	16.367	19.461	23.106	27.393	32.429	38.338
21	8.9492	10.804	13.021	15.668	18.822	22.575	27.034	32.324	38.591	46.005
22	9.9336	12.100	14.714	17.861	21.645	26.186	31.629	38.142	45.923	55.206
23	11.026	13.552	16.627	20.362	24.892	30.376	37.006	45.008	54.649	66.247
24	12.239	15.179	18.788	23.212	28.625	35.236	43.297	53.109	65.032	79.497
25	13 586	17.000	21.231	26.462	32.919	40.874	50.658	62.669	77.388	95.396

n	21%	22%	23%	24%	25%	26%	27%	28%	29%	30%
1	1.2100	1.2200	1.2300	1.2400	1.2500	1.2600	1.2700	1.2800	1.2900	1.3000
2	1.4641	1.4884	1.5129	1.5376	1.5625	1.5876	1.6129	1.6384	1.6641	1.6900
3	1.7716	1.8159	1.8609	1.9066	1.9531	2.0004	2.0484	2.0972	2.1467	2.1970
4	2.1436	2.2153	2.2889	2.3642	2.4414	2.5205	2.6015	2.6844	2.7692	2.8561
5	2.5937	2.7027	2.8153	2.9316	3.0518	3.1758	3.3038	3.4360	3.5723	3.7129
6	3.1384	3.2973	3.4628	3.6352	3.8147	4.0015	4.1959	4.3981	4.6083	4.8268
7	3.7975	4.0227	4.2593	4.5077	4.7684	5.0419	5.3288	5.6295	5.9447	6.2749
8	4.5950	4.9077	5.2389	5.5895	5.9605	6.3528	6.7675	7.2058	7.6686	8.1573
9	5.5599	5.9874	6.4439	6.9310	7.4506	8.0045	8.5948	9.2234	9.8925	10.605
10	6.7275	7.3046	7.9260	8.5944	9.3132	10.086	10.915	11.806	12.761	13.786
11	8.1403	8.9117	9.7489	10.657	11.642	12.708	13.863	15.112	16.462	17.922
12	9.8497	10.872	11.991	13.215	14.552	16.012	17.605	19.343	21.237	23.298
13	11.918	13.264	14.749	16.386	18.190	20.175	22.359	24.759	27.395	30.288
14	14.421	16.182	18.141	20.319	22.737	25.421	28.396	31.691	35.339	39.374
15	17.449	19.742	22.314	25.196	28.422	32.030	36.063	40.565	45.588	51.186
16	21.114	24.086	27.446	31.243	35.527	40.358	45.799	51.923	58.898	66.542
17	25.548	29.384	33.759	38.741	44.409	50.851	58.165	66.461	75.862	86.504
18	30.913	35.849	41.523	48.039	55.511	64.072	73.870	85.071	97.862	112.46
19	37.404	43.736	51.074	59.568	69.389	80.731	93.815	108.89	126.24	146.19
20	45.259	53.358	62.821	73.864	86.736	101.72	119.15	139.38	162.85	190.05
21	54.764	65.096	77.269	91.592	108.42	128.17	151.31	178.41	210.08	247.07
22	66.264	79.418	95.041	113.57	135.53	161.49	192.17	228.36	271.00	321.18
23	80.180	96.889	116.90	140.83	169.41	203.48	244.05	292.30	349.59	417.54
24	97.017	118.21	143.79	174.63	211.76	256.39	309.95	374.14	450.98	542.80
25	117.39	144.21	176.86	216.54	264.70	323.05	393.63	478.91	581.76	705.64

Future Value of an Annuity ($1):

$$FV_a = PMT \left[\sum_{t=1}^{n} (1 + i)^{n - t} \right]$$

where $\sum_{t=1}^{n} (1 + i)^{n - t} = FVAIF_{i,n}$ and is shown in the following table.

Period	1%	2%	3%	4%	5%	6%	7%	8%	9%	10%
1	1.000	1.000	1.000	1.000	1.000	1.000	1.000	1.000	1.000	1.000
2	2.010	2.020	2.030	2.040	2.050	2.060	2.070	2.080	2.090	2.100
3	3.030	3.060	3.091	3.122	3.152	3.184	3.215	3.246	3.278	3.310
4	4.060	4.122	4.184	4.246	4.310	4.375	4.440	4.506	4.573	4.641
5	5.101	5.204	5.309	5.416	5.526	5.637	5.751	5.867	5.985	6.105
6	6.152	6.308	6.468	6.633	6.802	6.975	7.153	7.336	7.523	7.716
7	7.214	7.434	7.662	7.898	8.142	8.394	8.654	8.923	9.200	9.487
8	8.286	8.583	8.892	9.214	9.549	9.897	10.260	10.637	11.028	11.436
9	9.368	9.755	10.159	10.583	11.027	11.491	11.978	12.488	13.021	13.579
10	10.462	10.950	11.464	12.006	12.578	13.181	13.816	14.487	15.193	15.937
11	11.567	12.169	12.808	13.486	14.207	14.972	15.784	16.645	17.560	18.531
12	12.682	13.412	14.192	15.026	15.917	16.870	17.888	18.977	20.141	21.384
13	13.809	14.680	15.618	16.627	17.713	18.882	20.141	21.495	22.953	24.523
14	14.947	15.974	17.086	18.292	19.598	21.015	22.550	24.215	26.019	27.975
15	16.097	17.293	18.599	20.023	21.578	23.276	25.129	27.152	29.361	31.772
16	17.258	18.639	20.157	21.824	23.657	25.672	27.888	30.324	33.003	35.949
17	18.430	20.012	21.761	23.697	25.840	28.213	30.840	33.750	36.973	40.544
18	19.614	21.412	23.414	25.645	28.132	30.905	33.999	37.450	41.301	45.599
19	20.811	22.840	25.117	27.671	30.539	33.760	37.379	41.446	46.018	51.158
20	22.019	24.297	26.870	29.778	33.066	36.785	40.995	45.762	51.159	57.274
21	23.239	25.783	28.676	31.969	35.719	39.992	44.865	50.422	56.764	64.002
22	24.471	27.299	30.536	34.248	38.505	43.392	49.005	55.456	62.872	71.402
23	25.716	28.845	32.452	36.618	41.430	46.995	53.435	60.893	69.531	79.542
24	26.973	30.421	34.426	39.082	44.501	50.815	58.176	66.764	76.789	88.496
25	28.243	32.030	36.459	41.645	47.726	54.864	63.248	73.105	84.699	98.346

Example The future value of $1.00 per year for the next 25 years, compounded at 10 percent is $98.35 ($1.00 × 98.346 = $98.35).

Period	11%	12%	13%	14%	15%	16%	17%	18%	19%	20%
1	1.000	1.000	1.000	1.000	1.000	1.000	1.000	1.000	1.000	1.000
2	2.110	2.120	2.130	2.140	2.150	2.160	2.170	2.180	2.190	2.200
3	3.342	3.374	3.407	3.440	3.472	3.506	3.539	3.572	3.606	3.640
4	4.710	4.779	4.850	4.921	4.993	5.066	5.141	5.215	5.291	5.368
5	6.228	6.353	6.480	6.610	6.742	6.877	7.014	7.154	7.297	7.442
6	7.913	8.115	8.323	8.535	8.754	8.977	9.207	9.442	9.683	9.930
7	9.783	10.089	10.405	10.730	11.067	11.414	11.772	12.141	12.523	12.916
8	11.859	12.300	12.757	13.233	13.727	14.240	14.773	15.327	15.902	16.499
9	14.164	14.776	15.416	16.085	16.786	17.518	18.285	19.086	19.923	20.799
10	16.722	17.549	18.420	19.337	20.304	21.321	22.393	23.521	24.709	25.959
11	19.561	20.655	21.814	23.044	24.349	25.733	27.200	28.755	30.403	32.150
12	22.713	24.133	25.650	27.271	29.001	30.850	32.824	34.931	37.180	39.580
13	26.211	28.029	29.984	32.088	34.352	36.786	39.404	42.218	45.244	48.496
14	30.095	32.392	34.882	37.581	40.504	43.672	47.102	50.818	54.841	59.196
15	34.405	37.280	40.417	43.842	47.580	51.659	56.109	60.965	66.260	72.035
16	39.190	42.753	46.671	50.980	55.717	60.925	66.648	72.938	79.850	87.442
17	44.500	48.883	53.738	59.117	65.075	71.673	78.978	87.067	96.021	105.930
18	50.396	55.749	61.724	68.393	75.836	84.140	93.404	103.739	115.265	128.116
19	56.939	63.439	70.748	78.968	88.211	98.603	110.283	123.412	138.165	154.739
20	64.202	72.052	80.946	91.024	102.443	115.379	130.031	146.626	165.417	186.687
21	72.264	81.698	92.468	104.767	118.809	134.840	153.136	174.019	197.846	225.024
22	81.213	92.502	105.489	120.434	137.630	157.414	180.169	206.342	236.436	271.028
23	91.147	104.602	120.203	138.295	159.274	183.600	211.798	244.483	282.359	326.234
24	102.173	118.154	136.829	158.656	184.166	213.976	248.803	289.490	337.007	392.480
25	114.412	133.333	155.616	181.867	212.790	249.212	292.099	342.598	402.038	471.976

Period	21%	22%	23%	24%	25%	26%	27%	28%	29%	30%
1	1.000	1.000	1.000	1.000	1.000	1.000	1.000	1.000	1.000	1.000
2	2.210	2.220	2.230	2.240	2.250	2.260	2.270	2.280	2.290	2.300
3	3.674	3.708	3.743	3.778	3.813	3.848	3.883	3.918	3.954	3.990
4	5.446	5.524	5.604	5.684	5.766	5.848	5.931	6.016	6.101	6.187
5	7.589	7.740	7.893	8.048	8.207	8.368	8.533	8.700	8.870	9.043
6	10.183	10.442	10.708	10.980	11.259	11.544	11.837	12.136	12.442	12.756
7	13.321	13.740	14.171	14.615	15.073	15.546	16.032	16.534	17.051	17.583
8	17.119	17.762	18.430	19.123	19.842	20.588	21.361	22.163	22.995	23.858
9	21.714	22.670	23.669	24.712	25.802	26.940	28.129	29.369	30.664	32.015
10	27.274	28.657	30.113	31.643	33.253	34.945	36.723	38.592	40.556	42.619
11	34.001	35.962	38.039	40.238	42.566	45.030	47.639	50.398	53.318	56.405
12	42.141	44.873	47.787	50.895	54.208	57.738	61.501	65.510	69.780	74.326
13	51.991	55.745	59.778	64.109	68.760	73.750	79.106	84.853	91.016	97.624
14	63.909	69.009	74.528	80.496	86.949	93.925	101.465	109.611	118.411	127.912
15	78.330	85.191	92.669	100.815	109.687	119.346	129.860	141.302	153.750	167.285
16	95.779	104.933	114.983	126.010	138.109	151.375	165.922	181.867	199.337	218.470
17	116.892	129.019	142.428	157.252	173.636	191.733	211.721	233.790	258.145	285.011
18	142.439	158.403	176.187	195.993	218.045	242.583	269.885	300.250	334.006	371.514
19	173.351	194.251	217.710	244.031	273.556	306.654	343.754	385.321	431.868	483.968
20	210.755	237.986	268.783	303.598	342.945	387.384	437.568	494.210	558.110	630.157
21	256.013	291.343	331.603	377.461	429.681	489.104	556.710	633.589	720.962	820.204
22	310.775	356.438	408.871	469.052	538.101	617.270	708.022	811.993	931.040	1067.265
23	377.038	435.854	503.911	582.624	673.626	778.760	900.187	1040.351	1202.042	1388.443
24	457.215	532.741	620.810	723.453	843.032	982.237	1144.237	1332.649	1551.634	1805.975
25	554.230	650.944	764.596	898.082	1054.791	1238.617	1454.180	1706.790	2002.608	2348.765

APPENDIX C **Present Value of One Dollar:**

$$PV_0 = FV_n \left[\frac{1}{(1 + i)^n} \right]$$

where $\dfrac{1}{(1 + i)^n} = PVIF_{i,n}$ and is shown in the following table.

n	1%	2%	3%	4%	5%	6%	7%	8%	9%	10%
1	0.99010	0.98039	0.97087	0.96154	0.95238	0.94340	0.93458	0.92593	0.91743	0.90909
2	0.98030	0.96117	0.94260	0.92456	0.90703	0.89000	0.87344	0.85734	0.84168	0.82645
3	0.97059	0.94232	0.91514	0.88900	0.86384	0.83962	0.81630	0.79383	0.77218	0.75131
4	0.96098	0.92385	0.88849	0.85480	0.82270	0.79209	0.76290	0.73503	0.70843	0.68301
5	0.95147	0.90573	0.86261	0.82193	0.78353	0.74726	0.71299	0.68058	0.64993	0.62092
6	0.94204	0.88797	0.83748	0.79031	0.74622	0.70496	0.66634	0.63017	0.59627	0.56447
7	0.93272	0.87056	0.81309	0.75992	0.71068	0.66506	0.62275	0.58349	0.54703	0.51316
8	0.92348	0.85349	0.78941	0.73069	0.67684	0.62741	0.58201	0.54027	0.50187	0.46651
9	0.91434	0.83675	0.76642	0.70259	0.64461	0.59190	0.54393	0.50025	0.46043	0.42410
10	0.90529	0.82035	0.74409	0.67556	0.61391	0.55839	0.50835	0.46319	0.42241	0.38554
11	0.89632	0.80426	0.72242	0.64958	0.58468	0.52679	0.47509	0.42888	0.38753	0.35049
12	0.88745	0.78849	0.70138	0.62460	0.55684	0.49697	0.44401	0.39711	0.35553	0.31683
13	0.87866	0.77303	0.68095	0.60057	0.53032	0.46884	0.41496	0.36770	0.32618	0.28966
14	0.86996	0.75787	0.66112	0.57747	0.50507	0.44230	0.38782	0.34046	0.29925	0.26333
15	0.86135	0.74301	0.64186	0.55526	0.48102	0.41726	0.36245	0.31524	0.27454	0.23939
16	0.85282	0.72845	0.62317	0.53391	0.45811	0.39365	0.33873	0.29189	0.25187	0.21763
17	0.84438	0.71416	0.60502	0.51337	0.43630	0.37136	0.31657	0.27027	0.23107	0.19784
18	0.83602	0.70016	0.58739	0.49363	0.41552	0.35034	0.29586	0.25025	0.21199	0.17986
19	0.82774	0.68643	0.57029	0.47464	0.39573	0.33051	0.27651	0.23171	0.19449	0.16351
20	0.81954	0.67297	0.55367	0.45639	0.37689	0.31180	0.25842	0.21455	0.17843	0.14864
21	0.81143	0.65978	0.53755	0.43883	0.35894	0.29415	0.24151	0.19866	0.16370	0.13513
22	0.80340	0.64684	0.52189	0.42195	0.34185	0.27750	0.22571	0.18394	0.15018	0.12285
23	0.79544	0.63414	0.50669	0.40573	0.32557	0.26180	0.21095	0.17031	0.13778	0.11168
24	0.78757	0.62172	0.49193	0.39012	0.31007	0.24698	0.19715	0.15770	0.12640	0.10153
25	0.77977	0.60953	0.47760	0.37512	0.29530	0.23300	0.18425	0.14602	0.11597	0.09230

Example   The present value of $1.00 received 5 years from now, discounted at 10 percent, is $0.62 ($1.00 × 0.62092 = $0.62).

n	11%	12%	13%	14%	15%	16%	17%	18%	19%	20%
1	0.90090	0.89286	0.88496	0.87719	0.86957	0.86207	0.85470	0.84746	0.84034	0.83333
2	0.81162	0.79719	0.78315	0.76947	0.75614	0.74316	0.73051	0.71818	0.70616	0.69444
3	0.73119	0.71178	0.69305	0.67497	0.65752	0.64066	0.62437	0.60863	0.59342	0.57870
4	0.65873	0.63552	0.61332	0.59208	0.57175	0.55229	0.53365	0.51579	0.49867	0.48225
5	0.59345	0.56743	0.54276	0.51937	0.49718	0.47611	0.45611	0.43711	0.41905	0.40188
6	0.53464	0.50663	0.48032	0.45559	0.43233	0.41044	0.38984	0.37043	0.35214	0.33490
7	0.48166	0.45235	0.42506	0.39964	0.37594	0.35383	0.33320	0.31392	0.29592	0.27908
8	0.43393	0.40388	0.37616	0.35056	0.32690	0.30503	0.28478	0.26604	0.24867	0.23257
9	0.39092	0.36061	0.33288	0.30751	0.28426	0.26295	0.24340	0.22546	0.20897	0.19381
10	0.35218	0.32197	0.29459	0.26974	0.24718	0.22668	0.20804	0.19106	0.17560	0.16151
11	0.31728	0.28748	0.26070	0.23662	0.21494	0.19542	0.17781	0.16192	0.14756	0.13459
12	0.28584	0.25667	0.23071	0.20756	0.18691	0.16846	0.15197	0.13722	0.12400	0.11216
13	0.25751	0.22917	0.20416	0.18207	0.16253	0.14523	0.12989	0.11629	0.10420	0.09346
14	0.23199	0.20462	0.18068	0.15971	0.14133	0.12520	0.11102	0.09855	0.08757	0.07789
15	0.20900	0.18270	0.15989	0.14010	0.12289	0.10793	0.09489	0.08352	0.07359	0.06491
16	0.18829	0.16312	0.14150	0.12289	0.10686	0.09304	0.08110	0.07078	0.06184	0.05409
17	0.16963	0.14564	0.12522	0.10780	0.09293	0.08021	0.06932	0.05998	0.05196	0.04507
18	0.15282	0.13004	0.11081	0.09456	0.08080	0.06914	0.05925	0.05083	0.04367	0.03756
19	0.13768	0.11611	0.09806	0.08295	0.07026	0.05961	0.05064	0.04308	0.03669	0.03130
20	0.12403	0.10367	0.08678	0.07276	0.06110	0.05139	0.04328	0.03651	0.03084	0.02608
21	0.11174	0.09256	0.07680	0.06383	0.05313	0.04430	0.03699	0.03094	0.02591	0.02174
22	0.10067	0.08264	0.06796	0.05599	0.04620	0.03819	0.03162	0.02622	0.02178	0.01811
23	0.09069	0.07379	0.06014	0.04911	0.04017	0.03292	0.02702	0.02222	0.01830	0.01509
24	0.08170	0.06588	0.05322	0.04308	0.03493	0.02838	0.02310	0.01883	0.01538	0.01258
25	0.07361	0.05882	0.04710	0.03779	0.03038	0.02447	0.01974	0.01596	0.01292	0.01048

n	21%	22%	23%	24%	25%	26%	27%	28%	29%	30%
1	0.82645	0.81967	0.81301	0.80645	0.80000	0.79365	0.78740	0.78125	0.77519	0.76923
2	0.68301	0.67186	0.66098	0.65036	0.64000	0.62988	0.62000	0.61035	0.60093	0.59172
3	0.56447	0.55071	0.53738	0.52449	0.51200	0.49991	0.48819	0.47684	0.46583	0.45517
4	0.46651	0.45140	0.43690	0.42297	0.40960	0.39675	0.38440	0.37253	0.36111	0.35013
5	0.38554	0.37000	0.35520	0.34111	0.32768	0.31488	0.30268	0.29104	0.27993	0.26933
6	0.31863	0.30328	0.28878	0.27509	0.26214	0.24991	0.23833	0.22737	0.21700	0.20718
7	0.26333	0.24859	0.23478	0.22184	0.20972	0.19834	0.18766	0.17764	0.16822	0.15937
8	0.21763	0.20376	0.19088	0.17891	0.16777	0.15741	0.14776	0.13878	0.13040	0.12259
9	0.17986	0.16702	0.15519	0.14428	0.13422	0.12493	0.11635	0.10842	0.10109	0.09430
10	0.14864	0.13690	0.12617	0.11635	0.10737	0.09915	0.09161	0.08470	0.07836	0.07254
11	0.12285	0.11221	0.10258	0.09383	0.08590	0.07869	0.07214	0.06617	0.06075	0.05580
12	0.10153	0.09198	0.08339	0.07567	0.06872	0.06245	0.05680	0.05170	0.04709	0.04292
13	0.08391	0.07539	0.06780	0.06103	0.05498	0.04957	0.04472	0.04039	0.03650	0.03302
14	0.06934	0.06180	0.05512	0.04921	0.04398	0.03934	0.03522	0.03155	0.02830	0.02540
15	0.05731	0.05065	0.04481	0.03969	0.03518	0.03122	0.02773	0.02465	0.02194	0.01954
16	0.04736	0.04152	0.03643	0.03201	0.02815	0.02478	0.02183	0.01926	0.01700	0.01503
17	0.03914	0.03403	0.02962	0.02581	0.02252	0.01967	0.01719	0.01505	0.01318	0.01156
18	0.03235	0.02789	0.02408	0.02082	0.01801	0.01561	0.01354	0.01175	0.01022	0.00889
19	0.02673	0.02286	0.01958	0.01679	0.01441	0.01239	0.01066	0.00918	0.00792	0.00684
20	0.02209	0.01874	0.01592	0.01354	0.01153	0.00983	0.00839	0.00717	0.00614	0.00526
21	0.01826	0.01536	0.01294	0.01092	0.00922	0.00780	0.00661	0.00561	0.00476	0.00405
22	0.01509	0.01259	0.01052	0.00880	0.00738	0.00619	0.00520	0.00438	0.00369	0.00311
23	0.01247	0.01032	0.00855	0.00710	0.00590	0.00491	0.00410	0.00342	0.00286	0.00239
24	0.01031	0.00846	0.00695	0.00573	0.00472	0.00390	0.00323	0.00267	0.00222	0.00184
25	0.00852	0.00693	0.00565	0.00462	0.00378	0.00310	0.00254	0.00209	0.00172	0.00142

APPENDIX D Present Value of an Annuity ($1):

$$PV_a = PMT \sum_{t=1}^{n} \left[\frac{1}{(1 + i)^t} \right]$$

where $\sum_{t=1}^{n} \left(\frac{1}{(1 + i)^t} \right) = PVAIF_{i,n}$ and is shown in the following table.

n	1%	2%	3%	4%	5%	6%	7%	8%	9%	10%
1	0.9901	0.9804	0.9709	0.9615	0.9524	0.9434	0.9346	0.9259	0.9174	0.9091
2	1.9704	1.9416	1.9135	1.8861	1.8594	1.8334	1.8080	1.7833	1.7591	1.7355
3	2.9410	2.8839	2.8286	2.7751	2.7233	2.6730	2.6243	2.5771	2.5313	2.4868
4	3.9020	3.8077	3.7171	3.6299	3.5459	3.4651	3.3872	3.3121	3.2397	3.1699
5	4.8535	4.7134	4.5797	4.4518	4.3295	4.2123	4.1002	3.9927	3.8896	3.7908
6	5.7955	5.6014	5.4172	5.2421	5.0757	4.9173	4.7665	4.6229	4.4859	4.3553
7	6.7282	6.4720	6.2302	6.0020	5.7863	5.5824	5.3893	5.2064	5.0329	4.8684
8	7.6517	7.3254	7.0196	6.7327	6.4632	6.2098	5.9713	5.7466	5.5348	5.3349
9	8.5661	8.1622	7.7861	7.4353	7.1078	6.8017	6.5152	6.2469	5.9852	5.7590
10	9.4714	8.9825	8.7302	8.1109	7.7217	7.3601	7.0236	6.7101	6.4176	6.1446
11	10.3677	9.7868	9.2526	8.7604	8.3064	7.8868	7.4987	7.1389	6.8052	6.4951
12	11.2552	10.5753	9.9539	9.3850	8.8632	8.3838	7.9427	7.6361	7.1607	6.8137
13	12.1338	11.3483	10.6349	9.9856	9.3935	8.8527	8.3576	7.9038	7.4869	7.1034
14	13.0038	12.1062	11.2960	10.5631	9.8986	9.2950	8.7454	8.2442	7.7861	7.3667
15	13.8651	12.8492	11.9379	11.1183	10.3796	9.7122	9.1079	8.5595	8.0607	7.6061
16	14.7180	13.5777	12.5610	11.6522	10.8377	10.1059	9.4466	8.8514	8.3125	7.8237
17	15.5624	14.2918	13.1660	12.1656	11.2740	10.4772	9.7632	9.1216	8.5436	8.0215
18	16.3984	14.9920	13.7534	12.6592	11.6895	10.8276	10.0591	9.3719	8.7556	8.2014
19	17.2261	15.2684	14.3237	13.1339	12.0853	11.1581	10.3356	9.6036	8.9501	8.3649
20	18.0457	16.3514	14.8774	13.5903	12.4622	11.4699	10.5940	9.8181	9.1285	8.5136
21	18.8571	17.0111	15.4149	14.0291	12.8211	11.7640	10.8355	10.0168	9.2922	8.6487
22	19.6605	17.6581	15.9368	14.4511	13.1630	12.0416	11.0612	10.2007	9.4424	8.7715
23	20.4559	18.2921	16.4435	14.8568	13.4885	12.3033	11.2722	10.3710	9.5802	8.8832
24	21.2435	18.9139	16.9355	15.2469	13.7986	12.5503	11.4693	10.5287	9.7066	8.9847
25	22.0233	19.5234	17.4131	15.6220	14.0939	12.7833	11.6536	10.6748	9.8226	9.0770

Example The present value of $1.00 received per year for the next 25 years, discounted at 10 percent, is $9.07 ($1.00 × 9.0770 = $9.07).

n	11%	12%	13%	14%	15%	16%	17%	18%	19%	20%
1	0.9009	0.8929	0.8850	0.8772	0.8696	0.8621	0.8547	0.8475	0.8403	0.8333
2	1.7125	1.6901	1.6681	1.6467	1.6257	1.6052	1.5852	1.5656	1.5465	1.5278
3	2.4437	2.4018	2.3612	2.3216	2.2832	2.2459	2.2096	2.1743	2.1399	2.1065
4	3.1024	3.0374	2.9745	2.9137	2.8550	2.7982	2.7432	2.6901	2.6386	2.5887
5	3.6959	3.6048	3.5172	3.4331	3.3522	3.2743	3.1993	3.1272	3.0576	2.9906
6	4.2305	4.1114	3.9976	3.8887	3.7845	3.6847	3.5892	3.4976	3.4098	3.3255
7	4.7122	4.5638	4.4226	4.2883	4.1604	4.0386	3.9224	3.8115	3.7057	3.6046
8	5.1461	4.9676	4.7988	4.6389	4.4873	4.3436	4.2072	4.0776	3.9544	3.8372
9	5.5370	5.3282	5.1317	4.9464	4.7716	4.6065	4.4506	4.3030	4.1633	4.0310
10	5.8892	5.6502	5.4262	5.2161	5.0188	4.8332	4.6586	4.4941	4.3389	4.1925
11	6.2065	5.9377	5.6869	5.4527	5.2337	5.0286	4.8364	4.6560	4.4865	4.3271
12	6.4924	6.1944	5.9176	5.6603	5.4206	5.1971	4.9884	4.7932	4.6105	4.4392
13	6.7499	6.4235	6.1218	5.8424	5.5831	5.3423	5.1183	4.9095	4.7147	4.5327
14	6.9819	6.6282	6.3025	6.0021	5.7245	5.4675	5.2293	5.0081	4.8023	4.6106
15	7.1909	6.8109	6.4624	6.1422	5.8474	5.5755	5.3242	5.0916	4.8759	4.6755
16	7.3792	6.9740	6.6039	6.2651	5.9542	5.6685	5.4053	5.1624	4.9377	4.7296
17	7.5488	7.1196	6.7291	6.3729	6.0472	5.7487	5.4746	5.2223	4.9897	4.7746
18	7.7016	7.2497	6.8399	6.4674	6.1280	5.8178	5.5339	5.2732	5.0333	4.8122
19	7.8393	7.3650	6.9380	6.5504	6.1982	5.8775	5.5845	5.3176	5.0700	4.8435
20	7.9633	7.4694	7.0248	6.6231	6.2593	5.9288	5.6278	5.3527	5.1009	4.8696
21	8.0751	7.5620	7.1016	6.6870	6.3125	5.9731	5.6648	5.3837	5.1268	4.8913
22	8.1757	7.6446	7.1695	6.7429	6.3587	6.0113	5.6964	5.4099	5.1486	4.9094
23	8.2664	7.7184	7.2297	6.7921	6.3988	6.0442	5.7234	5.4321	5.1668	4.9245
24	8.3481	7.7843	7.2829	6.8351	6.4338	6.0726	5.7465	5.4509	5.1822	4.9371
25	8.4217	7.8431	7.3300	6.8729	6.4641	6.0971	5.7662	5.4669	5.1951	4.9476

n	21%	22%	23%	24%	25%	26%	27%	28%	29%	30%
1	0.8264	0.8197	0.8130	0.8065	0.8000	0.7937	0.7874	0.7813	0.7752	0.7692
2	1.5095	1.4915	1.4740	1.4568	1.4400	1.4235	1.4074	1.3916	1.3761	1.3609
3	2.0739	2.0422	2.0114	1.9813	1.9520	1.9234	1.8956	1.8684	1.8420	1.8161
4	2.5404	2.4936	2.4483	2.4043	2.3616	2.3202	2.2800	2.2410	2.2031	2.1662
5	2.9260	2.8636	2.8035	2.7454	2.6893	2.6351	2.5827	2.5320	2.4830	2.4356
6	3.2446	3.1669	3.0923	3.0205	2.9514	2.8850	2.8210	2.7594	2.7000	2.6427
7	3.5079	3.4155	3.3270	3.2423	3.1611	3.0833	3.0087	2.9370	2.8682	2.8021
8	3.7256	3.6193	3.5179	3.4212	3.3289	3.2407	3.1564	3.0758	2.9986	2.9247
9	3.9054	3.7863	3.6731	3.5655	3.4631	3.3657	3.2728	3.1842	3.0997	3.0190
10	4.0541	3.9232	3.7993	3.6819	3.5705	3.4648	3.3644	3.2689	3.1781	3.0915
11	4.1769	4.0354	3.0918	3.7757	3.6564	3.5435	3.4365	3.3351	3.2388	3.1473
12	4.2785	4.1274	3.9852	3.8514	3.7251	3.6060	3.4933	3.3868	3.2850	3.1903
13	4.3624	4.2028	4.0530	3.9124	3.7601	3.6555	3.6381	3.4272	3.3224	3.2233
14	4.4317	4.2646	4.1082	3.9616	3.8241	3.6949	3.5733	3.4587	3.3507	3.2487
15	4.4890	4.3152	4.1530	4.0013	3.8593	3.7261	3.6010	3.4834	3.3726	3.2682
16	4.5364	4.3567	4.1894	4.0333	3.8874	3.7509	3.6228	3.5026	3.3896	3.2832
17	4.5755	4.3908	4.2890	4.0591	3.9099	3.7705	3.6400	3.5177	3.4028	3.2948
18	4.6079	4.4187	4.2431	4.0799	3.9279	3.7861	3.6536	3.5294	3.4130	3.3037
19	4.6345	4.4415	4.2627	4.0967	3.9424	3.7985	3.6642	3.5386	3.4210	3.3105
20	4.6567	4.4603	4.2786	4.1103	3.9539	3.8083	3.6726	3.5458	3.4271	3.3158
21	4.6750	4.4756	4.2916	4.1212	3.9631	3.8161	3.6792	3.5514	3.4319	3.3198
22	4.6900	4.4882	4.3021	4.1300	3.9705	3.8223	3.6844	3.5553	3.4356	3.3230
23	4.7025	4.4985	4.3106	4.1371	3.9764	3.8273	3.6885	3.5592	3.4384	3.3254
24	4.7128	4.5070	4.3176	4.1428	3.9811	3.8312	3.6981	3.5619	3.4406	3.3272
25	4.7213	4.5139	4.3232	4.1474	3.9849	3.8342	3.6943	3.5640	3.4423	3.3286

Areas under Normal Curve

$$Z = \frac{x_i - \bar{x}}{\sigma}$$

Standard Deviations $(Z)_{(1)}$	Area on One side of Expected Value$_{(2)}$	Area Outside Z on Same Side$_{(3)}$
0.0	0.0000	0.0000
0.1	0.0398	0.4602
0.2	0.0793	0.4207
0.3	0.1179	0.3821
0.4	0.1554	0.3446
0.5	0.1915	0.3085
0.6	0.2257	0.2743
0.7	0.2580	0.2420
0.8	0.2881	0.2119
0.9	0.3159	0.1841
1.0	0.3413	0.1587
1.1	0.3643	0.1357
1.2	0.3849	0.1151
1.3	0.4032	0.0968
1.4	0.4192	0.0808
1.5	0.4332	0.0668
1.6	0.4452	0.0548
1.7	0.4554	0.0446
1.8	0.4641	0.0359
1.9	0.4713	0.0287
2.0	0.4772	0.0228
2.1	0.4821	0.0179
2.2	0.4861	0.0139
2.3	0.4893	0.0107
2.4	0.4918	0.0082
2.5	0.4938	0.0062
2.6	0.4953	0.0047
2.7	0.4965	0.0035
2.8	0.4974	0.0026
2.9	0.4981	0.0019
3.0	0.4987	0.0013

Note (2) + (3) = 50 percent of area under the curve.

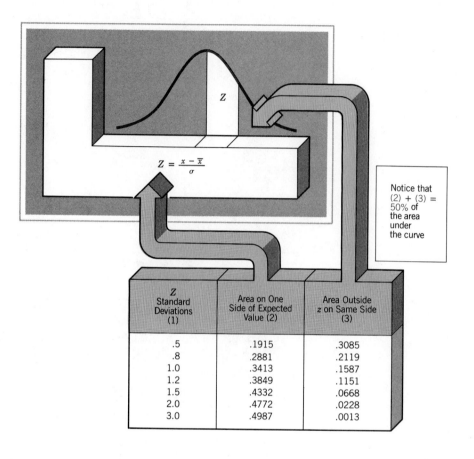

Z Standard Deviations (1)	Area on One Side of Expected Value (2)	Area Outside z on Same Side (3)
.5	.1915	.3085
.8	.2881	.2119
1.0	.3413	.1587
1.2	.3849	.1151
1.5	.4332	.0668
2.0	.4772	.0228
3.0	.4987	.0013

$$Z = \frac{x - \overline{x}}{\sigma}$$

Notice that (2) + (3) = 50% of the area under the curve

Index